Cambridge Patristic Texts

GENERAL EDITOR:—A. J. MASON, D.D.
MASTER OF PEMBROKE COLLEGE, CAMBRIDGE

THE LETTERS
AND OTHER REMAINS
OF
DIONYSIUS OF ALEXANDRIA

ΔΙΟΝΥΣΙΟΥ ΛΕΙΨΑΝΑ

THE LETTERS AND OTHER REMAINS

OF

DIONYSIUS OF ALEXANDRIA

EDITED BY

CHARLES LETT FELTOE, B.D.

SOMETIME FELLOW OF CLARE COLLEGE, CAMBRIDGE,
RECTOR OF FORNHAM ALL SAINTS AND WESTLEY, SUFFOLK

WIPF & STOCK · Eugene, Oregon

Wipf and Stock Publishers
199 W 8th Ave, Suite 3
Eugene, OR 97401

The Letters and Other Remains of Dionysius of Alexandria
By Feltoe, Charles Lett
ISBN 13: 978-1-60608-442-7
Publication date 11/11/10
Previously published by Cambridge University Press, 1904

PREFACE.

THE idea of editing (*inter alia*) the epistolary portion of these fragments was first put into my head some twenty years ago by the late Canon Bright, of Oxford, who was anxious to get someone to publish two volumes of early Christian letters (one Greek and one Latin), as being likely to prove useful to students of theology. At his suggestion, therefore, I did make a start on this project, and for a short time studied especially the Eusebian extracts from Dionysius the Great's letters; but for a variety of reasons I had soon to turn my attention to other more pressing concerns, and it was not till about two years ago that my mind reverted to the subject. In reading Dr Swete's most helpful and stimulating little book on *Patristic Study* I came upon this sentence (p. 55): "a careful study of his (Dionysius's) work and theological position would make an attractive contribution to the literature of Patristics." I at once consulted Dr Swete on the advisability of taking up this new suggestion and found that, owing to ill health, the Rev. M. A. Bayfield, a member of my own college, to whom the work had already been entrusted, had just withdrawn from the undertaking and Dr Mason was good enough to accept me in his place.

I soon found that the task of collecting, arranging and editing the numerous and multifarious fragments (often of considerable length) attributed to Dionysius of Alexandria was one of no small difficulty, and the longer I proceeded with the work the greater the difficulties seemed to be. A competent knowledge was required not only of Greek scholarship, Church History and Christian antiquities, but also of Hellenistic philosophy, of the developement of Doctrine and of Biblical exegesis, and my equipment in these various branches of theology was but slender. Indeed, were it not for the help I have received on many sides, I should either have abandoned the task in despair or have produced a vastly inferior and less serviceable book than I think is now the case. A large share, therefore, of any merit the book may possess is due to my generous assistants, and any blame wholly to myself.

First and foremost, I must acknowledge with gratitude the patient and unstinted help that Dr Mason (as Editor-in-chief) has always given me throughout in correcting my mistakes, in supplementing my deficiencies and in advising me on the general conduct of my work. It would be difficult to exaggerate the value of the services which he has rendered me.

The Introductions to the different sections of the fragments will more or less reveal the particular forms of help which the following have also given me from time to time, and for which I now beg to record my sincere thanks: the Rev. Dr Gifford, Dr E. Schwartz,

Dr H. Jackson, Mr N. McLean and the Rev. H. E. Symonds. To these I must now add the names of Mr Stanley A. Cook, who helped me with the Syriac fragments when Mr McLean was ill, and of the Rev. H. B. Waterfield, who has assisted me several times in various small researches and in other ways. Lastly, there is the staff of the University Press itself, who certainly deserve as much praise as anyone for their share in the production of the book.

Whether we have between us succeeded in presenting an adequate description of the man and of his writings will remain for others to determine. The worthiness of the theme and the excellence of our intentions are not open to doubt.

C. L. FELTOE.

FORNHAM ALL SAINTS,
July, 1904.

TABLE OF CONTENTS.

		PAGE
PREFACE		v
GENERAL INTRODUCTION		xi—xxxiv
JEROME de viris illustribus 69		xxxv

A. Letters . . . . 1—105

    I   πρὸς Φαβιανόν . . . . . 3—21

    II   πρὸς Γερμανόν . . . . . 21—36

    III   πρὸς Νοουάτον . . . . . 36—39

    IV   πρὸς Κορνήλιον 39, 40

    V   περὶ Βαπτίσματος . . . . 40—59

        1 πρὸς Στέφανον . . . . 44—49

        2 πρὸς Ξύστον . . . . . 49—52

        3 πρὸς Φιλήμονα . . . . 52—55

        4 πρὸς Διονύσιον 55, 56

        5 πρὸς Ξύστον . . . . . 56—59

    VI   πρὸς Κόνωνα . . . . . 59—62

    VII   περὶ Μετανοίας . . . . . 62—64

    VIII   πρὸς Δομέτιον καὶ Δίδυμον . . 64—69

    IX   πρὸς Ἑρμάμμωνα . . . . 69—78

    X   πρὸς τοὺς ἐν Ἀλεξανδρείᾳ ἀδελφούς . 79—84

    XI   πρὸς Ἱέρακα . . . . . 84—89

    XII   ἐκ τῆς β' Ἐπιστολῆς 90

    XIII   ἐκ τῆς δ' ἑορταστικῆς Ἐπιστολῆς . 90, 91

    XIV   πρὸς Βασιλείδην . . . . 91—105

B. περὶ Ἐπαγγελιῶν . . . . . . 106—126

Γ. περὶ Φύσεως . . . . 127—164

TABLE OF CONTENTS

		PAGE
Δ.	The Controversy between the two Dionysii	165—198
I	Διονυσίου τοῦ κατὰ ʽΡώμην ἐπιστολή	176—182
II	Ἔλεγχος καὶ Ἀπολογία	182—198
E.	Exegetical Fragments	
I	[ἐκ τῶν κατ' Ὠριγενοῦς]	199, 200
II	On Job	200—208
III	εἰς τὴν Ἀρχὴν τοῦ Ἐκκλησιαστοῦ	208—227
IV	On the Song of Solomon	228, 229
V	On Luke xxii 42 ff.	229—250
Z.	Miscellaneous Fragments	
I	On Acts v 4	251
II	On Rom. xi. 26	251
III	On the Epistle of James	252, 253
IV	On Revel. xxii 3	253
V	πρὸς Ἀφροδίσιον	253—256
VI	περὶ Γυμνασίου	256
VII	περὶ Γάμων	256, 257
VIII	From works unspecified	257—260

INDEXES

1	Biblical Quotations and References	261—266
2	Proper Names	267—270
3	Greek Words	271—283

GENERAL INTRODUCTION.

1. OF the many influential occupants of the chair of St Mark at Alexandria, of the many distinguished heads of the Catechetical School in that city, none seems to have been held in higher respect by the ancients than Dionysius. By common consent he is styled ὁ μέγας[1], while Athanasius (*de sent. Dion.* 6) calls him καθολικῆς ἐκκλησίας διδάσκαλος and Basil (*Ep.* II 188 *ad Amphiloch. περὶ κανόνων*) refers to him as κανονικός (a person of canonical authority)[2]. He took a prominent and important part in all the leading movements and controversies of the day and his opinions always carried great weight, especially in Eastern Christendom. His writings are not only referred to and quoted more freely than is the case with other authors by Eusebius (both in his *Ecclesiastical History* Bks. vi and vii and in his *Praeparatio Evangelica* Bks. vii and xiv and in the latter work side by side with great authors like Plato and Aristotle) but are also put to similar uses by Athanasius, Basil, John of Damascus and others. And though little, if anything, is known for certain of his

---

[1] E.g. Eus. *H. E.* vii praef., Pet. Alex. *Mystag.* (see n. 2 on p. xvii), Basil (*Ep.* II 188 *ad Amphiloch.*) etc.; in the MSS, however, extracts which are attributed to Δ. ὁ μέγας seem sometimes to belong to the Areopagite or some other Dionysius.

[2] For further light on this epithet see pp. 175 f.

personal story except what he himself has told us in his letters, and though nothing but fragments embodied in the works of others remains to us of his compositions, yet a careful study of those fragments and a comparison of them with other writings of the period will undoubtedly leave on the mind the impression that the verdict of the ancient world and even of his contemporaries is correct and that he is truly the Great St Denys.

2. The references to Dionysius's family and early years are extremely scanty and vague. *Hic erat Sabaita sapientissimus et ex gentis primoribus atque optimatibus* is the statement of the *Chronicon Orientale* (p. 94 ed. 1685). In the Scholia Maximi *ad Dion. Areopag.* he is called ὁ ἀπὸ ῥητόρων, and other writers (e.g. Nicetas and Anastasius Sinaita) make similar statements; and hence it has been inferred that like his contemporary Cyprian of Carthage Dionysius had been a rhetorician before his conversion. But this view is rejected by Dittrich[1] on the ground that there is a confusion between our Dionysius and a much later Alexandrian writer of the same name, who made scholia on the works of the Areopagite and wrote other treatises. On the other hand Dionysius's literary style is such that it might very well have been formed by the study and practice of rhetoric; while he has been thought himself to corroborate the statement of the *Chronicon Orientale* as to the high position of his family in his reply to Germanus (p. 35), where he refers to the ἀξιωμάτων ἀποθέσεις which he has suffered for the Faith. Again

[1] See Dittrich *D. der Grosse* p. 2 n. 3, and Harnack *Altchrist. Lit.* i 424. If this contention is correct, possibly a considerable number of the short sententious extracts doubtfully assigned to D. in the present collection come from this mediaeval writer.

what exactly is meant by the term *Sabaita*[1], must remain doubtful. The word suggests that he was of Arab descent; and yet the way in which Dionysius himself always distinguishes even the Αἰγύπτιοι (the Coptic inhabitants of Egypt) from the city-folk of Alexandria certainly suggests that he considers himself connected by education and residence, if not by birth, with the latter, who were of course largely of Greek origin: and if so, it would be rather a surprise to find that his family came from the remoter parts of Arabia.

3. As he was in all probability a priest and at least 30 years of age when he was raised to the headship of the Catechetical School in A.D. 231, and as he excused himself from attendance at the Council of Antioch in A.D. 264 on the ground of his age and infirmity[2], it is a fairly safe inference that Dionysius was born about or before A.D. 200, being thus nearly of an age with Cyprian of Carthage and only 10 or 15 years younger than his master, Origen.

4. The *Chronicon Orientale* assigns the reading of St Paul's letters as the cause of his conversion to Christianity (*causa vero eius ad fidem conversionis fuit lectio epistolarum Pauli*)[3] and proceeds to state how after their perusal he presented himself for baptism to Demetrius, then Bishop of Alexandria (*quibus lectis Demetrio sese sistit, qui comiter illum excipiens baptismatis*

[1] The Sabaeans were a tribe in the south of Arabia Felix, mentioned in the Book of Job and elsewhere. Dittrich quotes 'Herbelot B O V unter Sabi 715 "*Constantinus fertur a Sabaeis migrasse ad Christianos.*"' It is possible, as has been suggested to me, that the *Chron. Or.* may be claiming D. as a member of the Sabaite convent near Jerusalem, though of course there would be no ground for the claim.

[2] γῆρας ὁμοῦ καὶ ἀσθένειαν τοῦ σώματος αἰτιασάμενος, Eus. *H. E.* vii 27.

[3] So also the *Synaxarium Copticum* in Simon de Magistris p. CLVI (Dittrich).

aqua lustravit). Whether this was actually the case or not, we know from what he has himself told us in his letter to Philemon (p. 53) that both before and after baptism he was a diligent student of all that was written both for and against Christianity. "One of the brethren," he there says, "who was a presbyter urged me to desist (from reading heretical works) from fear that I should be contaminated by the filth of their wickedness: for he thought my soul would be injured and therein he spoke the truth, as I perceived. But a God-sent vision came and strengthened me, and a word was spoken to me and expressly commanded me saying 'Peruse all that you lay your hands on: for you are competent to correct and test each statement, and this was the original cause of your accepting the Faith.' So I accepted the vision, as according with the apostolic utterance which says to the more able, 'Be ye bankers of repute.'"

5. Whether in accordance with the common practice of the Eastern Church at that time[1] Dionysius was married or not, is a moot point. He addressed or dedicated his treatise περὶ Φύσεως to one Timotheus ὁ παῖς (Eus. *H. E.* vii 26. 2) and we read of οἱ παῖδες (of whom Timotheus was one) as accompanying him in his flight (p. 25). The natural inference is that he was at that time a widower (his wife not being mentioned) and that these were his sons; but Dittrich[2] considers them to have been his pupils, holding that he did not resign his post of Catechete on becoming Bishop, while others with less likelihood have considered them to have been his servants.

---

[1] Cf. Eus. *H.E.* vi 42. 3: vii. 30. 17.
[2] pp. 4 and 5: the whole question is fully discussed by G. Roch *Die Schrift des Alex. Bischofs, D. d. Gr. über die Natur* (Leipzig, 1882) pp. 24 and 25.

6. In 231 the Bishop Demetrius died, and Heraclas the head of the Catechetical School was elected into his place. The vacancy thus created at the School was filled by the appointment of Dionysius, who had himself been a pupil of the School under Origen[1]. With some show of reason it has been suggested that the treatise περὶ Φύσεως, in which for the first time a Christian undertook systematically to refute the atomistic theories of Epicurus and his followers, was composed while Dionysius held this important post[2]. His commentary on the beginning of Ecclesiastes may also belong to the same period[3]. Sixteen years later, in 247, upon the death of Heraclas, Dionysius succeeded him in the bishopric also as the 14th occupant of the see, possibly, as has been said above, without resigning his work of Catechete —at least for a time[4]. Philip the Arabian (of Bostra) had then been Emperor for three years, a position he was destined to retain for two years longer. Philip, like Alexander Severus before him, was a well-known favourer of the Christians[5]; and Dionysius himself bears witness to his rule having been εὐμενεστέρα ἡμῖν (p. 9). For a short time therefore the new Bishop and his flock were left in peace; but even before the death of Philip

---

[1] εἷς καὶ οὗτος τῶν Ὠριγένους γενόμενος φοιτητῶν, Eus. *H. E.* vi 29. 4: so Jerome *de virr. ill.* 69 *Origenis valde insignissimus auditor fuit.* The *Chronicon Orientale* gives a different and apparently an inaccurate account: *praefecit illum Hieroclas iudiciis ac sibi vicarium ob insignem eius sapientiam et ingenium constituit.*

[2] See Roch *op. cit.* p. 19 and Bardenhewer *Altkirch. Lit.* ii p. 174.

[3] See p. 210.

[4] See p. 92 where the suggestion is made that the letter πρὸς Βασιλείδην was written in the earlier years of D.'s episcopate.

[5] τοῦτον κατέχει λόγος Χριστιανὸν ὄντα ἐν ἡμέρᾳ τῆς ὑστάτης τοῦ πάσχα παννυχίδος τῶν ἐπὶ τῆς ἐκκλησίας εὐχῶν τῷ πλήθει μετασχεῖν ἐθελῆσαι κ.τ.λ., Eus. *H. E.* vi 34: Origen addressed letters to him and to Severa his wife, *ibid.* 36.

signs of the coming storm appeared. In the last year of his reign Dionysius tells Fabius, Bishop of Antioch (p. 6), that ὁ κακῶν τῇ πόλει ταύτῃ μάντις καὶ ποιητὴς ὅστις ἐκεῖνος ἦν stirred up the populace against the Christians in Alexandria, and several persons were cruelly martyred. This reign of terror lasted for some time (ἐπὶ πολύ), but was interrupted in the autumn of 249 by the revolution which caused the deposition and death of Philip and which set Decius on the throne in his stead. The respite was only too brief: "by the following January," says Benson (*Cyprian* p. 65), the edict of Decius against the Christians "was doing deadly execution." The Bishops of the various sees were at first singled out for special attention. Origen, though not a bishop, was included among the earlier victims— probably on account of his prominence as a scholar and teacher—being imprisoned at Tyre (A.D. 250—1) and cruelly tortured, but failing to obtain the martyr's crown itself.

7. The reason for Decius's reversal of his predecessor's policy towards the Christians has been diversely estimated. Eusebius attributes it simply to his hatred of Philip and all his ways. But this seems to be out of agreement with the facts. Decius had been very reluctant to oppose one who had been his master; and both Zosimus (i 21) and Vopiscus (*Aurel.* 42) give evidence that he was "as virtuous and capable as he was anti-Christian[1]." The view of Gibbon[2] therefore seems historically more accurate that Decius thought the much needed restoration of public morality would be best effected by strong support of the national religion.

[1] See Benson *Cyprian* pp. 64 and 65.
[2] *Decline and Fall*, chap. xvi.

GENERAL INTRODUCTION xvii

8. Whatever were the causes, the severity of the Decian persecution is undoubted, and it fell with full force on the Church at Alexandria. Sabinus was then the Prefect of Egypt, and he lost no time in carrying out the imperial edict upon Dionysius and his followers. Many endured tortures or death or both. Dionysius himself after waiting four days fled and was sought for by a *frumentarius* sent by Sabinus. A brief search was sufficient to discover him and he was carried off with four of his companions to Taposiris. But through a strange interposition of Providence (related in the Letter to Germanus pp. 26 and 27) he was rescued by a wedding party of rustic revellers and carried off into a place of safety in the Libyan desert, where he appears to have been left unmolested with two of his four companions (see p. 67), till the cessation of the persecution allowed him to return to the city. In after days Dionysius's action in fleeing on this occasion was violently attacked by a certain Bishop Germanus[1], perhaps one of his suffragans. Germanus boasted of his own braver conduct under persecution (πολλαῖς γε ταῖς ὁμολογίαις Γ. σεμνύνεται). Dionysius in his reply maintains that it was not of his own will nor yet without divine intimation that he had fled, and that he had suffered far more than Germanus for the Faith (pp. 24 and 35)[2]. Decius's rule was brought to a calamitous end in 251, but Gallus who succeeded

[1] D. speaks of ἡ Γερμανοῦ βία in his reply which Eusebius (*H. E.* vii 11) describes as addressed πρὸς Γ. τῶν κατ' αὐτὸν ἐπισκόπων κακῶς ἀγορεύειν αὐτὸν πειρώμενον.

[2] There is an interesting reference to the trials undergone by D. in the *Mystagogia* of his martyred successor, Peter of Alexandria, a fragment of which is given in Routh *Rell. Sacr.* iv p. 81 and which contains these words ὡς δὲ καὶ ὁ μέγας Διονύσιος κατακρυπτόμενος ἀπὸ τόπων εἰς τόπους, πρὸς τούτῳ καὶ Σαβελλίου θλίβοντος. For the last reference here to Sabellius see p. 165, but it seems as if the last words must be a mistake for πρὸς τοῦτο κ. Σαβείνου θλίβ.

him pursued the same policy against the Christians for another two years, when he too succumbed to an untimely fate.

9. For the next four years the Church of Alexandria enjoyed comparative rest and peace. In 253 Aemilianus[1], the Governor of Pannonia and Moesia, who had in that spring wrested the imperial power from Gallus, was in his turn, after four months' rule, defeated by Valerian and his son Gallienus and slain by the soldiery. The new Emperors (father and son) took no active measures against the Christians during the first four years of their reign—a fact which surprises us when it is considered that Valerian had been specially chosen to fill the office of "Censor" which Decius had revived. Possibly it was in some measure due to his "languid temperament[2]," as well as to his son's connexions with the Christians through his wife Cornelia Salonina. It was during these four years of peace, though chiefly during the last of them, that Dionysius took part in the controversy about heretical baptism to which that group of epistolary extracts belongs which we have given on pp. 44 ff.[3]: some account of the circumstances which gave rise to the controversy and the share taken in it by Dionysius will be found in the Introduction to that section (pp. 40 ff.).

10. Suddenly in the summer of 257 the Church was startled by the issue of an edict which revived the reign of terror and threw her into a state of persecution which lasted for more than three years. This unexpected change of policy towards the Christians is attributed by

[1] Not the Prefect of Egypt mentioned by D. p. 28; see notes *in loco*.

[2] Benson *Cyprian* p. 457 who quotes Treb. Poll. *Regilianus* in proof.

[3] The date of D.'s letter to Novatian (p. 38) is uncertain but it was probably written in 252 or 253.

GENERAL INTRODUCTION xix

Dionysius to the influence of Macrianus, who at one time held the office of *Rationalis* to the Emperor (ἐπὶ τῶν καθόλου λόγων βασιλέως p. 74). Though apparently a cripple in one leg, Macrianus was mentally and otherwise a person of considerable character[1] and ability: but he appears to have associated himself in some way with the soothsayers of Egypt (ὁ διδάσκαλος καὶ τῶν ἀπ' Αἰγύπτου μάγων ἀρχισυνάγωγος) and to have conceived a violent hatred against the Christians, if we may trust Dionysius (p. 72). Quite early in the proceedings which were instituted against the Christians at Alexandria in consequence of the edict, Dionysius with several of his clergy was brought before Aemilian the Prefect[2], and after examination—chiefly as to his loyalty to the Emperors, which his refusal to pay them divine honours rendered doubtful—was banished first to a place called Cephro (probably not far from Taposiris where he had been sent before) and then somewhere on the high road in the district called Colluthion. A full account of the circumstances which led to and attended this second period of exile is given on pp. 28 ff., an account which is valuable among other reasons because it is largely drawn from the official memoranda (ὑπομνήματα) of the Prefect's court.

11. The persecution of Valerian lasted till the autumn of the year 260 (42 months according to Dionysius's letter to Hermammon p. 78) and was then, on the disappearance of Valerian, stayed by the Edict of Peace which was issued by his son, Gallienus, now left alone upon the throne. Eusebius (*H. E.* vii 13) gives us a Greek version of what is apparently not the actual Edict but

[1] See Benson *Cyprian* p. 457.
[2] This Aemilian was the man who afterwards made one of the many attempts of the period to seize the imperial power: see p. 28.

the rescript applying it to Egypt: it is addressed to Dionysius, Pinna, Demetrius and the other bishops and runs as follows: "I have ordained that the benefit of my concession be enforced throughout the world, to the effect that men should withdraw from (i.e. not interfere with) your places of worship (τῶν τόπων τῶν θρησκευσίμων). And accordingly ye too may use the terms of my rescript, so that none interfere with you. And this which may with authority be carried out by you, has already been granted by me sometime ago (πρὸ πολλοῦ)[1]. And accordingly Aurelius Quirinius, who is in charge of the Exchequer[2], shall preserve this form now given by me." Further instructions were also issued permitting the Christians to have free access to their cemeteries—a privilege which they always highly prized (τὰ τῶν καλουμένων κοιμητηρίων ἀπολαμβάνειν ἐπιτρέπων χωρία).

12. It is practically certain that Dionysius returned to Alexandria, as soon as Gallienus's Edict was in operation there. But almost immediately fresh disturbances were felt in the city, followed by one of those frequent outbreaks of pestilence to which the East was always liable, and these hindered for a time his work of bringing the brethren together again. The disturbance is with good reason thought to have been that connected with the attempt of Macrianus to overturn the power of Gallienus in Egypt, though, as Gibbon has remarked, "after the captivity of Valerian and the insolence of his son had relaxed the authority of the laws, the Alexandrians abandoned themselves to the ungoverned

---

[1] This expression seems to suggest that it was one or two months before the Edict reached Egypt.

[2] ὁ τοῦ μεγίστου πράγματος προστατεύων (Lat. *summae rei procurator*): apparently the same office as that of ὁ ἐπὶ τῶν καθόλου λόγων above is meant.

rage of their passions, and their unhappy country was the theatre of a civil war, which continued (with a few short and suspicious truces) above 12 years[1]," and so it is almost impossible with certainty to identify any particular disturbance of this period[2].

13. For another five years Dionysius was spared to administer his charge and to benefit the Church at large with his prudent counsels. But, though attacks upon himself never seem to have troubled him very much, he had in this last period of his life to pass through one such attack, which probably grieved him more than all the rest, and the after-results of which lingered on till the days of Athanasius and Basil in the next century. This was in connexion with the Sabellian controversy, especially that phase of it which had recently arisen in the Pentapolis. The circumstances which had led to Dionysius's intervention and to the criticisms which were passed upon his utterances on the occasion will be found set out in the Introductions to the Letter of Dionysius of Rome and to the Ἔλεγχος καὶ Ἀπολογία. No doubt some of Dionysius's phrases in combating Sabellianism were open to objection; but the Bishop of Rome showed an imperfect appreciation of his illustrious namesake's point of view, and his attempted rebuke of the Alexandrian theology did little, if anything, to discredit its exponent in the eyes of his brother bishops. Indeed that his high repute in the eyes of the Church was still maintained, is shown by the fact that, when the Council of Antioch was being summoned to deal with the troubles connected with the heresies of Paul of Samosata, Dionysius was specially invited to attend. The letter which he sent in reply contained a statement of

---

[1] *Decline and Fall* chap. x.   [2] See however pp. 79 and 85.

his views on the matter (δι' ἐπιστολῆς τὴν αὐτοῦ γνώμην ἣν ἔχοι περὶ τοῦ ζητουμένου παραστήσας Eus. *H. E.* vii 27. 2)[1]. In 265, before the Council had finished its sessions, he passed to his well-earned rest.

14. From what has been said already about our author's various interests and activities, and even from the mere list of his recorded writings, it will be gathered that he was a person of remarkable versatility and at the same time unusually free from those snares of the versatile man, shallowness and inaccuracy. The expositions of Biblical passages attributed to him, though it is probable that they are not entirely genuine, are for the most part well worth reading and consideration, while his critical remarks on the Revelation of St John the Divine are deserving of higher praise. The long extracts, which remain, from his book περὶ Φύσεως, directed against the Epicureans, show him to have possessed on the whole a clear grasp of their tenets, together with much genuine humour and entire absence of bitterness of spirit in criticizing them. The letter to Basilides on several points of ecclesiastical order is a model of what such episcopal utterances should be, definitely stating what is the highest and best course, but leaving the decision to the individual conscience. His

---

[1] See also *ibid.* 30. 3, where Eusebius implies that D. disdained to have any dealings with the heresiarch himself in the matter (ἐπέστειλεν εἰς τὴν Ἀντιόχειαν, τὸν ἡγεμόνα τῆς πλάνης οὐδὲ προσρήσεως ἀξιώσας οὐδὲ πρὸς πρόσωπον γράψας αὐτῷ ἀλλὰ τῇ παροικίᾳ πάσῃ). In view of this statement the remarks of Theodoret *Haer. Fab.* ii 8 must be taken with caution: καὶ Διονύσιος μὲν ὁ τῆς Ἀλεξανδρέων (ἐκκλησίας) ἐπίσκοπος ἀνὴρ ἐπίσημος ἐν διδασκαλίᾳ γενόμενος ἀνεβάλετο μὲν τὴν ἐπιδημίαν διὰ τὴν τοῦ γήρως ἀσθένειαν· διὰ δὲ γραμμάτων ἐκείνῳ (sc. τῷ Παύλῳ τῷ Σαμοσατεῖ) παρῄνεσε τὰ προσήκοντα καὶ τοὺς συνεληλυθότας ἐπισκόπους εἰς τὸν ὑπὲρ τῆς εὐσεβείας παρέθηξε ζῆλον. A spurious letter of D. to Paul is given by Mansi *Conc. Coll.* I 1039 ff: see Dittrich *Dionysius d. Gr.* pp. 123 ff, and Harnack *Altchrist. Lit.* i 425.

GENERAL INTRODUCTION xxiii

general correspondence deals with a large variety of subjects: in some letters theological matters are discussed, like Novatianism, Sabellianism, and the baptism of heretics: in others there are descriptions of the martyrdoms of his time at Alexandria and his own personal experiences under persecution, all told with a vividness and a sobriety eminently characteristic of the man: others are addressed to persons or districts in his province, especially at Eastertide, treating of matters of local and temporary importance. In his controversy with the Sabellians, as we have remarked elsewhere, some of the expressions and figures he used were insufficiently guarded or explained, and so laid him open to criticism; but we must remember how much more easy it is for us, who have the benefit of after history and experience, to criticize and correct, than it was for Dionysius and his contemporaries to grope their way, as they slowly but surely did, under the Divine guidance, to a fuller knowledge and a more accurate statement of the Truth.

15. It is also to be noticed how very seldom, if ever, Dionysius offends against the principles of good taste (however fastidious), either when attacking opponents or when describing horrors or when dealing with the mysteries of the Faith. In controversy he always displays a moderation and convincing sweetness of tone, which is entirely admirable and all the more remarkable because his own convictions were strong and definite. This is especially to be observed in his treatment of Novatianus the intruder, in his criticism of the dead Nepos of Arsenoe, and (though to a less extent) in his defence of himself against the charges of Germanus. Even when he has to speak of one whom he believes to have done him wrong like the Prefect Aemilianus, or of one whom his soul abhors like Macrianus, his language

is mild in comparison with that of many in similar circumstances. So too when he has to describe the tortures and deaths of the martyrs or the ravages of pestilence, he indulges in but few ghastly or revolting details, though his narrative is always lively and thrilling. And once more when he treats of such a subject as the Incarnation of our Lord, there is a delicacy and restraint in his language which leaves nothing to be desired.

16. Dionysius's literary style is excellent, considering the age in which he lived, and so far confirms the truth of the statement that he had been a master of rhetoric before his conversion. He gives evidence of having read widely and to good purpose both in classical and in religious literature. As to the former he actually quotes from, or refers to, Homer, Hesiod, Thucydides, Aristotle, and Democritus, among others: but his language is really saturated with classical uses, and a large number of the words and phrases which he employs recall the best writers of antiquity[1]. Many of his compositions exhibit signs of much care in production, notably the περὶ Φύσεως and the two Paschal letters to Bishop Hierax and to the Alexandrians. Here, and to a somewhat less extent in the letter to Hermammon, he writes in a more rhetorical and elaborate manner than in most of the other fragments which are extant but even in these passages he is seldom fantastic or stilted or obscure, whilst in pure narrative or simple description (e.g. in the letters which record his own or others' sufferings and in the περὶ Ἐπαγγελιῶν) his language could hardly be more unaffected or better chosen. The classical scholar will naturally find certain

[1] To make a full list of these would be laborious and unnecessary but a few instances are ἀλιτήριος, ἐπεισκυκλεῖν, ἐπ' ἐμαυτοῦ βάλλεσθαι, ἐξομόρξασθαι, παλαμναῖοι δαίμονες, φυλοκρινεῖν, ὠμογέροντες.

marks of decadent Greek in his writings, but they are not sufficient to cause him any serious discomfort or confusion. It may be well however to mention some of the principal of them here, viz.: (1) the interchange of tenses, perfects and pluperfects for aorists and imperfects and *vice versâ* without any perceptible difference of meaning: (2) the tendency to use οὐ and μή indiscriminately: (3) a laxity as to cases (*a*) with prepositions (e.g. ἐπὶ τῆς οἰκίας 'at my house' p. 24), (*b*) in temporal phrases (e.g. ὅλον ἐνιαυτὸν προὔλαβεν 'anticipated by a whole year' p. 6, τεσσάρων ἡμερῶν 'during four days' p. 24 etc.). These are perhaps the most frequently occurring lapses from Attic Greek. Besides them however the student will occasionally find (1) the optative where he would expect the subjunctive and *vice versâ*, (2) a genitive absolute where the accusative would be more correct, and (3) αὐτός in the demonstrative sense, as in modern Greek (e.g. αὐτῆς ὥρας p. 24).

17. To what extent did Dionysius accept the conclusions of Origen, especially in the matter of biblical criticism and interpretation? The evidence, such as it is, is rather doubtful and conflicting. In the first place it is somewhat ominous, as Professor J. J. Blunt has pointed out[1], that, after the death of Bishop Demetrius, whose denunciations had caused the master's removal from Alexandria and his retirement to Caesarea, we hear of no effort on the part of Dionysius or of any other pupil to obtain his recall. This certainly suggests that, great as their regard and respect for him as a man and a scholar may have been, they either felt themselves powerless to reinstate him, or else considered his views and methods of advocating them detrimental to the

---

[1] *Christian Church* p. 304.

welfare of the Church at large. On the other hand it is pleasing to remember that Dionysius wrote an epistle to his old master on the subject of martyrdom[1], which was presumably designed to comfort him during his imprisonment at Tyre: a fragment of this is thought by Harnack[2] to be contained in the passages on Luke xxii given on pp. 231 ff. of this edition. We learn too on the authority of Stephen Gobar (quoted by Photius cod. 232) that after Origen's death Dionysius wrote a letter to Theotecnus, Bishop of Caesarea, in which he extolled his master's virtues. The chief methodical comments on the Bible of the authenticity of which we may be certain are those contained in the Eusebian fragments of the treatise περὶ 'Επαγγελιῶν (pp. 109 ff.). This was, we know, a direct reply to the "Ελεγχος 'Αλληγοριστῶν, in which Nepos of Arsenoe had thought to support his gross Chiliastic views by the Revelation of St John. The very title of the work impugned no doubt denotes that it had attacked the allegorizing tendency of Origen as a commentator, and especially on the subject of Chiliasm[3], and therefore we may with some amount of certainty infer that Dionysius's refutation of Nepos would support Origen's methods of interpreting Scripture; but the extracts preserved by Eusebius from the second book of the περὶ 'Επαγγελιῶν, which dealt with the Apocalypse, are almost wholly occupied in matters of authorship and textual criticism and therefore give no real clue as to his exact method of interpreting the subject-matter of the book. The requirements of the case in the letter πρὸς Βασιλείδην

---

[1] Eus. *H. E.* vi 46. 2.

[2] *Altchrist. Lit.* i 421: see also p. 230 of this edition.

[3] Cf. Orig. περὶ 'Αρχῶν II 11, and *Proleg. in cant. cantic.*; also Dittrich *op. cit.* p. 72.

do not call for a style of interpretation which would bring out either a correspondence or a disagreement with Origen's methods except so far as it is marked by the frank and free exercise of critical judgement. The commentary on the Beginning of Ecclesiastes, if, as seems likely, it is in part the work of Dionysius, is quite consistent in style of treatment with a general acceptance of his master's position: and the same may be said of the extracts on Job and on Luke xxii, though here we are on very doubtful ground with regard to authorship.

The indications of Dionysius's position from other sources are still uncertain and conflicting. Procopius of Gaza in his *Commentary on Genesis* chap. iii refers to our author as one of the ecclesiastical writers who have denied the allegorical interpretation of the "coats of skins" (*v.* 21), and this suggests a rejection of the Origenistic view. According to Procopius moreover it was in his Commentary on Ecclesiastes that Dionysius thus attacked his master, and one of the two short fragments assigned to that work by Pitra[1] is distinctly less allegorical than the rest. Again the extract quoted by Anastasius Sinaita and given on p. 199, if genuine as Harnack holds[2], is an unmistakeable claim on Dionysius's part for the literal understanding of another passage in Genesis (chap. ii *vv.* 8, 9) and Anastasius describes it as coming ἐκ τῶν κατὰ 'Ωριγένους. A very similar passage is assigned to Hippolytus in the *Sacred Parallels* of John Damascene (II 787 Le Quien), but the identical passage is found in Cod. Vat. Reg. 7 fol. 41 and in Cod. Synod. Mosq. 385 (10th cent.) ascribed to Dionysius of Alexandria without the words referring to Origen. Once more, the extract given on p. 228 in connexion with the

[1] Viz. that on p. 227 from *Spicil. Solesm.* vol. I p. XVI.   [2] *op. cit.* i 422.

Song of Solomon (viii 5 and i 4) definitely interprets "the coats of skins" in the way that according to Procopius Dionysius denied. Either then Procopius is mistaken or the last-named extract is not genuine or Dionysius changed his views in the course of his studies. In any case Anastasius has probably made a mistake in attributing to Dionysius any such systematic attack on Origen as his phrase ἐκ τῶν κατὰ Ὠριγένους implies. The references to Dionysius as a commentator in Jerome give us no more definite information: in *Ep.* 70. 4 to Magnus he extols his biblical knowledge and general erudition: in *Ep.* 48. 19 to Pammachius he mentions him as one of the authors who have written about Gen. vii 2: and in *Ep.* 49. 3 he mentions him among commentators who have discussed the question of marriage in connexion with 1 Cor. vii.

On the subject of Inspiration we have no ground for thinking that Dionysius adopted an independent position: his Biblical quotations are introduced with the phrases current amongst writers of the third century. In the Commentary on Luke xxii (p. 234) a sentence occurs which Dr Sanday (*Inspiration* p. 36) quotes as agreeing with the views of Origen and others on the complementary inspiration of the Four Evangelists (τὸ οὖν Πνεῦμα τὸ ἅγιον εἰς τοὺς εὐαγγελιστὰς κατανεμηθὲν τὴν πᾶσαν τοῦ Σωτῆρος ἡμῶν διάθεσιν ἐκ τῆς ἑκάστου φωνῆς συντίθησιν) but it is not certain that this (portion of the) fragment is genuine. The general impression therefore left upon us is that Dionysius reverted to the more sober methods of interpreting the Bible that prevailed throughout the Church of his day as a whole, though he approached his master's theories in his usual sympathetic spirit and availed himself of much that was valuable in them.

A table of actual quotations from or reminiscences of Biblical and Apocryphal passages is given on pp. 261 ff., from which it will be seen that they are fairly evenly distributed over the whole range of books. Occasionally the appositeness of the reference is rather questionable, but to a much less degree and much less frequently than is the case with many of the early Christian writers.

18. The earliest list of Dionysius's literary productions, except the scattered references to be found in the *Ecclesiastical History* of Eusebius, is that of Jerome (*de viris illustribus* 69) which we have printed in full on p. xxxv. But the student will find a complete modern list of them together with other valuable matter in Harnack *Altchrist. Lit.* vol. i pp. 409—427 and shorter accounts in Krüger *Early Christian Literature* (Eng. Trans.) and Bardenhewer *Altkirch. Lit.* vol. ii pp. 167—191. There are however several compositions mentioned by Eusebius of which nothing but the title now remains and which we may briefly discuss here.

(*a*) One of the letters mentioned by Eusebius (*H. E.* vii 9. 6) was addressed to Dionysius of Rome (the recipient of at least two other of his letters) and is described as ἡ περὶ Λουκιανοῦ. There was a Carthaginian presbyter of that name, concerning whom Cyprian had occasion to write to the Church at Rome about this time. This Lucian, who was well meaning but somewhat illiterate, had been a friend of Celerinus, and, like him, was a confessor in the Decian persecution; in that capacity he had afterwards granted *libelli* to many of the lapsed, and Cyprian felt called upon to express disapproval of his action (*Ep.* xxvii)[1]. It is quite possible that Dionysius also was brought into some relation with this man, which

[1] See Benson *Cyprian* pp. 70 and 93.

caused him to write to his Roman namesake. On the other hand the successor of Cornelius in the see of Rome (A.D. 253) for a few months bore the name of Lucius, which, as we know from other cases, might easily be confused with Lucianus. One of Cyprian's letters (*Ep.* lxi) addressed to him is still extant[1], and there is no reason why he may not have been the subject of Dionysius's letter. Harnack however (*Altchrist. Lit.* i pp. 411 and 527) inclines to the opinion that the well-known writer and martyr of Antioch is the person meant[2]. This Lucianus, we may note, was, like Dionysius himself, charged with fostering the rise of Arianism by his writings; but it seems to me hardly likely that so long as 50 years before his martyrdom (A.D. 312) he should have become sufficiently prominent to form the subject of a letter from the Bishop of Alexandria to the Bishop of Rome.

(*b*) An ingenious theory has recently been put forward by Dom Morin (*Revue Bénédictine* XVII 1900) that the ἐπιστολὴ διακονικὴ δι' Ἱππολύτου τοῖς ἐν Ῥώμῃ mentioned in Eus. *H. E.* vi 46. 5 was none other than the *Canones Hippolyti*, Rufinus's translation of the doubtful epithet (διακον.) being *de ministeriis*, and that the Canons were afterwards attributed to the church writer Hippolytus through a mistaken identification of the unknown bearer of the missive with the well known author. But Bardenhewer has pointed out[3] that the *Canones Hippolyti*, at least in their present form, belong to the fifth rather than the third century, and he considers that if they had an earlier origin, Hippolytus of Rome has a better claim to them than Dionysius of Alexandria.

---

[1] Benson *Cyprian* pp. 304—7 : cf. Eus. *H. E.* vii 2.
[2] So also Bardenhewer *Altkirch. Lit.* ii 188.
[3] *Altkirch. Lit.* ii 186.

At the same time it must be allowed that, though we should hesitate to accept the learned Benedictine's clever guess, the balance of probability is in favour of assigning to the *Canones Hippolyti* an Egyptian rather than a Roman origin.

(c) Several other letters on discipline are mentioned, and the contents of some of them briefly described, in the same chapter of Eusebius as that last mentioned (vi 46). First comes a letter τοῖς κατ' Αἴγυπτον περὶ Μετανοίας: in it, we are told, Dionysius sets forth his decisions about those who had fallen (i.e. lapsed) and draws up a list of penalties for their transgressions[1]. Then there is a private letter to Conon, an extract from which is perhaps given on pp. 60 ff. and another containing admonitions (ἐπιστρεπτική) to his flock at Alexandria. Moreover, besides the letter addressed to Origen περὶ Μαρτυρίου and that to Cornelius, Bishop of Rome, both of which we have dealt with elsewhere (pp. xxvi and 39), letters to the brethren at Laodicea, whose Bishop was then Thelymidres, and to the Armenians, whose Bishop was Meruzanes, are mentioned in connexion with the same subject of Repentance. And once more, after mentioning the ἐπιστολὴ διακονική already discussed, Eusebius speaks of several other letters to members of the Roman church which are briefly enumerated and described on p. 37. The large collection of Dionysian letters, from which the historian tells us he makes this selection for special mention, may well have been found by him in the Library at Caesarea, as Harnack (*op. cit.* 410) remarks.

(d) The two groups of Baptismal and of Paschal fragments are briefly treated of in their respective Introductions (pp. 40 ff. and 64 ff.). Apparently in con-

[1] ἐν ᾗ τὰ δόξαντα αὐτῷ περὶ τῶν ὑποπεπτωκότων παρατέθειται, τάξεις παραπτωμάτων διαγράψας. Jerome does not mention this letter in his list, nor yet apparently the ἐπιστολὴ ἐπιστρεπτική.

nexion with the latter group Eusebius followed by Jerome tells us of a letter περὶ Σαββάτου and another περὶ Γυμνασίου[1]. Nothing further is known or seems to have been conjectured about the former treatise. A short fragment from the latter will be found on p. 256; Bardenhewer suggests that it perhaps contained warnings against the games and shows of the heathen[2]. Eusebius (*H. E.* vii 26. 2) includes among the πολυεπεῖς λόγοι ἐν ἐπιστολῆς χαρακτῆρι γραφέντες not only the treatise περὶ Φύσεως but also ὁ περὶ Πειρασμῶν dedicated to Euphranor, who was one of the recipients of the Sabellian correspondence. A short extract possibly from this work is to be found on p. 252. On pp. 254 ff. and 257 are printed several more short extracts from works of Dionysius not named by either Eusebius or Jerome (viz. πρὸς Ἀφροδίσιον and περὶ Γάμων) and not otherwise known to us.

19. There are several fragments in Syriac and in Armenian attributed to our author, but of these only three, in the former language, appear to be genuine. One is simply a translation of the letter to Novatian which exists in its original Greek form (pp. 38 and 39): two others are, with the exception of one small portion, only known to us in this version (pp. 45 ff. and 48). The rest of the Syriac and all the Armenian extracts are justly condemned by Harnack (*op. cit.* 425 and 426) on internal grounds.

20. We hear of a church dedicated to St Denys in Alexandria at the beginning of the fourth century (Epiph. *Haer.* lxix), which was destroyed by fire in a tumult in the time of Athanasius (Soz. *Hist. Eccl.* iii 5: Philost. *Hist.* ii 11). But owing probably to the number of more or less famous Saints of his name, there is considerable confusion as to the date of his commemoration in the Kalendar. Oct. 3 and Nov. 17 are

[1] *H. E.* vii 22. 11.   [2] *op. cit.* 190.

the two most usual days, the former more especially in the East where he is honoured as ἱερόμαρτυς, though this date is not confined to the East (cf. Miss. Rom. 1474 (H.B.S.) p. xxii and Whytford's *Martiloge* (H.B.S.) p. 155). Whytford's entry (p. 179) under Nov. 17 is as follows: "In alexander ye feest of saynt Denyse a bysshop and martyr y^t by the emperours Valerian and Galien was by many tormentes put to deth": a statement which is of course not strictly accurate.

21. In conclusion we may observe that, considered as a man of action and a ruler of the Church, Dionysius's personality is no less striking than as a student, a writer and a thinker. He was clearly a strong yet conciliatory administrator of his province as Bishop of Alexandria, just as he had been a competent and successful teacher and director of sacred studies as head of the Catechetical School; one who in each capacity carried on and maintained the great traditions which he inherited from Pantaenus, Clement and Origen, from St Mark and his successors. And not only at home and within his own jurisdiction did he worthily 'magnify his office' and 'make full proof of his ministry,' but his influence made itself felt throughout Christendom. Bishops and clergy from all parts naturally turned to him in their difficulties for advice and guidance; and it is impossible not to feel that his wonderful breadth of judgement and his love of conciliation were of the greatest value to the Church of his day and will remain a model for imitation to each succeeding age. Men will always be tempted as they were in the third century to speak strongly and to act vehemently, where their spiritual beliefs are involved, and we may well pray that God will never fail to raise up amongst the rulers of His Church men of the type of St Denys the Great of Alexandria.

22. The first attempt at making a full collection of our author's remains was undertaken by Simon de Magistris, whose edition was published at Rome 1796. Since then the attempt has not been repeated, though Routh (*Reliquiae Sacrae* tom. iii and iv; Oxford 1846) and Migne (*Patr. Graec.* tom. x) published considerable portions with Latin notes, while Gallandius (*Biblioth. vett. patrum* app. to vol. xiv), Pitra, Mai and (more recently) Holl in vol. v of *Texte und Untersuchungen* (*neue Folge*) have printed a number of extracts whose claims to authenticity are of very varying degrees. Besides those books already mentioned on p. xxix, the student will do well to consult the following recent works:—(1) Förster *de doctrina et sententiis Dionysii*, Berolini 1865; (2) Dittrich *Dionysius der Grosse*, Freiburg i/B. 1867; (3) Roch *Dionysius der Grosse über die Natur*, Leipzig 1882. Dr Salmond has produced a serviceable translation of the fragments in T. & T. Clark's series, Edinburgh 1871, and to this must now be added Dr Gifford's, in his scholarly edition of Eus. *Praepar. Evang.*, Oxford 1903. For the general history of the period much valuable help will be found in Archbishop Benson's *Cyprian*, London 1897, P. Allard *Histoire des Persécutions* vols ii and iii, Paris 1886, and Aubé *L'Église et l'État dans la 2de moitié du 3me Siècle*.

Other works bearing on the special subjects of the different sections will be found mentioned either in the Introductions to those sections or in the notes on the text.

Hieronymi de viris illustribus 69.

Dionysius Alexandrinae episcopus urbis sub Heracla scholam κατηχήσεων presbyter tenuit et Origenis valde insignissimus auditor fuit. Hic in Cypriani et Africanae synodi dogma consentiens de haereticis rebaptizandis plurimas ad diversos misit epistolas quae usque hodie exstant. Et ad Fabium Antiochenae urbis episcopum scripsit de paenitentia et ad Romanos per Hippolytum alteram[1]: et ad Xystum qui Stephano successerat duas epistolas et ad Philemonem et ad Dionysium Romanae ecclesiae presbyteros duas et ad eundem Dionysium postea Romanae urbis episcopum et ad Novatianum causantem quod invitus Romae episcopus ordinatus esset, cuius epistolae hoc exordium est: Dionysius Novatiano fratri salutem. Si invitus, ut dicis, ordinatus es, probabis, cum volens recesseris. Est eius et ad Domitium et Didymum altera epistola et ἑορταστικαὶ de Pascha plurimae declamatorio sermone conscriptae[2] et ad Alexandrinam ecclesiam de exilio[3] et ad Hieracam in Aegypto episcopum et alia de mortalitate et de Sabbato et περὶ γυμνασίου et ad Hermammonem et alia de persecutione Decii et duo libri adversum Nepotem episcopum, qui mille annorum corporale regnum suis scriptis asserebat, in quibus et de Apocalypsi Iohannis diligentissime disputat: et adversus Sabellium et ad Ammonem Berenices episcopum et ad Telesphorum et ad Euphranorem. Et quattuor libri ad Dionysium Romanae urbis episcopum; ad Laodicenses[4] de paenitentia; ad Origenem de martyrio; ad Armenios[5] de paenitentia et de ordine delictorum. De natura ad Timotheum, de temptationibus ad Euphranorem. Ad Basilidem multae quoque epistolae, in quarum una asserit se etiam in Ecclesiastem coepisse scribere commentarios. Sed et adversus Paulum Samosatenum ante paucos dies quam moreretur insignis eius fertur epistola. Moritur duodecimo Gallieni anno.

[1] καὶ ἑτέρα τις ἐπιστολὴ τοῖς ἐν 'Ρώμῃ τοῦ Διονυσίου φέρεται διακονικὴ διὰ 'Ιππολύτου, Eus. *H. E.* vi 46. 5.

[2] τὰς φερομένας ἑορταστικὰς τοτηνικαῦτα συντάττει πανηγυρικωτέρους ἐν αὐταῖς περὶ τῆς τοῦ πάσχα ἑορτῆς ἀνακινῶν λόγους, Eus. *H. E.* vii 20.

[3] This is not apparently the ἄλλη ἐπιστρεπτικὴ πρὸς τὸ κατ' 'Αλεξάνδρειαν ποίμνιον αὐτοῦ of Eus. *H. E.* vi 46. 2.

[4] ὧν προΐστατο Θηλυμίδρης ἐπίσκοπος, *ibid.* 2.

[5] ὧν ἐπεσκόπευε Μερουζάνης, *ibid.* 2.

Διονυσίου λείψανα.

A. LETTERS.

THE text of the fragments in this section was originally based, so far as they are drawn from the *Historia Ecclesiastica* of Eusebius, on that of F. A. Heinichen (Leipzig 1868); but I had the benefit of consulting the Berlin text as it was going through the press, through the kindness of the editor of that work, Dr E. Schwartz, of Göttingen, and of Dr A. Harnack, the Head of the Commission for publishing the series in which it comes. In many cases therefore I have altered my text in accordance with Schwartz's: but as I was not in a position to adopt his names for the MSS employed, I have not altered Heinichen's nomenclature. A new element has however been introduced into the critical apparatus and as a rule where the vague term *nonnulli* occurs as an authority, it is meant that the Berlin reading is accepted and Heinichen's rejected. The student will find a full and interesting account of the MSS employed by Heinichen in Vol. I. pp. xi—xxix of his edition: a list of his abbreviations so far as they affect these extracts is transcribed:—

A   = codex Regius (xiii cent.)
B   = ,, Medicaeus (xvi cent.)
C   = ,, Mazarinaeus (x cent.)
C^a = ,, Castellanus
Cph   = Christophorsoni lectiones
D   = codex Fuketianus (xvi cent.)

E^a	=	codex Parisiensis 1431 (x or xi cent.)
E^b	=	„ „ 1437
F^a	=	„ Savilianus
F^b	=	„ Musei Britannici
G	=	„ Florentinus bibl. Laur. lxx 7 (x cent.)
G^a	=	margo Genevensis editionis
H	=	codex Florent. bibl. Laur. plut. lxx 20 (xi cent.)
J	=	„ bibl. Synod. Moscov. 51 (xi cent.)
K	=	„ „ regiae Dresd. (xii cent.)
L	=	„ „ Caes. Vindobon. 71 (42)
L^r	=	Laemmeri editio (1859—62)
M	=	codex Caes. Vindobon. 174 (332)
N	=	„ Venetus 337 (xv cent.)
Niceph	=	Nicephori Callisti Hist. Eccl. (A.D. 1333)
O	=	codex Venetus 338 (ix or x cent.)
P	=	„ „ 339 (xiv cent.)
Q	=	„ „ 452 (xiv or xv cent.)
R	=	„ Monacensis 380 (xiv cent.)
R^a	=	„ Vaticanus 399 antiquissimus
R^b	=	„ „ Ottob. 108 (xvi cent.)
R^c	=	„ „ 973 (xiv or xv cent.)
Ruf	=	Rufini translatio (circ. A.D. 360)
Schw	=	Schwegleri editio (A.D. 1852)
Steph	=	Stephani editio (xvi cent.)
Stroth	=	Strothii editio (A.D. 1779)
Sync	=	Syncelli Chronographia
Val	=	Valesii editio (A.D. 1659)
Zim	=	Zimmermanni editio (A.D. 1822)

⁂ Of these MSS Heinichen considers C K and R^a the best and O nearly as good as these. Brackets ( ) imply that Heinichen is not sure of the witness of the MSS quoted in these cases.

A. *LETTERS* 3

I

Πρὸς Φαβιανὸν Ἐπιστολή
(Eus. *H. E.* vi 41, 42 and 44)

These very considerable extracts are from Dionysius's Letter to Fabian (or Fabius) bishop of Antioch[1] and begin by describing somewhat fully the sufferings of several confessors and martyrs at Alexandria. Dionysius here explains what is not clear from the Letters to Germanus and to Domitius and Didymus, viz. that the attack upon the Christians had begun in Alexandria a whole year before the decree of Decius (Oct. A.D. 249). This he attributes to the machinations of some local agitator, whom with intentional obscurity he describes as ὁ κακῶν τῇ πόλει ταύτῃ μάντις καὶ ποιητής, ὅστις ἐκεῖνος ἦν. At Alexandria therefore the troubles of the Christians seem to have begun towards the end of A.D. 248, when Philip the Arabian who was popularly supposed to be half a Christian himself was still Emperor[2]. To this earlier persecution Dionysius assigns the martyrdoms of an old man Metras and of a woman Quinta who on two different occasions were stoned to death, and later on of an aged virgin Apollonia who was burnt, and of a certain Sarapion who was thrown to the ground from an upper window in his own house. Besides these four specified cases Dionysius implies that there were a number of smaller acts of cruelty inflicted. Then followed the revolution caused by Decius's overthrow of Philip and usurpation of the supreme power, which gave the Christians at Alexandria, he says, a brief respite.

But what they had suffered hitherto was as nothing to the reign of terror which set in with the promulgation of the new Emperor's edict. The secular historians of the period speak in the highest terms of Decius's ability and virtue, both as a man and as a ruler. But his very ability and old-fashioned standard of morality made him a stern and vigorous opponent of Christianity, and the blow fell with unerring precision on the Christian leaders. In other parts of the empire it was especi-

[1] Though bearing the Bishop's name it seems to have been addressed to the Church at Antioch as a body rather than to the Bishop as an individual; ἀδελφοί, p. 18, but on p. 17 ἀδελφέ.
[2] τῆς βασιλείας ἐκείνης τῆς εὐμενεστέρας ἡμῖν, p. 9.

1—2

ally the bishops who became the first victims, though the great Origen, who was only a presbyter, was included amongst the tortured confessors: at Alexandria there seems to have been a considerable number of well-to-do and prominent citizens[1] in the Christian ranks, and these were at once subjected to a rigorous test with the result, apparently, that they all sooner or later conformed to the requirements of the State. Of the rest some followed their example, some fled, and some resisted openly and suffered the consequences with conspicuous courage[2]. Dionysius gives an account of several such martyrs and confessors of various classes and ages and of both sexes, including the boy Dioscorus and several soldiers.

The persecution was not confined to the city but reached the country towns and villages, and Dionysius mentions two instances of this kind, one of a steward named Ischyrion who was martyred, the other of an aged bishop and his wife who fled to the hills and were never heard of again.

The criticisms which have been passed upon the trustworthiness of these, and, for that matter, of many other *Acta Martyrum*, need not trouble us much. Granted that both Decius and afterwards Valerian were by way of being capable governors and personally upright men and that there was much to be said for the policy which led them to persecute the Christians, granted also that some of Dionysius's descriptions are highly coloured and somewhat exaggerated, these two facts yet remain, that, as the event has proved, neither Decius nor Valerian (the two Emperors with whom we are mainly concerned) was able to read the signs of the times aright and to detect in Christianity the seed of a future world-power, and that, unless we give Dionysius and Eusebius the lie direct, a certain number of Christians were exiled, slain, or otherwise punished for their faith: and no one who is familiar with the records of sufferings made by one of the sufferers himself whether in ancient or in more modern times will expect to find an unimpassioned statement of the bare facts, to which even the scientific historian does not always confine himself. It is noteworthy too, as Allard (*Hist. des Perséc.* ii pp. 356, 357) has remarked, that the 'withholding of the rapid death by the

---

[1] τῶν περιφανεστέρων, p. 10, οἱ ἐν τῷ κόσμῳ προφανέστεροι, p. 67.

[2] Ces chutes si rapides et si faciles contrastent avec le courage montré par les fidèles d'Alexandrie pendant l'émeute de l'année précédente. Allard *Hist. des Perséc.* ii p. 354.

sword as a rule from all except the women, and the inflicting of various slow working and cruel tortures and deaths, as here recorded, are in accordance with what we know of the Egyptians' capacity for enduring pain and their insensibility to ordinary means of intimidation.'

The rest of the letter is concerned with the serious question of the Restoration of the Lapsed. The Church at Antioch was causing at the time some anxiety on the matter. Fabius himself was somewhat inclined, Eusebius tells us[1], to the Novatianist schism which dealt over-severely with the Lapsed, and both Cornelius bishop of Rome and Cyprian bishop of Carthage felt it necessary to communicate with him more than once with regard to it[2]. Dionysius with his usual conciliatory manner puts the subject in the form of questions on which he desires counsel and advice: 'as those who have now attained to the glory of martyrdom and are Christ's assessors in heaven, before they left us, accepted certain of those who had lapsed among us as penitents, are we to associate ourselves with their judgment or to reject it? We desire your opinion on the matter.' The inference obviously is that Dionysius would say that that judgment was accepted at Alexandria and that he suggested a like course at Antioch. It will be observed however that the case here discussed is only that of the weight to be allowed to the action of such confessors as had afterwards become martyrs in the strict sense and not of those who had never attained to that rank; Cyprian and others had to deal with the latter case. Dionysius then cites the example of Sarapion who in a miraculous way was permitted to show that his penitence was accepted by Christ and to survive until he had received the Holy Communion on his deathbed.

[1] ὑποκατακλινομένῳ πως τῷ σχίσματι, p. 19.
[2] See Benson *Cyprian* pp. 167, 168.

Ὁ δ' αὐτὸς (Διονύσιος) ἐν ἐπιστολῇ τῇ πρὸς Φαβιανὸν Ἀντιοχέων ἐπίσκοπον τῶν κατὰ Δέκιον μαρτυρησάντων ἐν Ἀλεξανδρείᾳ τοὺς ἀγῶνας τοῦτον ἱστορεῖ τὸν τρόπον·

(1) Οὐκ ἀπὸ τοῦ βασιλικοῦ προστάγματος ὁ διωγμὸς

4. *Through the machinations of an influential evil-wisher the persecution began at Alexandria some time before the promulgation of the*

Imperial edict.
ib. τοῦ βασιλ. προστάγμ.] viz. the decree of Decius which was first promulgated in the autumn of A.D. 249.

παρ' ἡμῖν ἤρξατο, ἀλλὰ γὰρ ὅλον ἐνιαυτὸν προὔλαβε, καὶ
φθάσας ὁ κακῶν τῇ πόλει ταύτῃ μάντις καὶ ποιητής, ὅστις
ἐκεῖνος ἦν, ἐκίνησε καὶ παρώρμησε καθ' ἡμῶν τὰ πλήθη
τῶν ἐθνῶν, εἰς τὴν ἐπιχώριον αὐτοὺς δεισιδαιμονίαν ἀναρ-
5 ριπίσας. οἱ δὲ ἐρεθισθέντες ὑπ' αὐτοῦ, καὶ πάσης ἐξου-
σίας εἰς ἀνοσιουργίαν λαβόμενοι, μόνην εὐσέβειαν τὴν
θρησκείαν τῶν δαιμόνων ταύτην ὑπέλαβον, τὸ καθ' ἡμῶν
φονᾶν. πρῶτον μὲν οὖν πρεσβύτην Μητρᾶν ὀνόματι
συναρπάσαντες καὶ κελεύσαντες ἄθεα λέγειν ῥήματα, μὴ

1 παρ ημιν] om A Steph post ηρξατο F^b ∥ 4 αυτους] αυτου E^{a}GHOL^r ∥
6 την θρησκ. τ. δαιμ. ταυτην] om G* (και θεραπειαν G^2) ∥ 8 μεν CF^a
Sync om AE^{a}F^{b}GHL^r ∥ Μητραν] Μετραν E^{a}K Val Stroth

1. ὅλον ἐνιαυτ. προὔλ.] 'anticipated it by a whole year.'
2. ὁ κακῶν...ἐκεῖνος ἦν] 'the prophet and poet of evil to this city whoever he was.' D. himself seems afraid to mention the name of the instigator: for he can hardly have been uncertain as to who he was. It is therefore impossible for us to tell now: perhaps it was Sabinus the prefect. Aubé's words are 'À la suite des prédications d'on ne sait quel prophète de carrefour, la populace s'était ruée sur les fidèles' (*L'Église et l'État dans la 2de moitié du 3me siècle* p. 120): Allard paraphrases thus: 'Un méchant devin, mauvais poète, excitait depuis longtemps contre nous les passions superstitieuses de la foule' (p. 265). Ποιητής is used elsewhere by D. to mean 'maker' in a general sense (p. 194 etc.), but here it probably has a double meaning.

4. αὐτούς]=τὰ πλήθη τῶν ἐθνῶν.
ib. δεισιδαιμονίαν] 'A neutral term, taking its colour from the spirit of the writer and the context' (F. Rendall on Acts xvii 22). Here it has evidently the sense of superstition: cf. Theophr. xvi ἀμέλει ἡ δεισιδαιμονία δόξειεν ἂν εἶναι δειλία πρὸς τὸ δαιμόνιον. Allard aptly compares Tac. *Hist.* i 11 *provinciam* (Egypt)...*superstitione ac lascivia*

discordem. The article (τὴν ἐπιχ. δεισιδ.) should be noticed as identifying the expression with the worship of Isis, Osiris and the like: cf. τὴν θρησκείαν τῶν δαιμόνων below.

ib. ἀναρριπίσας] 'having aroused them': the verb properly means 'to fan a flame' or 'rekindle a fire.'

5. πάσης ἐξουσ. λαβ.] 'availing themselves of all (lawful) authority for their unholy doings.' The phrase suggests that they enlisted the Prefect on their side, even if he was not the prime mover himself.

6. μόνην εὐσέβ....φονᾶν] 'considered that the only piety—the (appropriate) worship of their gods—was this, to thirst for our blood.' For the construction compare p. 52 ὄνησιν ... βδελύττεσθαι and p. 91 χάριν—κακόν. There is no need to omit τὴν θρ. τ. δαιμ. ταύτ. as Vales. and Stroth. propose, following G.

8. φονᾶν] is a desiderative verb, ('to desire bloodshed').

ib. *An old man Metras was the first victim: after cruel tortures he was stoned.*

9. συναρπάσαντες] 'carried off,' probably to the tribunal. The εἰδωλεῖον is specified in the next case, apparently in contradistinction to this case.

ib. ἄθεα λέγ. ῥήμ.] So below τὰ

πειθόμενον, ξύλοις τε παίοντες τὸ σῶμα καὶ καλάμοις ὀξέσι τὸ πρόσωπον καὶ τοὺς ὀφθαλμοὺς κεντοῦντες, ἀγαγόντες εἰς τὸ προάστειον κατελιθοβόλησαν. εἶτα πιστὴν γυναῖκα Κοίνταν καλουμένην ἐπὶ τὸ εἰδωλεῖον ἀγαγόντες ἠνάγκαζον προσκυνεῖν, ἀποστρεφομένην δὲ καὶ βδελυττο- 5
μένην ἐκδήσαντες τῶν ποδῶν, διὰ πάσης τῆς πόλεως κατὰ τοῦ τραχέος λιθοστρώτου σύροντες προσαρασσομένην τοῖς μυλιαίοις λίθοις, ἅμα καὶ μαστιγοῦντες, ἐπὶ τὸν αὐτὸν ἀγαγόντες κατέλευσαν τόπον. εἶθ' ὁμοθυμαδὸν ἅπαντες ὥρμησαν ἐπὶ τὰς τῶν θεοσεβῶν οἰκίας, καὶ οὓς ἐγνώριζον 10
ἕκαστοι γειτνιῶντας, ἐπεισπεσόντες ἦγον, ἐσύλων τε καὶ διήρπαζον, τὰ μὲν τιμιώτερα τῶν κειμηλίων νοσφιζόμενοι, τὰ δὲ εὐτελέστερα καὶ ὅσα ἐκ ξύλων ἐπεποίητο, διαρριπτοῦντες καὶ κατακαίοντες ἐν ταῖς ὁδοῖς, ἑαλωκυίας ὑπὸ πολεμίων πόλεως παρεῖχον θέαν. ἐξέκλινον δὲ καὶ ὑπ- 15
ανεχώρουν οἱ ἀδελφοί, κaὶ τὴν ἁρπαγὴν τῶν ὑπαρχόντων,

2 αγαγοντες] απαγαγοντες CF^a Sync επαγαγοντες F^b ‖ 3 ειτα AGH(OR^a) Steph Stroth επειτα cett. ‖ 4 ειδωλειον] ειδωλον AE^{ab}F^b *idola* Ruf ‖ 11 επεισπεσοντες] επισπευδοντες nonnulli ‖ 14 κατακαιοντες] *igni...cremarent* Ruf κατακλωντες nonnulli

τῆς ἀσεβείας κηρύγματα, τὰ δύσφημα ῥήματα, such words as Polycarp was called upon to utter: ὄμοσον τὴν Καίσαρος τύχην, αἶρε τοὺς ἀθέους, λοιδόρησον τὸν χριστόν (Eus. *H. E.* iv 15. 18 and 20). So Pliny (*Ep.* x 97) says that in Bithynia at the beginning of the second century the Christians were required *Christo maledicere*.

1. καλάμοις] 'bulrushes' from the river, whose points are sharp (ὀξέσι). These outrages were apparently perpetrated by the multitude as Metras was dragged along, not inflicted by the orders of the magistrate.

3. *A woman named Quinta was the next: they dragged her to the temple, and when she refused to bow down they hauled her through the streets and stoned her at the same place.*

8. μυλιαίοις] 'as large as millstones.'

9. *Then there was a general rush to plunder the Christians' houses.*

11. ἦγον] 'led to justice,' or possibly here 'plundered,' the last clause of the sentence ἑαλ....θέαν suggesting that D. has in his mind the old military phrase ἄγειν καὶ φέρειν.

12. τὰ μὲν τιμιώτ. κτλ.] The first of these participles (νοσφιζ.) goes with ἐσύλων τε καὶ διήρπαζον, the other two (διαρριπτ. καὶ κατακαί.) with παρεῖχον.

15. *No resistance was offered: one unhappy brother denied his Lord.*

ὁμοίως ἐκείνοις οἷς καὶ Παῦλος ἐμαρτύρησε, μετὰ χαρᾶς προcεΔέΖαντο. καὶ οὐκ οἶδ' εἴ τις, πλὴν εἰ μή πού τις εἰς ἐμπεσών, μέχρι γε τούτου τὸν κύριον ἠρνήσατο. ἀλλὰ καὶ τὴν θαυμασιωτάτην τότε παρθένον πρεσβῦτιν Ἀπολ-
5 λωνίαν διαλαβόντες, τοὺς μὲν ὀδόντας ἅπαντας, κόπτοντες τὰς σιαγόνας, ἐξήλασαν, πυρὰν δὲ νήσαντες πρὸ τῆς πόλεως ζῶσαν ἠπείλουν κατακαύσειν, εἰ μὴ συνεκφωνήσειεν αὐτοῖς τὰ τῆς ἀσεβείας κηρύγματα. ἡ δὲ ὑποπαραιτησαμένη βραχὺ καὶ ἀνεθεῖσα, συντόνως ἐπεπήδησεν εἰς τὸ
10 πῦρ καὶ καταπέφλεκται. Σαραπίωνά τε καταλαβόντες ἐφέστιον, σκληραῖς βασάνοις αἰκισάμενοι, καὶ πάντα τὰ ἄρθρα διακλάσαντες, ἀπὸ τοῦ ὑπερῴου πρηνῆ κατέρριψαν. οὐδεμία δὲ ὁδός, οὐ λεωφόρος, οὐ στενωπὸς ἡμῖν βάσιμος ἦν, οὐ νύκτωρ, οὐ μεθ' ἡμέραν, ἀεὶ καὶ πανταχοῦ πάντων

7 κατακαυσειν CF^{a}GHOR^a Sync Schw L^r κατακαυσαι AE^{a}F^{b}K ‖ 9 συντονως] συντομως AE^a Steph ‖ επεπηδησεν] επηδησεν AE^{a}F^b(OR^a) Steph Stroth L^r ‖ 12 πρηνη] πριvη R^a

1. Παῦλος ἐμαρτύρησε] Heb. x. 34. The Pauline attribution will not escape notice, in which D. apparently follows his master, Origen, and the Alexandrine tradition that at least the thoughts, if not the actual composition, are St Paul's (Eus. *H. E.* vi 25). But it is possible that in quoting loosely from memory D. forgets the particular epistle from which the quotation comes.

2. πλὴν...εἰς] The words seem to imply that D. knew for certain of one who was suspected of having denied the Lord.

3. ἐμπεσών] 'having fallen into their hands' or perhaps (for the simple verb πεσών) 'having lapsed.'

ib. Another notable case was that of the aged virgin Apollonia, whom after many cruelties they burnt to death.

6. νήσαντες] 'having piled up.'

8. τὰ τῆς ἀσεβ. κηρύγμ.] 'the proclamations' (or 'preachings') 'of impiety': see 11. on ἄθεα ῥήματα above.

ib. ὑποπαραιτ. βραχύ] 'having begged for a brief respite.'

10. *Sarapion was thrown headlong from the upper storey of his own house.*

ib. Σαραπίωνα] a common Egyptian name formed from the name of the god Sarapis, who was a later combination of the ancient deities Osiris and Apis. Another Christian of the same name is mentioned at the end of this very epistle.

13. *This terrible state of things filled the city, till the revolution of Decius turned the ferocity of our persecutors against one another.*

ib. ὁδός, λεωφόρος, στενωπός] 'high road, thoroughfare, byway' (or 'alley'): cf. p. 87.

A. LETTERS

κεκραγότων, εἰ μὴ τὰ δύσφημά τις ἀνυμνοίη ῥήματα,
τοῦτον εὐθέως δεῖν σύρεσθαί τε καὶ πίμπρασθαι. καὶ
ταῦτα ἐπὶ πολὺ μὲν ἤκμασε τοῦτον τὸν τρόπον, διαδεξα-
μένη δὲ τοὺς ἀθλίους ἡ στάσις καὶ ὁ πόλεμος ὁ ἐμφύλιος
τὴν καθ' ἡμῶν ὠμότητα πρὸς ἀλλήλους αὐτῶν ἔτρεψε. 5
καὶ σμικρὸν μὲν προσανεπνεύσαμεν, ἀσχολίαν τοῦ πρὸς
ἡμᾶς θυμοῦ λαβόντων, εὐθέως δὲ ἡ τῆς βασιλείας ἐκείνης
τῆς εὐμενεστέρας ἡμῖν μεταβολὴ διήγγελται, καὶ πολὺς ὁ
τῆς ἐφ' ἡμᾶς ἀπειλῆς φόβος ἀνετείνετο. καὶ δὴ καὶ
παρῆν τὸ πρόσταγμα, αὐτὸ σχεδὸν ἐκεῖνο οἷον τὸ προρρηθὲν 10
ὑπὸ τοῦ κυρίου παρὰ βραχὺ τὸ φοβερώτατον, ὡς, εἰ ΔΥΝΑΤΌΝ,
ϲκανδαλίϲαι καὶ τοὺϲ ἐκλεκτούϲ. πλὴν πάντες γε κατε-

3 ηκμασε τουτον τον τροπον BCDF^aGHR^{ab} Schw τουτον τον τροπον ηκμασε K τουτον ηκμασε (L^r ηκμαζε) τον τροπον cett ‖ 4 ο πολεμος] om o E^aF^bGH Sync ‖ 11 κυριου CF^aR^{ab} Schw add ημων AE^aF^bGHK κυριου η O Sync L^r ‖ παρα βραχυ AE^aF^bGHO Sync Steph L^r αποφαινον (-ων) nonnulli

1. τὰ δύσφ. ῥήμ.]: cf. n. above on ἄθεα ῥήματα.
3. διαδεξ. τ. ἀθλίους] 'having succeeded to the attentions of these unhappy men.'
4. ἡ στάσις] viz. the revolt of Decius in Oct. A.D. 249: see Allard *Hist. des Persec.* vol. ii p. 252.
6. *After a brief respite, the issue of the new Emperor's edict plunged us into as evil a plight as ever.*
ib.' ἀσχολίαν...λαβ.] Gen. abs. 'as they found no leisure for raging against us.' ἀσχολίαν λαβεῖν = μὴ σχολὴν λαβεῖν, the gen. τοῦ θυμοῦ depending on the idea of σχολή involved in ἀσχολία.
7. τῆς βασιλ. ἐκ.] i.e. the reign of Philip, who had favoured the Christians.
10. παρῆν τὸ πρόστ....τὸ φοβερώτατον] 'the edict (of Decius) was upon us, and that itself was almost to be compared with that which was foretold by the Lord, well nigh the most terrible (of all things)': a difficult sentence, though the general meaning is well given by Ruf. '*continuo namque crudelissima principum mittuntur edicta, quibus tanta adversum nos ferebatur immanitas ut secundum quod praedictum est a Domino, si fieri potest, scandalizarentur etiam electi.*' Ἐκεῖνο refers to τὸ πρόσταγμα. I have accepted the Berlin reading παρὰ βραχύ instead of ἀποφαῖνον (-ων), though the latter if it governs τὸ φοβερώτατον is much easier to translate, while παρὰ βραχύ seems out of place where it is, and merely a repetition of σχεδόν: Liddell and Scott assign the meaning 'scarcely' to the phrase, but that is surely impossible here. The reference is obviously to Matt. xxiv 24 and Mark xiii 22, but for σκανδαλίσαι the former has πλανᾶσθαι or πλανῆσαι and the latter ἀποπλανᾶν.

12. *The panic was general, but the attack was especially directed against those lay Christians who held any kind of official position under the Emperor. Some of these succumbed, though many remained steadfast.*

πτήχεσαν, καὶ πολλοὶ μὲν εὐθέως τῶν περιφανεστέρων οἱ
μὲν ἀπήντων δεδιότες, οἱ δὲ δημοσιεύοντες ὑπὸ τῶν πράξεων
ἤγοντο, οἱ δὲ ὑπὸ τῶν ἀμφ' αὐτοῖς ἐφείλκοντο, ὀνομαστί τε
καλούμενοι ταῖς ἀνάγνοις καὶ ἀνιέροις θυσίαις προσῄεσαν,
5 οἱ μὲν ὠχριῶντες καὶ τρέμοντες, ὥσπερ οὐ θύσοντες, ἀλλ'
αὐτοὶ θύματα καὶ σφάγια τοῖς εἰδώλοις ἐσόμενοι, ὡς ὑπὸ
πολλοῦ τοῦ περιεστῶτος δήμου χλεύην αὐτοῖς ἐπιφέρεσθαι,
καὶ δήλους μὲν εἶναι πρὸς πάντα δειλοὺς ὑπάρχοντας, καὶ
πρὸς τὸ τεθνάναι καὶ πρὸς τὸ θῦσαι, οἱ δέ τινες ἑτοιμό-
10 τερον τοῖς βωμοῖς προσέτρεχον, ἰσχυριζόμενοι τῇ θρασύ-
τητι τὸ μηδὲ πρότερον Χριστιανοὶ γεγονέναι. περὶ ὧν ἡ
τοῦ κυρίου πρόρρησις ἀληθεστάτη, ὅτι ΔΥϹΚΌΛΩϹ ϹΩΘΉ-
ϹΟΝΤΑΙ. τῶν δὲ λοιπῶν οἱ μὲν εἵποντο τούτοις ἑκατέροις, οἱ

3 αυτοις ACE^aGH αυτους F^{ab}G²KO Val Stroth

1. πολλοὶ μὲν κτλ.] Πολλοὶ μέν are
first subdivided into οἱ μὲν...δεδιότες,
οἱ δὲ...ἤγοντο and οἱ δὲ...προσῄεσαν :
these last are again subdivided into
οἱ μὲν...πρὸς τὸ θῦσαι and οἱ δέ τινες
...γεγονέναι. The remark περὶ ὧν
κτλ. probably applies to all these
περιφανέστεροι.
ib. τῶν περιφανεστ.] So p. 67 ol
ἐν τῷ κόσμῳ προφανέστεροι.
2. ἀπήντων] 'voluntarily obeyed
(the decree),' lit. 'went to meet
(it)': as opposed to ὑπὸ τ. πράξ.
ἤγοντο and ὑπὸ τ. ἀμφ' ἁ. ἐφείλκοντο.
ib. δημοσιεύοντες] 'being in a
public position.' Vales. quotes Aristides in laudat. funeb. Alex. 12 ὁπότε
μὴ δημοσιεύοι, ἢ παρὰ τοῖς δυνασταῖς
ἂν ἦν ἢ ἐν αὐτῷ τοῦ βασιλέως οἴκῳ,
but δημοσιεύειν is usually transitive,
e.g. in Greg. Naz. Or. Theol. i 2 (p. 3
ed. Mason) οἱ τὰ παλαίσματα δημοσιεύοντες. In Eus. H. E. ii 23. 25,
iii 3. 6, 10. 11 it is used in the
passive of the published scriptures.
ib. ὑπὸ τῶν πράξ. ἤγ.] 'were led
by their official duties': for this use
of πράξεις cf. Dem. 1414. 4 ἡ περὶ τὰς
πράξεις ἐπιστήμη and Aristides l.c. 17
τὰ δ' εἰς πράξεις τε καὶ πολιτείας κτλ.

In Eus. H. E. viii 11. 2 we have
the word in the sing. ἐπ' αὐτῆς τῆς
τοῦ καθολικοῦ πράξεως.
3. ὀνομαστί τε κτλ.] Their names
were called out from the official lists
of suspected persons that had been
prepared.
11. ἡ τοῦ κυρίου πρόρρησις] Matt.
xix 23 and 25. The reference, which
is very loosely made here, is to
πλούσιος in the original and suggests
that these renegades were conspicuous for wealth as well as for
worldly position.
13. Of the ordinary Christians
likewise not a few gave way, but
there were many signal instances of
steadfastness.
ib. τῶν δὲ λοιπῶν κτλ.] This sentence answers to πολλοὶ μὲν κτλ.
before and τῶν λοιπῶν is subdivided
into οἱ μὲν...ἑκατέροις, οἱ δὲ ἔφευγον
and οἱ δὲ ἡλίσκοντο.
ib. ἑκατέροις] The two classes are
οἱ μὲν...πρὸς τὸ θῦσαι and οἱ δέ τινες
...προσέτρεχον, unless ἑκατέροις is
used loosely of any one of the various
classes mentioned under the main
heading πολλοὶ μέν above.

A. LETTERS

δὲ ἔφευγον, οἱ δὲ ἡλίσκοντο. καὶ τούτων οἱ μὲν ἄχρι
δεσμῶν καὶ φυλακῆς χωρήσαντες, καί τινες καὶ πλείονας
ἡμέρας καθειρχθέντες, εἶτα καὶ πρὶν ἐπὶ δικαστήριον
ἐλθεῖν, ἐξωμόσαντο, οἱ δὲ καὶ βασάνοις ἐπὶ ποσὸν ἐγ-
καρτερήσαντες, πρὸς τὸ ἑξῆς ἀπεῖπον. οἱ δὲ στερροὶ καὶ 5
μακάριοι στῦλοι τοῦ κυρίου, κραταιωθέντες ὑπ᾽ αὐτοῦ, καὶ
τῆς ἰσχυρᾶς ἐν ἑαυτοῖς πίστεως ἀξίαν καὶ ἀνάλογον δύναμιν
καὶ καρτερίαν λαβόντες, θαυμαστοὶ γεγόνασιν αὐτοῦ τῆς
βασιλείας μάρτυρες. ὧν πρῶτος Ἰουλιανός, ἄνθρωπος
ποδαγρός, μὴ στῆναι, μὴ βαδίσαι δυνάμενος, σὺν ἑτέροις 10
δύο τοῖς φέρουσιν αὐτὸν προσήχθη, ὧν ὁ μὲν ἕτερος εὐθὺς
ἠρνήσατο, ὁ δ᾽ ἕτερος, Κρονίων ὀνόματι, ἐπίκλην δὲ
Εὔνους, καὶ αὐτὸς ὁ πρεσβύτης Ἰουλιανός, ὁμολογήσαντες
τὸν κύριον, διὰ πάσης τῆς πόλεως μεγίστης οὔσης, ὡς ἴστε,
καμήλοις ἐποχούμενοι καὶ μετέωροι μαστιγούμενοι, τέλος 15
ἀσβέστῳ πυρί, περικεχυμένου τοῦ δήμου παντός, κατε-
κάησαν. στρατιώτης τε αὐτοῖς ἀπαγομένοις παραστὰς

3 επι F^{ab}GHKOR^{ab} Sync Schw L^r εις cett ‖ 4 ελθειν F^{ab}GHKOR^{ab} Sync εισελθειν cett ‖ 7 εαυτοις] αυτοις OR^{ab}L^r ‖ 11 αυτον] om FK ‖ 16 πυρι] om nonnulli ‖ κατεκαησαν] κατεταкησαν nonnulli

1. καὶ τούτων] sc. τῶν ἁλισκομένων.
6. στῦλοι] Cf. Gal. ii 9. The title is freely applied in patristic writings to leading Christians: see Suicer *sub vocibus* πέτρος and στῦλος.
8. τῆς βασιλείας μάρτυρες] a rather curious expression, possibly a reminiscence of Acts xxviii 23 or of Rev. i 9.
9. *The case of Julian, a sufferer from gout, and one of his two bearers, Cronion: they both were tortured and burnt to death in public; the other bearer apostatized at once.*
11. προσήχθη] *inductus est*, was brought up for trial.
12. ἐπίκλην δὲ Εὔνους] 'surnamed Eunous (well-disposed),' perhaps the second was his baptismal name.
15. μετέωροι] i.e. while they were on the camels' backs.
16. ἀσβέστῳ πυρί] Cf. Matt. iii 12. D. seems to use the phrase simply to express 'fierce fire': see Heinichen's note *in loc.* Vales. quotes '*in menaio ad diem* 30 *Octobr., ubi mentio fit horum martyrum Juliani, Cronionis et Macarii, legitur*: ἀσβέστου ζέοντος κατ᾽ αὐτῶν ἐκχυθέντος,' as if D.'s phrase was considered equivalent to ἡ ἄσβεστος (τίτανος) = unslaked lime.
17. *Besas, a soldier who resisted Julian's persecutors, was beheaded.*
ib. στρατιώτης] Lower down (p. 15) we find a whole quaternion (σύνταγμα στρατιωτικόν) becoming champions of the Faith. For the special difficulties of soldiers in this connexion cf. Benson *Cyprian* pp. 62, 63.

καὶ τοῖς ἐφυβρίζουσιν ἐναντιωθείς, ἐκβοησάντων ἐκείνων
προσαχθεὶς ὁ ἀνδρειότατος ὁπλόμαχος τοῦ θεοῦ Βησᾶς,
κἂν τῷ μεγάλῳ πολέμῳ τῷ περὶ τῆς εὐσεβείας ἀριστεύσας,
ἀπετμήθη τὴν κεφαλήν. καί τις ἕτερος τὸ μὲν γένος
5 Λίβυς, τὴν δὲ προσηγορίαν ἅμα καὶ τὴν εὐλογίαν ἀληθὴς
Μάκαρ, προτροπῆς αὐτῷ πολλῆς ὑπὸ τοῦ δικαστοῦ πρὸς
ἄρνησιν γενομένης, οὐχ ὑπαχθείς, ζῶν καταπέφλεκται.
Ἐπίμαχός τε μετ' αὐτοὺς καὶ Ἀλέξανδρος μετὰ πολὺν ὂν
ἔμειναν δεσμῶται χρόνον, μυρίας διενεγκόντες ἀλγηδόνας,
10 ξυστῆρας, μάστιγας, πυρὶ ἀσβέστῳ καὶ οὗτοι διεχύθησαν.
καὶ σὺν αὐτοῖς γυναῖκες τέσσαρες· Ἀμμωνάριόν τε ἁγία
παρθένος, πάνυ φιλονείκως αὐτὴν ἐπὶ πλεῖστον τοῦ δικαστοῦ βασανίσαντος, ἅτε προαποφηναμένην, ὅτι μηδὲν ὧν

2 Βησᾶς] om O(Rᵃ) Ruf Lʳ ‖ 6 Μάκαρ] *Macarius* Ruf ‖ 8 πολυν] ου
πολυν A Steph ‖ 9 εμειναν] ενεμειναν AEᵃK ‖ 11 Αμμωναριον] Αμμωναρια
FᵇO Sync Ruf Nic ‖ 13 οτι] ως A Steph ‖ μηδεν] μηδεν αν K

2. Βησᾶς] The name (*gen.* Βη-
σᾶτος) occurs in Papyri Oxyrh.
vol. iii pp. 194 and 230 (2nd cent.).
Besas occurs also in Ammian. Marc.
xix 12 pp. 227 ff. (Vales.). For the
circumstances attending the martyrdom of Besas we may compare the
case of Alban as given by Bede
Hist. Eccl. i 7.

4. *A Libyan named Macar was
burned alive.*

5. ἀληθὴς Μάκαρ] with an evident allusion to Matt. v 11 and Luke
vi 22. Rufinus gives the name as
Macarius. The ancients were ex-
ceedingly fond of these plays upon
names, and instances occur in all
kinds of literature (secular and religious).

8. *Epimachus and Alexander
endured a similar fate.*

10. ξυστῆρας] Lat. *ungulas*, iron
claws with which the flesh was torn
off. In Eus. *de mart. Pal.* vii 6 the
word seems used of the persons who
applied the torture, ταῖς κατὰ τῶν
πλευρῶν αὐτοῦ δι' ἐπιμόνων καὶ φιλο-
νείκων ξυστήρων (βασάνοις).

ib. διεχύθησαν] 'were consumed'
(lit. dissolved). In Herod. iii 16
the verb is used of a mummy crum-
bling away. Here Allard (*Hist. des
Persée.* ii p. 375) translates it 'con-
sumés par ce liquide incendie (de
chaux vive),' taking ἀσβέστῳ πυρί
in the sense mentioned above (p.
11).

11. *Four women also suffered martyrdom with them: Ammonarion a
virgin, the aged Mercuria, Dionysia
the mother of many children (and a
second Ammonarion).*

ib. γυναῖκες τέσσαρες] Only three
are mentioned by name in the existing Greek text; but Rufinus adds
the words *et alia Ammonaria*: hence
Heinichen following Valesius's suggestion inserts the Greek equivalent
in his text.

Ἀμμωνάριον] occurs as a woman's
name in Papyri Oxyrh. vol. i p. 158
and ii p. 248.

A. LETTERS

ἐκεῖνος κελεύοι φθέγξαιτο, ἀληθεύσασα τὴν ἐπαγγελίαν
ἀπήχθη· αἱ δὲ λοιπαί, ἡ σεμνοτάτη πρεσβῦτις Μερκουρία,
καὶ ἡ πολύπαις μέν, οὐχ ὑπὲρ τὸν κύριον δὲ ἀγαπήσασα
ἑαυτῆς τὰ τέκνα Διονυσία [καὶ Ἀμμωνάριον ἑτέρα], καται-
δεσθέντος εἰς ἀνήνυτον ἔτι βασανίζειν καὶ ὑπὸ γυναικῶν 5
ἡττᾶσθαι τοῦ ἡγεμόνος, σιδήρῳ τεθνᾶσι, μηκέτι βασάνων
πεῖραν λαβοῦσαι· τὰς γὰρ ὑπὲρ πασῶν ἡ πρόμαχος
Ἀμμωνάριον ἀνεδέδεκτο βασάνους. Ἥρων δὲ καὶ Ἀτὴρ
καὶ Ἰσίδωρος Αἰγύπτιοι καὶ σὺν αὐτοῖς παιδάριον ὡς
πεντεκαιδεκαέτης ὁ Διόσκορος παρεδόθησαν. καὶ πρῶτον 10

1 φθέγξαιτο] φθέγξεται E^a φεγξεται AE^b pro φθέγξεται ‖ 2 σεμνοτατη
CF^{ab}GHK Sync *anus venerabilis* Ruf σεμνοπρεπεστατη AE^a ‖ 4 και Αμμ.
ετερα=*et alia Ammonaria* Ruf sed desunt in omnibus codd ‖ 8 βασανους
CF^aGHKR^{ab} om AE^aF^bO Sync L^r ‖ Ατηρ] Αστηρ Sync Nic *Arsinus*
Ruf

1. φθέγξαιτο] Strictly this should mean 'had said,' but the necessary sense is 'would say'; D. often omits ἂν where classical usage requires it.

ib. ἀληθεύσ. τὴν ἐπ.] 'verified her promise'; the transitive use of ἀληθεύειν is illustrated by Liddell and Scott: we have ἐπαληθ. with accus. on p. 75.

2. ἀπήχθη] 'was led off' (to punishment).

6. τοῦ ἡγεμόνος] sc. the Prefect: see n. p. 30.

8. *Three Egyptians, Heron, Ater and Isidore, and with them Dioscorus, a boy of 15, were given up: the men were cruelly tortured and burnt; Dioscorus after a strict examination, in which he stood his ground nobly, was let go and is still with us.*

ib. Ἀτήρ] The name is variously given (see crit. appar. above), until in the Roman Martyrology it becomes *Arsenius*. 'The xiiij daye of December... At alexander the feest of saynt Heron, saynt Arseny, saynt Ysidour and a childe called saynt Dioscour that by myracle was delyvered for that tyme where the other after many turmentes were brent.' Whytford's *Martiloge* (H.B.S.) p. 193.

9. Αἰγύπτιοι] D. always uses this word to distinguish the natives of Egypt proper from the Alexandrians who were largely of Greek extraction and from the Libyans. Interesting illustrations of this distinction are furnished by the recently edited *papyri*, e.g. Amherst Papyri, vol. ii p. 33 (2nd century B.C.) καὶ ἐν τῇ πόλει ἠναγκάσθην ὑπὸ τῶν Αἰγυπτίων ἀποστατῶν ἐνέγκαι τὰς συγγραφάς, Oxyrrhynchus Papyri vol. i p. 72 οἱ μὲν ἐν τῇ πόλει πραγματευόμενοι ἀπὸ Φαρμοῦθι νεομηνίας, οἱ δὲ ἐν Αἰγύπτῳ ὁμοίως ἀπὸ Παχών, cp. infra οἱ ἀπὸ τῆς Αἰγύπτου νομικοί, vol. ii p. 161 l. 33 ὁ τῶν Αἰγυπτίων νόμος, l. 34 ἐξ Αἰγυπτιακῶν προσώπων, l. 40 τὰ πρόσωπα Αἰγύπτια ὄντα, p. 215 καὶ μηδένα ἕτερον οἰκεῖν παρ' ἐμοὶ μήτε ἐπίξενον μήτε Ἀλεξανδρέα μηδὲ ἀπελεύθερον μήτε Ῥωμανὸν μηδὲ Αἰγύπτιον.

10. παρεδόθησαν] 'were given up (by others).'

τὸ μειράκιον λόγοις τε ἀπατᾶν ὡς εὐπαράγωγον καὶ βασάνοις καταναγκάζειν ὡς εὐένδοτον πειρωμένου, οὔτε ἐπείσθη οὔτε εἶξεν ὁ Διόσκορος. τοὺς δὲ λοιποὺς ἀγριώτατα καταξήνας, ἐγκαρτερήσαντας πυρὶ καὶ τούτους παρα-
5 δέδωκε· τὸν δὲ Διόσκορον ἐλλαμπρυνάμενόν τε δημοσίᾳ, καὶ σοφώτατα πρὸς τὰς ἰδίας πεύσεις ἀποκρινάμενον θαυμάσας παρῆκεν, ὑπέρθεσιν φήσας εἰς μετάνοιαν αὐτῷ διὰ τὴν ἡλικίαν ἐπιμετρεῖν. καὶ νῦν ὁ θεοπρεπέστατος σὺν ἡμῖν ἐστὶ Διόσκορος, εἰς μακρότερον τὸν ἀγῶνα καὶ
10 διαρκέστερον μείνας τὸν ἆθλον. Νεμεσίων δέ τις, κἀκεῖνος Αἰγύπτιος, ἐσυκοφαντήθη μέν, ὡς δὴ σύνοικος λῃστῶν, ἀπολυσάμενος δὲ ταύτην παρὰ τῷ ἑκατοντάρχῳ τὴν ἀλλοτριωτάτην κατ' αὐτοῦ διαβολήν, καταμηνυθεὶς ὡς Χριστιανός, ἧκε δεσμώτης ἐπὶ τὸν ἡγούμενον. ὁ δὲ ἀδικώ-
15 τατος διπλαῖς αὐτὸν ἢ τοὺς λῃστὰς ταῖς τε βασάνοις καὶ ταῖς μάστιξι λυμηνάμενος, μεταξὺ τῶν λῃστῶν κατέφλεξε, τιμηθέντα τὸν μακάριον τῷ τοῦ χριστοῦ παραδείγματι.

4 παραδεδωκε CF*KR** παρεδωκε AE*F*OL* ‖ 12 απολυσαμενος BCDF**GHKR** Schw αποδυσαμενος AE*O Sync *quo crimine abluto* Ruf ‖ 13 κατ αυτου] om E*F*L*

2. πειρωμένου] sc. τοῦ ἡγεμόνος.
4. καταξήνας] 'having torn their flesh,' with ξυστῆρες, etc.
5. δημοσίᾳ...πρὸς τ. ἰδ. π.] i.e. at a public examination and in the course of private questionings.
7. παρῆκεν] 'pardoned' (Lat. *condonavit*).
8. καὶ νῦν ὁ θ. σὺν ἡμῖν ἐστὶ Δ.] i.e. some time between the end of the Decian persecution and the recrudescence of troubles under Valerian. Nothing further is known of Dioscorus: the presbyter of that name (p. 67) is doubtless another person.
10. *Another Egyptian, Nemesion, was first brought up before the centurion on a false charge of brigandage and acquitted, and then taken before the prefect as a Christian. He was burnt between two thieves after the example of his Master, after enduring twice as many torments as they.*
11. ἐσυκοφαντήθη] 'maliciously informed against' (Lat. *iniuste deferebatur*): cf. p. 193 τίς τῶν συκοφαντῶν and p. 56 Χριστὸν ὡς ἀνηλεῆ συκοφαντοῦντι.
12. τῷ ἑκατοντάρχῳ] viz. to the military officer for the martial offence of brigandage, whereas he is taken before the Prefect on the civil charge of being a Christian, which meant sedition.
15. διπλαῖς...ἢ] 'twice as many... as.' Διπλοῦς used (like διπλάσιος) as a comparative is quite a classical construction.
17. τῷ τ. χρ. παραδείγμ.] Cf. Matt. xxvii 38, Mark xv 27, Luke xxiii 33, John xix 18. The expression ('being honoured, happy man, by the

A. LETTERS 15

ἀθροον δέ τι σύνταγμα στρατιωτικόν, Ἄμμων καὶ Ζήνων
καὶ Πτολεμαῖος καὶ Ἰγγένης, καὶ σὺν αὐτοῖς πρεσβύτης
Θεόφιλος, εἱστήκεισαν πρὸ τοῦ δικαστηρίου· κρινομένου
δή τινος ὡς Χριστιανοῦ καὶ πρὸς ἄρνησιν ἤδη ῥέποντος,
ἐπρίοντο οὗτοι παρεστηκότες, καὶ τοῖς τε προσώποις 5
ἐνένευον, καὶ τὰς χεῖρας ἀνέτεινον καὶ συνεσχηματίζοντο
τοῖς σώμασιν. ἐπιστροφῆς δὲ πάντων πρὸς αὐτοὺς γενομένης, πρίν τινας αὐτῶν ἄλλους λαβέσθαι, φθάσαντες ἐπὶ
τὸ βάθρον ἀνέδραμον, εἶναι Χριστιανοὶ λέγοντες, ὡς τόν τε
ἡγεμόνα καὶ τοὺς συνέδρους ἐμφόβους γενέσθαι, καὶ τοὺς 10
μὲν κρινομένους εὐθαρσεστάτους ἐφ' οἷς πείσονται φαί-
νεσθαι, τοὺς δὲ δικάζοντας ἀποδειλιᾶν. καὶ οὗτοι μὲν ἐκ

11 ευθαρσεστατους] ευθαρσοτατους CF^aGH ‖ 12 δικαζοντας AE^aGHO
Sync δοκιμαζοντας CF^aKR^{ab} δικαστας Nic *persecutoribus* Ruf

example of the Christ') is a condensed one after D.'s manner; 'by
the example' = 'by being allowed to
follow the example.' The honour
of thus being allowed to imitate
Christ in their death is often alluded to in the Acts of the Martyrs
e.g. it is recorded of Probus in the
time of Diocletian that when they
pierced his hands with hot nails,
he exclaimed δόξα σοι κύριε Ἰησοῦ
Χριστέ, ὅτι καὶ τὰς ἐμὰς χεῖρας κατη-
ξίωσας ἡλωθῆναι ὑπὲρ τοῦ ὀνόματός
σου (Ruinart *Acta Sinc.* p. 440): cf.
ibid. pp. 60, 70 etc.

1. *Four soldiers, Ammon, Zeno,
Ptolemaeus and Ingenuus, and with
them an old man Theophilus, were
standing before the tribunal when a
Christian was being examined. Their
feelings were so aroused that they drew
attention on themselves, but before
they could be seized they leapt upon
the prisoner's stand, shouting out
that they were Christians, to the encouragement of the accused and the
terror of the Council. They were
then carried off to martyrdom.*

ib. σύνταγμα στρατιωτικόν] 'tur-
mam militum' Ruf. 'The xx daye
of December... At Alexander the
feest of saynt Ammony, saynt Zenony,
saynt Tholomy, Saint Ingeny and
saynt Theophyly all martyrs that
for confortynge a martyr that faynted
in his turmentes were all taken and
after greuous turmentes put to
death.' Whytford's *Martiloge*
(H.B.S.) p. 196.

2. Ἰγγένης] Lat. *Ingenuus*.

5. ἐπρίοντο] 'were provoked':
the compound διαπρίεσθαι is found
in this sense in Acts v 33 and vii 54,
but the simple verb is also so used
in the Classics.

6. συνεσχημ. τ. σώμ.] 'expressed
their feelings by their bodily ges-
tures.' The middle verb (συσχηματίζεσθαι) occurs with the dative twice
in N.T. (Rom. xii 2 and 1 Pet. i 14),
but the dative is differently used
there.

9. τὸ βάθρον] Lat. *catasta* or
ambo ('*subsellium in quo sedebat
reus*' Vales.).

10. τοὺς συνέδρους] These were the
assessores (πάρεδροι) who formed the
Prefect's *concilium*: cf. Acts xxv 12
and see Le Blant *Actes des Martyrs* pp. 53, 54.

δικαστηρίων ἐνεπόμπευσαν καὶ ἠγαλλιάσαντο τῇ μαρτυρίᾳ, θριαμβεγοντοc αὐτοὺς ἐνδόξως τοῦ θεοῦ.

(2) Ἄλλοι δὲ πλεῖστοι κατὰ πόλεις καὶ κώμας ὑπὸ τῶν ἐθνῶν διεσπάσθησαν, ὧν ἑνὸς παραδείγματος ἕνεκεν ἐπιμνησθήσομαι. Ἰσχυρίων ἐπετρόπευέ τινι τῶν ἀρχόντων ἐπὶ μισθῷ. τοῦτον ὁ μισθοδότης ἐκέλευσε θῦσαι, μὴ πειθόμενον ὕβριζεν, ἐμμένοντα προεπηλάκιζεν· ὑφισταμένου, βακτηρίαν μεγίστην λαβών, διὰ τῶν ἐντέρων καὶ τῶν σπλάγχνων διώσας ἀπέκτεινε. τί δεῖ λέγειν τὸ πλῆθος τῶν ἐν ἐρημίαιc καὶ ὄρεcι πλανηθέντων, ὑπὸ λιμοῦ καὶ δίψης καὶ κρύους καὶ νόσων καὶ ληστῶν καὶ θηρίων διεφθαρμένων; ὧν οἱ περιγενόμενοι τῆς ἐκείνων εἰσὶν ἐκλογῆς καὶ νίκης μάρτυρες. ἓν δὲ καὶ τούτων εἰς δήλωσιν ἔργον παραθήσομαι. Χαιρήμων ἦν ὑπέργηρως τῆς Νείλου

3 δὲ] τε Rᵃ ‖ 6 εκελευσε CFᵃᵇGHKORᵃ Sync Schw Lʳ εκελευε cett ‖ 12 περιγενομενοι] υπεργενομενοι Val sed sine ullis codd ut videtur

1. ἐνεπόμπευσαν] 'walked in brave procession.'
2. θριαμβεύοντος] carries on the metaphor of ἐνεπόμπευσαν, 'God then giving them a glorious triumph.' Cf. 2 Cor. ii 14: the use of θριαμβεύειν in Col. ii 15 is in a different connexion. Field's *Notes on Trans. of N.T.* p. 181 should be consulted. Ruf.'s version here, *deo ita triumphante per sanctos suos*, is loose and inaccurate.
3. *There were many other examples from the towns and villages: one of whom was Ischyrion, a steward, slain by his master's own hand for refusing to sacrifice.*
4. διεσπάσθησαν] 'were torn asunder': but the only case he adduces was not actually so treated, though fatally injured in his body.
5. ἐπετρόπευε]'acted as steward' (ἐπίτροπος, Lat. *procurator*): see Becker's *Gallus* pp. 204, 205.
6. ὁ μισθοδότης] i.e. the master here, who was τῶν ἀρχόντων τις, the word being purposely used in connexion with ἐπὶ μισθῷ above, to show the hold he had over his steward. The word usually signifies 'a paymaster.'
7. ὑφισταμένου] gen. abs. 'when he stood his ground.'
9. *A large number fled to the deserts and mountains and were no more heard of; some perished from various causes and among them probably Chaeremon, the aged bishop of Nilopolis, and his wife; others were captured by Saracens, and either retained by them or ransomed at high prices. All this shows the extent of our calamities.*
10. τῶν ἐν ἐρ. κ. ὄρ. πλανηθ.] Cf. Heb. xi 38.
12. ὧν οἱ περιγεν. κτλ.] 'the survivors of whom bear witness to their election and victory.' Ἐκλογῆς suggests that they showed themselves worthy of being among the elect (i.e. Christians).
14. τῆς Νείλου καλ....πόλεως] Nilo-

A. LETTERS

καλουμένης ἐπίσκοπος πόλεως. οὗτος εἰς τὸ Ἀράβιον ὄρος ἅμα τῇ συμβίῳ ἑαυτοῦ φυγὼν οὐκ ἐπανελήλυθεν, οὐδὲ ἐδυνήθησαν ἰδεῖν οὐκέτι καίτοι πολλὰ διερευνησάμενοι οἱ ἀδελφοί, οὔτε αὐτοὺς οὔτε τὰ σώματα εὗρον. πολλοὶ δὲ οἱ κατ' αὐτὸ τὸ Ἀραβικὸν ὄρος ἐξανδραποδισθέντες ὑπὸ 5 βαρβάρων Σαρακηνῶν· ὧν οἱ μὲν μόλις ἐπὶ πολλοῖς χρήμασιν ἐλυτρώθησαν, οἱ δὲ μέχρι καὶ νῦν οὐδέπω. καὶ ταῦτα διεξῆλθον οὐ μάτην, ἀδελφέ, ἀλλ' ἵνα εἰδῇς ὅσα καὶ ἡλίκα δεινὰ παρ' ἡμῖν συνέβη· ὧν οἱ μᾶλλον πεπειραμένοι πλείονα ἂν εἰδεῖεν. 10

Εἶτα τούτοις ἐπιφέρει μετὰ βραχέα λέγων·

1 επισκοπος πολεως] πολεως επισκοπος AE^aF^b Steph Stroth L^r ‖ Αραβιον] Αραβων F^aK Αραβικον F^b ‖ 3 εδυνηθησαν CF^aKOR^{ab} Schw L^r ηδυν. cett ‖ 4 ευρον BCDF^{ab}GHKR^{ab} om AE^a αυτων Sync *nec ipsos ultra quisquam neque corpora eorum potuit invenire* Ruf ‖ 6 ων οι μεν] om ων nonnulli ‖ 7 ελυτρωθησαν KOR^{ab}L^r ελυτρωθηντο cett ‖ και νυν CF^aGHKOR^{ab} Schw L^r om και cett

polis, mod. *Illahûn*, on the W. of the Nile, some 50 miles below Memphis.

1. τὸ Ἀράβιον ὄρος] apparently the range of hills to the E. of the Nile, which Herod. (ii 8) calls by this name, but which Ptolemy and others call Τρωικόν.

2. ἅμα τῇ συμβίῳ] On the marriage of the clergy at this time see Bingham's *Antiqq.* Bk IV chap. v § 5. Σύμβιος ὁ and ἡ is used of husband and wife in later Greek.

ib. οὐκ ἐπανελήλυθεν] 'never returned.' It is impossible to give an exact force to the perfect here or elsewhere. D. constantly uses perfects and pluperfects almost indiscriminately with aorists and imperfects, as the reader will find. The rise of monasticism is traced by some to such fugitive Christians, who never returned from the Egyptian deserts; but the suggestion in the case of Chaeremon is that he perished.

4. οὔτ' αὐτ. οὔτε τὰ σώμ.] a curious expression to convey the idea of 'neither alive nor dead.'

5. κατ' αὐτὸ τὸ Ἀρ. ὄρος] 'on those very Arabian hills.' For this later use of αὐτός see p. 24 n.; here αὐτὸ τό is virtually equivalent to the classical τὸ αὐτό.

ib. ἐξανδραποδισθέντες] Cf. p. 26.

6. Σαρακηνῶν] This is probably the earliest extant mention of the Saracens—at least by that name. Of secular historians Ammianus Marcellinus a century later mentions them in connexion with the reign of Marcus Aurelius (A.D. 147—180), and Spartianus a little later than D.; see Gibbon *Decline and Fall* chap. L. They seem however to be identical with the Σκηνῖται Ἄραβες mentioned by Strabo.

9. ὧν οἱ μ. πεπειρ. κτλ.] 'of which those who have had more experience will know of more cases' (i.e. than D.): for this use of πεπειραμένοι cf. Thucyd. ii 44.

F. 2

(3) Αὐτοὶ τοίνυν οἱ θεῖοι μάρτυρες παρ' ἡμῖν, οἱ νῦν τοῦ χριστοῦ πάρεδροι καὶ τῆς βασιλείας αὐτοῦ κοινωνοὶ καὶ μέτοχοι τῆς κρίσεως αὐτοῦ καὶ συνδικάζοντες αὐτῷ, τῶν παραπεπτωκότων ἀδελφῶν τινὰς ὑπευθύνους τοῖς τῶν 5 θυσιῶν ἐγκλήμασι γενομένους προσελάβοντο, καὶ τὴν ἐπιστροφὴν καὶ μετάνοιαν αὐτῶν ἰδόντες, δεκτήν τε γενέσθαι δυναμένην τῷ μὴ Βογλομένῳ καθόλου τὸν θάνατον τοῦ ἁμαρτωλοῦ ὡς τὴν μετάνοιαν δοκιμάσαντες εἰσεδέξαντο καὶ συνήγαγον καὶ συνέστησαν, καὶ προσευχῶν αὐτοῖς καὶ 10 ἑστιάσεων ἐκοινώνησαν. τί οὖν ἡμῖν, ἀδελφοί, περὶ τούτων συμβουλεύετε; τί ἡμῖν πρακτέον; σύμψηφοι καὶ ὁμογνώμονες αὐτοῖς καταστῶμεν, καὶ τὴν κρίσιν αὐτῶν καὶ τὴν

12 και την χαριν] η την χ. AE^a Steph Stroth

1. *The martyrs, while still on earth, befriended and held communion with those who had lapsed but shown signs of penitence for their apostasy. Ought we to ratify their judgement or reverse it?*
ib. παρ' ἡμῖν] Supply ἔτι ὄντες, 'whilst still amongst us.'
ib. νῦν τ. χρ. πάρεδροι] The opinion that those who suffered martyrdom for Christ at once passed to heaven and became partners of His throne (based upon passages like Matt. xix 28, 1 Cor. vi 2, 3) was general amongst the early Fathers (e.g. Tert. *de resurr. carnis* 43, *de anima* 55).
2. τῆς βασ. αὐτ. κοιν.] Cf. Rev. iii 21.
4. ὑπευθ....γεν.] 'who had rendered themselves liable to the charge of having done sacrifice.'
5. προσελάβοντο] 'espoused their cause,' 'befriended': cf. Rom. xiv 1, 3.
ib. τὴν ἐπιστρ.... δοκιμάσαντες] 'and seeing their conversion and repentance and approving it as fit to be accepted by Him who desireth not at all the death of the sinner so much as his repentance.' The reference is to Ezek. xviii 23, xxxiii 11 and 2 Pet. iii 9; καθόλου seems to represent the θελήσει θελήσω of the first passage; ὡς is in accordance with the LXX text of Ezek.=τοσοῦτον ὡς: τὴν μετάνοιαν comes from 2 Pet. iii 9 rather than from Ezek.
9. συνήγαγον] 'summoned them to assemblies (of the brethren)': cf. p. 29; but the word is not to be pressed as if they assumed episcopal authority.
ib. συνέστησαν] 'introduced or commended them (to the brethren)': cf. Rom. xvi 1 and 2 Cor. iii 1 (συστατικαὶ ἐπιστολαί).
ib. προσευχ. αὐτ. κ. ἑστιάσ. ἐκοιν.] Vales. considers that this only implies restoration to communion with the brethren in their private prayers and social gatherings, restoration to public communion at the Holy Eucharist being ultimately within the province of the Bishop. This latter statement is of course true (see below, note on ἐδεῖτο), but the action of the martyrs must, I think, have been taken with a view to communion in its full sense and the necessary stages of this restoration were so well known as to be taken for granted.
10. τί...συμβουλεύετε;] For the point raised see Introduction to this Letter, p. 5.
12. αὐτοῖς] i.e. τοῖς θείοις μάρτυσι.

A. LETTERS

χάριν φυλάξωμεν, καὶ τοῖς ἐλεηθεῖσιν ὑπ' αὐτῶν χρηστευσώμεθα; ἢ τὴν κρίσιν αὐτῶν ἄδικον ποιησώμεθα, καὶ δοκιμαστὰς αὐτοὺς τῆς ἐκείνων γνώμης ἐπιστήσωμεν, καὶ τὴν χρηστότητα λυπήσωμεν, καὶ τὴν τάξιν ἀνασκευάσωμεν;

Ταῦτα δὲ εἰκότως ὁ Διονύσιος παρατίθεται, τὸν περὶ τῶν ἐξησθενηκότων κατὰ τὸν τοῦ διωγμοῦ καιρὸν ἀνακινῶν λόγον.

Τῷ δ' αὐτῷ τούτῳ Φαβίῳ ὑποκατακλινομένῳ πως τῷ σχίσματι καὶ Διονύσιος ὁ κατ' Ἀλεξάνδρειαν ἐπιστείλας, πολλά τε καὶ ἄλλα περὶ μετανοίας ἐν τοῖς πρὸς αὐτὸν γράμμασι διελθών, τῶν τε κατ' Ἀλεξάνδρειαν ἔναγχος τότε μαρτυρησάντων τοὺς ἀγῶνας διιών, μετὰ τῆς ἄλλης ἱστορίας πρᾶγμά τι μεστὸν θαύματος διηγεῖται, ὃ καὶ αὐτὸ ἀναγκαῖον τῇδε παραδοῦναι τῇ γραφῇ, οὕτως ἔχον·

(4) Ἓν δέ σοι τοῦτο παράδειγμα παρ' ἡμῖν συμβεβηκὸς ἐκθήσομαι. Σαραπίων τις ἦν παρ' ἡμῖν πιστὸς γέρων, ἀμέμπτως μὲν τὸν πολὺν διαβιώσας χρόνον, ἐν δὲ τῷ πειρασμῷ πεσών. οὗτος πολλάκις ἐδεῖτο, καὶ οὐδεὶς προσεῖχεν αὐτῷ, καὶ γὰρ ἐτεθύκει· ἐν νόσῳ δὲ γενόμενος τριῶν ἑξῆς ἡμερῶν ἄφωνος καὶ ἀναίσθητος διετέλεσε.

2 αδικον] αδεκτον AE^a Steph Stroth ‖ 7 σχισματι] σχηματι E^aF^bGH ‖ 14 Σαραπιων] Σεραπιων RL^r

3. αὐτούς]=ἡμᾶς αὐτούς: cf. p. 61.
4. τὴν τάξιν ἀνασκευάσωμεν;] 'shall we reverse their arrangement?' (hardly 'overturn the established order,' as Salmond, which is not in question here).
13. *An instance cited which had come under D.'s own cognizance. Sarapion, an old man, after a long and blameless life, fell under temptation and sacrificed. No one listened to his entreaties for restoration. At last he fell sick unto death: rallying a little on the fourth day, he sent his young grandson to ask the presbyter to come and absolve him. It was night, and the presbyter also was sick, but, acting upon D.'s recent instructions to the clergy in such cases, he gave the lad some of the consecrated Bread and told him to moisten it and put it in the sick man's mouth. This he did and shortly afterwards Sarapion expired, a clear sign that his life had been spared till his sin should be forgiven him in the act of Communion.*

16. ἐδεῖτο] sc. to be received back to communion. The request of the laity and the consent of the Bishop or *vice versa* were necessary for this, unless (as here) the penitent was in extreme danger: cf. Cypr. *Ep.* lxiiii 1 (ed. Hartel) *quae res nos satis movit, recessum esse a decreti nostri auctoritate, ut ante legitimum et plenum tempus satisfactionis et sine petitu et conscientia plebis, nulla infirmitate urgente ac necessitate cogente, pax ei concederetur.*

18. ἀναίσθητος] act. 'unconscious,' 'insensible.'

βραχὺ δὲ ἀνασφήλας τῇ τετάρτῃ προσεκαλέσατο τὸν
θυγατριδοῦν· καὶ Μέχρι τίνος, φησίν, ὦ τέκνον, με κατέχετε; δέομαι, σπεύσατε καί με θᾶττον ἀπολύσατε· τῶν
πρεσβυτέρων μοί τινα κάλεσον. καὶ ταῦτα εἰπών, πάλιν
5 ἦν ἄφωνος. ἔδραμεν ὁ παῖς ἐπὶ τὸν πρεσβύτερον· νὺξ δὲ
ἦν, κἀκεῖνος ἠσθένει. ἀφικέσθαι μὲν οὖν οὐκ ἐδυνήθη,
ἐντολῆς δὲ ὑπ' ἐμοῦ δεδομένης, τοὺς ἀπαλλαττομένους τοῦ
βίου, εἰ δέοιντο, καὶ μάλιστα εἰ καὶ πρότερον ἱκετεύσαντες
τύχοιεν, ἀφίεσθαι, ἵν' εὐέλπιδες ἀπαλλάττωνται, βραχὺ
10 τῆς εὐχαριστίας ἔδωκεν τῷ παιδαρίῳ, ἀποβρέξαι κελεύσας

2 με] ante φησιν AE^aR Nic Steph Stroth om F^bOL^r ‖ κατεχετε
AE^aF^bRO Nic *detinetis* Ruf κατεχεις BCDF^aGHKR^ab ‖ 6 ουν] om OL^r
venire non potuit Ruf ‖ 9 τυχοιεν] add των θειων δωρων της μεταδοσεως
αξιουσθαι και ουτως DF^aG (marg) H (marg) om ABCE^aF^bO Sync ‖
βραχυ] add τι R ‖ 10 εδωκεν] επεδωκεν AE^a Steph Val εδωκεν cett

1. ἀνασφήλας] 'having recovered from his coma.'
2. κατέχετε, ἀπολύσατε] The plurals are to be noticed in contradistinction to the singular (κάλεσον) which follows: 'you' = 'all you who are concerned in my case,' 'thou' = ὁ θυγατριδοῦς, ὁ παῖς.
7. ἐντολῆς ὑπ' ἐμοῦ δεδομ.] See extract on p. 60.
8. εἰ...ἱκετεύσαντες τύχοιεν] 'if they chanced to have made supplication (for it).'
9. ἀφίεσθαι] 'should be absolved.'
ib. βραχὺ τῆς εὐχαρ.] Scudamore (*Not. Euchar.* p. 885) thinks it 'natural to suppose that' the reserved Sacrament was in this, as in other cases, 'kept in the Church itself'; but as the priest was too sick to go out, it seems more likely that he kept it in his own house. As to the question whether βραχὺ τῆς εὐχαρ. was the consecrated Bread only or 'the Body steeped in the Blood and then dried,' the student may again with advantage consult Scudamore pp. 879—81.

'We know,' he says, 'that this' (sc. steeping the Bread in the Wine and then drying it) 'was done at Alexandria at a later period and is done there still; but we may doubt whether the custom had been introduced as early as the middle of the 3rd century.'

10. ἔδωκεν τῷ παιδαρίῳ] Justin Martyr (*Apol.* i 65) speaks of the deacon as carrying away the Eucharist to the absent. We are told too of a Christian of Rome named Tharsicius in A.D. 257, whose murderers found him 'carrying about him the sacraments of the Lord's body' (Damasus *Carm.* 35 and Surius Aug. 2 *Acta Stephani* p. 13). Here we have a boy allowed in case of need to carry a portion of the Eucharist to the sick man's house. 'In the West this office was early restrained to priests....The existence of several prohibitions however seems to imply that there was great laxity on this point as time passed on.' Scudamore *Not. Euchar.* p. 884

ib. ἀποβρέξαι ... ἐπιστάξαι] 'to moisten it' (prob. with water) 'and

καὶ τῷ πρεσβύτῃ κατὰ τοῦ στόματος ἐπιστάξαι. ἐπανῆκεν ὁ παῖς φέρων· ἐγγύς τε γενομένου, πρὶν εἰσελθεῖν, ἀνενέγκας πάλιν ὁ Σαραπίων· Ἧκες, ἔφη, τέκνον; καὶ ὁ μὲν πρεσβύτερος ἐλθεῖν οὐκ ἠδυνήθη, σὺ δὲ ποίησον ταχέως τὸ προσταχθέν, καὶ ἀπάλλαττέ με. ἀπέβρεξεν ὁ παῖς 5 καὶ ἅμα τε ἐνέχεε τῷ στόματι, καὶ μικρὸν ἐκεῖνος καταβροχθίσας εὐθέως ἀπέδωκε τὸ πνεῦμα. ἆρ' οὐκ ἐναργῶς διετηρήθη καὶ παρέμεινεν, ἕως λυθῇ, καὶ τῆς ἁμαρτίας ἐξαλειφθεὶς ἐπὶ πολλοῖς οἷς ἔπραξε καλοῖς ὁμολογηθῆναι δυνηθῇ; 10

Ταῦτα ὁ Διονύσιος.

1 επισταξαι] αυτου σταξαι R ‖ 3 ανενεγκας] ανανευσας ORLʳ *respiciens* Ruf ‖ 6 καταβροχθισας] καταβροχθησας R

to drop it' (as a liquid or the liquid from it) 'into the mouth.' Ἐπιστάξαι is lower down altered to ἐνέχεε.

3. ἀνενέγκας] intrans. 'having revived,' quite a classical use of the act. for the passive: e.g. Herod. iii 22 εἰ μὴ τῷ πόματι ἀνέφερον. Ruf. seems to have read ἀνανεύσας with OR.

6. καταβροχθίσας] 'having swallowed.' καταβροχθίζειν is a later form derived from καταβρέχειν.

ib. καὶ ἅμα τε...καί] Lat. *et simul ac* ('and as soon as').

8. τῆς ἁμαρτ. ἐξαλειφθ.] Cf. Acts iii 19.

9. ὁμολογηθῆναι] It seems best to take this as meaning 'to be acknowledged (by the Lord)' with a reference to Matt. x 32, though ὁμολογεῖν is there constructed not with a direct accus. but with ἔν τινι. Others have taken it as dep. = *confiteri*, Christophorsonus *in numerum confessorum referri*.

II

Πρὸς Γερμανὸν Ἐπιστολή

(Eus. *H. E.* vi 40, vii 11. 1—19)

A certain Bishop Germanus had accused Dionysius of a great dereliction of duty under stress of persecution: he appears to have charged him, in somewhat violent terms[1], with having neglected to convene the brethren for exhortation etc.,

[1] ὁμόσε χωρήσω τῇ Γερμανοῦ βίᾳ, p. 28.

when persecution broke out, and with consulting his own safety rather than the general weal by hasty flight. The two groups of fragments which follow are given by Eusebius at two separate points in his Ecclesiastical History and deal with two different stages in Dionysius's episcopate.

The first group of fragments refers to what took place when the persecution broke out at Alexandria towards the end of A.D. 249 under Decius. At that time Dionysius acknowledges that he and his household took to flight but not till he had waited four days at his house, expecting the emissary of the Governor Sabinus: and even then against his will and only in obedience to some Divine intimation, the exact nature of which he does not specify. He was however pursued by the soldiers and carried off to Taposiris under arrest: the strange tale of his escape from that place through the instrumentality of Timotheus (ὁ παῖς) will be found narrated with much liveliness in the text: and with that escape the first set of fragments ends. We are left to infer from this extract that the Roman authorities took no further steps to recover their prisoner, while from the letter to Domitius and Didymus we gather that he remained in exile[1] till the persecution subsided in A.D. 253 and it was safe for him to return to Alexandria and resume the charge of his flock. The point of Dionysius's narrative so far is apparently to show that he displayed no undue haste in taking to flight on this earlier occasion and that nothing but a Divine interposition saved him from being brought up before the Governor. On the other hand the fact that the authorities so soon relinquished their pursuit does not show excessive zeal on their part in the cause of persecution.

The second group of fragments is concerned with the public examination of Dionysius with four or five of his companions before the Governor, Aemilian, some four years later, when Valerian had decided to revive the persecution of Christians (A.D. 257). This extract is of special value because Dionysius appears to quote the *ipsissima verba* of the official record of the trial. It is extremely interesting to observe how reasonable and patient the Prefect thinks he is in dealing with these well-meaning but unreasonable and therefore dangerous Christians:—I have discoursed to you before, he says, on the clemency of the Emperors and you have only now to follow a natural course and show your loyalty to them by an act of homage to their deities. If you will only do that, you can worship as

[1] ἐν ἐρήμῳ καὶ αὐχμηρῷ τῆς Λιβύης τόπῳ κατακεκλείσμεθα, p. 67.

A. LETTERS 23

many other gods as you like. Dionysius's reply is inexplicable to him:—We are perfectly loyal folk, he says in effect, and thoroughly believe that the Emperors are under the protection of Divine power but there is only one God, who protects them and us and we cannot worship any other. In that case, the Prefect replies, you shall not remain in Alexandria but shall be banished to a remote place in accordance with the Emperors' instructions: and you shall have no opportunity nor permission to conduct public services or to convene assemblies of your people. Whereupon, ill as he was, Dionysius had, without a day's delay, to hurry off into exile first at Cephro and then in the district called Colluthion. In both places, however, he was able to hold assemblies of the brethren and to conduct services, while the assemblies in the city were not discontinued: and thus in spite of all his losses and privations (such as Germanus himself could never have felt) he was able to continue a large portion of his episcopal duties throughout. The last is the main point which Dionysius wishes to make in refutation of his accuser's charge, and though the more general questions raised by the quotations from the official record are, I think, of greater importance and interest to us to-day, yet to the fair-minded student Dionysius's defence of his conduct as Bishop of so important a see under stress of persecution is of considerable interest, the more especially when we remember that it forms the reason why Eusebius included these particular extracts in his history and thus earned our gratitude on the wider issue.

Τά γέ τοι κατὰ Διονύσιον ἐκ τῆς πρὸς Γερμανὸν ἐπιστολῆς αὐτοῦ παραθήσομαι, ἔνθα τοῦτον περὶ ἑαυτοῦ λέγων ἱστορεῖ τὸν τρόπον·

(1) Ἐγὼ δὲ καὶ ἐνώπιον τοῦ θεοῦ λαλῶ, καὶ αὐτὸς οἶδεν εἰ ψεύδομαι· οὐδὲ μίαν ἐπ' ἐμαυτοῦ βαλλόμενος οὐδὲ 5

4 και ενωπ. om και B Val ‖ 5 ει E^aH(OR^a)L^r: οτι ου cett ‖ ουδε μιαν BCD Val L^r ουδεμιαν cett ‖ εμαυτου omnes codd et edd exceptis BC (εμαυτον) εμαυτω D Sync ‖ βαλλομενος] βουλομενος AE^a Steph βαλομενος L^r tacite

4. *Account of D.'s flight on the first intimation of the Decian persecution and of Sabinus the Prefect sending a frumentarius to search for him. The hand of God was plainly visible in all this.*
ib. ἐνώπιον τοῦ θεοῦ...εἰ ψεύδ.] Cf. Gal. i 20.
5. οὐδὲ μίαν ἐπ' ἐμ. βαλλ.] 'not at all on my own judgement.' The

ἀθεεὶ πεποίημαι τὴν φυγήν. ἀλλὰ καὶ πρότερον τοῦ κατὰ
Δέκιον προτεθέντος διωγμοῦ Σαβῖνος αὐτῆς ὥρας φρου-
μεντάριον ἔπεμψεν εἰς ἀναζήτησίν μου, κἀγὼ μὲν τεσσάρων
ἡμερῶν ἐπὶ τῆς οἰκίας ἔμεινα, τὴν ἄφιξιν τοῦ φρουμενταρίου
5 προσδοκῶν. ὁ δὲ πάντα μὲν περιῆλθεν ἀνερευνῶν, τοὺς
ποταμούς, τὰς ὁδούς, τοὺς ἀγρούς, ἔνθα κρύπτεσθαί με ἢ
βαδίζειν ὑπενόησεν, ἀορασίᾳ δὲ εἴχετο, μὴ εὑρίσκων τὴν

5 τοὺς ποταμοὺς τὰς ὁδοὺς CFᵃKRᵃᵇ Schw τὰς ὁδοὺς τοὺς ποτ. cett

phrase βάλλεσθαι ἐπί with gen. (not dat. or accus.) is found several times in Herodotus (e.g. iii 71, 155, iv 160 etc.). For the absolute use of the fem. accus. μίαν cf. Aesch. *Ag.* 1345 δευτέραν πεπληγμένος, Aristoph. *Vesp.* 595 μίαν δικάσαντας etc.

1. ἀθεεί] 'without Divine intimation' or 'guidance': so below κελεύσαντός μοι μεταστῆναι τοῦ θεοῦ and τῆς τοῦ θεοῦ προνοίας ἔργον.

ib. πεποίημαι] 'I made good.'

ib. καὶ πρότερον] 'on a former occasion also' (as well as on the occasion of the flight just mentioned). He means that he is going to review his conduct, not only during the persecution of Valerian, but also during the Decian.

ib. τοῦ κ. Δ. προτεθ. διωγμοῦ] is gen. abs. and not governed as some have thought by πρότερον.

2. Σαβῖνος] was the Prefect of Egypt under Decius: so below τὰ ἐπὶ Δεκίου καὶ Σαβίνου συμβάντα μοι (p. 36).

ib. αὐτῆς ὥρας] 'at that very hour,' i.e. as soon as ever the persecution under Decius had been decided upon. For this use of αὐτός cf. *Evang. Petri* § 5 and *Clem. Hom.* xx 16 quoted by Robinson (*Study of the Gospels* p. 106) with reference to Luke x 21. 'Here,' he says, 'αὐτός is used, as it is in modern Greek, as a demonstrative pronoun.'

ib. φρουμεντάριον] Lat. *frumentarius*, a kind of soldier employed on secret service by the Emperors and their provincial Governors. They were finally abolished by Constantine. The name is a strange one for such service: perhaps they were so called 'because it was their duty to collect information in the same way as it was the duty of other officers called by the same name to collect corn' (Smith's *Dict. of Class. Antiqq.*), or possibly because the same person who collected corn was also sometimes employed to collect information. See Allard *Hist. des Perséc.* vol. ii p. 361 n.

3. τεσσάρων ἡμερῶν] not 'within four days,' as in classical Greek, but 'for a period of four days': so τριῶν ἑξῆς ἡμερῶν (p. 19).

4. ἐπὶ τῆς οἰκίας] 'at my house,' not 'on my housetop,' or 'homewards,' as in classical Greek.

5. τοὺς ποταμούς] i.e. some of the various streams which form the Delta of the Nile, as Allard *Hist. des Perséc.* vol. ii p. 361 n., has pointed out. These were of course highways for traffic.

7. μὴ εὑρίσκων] 'never lighting on my house.' The student must not expect always to find a hypothetical force in μή with a participle in later Greek. This force was probably more or less confined to Attic Greek and is not essential to the particle.

A. LETTERS 25

οἰκίαν· οὐ γὰρ ἐπίστευσεν οἴκοι με διωκόμενον ἔχειν. καὶ μόλις μετὰ τὴν τετάρτην ἡμέραν κελεύσαντός μοι μεταστῆναι τοῦ θεοῦ καὶ παραδόξως ὁδοποιήσαντος ἐγώ τε καὶ οἱ παῖδες καὶ πολλοὶ τῶν ἀδελφῶν ἅμα συνεξήλθομεν. καὶ ὅτι τῆς τοῦ θεοῦ προνοίας ἔργον ἐκεῖνο γέγονε, τὰ ἐξῆς 5 ἐδήλωσεν, ἐν οἷς τάχα τισὶ γεγόναμεν χρήσιμοι.

Εἶτά τινα μεταξὺ εἰπὼν τὰ μετὰ τὴν φυγὴν αὐτῷ συμβεβηκότα δηλοῖ, ταῦτα ἐπιφέρων·

(2) Ἐγὼ μὲν γὰρ περὶ ἡλίου δυσμὰς ἅμα τοῖς σὺν ἐμοὶ γενόμενος ὑπὸ τοῖς στρατιώταις εἰς Ταπόσιριν ἤχθην, ὁ δὲ 10 Τιμόθεος κατὰ τὴν τοῦ θεοῦ πρόνοιαν ἔτυχε μὴ παρὼν μηδὲ καταληφθείς. ἐλθὼν δὲ ὕστερον εὗρε τὸν οἶκον ἔρημον, καὶ φρουροῦντας αὐτὸν ὑπηρέτας, ἡμᾶς δὲ ἐξηνδραποδισμένους.

1 επιστευσεν BCDFªORᵃᵇLʳ Schw επιστευεν cett ‖ εχειν BCDFªKRᵃᵇ Schw μενειν cett ‖ 10 γενομενος] γενομενοις FªGH Sync

1. ἔχειν] intrans., to be taken with οἴκοι, 'to keep at home.'
2. κελ. μοι μεταστ.] Κελεύειν with dat. and inf. seems to have been an Epic usage revived in later Greek.
4. οἱ παῖδες] probably 'my sons,' not, as others have held, 'my pupils' (i.e. of the Catechetical School), nor 'my servants.' We know that the Egyptian clergy were often married men at this time (see e.g. p. 17 ἅμα τῇ συμβίῳ), and, though D.'s wife is never mentioned, it is the most natural inference that these were his children, and perhaps that he was now a widower: see General Introduction, p. xii.
6. τισὶ γεγ. χρήσιμοι] a modest way of saying that his life was spared for future usefulness on behalf of the Church.
9. *D. and his companions are captured and taken to Taposiris. Timothy happened to be elsewhere at the time.*

10. ὑπὸ τοῖς στρατ.] is here to be taken with γενόμενος, 'having fallen into the hands of the soldiers': cf. p. 254 ὑπὸ τοῖς ἐχθροῖς...ἐστίν.
ib. Ταπόσιριν] mod. *Abusîr*, a town (πολίχνιον) some 25 miles S.W. of Alexandria, close to the sea-coast, and at the end of a long arm of the lake Mareotis.
11. Τιμόθεος] one of the παῖδες mentioned above: D. addressed his book περὶ Φύσεως to him (Eus. *H. E.* vii 26).
12. τὸν οἶκον] i.e. the house from which D. had fled at Alexandria.
13. ὑπηρέτας] probably 'municipal servants,' while the prisoners themselves were in charge of soldiers: cf. p. 67 ἀπαγομένους ὑπὸ ἑκατοντάρχου καὶ στρατηγῶν καὶ τῶν σὺν αὐτοῖς στρατιωτῶν καὶ ὑπηρετῶν.
ib. ἡμᾶς δὲ ἐξηνδραποδ.] 'and (heard) that we had been carried off prisoners (to Taposiris)' (lit. 'reduced to utter slavery'), rather a strong word to use for an ordinary

Καὶ μεθ' ἕτερά φησι·

(3) Καὶ τίς ὁ τῆς θαυμασίας οἰκονομίας αὐτοῦ τρόπος; τὰ γὰρ ἀληθῆ λεχθήσεται. ἀπήντα τις τῶν χωρικῶν ὑποφεύγοντι τῷ Τιμοθέῳ καὶ τεταραγμένῳ, καὶ τὴν αἰτίαν τῆς
5 ἐπείξεως ἐπύθετο. ὁ δὲ τἀληθὲς ἐξεῖπε, κἀκεῖνος ἀκούσας (ἀπῄει δὲ εὐωχησόμενος γάμους· διαπαννυχίζειν γὰρ αὐτοῖς ἐν ταῖς τοιαύταις συνόδοις ἔθος), εἰσελθὼν ἀπήγγειλε τοῖς κατακειμένοις. οἱ δὲ ὁρμῇ μιᾷ καθάπερ ὑπὸ συνθήματι πάντες ἐξανέστησαν, καὶ δρόμῳ φερόμενοι τάχιστα ἧκον,
10 ἐπεισπεσόντες τε ἡμῖν ἠλάλαξαν, καὶ φυγῆς εὐθέως τῶν φρουρούντων ἡμᾶς στρατιωτῶν γενομένης ἐπέστησαν ἡμῖν, ὡς εἴχομεν ἐπὶ τῶν ἀστρώτων σκιμπόδων κατακείμενοι. κἀγὼ μέν, οἶδεν ὁ θεός, ὡς λῃστὰς εἶναι πρότερον ἡγούμενος ἐπὶ σύλησιν καὶ ἁρπαγὴν ἀφικομένους, μένων ἐπὶ

3 απηντα BCDFᵃK Val Stroth απηντατο GRᵃᵇ Sync Schw Val απηντετο AEᵃHO Steph L^r απηντα τοτε F^b ‖ χωρικων BCDRᵃᵇ Schw χορητικων K χωριτων cett ‖ 7 εν—συνοδοις om L^r tacite ‖ 8 οι δε] om δε A Steph Val ‖ υπο συνθηματι AF^bGO Steph L^r απο συνθηματος BCDFᵃHK Val Hein υπο συνθηματος Eᵃ ‖ 10 επεισπεσοντες AEᵃF^bG επισπευδοντες CFᵃHK Sync Val

arrest: perhaps the ἐξ in this instance only suggests the idea of 'removal' or 'change of condition.' Cf. p. 17.

2. *The story of D.'s strange rescue by the peasants who were assembled at a wedding feast, through one of the guests meeting Timothy and hearing that he was in the soldiers' hands.*

ib. αὐτοῦ] sc. τοῦ θεοῦ.

3. τις τῶν χωρικῶν] 'a rustic,' not 'one of the inhabitants' or 'natives,' as some take the words. 'Si mal disposés que les habitants des campagnes égyptiennes fussent à l'égard des fidèles, ils n'avaient guère moins d'antipathie pour les représentants de l'autorité romaine.' Allard *Hist. des Perséc.* vol. ii p. 360. Allard also quotes (p. 363) a passage from Apuleius *Metamorphoses* lib. ix, in illustration of the peasants siding against the soldiery.

ib. ὑποφεύγοντι] Whether Timothy was making off to join D. at Taposiris or was fleeing in another direction, is not clear.

7. τοῖς κατακειμένοις] 'to those reclining (at the feast)': down below κατακείμενοι = 'lying down' in the ordinary sense.

10. ἠλάλαξαν] In 1 Cor. xiii 1 the word is applied to κύμβαλον, 'loud clanging,' but here it has its older meaning of 'yelling' (as of persons in battle).

12. σκιμπόδων] 'wooden bedsteads,' such as the poorer classes or the ascetics would use. Socrates slept on one (Plat. *Protag.* 310 C; Aristoph. *Nub.* 709).

τῆς εὐνῆς, ἧς ἤμην γυμνὸς ἐν τῷ λινῷ ἐσθήματι, τὴν δὲ
λοιπὴν ἐσθῆτα παρακειμένην αὐτοῖς ὤρεγον. οἱ δὲ ἐξ-
ανίστασθαί τε ἐκέλευον καὶ τὴν ταχίστην ἐξιέναι. καὶ
τότε συνείς, ἐφ᾽ ᾧ παρῆσαν, ἀνέκραγον δεόμενος αὐτῶν καὶ
ἱκετεύων ἀπιέναι καὶ ἡμᾶς ἐᾶν, εἰ δὲ βούλονταί τι χρηστὸν 5
ἐργάσασθαι, τοὺς ἀπάγοντάς με φθάσαι καὶ τὴν κεφαλὴν
αὐτοὺς τὴν ἐμὴν ἀποτεμεῖν ἠξίουν. καὶ τοιαῦτα βοῶντος,
ὡς ἴσασιν οἱ κοινωνοί μου καὶ μέτοχοι πάντων γενόμενοι,
ἀνίστασαν πρὸς βίαν, κἀγὼ μὲν παρῆκα ἐμαυτὸν ὕπτιον
εἰς τοὔδαφος, οἱ δὲ διαλαβόντες χειρῶν καὶ ποδῶν σύροντες 10
ἐξήγαγον. ἐπηκολούθουν δέ μοι οἱ τούτων πάντων γενόμενοι μάρτυρες, Γάιος, Φαῦστος, Πέτρος, Παῦλος, οἳ καὶ
ὑπολαβόντες με φοράδην ἐξήγαγον τοῦ πολιχνίου καὶ ὄνῳ
γυμνῷ ἐπιβιβάσαντες ἀπήγαγον.

Ταῦτα περὶ ἑαυτοῦ ὁ Διονύσιος. 15

Περὶ δὲ τοῦ κατ᾽ αὐτὸν διωγμοῦ σφοδρότατα πνεύσαντος οἷα σὺν
ἑτέροις ὁ αὐτὸς διὰ τὴν εἰς τὸν τῶν ὅλων θεὸν εὐσέβειαν ὑπέστη, δηλώ-
σουσιν αἱ αὐτοῦ φωναί, ἃς πρὸς Γερμανὸν τῶν κατ᾽ αὐτὸν ἐπισκόπων

1 ης] om E^aF^bG Sync || 8 μου] μοι R^a || 10 χειρων] add των K || 11 γενο-
μενοι CF^aKR^{ab} Steph Val Schw om AE^aF^bGH || 13 εξηγαγον] επηγαγον K ||
14 απηγαγον] ανηγαγον Hein

1. ἧς] elliptical for ἐφ᾽ ἧς.
ib. ἤμην] acc. to Cobet (*Var. Lect.* 57) a Macedonian form of the imperf. of εἰμί, but found in Xen. *Cyr.* vi 1. 9 etc. as well as in N.T.
ib. γυμνός] explained by the words which follow (ἐν τῷ λινῷ ἐσθήμ.), 'undressed, save for my linen undergarment (or χιτών).' Cf. Mark xiv 52.
ib. τὴν δὲ λοιπήν] The δέ here is strictly superfluous, as only a participle (μένων) has preceded it, and ὤρεγον is the predicate of the sentence: the omission of ἧς after εὐνῆς, which has considerable MSS authority, would simplify the sentence.
3. τὴν ταχίστην] 'as quickly as possible': cf. note on μίαν, p. 24.
4. ἐφ᾽ ᾧ παρῆσαν] seems certainly a reminiscence of Matt. xxvi 50, and so far supports the dat. (ἐφ᾽ ᾧ) as against the accus. (ἐφ᾽ ὅ) accepted by Westcott and Hort.
7. βοῶντος] sc. μου gen. abs., though more strictly it should have been accus. after ἀνίστασαν.
12. Γάιος, Φαῦστος, Πέτρος, Παῦλος] The same four are mentioned as his companions on this occasion in the letter to Domitius and Didymus, p. 67.
13. φοράδην] 'in their arms,' or perhaps 'rapidly,' not *in sella*, as Vales. translates it.
14. γυμνῷ] 'bare backed,' 'unsaddled.'

κακῶς ἀγορεύειν αὐτὸν πειρώμενον ἀποτεινόμενος, τοῦτον παρατίθεται τὸν τρόπον·

(4) Εἰς ἀφροσγΝΗΝ δὲ κινδυνεύω πολλὴν καὶ ἀναισθησίαν ὄντως ἐμπεσεῖν, εἰς ἀνάγκην συμβιβαζόμενος τοῦ διηγεῖσθαι τὴν θαυμαστὴν περὶ ἡμᾶς οἰκονομίαν τοῦ θεοῦ. ἀλλ᾽ ἐπεὶ μγcτΗριόν, φησι, Βαcιλέως κργψαι καλόν, τὰ δὲ ἔργα τοῦ θεοῦ ἀνακαλγπτειν ἔνδοξον, ὁμόσε χωρήσω τῇ Γερμανοῦ βίᾳ. ἧκον πρὸς Αἰμιλιανὸν οὐ μόνος· ἠκολούθησαν δέ μοι συμπρεσβύτερός τέ μου Μάξιμος, καὶ διάκονοι Φαῦστος, Εὐσέβιος, Χαιρήμων· καί τις τῶν ἀπὸ Ῥώμης παρόντων ἀδελφῶν ἡμῖν συνεισῆλθεν. Αἰμιλιανὸς δὲ οὐκ εἶπέ μοι

6 επει AE^aF^b Nic Steph Stroth επειδη cett || 7 ανακαλυπτειν] CF^abGHO ανακηρυττειν E^a ανακρυπτειν A

3. *Account of D. with four or five others being brought before Aemilian the prefect, and being charged not to hold meetings of the brethren.*
ib. Εἰς ἀφροσύνην...εἰς ἀνάγκην] Cf. 2 Cor. xi 1, 17, 21, xii 6, 11.
ib. ἀναισθησίαν] 'want of right feeling': on p. 52 the word is applied to the Sabellians' want of perception about the Holy Spirit.
6. μυστήριον κτλ.] Tob. xii 7 (ἐνδόξως B).
7. τῇ Γερμανοῦ βίᾳ] a poetic periphrase, = 'our violent accuser, Germanus.'
8. Αἰμιλιανόν] The Prefect of Egypt of this name, to whom this extract refers, must not be confused with the Aemilian, who, as governor of Pannonia and Moesia, after defeating the Goths (A.D. 253), was declared Emperor in place of the murdered Gallus at the dictation of his army, and wore the purple for a brief four months, till Valerian in his turn, having defeated and put him to death, assumed the imperial power. Our Aemilian in 260 or thereabouts tried unsuccessfully to seize the supreme power in Egypt: Treb. Pollio (*Thirty Tyrants* 22, 23) calls him *ducem*, which seems to denote 'Sirdar' rather than 'Khedive,' and distinguishes him from *curator quidam, qui Alexandriam tum regebat*, but his authority is no greater than that of the present passage.
ib. συμπρεσβύτερός μου] Cf. 1 Pet. v 1 etc. and p. 50; also Eus. *H. E.* v 16. 5 παρόντος καὶ τοῦ συμπρεσβυτέρου ἡμῶν Ζωτικοῦ τοῦ Ὀτρηνοῦ, and vii 20 ἄλλην τοῖς κατ᾽ Ἀλεξάνδρειαν συμπρεσβυτέροις ἐπιστολὴν διαχαράττει (Διονύσιος). The Latin equivalent *compresbyter* occurs frequently in Cyprian's letters: see Watson *Studia Bibl. et Eccl.* iv pp. 258, 259.
9. Μάξιμος] Cf. p. 67: he succeeded D. as the 14th Bishop of Alexandria.
ib. Φαῦστος] suffered martyrdom in the persecution of Diocletian in extreme old age (Eus. *H. E.* vii 12. 26, viii 13. 7): prob. he is the same as the Φαῦστος who was one of D.'s companions in exile (p. 27).
10. Εὐσέβιος] afterwards became bp of Laodicea in Syria (A.D. 269).
ib. καί τις τῶν ἀπὸ Ῥ. παρ. ἀδ.] His name (Marcellus) is given below, while Eusebius's name is there omitted.

A. LETTERS

προηγουμένως· Μὴ σύναγε. περιττὸν γὰρ ἦν αὐτῷ τοῦτο
καὶ τὸ τελευταῖον, ἐπὶ τὸ πρῶτον ἀνατρέχοντι. οὐ γὰρ
περὶ τοῦ μὴ συνάγειν ἑτέρους ὁ λόγος ἦν αὐτῷ, ἀλλὰ περὶ
τοῦ μηδ' αὐτοὺς ἡμᾶς εἶναι Χριστιανούς, καὶ τούτου προσ-
έταττε πεπαῦσθαι, εἰ μεταβαλοίμην ἔγωγε καὶ τοὺς 5
ἄλλους ἔψεσθαί μοι νομίζων. ἀπεκρινάμην δὲ οὐκ ἀπεοικότως οὐδὲ μακρὰν τοῦ· Πειθαρχεῖν δεῖ θεῷ μᾶλλον ἢ
ἀνθρώποις, ἀλλ' ἄντικρυς διεμαρτυράμην, ὅτι τὸν θεὸν τὸν
ὄντα μόνον καὶ οὐδένα ἕτερον σέβω οὐδ' ἂν μετατεθείμην
οὐδὲ παυσαίμην ποτέ, Χριστιανὸς ὤν. ἐπὶ τούτοις ἐκέ- 10
λευσεν ἡμᾶς ἀπελθεῖν εἰς κώμην πλησίον τῆς ἐρήμου
καλουμένην Κεφρώ. αὐτῶν δὲ ἐπακούσατε τῶν ὑπ' ἀμ-

1 ην αυτω τουτω C^aF^bGHR^{ab} Schw τουτο ην αυτω cett ‖ 6 απεοικοτως] απεικοτως O Val L^r ‖ 7 μακραν του AE^aF^bG*HO Stroth L^r om του cett ‖ 9 σεβω AE^aO Steph L^r σεβων cett ‖ 10 ων] ειναι (OR^{ab})L^r ‖ 12 δε] τε CF^{ab}GHR^{ab}

1. προηγουμένως] 'at the start,' *prima fronte* (Vales.).

ib. Μὴ σύναγε] sc. τοὺς ἀδελφούς.

ib. περιττὸν γὰρ κτλ.] 'for that was superfluous and the last thing (to insist on), since he was going back to the very beginning of the matter.' The expression is condensed and therefore somewhat obscure: perhaps D. is making use of a proverbial phrase for 'putting the cart before the horse.' For the dat. ἀνατρέχοντι cf. the common phrase ξυνελόντι εἰπεῖν.

5. εἰ μεταβαλοίμην ἔγωγε] 'if I should change my mind': cf. Eus. *H. E.* v 21. 4 τοὺς ἅπαξ εἰς δικαστήριον παριόντας καὶ μηδαμῶς τῆς προθέσεως μεταβαλλομένους. Further down we have μετατεθείμην in the same sense. As an illustration of the policy involved cf. *Passio S. Philippi ep. Heracleae* (Ruinart *Acta Sinc.* p. 368, ed. 1731) *Ait Bassus, 'si Philippus ad sacrificium fuerit adductus, sequeris auctorem?' respondit Hermes, 'nec ego sequar nec ille vincetur.'*

6. οὐκ ἀπεοικ. οὐδὲ μακρ. τοῦ] 'not unsuitably nor yet very differently from (the words of the Apostles)': οὐκ ἀπεοικότως is a Thucydidean expression. If τοῦ is omitted μακράν would seem rather to mean 'at any length' than (as Vales. approved by Hein.) '*longe arcessita responsione.*'

7. Πειθαρχεῖν δεῖ κτλ.] Acts v 29.

8. ἄντικρυς] 'outright,' 'in plain language.'

12. Κεφρώ] an otherwise unknown village on the borders of the Libyan desert, perhaps named after Kephren, the brother and successor of Cheops, whose pyramids lie together at Gizeh: see Benson *Cyprian* pp. 463, 464.

ib. Quotations from the official account of the proceedings, showing the nature of the demands made upon the accused and of their reply. D. was in consequence banished first to Cephro and then to 'the parts of Colluthion.'

φοτέρων λεχθέντων ὡς ὑπεμνηματίσθη· Εἰσαχθέντων Διονυσίου καὶ Φαύστου καὶ Μαξίμου καὶ Μαρκέλλου καὶ Χαιρήμονος, Αἰμιλιανὸς διέπων τὴν ἡγεμονίαν εἶπε· Καὶ ἀγράφως ὑμῖν διελέχθην περὶ τῆς φιλανθρωπίας τῶν
5 κυρίων ἡμῶν ᾗ περὶ ὑμᾶς κέχρηνται. δεδώκασι γὰρ ἐξουσίαν ὑμῖν σωτηρίας, εἰ βούλοισθε ἐπὶ τὸ κατὰ φύσιν τρέπεσθαι καὶ θεοὺς τοὺς σώζοντας αὐτῶν τὴν βασιλείαν προσκυνεῖν, ἐπιλαθέσθαι τε τῶν παρὰ φύσιν. τί οὖν φατὲ πρὸς ταῦτα; οὐδὲ γὰρ ἀχαρίστους ὑμᾶς ἔσεσθαι περὶ τὴν
10 φιλανθρωπίαν αὐτῶν προσδοκῶ, ἐπειδήπερ ἐπὶ τὰ βελτίω ὑμᾶς προτρέπονται. Διονύσιος ἀπεκρίνατο· Οὐ πάντες πάντας προσκυνοῦσι θεούς, ἀλλ' ἕκαστοί τινας, οὓς νομί-

6 βούλοισθε AE[a]KO βούλεσθε BCDGH R[ab] βούλεσθαι F[a]

1. ὡς ὑπεμνηματίσθη] i.e. as the proceedings are given in the official records (ὑπομνήματα, *acta publica*): cf. 1 Esdr. vi 23 ὑπομνημάτιστο τάδε. Eus. uses the verb several times in his History to express the recording of facts or the like in general.

3. διέπων τὴν ἡγεμονίαν] apparently the official phrase to describe the Prefect of Egypt, who was a kind of personal viceroy of the Emperor: on p. 13 D. calls him ἡγεμών. For similar phrases cf. Alexander of Jerusalem about his predecessor Narcissus ὁ πρὸ ἐμοῦ διέπων τὸν τόπον τῆς ἐπισκοπῆς τοῦ ἐνθάδε (Eus. *H. E.* vi 11. 3), and Τραιανοῦ τὰ Ῥωμαίων σκῆπτρα διέποντος *Acta S. Eustathii* 1 (*Anal. Boll.* iii p. 66).

4. ἀγράφως] 'orally,' 'in the course of conversation': cf. p. 110 ἡ ἄγραφος ὁμιλία. The preceding καί suggests that some written communication had been made to the accused, or does it refer to the terms of the imperial edict?

ib. περὶ τῆς φιλανθρωπίας] The same word is repeated below (l. 10), while lower down it is changed to the equivalent πραότητος. The stress which Aemilian lays on the imperial leniency and humanity is an additional proof of his inability to understand the Christian's position.

6. ἐπὶ τὸ κατὰ φ. τρέπ.] 'adopt a natural line of conduct,' explained by the next phrase καὶ θ. τ. σ. αὐτ. τ. βασ. προσκυνεῖν. 'It is quite touching to see...how the magistrates always think the pantheon gods are the natural ones for all men.' Benson *Cyprian* p. 462 n.

8. τῶν παρὰ φύσιν] sc. θεῶν. Of course the plural only shows Aemilian's misunderstanding of the Christian position.

9. ἀχαρίστους] Probably from Aemilian's point of view the thing for which the Christians ought to have been 'grateful' was that the Emperors were willing to forgive their *past* errors if they would now comply with what was required: cf. Trajan's rescript: '*ut...quamvis suspectus in praeteritum fuerit, veniam ex paenitentia impetret.*'

12. οὓς νομίζουσι[ν]] sc. θεοὺς εἶναι. The student will remember that the accusation against Socrates was that οὐ νομίζει οὓς ἡ πόλις νομίζει θεούς (Xen. *Mem.* i 1. 1; Plat. *Apol.* 10).

ζουσιν. ἡμεῖς τοίνυν τὸν ἕνα θεόν, τὸν δημιουργὸν τῶν
ἁπάντων, τὸν καὶ τὴν βασιλείαν ἐγχειρίσαντα τοῖς θεοφιλεστάτοις Οὐαλεριανῷ καὶ Γαλλιηνῷ σεβαστοῖς, τοῦτον
καὶ σέβομεν καὶ προσκυνοῦμεν, καὶ τούτῳ διηνεκῶς ὑπὲρ
τῆς βασιλείας αὐτῶν, ὅπως ἀσάλευτος διαμένῃ, προσ- 5
ευχόμεθα. Αἰμιλιανὸς διέπων τὴν ἡγεμονίαν αὐτοῖς εἶπεν·
Τίς γὰρ ὑμᾶς κωλύει καὶ τοῦτον, εἴπερ ἐστὶ θεός, μετὰ τῶν
κατὰ φύσιν θεῶν προσκυνεῖν; θεοὺς γὰρ σέβειν ἐκελεύσθητε, καὶ οὓς πάντες ἴσασι. Διονύσιος ἀπεκρίνατο· Ἡμεῖς
οὐδένα ἕτερον προσκυνοῦμεν. Αἰμιλιανὸς διέπων τὴν ἡγε- 10
μονίαν αὐτοῖς εἶπεν· Ὁρῶ ὑμᾶς ὁμοῦ καὶ ἀχαρίστους ὄντας
καὶ ἀναισθήτους τῆς πραότητος τῶν σεβαστῶν ἡμῶν.
διόπερ οὐκ ἔσεσθε ἐν τῇ πόλει ταύτῃ, ἀλλὰ ἀποσταλήσεσθε
εἰς τὰ μέρη τῆς Λιβύης, καὶ ἐν τόπῳ λεγομένῳ Κεφρώ·
τοῦτον γὰρ τὸν τόπον ἐξελεξάμην ἐκ τῆς κελεύσεως τῶν 15
σεβαστῶν ἡμῶν. οὐδαμῶς δὲ ἔξεσται οὔτε ὑμῖν οὔτε
ἄλλοις τισίν, ἢ συνόδους ποιεῖσθαι, ἢ εἰς τὰ καλούμενα

1 τον δημιουργον CK Schw *deum qui coelum fecisset et terram* Ruf και δημιουργον cett ‖ 2 εγχειρισαντα F^b KOR^ab Steph Stroth Schw L^r εγχειρησαντα cett ‖ 12 ημων] om O Steph L^r ‖ 13 αποσταλησεσθε] αποστησεσθε CL^r ‖ 14 και εν—τουτον γαρ] om KR^a Steph ‖ 17 η] om AE^aF^aK add cett codd L^r Schw

3. Οὐαλεριανῷ καὶ Γαλλιηνῷ] Valerian associated his son Gallienus with him in the empire on his accession (A.D. 253), and for the first four years of their reign the Christians had been left in peace; hence perhaps the epithet θεοφιλεστάτοις here, though it may only represent the formal epithet *pius* as applied to Emperors.
4. ὑπὲρ τῆς βασιλ....προσευχόμ.] For this laudable custom, which is in accordance with the Apostle's injunction (1 Tim. ii 2), cf. Tert. *Apol.* chaps. 30—32; Orig. *c. Cels.* viii 73; Just. Mart. *Apol.* i 17; Arnob. iv 36: also *Acta Apollonii* (Klette *Texte und Untersuchungen*

xv 2) καθ' ἡμέραν κατὰ πρόσταγμα δικαίας ἐντολῆς εὐχόμεθα τῷ κατοικοῦντι ἐν οὐρανοῖς θεῷ ὑπὲρ τοῦ βασιλεύοντος ἐν τῷδε τῷ κόσμῳ Κομόδου; Theoph. *ad Autolyc.* i 11 τοιγαροῦν μᾶλλον τιμήσω τὸν βασιλέα, οὐ προσκυνῶν αὐτῷ, ἀλλ' εὐχόμενος ὑπὲρ αὐτοῦ; and *Acta Cypriani*: *Huic Deo nos Christiani deservimus: hunc deprecamur diebus ac noctibus pro nobis et pro omnibus hominibus et pro incolumitate ipsorum imperatorum*.
14. ἐν τόπῳ] sc. ἔσεσθε, supplied from οὐκ ἔσεσθε above.
17. εἰς τὰ καλ. κοιμ. εἰσιέναι] This restriction was constantly enforced by persecuting Emperors,

κοιμητήρια εἰσιέναι. εἰ δέ τις φανείη ἢ μὴ γενόμενος εἰς τὸν τόπον τοῦτον ὃν ἐκέλευσα, ἢ ἐν συναγωγῇ τινὶ εὑρεθείη, ἑαυτῷ τὸν κίνδυνον ἐπαρτήσει. οὐ γὰρ ἐπιλείψει ἡ δέουσα ἐπιστρέφεια. ἀποστῆτε οὖν ὅπου ἐκελεύσθητε. καὶ νοσ-
5 οῦντα δέ με κατήπειξεν, οὐδὲ μιᾶς ὑπέρθεσιν δοὺς ἡμέρας. ποίαν οὖν ἔτι τοῦ συναγαγεῖν ἢ μὴ συναγαγεῖν εἶχον σχολήν;

Εἶτα μεθ' ἕτερά φησιν·

(5) Ἀλλ' οὐδὲ τῆς αἰσθητῆς ἡμεῖς μετὰ τοῦ κυρίου
10 συναγωγῆς ἀπέστημεν, ἀλλὰ τοὺς μὲν ἐν τῇ πόλει σπου-

6 συναγαγειν CHR^ab Schw συναγειν cett ‖ συναγαγειν 2° CF^aKR^ab Schw συναγειν cett ‖ 10 σπουδαιοτερον] -ους nonnulli

because the graves in which martyrs were buried were a favourite resort for prayer and worship: see Duchesne *Origines du culte Chrétien* p. 387 (1889); Benson *Cyprian* pp. 481 foll. Gallienus removed the restriction in A.D. 260, τὰ τῶν καλουμένων κοιμητηρίων ἀπολαμβάνειν ἐπιτρέπων χωρία (Eus. *H. E.* vii 13. 3). For a clear statement of the origin of this beautiful name for graveyards cf. Chrys. *Hom.* lxxxi 5 διὰ τοῦτο καὶ αὐτὸς ὁ τόπος κοιμητήριον ὠνόμασται, ἵνα μάθῃς ὅτι οἱ τετελευτηκότες καὶ ἐνταῦθα κείμενοι οὐ τεθνήκασιν ἀλλὰ κοιμῶνται καὶ καθεύδουσι.

1. μὴ γενόμ. εἰς τ. τόπον] 'not to have arrived at the place': they were to convey themselves there on parole, not to be taken under custody.

2. συναγωγῇ] Possibly Aemilian uses a word to describe Christian meeting-houses which he had learnt from the numerous Jews of Alexandria to be customary among themselves. It is however not an unnatural noun to describe the congregation or the place where the congregation is assembled (συνάγεται) for service (σύναξις), and is often equivalent to ἐκκλησία in early Christian writings (e.g. in James ii 2). Clem. Alex. *Strom.* vi combines the two words ἡ τοῦ λόγου δύναμις, ῥῆμα Κυρίου φωτεινόν, ἀλήθεια οὐρανόθεν ἄνωθεν ἐπὶ τὴν συναγωγὴν ἐκκλησίας ἀφιγμένη. On p. 72 we have even a heathen sarcastically described as ἀρχισυνάγωγος τῶν ἀπ' Αἰγύπτου μάγων.

3. ἐπαρτήσει] from ἐπαρτᾶν 'to suspend over.' Perhaps we should read ἐπαρτίσει ('will prepare').

4. ἐπιστρέφεια] 'attention (by way of punishment),' Lat. *animadversio*: cf. Eus. *H. E.* vii 30. 21 παιδείας ἕνεκα καὶ ἐπιστροφῆς.

6. ποίαν...σχολήν;] The question is in indignant protest against Germanus's accusation: see Introduction, p. 23.

9. *D. found unexpectedly good opportunities in his exile, not only for continuing, but also for extending his work and influence as bishop.*

ib. Ἀλλ' οὐδὲ...συνών] 'but we did not abstain even from the visible (αἰσθητῆς) assembling of ourselves together in the Lord's presence, but those who were in the city (i.e. in Alexandria) I the more earnestly urged to meet together, as if I were

A. 'LETTERS

δαιότερον συνεκρότουν ὡς συνών, ἀπὼν μὲν τῷ ϲώματι, ὡς
εἶπεν, παρὼν δὲ τῷ πνεύματι. ἐν δὲ τῇ Κεφροῖ καὶ πολλὴ
συνεδήμησεν ἡμῖν ἐκκλησία, τῶν μὲν ἀπὸ τῆς πόλεως ἀδελφῶν ἑπομένων, τῶν δὲ συνόντων ἀπ' Αἰγύπτου. κἀκεῖ θγραν
ἡμῖν ὁ θεὸς ἀνέῳξε τοῦ λόγου. καὶ τὸ μὲν πρῶτον ἐδιώχ- 5
θημεν, ἐλιθοβολήθημεν, ὕστερον δέ τινες οὐκ ὀλίγοι τῶν
ἐθνῶν τὰ εἴδωλα καταλιπόντες ἐπέϲτρεψαν ἐπὶ τὸν θεόν.
οὐ πρότερον δὲ παραδεξαμένοιϲ αὐτοῖς τότε πρῶτον δι' ἡμῶν
ὁ λόγοϲ ἐπεϲπάρη. καὶ ὥσπερ τούτου ἕνεκεν ἀπαγαγὼν
ἡμᾶς πρὸς αὐτοὺς ὁ θεός, ἐπεὶ τὴν διακονίαν ταύτην 10
ἐπληρώϲαμεν, πάλιν ἀπαγήοχεν. ὁ γὰρ Αἰμιλιανὸς εἰς
τραχυτέρους μέν, ὡς ἐδόκει, καὶ Λιβυκωτέρους ἡμᾶς μετα-
στῆσαι τόπους ἐβουλήθη, καὶ τοὺς πανταχόσε εἰς τὸν

---

1 ως ειπεν G*HO Stroth L^r ως ειπεν ο αποστολος DF^aG^2 ως ειπειν BCK
Schw Hein ως ειπον AE^aF^b Steph Val ‖ 4 συνοντων] συνιοντων KR^ab ‖
6 δε BCDF^aGHOR^abL^r γαρ cett ‖ 11 απαγηοχεν] απαγιοχεν E^a απα-
γεωχεν G*H απηγειοχεν G^2 ‖ 12 ως] ωσπερ nonnulli

---

still present with them.' συνεκρότουν is a stronger expression for
συνῆγον here, and suggests that D.
either left instructions on the matter
before departing, or found opportunities of sending messages to them
from exile: cf. p. 160 for a slightly
different use of the word, and Eus.
H. E. v 23. 2 σύνοδοι δὴ καὶ συγ-
κροτήσεις ἐπισκόπων ἐπὶ ταὐτὸν ἐγένοντο.

1. ὡς εἶπεν] sc. 1 Cor. v 3. The
variations in the MSS are interesting,
but the reading of the text is that
adopted in the new Berlin edition.

4. ἀπ' Αἰγύπτου] 'from (other
parts of) Egypt': cf. note on p.
13.

ib. θύραν ἡμῖν κτλ.] Cf. Col.
iv 3.

7. ἐπέστρεψαν ἐπὶ τὸν θεόν] Cf.
Acts xiv 15; 1 Thess. i 9.

9. ὁ λόγος ἐπεσπάρη] Cf. Luke
viii 11, 13.

10. τὴν διακ....ἐπληρ.] Cf. Acts
xii 25.

11. ἀπαγήοχεν] a later form of
the perf. of ἄγω, which however is
found in compounds (as here) even
in Attic Gk.

12. Λιβυκωτέρους] 'more Libyan-
like' (a use of the adj. probably
coined by D.).

13. τοὺς πανταχόσε...συρρεῖν] 'he
bade those (who were scattered) in
every direction to draw together to
the Mareotis.' With τοὺς πανταχόσε we must supply some participle
like διασκορπισθέντας unless the adv.
is loosely used for πανταχόθεν (or
πανταχοῦ); so below ὅποι ποτὲ οὗτός
ἐστι, and p. 44 αἱ πανταχόσε ἐκκλησίαι.

ib. εἰς τὸν Μαρεώτην] (sc. νομόν).
From this we gather that Cephro
was outside the Mareotis, while the
parts of Colluthion to which D. was
removed were within its borders.

Μαρεώτην ἐκέλευσε συρρεῖν, κώμας ἑκάστοις τῶν κατὰ χώραν ἀφορίσας, ἡμᾶς δὲ μᾶλλον ἐν ὁδῷ καὶ πρώτους καταληφθησομένους ἔταξεν. ᾠκονόμει γὰρ δηλονότι καὶ παρεσκεύαζεν, ἵνα, ὁπόταν βουληθείη συλλαβεῖν, πάντας
5 εὐαλώτους ἔχοι. ἐγὼ δὲ ὅτε μὲν εἰς Κεφρὼν κεκελεύσμην ἀπελθεῖν, καὶ τὸν τόπον ἠγνόουν ὅποι ποτὲ οὗτός ἐστιν, οὐδὲ τὸ ὄνομα σχεδὸν πρότερον ἀκηκοώς· καὶ ὅμως εὐθύμως καὶ ἀταράχως ἀπῄειν. ἐπεὶ δὲ μετασκηνώσειν εἰς τὰ Κολλουθίωνος ἀπηγγέλη μοι, ἴσασιν οἱ παρόντες ὅπως
10 διετέθην. ἐνταῦθα γὰρ ἐμαυτοῦ κατηγορήσω. τὸ μὲν πρῶτον ἠχθέσθην καὶ λίαν ἐχαλέπηνα· καὶ γὰρ εἰ γνωριμώτεροι καὶ συνηθέστεροι ἐτύγχανον ἡμῖν οἱ τόποι, ἀλλ' ἔρημον μὲν ἀδελφῶν καὶ σπουδαίων ἀνθρώπων ἔφασκον εἶναι τὸ χωρίον, ταῖς δὲ τῶν ὁδοιπορούντων ἐνοχλήσεσι
15 καὶ λῃστῶν καταδρομαῖς ἐγκείμενον. ἔτυχον δὲ παραμυθίας, ὑπομνησάντων με τῶν ἀδελφῶν, ὅτι γειτνιᾷ μᾶλλον τῇ πόλει, καὶ ἡ μὲν Κεφρὼν πολλὴν ἡμῖν ἦγεν ἀδελφῶν τῶν ἀπ' Αἰγύπτου τὴν ἐπιμιξίαν, ὡς πλατύτερον ἐκκλησιάζειν δύνασθαι, ἐκεῖ δὲ πλησιαίτερον οὔσης τῆς πόλεως
20 συνεχέστερον τῆς τῶν ὄντως ἀγαπητῶν καὶ οἰκειοτάτων καὶ φιλτάτων ὄψεως ἀπολαύσομεν. ἀφίξονται γὰρ καὶ

15 ἐγκειμενον] εκκειμ. nonnulli ǁ 16 γειτνια] γειτνιωη Schw Berlin

1. τῶν κατὰ χώραν ἀφ.] 'assigning to each party one of the villages of the district': with τῶν κ. χ. supply κωμῶν.
2. ἡμᾶς δὲ μᾶλλον κτλ.] 'but us he put more on the road and (so arranged) that we should be the first to be arrested.' Benson suggests that the ὁδός was perhaps the highroad to Cyrene.
4. ὁπόταν βουληθείη] The opt. with ὁπόταν is of course not a classical construction: cf. p. 53 οἷς ἂν... λάβοις.
6. ὅποι ποτὲ οὗτ. ἐστ.] 'in whatever direction the place lay': see above on πανταχόσε.

8. τὰ Κολλουθίωνος] 'nearer Alexandria and a frequented station (probably a night station)...on a high road,' Benson Cyprian p. 464. The exact situation is not now known. We meet with the personal name Κόλλουθος in Church history.
13. ἔφασκον] retains here its classical sense of 'maintaining' and 'asserting,' not mere 'saying.'
17. καὶ ἡ μὲν Κ. κτλ.] This was what the brethren said to comfort D.
18. ἐπιμιξίαν] 'opportunity of intercourse with': cf. p. 152.
ib. ὡς πλατύτερον ἐκκλησιάζειν δύνασθαι] 'so as to be able to draw my congregations from a wider

A. LETTERS

ἀναπαύσονται, καὶ ὡς ἐν προαστείοις πορρωτέρω κειμένοις
κατὰ μέρος ἔσονται συναγωγαί. καὶ οὕτως ἐγένετο.

Καὶ μεθ' ἕτερα περὶ τῶν συμβεβηκότων αὐτῷ αὖθις ταῦτα γράφει·

(6) Πολλαῖς γε ταῖς ὁμολογίαις Γερμανὸς σεμνύνεται.
πολλά γε εἰπεῖν ἔχει καθ' ἑαυτοῦ γενόμενα. ὅσας ἀριθ- 5
μῆσαι δύναται περὶ ἡμῶν ἀποφάσεις, δημεύσεις, προγραφάς,
ὑπαρχόντων ἁρπαγάς, ἀξιωμάτων ἀποθέσεις, δόξης κοσμικῆς
ὀλιγωρίας, ἐπαίνων ἡγεμονικῶν καὶ βουλευτικῶν κατα-
φρονήσεις καὶ τῶν ἐναντίων ἀπειλῶν, καὶ καταβοήσεων

4 πολλαῖς γε] add τοι nonnulli || 5 ὅσας] ὅσα DF^bGH Val

area,' i.e. to extend the influence of Christianity in the district. Ἐκκλησιάζειν is generally used with an accus. of the person summoned.

1. ἀναπαύσονται] 'stay the night' (Benson, *l.c.*), whereas at Cephro visitors 'had to take up their abode there' (συνεδήμησεν).

ib. ἐν προαστείοις] See Bingham *Antiqq.* Bk ix chap. 2 § 3, where it is shown that the term προάστειον includes a much wider district round a town than our 'suburb': e.g. Canopus, 12 miles distant from Alexandria, is called by this name in the Acts of Chalcedon III iv.

2. κατὰ μέρος...συναγωγαί] 'district-meetings': for συναγωγαί see note above (p. 32). The brethren who lived on the outskirts of a city like Alexandria were not bound to attend the mother church, but had, as it were, chapels of ease in their own vicinities.

4. *Germanus's charges therefore against D. of cowardice and unfaithfulness under persecution break down: in fact D.'s sufferings for the truth's sake are infinitely greater than those of Germanus.*

ib. ταῖς ὁμολογίαις] sc. open confessions of faith, which had caused him persecution.

5. ὅσας ἀριθμ. κτλ.] The question is put in a condensed form; lit. 'as many condemnations etc. as he can reckon up in our case,' i.e. 'can he reckon up as many condemnations etc. in his own case as I can in mine?'

6. ἀποφάσεις] 'condemnations.' Hesych. ἀπόφασις· κρίσις, ψῆφος, δίκη. See Suicer *s.v.*

ib. δημεύσεις] 'confiscations,' Lat. *publicationes.*

ib. προγραφάς] 'sales by public auction,' Lat. *proscriptiones.*

7. ὑπαρχόντων ἁρπ.] Cf. Heb. x 34.

ib. ἀξιωμάτων ἀποθέσεις] 'loss of dignities'; *hinc patet D. Alex. splendido genere ortum fuisse* (Vales.): see General Introduction, p. xii.

8. ἐπαίνων ἡγεμον. καὶ βουλ.] 'commendations by Prefects (ἡγεμόνες) and Councillors (βουλευταί).' Augustus had wished Alexandria to be governed by a Prefect without any *decuriones* (βουλευταί): cf. Tac. *Hist.* i 11. 1, *Ann.* ii 59. But Severus had granted them a Senate (Dio. li.; Spart.). For the ideas suggested by the word ἐπαίνων in this connexion cf. Rom. xiii 3 and 1 Pet. ii 14: it would be a mistake not to recognize that at least in theory and substantially in practice the Roman official in the provinces realized the twofold nature of his office 'for the punishment of evil doers and the praise of them that do well.'

καὶ κινδύνων καὶ διωγμῶν καὶ πλάνης καὶ στενοχωρίας καὶ ποικίλης θλίψεως ὑπομονήν, οἷα τὰ ἐπὶ Δεκίου καὶ Σαβίνου συμβάντα μοι, οἷα μέχρι νῦν Αἰμιλιανοῦ; ποῦ δὲ Γερμανὸς ἐφάνη; τίς δὲ περὶ αὐτοῦ λόγος; ἀλλὰ τῆς πολλῆς
5 ἀφροσύνης, εἰς ἣν ἐμπίπτω διὰ Γερμανόν, ὑφίεμαι, διὸ καὶ τὴν καθ᾿ ἕκαστον τῶν γενομένων διήγησιν παρίημι τοῖς εἰδόσιν ἀδελφοῖς λέγειν.

1. διωγμῶν κτλ.] Cf. Rom. viii 35 etc.
3. οἷα μέχρι νῦν Αἰμιλιανοῦ] 'such as up to the present time (are the things which have happened to me under) Aemilian.' This implies that Aemilian was still in office when D. wrote the letter.
5. ἀφροσύνης] See above p. 28.
ib. ὑφίεμαι] 'I withdraw from.'

III

Πρὸς Νοουάτον Ἐπιστολή

(Eus. *H. E.* vi 45)

Early in A.D. 251 Cornelius had been canonically elected Bishop of Rome in place of the martyred Fabius, and almost immediately afterwards the party of severity in the city, stimulated by Novatus the disobedient priest of Carthage, had set up Novatian as his rival and had even persuaded three country Bishops to lay their hands upon him. 'Thus was commenced the Novatianist or Purist schism which deepened its unforgivingness' (viz. in the matter of the Lapsed) 'at last to heresy; which planted bishops in all the leading sees from Spain to Pontus, and made the mountaineers of Phrygia almost its own; which, first allowed and then proscribed by Constantine, supported by Julian, supported by Theodosius, and forbidden by his two sons, lasted on at least until the end of the sixth century' (Benson *Cyprian* p. 141). This consecration was formally announced to the occupants of the principal sees of Christendom and the announcement was accompanied by letters from Novatian in which he explained that the position had been forced upon him[1]. Here we have Dionysius's reply

[1] ὡς δὴ πρὸς αὐτῶν ἐπὶ τοῦτ᾿ ἐλθεῖν ἐκβεβιασμένος (p. 38).

A. *LETTERS* 37

to that letter, in which, with an evident desire to conciliate as usual, he reasons firmly but kindly with Novatian, showing him that retreat is the only possible way of escape for him from his false position, whatever the direct consequences to himself might be. When we consider what Dionysius actually thought of the mischief which Novatian was doing (as revealed in his letter to Dionysius Romanus p. 55), this private letter of expostulation is, as Benson remarks (p. 142), 'surely a pattern of controversial sweetness.'

Eusebius informs us (*H. E.* vi 46) that Cornelius also wrote to Dionysius denouncing the action of Novatian, and that Dionysius replied to him, but the contents of the letter on that subject, which it would have been interesting to compare with the present text, are not given except the single sentence printed in the succeeding section (IV): it is stated however that Dionysius mentions that he has been invited to the synod of Antioch, where an attempt has been made to establish the schism of Novatian[1].

The same chapter in Eusebius mentions other communications of Dionysius with the Roman Church on the same matter, viz. the ἐπιστολὴ διακονικὴ[2] διὰ Ἱππολύτου, another περὶ εἰρήνης, a third περὶ μετανοίας, and three letters to the Confessors at Rome, one while they were still adherents of Novatian and two when they had returned to the Church[3].

A Syriac version of this letter exists in the Codd. Brit. Mus. Add. 12155 fol. 111ᵃ and 14533 fol. 176ᵇ, which has been printed by Pitra *Analecta Sacra* vol. iv p. 169.

---

[1] See Introductions to πρὸς Φαβιανὸν ἐπιστολή, p. 5, and to πρὸς Κορνήλιον ἐπιστολή, p. 39.

[2] There has been much dispute as to the meaning of this epithet: Benson (*Cyprian* pp. 171, 172) has collected several of the meanings suggested: e.g. = εἰρηνική (Bp Chr. Wordsworth), 'concerned with the arrangements of deacons' (Bp Lightfoot), 'serviceable' or 'containing practical advice' (M. Larpent). One of the latest hypotheses, which has gained some general support, is that of Dom Morin (*Revue Bénéd.* July 1900) that this 'diaconic letter by the hand of Hippolytus' is none other than 'the Canons of Hippolytus.' See General Introduction, p. xxx.

[3] τοῖς ἐκεῖσε ὁμολογηταῖς, ἔτι τῇ τοῦ Νοουάτου συμφερομένοις γνώμῃ, τοῖς δὲ αὐτοῖς τούτοις ἑτέρας δύο μετατιθεμένοις ἐπὶ τὴν ἐκκλησίαν.

Ἴδωμεν δὲ ὁ αὐτὸς ὁποῖα καὶ τῷ Νοουάτῳ διεχάραξε, ταράττοντι τηνικάδε τὴν Ῥωμαίων ἀδελφότητα. ἐπειδὴ οὖν τῆς ἀποστασίας καὶ τοῦ σχίσματος πρόφασιν ἐποιεῖτο τῶν ἀδελφῶν τινάς, ὡς δὴ πρὸς αὐτῶν ἐπὶ τοῦτ' ἐλθεῖν ἐκβεβιασμένος, ὅρα τίνα τρόπον αὐτῷ
5 γράφει·

Διονύσιος Νοουάτῳ τῷ ἀδελφῷ χαίρειν.

Εἰ ἄκων, ὡς φῄς, ἤχθης, δείξεις, ἐὰν ἀναχωρήσῃς ἑκών. ἔδει μὲν γὰρ καὶ πᾶν ὁτιοῦν παθεῖν ὑπὲρ τοῦ μὴ διακόψαι τὴν ἐκκλησίαν τοῦ θεοῦ, καὶ ἦν οὐκ ἀδοξοτέρα τῆς
10 ἕνεκεν τοῦ μὴ εἰδωλολατρῆσαι γινομένης ἡ ἕνεκεν τοῦ μὴ σχίσαι μαρτυρία, κατ' ἐμὲ δὲ καὶ μείζων. ἐκεῖ μὲν γὰρ ὑπὲρ μιᾶς τις τῆς ἑαυτοῦ ψυχῆς, ἐνταῦθα δὲ ὑπὲρ ὅλης τῆς ἐκκλησίας μαρτυρεῖ. καὶ νῦν δὲ εἰ πείσαιο ἢ βιάσαιο τοὺς ἀδελφοὺς εἰς ὁμόνοιαν ἐλθεῖν, μεῖζον ἔσται σοι τοῦ
15 σφάλματος τὸ κατόρθωμα, καὶ τὸ μὲν οὐ λογισθήσεται,

6 Νοουατω] Νοουατιανω E Hieron (de virr. ill. 69) Νααυατιανω Nic Sync ‖ τω αδ.] om τω nonnulli ‖ 7 εαν CF^{a}GR^{ab} Val Schw αν AE^a Steph Stroth om cett ‖ αναχωρησης] αναχωρησας F^{b}GHORL^r ‖ 9 της] του R ‖ 13 πεισαιο CKR^{ab} Val πεισαις AE^{a}F^{b}G^{2}H Steph Stroth Schw πεισης R πεισεις Nic πεισας F^{a}OL^r ‖ η] om L^r tacite

6. *You will show that your promotion was against your will, by willingly retiring now. Better endure anything than rend the unity of the Church. And now if you will somehow restore harmony, your reparation will be of greater account than your mistake: and if you fail with your supporters, at least you will save your own soul. Farewell.*

ib. Νοουάτῳ] The confusion between names ending in -*us* and in -*anus* constantly recurs and esp. in the case of Novatian (of Rome) and Novatus (of Carthage).

7. ἤχθης] 'thou wert promoted' (Benson), but 'thou wert carried on' (Salmond) seems more probable. Cp. ἤγοντο, p. 10.

11. μαρτυρία] must mean 'martyrdom' in the strict sense (so Ruf. *sustinere martyrium ne scindatur ecclesia*), though one may doubt whether Novatian was ever really likely to endure such a fate for withdrawing from his position.

ib. κατ' ἐμέ] 'in my opinion.'

13. εἰ πείσαιο] I have retained this reading, though it is doubtful if the middle can mean anything but 'be persuaded': Benson and Salmond seem to have adopted the well-supported variant πείσαις which certainly simplifies the passage.

14. μεῖζ. ἔστ. τοῦ σφάλμ. τὸ κατόρθ.] 'the recovery of your standing will be greater than your fall.' Κατόρθωμα = 'success' generally, esp. moral success, i.e. a right action (e.g. Eus. *H. E.* iv 3. 5; v 10. 4; vi 3. 6) but here D. evidently means in his favourite manner to play on

A. *LETTERS* 39

τὸ δὲ ἐπαινεθήσεται. εἰ δὲ ἀπειθούντων ἀδυνατοίης,
cώzωn cŵze thn ceaytoŷ ψychn. ἐρρῶσθαί σε ἐχόμενον
τῆς εἰρήνης ἐν κυρίῳ εὔχομαι.

Ταῦτα καὶ πρὸς τὸν Νοουάτον.

4 ταυτα—Νοουατον] *haec eadem etiam Novatianis* (vel *Novatiano*) *scripsit* Ruf

the contrast between the two words
(κατόρθ. and σφάλμα).

1. ἀπειθούντων] Gen. abs.
2. σώζων...ψυχήν] Gen. xix 17.

IV

Πρὸς Κορνήλιον Ἐπιστολή

(Eus. *H. E.* vi 46. 4)

The Alexander to whom this extract refers had been a bishop in Cappadocia, but when on a visit to Jerusalem he was elected coadjutor to the aged Narcissus, Bishop of that see, and eventually succeeded him. He was one of Origen's distinguished pupils and joined with Theoctistus, Bishop of Caesarea (in Palestine), in advancing him to the priesthood. Eusebius gives us short extracts from his letters to the churches of Antinoia (in Egypt?) and of Antioch and also from the joint letter which he and Theoctistus wrote to Demetrius, Bishop of Alexandria, about Origen. Jerome mentions other letters of his and among them one to Origen himself. Alexander twice made a bold confession of Christianity in the Governor's court at Caesarea and, as we read here, died at last in prison[1].

Dionysius's letter was addressed to Cornelius, Bishop of Rome, in reply to one from him on the subject of Novatian (see above, p. 37). It was despatched after Demetrian had succeeded Fabian at Antioch (i.e. about A.D. 253). In the same letter Dionysius also mentioned that he had been invited by the bishops of Asia Minor to the Synod which was to meet at Antioch ἔνθα τοῦ Νοουάτου κρατύνειν τινὲς ἐπεχείρουν τὸ σχίσμα.

[1] See Eus. *H. E.* vi 8; 11; 19; and 39: Jerom. *de virr. ill.* 62: Krüger *Early Christian Literature* (Eng. Trans.) pp. 247 ff.

Γράφει δὲ καὶ περὶ τοῦ ἐν Ἱεροσολύμοις αὐτοῖς ῥήμασι φάσκων·
Ὁ μὲν γὰρ θαυμάσιος Ἀλέξανδρος ἐν φρουρᾷ γενόμενος
μακαρίως ἀνεπαύσατο.

2 θαυμάσιος AE^{ab}O Steph L^r *admirabilis* Ruf μακάριος BCDF^aGHKR^{ab}

2. θαυμάσιος] The epithet μακάριος is well supported in the MSS but it seems strange that it should have been altered to θαυμάσιος: on the other hand the μακαρίως that follows loses some of its point if D. actually wrote θαυμάσιος.

V

Περὶ Βαπτίσματος

The group of letters under this heading are addressed to the Church of Rome or to individual members of that Church and deal with the question of the validity of heretical baptism[1]. Up till now various parts of Christendom had followed various customs on this matter without much controversy—in spite of Eusebius' statement quoted below. In Asia Minor and in Africa heretical baptism was not recognized, while in the West baptism with water in the name of the Trinity or of Christ was held valid by whomsoever performed. Before the middle of the third century however the difference of practice gradually became more and more a matter of controversy. In or about A.D. 230 two synods were held one after the other at Iconium and at Synnada, which confirmed the opinion that baptism by heretics was invalid: and some twenty-five years later on Cyprian of Carthage convened several synods in North Africa which arrived at the same conclusion. Thereupon a violent quarrel arose between Cyprian and Stephen the Bishop of Rome, which became perhaps all the keener because of the former alliance and cooperation between Cyprian and Stephen's predecessor, Cornelius, in combating Novatianism; and severe language was used on both sides. Other leading

---

[1] Eus. *H. E.* vii 2 ζητήματος οὐ σμικροῦ τηνικάδε ἀνακινηθέντος, εἰ δέοι τοὺς ἐξ οἵας δ᾽ οὖν αἱρέσεως ἐπιστρέφοντας διὰ λουτροῦ καθαίρειν, παλαιοῦ γέ τοι κεκρατηκότος ἔθους ἐπὶ τῶν τοιούτων μόνῃ χρῆσθαι τῇ διὰ χειρῶν ἐπιθέσεως εὐχῇ.

A. LETTERS 41

Churchmen of the period were naturally drawn into the dispute: among them Firmilian of Caesarea in Cappadocia and Dionysius of Alexandria, who with characteristic sagacity steered a middle course and advised that the older spirit of toleration should be maintained, the circumstances of different churches requiring different methods[1].

The first of the fragments here reproduced belongs probably to the year 254 and was addressed to Stephen of Rome: the whole letter seems to have been a long one[2] and the fragment which Eusebius embodies occurred towards the end of it[3]. In it he refers to the subsiding of the Novatianist schism and the restoration of peace among the churches of Christendom, which Eusebius mistakes for an allusion to the cessation of persecution[4]. By mentioning the distinguished prelates who had taken part in producing this welcome state of things and by subtly referring to the generosity of the Roman Church to their poorer brethren in Syria and Arabia, Dionysius evidently hopes to moderate the vehemence and imperiousness of Stephen's methods, which, as the next letter shows, had gone the length of threatening to excommunicate the offending churches.

The next fragment in all probability formed part of the same letter, and occurred at an earlier point in it. The Syriac version of it here given is put together out of two MSS in the British Museum, neither of which contains the whole. Part is contained in MS Add. 17214, beginning at the end of fol. 73 *r.*, col. 2: this is denoted by the letter A in the textual notes. Part is contained in Add. 12156, fol. 3 *r.*, col. 1: this is denoted by the letter B. The extract is given from these two sources by Pitra in his *Analecta Sacra*, vol. iv. Mr N. McLean of Christ's College has very kindly examined the MSS afresh and constructed the text as now presented together with the critical annotations, and has also furnished the accom-

---

[1] Jerome's description (*de virr. ill.* 69) of D. as *in Cypriani et Africanae synodi dogma consentiens* is inaccurate and misleading: see Benson *Cyprian* p. 356. Dionysius's position admitted Montanist baptism which scandalized Basil (*Ep.* II. 188 *ad Amphiloch.*): τίνα οὖν λόγον ἔχει τὸ τούτων βάπτισμα ἐγκριθῆναι τῶν βαπτιζόντων εἰς Πατέρα καὶ Υἱὸν καὶ Μοντανὸν ἢ Πρίσκιλλαν;

[2] πλεῖστα...ὁμιλήσας, p. 44.

[3] τελευτῶν δηλοῖ.

[4] τοῦ διωγμοῦ λελωφηκότος.

panying translation. The original of one sentence of the extract is preserved in Cod. Vatic. 1521, fol. 591, in a catena upon Deuteronomy (see Simon de Magistris, p. 200). The contents, as Harnack says (*Altchr. Litteratur* i 425), are wholly in keeping with what we know of Dionysius and his attitude in this question.

Our ground in dealing with the other Syriac fragment is less sure. Like the foregoing, it is given by Pitra, and has been edited for this volume by Mr McLean. It is found in three British Museum MSS, viz. Add. 12155, fol. 90 v., col. 1 (here called A), Add. 14536, fol. 14 v. (= B), and Add. 14493, fol. 155 v. (= C). As Harnack observes, the juxtaposition of the names 'Dionysius (or Dionysianus) and Stephen' as presidents of the Church of Rome in itself awakes suspicion. No epistle bearing that address was known to Eusebius, nor is it likely that in a letter addressed to them jointly the name of Stephen would have come second. The difficulty, such as it is, however, may be got over by supposing that the extract comes from the letter which Dionysius tells us that he wrote to Dionysius of Rome and Philemon at the time when they were of the same opinion as Stephen. With regard to the contents of the extract, we need not be surprised if Dionysius took the line which is attributed to him in it. The foregoing extract shows that the heresies which he considered to invalidate baptism were of a very fundamental kind, and such as might well produce the kind of liturgical variations from Church usage which are contemplated in the letter to Xystus (p. 57). It is not at all incredible that he was willing to admit the validity of baptisms administered in the name of the Trinity, even if administered by unauthorised persons.

The second Eusebian letter was addressed to Stephen's successor (Xystus[1]) in the see of Rome and together with all the other letters of the group belongs to the year 257. The first of the three fragments preserved by Eusebius mentions (though not by name) the largely attended synods which, as Dionysius had discovered, had dealt with the present question (viz. those of Iconium and Synnada) and the decisions they had arrived at. The second fragment alludes quite briefly to the correspondence which Dionysius had had on a former occasion and again now with the Roman presbyters Dionysius and Philemon who

---

[1] This was Xystus (or Sixtus) II, who was Bishop from Aug. 257 till the following August, when he was martyred.

A. LETTERS 43

had been won over from the side of Stephen. The third fragment refers entirely to the Sabellian heresy and need not here be dealt with: see pp. 165 ff.

The third letter (to Philemon) and the fourth (to Dionysius of Rome), from which our next extracts come, are probably two of those mentioned above. The fragment to Philemon is longer than most of the others and its contents are of importance, though Philemon seems to have held no higher office at Rome than that of presbyter. Not only does it give an interesting personal incident connected with Dionysius's conversion[1], but it informs us about his predecessor (Heraclas's) methods of dealing with penitent apostates, and also refers (by name) to those synods or councils of Asia Minor and Africa mentioned above and his refusal to set aside their decisions in the interests of peace.

The Dionysius of the fourth letter is the Roman presbyter who not long after[2] (viz. in A.D. 259) succeeded Xystus II in the chair of St Peter and whose fragment on Sabellianism we have printed on pp. 177 ff. Eusebius says that the present letter shows our Dionysius's estimate of his Roman namesake's eloquence and general ability[3]. The short extract which Eusebius proceeds to give has reference rather to the hateful nature and consequences of Novatianism than to heretical baptism proper, but it is valuable as a revelation of Dionysius's wonderful breadth of view in theological matters.

The fifth letter is again addressed to Xystus: in it, after writing at some length about the situation in general, he consults the Bishop of Rome about a case of heretical baptism which had come before his notice and caused him some perplexity: and the passage in which he describes the case is preserved by Eusebius. Here again the nobility of Dionysius's nature is to be observed as evidenced especially by the opening phrase of the fragment. At the end of the extract Eusebius mentions yet a sixth letter on the subject which was addressed by Dionysius and his diocese to this same Xystus and the Church of Rome[4].

[1] See General Introduction, p. xiv.
[2] οὐκ εἰς μακρόν, p. 55.
[3] λόγιός τε καὶ θαυμάσιος, p. 55.
[4] παροικίας...ἐκκλησίᾳ, p. 59.

I

Τῶν περὶ βαπτίσματος ἐπιστολῶν
Ἡ πρώτη—πρὸς Στέφανον

(Eus. *H. E.* vii 4 and 5. 1 and 2)

Πλεῖστα δὴ οὖν (τῷ Στεφάνῳ) περὶ τούτου διὰ γραμμάτων ὁ Διονύσιος ὁμιλήσας, τελευτῶν δηλοῖ ὡς ἄρα τοῦ διωγμοῦ λελωφηκότος αἱ πανταχόσε ἐκκλησίαι τὴν κατὰ Νοουάτον ἀποστραφεῖσαι νεωτεροποιίαν εἰρήνην πρὸς ἑαυτὰς ἀνειλήφεσαν. γράφει δὲ ὧδε·

5 (1) Ἴσθι δὲ νῦν, ἀδελφέ, ὅτι ἥνωνται πᾶσαι αἱ πρότερον διεσχισμέναι κατά τε τὴν ἀνατολὴν ἐκκλησίαι καὶ ἔτι προσωτέρω. καὶ πάντες εἰσὶν ὁμόφρονες οἱ πανταχοῦ προεστῶτες, χαίροντες καθ᾽ ὑπερβολὴν ἐπὶ τῇ παρὰ προσδοκίαν εἰρήνῃ γενομένῃ, Δημητριανὸς ἐν Ἀντιοχείᾳ,
10 Θεόκτιστος ἐν Καισαρείᾳ, Μαζαββάνης ἐν Αἰλίᾳ, Μαρῖνος

6 και ετι προσωτερω] om DF^a duobus punctis includunt BC ‖ 10 Μαζαββανης] (OR^a) Ruf L^r Μαζαβανης cett

5. *All the churches of the East that were divided are now united and rejoice in the unexpected restoration of peace. All alike join in praising God for this happy turn of affairs.*

6. καὶ ἔτι προσωτέρω] From the omission of these words in two MSS while two others put them between two stops, Vales. surmised that they were D.'s abbreviation ('and so forth') for a full list; but, if they may be translated 'and even further afield' (than what we ordinarily mean by the East), the churches of Mesopotamia and Osroene are perhaps meant: cf. τῶν ἐξῆς ὁμορούντων ἐθνῶν below, p. 50.

8. καθ᾽ ὑπερβολὴν ἐπὶ τῇ παρὰ προσδοκίαν εἰρ.] The greatness of the joy is accounted for by the surprise at peace being restored, whilst the surprise was perhaps due to the violence of the language and other measures which had been employed both by Stephen and by Cyprian: cf. Firmilian's words addressed to Stephen in his letter to Cyprian, *lites et dissensiones quantas parasti per ecclesias totius mundi?* (Cypr. *Ep.* cxxv 24 ed. Hartel). For Eusebius's mistake in identifying this peace with the cessation of persecution see Introduction p. 41: cf. also p. 85 for similar mistakes of Eusebius.

10. Καισαρείᾳ] sc. in Palestine (also called *Stratonis turris*).

ib. Αἰλίᾳ] i.e. *Capitolina*. Hadrian's colony on Mount Sion was so named (A.D. 132). Ruf. here substitutes the name Jerusalem for Aelia. Eus. himself almost always speaks of the Bishops of Jerusalem, not of Aelia (see however *de mart. Pal.* xi 4), but even so late as the

A. LETTERS 45

ἐν Τύρῳ, κοιμηθέντος Ἀλεξάνδρου, Ἡλιόδωρος ἐν Λαο-
δικείᾳ ἀναπαυσαμένου Θηλυμίδρου, Ἕλενος ἐν Ταρσῷ καὶ
πᾶσαι αἱ τῆς Κιλικίας ἐκκλησίαι, Φιρμιλιανὸς καὶ πᾶσα
Καππαδοκία. τοὺς γὰρ περιφανεστέρους μόνους τῶν
ἐπισκόπων ὠνόμοσα, ἵνα μήτε μῆκος τῇ ἐπιστολῇ μήτε 5
βάρος προσάψω τῷ λόγῳ. αἱ μέντοι Συρίαι ὅλαι καὶ
ἡ Ἀραβία, οἷς ἐπαρκεῖτε ἑκάστοτε καὶ οἷς νῦν ἐπεστεί-
λατε, ἥ τε Μεσοποταμία, Πόντος τε καὶ Βιθυνία καὶ
συνελόντι εἰπεῖν ἀγαλλιῶνται πάντες πανταχοῦ τῇ ὁμο-
νοίᾳ καὶ φιλαδελφίᾳ, δοξάζοντες τὸν θεόν. 10

Ταῦτα μὲν ὁ Διονύσιος.

[Syriac text, 4 lines]

1 κοιμηθ. Ἀλεξ.] cum εν Αιλια iungunt Ruf Stroth Val Zimmermann
‖ 3 Φιρμιλιανος] Φιρμιλλιανος F^bGH Schw Φιρμιλιανος cett ‖ 7 επαρκειτε]
επαρκειται F^bOL^r

days of Constantine the older and more glorious name does not seem to have been generally restored to the see (e.g. Concil. Nic. canon vii): see Heinichen's note *in loc.*

1. κοιμηθ. Ἀλεξ.] There seems no doubt that this clause belongs to the succession in Aelia not at Tyre: cf. p. 40, and Eus. *H. E.* vi 39. 2 and 3.

3. Φιρμιλιανός] Bishop of Caesarea in Cappadocia (†A.D. 260), one of Origen's distinguished pupils: he took a prominent part against Paul of Samosata and on the baptismal controversy sided with Cyprian. See his letter preserved in Cyprian's correspondence.

7. οἷς ἐπαρκεῖτε ἑκάστοτε] 'whose needs ye from time to time supply,' cf. 1 Tim. v 10, 16 etc. The adroit reference to the wonted liberality of the Roman Church in material matters is to be noted: see Salmon *Infallibility* p. 375, where attention is drawn to the curious coincidence that this liberality is specially connected with the names of three Dionysii, viz. D. of Corinth (Eus. *H. E.* iv 23), D. of Alex. (in the present instance), and D. of Rome who freed captives in Cappadocia (Basil Magnus *ad Damasum Ep.* 70).

ib. οἷς νῦν ἐπεστείλ.] see below.

9. ἀγαλλ. πάντες παντ.] Benson sees a subtle reference in the list of churches named to the list given in Acts ii 9, 10: 'the chord which plainly he hopes to touch in Stephen's heart is the near fulfilment of the Pentecostal foreshadowing' (p. 357).

(2) Ἐπ' ἐκείνοις μὲν εἴπερ τις τὸ ἀσεβὲς περὶ θεοῦ ἐφθέγξατο, λιθοβολεῖσθαι τὸν τοιοῦτον ὁ νόμος ἐκέλευσεν· ἡμεῖς δὲ τοῖς στερροῖς τῆς πίστεως ἡμῶν λόγοις καταλεύσωμεν.

ܐܢ ܗܘ ܕܐܢܫ ܡܢ ܡܕܡ ܕܪܫܝܥ ܡܡܠܠ ܥܠ ܐܠܗܐ: ܐܡܝܢܐ ܕܗܠܝܢ ܕܐܡܪܝܢ ܠܗ ܠܐ ܡܪܓܡܢܐ: ܐܦ ܕܢܠܬܐ ܕܐܠܗ̈ܐ ܐܚܪ̈ܢܐ ܐܢܫ ܡܡܠ. ܕܢܬܪܓܡ ܗܘ ܕܐܡܪ ܗܘ ܟܕ ܢܦܘܩܐ. ܚܢܢ ܕܝܢ ܠܗܠܝܢ ܒܡ̈ܠܐ ܚܠܝܨ̈ܬܐ ܕܗܝܡܢܘܬܐ ܪ̈ܓܡܝܢ. ܐܦ ܐܠܐ ܐܢܫ ܠܐܪ̈ܥܐ[1] ܕܡܫܝܚܐ ܡܢ[2] ܠܐ ܡܡܠܠ. ܐܦ ܡܫܠܛ ܘܡܡܠܟ[3]: ܐܦ ܕܠܐ ܐܬܘܗܝ ܐܠܗܐ: ܐܦ ܕܠܐ ܗܘܐ ܒܪܢܫܐ: ܐܦ ܕܠܐ ܡܝܬ ܐܦ ܕܠܐ ܡܢ: ܐܦ ܕܠܐ ܐܬܐ ܕܢܕܘܢ ܚ̈ܝܐ ܘܡ̈ܝܬܐ: ܐܦ ܡܕܡ ܐܚܪܢܐ ܡܡܠܠ[4] ܠܒܪ ܡܢ ܡܟܐ ܕܡܟܪܙܝܢ[5]. ܢܗܘܐ ܚܪܡ ܐܡܪ ܦܘܠܘܣ. ܐܦ ܐܠܐ[6] ܗܘ ܠܒܠܬܐ ܕܡܠܠ[7] ܡܢܬܐ ܕܡܫܪܐ[8] ܛܠܡ. ܗܢܐ ܡܢ ܒܗܘ ܟܡ ܡܢܬܐ ܢܬܦܫܩ. ܡܛܠ ܗܠܝܢ ܓܝܪ: ܡܛܠ ܕܒܫܠܡܘܬܐ ܢܗܘܐ ܐܝܬ ܠܗ ܫܪ̈ܪܐ[9]: ܒܪ̈ܬܐ ܠܗ ܒܪ̈ܬܐ: ܐܦܣܩܘܦܐ ܒܝܬ[10] ܠܗ ܐܦܣܩܘܦܐ: ܡܫ̈ܡܫܢܐ ܠܗ ܡܫ̈ܡܫܢ. ܒܝܕ ܦܘܬܐ[11] ܡܡܠܠܝܢ[12]. ܥܠ ܕܝܢ ܕܒ̈ܢܝܐ

[1] Here begins B, with ܐܢ ܗܘ ܕܠܐܪ̈ܥܐ preceded by the title ܕܛܘܒܢܐ ܕܝܘܢܘܣܝܘܣ ܪܝܫܐ ܕܐܦܝܣܩܘܦܐ ܕܐܠܟܣܢܕܪܝܐ. ܡܢ ܐܓܪܬܐ ܕܠܘܬ ܣܛܦܢܘܣ ܪܝܫܐ ܕܐܦܝܣܩܘܦܐ ܕܪܗܘܡܐ.

[2] B inserts here ܐܢܫ [3] B ܘܡܡܠܠ [4] B ܐܚܪܢ ܡܡܠܠ

[5] B ܕܐܡܪܝܢ [6] B ܘܐܠܐ [7] B ܕܥܠ [8] B here inserts ܐܢܫ

[9] ܗܢܐ ܡܢ ܒܗܘ—ܫܪ̈ܪܐ] B ܗܢܐ ܒܡ̈ܢܬܐ ܡܢ ܒܗܘ ܢܬܦܫܩ. ܥܠ ܗܠܝܢ ܓܝܪ. ܡܛܠ ܕܗܘܝܢ ܐܝܬܝܢ ܒܫܠܡܘܬܐ

[10] B ܘܐܦܣܩܘܦܐ (omitting ܒܝܬ) [11] B ܒܐܦܝܦܘܬܐ

[12] End of the extract in A.

ܘܣܘܥܪ̈ܢܐ. ܕܥܠ ܗܠܝܢ ܕܥܠ ܐܢܫ ܐܢܫ: ܕܐܝܟܢܐ
ܠܗܘ ܕܡܢ ܠܒܪ ܡܬܩܪܒ ܘܠܐ ܠܡܩܒܠܘ. ܘܐܝܟܢܐ ܠܗܘ
ܕܡܢ ܠܓܘ. ܠܡܬܚܕܘܬܗ ܠܐܝܠܝܢ ܕܡܫܚܢ ܒܪܘܚܐ ܕܥܠ ܐܝܬ
ܡܣܒܡܢ ܗܘ. ܐܝܠܝܢ ܕܒܦܢܩܝܬܐ ܐܠܗܝܬܐ ܡܬܟܬܒܢܐ
ܡܕܐ ܡܣܒܪܝܢ.. ܒܕ ܕܝܕܥܐ ܕܠܘܬܗܘܢ ܐܝܠܝܢ ܕܡܣܒܪܝܢ ܗܘܝܢ
ܠܒܪ̈ܢܫܐ ∴

Of the holy Dionysios, chief bishop of Alexandria, from the letter to Stephanos, chief bishop of Rome, concerning baptism, the one which begins "The things which were done aforetime, our reverend brother, I have made known unto thee."

If so be that any man speak a wicked thing of God, like those who call him unpitying[1], or any man bring in the fear of other gods, the law has commanded that such a one be stoned[2]: but we would stone these men with sound words of faith. [3]Or if a man receive not at all the mystery[4] of Christ, or alter and distort,—(saying) that he is not God, or that he did not become a man, or that he did not die, or that he did not rise, or that he will not come to judge the quick and the dead,—or preach anything else apart from what we preached, let him be a curse, says Paul. Or if so be he have wronged the word concerning the resurrection of the flesh, let him be already reckoned with the dead. For we speak in carefulness concerning [5]these things,—in order that we may be in agreement one to another, churches to churches, bishops to bishops, priests to priests[6]. And in regard to causes and affairs about matters which concern individual men,—how it is right to receive him who approaches from without, and how

[1] Cp. the letter to Dionysius p. 56, ὡς ἀνηλεῆ συκοφαντοῦντι.

[2] Lev. xxiv 13—16.

[3] Here begins the extract in B "If so be a man receive not": the preceding title is "Of the blessed Dionysios, chief bishop of Alexandria, from the letter to Stephanos, chief bishop of Rome."

[4] The word here used represents μυστήριον, denoting (as μυστήριον often does) the Christian revelation.

[5] B "in zeal concerning."

[6] Here ends the extract in A.

48 *DIONYSIUS OF ALEXANDRIA*

him who comes from within[7]—we counsel to obey those who stand at the head of every place, who by Divine election[8] are put into this ministration,—leaving to our Lord the judgment of all things which they do[9].

---

[7] The former are converts from heathenism, or perhaps from heresy; the latter appear to be Christians who have lapsed.

[8] The word here translated 'election' is the Greek χειροτονία in Syriac letters. It might accordingly be rendered either 'election' or 'ordination.'

[9] Cf. Cyprian, *Ep.* lv 29 and πρὸς Κόνωνα p. 61.

[Syriac text]

A. *LETTERS*

[1]Of the holy Dionysios[2] of Alexandria, from the letter to Dionysios and Stephanos, who presided over the church of the Romans[3].

Those who were baptised in the name of the three persons[4], —the Father, the Son, and the Holy Spirit—though they were baptised by heretics who confess the three persons[5], shall not be re-baptised. But those who are converted from other heresies shall be perfected by the baptism of the holy church[6].

[1] In C the title runs—"And after a little time Dionysios, who was pastor of the church of Alexandria at that time, wrote to his namesake Dionysianos and to Stephanos of the holy church of Rome, making decision and saying other things as follows." [2] B adds "bishop." [3] B "of Rome." [4] C inserts "and confess the three persons." [5] The concessive force of the word "though" stops short of the relative clause; the meaning of the sentence might be rendered thus:—"though they were baptized by heretics, so long as those heretics confess the three persons." C omits "who confess the three persons." [6] C "of the church in every way." The same MS adds "This opinion was adopted also by the 318 holy fathers who assembled at Nicæa, and by those who after them were pastors of the church. Those who assembled in Africa in the days of Cyprian, having regard to the name 'heresy,' applied a single remedy [viz. re-baptism in every case]—the contemporaries of the great Dionysius: but those after him distinguished the forms of sickness, and to all of them applied the remedy which suited them."

2

Ἡ δευτέρα—πρὸς Ξύστον

(Eus. *H. E.* vii 5. 3—6 and 6)

Στέφανον δ' ἐπὶ δυσὶν ἀποπλήσαντα τὴν λειτουργίαν ἔτεσι Ξύστος διαδέχεται. τούτῳ δευτέραν ὁ Διονύσιος περὶ βαπτίσματος ἐγχαράξας ἐπιστολὴν ὁμοῦ τὴν Στεφάνου καὶ τῶν λοιπῶν ἐπισκόπων γνώμην τε καὶ κρίσιν δηλοῖ, περὶ τοῦ Στεφάνου λέγων ταῦτα·

(1) Ἐπεστάλκει μὲν οὖν πρότερον καὶ περὶ Ἑλένου 5

5. *Stephen had previously informed the various bishops of Asia Minor that he would have no dealings with them if they rebaptized heretics. This is an important matter in view of the* canons that have already been passed on the subject in large synods of the Bishops. I have written to him myself.

ib. Ἐπεστάλκει] sc. ὁ Στέφανος.

F. 4

καὶ περὶ Φιρμιλιανοῦ καὶ πάντων τῶν τε ἀπὸ Κιλικίας καὶ Καππαδοκίας καὶ δῆλον ὅτι Γαλατίας καὶ πάντων τῶν ἑξῆς ὁμορούντων ἐθνῶν, ὡς οὐδὲ ἐκείνοις κοινωνήσων διὰ τὴν αὐτὴν ταύτην αἰτίαν, ἐπειδὴ τοὺς αἱρετικούς, φησίν, 5 ἀναβαπτίζουσι. καὶ σκόπει τὸ μέγεθος τοῦ πράγματος. ὄντως γὰρ δόγματα περὶ τούτου γέγονεν ἐν ταῖς μεγίσταις τῶν ἐπισκόπων συνόδοις, ὡς πυνθάνομαι, ὥστε τοὺς προσ- ιόντας ἀπὸ αἱρέσεων, προκατηχηθέντας, εἶτα ἀπολού- σασθαι καὶ ἀνακαθαίρεσθαι τὸν τῆς παλαιᾶς καὶ ἀκαθάρτου 10 ζύμης ῥύπον. καὶ περὶ τούτων αὐτοῦ πάντων δεόμενος ἐπέστειλα.

Καὶ μεθ' ἕτερά φησι·

(2) Καὶ τοῖς ἀγαπητοῖς δὲ ἡμῶν καὶ συμπρεσβυτέροις Διονυσίῳ καὶ Φιλήμονι, συμψήφοις πρότερον Στεφάνου

---

1 Φιρμιλιανου] Φιρμιλλ. F[b]GH Schw || τε—των εξης om Nic et Ruf || απο] om της post απο CF[a]GHOR[ab] Schw L[r] || 2 δηλον οτι AE[a]GH(OR[ab]) Sync Steph L[r] om BCDF[a]K Val Stroth Schw || 8 αιρεσεων E[a]F[b]KOR[ab] Nic Ruf Stroth Schw αιρεσεως CF[a]G Steph Val || απολου- σασθαι] -εσθαι O Sync Steph Stroth L[r] -σασθαι cett

---

2. δῆλον ὅτι] seems inserted to lay stress on the fact that not only Helenus's and Firmilian's sees in Cilicia and Cappadocia but also Galatia and other neighbouring districts were included.

3. ὡς οὐδὲ ἐκ. κοινωνήσων] Probably a reference to Cyprian had preceded. The phrase only shows that Stephen had threatened to excommunicate these churches, not that he actually did so: see Benson *op. cit.* p. 354.

6. ἐν ταῖς μεγ. συνόδ.] e.g. those of Iconium and Synnada (circ. A.D. 230): see p. 55. In writing to Stephen D. seems to have known nothing of these councils which required or at least accepted the rebaptism of heretics. D. may also be referring to the three much more recent councils of Cyprian on rebaptism which had been held at Carthage between A.D. 254 and 256 (i.e. since his letter to Stephen above): see below οἱ ἐν Ἀφρικῇ, p. 54.

7. ὡς πυνθάνομαι] So to Philemon, p. 54 μεμάθηκα. By this time (A.D. 257) D. had by patient inquiry found out much more than he had known at first of what was necessary to be known before coming to a decision.

8. ἀπολούσασθαι] prob. used absolutely as in 1 Cor. vi 11.

9. ἀνακαθαίρεσθαι κτλ.] Cf. 1 Cor. v 7, 8.

10. αὐτοῦ] gov. by δεόμενος, ἐπέστειλα being used absolutely here.

13. *I have also written more than once to Dionysius and Philemon, who at one time sided with Stephen.*

ib. συμπρεσβυτέροις] See p. 28 n.

14. Φιλήμονι] See p. 42.

A. *LETTERS* 51

γενομένοις, καὶ περὶ τῶν αὐτῶν μοι γράφουσι, πρότερον
μὲν ὀλίγα καὶ νῦν δὲ διὰ πλειόνων ἐπέστειλα.

'Αλλὰ ταῦτα μὲν περὶ τοῦ δηλουμένου ζητήματος.

Σημαίνων δὲ ἐν ταὐτῷ καὶ περὶ τῶν κατὰ Σαβέλλιον αἱρετικῶν
ὡς κατ' αὐτὸν ἐπιπολαζόντων ταῦτά φησι· 5

(3) Περὶ γὰρ τοῦ νῦν κινηθέντος ἐν τῇ Πτολεμαΐδι τῆς
Πενταπόλεως δόγματος, ὄντος ἀσεβοῦς καὶ βλασφημίαν
πολλὴν ἔχοντος περὶ τοῦ παντοκράτορος θεοῦ κὰὶ πατρὸς
τοῦ κυρίου ἡμῶν Ἰησοῦ Χριστοῦ, ἀπιστίαν τε πολλὴν ἔχοντος
περὶ τοῦ μονογενοῦς παιδὸς αὐτοῦ καὶ πρωτοτόκου πάσης 10

4 εν ταυτω BCDF^{ab}GHK(OR^{ab}) επ αυτω AE Steph probante Val ||
8 εχοντος] περιεχοντος CGH*K Nic || θεου και πατρος] θεου πατρος και
CF^{ab}GKOR^{ab} Sync L^r θεου πατρος και AE^a Steph Val om και post
πατρος H Nic (apud quem του πατρος) Schw || 9 εχοντος] om F^bGH
Nic Schw || 10 και BCDF^{ab}GHK Sync Val Schw του cett

1. γράφουσι] The imperf. part. ('were correspondents of mine' Benson) following upon the aor. (γενομένοις) is to be noticed: it indicates either that they wrote more than once or that the time of their writing was subsequent to their quitting the side of Stephen.

6. *Concerning the recent false teaching in Ptolemaïs about the Incarnation and the Holy Spirit I have already written as instructively as I could: I send you copies of my letters.*

ib. Πτολεμαΐδι] on the N.W. coast of Cyrenaica, one of the five chief cities which gave its name to the Libyan Pentapolis. Sabellius, whose heresy (δόγμα) consisted of 'a denial of the three Persons in the Trinity and the belief that the Person of the Father who is one with the Son was incarnate in Christ' (Browne *on the XXXIX Articles* p. 23), was a native of this district: see further, pp. 165 ff. His follower, Paul of Samosata, appears to have considered Christ an emanation rather than the incarnation of the Father: 'he spoke of the Son of God as being an unsubsisting knowledge or energy, ἐπιστήμη ἀνυπόστατος. In opposition to which the Fathers of the Council of Antioch (A.D. 264) speak of Him as ζῶσαν ἐνέργειαν καὶ ἐνυπόστατον, a living and substantial energy' (*ib.* p. 24).

8. θεοῦ καὶ πατρός] It seems practically certain that this is the right reading, though the MS evidence in favour of θεοῦ πατρὸς καὶ is overwhelming: the αὐτοῦ after παιδός in the next clause makes it clear that D. has spoken only of God the Father in this clause, whereas the rejected reading must mean 'God the Father and our Lord Jesus Christ.' The phrase occurs in 2 Cor. i 2, Eph. i 3, 1 Pet. i 3 and other places.

10. περὶ τοῦ μονογ....λόγου] It was D.'s treatment of this subject which afterwards gave Arius, the heresiarch of Alexandria, an opening for claiming his teaching in support of his own tenets, though there is no Arian suggestion in this particular phrase.

ib. πρωτοτόκ. π. κτ.] Col. i 15.

4—2

κτίcεωc, τοῦ ἐνανθρωπήσαντος Λόγου, ἀναισθησίαν δὲ τοῦ ἁγίου πνεύματος, ἐλθόντων ἑκατέρωθεν πρὸς ἐμὲ καὶ προγραμμάτων καὶ τῶν διαλεξομένων ἀδελφῶν, ἐπέστειλά τινα ὡς ἐδυνήθην, παρασχόντος τοῦ θεοῦ, διδασκαλικώ-
5 τερον ὑφηγούμενος, ὧν τὰ ἀντίγραφα ἔπεμψά σοι.

3

Ἡ τρίτη—πρὸς Φιλήμονα
(Eus. *H. E.* vii 7)

Καὶ ἐν τῇ τρίτῃ δὲ τῶν περὶ βαπτίσματος, ἣν Φιλήμονι τῷ κατὰ Ῥώμην πρεσβυτέρῳ ὁ αὐτὸς γράφει Διονύσιος, ταῦτα παρατίθεται·

(1) Ἐγὼ δὲ καὶ τοῖς συντάγμασι καὶ ταῖς παραδόσεσι τῶν αἱρετικῶν ἐνέτυχον, χραίνων μέν μου πρὸς ὀλίγον
10 τὴν ψυχὴν ταῖς παμμιάροις αὐτῶν ἐνθυμήσεσιν, ὄνησιν δ᾽ οὖν ἀπ᾽ αὐτῶν ταύτην λαμβάνων, τὸ ἐξελέγχειν αὐτοὺς παρ᾽ ἐμαυτῷ καὶ πολὺ πλέον βδελύττεσθαι. καὶ δή

2 προγραμματων] των γραμμ. Nic

1. ἀναισθησίαν] 'want of perception concerning,' or perhaps 'want of experience' of the Holy Spirit's influence.
2. ἑκατέρωθεν] 'from both parties' in the dispute.
ib. προγραμμάτων] 'official communications' from those in authority as opposed to personal interviews with individual brethren (τῶν διαλεξ. ἀδελφ.). For this use of the word cf. Eus. *H. E.* vii 13. 1 ἀνῄεσί τε αὐτίκα διὰ προγραμμάτων τὸν καθ᾽ ἡμῶν διωγμόν, viii 16. 1 etc.
3. ἐπέστειλά τινα] Perhaps he refers to the letters to Ammonius, Bishop of Bernice, Telesphorus, Euphranor and Euporus mentioned by Eus. *H. E.* vii 26. Athanasius appears only to mention one joint letter to Ammonius and Euphranor on this subject, see p. 166.
4. διδασκ. ὑφηγ.] 'giving a somewhat methodical explanation of the matter.'
8. *I was accustomed to read all sorts of heretical writings for my information. One of the brethren warned me of the risk of pollution which I ran. But a Divine intimation distinctly enjoined me to continue my practice, as I was competent to sift what was written without harm to my own faith.*
ib. συντάγμασι...παραδόσεσι] Both these terms must refer to *written* documents, as D. says he read (ἐνέτυχον) them. The former probably denotes a more systematic and scientific class of composition than the latter. For the various uses of the word παράδοσις see a valuable note in Heinichen (Index II pp. 507 ff. *s.v. Traditio*).
11. τὸ ἐξελέγχειν...καὶ...βδελύττ.] For the constr. cf. p. 6 τὸ καθ᾽ ἡμῶν φονᾶν.

A. LETTERS 53

τινὸς ἀδελφοῦ τῶν πρεσβυτέρων με ἀπείργοντος καὶ δε-
διττομένου συμφύρεσθαι τῷ τῆς πονηρίας αὐτῶν βορ-
βόρῳ· λυμανεῖσθαι γὰρ τὴν ψυχὴν τὴν ἐμαυτοῦ, καὶ
ἀληθῆ γε λέγοντος, ὡς ᾐσθόμην· ὅραμα θεόπεμπτον
προσελθὸν ἐπέρρωσέ με, καὶ λόγος πρός με γενόμενος 5
προσέταξε διαρρήδην λέγων· Πᾶσιν ἐντύγχανε οἷς ἂν εἰς
χεῖρας λάβοις· διευθύνειν γὰρ ἕκαστα καὶ δοκιμάζειν
ἱκανὸς εἶ, καί σοι γέγονε τοῦτο ἐξ ἀρχῆς καὶ τῆς πίστεως
αἴτιον. ἀπεδεξάμην τὸ ὅραμα, ὡς ἀποστολικῇ φωνῇ συν-
τρέχον τῇ λεγούσῃ πρὸς τοὺς δυνατωτέρους· Γίνεcθε 10
δόκιμοι τραπεζῖται.

Εἶτά τινα περὶ πασῶν εἰπὼν τῶν αἱρέσεων, ἐπιφέρει λέγων·

(2) Τοῦτον ἐγὼ τὸν κανόνα καὶ τὸν τύπον παρὰ

2 συμφυρεσθαι F^bGHK Sync *polluerer* Ruf Stroth Schw L^r Val (ex coniectura) συμφερεσθαι cett

1. ἀδελφοῦ τῶν πρεσβ.] This is a pleasing illustration of the terms on which D. was with his clergy. His confession that the presbyter was right is a sign of the fair and sympathetic hearing which he gave to the writings against which he had been warned.

5. λόγος πρός με γενόμ.] Cf. above p. 24 οὐκ ἀθεεί etc. Heinichen appositely quotes (1) the voice *de vicina domo cum cantu dicentis et crebro repetentis quasi pueri an puellae nescio*, *Tolle, lege*, which Augustine says he heard at a critical moment of his conversion (*Conf.* viii ch. 12 § 29); and (2) the φωνὴ ἐξ οὐρανοῦ, "Ἴσχυε καὶ ἀνδρίζου, which came to Polycarp, as he was led into the arena (Eus. *H. E.* iv 15. 17). Cf. also Jerome *Ep.* 22 *ad Eustochium* c. 30.

6. διαρρήδην] 'expressly,' 'in so many words.'

ib. οἷς ἂν...λάβοις] For the construction cf. p. 34 ὁπόταν βουληθείη.

8. ἐξ ἀρχῆς] See General Introduction, p. xiv.

9. ἀποστολικῇ φωνῇ] The epithet is somewhat strange as this common apocryphal saying is usually attributed to our Lord: see Westcott *Introduction to Gospels* p. 454, Resch *Agrapha* pp. 116 ff. Trans. the phrase: 'approve yourselves good bankers (or traders).' The exhortation in a negative form is found, as Heinichen (tom. ii p. 694) has pointed out, in *Cebetis Tabula* (circ. B.C. 400) μὴ γίνεσθε ὅμοιοι τοῖς κακοῖς τραπεζίταις and in Max. Tyr. ii 2. Cf. 1 Thess. v 21. It is remarkable that another positive command of Christianity (Mark vii 12) is found elsewhere (e.g. in Tobit iv 15) in a negative form, just as generally the 'thou shalt not' of the Mosaic decalogue becomes 'thou shalt' in the Sermon on the Mount.

13. *This canon I received from my predecessor Heraclas: that those who after orthodox baptism had consorted with heretics should not be admitted to Communion, until they had made a public acknowledgement of their errors, but that no rebaptism should be required of them.*

ib. Τοῦτον ἐγὼ τὸν κανόνα κτλ.] D.'s citation of Heraclas's canon in

τοῦ μακαρίου πάπα ἡμῶν Ἡρακλᾶ παρέλαβον. τοὺς γὰρ προσιόντας ἀπὸ τῶν αἱρέσεων, καίτοι τῆς ἐκκλησίας ἀποστάντας, μᾶλλον δὲ οὐδὲ ἀποστάντας, ἀλλὰ συνάγεσθαι μὲν δοκοῦντας, καταμηνυθέντας δὲ ὡς προσφοιτῶντάς
5 τινι τῶν ἑτεροδιδασκαλούντων, ἀπελάσας τῆς ἐκκλησίας, δεομένους οὐ προσήκατο, ἕως δημοσίᾳ πάντα ὅσα ἀκηκόεσαν παρὰ τοῖς ἀντιδιατιθεμένοις, ἐξέφρασαν, καὶ τότε συνήγαγεν αὐτούς, οὐ δεηθεὶς ἐπ' αὐτῶν ἑτέρου βαπτίσματος· τοῦ γὰρ ἁγίου πρότερον παρ' αὐτοῦ τετυχήκεσαν.
10 Πάλιν δὲ ἐπιπολὺ γυμνάσας τὸ πρόβλημα ταῦτα ἐπιλέγει·

(3) Μεμάθηκα καὶ τοῦτο, ὅτι μὴ νῦν οἱ ἐν Ἀφρικῇ μόνον τοῦτο παρεισήγαγον, ἀλλὰ καὶ πρὸ πολλοῦ κατὰ τοὺς

6 ακηκοεσαν OR^{ab} Schw L^r ακηκοασι cett ‖ 9 αγιου] add πνευματος B Steph Val om cett ‖ 11 τουτο] om L^r tacite

this connexion seems to imply that he had not yet quite clearly grasped the point at issue in his own time.

1. πάπα] Πάπας (πάππας) Lat. *papa* is a colloquial form of πατήρ, applied to the bishop (and even to the inferior clergy sometimes) in the first ages. Neither the exclusive claim of the Bishop of Rome to the title nor the theory that it originated with the Bishop of Alexandria has any historical ground. Tert. *de pud.* 13 applies it generally to any bishop; it is given to Cyprian of Carthage (a contemporary of Heraclas) and so on. See Benson *Cyprian* p. 29 ff.

3. ἀποστάντας] Heraclas was dealing here not with those who had received heretical baptism but with those who were actually or were reputed perverts: see p. 50. In the letter to Xystus, p. 57, we have a case of heretical baptism pure and simple discussed.

8. συνήγαγεν] 'admitted them to assemblies' (cf. προσήκατο above): so p. 18, like συνάγεσθαι above.

9. τοῦ ἁγίου] Some understand πνεύματος, others βαπτίσματος, as omitted; but perhaps it is simplest to understand τὸ ἅγιον as used abs. = 'the holy gift': cf. Matt. vii 6, Luke i 35 and Heb. ix 1. Cyprian uses *sanctum* (of the Holy Eucharist) much in the same way *de laps.* 26 *sancto fugiente*.

11. *I have ascertained that this policy (of rebaptism) has been introduced not only in the African Church, but also in many other churches and synods, e.g. those of Iconium and Synnada.*

ib. Μεμάθηκα] Cf. p. 50 ὡς πυνθάνομαι.

ib. ὅτι μή] The μή here would simply be οὐ in classical Greek: the use of ὅτι μή ('except') after negatives is of course not in question.

ib. οἱ ἐν Ἀφρικῇ] i.e. the church in Africa Proconsularis of which Carthage was the metropolis and Cyprian the Metropolitan: see note on p. 50 above.

12. πρὸ πολλοῦ] The Synods, to which D. refers, had been held some 25 years before (in A.D. 230).

A. LETTERS

πρὸ ἡμῶν ἐπισκόπους ἐν ταῖς πολυανθρωποτάταις ἐκκλησίαις καὶ ταῖς συνόδοις τῶν ἀδελφῶν, ἐν Ἰκονίῳ καὶ Συννάδοις, καὶ παρὰ πολλοῖς τοῦτο ἔδοξεν· ὧν τὰς βουλὰς ἀνατρέπων εἰς ἔριν αὐτοὺς καὶ φιλονεικίαν ἐμβαλεῖν οὐχ ὑπομένω. Οὐ γὰρ μετακινήσεις, φησίν, ὅρια τοῦ πλησίον σου, 5 ἃ ἔθεντο οἱ πατέρες σου.

4

Ἡ τετάρτη—πρὸς Διονύσιον τὸν κατὰ Ῥώμην
(Eus. *H. E.* vii 7. 6 and 8)

Ἡ τετάρτη αὐτοῦ τῶν περὶ βαπτίσματος ἐπιστολῶν πρὸς τὸν κατὰ Ῥώμην ἐγράφη Διονύσιον, τότε μὲν πρεσβείου ἠξιωμένον, οὐκ εἰς μακρὸν δὲ καὶ τὴν ἐπισκοπὴν τῶν ἐκεῖσε παρειληφότα· ἐξ ἧς γνῶναι πάρεστιν, ὅπως καὶ αὐτὸς οὗτος λόγιός τε καὶ θαυμάσιος 10 πρὸς τοῦ κατ᾽ Ἀλεξάνδρειαν Διονυσίου μεμαρτύρηται. γράφει δὲ αὐτῷ μεθ᾽ ἕτερα τῶν κατὰ τὸν Νοουάτον μνημονεύων ἐν τούτοις·

Νοουατιανῷ μὲν γὰρ εὐλόγως ἀπεχθανόμεθα, διακόψαντι τὴν ἐκκλησίαν καί τινας τῶν ἀδελφῶν εἰς ἀσεβείας καὶ βλασφημίας ἑλκύσαντι καὶ περὶ τοῦ θεοῦ 15 διδασκαλίαν ἀνοσιωτάτην ἐπεισκυκλήσαντι καὶ τὸν

4 αυτους] post εριν CF^{ab}GHR^a Sync Schw post φιλον. cett ‖ εμβαλειν] εμβαλλειν GH(OR^a) Nic L^r ‖ 13 Νοουατιανω] Ναυατ. AE^aO Nic Sync L^r Νοουατ. cett

2. Ἰκονίῳ] mod. *Konieh*, the chief city of Lycaonia: see Acts xiii and xiv.
ib. Συννάδοις] an important town in Phrygia (Salutaris): see Benson *Cyprian* p. 340 note 3. Eus. (*H. E.* vi 19. 18) quotes from a letter of Alexander of Jerusalem and Theoctistus of Caesarea which mentions the Bishops (Celsus and Atticus) of these two towns as prominent in employing lay-preachers.
3. παρὰ πολλοῖς] 'amongst many (brethren)' as contrasted with the single church of Africa (οἱ ἐν Ἀφρικῇ).

4. αὐτούς] refers to the same persons as πολλοῖς above and ὧν.
5. οὐ γὰρ κτλ] Deut. xix 14 (ἐστησαν LXX).
13. We do well to abhor Novatian's methods which mar the unity of the Church, mislead certain of the brethren, introduce impious teaching about both God the Father and God the Son, nullify Holy Baptism and destroy the penitent's hope of the Holy Ghost's return.
16. ἐπεισκυκλήσαντι] vox a re scenica petita Hein.; cf. ἐκκύκλημα and εἰσκυκλεῖν. Here it seems to

χρηστότατον κύριον ἡμῶν Ἰησοῦν Χριστὸν ὡς ἀνηλεῆ συκοφαντοῦντι, ἐπὶ πᾶσι δὲ τούτοις τὸ λουτρὸν ἀθετοῦντι τὸ ἅγιον καὶ τήν τε πρὸ αὐτοῦ πίστιν καὶ ὁμολογίαν ἀνατρέποντι, τό τε πνεῦμα τὸ ἅγιον ἐξ αὐτῶν, εἰ καί τις ἦν
5 ἐλπὶς τοῦ παραμεῖναι ἢ καὶ ἐπανελθεῖν πρὸς αὐτούς, παντελῶς φυγαδεύοντι.

5

Ἡ πέμπτη—πρὸς Ξύστον

(Eus. *H. E.* vii 9)

Καὶ ἡ πέμπτη δὲ αὐτῷ πρὸς τὸν Ῥωμαίων ἐπίσκοπον Ξύστον ἐγέγραπτο, ἐν ᾗ πολλὰ κατὰ τῶν αἱρετικῶν εἰπὼν τοιοῦτόν τι γεγονὸς κατ' αὐτὸν ἐκτίθεται λέγων·

10 Καὶ γὰρ ὄντως, ἀδελφέ, καὶ συμβουλῆς δέομαι, καὶ

5 η και] om και CF[a] || 10 και συμβ.] om και AE[a] Steph Val

mean 'to bring in the unexpected,' 'to spring something on one.' Liddell and Scott translate and give exx. of the meaning 'to roll in one thing after another,' but this force of the prep. ἐπί seems not to be present here. Hein. and Schwegler give other exx. in the Indices of their editions.

1. χρηστότατον] Cf. 1 Pet. ii 3.
ib. συκοφαντοῦντι] See above, p. 14.
3. πρὸ αὐτοῦ] sc. τοῦ λουτροῦ. A confession of faith has always been required before baptism either from the person himself or (in the case of infants) from their sponsors: see for instance Cypr. *Ep.* lxx ch. 2 (ed. Hartel) and Justin M. *Apol.* 1.
4. ἐξ αὐτῶν] sc. τῶν βαπτισθέντων.
ib. ἐξ αὐτῶν...φυγαδεύοντι] 'altogether banishes the Holy Spirit from them, even though there were some hope of His remaining with them or even of His returning to them.' Vales. is troubled at the difficulty of the Holy Spirit's remaining with the lapsed and rather thinks it must refer to the faithful who fall into other sin than that of apostasy, or perhaps to those who, when they apostatized, were *mente capti aut mirrata potione sopiti*. But D. is only showing here as elsewhere the breadth of his view of God. As to the possibility of a *return* of the Holy Spirit after departure, see Mason *Relation of Confirmation to Baptism* p. 280.

10. *I desire your advice in a case which has come before me: an ancient disciple after being present at a public Baptism came to me in tears and told me that the Baptism he had received among the heretics was something quite different from this, being full of impiety and blasphemy: he begged me to give him the Baptism of the Church; but I dared not do so, as he had long been a regular communicant and I bade him take courage and resume his communions: but nothing will console him or induce him to approach the Holy Table.*

ib. συμβουλῆς δέομαι] The open-

A. LETTERS

γνώμην αἰτῶ παρὰ σοῦ, τοιούτου τινός μοι προσελθόντος
πράγματος, δεδιὼς μὴ ἄρα σφάλλομαι. τῶν γὰρ συναγο-
μένων ἀδελφῶν πιστὸς νομιζόμενος ἀρχαῖος, καὶ πρὸ τῆς
ἐμῆς χειροτονίας, οἶμαι δὲ καὶ πρὸ τῆς τοῦ μακαρίου
Ἡρακλᾶ καταστάσεως, τῆς συναγωγῆς μετασχών, τοῖς 5
ὑπόγυιον βαπτιζομένοις παρατυχὼν καὶ τῶν ἐπερωτήσεων
καὶ τῶν ἀποκρίσεων ἐπακούσας, προσῆλθέ μοι κλαίων
καὶ καταθρηνῶν ἑαυτὸν καὶ πίπτων πρὸ τῶν ποδῶν μου,
ἐξομολογούμενος μὲν καὶ ἐξομνύμενος τὸ βάπτισμα, ὃ
παρὰ τοῖς αἱρετικοῖς βεβάπτιστο, μὴ τοῦτο εἶναι μηδὲ 1
ὅλως ἔχειν τινὰ πρὸς τοῦτο κοινωνίαν· ἀσεβείας γὰρ
ἐκεῖνο καὶ βλασφημιῶν πεπληρῶσθαι· λέγων δὲ πάνυ τι
τὴν ψυχὴν νῦν κατανενύχθαι, καὶ μηδὲ παρρησίαν ἔχειν

2 σφάλλομαι CF^aGHR^{ab} παρασφαλλ. F^b σφαλλωμαι AE^a Nic Steph Val Schw L^r ǁ 3 αδελφων] add τις Nic *frater quidam* Ruf ǁ 4 προ] om E^aF^bGH Steph ǁ 7 των αποκρ.] om των AE^aGH Steph Stroth Schw ǁ 10 τουτο AE^a (OR^{ab}) Steph L^r τοιουτον nonnulli ǁ 13 νυν] om AE^aF^b Nic Ruf Steph Stroth

ing phrases of this fragment bring out clearly the highly conscientious and humble as well as the conciliatory and sympathetic elements in D.'s character.

3. ἀρχαῖος] Cf. Acts xxi 16 ἀρχαίῳ μαθητῇ.

4. χειροτονίας] 'ordination' (as bishop); in the next clause κατα-στάσεως = 'appointment' (as bishop). Χειροτονία καλεῖται ἡ τῆς καθιερώ-σεως τοῦ ἱερᾶσθαι λαχόντος τελεσι-ουργία τῶν εὐχῶν καὶ τοῦ Ἁγίου Πνεύ-ματος ἐπίκλησις ἀπὸ τοῦ τὸν ἀρχιε-ρέα τείνειν τὴν χεῖρα εὐλογοῦντα τὸν χειροτονούμενον, πάλαι δὲ καὶ αὐτὴ ἡ ψῆφος χειροτονία ὠνόμαστο, Zonaras quoted by Walcott *On the English Ordinal* p. 35. This derivation is however less probable than that from the use of the word χειρο-τονεῖν at Athens to express election by show of hands. The act of Imposition of hands is strictly χειροθεσία or χειρεπιθεσία rather than χειρο-τονία.

5. συναγωγῆς] See note on p. 57.
6. ὑπόγυιον] adv. 'recently'; the usual form is ὑπογυίως or ὑπογύως.
ib. τῶν ἐπερωτ. καὶ τῶν ἀποκρίσ.] i.e. the questions put by the minister and the answers given by the candidates before Baptism.

9. ὃ] cognate accus. after βε-βάπτιστο.

10. μὴ τοῦτο εἶναι] 'not to be (identical with) this (sc. orthodox Baptism)': I have rejected the reading τοιοῦτον ('like what he then witnessed') with the Berlin editor. The wide difference which the man saw between the rite of the Church and that which he had received is to be noted. It is strange that so old a believer should never have noticed it before, but Baptism was almost entirely confined in those days to Easter and Whitsuntide and he may not have been present on any such occasion.

13. τὴν ψυχὴν...κατανενύχθαι] 'to be sore pricked in the soul.'

ἐπᾶραι τοὺς ὀφθαλμοὺς πρὸς τὸν θεόν, ἀπὸ τῶν ἀνοσίων
ἐκείνων ῥημάτων καὶ πραγμάτων ὁρμώμενος, καὶ διὰ
τοῦτο δεόμενος τῆς εἰλικρινεστάτης ταύτης καθάρσεως
καὶ παραδοχῆς καὶ χάριτος τυχεῖν. ὅπερ ἐγὼ μὲν οὐκ
5 ἐτόλμησα ποιῆσαι, φήσας αὐτάρκη τὴν πολυχρόνιον αὐτῷ
κοινωνίαν εἰς τοῦτο γεγονέναι. εὐχαριστίας γὰρ ἐπακού-
σαντα καὶ συνεπιφθεγξάμενον τὸ Ἀμήν, καὶ τραπέζῃ
παραστάντα καὶ χεῖρας εἰς ὑποδοχὴν τῆς ἁγίας τροφῆς
προτείναντα, καὶ ταύτην καταδεξάμενον καὶ τοῦ σώματος
10 καὶ τοῦ αἵματος τοῦ κυρίου ἡμῶν Ἰησοῦ Χριστοῦ μετα-
σχόντα ἱκανῷ χρόνῳ, οὐκ ἂν ἐξ ὑπαρχῆς ἀνασκευάζειν

10 Ιησου Χριστου] om AE^{a}F^{b}OL^r || 11 υπαρχης] AE^a Steph Val

1. ἐπᾶραι τ. ὀφθ.] cf. Luke xviii 13.
2. ὁρμώμενος] The participle gives the reason why he felt as he did, viz. 'because he had started (his religious life) with such unholy words and rites.'
4. παραδοχῆς] From its position between καθάρσεως and χάριτος this probably means 'reception' (of the Holy Ghost): otherwise it might be taken to mean 'reception' (into the Church) or 'acceptance' (by God): the word does not seem to be used quite for 'adoption,' as Vales. suggests.
7. Ἀμήν] Cf. 1 Cor. xiv 16 and Just. Mart. *Apol.* i οὗ συντελέσαντες τὰς εὐχὰς καὶ τὴν εὐχαριστίαν πᾶς ὁ παρὼν λαὸς ἐπευφημεῖ λέγων Ἀμήν. The Amen is either that after the Consecration of the Elements or at the Reception of them. See the quotation from Cyril of Jerus. below.
ib. τραπέζῃ παραστάντα] For this use of τράπεζα, which is rare in ante-Nicene times, cf. p. 103, and *Can. Hipp.* xix § 143 *stans ad mensam*, and for the posture (παραστάντα), see Scudamore, *Not. Euchar.* p. 637, who quotes, besides this passage, Cyril of Jerus. *Catech.*

Myst. v § 22 and Chrys. *Hom.* xx *in* 2 Cor. ix 15 to show that the primitive posture (as it is still the posture in the East) at the Reception of the Elements was standing.
8. χεῖρας...προτείναντα] Cyril of Jerus. *Catech. Myst.* v §§ 21 and 22 gives exact directions for the position of the hands: προσιὼν οὖν μὴ τεταμένοις τοῖς τῶν χειρῶν καρποῖς προσέρχου, μηδὲ διῃρημένοις τοῖς δακτύλοις· ἀλλὰ τὴν ἀριστερὰν θρόνον ποιήσας τῇ δεξιᾷ ὡς μελλούσῃ βασιλέα ὑποδέχεσθαι καὶ κοιλάνας τὴν παλάμην δέχου τὸ σῶμα, ἐπιλέγων τὸ Ἀμήν...εἶτα μετὰ τὸ κοινωνῆσαί σε τοῦ σώματος Χριστοῦ προσέρχου καὶ τῷ ποτηρίῳ τοῦ αἵματος, μὴ ἀνατείνων τὰς χεῖρας ἀλλὰ κύπτων καὶ τρόπῳ προσκυνήσεως καὶ σεβάσματος λέγων τὸ Ἀμήν. The phrase εἰς ὑποδοχήν in D. compared with the ὑποδέχεσθαι in Cyril shows that Warren (*Liturgy of the Ante-Nicene Church* p. 127) is mistaken in thinking that this is a 'trace of a custom at Alexandria—a custom not universally followed even there — of permitting the communicants to approach the holy table and to take each for themselves a portion of the consecrated Eucharist: Clem. Alex. *Strom.* i 1 (= P. G. viii 691).'

ἔτι τολμήσαιμι· θαρσεῖν δὲ ἐκέλευον, καὶ μετὰ βεβαίας πίστεως καὶ ἀγαθῆς ἐλπίδος τῇ μετοχῇ τῶν ἁγίων προσιέναι. ὁ δὲ οὔτε πενθῶν παύεται, πέφρικέ τε τῇ τραπέζῃ προσιέναι, καὶ μόλις παρακαλούμενος συνεστάναι ταῖς προσευχαῖς ἀνέχεται. 5

Ἐπὶ ταῖς προειρημέναις φέρεταί τις καὶ ἄλλη τοῦ αὐτοῦ περὶ βαπτίσματος ἐπιστολή, ἐξ αὐτοῦ καὶ ἧς ἡγεῖτο παροικίας Ξύστῳ καὶ τῇ κατὰ Ῥώμην ἐκκλησίᾳ προσπεφωνημένη, ἐν ᾗ διὰ μακρᾶς ἀποδείξεως τὸν περὶ τοῦ ὑποκειμένου ζητήματος παρατείνει λόγον.

1 ετι τολμ.] επιτολμ. F^aGHOR^{ab}L^r ‖ 2 ελπιδος AE^aF^bGHO Sync συνειδησεως BCDF^aK(R^{ab}) Ruf Nic Stroth Schw

4. συνεστάναι ταῖς προσευχαῖς] sc. as one of the *Consistentes* (the last order of penitents) to stay and join in the prayers of the Church after the dismissal of the catechumens and other penitents but not to make his oblation or communicate. Cf. Can. Nic. xi χωρὶς προσφορᾶς κοινωνήσουσι τῷ λαῷ τῶν προσευχῶν. We may notice that the position of standing is still implied in both συνεστάναι and *Consistentes*.

VI

Πρὸς Κόνωνα Ἐπιστολή

(Pitra *Spic. Sol.* i 15 = Bodl. Cod. Bar. cxcvi fol. 75)

Eus. *H. E.* vi 46. 2 tells us πρὸς Κόνωνα (τῆς Ἑρμουπολιτῶν[1] δὲ παροικίας ἐπίσκοπος ἦν οὗτος) ἰδία τις περὶ μετανοίας αὐτοῦ (sc. Διονυσίου) φέρεται γραφή. This letter has sometimes been referred to as a Canon from faulty MSS of Jerome (*de virr. illust.* 69) which insert the words *item canonem de paenitentia* after *ad Laodicenses de paenitentia* (p. xxxiv)[2]. The codex from which the fragment before us is taken is dated A.D. 1062; to

[1] *Hermopolis minor* was a town on the Nile not far from Alexandria; another town of the name (called *maior*) existed much farther up the river, about half way between Memphis and Thebes. The former is probably meant.
[2] Harnack (*Altchrist. Lit.* i 414) leaves out the clause altogether: Pitra appears to think that *item canonem* stands for *et ad Cononem*.

it is added a scholium (or epitome) by Alexander Aristaeus of the tenth century. The whole of the extract should be compared with Cyprian's Letter LV chaps. 23 and 29: and it may be added that the wording of it, which is in accordance with Dionysius's abundantly illustrated broad-mindedness, bears just sufficient resemblance to the passage given on p. 20 to suggest that in it we have the ἐντολὴ ὑπ' ἐμοῦ δεδομένη there mentioned[1].

The text of Bar. cxcvi fol. 75 has been subjected to a fresh collation by the Rev. H. E. Symonds, who discovers that two of the four emendations suggested by Pitra are actually in the text already, viz. δεσμῶται (not δεσμῶνται) and ἐπιμένοιεν (not ἐπιμένοι ἐν), whilst the other two, γινομένου for γενομένου and τοὺς ὅρους for ὅρους, are not necessary.

[1] E.g. τοῦ βίου εἰ δέοιντο in both passages: ἀφέσεως τυχεῖν ‖ ἀφίεσθαι: βεβαίαν τὴν εὐδοκίαν ‖ εὐέλπιδες.

Καὶ τοὺς πρὸς τῇ ἐξόδῳ γινομένους τοῦ βίου, εἰ δέοιντο καὶ ἱκετεύοιεν ἀφέσεως τυχεῖν πρὸ ὀφθαλμῶν ἔχοντες εἰς ἣν ἀπίασι κρίσιν, λογιζόμενοι ἃ πείσονται δεσμῶται καὶ κατάδικοι παραδοθέντες, πιστεύοντες δέ, εἰ ἐντεῦθεν λυ-
5 θεῖεν, ἄνεσιν ἕξειν καὶ κουφισμὸν τῆς ἐκεῖ τιμωρίας· ἀληθῆ γὰρ εἶναι καὶ βεβαίαν τὴν εὐδοκίαν τοῦ κυρίου· καὶ τούτους ἐλευθέρους παραπέμπειν τῆς θεοπρεποῦς ἐστὶ φιλανθρωπίας. εἰ μέντοι μετὰ τοῦτο ἐπιμένοιεν τῷ βίῳ, δεσμεύειν μὲν αὖθις καὶ ἐπαχθίζειν ταῖς ἁμαρτίαις οὐκ
10 ἀκόλουθόν μοι φαίνεται. τοὺς γὰρ ἅπαξ ἀφειμένους, καὶ

1. *It is but right that absolution should be granted to those who being near to death ask for it and show true penitence and faith. But in the event of their recovery to seek to withdraw that absolution, unless they lapse into sin again, is quite inconsistent with proper views of grace.*

3. δεσμῶται] sc. *quos delictorum catena constringit* (to quote the language of the ancient Gregorian collect).

4. ἐντεῦθεν] for ἐνταῦθα 'in this world,' opp. to ἐκεῖ which follows.

6. ἀληθῆ γὰρ κτλ.] 'for the approval of the Lord' (i.e. as expressed by the absolution of the Church) 'is real and sure'; for εὐδοκία ('approval') cf. Matt. iii 17, Luke ii 14.

7. καὶ τούτους] 'these also' (sc. τοὺς πρὸς τῇ ἐξ. γιν. τ. β. above). Others must have been mentioned by D. in an earlier part of the letter.

ib. θεοπρεποῦς] Cf. pp. 94 and 156.

A. LETTERS

τῷ θεῷ συστάντας, καὶ πάλιν τῆς θείας χάριτος κοινωνοὺς
ἀποφανθέντας, καὶ ὡς ἐλευθέρους πρὸς τὸν κύριον ἀπε-
σταλμένους, μηδενὸς ἐν τῷ μεταξὺ ὑπ' αὐτῶν ἑτέρως
γενομένου, πάλιν ἀνθυπάγειν τοῖς ἁμαρτήμασιν ἀλογώ-
τατον. εἶτα τῷ μὲν θεῷ τῆς ἡμετέρας κρίσεως ὅρους 5
δώσομεν φυλαχθησομένους ὑπ' αὐτοῦ, ἑαυτοῖς δὲ τούτους
οὐ τηρήσομεν, κατεπαγγελλόμενοι μὲν τὴν χρηστότητα
τοῦ κυρίου, ἀφαιρούμενοι δὲ τὴν ἑαυτῶν; εἰ μέντοι φαίνοιτό τις μετὰ τὸ ῥαῖσαι πλείονος ἐπιστροφῆς δεόμενος,

1. τῷ θεῷ συστάντας] 'being reconciled to God'; the phrase can hardly have reference to the technical sense of Συνιστάμενοι which occurs on p. 59.

2. ἀποφανθέντας] 'having been pronounced' by the official act of the Church or perhaps simply 'having been made' or 'constituted.'

ib. ὡς ἐλευθ. πρὸς τὸν κύριον ἀπεσταλμ.] 'dispatched as free men to appear before the Lord' (viz. under the impression that they were going to die) : the use of the word ἀποστέλλεσθαι in this connexion (i.e. without the idea of mission or commission) is strange : but compare παραδοθέντες and παραπέμπειν above.

3. μηδενὸς...ἑτέρως γενομ.] neut. 'if nothing wrong has been done by them in the meantime.' Alex. Arist. paraphrases the sentence μηδὲν ἐν τ. μ. ἐργασαμένους. Pitra's suggestion γινομ. seems to spoil the sense. For ἑτέρως as an euphemism (=κακῶς) see Lexicons.

4. ἀνθυπάγειν τ. ἁμαρτ.] In Thuc. iii 70 the verb is used strictly ('to indict in turn'), and so here we might translate 'to indict for their sins' (which, however, would rather require the genitive). But the meaning is rather 'to bring back into bondage to their sins,' as above we have δεσμεύειν καὶ ἐπαχθίζειν.

5. Surely we shall not thus impose limits on the goodness of God. But if any one after recovery shows that he needs a long course of penance, we must urge him to consent to undergo this to his own and the general advantage : if he refuse, we must have recourse to a second excommunication.

ib. εἶτα] 'after thus pledging ourselves to them.'

ib. τῷ μὲν θεῷ...οὐ τηρήσομεν] 'shall we impose on God the limits of our judgement, which He is bound to keep, while we observe them not for ourselves?' Ἑαυτοῖς =ἡμῖν αὐτοῖς.

7. τὴν χρηστότητα τ. κυρ.] Cf. 1 Pet. ii 3 quoted from Ps. xxxiii (xxxiv) 9 : for κατεπαγγελλ. see p. 110.

9. μετὰ τὸ ῥαῖσαι] 'after getting better' (in bodily health) : ῥαΐζειν is a medical term from ῥᾴδιος, ῥᾴων.

ib. ἐπιστροφῆς] 'attention,' 'treatment' : the word occurs in Thuc. iii 71 shortly after the word ἀνθυπάγ. noticed above ; μηδὲν ἀνεπιτήδειον πράσσειν, ὅπως μή τις ἐπιστροφὴ γένηται, where some translate 'reaction' and others 'punishment.' See n. on ἐπιστρέφεια p. 32 and cf. the epithet ἐπιστρεπτική applied to one of D.'s letters by Eus. *H. E.* vi 46. 2.

ἑκοντὶ συμβουλεύομεν ταπεινοῦν καὶ κακοῦν καὶ συστέλλειν ἑαυτόν, εἴς τε τὸ ἑαυτοῦ συμφέρον ἀφορῶντα, καὶ τὸ
πρὸς τοὺς λοιποὺς εὐπρεπὲς καὶ πρὸς τοὺς ἔξωθεν ἀνεπί-
ληπτον. καὶ πειθόμενος μὲν ὀνήσεται· εἰ δὲ ἀπειθοίη
5 καὶ ἀντιλέγοι, τότε δὴ καὶ τοῦτο ἔγκλημα ἔσται ἱκανὸν
πρὸς ἀφορισμὸν δεύτερον.

Τοὺς προσδοκίᾳ θανάτου λυθέντας τῆς ἀκοινωνησίας ἄλογον, ἂν
ἐπιβιῴεν, αὖθις δεσμεῖν, μηδὲν ἐν τῷ μεταξὺ ἐργασαμένους. Εἰ μέντοι
μετὰ τὸ ῥαῖσαι φαίνοιτό τις πλείονος δεόμενος ἐπιστροφῆς, καὶ νου-
10 θετούμενος ταπεινοῦν καὶ κακοῦν καὶ συστέλλειν ἑαυτὸν μὴ πείθοιτο,
ἀλλ' ἀντιλέγοι, τοῦτο αὐτῷ ἔγκλημα πρὸς δεύτερον ἀφορισμόν. Alex-
andri Aristaei scholium.

1. ἑκοντί] adv. 'of his own accord,' to be taken with the infinitives
ταπεινοῦν, etc.
ib. συμβουλεύομεν] 'we advise
him': we might perhaps have expected -ωμεν, as D. is instructing
Conon how to act, not stating his
own practice.
ib. συστέλλειν] lit. 'to shorten
sail' and so 'to draw in,' 'to
abase.'

3. πρὸς τοὺς λοιπούς] sc. Χριστιανούς.
ib. πρὸς τοὺς ἔξωθεν] Cf. 1 Tim.
iii 7, Col. iv 5, 1 Thess. iv 12.
ib. ἀνεπίληπτον] Cf. 1 Tim. v 7.
5. καὶ τοῦτο κτλ.] 'this also will
be a sufficient charge for a second
excommunication' (just as the former
charge was for the first). Ἀφορισμός = 'excommunication,' for which
ἀκοινωνησία is the later word.

VII

Ἐκ τῶν περὶ Μετανοίας

I

Mai, who printed this fragment from a Vat. MS (in *Class. Auct.* x 484)[1], refers it to one of the three treatises on Penitence mentioned by Jerome (*de virr. illust.* 69) as addressed
to Fabius of Antioch, to the Laodiceans, and to the Armenians
respectively: but Benson (*Cyprian* p. 164) inclines to the
view that it comes from the letter 'to the Confessors while
still adherents of Novatian,' because 'its peculiar touches on

[1] Pitra (*Mon. Jur. Eccl. Graec.* i 540) joined it to the extract πρὸς
Κόνωνα (pp. 60 ff.).

A. LETTERS

Peace' indicate 'a context on that topic'; this is the letter mentioned by Eus. *H. E.* vi 46 ἔτι δὲ τῇ τοῦ Νοουάτου συμφερομένοις γνώμῃ.

Νῦν δὲ τοὐναντίον ποιοῦμεν ἡμεῖς· ὃν γὰρ ὁ χριστὸς ἀγαθὸς ὢν ἐπὶ τὰ ὄρη πλανώμενον ἐπιζητεῖ, καὶ ἀποφεύγοντα προσκαλεῖται, καὶ εὑρεθέντα μόλις ἐπὶ τῶν ὤμων αἴρει, τοῦτον προσιόντα θρασέως ἀπολακτίζομεν. ἀλλὰ μὴ οὕτω κακῶς περὶ ἑαυτῶν βουλευώμεθα, μηδὲ εἰς 5 αὑτοὺς ὠθῶμεν τὸ ξίφος· οἱ μὲν γὰρ ἀδικεῖν τινὰς ἢ τοὐναντίον εὐεργετεῖν ἐπιχειροῦντες ἐκείνους μὲν οὐ πάντως ἔδρασαν ὅπερ ἠθέλησαν, ἑαυτοῖς δὲ κακίαν ἢ ἀγαθότητα συνοικίσαντες ἢ θείων ἀρετῶν ἢ ἀτιθάσων παθῶν ἔκπλεοι ἔσονται. καὶ οὗτοι μὲν ἀγγέλων ἀγαθῶν 10 ὀπαδοὶ καὶ συνοδοιπόροι, καὶ ἐνθάδε καὶ ἐκεῖ, ξὺν πάσῃ εἰρήνῃ καὶ ἐλευθερίᾳ πάντων κακῶν, εἰς τὸν ἀεὶ ὄντα αἰῶνα τὰς μακαριωτάτας ἀποκληρώσονται λήξεις, καὶ μετὰ Θεοῦ ἀεὶ ἔσονται, τὸ πάντων ἀγαθὸν μέγιστον· οὗτοι δὲ ἀποπεσοῦνται τῆς θείας ἅμα καὶ τῆς ἑαυτῶν 15

9 ατιθασων] ατιθασσων Migne

1. *Let us not act contrary to the Good Shepherd, who with infinite care brings back the lost sheep to the fold. To be too severe with penitents is bad policy even for ourselves. For the harm or good we do to others affects ourselves as well as them: and those who benefit others will now and hereafter be partakers with the angels of bliss in God's Presence: and those who injure others will lose all peace and have their lot with devils. So let us be gentle in receiving penitents.*

ib. ὃν γὰρ κτλ.] The reference is to Luke xv 4–7: it will be noticed that the epithet (ἀγαθός) is not St John's in the tenth chapter of his gospel (καλός). The words πλαν. ἐπὶ τὰ ὄρη are a touch derived from Ezek. xxxiv 6 (cf. 1 Kings xxii 17).

7. οὐ πάντως] 'not at all,' as in classical Greek.

9. ἀτιθάσων παθῶν] 'wild affections': the epithet denotes originally animals that have not been domesticated or tamed.

10. ἀγγέλων] The more usual thought is that we shall be associated hereafter with the saints rather than with the angels: but here the ἐνθάδε governs the writer's thoughts, and perhaps he has Tob. vi 6 in view.

13. λήξεις] derived from λαγχάνειν 'they shall be allotted the most blessed inheritances for ever.'

14. τὸ πάντ. ἀγ. μέγ.] in apposition to the whole sentence.

εἰρήνης, καὶ ἐνθάδε καὶ μετὰ θάνατον ἅμα τοῖς παλαμναίοις ἔσονται δαίμοσι. μὴ οὖν ἀποπεμπώμεθα τοὺς ἐπιστρέφοντας, ἀλλ' ἀσμένως δεχώμεθα, καὶ τοῖς ἀπλάνεσιν ἐναριθμῶμεν, καὶ τὸ ἐλλεῖπον ἀναπληρῶμεν.

2

Holl (*Fragmente Vornikänischer Kirchenväter aus dem Sacra Parallela* 380) gives this fragment in full from the *Sacra Parallela Rupefucald.* fol. 246. Pitra (*Mon. Jur. Eccl. Graec.* i 550) prints it from Cod. Barb. i 158 fol. 169 without the last twelve words and assigns it to Dionysius's letter περὶ Μετανοίας πρὸς Κόνωνα. According to Harnack (*Altchrist. Lit.* i 420) it is ascribed to Dionysius of Halicarnassus in Maxim. Confess. *Serm. per excerpta* xix (*Opp.* II p. 593).

5   Τὸ ὀργίζεσθαι παρ' ἡμῖν ἄχρι τοῦ παύειν τὰ ἁμαρτήματα περιορισθήσεται· ὀργίzεϲθε γάρ, φησι, κἀὶ μὴ ἁμαρτάνετε. καὶ τὸ ἀκριβῶς κριτικὸν παραιτητέον τοῦ Ἐκκλησιαστοῦ συμβουλεύοντος· Μὴ γίνογ δίκαιος πολύ.

1. τοῖς παλαμναίοις...δαίμοσι] an expression borrowed from the classics where it means 'avenging deities': here 'tormenting devils': see Liddell and Scott *s.v.*
5. Τὸ ὀργίζ....περιορισθ.] 'the being angry shall be restricted amongst ourselves, until (the wrong-doer) ceases his wrong-doings' (i.e. our anger must cease, so soon as a man reforms his ways).
6. ὀργίζ. καὶ μὴ ἁμαρτάν.] Ps. iv 5.
7. τὸ ἀκριβ. κριτ.] 'censoriousness in judgement.'
8. Μὴ γίν.—πολύ] Eccl. vii 17.

VIII

Πρὸς Δομέτιον καὶ Δίδυμον Ἐπιστολή

(Eus. *H. E.* vii 11. 20—25)

This is apparently an extract from one of Dionysius's Paschal letters, so far as we can gather from Eus. *H. E.* vii 20 τούτων (sc. τῶν φερομένων ἑορταστικῶν ἐπιστολῶν) τὴν μὲν Φλαουίῳ προσφωνεῖ, τὴν δὲ Δομετίῳ καὶ Διδύμῳ, ἐν ᾗ καὶ κανόνα ἐκτίθεται ὀκταετηρίδος, ὅτι μὴ ἄλλοτε ἢ μετὰ τὴν ἐαρινὴν ἰσημερίαν προσήκοι

A. *LETTERS* 65

τὴν τοῦ πάσχα ἑορτὴν ἐπιτελεῖν παριστάμενος. The fact that both here and in the words with which he introduces the extract itself (as given below) Eusebius puts the article before ἐπιστολή implies that there was but one such letter.

The Bishop of Alexandria year by year issued a pastoral letter to his flock about Eastertide. Thus the Council of Ephesus (A.D. 431) mentions the 5th and 6th ἐπιστολαὶ ἑορταστικαί of Theophilus Alex. (circ. A.D. 385): Cyril Alex. (circ. A.D. 412) wrote 30 Paschal Homilies which appear to have been of the same nature: Jerome mentions the ἐπιστολαὶ ἑορταστικαί of Athanasius (circ. 330), one of which is still extant: see Suicer *s.v.* From Eus. *H. E.* vii 1; 20; 21. 1, 2; 22. 1, 11, 12 we seem to make out a list of eight such letters of Dionysius, viz. (1) To Domitius and Didymus, (2) To Flavius, (3) To the Presbyters in Alexandria, (4) To 'others' unspecified, (5) To the Alexandrians before Easter A.D. 262, (6) To Hierax, (7) To Hermammon, (8) To the Brethren (in Egypt?) after the plague: of these we possess fragments in the case of (1), (5), (6), and (7); besides which we have two fragments of uncertain origin.

The persecution referred to (τῶν ἀμφὶ τὸν διωγμόν) is not that of Valerian, of which Dionysius speaks at some length in the second part of the letter πρὸς Γερμανόν, but that which was instituted by Decius and which is described in the first part of that letter. Eusebius is at fault in confusing the matter by quoting this extract in close connexion with the second rather than with the first part.

This extract adds one important detail to the account given in the letter to Germanus of Dionysius's first exile: for it tells us how that when he had been carried off by the rustic revellers he (with Gaius and Peter only) remained shut up (for some four years?) in a dreary spot in the Libyan desert three days' journey from Paraetonium.

The brief references here made to the Christian martyrs at Alexandria under the Decian persecution are supplemented by the fuller accounts furnished in Dionysius's Letter to Fabian, while the interesting glimpse we get of the personal labours of the city clergy amongst those who were imprisoned for their faith and in burying the dead at the same period agrees with what we read at greater length in the Letter to the Alexandrians, which refers to similar labours at a later period.

We have no information as to who Domitius and Didymus were: but they were not familiar with the persons composing the Church of Alexandria. It is evident that the letter was written while the Decian persecution was still raging in Alexandria, in answer to an inquiry which Domitius and Didymus had made ὅπως διάγομεν, probably from Dionysius's lonely place of banishment and when he had already been there some time.

Ὁ δ' αὐτὸς καὶ ἐν τῇ πρὸς Δομέτιον καὶ Δίδυμον ἐπιστολῇ τῶν ἀμφὶ τὸν διωγμὸν αὖθις μνημονεύει ἐν τούτοις·

(1) Τοὺς δὲ ἡμετέρους πολλούς τε ὄντας καὶ ἀγνῶτας ὑμῖν περισσὸν ὀνομαστὶ καταλέγειν· πλὴν ἴστε ὅτι ἄνδρες
5 καὶ γυναῖκες, καὶ νέοι καὶ γέροντες, καὶ κόραι καὶ πρεσβύτιδες, καὶ στρατιῶται καὶ ἰδιῶται, καὶ πᾶν γένος καὶ πᾶσα ἡλικία, οἱ μὲν διὰ μαστίγων καὶ πυρός, οἱ δὲ διὰ σιδήρου τὸν ἀγῶνα νικήσαντες τοὺς στεφάνους ἀπειλήφασι. τοῖς δὲ οὐ πάμπολυς αὐτάρκης ἀπέβη χρόνος,
10 εἰς τὸ φανῆναι δεκτοὺς τῷ κυρίῳ, ὥσπερ οὖν ἔοικε μηδὲ ἐμοὶ ὁ μέχρι νῦν. διόπερ εἰς ὃν οἶδεν αὐτὸς ἐπιτήδειον καιρὸν ὑπερέθετό με ὁ λέγων· Καιρῷ δεκτῷ ἐπήκογςά coy, καὶ ἐν ἡμέρᾳ ςωτηρίας ἐβοήθηςά coi. τὰ γὰρ καθ' ἡμᾶς ἐπειδὴ πυνθάνεσθε καὶ βούλεσθε δηλωθῆναι ὑμῖν, ὅπως
15 διάγομεν, ἠκούσατε μὲν πάντως, ὅπως ἡμᾶς δεσμώτας

4 πλὴν...ὅτι] πλὴν τε nonnulli ‖ 8 νικησαντες] τελεσαντες OL^r ‖ 9—11 αυταρκης...νυν] αυταρκης δε απεβη χρονος ο μεχρι νυν εις το φανηναι O om o nonnulli ‖ 11 οιδεν] ειδεν KF^a

3. *All sorts and conditions of Christians were included in the list of those who suffered in the* (*Decian*) *persecution.*

6. ἰδιῶται] here 'civilians,' as opposed to 'soldiers'; cf. Thucyd. vi 72 ἰδιώτας, ὡς εἰπεῖν, χειροτέχναις ἀνταγωνισαμένους, Arist. *Eth. Nic.* III xi 7, 8 μάχονται καὶ ἀθληταὶ ἰδιώταις.

9. οὐ πάμπ. αὐτ. ἀπ. χρ.] 'even a very long period did not prove sufficient,' i.e. they have not been deemed worthy of the martyr's crown yet.

10. ὥσπερ οὖν κτλ.] 'as in fact seems to be the case with me even now.' With ἔοικε supply αὐτάρκης εἶναι and with ὁ μέχρι νῦν supply χρόνος. Μηδέ would have been οὐδέ in class. Gk. The context seems to suggest that D.'s exile had already lasted some time.

12. καιρῷ δεκτῷ κτλ.] Is. xlix 8: cf. 2 Cor. vi 2.

13. *A brief account of Dionysius's own experiences in his first exile.*

A. LETTERS

ἀπαγομένους ὑπὸ ἑκατοντάρχου καὶ στρατηγῶν καὶ τῶν σὺν αὐτοῖς στρατιωτῶν καὶ ὑπηρετῶν, ἐμέ τε καὶ Γάιον καὶ Φαῦστον καὶ Πέτρον καὶ Παῦλον, ἐπελθόντες τινὲς τῶν Μαρεωτῶν ἄκοντας καὶ μηδὲ ἑπομένους βίᾳ τε σύροντες ἀφήρπασαν. ἐγὼ δὲ νῦν καὶ Γάιος καὶ Πέτρος, 5 μόνοι, τῶν ἄλλων ἀδελφῶν ἀπορφανισθέντες, ἐν ἐρήμῳ καὶ αὐχμηρῷ τῆς Λιβύης τόπῳ κατακεκλείσμεθα, τριῶν ἡμερῶν ὁδὸν τοῦ Παραιτονίου διεστηκότες.

Καὶ ὑποκαταβὰς φησιν·

(2) Ἐν δὲ τῇ πόλει καταδεδύκασιν, ἀφανῶς ἐπισκεπ- 10 τόμενοι τοὺς ἀδελφούς, πρεσβύτεροι μέν, Μάξιμος, Διόσκορος, Δημήτριος καὶ Λούκιος· οἱ γὰρ ἐν τῷ κόσμῳ προφανέστεροι Φαυστῖνος καὶ Ἀκύλας ἐν Αἰγύπτῳ πλα-

1 απαγομενους] αγομενους AG^a Steph L^r ‖ στρατηγων] στρατηγου F^b ‖ 3 Φαυστον et Παυλον] om Ruf ‖ 4 βια τε] add και AE^aO Steph L^r ‖ 12 και Λουκιος] om και AE^aF^bGHO Steph Schw L^r add cett

1. στρατηγῶν] viz. *duumviri*, attended by their ὑπηρέται, whilst the soldiers mentioned belonged to the centurion (ἑκατόνταρχος). Cf. Acts xvi 20, 35 where we read of στρατηγοί (*Journal of Theol. Stud.* i pp. 114, 434) with ῥαβδοῦχοι (lictors) at Philippi; Athan. *ad Sol. Ep.* 63 διὰ τῶν στρατιωτῶν καὶ τοῦ στρατηγοῦ Γοργονίου.

3. τινὲς τῶν Μαρεωτῶν] see p. 26.

6. τῶν ἄλλων] including Timothy, who had been the means of his rescue.

7. κατακεκλείσμεθα] The perf. is prob. (as usual) not to be pressed, though it would yield a satisfactory sense here, 'we have been shut up' (viz. in this place where we now are).

8. τοῦ Παραιτονίου] mod. *Kasr Medjed*, a town of Libya Marmarica on the sea coast some 150 miles W. of Alexandria.

10. *The conduct of the city clergy in their care for the sick and the dead amongst those Christians who suffered imprisonment or martyrdom for the Faith was most noble and honourable.*

10. καταδεδύκασιν] 'concealed themselves': cf. Plat. *Rep.* 579 B καταδεδυκὼς ἐν τῇ οἰκίᾳ.

11. Μάξιμος] appears not to have then given signs of his future eminence, not being included amongst οἱ ἐν τῷ κόσμῳ προφανέστεροι: see p. 28, but perhaps this phrase indicates social or political position rather than ecclesiastical.

ib. Διόσκορος] not of course the boy mentioned p. 13.

12. οἱ ἐν τῷ κ. προφανέστ.] seems to be an equivalent phrase to τῶν περιφανεστέρων in the letter to Fabian, p. 10, of whom we read that some fled: Faustinus and Aquila were probably of this number.

13. ἐν Αἰγύπτῳ] i.e. in other parts of Egypt as opposed to Alexandria and to Libya. Cf. n. on p. 13.

5—2

νῶνται· διάκονοι δὲ οἱ μετὰ τοὺς ἐν τῇ νόσῳ τελευτήσαντας
ὑπολειφθέντες Φαῦστος, Εὐσέβιος, Χαιρήμων· Εὐσέβιος
ὃν ἐξ ἀρχῆς ὁ θεὸς ἐδυνάμωσε καὶ παρεσκεύασε τὰς
ὑπηρεσίας τῶν ἐν ταῖς φυλακαῖς γενομένων ὁμολογητῶν
5 ἐναγωνίως ἀποπληροῦν καὶ τὰς τῶν σωμάτων περιστολὰς
τῶν τελείων καὶ μακαρίων μαρτύρων οὐκ ἀκινδύνως ἐκ-
τελεῖν. καὶ γὰρ μέχρι νῦν οὐκ ἀνίησιν ὁ ἡγούμενος, τοὺς
μὲν ἀναιρῶν, ὡς προεῖπον, ὠμῶς τῶν προσαγομένων, τοὺς
δὲ βασάνοις καταξαίνων, τοὺς δὲ φυλακαῖς καὶ δεσμοῖς
10 ἐκτήκων, προστάσσων τε μηδένα τούτοις προσιέναι, καὶ

1 δε] τε BCDF^{ab} ‖ νοσω] νησω nonnulli *ex diaconis quosdam in insula post poenas confessionis esse defunctos* Ruf tanquam νησω legens ‖ 3 εξ αρχης] εξαρχης R^{ab}

1. ἐν τῇ νόσῳ] Ruf.'s *in insula* is accepted as the right rendering by the new Berlin edition. If the reading of the text is retained, the epidemic referred to is probably that which devastated North Africa in the time of Gallus and Volusianus (A.D. 252) but not apparently the same as that described by D. pp. 80 ff., which occurred some years later. If νήσῳ be right, what is the island referred to?

2. Φαῦστος] If this is the same as the Faustus mentioned above, he must have returned to Alexandria, when D. went into exile: see p. 28.

ib. Εὐσέβιος] see p. 28.

5. ἐναγωνίως] 'energetically.'

ib. τὰς τῶν σωμ. περιστ.] For the contrast between the care of Christians for their dead even during a time of pestilence and the indifference of the heathen, see pp. 81 ff. In Eus. *H. E.* vii 17 we have the case of Astyrius, a Roman senator, who attended the funeral of Marinus the martyr at Caesarea in Palestine and decked the body out in costly and fine attire. In Egypt they seem to have preferred linen cloths for the purpose (Athan. *vita Anton.* c. 90).

6. τῶν τελείων...μαρτ.] The epithet τέλειοι is used of believers generally in the N. T. (Matt. v 48, 1 Cor. ii 6, xiv 20, Phil. iii 15, Col. i 28, iv 12, Heb. v 14, James i 4, iii 2): but in accordance with Solon's dictum δεῖ ἐς τὸ τέλος σκοπεῖν in judging a man's perfection, D. uses the word here in connexion with martyrdom, as τελειοῦται is in fact used by Eusebius of one of these martyrs, Faustus (*H. E.* vii 12. 26): and in that connexion τελειοῦν and τελείωσις are frequently found in the Fathers (see Suicer *sub vocibus*). In the account of the martyrdoms at Lugdunum (Eus. *H. E.* v 2. 5) St Stephen is called ὁ τέλειος μάρτυς and on p. 81 D. speaks again of οἱ τέλειοι μάρτυρες: cf. Eus. *H. E.* viii 13. 17.

7. ὁ ἡγούμενος] the Prefect (ἡγεμών): see pp. 13 and 30.

8. τῶν προσαγομένων] 'of those brought up before him': so προσαχθείς, p. 12.

9. καταξαίνων] 'tearing in pieces' with ξυστῆρες or the like: see Tert. *Apol.* c. 30 and Cypr. *de laps.* c. 13 for lists of instruments with which torture was inflicted.

A. LETTERS 69

ἀνερευνῶν μή τις φανείη. καὶ ὅμως ὁ θεὸς τῇ προθυ-
μίᾳ καὶ λιπαρίᾳ τῶν ἀδελφῶν διαναπαύει τοὺς πεπιεσ-
μένους.

Καὶ τοσαῦτα μὲν ὁ Διονύσιος.

2 λιπαρια AE^aGH λιπαρεια CF^{ab}R^{ab} Val Schw ‖ 4 ο Διονυσιος] add
και εν ταυτη τεθειται τη γραφη CF^aKR^{ab} Steph Val Stroth om cett

1. ἀνερ. μή τις φαν.] 'making strict search lest any should show himself (in the prisons).'
2. λιπαρίᾳ] 'steadfastness' acc. to Heinichen (and Liddell and Scott), 'benignitate' (Vales.): cf.

Eus. H. E. ix 1. 4 λιπαρωτάτῃ καὶ καθωσιωμένῃ σπουδῇ.
ib. διαναπαύει] 'allows to rest a while,' or perhaps 'in the meantime refreshes.'

IX

Πρὸς Ἑρμάμμωνα (ἑορταστικὴ) Ἐπιστολή

(Eus. *H. E.* vii 1, 10, 23)

This is reputed one of the Paschal letters of Dionysius[1] and was meant for τοῖς κατ' Αἴγυπτον ἀδελφοῖς generally, though it was specially addressed to an otherwise unknown person named Hermammon. It was probably written before the Easter of A.D. 262[2] towards the end of the ninth year of Gallienus: Eusebius tells us that it contained first a long account περὶ τῆς Δεκίου καὶ τῶν μετ' αὐτὸν κακοτροπίας and then went on to make mention τῆς κατὰ τὸν Γαλλιηνὸν εἰρήνης. The remains, which are imbedded in Eusebius's History, include (1) a brief reference to the continuance of persecution under Gallus, who succeeded to the empire on the death of Decius and his sons in A.D. 251: (2) a somewhat longer account of the change of policy towards the Christians adopted by Valerian under the influence of his favourite Macrianus, together with the story of the latter's brief usurpation of the Empire: (3) a highly-coloured description of the welcome restoration of Gallienus to power and of his Edict of Peace towards the Christians, which would inspire them to keep the Easter festival with special rejoicings that year. Several obscure points of history are raised in the course of

[1] See p. 65.   [2] See note on p. 78.

these extracts, and the student will find what help can be given to their elucidation in the notes to the text. Only one other point need be mentioned here and it is this: that though Dionysius deals at some length with the abortive effort of Macrianus and his two sons to secure the Empire on the disappearance of Valerian (A.D. 260), he appears to have made no mention of the four months' rule of Aemilian in 253, which intervened between the end of Gallus's and the beginning of Valerian's reign. The explanation of the omission probably is that the latter episode was brought about at a distance from Egypt, in Pannonia and Moesia, where Aemilian had been Governor, while the former directly affected Dionysius and his diocese.

Γράφων γέ τοι ὁ Διονύσιος Ἑρμάμμωνι περὶ τοῦ Γάλλου ταῦτα φάσκει·

(1) Ἀλλ' οὐδὲ Γάλλος ἔγνω τὸ Δεκίου κακόν, οὐδὲ προεσκόπησε τί ποτ' ἐκεῖνον ἔσφηλεν, ἀλλὰ πρὸς τὸν αὐτὸν
5 πρὸ τῶν ὀφθαλμῶν αὐτοῦ γενόμενον ἔπταισε λίθον. ὅς, εὖ φερομένης αὐτῷ τῆς βασιλείας καὶ κατὰ νοῦν χωρούντων τῶν πραγμάτων, τοὺς ἱεροὺς ἄνδρας τοὺς περὶ τῆς εἰρήνης αὐτοῦ καὶ τῆς ὑγιείας πρεσβεύοντας πρὸς τὸν θεὸν ἤλασεν. οὐκοῦν σὺν ἐκείνοις ἐδίωξε καὶ τὰς ὑπὲρ ἑαυτοῦ
10 προσευχάς.

Ταῦτα μὲν οὖν περὶ τοῦδε.

Αὖθις δὴ οὖν ὁ Διονύσιος οἷα καὶ περὶ (Οὐαλεριανοῦ) διέξεισιν,

6 κατα νουν] κατα ρουν A Steph *ex sententia* Ruf ‖ 9 εαυτου] αυτου AE^{a}F^b(OR^a) Steph L^r

3. *Gallus made the same mistake as Decius and persecuted those whose prayers would have been his chief support.*
 ib. οὐδὲ...ἔγνω] 'failed to understand.'
 ib. τὸ Δεκίου κακόν] 'the flaw in Decius's policy' or 'the mischief that befell Decius.'
 5. ὅς] i.e. Gallus.
 6. κατὰ νοῦν] 'according to his mind'; cf. Eus. *H. E.* x 8. 7 κατὰ γνώμην αὐτῷ χωροῦσαν. The reading of A adopted by Steph. κατὰ ῥοῦν ('swimmingly') is found in Plat. *Rep.* 492 C and Chrysostom (tom. xii p. 314 A) κατὰ ῥοῦν τῶν πραγμάτων φερομένων.
 8. πρεσβεύοντας] 'interceding': πρεσβεύειν (which with an accus. = to proclaim, as an ambassador) is used with the gen. with or without περί or ὑπέρ in the sense of 'intercede,' here 'with God,' elsewhere 'with man': cf. 2 Cor. v 20; Eph. vi 20, etc.
 9. ἤλασεν] 'drove into exile,' as Hein., not 'persecuted' as Vales.

A. *LETTERS* 71

ἐκ τῆς πρὸς Ἑρμάμμωνα ἐπιστολῆς μαθεῖν ἐστίν, ἐν ᾗ τοῦτον ἱστορεῖ τὸν τρόπον·

(2) Καὶ τῷ Ἰωάννῃ δὲ ὁμοίως ἀποκαλύπτεται. Καὶ ἐΔΌΘΗ γὰρ ἀγτῷ, φησί, ϲτΌΜΑ ΛΑΛΟγ̂Ν ΜεγάΛΑ καὶ ΒΛΑϲφΗΜίΑΝ, καὶ ἐΔΌΘΗ ἀγτῷ ἐξογϲίΑ καὶ ΜΗ̂ΝεϲΤεϲϲΑΡάκΟΝΤΑ Δγό. ἀμφό- 5
τερα δὲ ἔστιν ἐπὶ Οὐαλεριανοῦ θαυμάσαι, καὶ τούτων μάλιστα τὰ πρὸς αὐτοῦ ὡς οὕτως ἔσχε συννοεῖν, ἕως ἤπιος

4 βλασφημιαν] -μα G²H Sync *blasphemias* Ruf || 7 τα] om Eᵃ FᵇLʳ || προς FᵃOLʳ πρωτα GH προ cett Ruf || ουτως] ουτος Fᵃ Stroth Schw Hein ουτως cett codd et Sync || εως BCKRᵃᵇ Val Stroth Schw εως γαρ DFᵃ ως γαρ G² ως μεν AEᵃᵇFᵇG*HO Steph Lʳ Hein

3. *The change in Valerian's policy towards the Christians is most surprising: none of his predecessors had treated us more kindly than he at first.*
ib. Ἰωάννῃ] 'not in D.'s opinion the evangelist, as appears from his book περὶ Ἐπαγγελιῶν, p. 119.' Hort. [The notes marked 'Hort' are from a specimen page prepared for these Patristic texts drawn up on this passage by the late Dr Hort.]
ib. ὁμοίως] 'a reference to Dan. vii 8, 25 ff. had probably preceded.' Hort.
ib. Καὶ ἐδόθη κτλ.] Revel. xiii 5. 'The text seems to be ill preserved. The three readings of βλασφημ. in the MSS of Eusebius are found also in MSS of the N.T., the best attested here being the worst attested there. Καὶ μῆνες is an unsupported corruption of ποιῆσαι μῆνας.' Hort.
5. ἀμφότερα] both the 'gifts' just mentioned (sc. a blasphemous tongue and power to use it against the Christians for 42 months). 'For the first see p. 73. The 42 months for the duration of the second, according to D.'s interpretation of it, may with some difficulty be adjusted to our imperfect historical data. Valerian's first edict of persecution was issued in the summer of 257. His capture by the Persians is usually placed in 259, but may also

be reasonably referred to 260, and his latest coins belong to the year beginning in the autumn of 260 (Clinton *F. R.* i 284 f.).' Hort.
6. τούτων μάλιστα] 'and more especially of these two things'; "what follows is implied in the sense of the clause about the second 'gift.'" Hort.
7. τὰ πρὸς αὐτοῦ] is the subject of ὡς οὕτως ἔσχε: 'it is to be observed how his prosperity lasted as long as'; "lit. 'observe about the state of things favourable to him how it had this character as long as.' Συννοέω like συνοράω expresses the mental perception accompanying or following a comprehensive glance. Πρός has sufficient authority, and has doubtless been overlooked in some MSS: the reading πρό gives a plausible but impossible sense " ('the state of things before Valerian'). "Even in early writers πρός with a gen. sometimes means 'on the side of,' 'favourable to' (Kühner *Gr.* ii 448), and still more in later writers, e.g. especially Aristides. Οὕτως, sc. πρὸς αὐτοῦ, a clumsy rather than difficult phrase, though εἶχε would have been easier than ἔσχε: the aor. was probably used to state a fact respecting the whole period of prosperity." Hort.
ib. ἕως] The reading ὡς μέν is well-supported and, if adopted,

καὶ φιλόφρων ἦν πρὸς τοὺς ἀνθρώπους τοῦ θεοῦ. οὐδὲ
γὰρ ἄλλος τις οὕτω τῶν πρὸ αὐτοῦ βασιλέων εὐμενῶς καὶ
δεξιῶς πρὸς αὐτοὺς διετέθη, οὐδ' οἱ λεχθέντες ἀναφανδὸν
Χριστιανοὶ γεγονέναι, ὡς ἐκεῖνος οἰκειότατα ἐν ἀρχῇ καὶ
5 προσφιλέστατα φανερὸς ἦν αὐτοὺς ἀποδεχόμενος. καὶ
πᾶς τε ὁ οἶκος αὐτοῦ θεοσεβῶν πεπλήρωτο, καὶ ἦν ἐκκλησία Θεοῦ. ἀποσκευάσασθαι δὲ παρέπεισεν αὐτὸν ὁ
διδάσκαλος καὶ τῶν ἀπ' Αἰγύπτου μάγων ἀρχισυνάγωγος,

5 φανερός] -ως O Sync Steph Stroth L^r ∥ 6 πᾶς τε BCDF^{ab}GH(OR^{ab})
Schw L^r om τε cett ∥ 7 θεοῦ] τοῦ θ. R^{ab}

would make the clause ὡς...τοῦ
θεοῦ an exegesis of ὡς οὕτως ἔσχε
('viz. that he was gentle and well
disposed to the men of God'), but it
would not easily fit in with either
τὰ πρὸς αὐτοῦ or τὰ πρὸ αὐτοῦ: there
would be no difficulty however in
the loose use of μέν without a δέ to
follow in D.'s style; see p. 80.

1. τ. ἀνθρ. τ. θεοῦ] 'in the O.T.
and probably in the N.T. (1 Tim.
vi 11; 2 Tim. iii 17: cf. 2 Pet. i 21)
God's prophets: and so in Eus. *Vit.
Const.* iii 152 the bishops: here
God's true worshippers, i.e. the
Christians.' Hort.

3. οἱ λεχθέντες] 'doubtless Alexander Severus (cf. Eus. *H. E.* iv
21. 3 and 28; Lampr. *Al. Sev.*
29, 43, 45, 49, 51; Oros. vii 19)
and Philip the Arabian (Eus. *H. E.*
vi 34. 1 κατέχει λόγος).' Hort.

7. *His infamous minister Macrianus is responsible for the change
by his gross misrepresentations about
our habits and practices.*

ib. ἀποσκευάσασθαι] 'to abandon
the position,' lit. 'to pack up one's
goods with a view to removal.'

8. ὁ διδάσκ. καὶ...ἀρχισυν.] This
is doubtless the same man as the
Macrianus mentioned further on.
The words τῶν ἀπ' Αἰγ. μάγων
contain a reference to Ex. vii 11 ff.,
though the word μάγος does not
actually occur in that connexion (σο-
φισταί, ἐπαοιδοί). That the Egyptians as well as the Chaldaeans
were much addicted to the magic
art we know from other sources.
Macrianus does not seem to have
been literally a magician himself:
D.'s language is probably extra-
vagant and satirical (see Benson
Cyprian p. 451). Valerian made
Macrianus his Pretorian Prefect
and reposed such confidence in him
as led to his defeat by Sapor and
the Persians in A.D. 260. The
Emperor's own words about him
(in Pollio) are *bellum Persicum
gerens Macriano totam rem publicam
tradidi quidem a parte militari*, but
nevertheless Gibbon considers him
to have been a worthless minister.
The epithets διδάσκαλος and ἀρχισυνάγωγος are both somewhat obscure in their application. Probably
the sinister suggestion of the former
is that he had constituted himself
the Emperor's tutor in magic or in
the persecuting spirit, while in the
latter there seems to be some allusion
to the large Jewish colony which
still flourished at Alexandria and
which would gladly have seen the
Christians put down. The ἀρχισυνάγωγος of the Alexandrian Jews is sa-
tirically mentioned by the Emperor
Hadrian in a letter to Servian quoted

A. *LETTERS* 73

τοὺς μὲν καθαροὺς καὶ ὁσίους ἄνδρας κτίννυσθαι καὶ
διώκεσθαι κελεύων, ὡς ἀντιπάλους καὶ κωλυτὰς τῶν
παμμιάρων καὶ βδελυκτῶν ἐπαοιδῶν ὑπάρχοντας (καὶ
γὰρ εἰσὶ καὶ ἦσαν ἱκανοί, παρόντες καὶ ὁρώμενοι καὶ
μόνον ἐμπνέοντες καὶ φθεγγόμενοι, διασκεδάσαι τὰς τῶν 5
ἀλιτηρίων δαιμόνων ἐπιβουλάς), τελετὰς δὲ ἀνάγνους καὶ
μαγγανείας ἐξαγίστους καὶ ἱερουργίας ἀκαλλιερήτους ἐπιτελεῖν ὑποτιθέμενος, παῖδας ἀθλίους ἀποσφάττειν, καὶ
τέκνα δυστήνων πατέρων καταθύειν, καὶ σπλάγχνα νεο-

by Vopiscus *Saturn*. Further on in this letter Macrianus is said to have had no understanding of the workings of Providence (πρόνοια) nor of κρίσις, which perhaps means that he was tainted with Epicureanism as well.

1. τοὺς καθαροὺς καὶ ὁσίους ἄνδ.] Christians generally are meant but, as the words following suggest, the Christian exorcists with their special powers over demons are particularly in his mind: Benson *op. cit.* p. 458. Whether exorcists were by this time separated off into one of the inferior orders of the clergy at Alexandria is doubtful: the order existed at Rome (Eus. *H. E.* vi 43) but in the East their powers were looked upon as too supernatural and extraordinary to depend upon human ordination; see Duchesne *Origines du c. chrét.* p. 331, and Bingham *Antiqq.* III iv §§ 1—5.

4. ἱκανοί, παρόντες κτλ.] 'able, by being present and seen and merely breathing on them and uttering words.' This description of the miraculous powers still retained by exorcists (εἰσὶ καὶ ἦσαν) is sufficiently remarkable: but cf. Min. Fel. *Oct.* xxvii, Tert. *Apol.* 23, etc.

5. ἐμπνέοντες] Lat. *insufflantes*.
ib. φθεγγόμενοι] 'uttering' esp. the name of the Lord Jesus, cf. Acts xix 13, and Chrysost. tom. ii p. 494 A, B.

6. ἀλιτηρίων δαιμ.] The epithet is properly applied to offenders against the gods not to the gods themselves; but the same phrase occurs in the Panegyric quoted by Eus. *H. E.* x 4. 13 δαιμόνων ἀλιτηρίων πλάναις: cf. Eus. *Dem. Evang.* iv 10; Zosim. *Hist.* v 34, vi 41. On p. 64 we have τοῖς παλαμναίοις δαίμοσιν.

ib. τελετάς] lit. 'initiatory rites.'
7. μαγγαν. ἐξαγ.] 'detestable juggleries.'

ib. ἱερουργ. ἀκαλλιερήτους] The epithet, which is found several times in Aeschines, occurs together with several other of the expressions here used in Eus. *H. E.* ix 3 and is there applied to μυήσεις. Καλλιερεῖν (Lat. *litare*) is 'to obtain favourable omens by sacrifice': hence ἀκαλλιέρητος as applied to sacrifices would mean such as could obtain no favourable omens and so something more reprehensible than merely 'vain,' 'futile' (Hein.), rather 'disapproved' or 'abhorred (by God).'

8. ὑποτιθέμενος] 'suggesting to him the adoption of': ὑποτίθεσθαι (mid.) often has some such meaning.

ib. παῖδας ἀθλ. ἀποσφάττ.] This is just the accusation brought against Christians themselves: see for instance Min. Fel. *Oct.* ix 7; Tert. *Apolog.* chaps. 7 to 9; Eus. *H. E.* v 1. 14, etc.

γενῆ διαιρεῖν, καὶ τὰ τοῦ θεοῦ διακόπτειν καὶ καταχορδεύειν πλάσματα, ὡς ἐκ τούτων εὐδαιμονήσοντας.

Καὶ τούτοις γε ἐπιφέρει λέγων·

(3) Καλὰ γοῦν αὐτοῖς Μακριανὸς τῆς ἐλπιζομένης
5 βασιλείας προσήνεγκε χαριστήρια, ὃς πρότερον μὲν ἐπὶ
τῶν καθόλου λόγων λεγόμενος εἶναι βασιλέως, οὐδὲν
εὔλογον οὐδὲ καθολικὸν ἐφρόνησεν, ἀλλ' ὑποπέπτωκεν
ἀρᾷ προφητικῇ τῇ λεγούσῃ· Οὐαὶ τοῖс προφητεύουсιν
ἀπὸ καρδίας αὐτῶν, καὶ τὸ καθόλου μὴ βλέπουсιν. οὐ γὰρ
10 συνῆκε τὴν καθόλου πρόνοιαν, οὐδὲ τὴν κρίσιν ὑπείδετο
τοῦ πρὸ πάντων καὶ διὰ πάντων καὶ ἐπὶ πᾶсιν. διὸ καὶ

1 διακόπτειν] κατακοπτειν CF^{a}GR^{ab} Sync Val διακ. cett ‖ 2 ευδαιμονησοντας BCDF^{ab}GHK(OR^{ab}) ευδαιμονησαντας AE^a ευδαιμονησοντα Nic ‖ 4 Μακριανος] Μακρινος AE^{a}F^b Nic Sync

1. *καταχορδεύειν*] 'to mince up,' 'cut into pieces': τὰ τ. θ. πλάσματα 'beings who are God's creation.'

2. *εὐδαιμονήσοντας*] The plural is apparently used in forgetfulness that the subject is singular (sc. αὐτόν = τὸν Οὐαλεριανόν).

4. *Macrianus thought to serve his ambitious ends by propitiating the demons: for he did not realize that the Almighty overrules all things and will bring us into judgement for our works.*

ib. Καλὰ...χαριστήρια] This can hardly mean (as Vales. explains the passage) that, as Macrianus had attained his hope of empire by the assistance of the demons, he made the best return he could to them by setting Valerian against the Christians; for ἐλπιζομένης is present not past. It would seem therefore as if the reference is to some action of Macrianus *before* he had attained his hope, when he was still hoping, and then χαριστήρια must mean offerings to propitiate favours to come, not thank offerings (its usual meaning). In any case αὐτοῖς = τοῖς δαίμοσι, not τοῖς βασιλεῦσι as some have thought.

5. *ἐπὶ τῶν καθόλου λόγων*] lit. 'in charge of (the Emperor's) general accounts.' This, like καθολικός and various similar expressions, is used to describe the office of the imperial *Rationalis* or *Procurator summae rei*. Under which Emperor Macrianus held this office does not appear. It is impossible to reproduce the play upon the phrase intended by the εὔλογον and καθολικόν, τὸ καθόλου and τὴν καθόλου πρόνοιαν. There is a further allusion to the use of καθόλου and καθολικός in the ecclesiastical sense of 'catholic,' as is shown by τῆς καθολ. ἐκκλησ. in the next sentence.

8. Οὐαὶ τοῖς προφητ. κτλ.] Ezek. xiii 3: here τὸ καθόλου is adverbial ('altogether,' 'at all'), whereas D. takes it to mean 'they see not that which is universal,' viz. the signs of God's government of the world.

9. *οὐ γὰρ...ὑπείδετο*] 'he did not understand the (workings of) Universal Providence nor suspect the (approach of) Judgement': τὴν κρίσιν sc. in reference to the accounts which it was Macrianus' duty to present to the Emperor.

11. *πρὸ πάντων κτλ.*] Cf. Eph. iv 6 and Col. i 17. This quotation again emphasizes the καθόλου.

A. LETTERS

τῆς μὲν καθολικῆς αὐτοῦ ἐκκλησίας γέγονε πολέμιος,
ἠλλοτρίωσε δὲ καὶ ἀπεξένωσεν ἑαυτὸν τοῦ ἐλέους τοῦ
θεοῦ, καὶ ὡς πορρωτάτω τῆς ἑαυτοῦ σωτηρίας ἐφυγά-
δευσεν, ἐν τούτῳ τὸ ἴδιον ἐπαληθεύων ὄνομα.

Καὶ πάλιν μεθ' ἕτερά φησιν·

(4) Ὁ μὲν γὰρ Οὐαλεριανὸς εἰς ταῦτα ὑπὸ τούτου προαχθείς, εἰς ὕβρεις καὶ ὀνειδισμοὺς ἐκδοθεὶς κατὰ τὸ ῥηθὲν
πρὸς Ἡσαΐαν· Καὶ οὗτοι ἐξελέξαντο τὰς ὁδοὺς αὐτῶν καὶ
τὰ βδελύγματα αὐτῶν, ἃ ἡ ψυχὴ αὐτῶν ἠθέλησε, καὶ ἐγὼ
ἐκλέξομαι τὰ ἐμπαίγματα αὐτῶν καὶ τὰς ἁμαρτίας ἀνταπο-
δώσω αὐτοῖς. οὗτος δὲ τῇ βασιλείᾳ παρὰ τὴν ἀξίαν ἐπι-
μανείς, καὶ τὸν βασίλειον ὑποδῦναι κόσμον ἀδυνατῶν
ἀναπήρῳ τῷ σώματι, τοὺς δύο παῖδας τὰς πατρῴας

3 σωτηριας] εκκλησιας B Steph

3. ἐφυγάδευσεν] sc. ἑαυτόν. D. always uses this verb transitively; see pp. 56 and 155.

4. τὸ ἴδιον ἐπαλ. ὄνομα] sc. Μακριανός, as if from μακρός (far), a derivation for which we should hesitate to vouch.

6. *So then Valerian was led into the disgrace that befel him through being persuaded to persecute the Christians.*

ib. ὑπὸ τούτου προαχθείς] 'being persuaded by this man (viz. by Macrianus) to this policy': see note on προέμενος further on.

7. ἐκδοθείς] D. forgets that he has left this clause incomplete, and proceeds as if he had written ἐξεδόθη. For the ὕβρεις καὶ ὀνειδισμούς which Sapor the Persian King is said to have inflicted on his fallen foe, see Gibbon *Decline and Fall* chap. x: 'We are told that Valerian in chains, but invested with the imperial purple, was exposed to the multitude, a constant spectacle of fallen greatness: and that whenever the Persian monarch mounted on horseback, he placed his foot on the neck of a Roman Emperor ... It is at least certain, that the only Emperor of Rome who had ever fallen into the hands of the enemy languished away his life in hopeless captivity.'

8. Καὶ οὗτοι κτλ.] Is. lxvi 3, 4: the readings οὗτοι (for αὐτοί), ἃ (which B omits) and ἐκλέξομαι (for ἐκδεξ.) are those of ℵAQ, except that ℵ reads ἐκλέξωμαι.

11. *But Macrianus, through physical infirmity being unable to act alone, associated his two sons with him in the throne and thus dragged them into the consequences of his villainy.*

ib. οὗτος δέ] sc. ὁ Μακρ.

ib. τῇ βασ. παρὰ τ. ἀξ. ἐπιμανείς] 'in his mad lust after the imperial power for which he had no qualifications': ἐπιμαίνεσθαι c. *dat.* in this sense is quite classical.

12. τὸν βασίλ. ὑποδ. κόσμ.] 'to assume the imperial insignia.'

13. ἀναπήρῳ τ. σώμ.] So Zonaras *Annal.* xii 24 θάτερον πεπήρωτο τῶν σκελῶν.

ib. τοὺς δύο παῖδας] sc. Macrianus junior and Quietus: 'his martial sons were patterns of discipline,' Benson *Cyprian* p. 457.

ἀναδεξαμένους ἁμαρτίας προεστήσατο. ἐναργὴς γὰρ ἐπὶ τούτων ἡ πρόρρησις ἦν εἶπεν ὁ θεός· Ἀποδιδοὺς ἁμαρτίας πατέρων ἐπὶ τέκνα ἕως τρίτης καὶ τετάρτης γενεᾶς τοῖς μισοῦσί με. τὰς γὰρ ἰδίας πονηρὰς ἐπιθυμίας, ὧν
5 ηὐτύχει, ταῖς τῶν υἱῶν κεφαλαῖς ἐπιβαλών, εἰς ἐκείνους τὴν ἑαυτοῦ κακίαν καὶ τὸ πρὸς τὸν θεὸν μῖσος ἐξωμόρξατο.

Καὶ περὶ μὲν τοῦ Οὐαλεριανοῦ τοσαῦτα ὁ Διονύσιος.

Ἑρμάμμωνι δὲ πάλιν καὶ τοῖς κατ' Αἴγυπτον ἀδελφοῖς δι' ἐπι-
10 στολῆς ὁμιλῶν, πολλά τε ἄλλα περὶ τῆς Δεκίου καὶ τῶν μετ' αὐτὸν διεξελθὼν κακοτροπίας, τῆς κατὰ τὸν Γαλλιηνὸν εἰρήνης ἐπιμιμνήσκεται. οὐδὲν δὲ οἷον τὸ καὶ τούτων ὧδέ πως ἐχόντων ἀκοῦσαι·

(5) Ἐκεῖνος μὲν οὖν τῶν πρὸ αὐτοῦ βασιλέων τὸν μὲν προέμενος, τῷ δὲ ἐπιθέμενος, παγγενῆ ταχέως καὶ πρόρ-

5 ηυτυχει BCDF^aGHKR^{ab} Schw ητυχει AE^aF^b Sync Steph Val Stroth ει τυχοι OL^r ‖ 13 προ] om nonnulli ‖ αυτου] εαυτου AE^aF^b Steph Stroth L^r ‖ 14 παγγενη] -ει F^bGH -ι E^a

1. ἀναδεξαμένους] 'having become liable for': we should certainly have expected the fut. (ἀναδεξομ.) here.
2. ἀποδιδοὺς κτλ.] Exod. xx 5.
4. ὧν ηὐτύχει] This, which is the best supported reading, yields the most satisfactory sense. 'Having gained his own wicked desires (sc. the Empire), he associated his sons in the position and thus made them partners in his wickedness.' Ὧν ἠτύχει ('which he had failed in') would refer to his bodily infirmities, which spoilt his enjoyment of the supremacy which he had gained. Εἰ τύχοι (si votorum compos fuisset, Laemmer) has little to be said for it.
6. ἐξωμόρξατο] 'wiped off'; a favourite word with Euripides; for D.'s special use of it here cf. Bacch. 337, parodied by Arist. Ach. 843. Cf. p. 83, περίψημα. The two Macriani, father and son, were after a brief reign, if reign it could be called, defeated and slain in Illyricum by Aureolus, another usurper, and Quietus was put to death in the East by Odenathus, the husband of Zenobia of Palmyra.

13. And now Macrianus has disappeared root and branch and Gallienus is restored to power, and his glory shines like the sun which emerges from a bank of clouds.

ib. Ἐκεῖνος] sc. ὁ Μακρ.

ib. τὸν μὲν προέμενος] This has usually been taken to mean that Macrianus 'betrayed' Valerian to Sapor, the Persian king, who captured him, but Benson is probably right (Cyprian pp. 458 and 556) in referring προέμενος here ('having incited' or 'urged on') and προαχθείς above merely to his bad influence on Valerian, which led ultimately to his ruin.

14. τῷ δὲ ἐπιθέμενος] i.e. Macrianus attacked Gallienus after Valerian's disappearance.

ib. παγγενῆ] 'with all his family.'

A. *LETTERS* 77

ρίζος ἐξηφανίσθη· ἀνεδείχθη δὲ καὶ συνανωμολογήθη παρὰ
πάντων ὁ Γαλλιηνός, παλαιὸς ἅμα βασιλεὺς καὶ νέος, πρῶτος ὢν καὶ μετ' ἐκείνους παρών. κατὰ γὰρ τὸ ῥηθὲν πρὸς
τὸν προφήτην Ἡσαΐαν· Τὰ ἀπ' ἀρχῆς ἰδοὺ ἥκασι, καὶ καινὰ
ἃ νῦν ἀνατελεῖ. ὥσπερ γὰρ νέφος τὰς ἡλιακὰς ἀκτῖνας 5
ὑποδραμὸν καὶ πρὸς ὀλίγον ἐπηλυγάσαν ἐσκίασεν αὐτὸν
καὶ ἀντ' αὐτοῦ προεφάνη, εἶτα παρελθόντος ἢ διατα-
κέντος τοῦ νέφους ἐξεφάνη πάλιν ἐπανατείλας ὁ ἥλιος ὁ
προανατείλας, οὕτω προστὰς καὶ προσπελάσας ἑαυτὸν
ὁ Μακριανὸς τῆς ἐφεστώσης Γαλλιηνοῦ βασιλείας, ὁ μὲν 10
οὐκ ἔστιν, ἐπεὶ μηδὲ ἦν, ὁ δ' ἔστιν ὁμοίως ὥσπερ ἦν.
καὶ οἷον ἀποθεμένη τὸ γῆρας ἡ βασιλεία, καὶ τὴν προ-
οῦσαν ἀνακαθηραμένη κακίαν, ἀκμαιότερον νῦν ἐπανθεῖ,
καὶ πορρώτερον ὁρᾶται καὶ ἀκούεται καὶ διαφοιτᾷ πανταχοῦ. 15

Εἶθ' ἑξῆς καὶ τὸν χρόνον, καθ' ὃν ταῦτ' ἔγραφε, διὰ τούτων
σημαίνει·

8 επαναт. ο ηλιος ο προαναт. CKR^{ab} Val Stroth Schw om ο post ηλιος F^a
επαναт. ο προεπαναт. ηλιος F^b επαναт. ο προαναт. ηλ. AE^aGHOL^r επαναт.
η προαναт. ηλ. Nic ∥ 9 προσπελασας ABCDE^aF^bGHKO προπελ. AF^a
Steph ∥ 10 Μακριανος] -ινος AE^aF^b Nic Steph ∥ 11 ωσπερ ην] om CF^aKR^{ab}

The same adv. is used in Eus. *H.E.*
vi 21. I and in *Mart. Pal.* viii 10 we
have παμμιγῆ.

1. ἀνεδείχθη] perhaps specially
used as opp. to ἐξηφανίσθη: cf.
ἐξεφάνη πάλιν...ὁ ἥλιος below: but
ἀναδεικνύναι is used in the technical
sense of to 'proclaim' or 'make'
(Lat. *designare*) and that may be all
it means here.

4. Τὰ ἀπ' ἀρχῆς κτλ.] Is. xlii 9
(but D. has changed ἐγὼ ἀναγγέλλω
into νῦν ἀνατελεῖ of xliii 19). Τὰ
ἀπ' ἀρχῆς, 'the things formerly
predicted,' i.e. in connexion with
the appearance of Cyrus; καινά, i.e.
his triumph and the conversion of
the world to Jehovah's worship:
the application of this to the restoration of Gallienus is somewhat too

fanciful for our modern ideas.

6. ὑποδραμόν] i.e. 'having over-
cast' (as we say) or 'intercepted.'
ib. ἐπηλυγάσαν] 'having screened.'
ib. αὐτὸν κ. ἀντ' αὐτοῦ] i.e. τὸν
ἥλιον καὶ ἀντὶ τοῦ ἡλίου.

9. προσπελάσας ἑαυτόν] 'having
gained access for himself': we find
προσπελάσαι with gen. in Soph.
O.T. 1101 Πανὸς προσπελασθεῖσ'
(acc. to Dindorf's reading): προ-
πελάσας here is an obvious emendation of the copyist.

11. ἐπεὶ μηδὲ ἦν] Cf. Eus. *H.E.* x
4. 29 οἱ μὲν οὐκ εἰσὶν οἱ θεομισεῖς,
ὅτι μηδὲ ἦσαν: also iv 25. 3. On
p. 146 we have αἱ μηδ' οὖσαι (ἄτομοι).
Thus μηδὲ εἶναι seems to be a later
equivalent for μηδὲν εἶναι.

(6) Καί μοι πάλιν τὰς ἡμέρας τῶν βασιλικῶν ἐτῶν ἔπεισι σκοπεῖν. ὁρῶ γάρ, ὡς ὀνομασθέντες μὲν οἱ ἀσεβέστατοι μετ' οὐ πολὺ γεγόνασιν ἀνώνυμοι, ὁ δὲ ὁσιώτερος καὶ φιλοθεώτερος ὑπερβὰς τὴν ἑπταετηρίδα, νῦν ἐνιαυτὸν 5 ἔνατον διανύει, ἐν ᾧ ἡμεῖς ἑορτάϲωμεν.

2 επεισι σκοπειν] επισκοπειν GHOL^r

1. *Let us then keep the festival in the happy consideration that the impious have been brought to naught and our godly Emperor is now come to his own again.*

ib. Καί μοι...ἔπεισι] 'it occurs to me.'

2. ὀνομασθέντες] 'named with honour': see Liddell and Scott *s.v.*

3. ὁσιώτερος καὶ φιλοθεώτερος] For much valuable information about 'this incomprehensible Emperor,' who had formerly been associated with his father Valerian on the throne, the student may consult Benson *Cyprian* pp. 300, 301 and 458. His wife, Cornelia Salonina, appears to have been a Christian, whatever he himself may have been: and 'it is possible that D. knew nothing of the' scandals about his 'personal life.'

4. ὑπερβὰς...διανύει] 'having completed the seven years' period is now passing through his ninth year.' The commentators explain this strange note of time in this way: that Gallienus was associated with his father on the throne for seven years (A.D. 253—260): then Macrianus held the power (in Egypt) for a year, but in his ninth year (about midsummer A.D. 261) Gallienus regained the imperial power: hence the Easter to which this letter refers (ἑορτάσωμεν) must be that of A.D. 262. If so, it must have been written some little time after Gallienus' original Edict of Peace (Oct. A.D. 260) and indeed Benson (*Cyprian* p. 458 n.) shows that the Greek translation given by Eus. *H.E.* vii 13 is the Rescript applying the Edict to Egypt and not the Edict itself. In which case the usurpation of Macrianus may have delayed the issue of the imperial decree in Egypt for some time: and yet D. has implied earlier in this letter that the persecution of Valerian lasted only 42 months (i.e. from before or about midsummer A.D. 257 till late in A.D. 260) and his language throughout seems to suggest that the welcome change in the imperial policy has quite recently been brought about.

5. ἑορτάσωμεν] 'let us keep the feast' (of Easter): cf. 1 Cor. v 8. This is really the only indication that the letter is one of the Paschal series.

A. LETTERS

X

Πρὸς τοὺς ἐν 'Αλεξανδρείᾳ ἀδελφοὺς (ἑορταστικὴ)
'Επιστολή

(Eus. *H. E.* vii 22)

This letter was apparently addressed by Dionysius to the members of his own flock at Alexandria in connexion with the same Easter as that referred to in the Letters to Hermammon and to Hierax. The extract preserved by Eusebius gives some account of one of those outbreaks of civil war and pestilence which were so common in that city and country. There is little doubt that the πόλεμος mentioned by Dionysius is the rising of Macrianus of which we have already spoken (pp. 75 f.) and which, as the succeeding letter to Hierax (*q.v.*) seems also to imply, was followed by a devastating plague. Dionysius had by this time returned from exile[1] and he speaks here with admiration of the devoted ministrations of the brethren to one another in the time of sickness and death, which formed a noble contrast to the cowardice and selfishness displayed by the heathen. On an earlier occasion also the clergy of the city had acted with similar devotedness (see the letter to Domitius and Didymus, p. 68), but here Dionysius lays special stress on the fact that τῶν ἀπὸ τοῦ λαοῦ λίαν ἐπαινούμενοι were associated with the clergy in the performance of these good offices.

[1] See p. 85, ἐπιλαβούσης...ὡμίλει (Eus. *H. E.* vii 21). It will be noticed that in this sentence Eusebius mentions that the letter we are now dealing with was rendered necessary by the disordered state of the city, which prevented Dionysius from exercising his ordinary methods of episcopal oversight with his flock, whereas the extract given contains no such expressions on the part of Dionysius; on the other hand the extract from the Paschal Letter to Hierax, which Eusebius intrudes between the sentence introducing the present extract and the extract itself, contains in its opening sentences certain phrases which Eusebius may have misunderstood as referring to his difficulties at home (e.g. τὰ ἐμαυτοῦ σπλάγχνα.. φαίνεται, as if this all referred to the Alexandrian brethren, not the Egyptian: so too εἰς τὴν ὑπεροψίαν compared with ὥσπερ τις ὑπερόριος). Perhaps also the στάσις which Eusebius connects with the Hierax extract, really belongs to the Alexandrian extract, which says something about it, whereas the other does not.

Μετὰ ταῦτα λοιμικῆς τὸν πόλεμον διαλαβούσης νόσου, τῆς τε ἑορτῆς πλησιαζούσης, αὖθις διὰ γραφῆς τοῖς ἀδελφοῖς ὁμιλεῖ, τὰ τῆς συμφορᾶς ἐπισημαινόμενος πάθη διὰ τούτων·

(1) Τοῖς μὲν ἄλλοις ἀνθρώποις οὐκ ἂν δόξειε καιρὸς ἑορτῆς εἶναι τὰ παρόντα. οὐδὲ ἔστιν αὐτοῖς οὔτε οὗτος οὔτε τις ἕτερος, οὐχ ὅπως τῶν ἐπιλύπων, ἀλλ' οὐδ' εἴ τις περιχαρὴς ὃν οἰηθεῖεν μάλιστα. νῦν μέν γε θρῆνοι πάντα, καὶ πενθοῦσι πάντες, καὶ περιηχοῦσιν οἰμωγαὶ τὴν πόλιν διὰ τὸ πλῆθος τῶν τεθνηκότων καὶ τῶν ἀποθνησκόντων ὁσημέραι. ὡς γὰρ ἐπὶ τῶν πρωτοτόκων τῶν Αἰγυπτίων γέγραπται, οὕτως καὶ νῦν ἐγενήθη κραυγὴ μεγάλη. οὐ γὰρ ἔστιν οἰκία, ἐν ᾗ οὐκ ἔστιν ἐν αὐτῇ τεθνηκώς· καὶ ὄφελόν γε εἷς. πολλὰ μὲν γὰρ καὶ δεινὰ καὶ τὰ πρὸ τούτου

6 επιλυπων BCF^aKR^{ab} Val Stroth Schw επιλοιπων cett ‖ 7 ον οιηθειεν] ων οιηθειη Nic ‖ 13 γε εις. πολλα C^aF^b Stroth Turneb γε· εις πολλα A Nic γε· επι πολλα OL^r γε· πολλα BCDE^aK Val Schw

4. *There is little appearance of festival in our present state. Our many former troubles from persecution have since been greatly increased and added to.*

ib. Τοῖς μὲν ἄλλ.] This μέν and several others in the passage have no corresponding δέ.

6. ἐπιλύπων] This is obviously the right reading: ἐπιλοίπων would be tautological after τις ἕτερος and in no way antithetical to the περιχαρής which follows. 'Nor indeed is this nor any other a season of true festival to them: I speak not of occasions obviously sorrowful but even of such as they may think most joyful' (lit. 'if there is any joyful season which they might think particularly so').

8. περιηχοῦσιν...τὴν πόλιν] The same construction is found in Plut. *Mor.* 2. 720 D θόρυβος περιηχεῖ τὴν οἰκίαν.

11. ἐγενήθη...τεθνηκώς] Exod. xii 30.

12. καὶ ὄφελόν γε εἷς. πολλὰ κτλ.] I have adopted this reading, which is that of the Berlin edition, with much diffidence: 'I would there were but one (dead in a house). For the evils that have before now fallen on us are also many and grievous.' The other readings are less satisfactory: (1) ὄφ. γε· εἰς (or ἐπὶ) πολλά requires the removal of the full stop after συμβεβηκότα and then τὰ πρὸ τ. συμβεβηκ. will become the subject of ἤλασαν (for ἤλασεν): 'for the former events drove us upon many (other) grievous ills'; but the ambiguity of the phrase καὶ ὄφελόν γε still remains: (2) ὄφελόν γε· πολλά would yield good sense if we took ὄφελον as looking back to the beginning of the fragment, answering the τοῖς μὲν ἄλλοις: 'and yet I hope it may be (a festival to us): for even before now many grievous things happened to us, which we did not allow to interfere with our keeping of the festival'; but this is, I think, too far fetched. Others take καὶ ὄφελόν γε to mean 'I would that this were all.'

A. LETTERS

συμβεβηκότα. πρῶτον μὲν ἡμᾶς ἤλασαν, καὶ μόνοι
πρὸς ἁπάντων διωκόμενοι καὶ θανατούμενοι ἑορτάσαμεν
καὶ τότε, καὶ πᾶς ὁ τῆς καθ' ἕκαστον θλίψεως τόπος
πανηγυρικὸν ἡμῖν γέγονε χωρίον, ἀγρός, ἐρημία, ναῦς,
πανδοχεῖον, δεσμωτήριον, φαιδροτάτην δὲ πασῶν ἤγαγον 5
ἑορτὴν οἱ τέλειοι μάρτυρες εὐωχηθέντες ἐν οὐρανῷ. μετὰ
δὲ ταῦτα πόλεμος καὶ λιμὸς ἐπέλαβεν, ἃ τοῖς ἔθνεσι
συνδιηνέγκαμεν, μόνοι μὲν ὑποστάντες ὅσα ἡμῖν ἐλυμή-
ναντο, παραπολαύσαντες δὲ καὶ ὧν ἀλλήλους εἰργάσαντό
τε καὶ πεπόνθασι· καὶ τῇ Χριστοῦ πάλιν ἐνηυφράν- 10
θημεν εἰρήνῃ, ἣν μόνοις ἡμῖν δέδωκε. βραχυτάτης δὲ
ἡμῶν τε καὶ αὐτῶν τυχόντων ἀναπνοῆς, ἐπικατέσκηψεν
ἡ νόσος αὕτη, πρᾶγμα φόβου τε παντὸς φοβερώτερον
ἐκείνοις, καὶ συμφορᾶς ἡστινοσοῦν σχετλιώτερον, καὶ ὡς
ἴδιός τις αὐτῶν ἀπήγγειλε συγγραφεύς, πρᾶγμα μόνον δὴ 15

3 εκαστον] εαυτους OL^r ‖ 7 λιμος] λοιμος R^{ab} ‖ 8 ελυμηναντο] -ατο K ‖
11 δεδωκε CF^{ab}GHR^{ab} Schw εδωκε cett ‖ 13 τε] inter πραγμα et φοβου R^a

1. ἤλασαν] 'drove us into exile,' as on p. 70.
3. πᾶς ὁ τῆς...χωρίον] 'every place where each particular affliction had befallen us became the scene of our festal assembly.' πανηγυρικόν cf. Eus. *H.E.* vii 20, where D. is described as πανηγυρικωτέρους ἀνακινῶν λόγους in his Paschal letters.
6. οἱ τέλειοι μάρτυρες] See p. 68, note.
ib. *War and famine ensued, which the Gentiles had to endure in common with us.*
7. πόλεμος...πεπόνθασι] 'war and famine seized us, which we endured in common with the Gentiles, having undergone alone all the injuries they had inflicted on us, and then having to share on one another and suffered.' For συνδιηνέγκ. cf. Herod. i 18 οἱ Μιλήσιοι τοῖσι Χίοισι τὸν πρὸς Ἐρυθραίους πόλεμον συνδιήνεικαν.

Παραπολαύειν properly means 'to have the benefit of (something) besides'; here in a bad sense 'to have the disadvantage of (something) besides.'
8. ὅσα ἡμῖν ἐλυμήναντο] '*quanta nobis nocuerunt*': the construction of λυμαίνεσθαι with either the dat. of the person or the neut. pl. adj. is common in Greek but not apparently the combination of the two constructions: see Liddell and Scott s. v.
10. πάλιν] 'again,' as in the time of persecution.
11. ἣν...δέδωκε] The reference is to John xiv 27.
ib. *And now after a very brief respite, they and we are visited with this terrible scourge of plague and sickness.*
14. ὡς ἴδιός τις αὐτ. ἀπήγγ. συγγρ.] The expression sounds as if it referred to some local contemporary historian, but as a matter of fact

τῶν πάντων ἐλπίδος κρεῖσσον γενόμενον· ἡμῖν δὲ οὐ
τοιοῦτο μέν, γυμνάσιον δὲ καὶ δοκίμιον οὐδενὸς τῶν ἄλλων
ἔλαττον. ἀπέσχετο μὲν γὰρ οὐδὲ ἡμῶν, πολλὴ δὲ ἐξῆλθεν
εἰς τὰ ἔθνη.

5 Τούτοις ἑξῆς ἐπιφέρει λέγων·

(2) Οἱ γοῦν πλεῖστοι τῶν ἀδελφῶν δι' ἡμῶν ὑπερβάλ-
λουσαν ἀγάπην καὶ φιλαδελφίαν ἀφειδοῦντες ἑαυτῶν καὶ
ἀλλήλων ἐχόμενοι, ἐπισκοποῦντες ἀφυλάκτως τοὺς νοσοῦν-
τας, λιπαρῶς ὑπηρετούμενοι, θεραπεύοντες ἐν Χριστῷ,
10 συναπηλλάττοντο ἐκείνοις ἀσμενέστατα, τοῦ παρ' ἑτέρων
ἀναπιμπλάμενοι πάθους καὶ τὴν νόσον ἐφ' ἑαυτοὺς ἕλκον-
τες ἀπὸ τῶν πλησίον καὶ ἑκόντες ἀναμασσόμενοι τὰς ἀλγηδόνας. καὶ πολλοὶ νοσοκομήσαντες καὶ ῥώσαντες ἑτέρους,
ἐτελεύτησαν αὐτοί, τὸν ἐκείνων θάνατον εἰς ἑαυτοὺς μετα-
15 στησάμενοι, καὶ τὸ δημῶδες ῥῆμα, μόνης ἀεὶ δοκοῦν

1 των παντων OR^{ab}L^r της π. cett ∥ 3 πολλη] πολυ A Steph ∥ 6 δι] δια
omissis υπερβαλλ. αγ. και OL^r ∥ 10 εκεινοις ασμενεστατα,] εκεινοις, ασμ. AO
Steph L^r ∥ 12 πλησιον] -ιων nonnulli

D. is quoting Thucyd. ii 64. 1 from
Pericles's speech about the plague at
Athens.
1. ἡμῖν δὲ οὐ τοι. μέν] i.e. to us
it was beyond neither endurance nor
expectation.
2. γυμνάσιον] 'discipline' (lit.
'training ground'): so Eus. *H. E.*
vii 22. 11 says that D. wrote a letter
περὶ Γυμνασίου, a supposed fragment
of which we give, p. 256.
3. πολλὴ δὲ ἐξῆλθ. εἰς τὰ ἔθνη]
'it went forth in great force against
the Gentiles': this (which is quite
a classical use of πολύς: e.g. Eur.
Bacch. 300 ὅταν πολὺς ὁ θεὸς ἔλθῃ)
is to be distinguished from the use
noted on p. 120 πολὺς ὀνομάζεται and
p. 122 εὑρήσει πολλὴν τὴν ζωήν.
6. *The devoted way in which the
majority of our brethren have faced
their own sickness and death, and
have nursed others in like circumstances and carried out their burial,
has shown the reality and depth of
their Christian love.*
ib. Οἱ γ. πλεῖστοι τ. ἀδ.] See p. 68
for an earlier instance of such devoted behaviour.
8. ἀφυλάκτως] 'without thought
of their own peril' (Salmond).
9. λιπ. ὑπηρετούμενοι] The reci-
procal use of the middle, 'diligently
tending one another': another of
the many instances in this letter of
D.'s polished, classical style.
12. ἀναμασσ. τὰς ἀλγηδ.] lit. 'wi-
ping off their troubles on themselves'
(i.e. taking the consequences of as-
sisting others): another classical
reminiscence; ἀναμάσσειν τι τῇ κεφαλῇ ('to become responsible for
some action') is found in Hom. *Od.*
xix 92, Herod. i 155, etc.
14. μεταστησάμενοι] 'having trans-
ferred': not quite a classical use

A. LETTERS

φιλοφροσύνης ἔχεσθαι, ἔργῳ δὴ τότε πληροῦντες, ἀπιόντες
αὐτῶν περίψημα. οἱ γοῦν ἄριστοι τῶν παρ' ἡμῖν ἀδελφῶν
τοῦτον τὸν τρόπον ἐξεχώρησαν τοῦ βίου, πρεσβύτεροί τέ
τινες καὶ διάκονοι καὶ τῶν ἀπὸ τοῦ λαοῦ λίαν ἐπαινούμενοι, ὡς καὶ τοῦ θανάτου τοῦτο τὸ εἶδος διὰ πολλὴν 5
εὐσέβειαν καὶ πίστιν ἰσχυρὰν γενόμενον μηδὲν ἀποδεῖν
μαρτυρίου δοκεῖν. καὶ τὰ σώματα δὲ τῶν ἁγίων ὑπτίαις
χερσὶ καὶ κόλποις ὑπολαμβάνοντες, καθαιροῦντές τε
ὀφθαλμοὺς καὶ στόματα συγκλείοντες, ὠμοφοροῦντές τε
καὶ διατιθέντες, προσκολλώμενοι, συμπλεκόμενοι, λουτροῖς 10
τε καὶ περιστολαῖς κατακοσμοῦντες, μετὰ μικρὸν ἐτύγχανον τῶν ἴσων, ἀεὶ τῶν ὑπολειπομένων ἐφεπομένων τοῖς

2 αυτων] add παντων BCDF^a Val Stroth om AE^{a}F^{b}GHKOR^{ab} Ruf Steph Schw L^r ‖ 6 γενομενον CF^{a}KR^{ab} Nic Schw γινομ. cett ‖ 8–10 καθαιρουντες τε...διατιθεντες] desunt in KR^a ‖ 9 οφθαλμους] praeponunt τους AE^a Steph Val Stroth ‖ 12 εφεπομενων] om O

of the word: see Liddell and Scott s. v.

1. ἀπιόντες αὐτῶν περίψημα] A condensed phrase 'becoming their expiatory substitutes in their departure (from this life)': cf. 1 Cor. iv 13, whence πάντων has crept into some MSS. Αὐτῶν=those other sick folk from tending whom they caught the fatal sickness. For περίψ. Suidas gives κατάμαγμα, ἀπολύτρωσις. Οὕτως ἐπέλεγον τῷ κατ' ἐνιαυτὸν συνέχοντι τῶν κακῶν· Περίψημα ἡμῶν γενοῦ, ἤτοι σωτηρία καὶ ἀπολύτρωσις, καὶ οὕτως ἐνέβαλον τῇ θαλάσσῃ ὡσὰν τῷ Ποσειδῶνι θυσίαν ἀποτιννύντες. The words κάθαρμα and ἀνάθεμα (Rom. ix 3) are used in the same way: cf. also ἀπεσκυβαλίζοντο below. Cf. Schol. ad Aristoph. Plut. 454. Valesius thinks that at Alexandria ἐγώ εἰμι περίψημά σου ('I am your obedient servant') was a colloquial and complimentary phrase (δημῶδες ῥῆμα) which became a reality for the Christians in the fullest significance of the word. Heinichen rightly rejects another suggestion of Vales. that περίψ. was a heathen term of contempt for Christians, as inconsistent with D.'s description of it as μόνης ἀεὶ δοκοῦν φιλοφροσύνης ('compliment,' 'friendly feeling') ἔχεσθαι. See Heinichen's Excursus on the phrase (pp. 710, 711).

5. ὡς]=ὥστε as often in D.

9. ὠμοφοροῦντες] 'bearing on their shoulders': the word is used by Joseph. Ant. Jud. iii 2. 7 of the embroidered linen girdle of the priest, the ends of which he threw over his left shoulder and wore there at the time of sacrifice so that they might not hinder his movements. The form ὁμοφοροῦντες (in Migne, P. G. x 1337, trans. by Salmond) is simply a misprint.

10. διατιθέντες] Lat. componentes, 'laying them out.'

11. περιστολαῖς] See above, p. 68.

πρὸ αὐτῶν. τὰ δέ γε ἔθνη πᾶν τοὐναντίον. καὶ νοσεῖν
τε ἀρχομένους ἀπωθοῦντο, καὶ ἀπέφευγον τοὺς φιλτάτους,
κἂν ταῖς ὁδοῖς ἐρρίπτουν ἡμιθνῆτας, καὶ νεκροὺς ἀτάφους
ἀπεσκυβαλίζοντο, τὴν τοῦ θανάτου διάδοσιν καὶ κοινωνίαν
5 ἐκτρεπόμενοι, ἣν οὐκ ἦν καὶ πολλὰ μηχανωμένοις ἐκκλῖναι
ῥᾴδιον.

Μετὰ δὲ καὶ ταύτην τὴν ἐπιστολήν, εἰρηνευσάντων τῶν κατὰ
τὴν πόλιν, τοῖς κατὰ τὴν Αἴγυπτον ἀδελφοῖς ἑορταστικὴν αὖθις
ἐπιστέλλει γραφήν, καὶ ἐπὶ ταύτῃ ἄλλας διαφόρους πάλιν διατυ-
10 ποῦται.

1 νοσειν τε] τε add CF^aKR^{ab} Schw om cett ‖ 3 καν] και CF^aR^{ab} ‖
7 και ταυτην] om και AE^aF^bK Val Stroth om cett ‖ 8 κατα την Αιγυπτον]
om AE^aF^bK Val Stroth add cett ‖ 9 διαφορους] om AE^a Steph

1. *The Gentiles on the other hand have displayed much selfishness and cowardice in their treatment of the sick and dead.*
ib. πᾶν τοὐναντίον] sc. ἐποίησαν or ἦσαν.
4. *ἀπεσκυβαλίζ.*] 'treated as vile refuse': cf. Phil. iii 8. Hein. quotes Eus. *de laud. Const.* xvi 11, where the phrase σκυβάλων ἐκβλητότερον occurs, in allusion to the saying of Heraclitus νέκυες κοπρίων ἐκβλητότεροι.
ib. τὴν τ. θαν. διάδ. καὶ κοιν.] 'the spreading and communication of the fatal disease': Salmond's 'communication and intercourse with death' is impossible.

XI

Πρὸς Ἱέρακα τῶν κατ' Αἴγυπτον ἐπίσκοπον ἑορταστικὴ Ἐπιστολή

(Eus. *H. E.* vii 21)

This is another of the Paschal Letters of Dionysius and has reference to the same Easter as those to Hermammon and to the Alexandrians (A.D. 262), though written somewhat later than the last named letter. Eusebius tells us it was addressed to Hierax bishop τῶν κατ' Αἴγυπτον[1], i.e. of some outlying district in his province. He further says that in the letter τῆς κατ'

[1] Nepos is also styled ἐπίσκοπος τῶν κατ' Αἴγυπτον, p. 108.

A. LETTERS

αὐτὸν[1] τῶν Ἀλεξανδρέων στάσεως μνημονεύει διὰ τούτων: but in the extract which he proceeds to give no mention of this revolution actually occurs, and hence it has been conjectured that Eusebius has by mistake copied the wrong letter, being perhaps misled by its opening words[2]. A mistake of this kind has been made elsewhere (*H. E.* iv 10), where the heading of the chapter mentions the bishops of Alexandria, while the text itself has nothing to do with them[3]. Anyhow the extract, as we have it, deals almost entirely with the devastations of the plague in Egypt, which broke out afresh after the revolt and overthrow of Macrianus (A.D. 261) and which was possibly in part due to the number of unburied corpses lying about in the city. In it Dionysius (1) makes interesting though rather far-fetched references to Old Testament history, especially in connexion with Egypt and the Nile: (2) very rhetorically describes the disastrous effects of the plague: and (3) laments the decrease in the population which it had caused.

[1] κατ' αὐτόν = 'in his time.'
[2] See note on p. 86 for further discussion of the point.
[3] See also pp. 44 and 65, where other mistakes of the historian are noted.

Ἐπιλαβούσης δὲ ὅσον οὔπω τῆς εἰρήνης ἐπάνεισι μὲν (ὁ Διονύσιος) εἰς τὴν Ἀλεξάνδρειαν, πάλιν δ' ἐνταῦθα στάσεως καὶ πολέμου συστάντος, ὡς οὐχ οἷόν τε ἦν αὐτῷ τοὺς κατὰ τὴν πόλιν ἅπαντας ἀδελφοὺς ἐς ἑκάτερον τῆς στάσεως μέρος διῃρημένους ἐπισκοπεῖν, αὖθις ἐν τῇ τοῦ πάσχα ἑορτῇ ὥσπερ τις ὑπερόριος ἐξ αὐτῆς τῆς Ἀλεξανδρείας διὰ 5 γραμμάτων αὐτοῖς ὡμίλει. καὶ Ἱέρακι δὲ μετὰ ταῦτα τῶν κατ' Αἴγυπτον ἐπισκόπῳ ἑτέραν ἑορταστικὴν ἐπιστολὴν γράφων, τῆς κατ' αὐτὸν τῶν Ἀλεξανδρέων στάσεως μνημονεύει διὰ τούτων·

Ἐμοὶ δὲ τί θαυμαστὸν εἰ πρὸς τοὺς πορρωτέρω παροικοῦντας χαλεπὸν τὸ κἂν δι' ἐπιστολῶν ὁμιλεῖν, ὅτε καὶ τὸ 10

9 παροικουντας CF^aGHKOR^{ab} Val Schw L^r κατοικ. cett

9. What wonder that it is difficult for me to correspond with those at a distance when I find it difficult to communicate even by letter with my own fellow-citizens. At present it is easier to cross from the East to the West than to pass from one part of Alexandria to another.

10. κἂν] practically equivalent to καί, here (as often) = 'even.'

πρὸς ἐμαυτὸν αὐτῷ μοι διαλέγεσθαι καὶ τῇ ἰδίᾳ ψυχῇ
συμβουλεύεσθαι καθέστηκεν ἄπορον; πρὸς γοῦν τὰ ἐμαυτοῦ
cπλάγχνα, τοὺς ὁμοσκήνους καὶ συμψύχους ἀδελφοὺς καὶ τῆς
αὐτῆς πολίτας ἐκκλησίας ἐπιστολιμαίων δέομαι γραμμά-
5 των, καὶ ταῦθ' ὅπως διαπεμψαίμην, ἀμήχανον φαίνεται.
ῥᾷον γὰρ ἄν τις οὐχ ὅπως εἰς τὴν ὑπερορίαν, ἀλλὰ καὶ ἀπ'
ἀνατολῶν ἐπὶ δυσμὰς περαιωθείη, ἢ τὴν Ἀλεξάνδρειαν
ἀπ' αὐτῆς τῆς Ἀλεξανδρείας ἐπέλθοι. τῆς γὰρ ἐρήμου τῆς
πολλῆς ἀτριβοῦς ἐκείνης, ἣν ἐν δυσὶ γενεαῖς διώδευσεν ὁ
10 Ἰσραήλ, ἄπειρος μᾶλλον καὶ ἄβατός ἐστιν ἡ μεσαιτάτη
τῆς πόλεως ὁδός, καὶ τῆς θαλάσσης, ἣν ἐκεῖνοι ῥαγεῖσαν

4 πολίτας ἐκκλ.] ἐκκλ. πολίτας AEa Steph πολιτείας και εκκλ. Nic Lr ||
6 υπεροριαν] -ιον CFabKRab Steph Val Stroth Schw -ιαν cett || 9 πολλης
ατριβους BCDFaKORab Schw Lr π. και ατρ. cett || 10 απειρος] απορος
DFaG Nic Stroth || 11 της πολεως] των πολεων AGa || οδος, και] οδος· και
Hein

1. αὐτῷ μοι] = ἐμαυτῷ dependent on καθέστ. ἄπορον. The cause of the difficulty is obviously that the disordered state of the city makes him incapable of concentrated thought.

2. τὰ ἐμ. σπλάγχνα] Cf. Philem. 12.

3. ὁμοσκήνους] well translated 'contubernales' by Vales.: 'tent-fellows,' 'those of my own house.'

4. ἐπιστολιμ. δέομ. γραμμ.] 'I am obliged to correspond by letter': the expression ἐπιστολ. γράμμ. occurs in Philo 2. 533.

7. ἤ...ἐπέλθοι] 'than he would visit one part of Alexandria from another.'

8. *The highways of the city are flooded with blood, and the channels of the overflowing Nile itself are choked with dead bodies, as in the days of Moses.*

9. ἐν δυσὶ γενεαῖς] D. reckons twenty years for a generation instead of the usual thirty.

10. ἄπειρος] probably equivalent to ἀπέρατος 'not to be traversed' here, rather than 'interminable,' which would be a very exaggerated way to describe a street: ἄπορος is an obvious emendation of a copyist.

ib. ἡ μεσαιτάτη τῆς πόλ. ὁδ.] 'the central street of the city.' The reading τῶν πόλεων is defended by some on the ground that ἡ στάσις had divided the city into two, but apart from the fancifulness of such an interpretation it is, as we have seen p. 85, doubtful whether the letter refers to ἡ στάσις at all, except so far as the pestilence was the result of it, as indeed the expressions τῶν ἐν αὐτοῖς φόνων and αἵματι καὶ φόνοις καὶ καταποντισμοῖς imply.

11. καὶ τῆς θαλάσσης] coordinate with τῆς ἐρήμου and like it dependent on ἄπειρος μᾶλλον.

ib. ῥαγεῖσαν κ. διατειχισθ.] 'parted asunder and walled up, so that there was a passage through': the words represent ἐσχίσθη τὸ ὕδωρ...καὶ τὸ ὕδωρ αὐτοῖς τεῖχος ἐκ δεξιῶν καὶ τεῖχος ἐξ εὐωνύμων, Exod. xiv 21, 22.

A. LETTERS 87

καὶ διατειχισθεῖσαν ἔσχον ἱππήλατον. καὶ ὧν ἐν τῇ
λεωφόρῳ κατεποντίσθησαν Αἰγύπτιοι, οἱ γαληνοὶ καὶ
ἀκύμαντοι λιμένες γεγόνασιν εἰκών, πολλάκις φανέντες
ἀπὸ τῶν ἐν αὐτοῖς φόνων οἷον ἐρυθρὰ θάλασσα. ὁ δ'
ἐπιρρέων ποταμὸς τὴν πόλιν ποτὲ μὲν ἐρήμου τῆς ἀνύδρου 5
ξηρότερος ὤφθη, καὶ μᾶλλον αὐχμώδης ἐκείνης, ἣν δια-
πορευόμενος ὁ Ἰσραὴλ οὕτως ἐδίψησεν, ὡς Μωυσοῦ μὲν
καταβοᾶν, ῥυῆναι δ' αὐτοῖς παρὰ τοῦ θαυμάcιa ποιοῦντος
μόνου ἐκ πέτρας ἀκροτόμου ποτόν· ποτὲ δὲ τοσοῦτον
ἐπλήμμυρεν, ὡς πᾶσαν τὴν περίχωρον τάς τε ὁδοὺς καὶ 10
τοὺς ἀγροὺς ἐπικλύσαντα, τῆς ἐπὶ Νῶε γενομένης τοῦ
ὕδατος φορᾶς ἐπαγαγεῖν ἀπειλήν. ἀεὶ δὲ αἵματι καὶ φόνοις
καὶ καταποντισμοῖς κάτεισι μεμιασμένος, οἷος ὑπὸ Μωυσεῖ

1 ιππηλατον. και] ιππηλατον, και Hein ∥ 7 Μωυσου BCK(R^{ab}) Val
Schw Μωυση ADF^{a}GH Steph Stroth Μωυσει F^{b} Μωση E^{a}O Nic L^{r} ∥
9 τοσουτον] -ος AE^{a} Nic L^{r} ∥ 12 αιματι] -σι K ∥ 13 Μωυσει CF^{b}HK(R^{ab})
Val Stroth Schw Μωσει AE^{a} Steph Μωυση F^{a} Μωυσου G^{2} Μωση O
Nic L^{r}

1. ἱππήλατον...λεωφόρῳ] 'carriage road...high road': these are both nouns substantive. Hesych. ἱππήλατος· πλατεῖα ὁδὸς καὶ λεία: cf. Pollux I 12 220 τὰς μὲν εὐρυτέρας ὁδοὺς λεωφόρους καὶ ἁμαξιτοὺς ἂν καλοῖς καὶ ἁμαξηλάτους καὶ ἱππηλάτους. Cf. above, p. 8.

ib. καὶ ὧν] We must supply λιμένων from οἱ γαλ. κ. ἀκύμ. λιμένες: 'in whose passage the Egyptians were drowned.'

3. λιμένες] Does this refer to the well-protected harbours of Alexandria (in the proper sense) or to the lake Mareotis? The epithets γαληνοί and ἀκύμαντοι seem almost too strong to apply to anything but land-locked waters, but the canal mentioned in the next note did not flow into the lake.

5. ἐπιρρέων ποτ. τὴν πόλιν] D. seems in this passage to be describing some unusual variations in the periodical rising and subsiding of the Nile. No mouth of the Nile passed nearer to Alexandria than the Canobic, but a canal cut from the river flowed at the back of the city between it and the Lake Mareotis into one of the harbours of the city: this must be the ποταμὸς ἐπιρρέων τὴν πόλιν which was, we may suppose, so affected by the variations in the Nile that year as to be rightly here described as ποτὲ μὲν ξηρότερος ὤφθη, ποτὲ δὲ τοσ. ἐπλήμμ. ὡς κτλ.

8. παρὰ τοῦ θαυμ....μόνου] Cf. Ps. lxxvi (lxxvii) 15, cxxxv (cxxxvi) 4.

9. ἐκ πέτρ. ἀκροτόμ.] Wisd. xi 4.

12. ἀεὶ δὲ κτλ.] The meaning is that whenever it runs at all—flood or no flood—it runs polluted with blood and slaughter and drowned corpses (καταποντισμοῖς).

γέγονε τῷ Φαραώ, μεταβαλὼν εἰς αἷμα καὶ ἐπόζεσας. καὶ
ποῖον γένοιτ' ἂν τοῦ πάντα καθαίροντος ὕδατος ὕδωρ ἄλλο
καθάρσιον; πῶς ἂν ὁ πολὺς καὶ ἀπέραντος ἀνθρώποις
Ὠκεανὸς ἐπιχυθεὶς τὴν πικρὰν ταύτην ἀποσμήξαι θάλασ-
5 σαν; ἢ πῶς ἂν ὁ μέγας ποταμὸς ὁ ἐκπορευόμενος ἐξ Ἐδέμ,
τὰς τέσσαρας ἀρχὰς εἰς ἃς ἀφορίζεται μετοχετεύσας εἰς μίαν
τοῦ Γηών, ἀποπλύναι τὸ λύθρον; ἢ πότε ὁ τεθολωμένος
ὑπὸ τῶν πονηρῶν πανταχόθεν ἀναθυμιάσεων ἀὴρ εἰλι-
κρινὴς γένοιτο; τοιοῦτοι γὰρ ἀπὸ τῆς γῆς ἀτμοὶ καὶ ἀπὸ
10 θαλάσσης ἄνεμοι, ποταμῶν τε αὖραι καὶ λιμένων ἀνιμή-
σεις ἀποπνέουσιν, ὡς σηπομένων ἐν πᾶσι τοῖς ὑποκειμένοις
στοιχείοις νεκρῶν ἰχῶρας εἶναι τὰς δρόσους. εἶτα θαυμά-
ζουσι καὶ διαποροῦσι, πόθεν οἱ συνεχεῖς λοιμοί, πόθεν αἱ

2 αλλο καθαρσιον] καθαρσιον αλλο CF^{a}R^{ab} Schw || 7 το] τον E^{a}F^{b}GH ||
11 εν] om O

1. μεταβαλὼν κτλ.] Cf. Exod. vii
20, 21. Μεταβαλ. (sc. ὁ ποταμός) is
here intrans. Perhaps D. took it as
intrans. in Exodus also.
*ib. Not even Ocean or the great
river of Eden could wash away all
this pollution, which has produced
noxious vapours and miasmatic exhalations everywhere.*
2. τ. πάντ. καθ. ὑδ.] Cf. Eur.
Iph. Taur. 1193 θάλασσα κλύζει
πάντα τἀνθρώπων κακά.
4. Ὠκεανός] Cf. *Macbeth* II ii
'Will all great Neptune's ocean
wash this blood Clean from my
hand? No: this my hand will
rather The multitudinous seas in-
carnadine, Making the green one
red.'
5. πῶς ἂν ὁ μέγ. ποτ. κτλ.]
'how could the great river that go-
eth out of Eden wash away the
pollution, though it were to divert
the four heads into which it is divided into the single head of the
Gihon?' Cf. Gen. ii 10 ff. The
name Gihon is here evidently taken
by D. to mean the Nile as in the
later Jewish writers, Αἰθιοπία (Cush)
being identified with Egypt.

8. ἀναθυμιάσεων] 'exhalations':
the technical sense of 'incense
smoke' (from θυμιᾶν) seems never
to belong to this compound.
10. ἀνιμήσεις] 'reeking vapours,'
from ἀνιμᾶν 'to rise' (of vapour).
11. ὡς (=ὥστε) σηπομ. κτλ.] 'so
that for dew we have the impure
fluids of corpses rotting in all their
component elements.'
12. στοιχείοις] sc. the various elements of which a human body is
composed, unless we should trans.
ἐν π. τ. ὑποκ. στοιχ. 'in all (the four)
constituent elements (of the world),'
i.e. all the four elements are charged
with the corruption, but no mention
has been made of πῦρ (one of the
four) and ὑποκειμ. seems hardly in
place.
ib. ἰχῶρας] In Homer ἰχώρ is
that which flows in the veins of
the gods for blood: in later writers
it means any juice or fluid, and in
Hipp. (*V. C.* 911) it means pus.
*ib. It is not surprising then that
so much disease and death should
be rife among us as materially to
diminish the population of all ages.*
13. οἱ συνεχεῖς λοιμοί] The Roman

A. LETTERS

χαλεπαὶ νόσοι, πόθεν αἱ παντοδαπαὶ φθοραί, πόθεν ὁ
ποικίλος καὶ πολὺς τῶν ἀνθρώπων ὄλεθρος, διὰ τί μηκέτι
τοσοῦτο πλῆθος οἰκητόρων ἡ μεγίστη πόλις ἐν αὐτῇ φέρει,
ἀπὸ νηπίων ἀρξαμένη παίδων μέχρι τῶν εἰς ἄκρον γεγη-
ρακότων, ὅσους ὠμογέροντας οὓς ἐκάλει πρότερον ὄντας 5
ἔτρεφεν, ἀλλ' οἱ τεσσαρακοντοῦται καὶ μέχρι τῶν ἑβδομή-
κοντα ἐτῶν τοσοῦτο πλείονες τότε, ὥστε μὴ συμπληροῦσθαι
νῦν τὸν ἀριθμόν, αὐτῶν προσεγγραφέντων καὶ συγκαταλε-
γέντων εἰς τὸ δημόσιον σιτηρέσιον τῶν ἀπὸ τεσσαρεσκαίδεκα
ἐτῶν μέχρι τῶν ὀγδοήκοντα, καὶ γεγόνασιν οἷον ἡλικιῶται 10
τῶν πάλαι γεραιτάτων οἱ ὄψει νεώτατοι. καὶ οὕτω
μειούμενον ἀεὶ καὶ δαπανώμενον ὁρῶντες τὸ ἐπὶ γῆς ἀνθρώπων γένος, οὐ τρέμουσιν, αὐξομένου καὶ προκόπτοντος τοῦ
παντελοῦς αὐτῶν ἀφανισμοῦ.

3 τοσουτο ACE^aGHR^{ab} -ον F^{ab}KO || πληθος] om OL^r || 7 τοσουτο ACE^a Steph Schw L^r -ον F^{ab}GHKR^{ab} Nic Val -ων O || πλειονες] πλεονες R^{ab}

Empire was a constant prey to the ravages of pestilence, just as medieval Europe was.

5. ὠμογέροντας] here evidently = 'hale old men' as in Hom. *Il.* xxiii 791, and as Vergil *Aen.* vi 304 describes Charon *iam senior, sed cruda deo viridisque senectus*: cf. Tac. *Agric.* 29. On the other hand in Hom. *Od.* xv 357 and Hes. Ἔργ. κ. Ἡμ. 703 ὠμὸν γῆρας seems to mean 'cruel or untimely old age.' Hesych. gives two slightly different shades of meaning to ὠμογέρων: οἱ μὲν τὸν ἀρξάμενον γηράσκειν, ἔτι δὲ ἰσχύοντα· οἱ δὲ τὸν μὴ λευκαινόμενον τὴν κεφαλήν, ὄντα δὲ πρεσβύτην. Ammonius makes ὠμογέρων equivalent to προβεβηκώς and γέρων. Vales. maintains that at Alexandria those who were between the age of 40 and 70 were called by this name, but, though Hein. does not reject this opinion, it seems to be merely a deduction from the mention in Cod. Theodos. i of officers in that city called ἀρχιγέροντες: cf. Greg.

Naz. *Or. de Athan.* xxi.

8. αὐτῶν] to be taken with τῶν ἀπὸ τεσσ. ἐτ. μέχρι τῶν ὀγδοήκ. 'even when all from 14 to 80 are enrolled and put together.'

9. τὸ δημ. σιτηρέσιον] Evidently at Alexandria (the capital of that country which was the chief granary of Rome), as at Rome itself, either the necessitous citizens or, as Vales. thinks, all between 40 and 70 received doles of corn. If the latter was the case, it was more like the Athenian practice of feeding at the public expense ἐν πρυτανείῳ those who were meritorious servants of the State. Σιτηρέσιον is used by D. in a general sense on p. 152 ('food-supply'): later writers use the word for church doles and esp. for grants to clergy, widows and virgins (e.g. Theodoret i 11, Sozom. v 5).

12. δαπανώμενον] Cf. Greg. Naz. *Theol. Or.* v 10 (p. 157, Mason) ὑφ' ἑαυτοῦ δαπανώμενον καὶ τικτόμενον (of the phoenix) and 2 Macc. i 23 δαπανωμένης τῆς θυσίας.

XII

Ἐκ τῆς β΄ Ἐπιστολῆς

(Holl *Fragmente* 378)

Holl makes no suggestion as to the source of this fragment. Pitra (*Anal. Sacr.* II xxxvii) conjectures that it is from the second letter of the series in which the next fragment is said to be from the fourth. If so we are right in connecting it with the Paschal Letters of Dionysius.

Τίς ἄλλη πρεπωδεστέρα κατάστασις ἑορτῆς ἢ τὸ ἄφοβον καὶ ἄλυπον καὶ ἀνειμένον διαμένειν; φόβον δὲ πάλιν λέγω, οὐ τὸν σοφόν, ἀλλὰ τὸν ἄλογον· φόβος γὰρ Κυρίογ τέρψει καρδίαν.

1. κατάστασις ἑορτῆς] 'state (of mind) for a festival': the gen. ἑορτῆς is a curious one = ἑορτάζοντός τινος or εἰς ἑορτήν.

2. ἀνειμένον] 'free from care' (or the like), Lat. *securus*: a classical use.

3. φόβος...καρδίαν] Ecclus. i 12.

XIII

Ἐκ τῆς δ΄ ἑορταστικῆς Ἐπιστολῆς

(Holl *Fragmente* 377)

This fragment is from the *Sacra Parallela Rupefucald.* fol. 70 and 71. Which of the Paschal Letters is meant by 'the fourth,' is quite uncertain. From Eus. *H. E.* vii 20 we might conjecture that it was the last of the four written ἔτι τοῦ διωγμοῦ συνεστῶτος, i.e. between A.D. 258 and 261, which he describes as addressed ἑτέροις ὁμοῦ διαφόρως (a vague and obscure phrase). The style of the present extract is a little sententious and involved for Dionysius, but the classical expressions εὖ πάσχειν as passive of εὖ ποιεῖν, καθικέτευσεν (gnomic aor.), στέργοντα etc. are very much like him. The main thought (of the cunning devices by which Love wins her way) is one of much beauty.

A. *LETTERS* 91

Ἡ ἀγάπη προπηδᾷ πάντως τι ὀνῆσαι καὶ ἄκοντα
θηρωμένη· καὶ πολλάκις ὀκνοῦντά τινα ὑπ' αἰδοῦς, καὶ
διὰ τὸ μὴ βούλεσθαι βαρὺν ἑτέρῳ γενέσθαι τὸ εὖ πάσχειν
παραιτούμενον, καὶ μᾶλλον αὐτὸν δυσφορεῖν στέργοντα
τοῖς ἰδίοις ἀλγεινοῖς, ὑπὲρ τοῦ μὴ πράγματά τινι καὶ 5
ὄχλησιν παρασχεῖν. ὁ πλήρης ἀγάπης καθικέτευσεν ἀνα-
σχέσθαι, καὶ ὑπομένειν ὡς ἀδικούμενον καὶ ἐπικουρούμενον,
καὶ χάριν ἄλλῳ μεγίστην, οὐχ ἑαυτῷ, παρασχεῖν τὸ
ἑαυτοῦ δι' ἐκείνου λωφῆσαι κακόν.

9 λωφῆσαι] λοφ. Holl

1. προπηδᾷ] Cf. p. 197 ὁ νοῦς προπηδῶν.
4. αὐτόν] 'himself.'
ib. δυσφορεῖν...τοῖς ἰδ. ἀλγ.] 'to
put up with his own disagreeables.'
Δυσφορεῖν with the dat. usually
means 'to be irritable under': here
it more nearly approaches the
meaning with the direct accus.

(*aegre ferre*).
7. καὶ ἐπικουρούμενον] perhaps
'even when helped.'
8. τὸ...κακόν] The article (τό)
goes apparently with λωφῆσαι (not
with ἑαυτοῦ κακόν): cf. τὸ καθ' ἡμῶν
φονᾶν (p. 6): the whole expression is exegetic of χάριν...παρα-
σχεῖν.

XIV

Πρὸς Βασιλείδην

This is one of several letters which, according to Eus. *H. E.* vii 22. 3 and Jerome *de virr. ill.* 69, Dionysius addressed to Basilides[1] Bishop of the churches in the Pentapolis (Cyrenaica)[2]. If genuine, as there seems no reason to doubt, it and the letter to Novatian are the only two pieces of his which have come down to us entire. As its contents are of the nature of Canons and were so entertained and accepted at the (3rd) Council of Constantinople *in Trullo* (A.D. 680), it is included in the collections of Canonical Letters, together

[1] In another of them Eusebius tells us he mentions that he has written a commentary on the Beginning of Ecclesiastes: see p. 208.

[2] It was in this district that that outbreak of Sabellianism had occurred which led to the proceedings connected with D.'s treatise Ἔλεγχος καὶ Ἀπολογία: see pp. 165 ff.

with the ancient commentaries of Zonaras and Balsamon upon the text. Dionysius speaks of Basilides both at the beginning and at the end of the letter in terms of affection[1] and high respect for his abilities[2] and his faithful discharge of duty[3]. And his replies to the various points raised are characterised by his usual conciliatory and broad-minded spirit, while at the end he makes a special point of remarking (1) that he appreciates his inquirer's good intention in applying to him and (2) that his response to the invitation is to be taken as coming not so much from master[4] to pupil as from a friend consulted by a friend. The date of the letter is uncertain though it has been assigned to so late a year as A.D. 262, after Dionysius's return to Alexandria[5], but possibly the touch in διδάσκαλος may refer to Dionysius's position, as head of the Catechetical School, which he has been thought to have retained at least for a time after his elevation to the Bishopric: and if so, it is more likely to be a reference to a post still held or only recently vacated, and this will give us an earlier date.

Basilides appears to have asked for Dionysius's ruling on four points, all of them perhaps suggested by what had been brought to his notice at an Easter lately kept.

The first is as to the proper hour for bringing the Paschal Fast to a close. We gather nothing certain during the discussion about the length of Lent in those days and in those parts: Dionysius concerns himself only with the last six days before Easter and of these chiefly with the last few hours, as the question asked demanded, and he does not tell us whether the Fast began before or only with Holy Week. But in answering the question put much of interest transpires. Some of the brethren in the Pentapolis held that they should conform to the Roman usage and fast till cockcrow, the technical term for which was ὑπέρθεσις (*superpositio*), while the general usage of the district was to end the Fast earlier. Dionysius replies that it is impossible to fix the hour of our Lord's Resurrection exactly from the Bible narrative[6] and that this would be necessary, if he is to lay down a hard and fast rule upon the point.

---

[1] υἱὲ ἀγαπητέ.   [2] λογιώτατε, συνετώτατε.

[3] συλλειτουργῷ, θεοπρεπεῖ, πιστότατε.

[4] οὐχ ὡς διδάσκαλος.

[5] Basnage *Annal. Pol. Eccl.* ii 340, quoted by Routh.

[6] So too Theophylact *Comm. in Marc.* xvi 9 τίς γὰρ οἶδε πότε ἀνέστη; (quoted by Routh).

He then proceeds to examine the accounts given in the four Gospels, because he says we may be sure that they really agree in spite of slight apparent discrepancies. He comes to the conclusion that according to St Matthew and St John the women who visited the tomb arrived at a late hour in the night and found Him risen, while according to St Luke and St Mark those who came with spices arrived somewhat later and also found Him risen: hence we know that it was at some very early hour on Easter morning that He rose, and nothing more precise can be said. Consequently those who give up even before midnight are not so far to be commended and those who continue till cockcrow are so far praiseworthy. At the same time it depends upon how men have spent the preceding six days, whether they are wholly to be commended or not. It would be much easier to keep the last two days rigorously than to keep the whole six, four, or three, moderately, and it is quite possible that in the case of the longer fast men's powers of endurance may become exhausted earlier than they hoped. As the notes will reveal, Dionysius's attempt to reconcile the Gospel narratives is not always clear nor wholly successful; but it is, like all his efforts, honest and worth considering and was indeed accepted by the Trullan Council (canon 89) together with his ruling on the practical point.

On the other three points raised by Basilides it is sufficient to refer the reader to the text and notes.

In preparing the text of this epistle, I have had the assistance of my friend, the Rev. H. E. Symonds of Queen's College, Oxford. He has kindly collated Routh's text (*Rell. Sacr.* tom. iii pp. 223 ff.) with several of the Bodleian MSS, viz. these:—

Bar. 26 (saec. xi ineuntis).
Laud. (Gr.) 39 (forsan saec. xi ineuntis) = Routh's Bodl. 715.
Bar. 196 (anno 1043 exarata).
Bar. 185 (saec. xi exeuntis).
Misc. 170 (saec. xi) 'olim Rawlinsoni 625' (Routh).
Bar. 86 (saec. xii exeuntis).
Bar. 158 (saec. xv).

Of these there seems to be considerable similarity between the witness of Bar. 26 and 86, except that the many misspellings of the former are usually corrected in the latter.

For the two Coislin MSS 37 and 122 I am dependent on

Routh, and also for the readings of the *Pedalion Graecorum* (Lipsiae 1801) and Balsamon (saec. xiii). Routh also frequently refers to the Commentary of Zonaras (saec. xii), *Sylloge Canonum* (Venetiis 1787) and the *Synodicum* of Bishop Beveridge (1672).

Διονύσιος Βασιλείδη τῷ ἀγαπητῷ μου υἱῷ καὶ ἀδελφῷ καὶ συλλειτουργῷ καὶ θεοπρεπεῖ, ἐν Κυρίῳ χαίρειν.

(α') Ἐπέστειλάς μοι, πιστότατε καὶ λογιώτατε υἱέ μου, πυνθανόμενος καθ' ἣν ὥραν ἀπονηστίζεσθαι δεῖ τῇ τοῦ
5 πάσχα περιλύσει. τινὰς μὲν γὰρ τῶν ἀδελφῶν λέγειν φῄς, ὅτι χρὴ τοῦτο ποιεῖν πρὸς τὴν ἀλεκτοροφωνίαν· τινὰς δέ, ὅτι ἀφ' ἑσπέρας χρή. οἱ μὲν γὰρ ἐν Ῥώμῃ ἀδελφοί, ὥς

2 και συλλ. Bar 196 86 Misc 170 Coisl 37 et 122 om και Bar 26 185 Laud 39 και θεοπρεπει Laud 39 Bar 185 Coisl 37 et 122 om και Bar 196 om και θεοπρ. Bar 26 θεοπειθει Bar 86 ‖ 5 περιλυσει] ημερα Bar 158

2. καὶ συλλ. καὶ θεοπρ.] With some hesitation I have inserted καί thrice over in the text though the third makes θεοπρ. coordinate with υἱῷ, ἀδελφῷ and συλλειτουργῷ, which is somewhat awkward.

3. *You ask whether you should follow the Roman practice of waiting till cockcrow before ending the Lenten fast or the practice of those who break it earlier.*

ib. λογιώτατε] 'most learned' or 'most eloquent,' see p. 124.

4. ἀπονηστίζεσθαι] 'to conclude the fast.' Hesych. ἀπονηστίσασθαι· τὸ ἀπὸ νηστείας ἐπὶ πρώτην (ἐδωδὴν) ἐλθεῖν: cf. Apost. Const. v 12, 18, etc. This breaking of the fast would, of course, properly consist in receiving the Easter Communion.

ib. τῇ τοῦ π. περιλύσει] Περιλύειν (or καταπαύειν) is the regular expression in Cyril of Alexandria's Homilies *de Fest. Pasch.* for ending the Lenten fast: cf. Eus. *H. E.* v 23 τὰς τῶν ἀσιτιῶν ἐπιλύσεις ποιεῖ-σθαι...τὰς νηστείας ἐπιλύεσθαι. Τὸ πάσχα (as in Lat. *pascha*) often refers to the fast which preceded Easter as well as the feast itself. Gunning *On the Lenten Fast* quotes several instances of the truth of the ancient saying *pascha includit ieiunia* (e.g. Tert. *de ieiun.* ii 13 and 14 *praeter pascha ieiunantes... numquam nisi in pascha ieiunandum*; Tim. Alex. τὸ πάσχα νηστεύειν, etc.), and Bingham *Antiqq.* Bk. xx chap. v § 1 shows that the week before Easter was often distinguished as πάσχα σταυρώσιμον and Easter week itself as πάσχα ἀναστάσιμον.

6. πρὸς τὴν ἀλεκτ.] 'at cockcrow' (*ad galli cantum*), i.e. at 3 a.m. on Easter day, the traditional hour of our Lord's Resurrection, esp. in the West: cf. Mark xiii 35. The Can. Hipp. (§ 255) make no actual mention of the fast but it is implied in the words *nemo igitur illa nocte dormiat usque ad auroram*.

7. ἀφ' ἑσπέρας] i.e. at 6 p.m. on the previous day.

A. LETTERS

φασι, περιμένουσι τὸν ἀλέκτορα· περὶ δὲ τῶν ἐνταῦθα
ἔλεγες ὅτι τάχιον. ἀκριβῆ δὲ ὅρον ἐπιτιθέναι ζητεῖς, καὶ
ὥραν πάνυ μεμετρημένην· ὅπερ καὶ δύσκολον καὶ σφαλερόν
ἐστι. τὸ μὲν γὰρ ὅτι μετὰ τὸν τῆς ἀναστάσεως τοῦ κυρίου
ἡμῶν καιρὸν χρὴ τῆς ἑορτῆς καὶ τῆς εὐφροσύνης ἐν- 5
άρχεσθαι, μέχρις ἐκείνου τὰς ψυχὰς ταῖς Νηστείαις ταπεινοῦν-
τας, ὑπὸ πάντων ὁμοίως ὁμολογηθήσεται. κατεσκεύασας
δὲ δι' ὧν ἔγραψάς μοι πάνυ ὑγιῶς καὶ τῶν θείων εὐαγγελίων
ᾐσθημένως, ὅτι μηδὲν ἀπηκριβωμένον ἐν αὐτοῖς περὶ τῆς
ὥρας καθ' ἣν ἀνέστη φαίνεται. διαφόρως μὲν γὰρ οἱ 10
εὐαγγελισταὶ τοὺς ἐπὶ τὸ μνημεῖον ἐλθόντας ἀνέγραψαν
κατὰ καιροὺς ἐνηλλαγμένους, καὶ πάντες ἀνεστηκότα ἤδη

2 επιτιθ. ζητ.] επιζητεις επιτιθεναι Misc 170 ‖ 3 σφαλερον] φανερον επισφαλισμα Bar 158 ‖ 4 εστι] om Bar 86 ‖ το μεν γαρ] οτι μεν γαρ Bar 26 Misc 170 ‖ μετα τον] κατα τον Misc 170 om τον Bar 26* ‖ 5 ημων] om Misc 170 ‖ χρη]+ημας Misc 170 ‖ και της ευφροσ.] om Bar 158 ‖ 6 ταις νηστ. ταπειν.] ταπειν. ταις νηστ. Misc 170 ‖ 7 κατεσκευασας] κατασκ. Bar 26 ‖ 8 δι ων] και δι ων Bar 158 ‖ ευαγγελιων] -ιστων Ped Bals Edd ‖ 9 ησθημενως Laud 39 Bar 196 185 86 158 -ενος Bar 26 Misc 170 Routh αισθομενος Ped Edd ‖ μηδεν] μη δ εν Bar 86 ‖ απηκριβωμενον] -ομενον Bar 26 ‖ 10 φαινεται] φεινεται Bar 26 ‖ 12 ανεστηκοτα] ανασταντα Bar 86

1. περὶ δὲ τῶν ἐνταῦθα] sc. ἐν τῇ Πενταπόλει.
2. τάχιον] sc. ἀπονηστίζονται: this form of the adv. (which here = 'sooner' or 'earlier') is found four or five times in N.T.
ib. But the definite rule you ask for is not easy to give, because, as you yourself perceive, the Gospels say nothing definite about the hour of the Resurrection.
6. τὰς ψυχ. ... ταπεινοῦντας] Cf. Ps. xxxiv (xxxv) 13, Lev. xvi 29, etc.
7. κατεσκεύασας κτλ.] 'but by what you have written to me you have very soundly and with a good insight into the Divine Gospels established the fact that, etc.' Κατασκευάζειν 'to build up (or 'construct') an argument' opp. to ἀνασκευάζειν is found in Arist. *Rhet.*

ii 24. 4 ἄλλος δὲ τόπος τὸ δεινώσει κατασκευάζειν ἢ ἀνασκευάζειν: cf. *ibid.* 26. 2. The adv. ᾐσθημένως is well-supported by the MSS: the participle (-ενος) is obviously a correction.
10. Moreover the four evangelists differ from one another both as to the general expressions they use about the time and as to the visitants to the tomb.
ib. διαφόρως] is explained immediately afterwards by κατὰ καιροὺς ἐνηλλαγ. Ἐνηλλαγμένους means simply 'different' here, for which we might expect διηλλαγμένους. Eus. *H. E.* viii. 3. 1 has a curious illustration of this use, ἕκαστος εἴδη διάφορα βασάνων ἐνήλλαττεν, a phrase which becomes in *de Mart. Pal.* 1. 3 ἐκ. εἴ. δ. β. διήλλαττον.
12. πάντες] These may be either

τὸν κύριον ἔφασαν εὑρηκέναι· καὶ ὀψὲ cαββάτων, ὡς ὁ
Ματθαῖος εἶπε· καὶ πρωΐας ἔτι σκοτίας οὔσης, ὡς ὁ Ἰωάννης
γράφει· καὶ ὄρθρου βαθέος ὡς ὁ Λουκᾶς· καὶ λίαν πρωῒ
ἀνατείλαντος τοῦ ἡλίου, ὡς ὁ Μάρκος. καὶ πότε μὲν ἀνέστη,
5 σαφῶς οὐδεὶς ἀπεφήνατο· ὅτι δὲ ὀψὲ cαββάτων τῇ ἐπι-
φωσκούσῃ μιᾷ cαββάτων μέχρις ἀνατολῆς ἡλίου τῆς μιᾶς
σαββάτων οἱ ἐπὶ τὸ μνημεῖον παραγενόμενοι οὐκέτι κείμενον
αὐτὸν ἐν αὐτῷ κατέλαβον, τοῦτο ἀνωμολόγηται. καὶ
μηδὲ διαφωνεῖν μηδὲ ἐναντιοῦσθαι τοὺς εὐαγγελιστὰς πρὸς
10 ἀλλήλους ὑπολάβωμεν· ἀλλ᾽ εἰ καὶ μικρολογία τις εἶναι
δόξει περὶ τὸ ζητούμενον, εἰ συμφωνοῦντες πάντες ἐν
ἐκείνῃ τῇ νυκτὶ τὸ τοῦ κόσμου φῶς τὸν κύριον ἡμῶν
ἀνατεταλκέναι περὶ τὴν ὥραν διαφέρονται, ἀλλ᾽ ἡμεῖς
εὐγνωμόνως τὰ λεχθέντα καὶ πιστῶς ἁρμόσαι προθυμή-
15 θωμεν.

1 εφασαν] ante ηδη Bar 158 ‖ 2 ειπε] φησι Bar 86 ‖ πρωιας] πρὸιας Bar 26 ‖ ο Ιωαννης] om ο Misc 170 ‖ 4 του ηλιου] om του Laud 39 ‖ ως ο Μαρκος] και ο Μαρκ. Edd ‖ 5 τη επιφ. μια σαββ. Laud 39 Bar 196 185 Misc 170 (μιας) om Bar 26 τη επιφ. εις μιαν σαββ. Bar 86 158 Coisl 122 ‖ 6–7 μεχρις ...σαββατων] om Bar 86 μεχρης Misc 170 ‖ 7 οι επι] om οι Misc 170 ‖ το μνημ.] om το Bar 26 ‖ 8 αυτον] post κατελαβον Misc 170 ‖ ανωμολογηται] ανομολ. Bar 26 ‖ και μηδε] και μητε Bar 86 ‖ 9 διαφωνειν] διαφωνιαν Bar 86 ‖ 11 ει συμφωνουντες παντες] ως μη συμφωνουντων παντων Bar 26 Misc 170* ως μη συμφωνουντες Bar 86 ‖ εν εκεινη] εκεινω Misc 170* εν εκεινη Misc 170² ‖ 12 ημων] om Bar 26* ‖ 13 την ωραν] αυτην ωρ. Bar 26 την αυτην ωρ. Bar 86 ‖ διαφερονται] και εν τουτω διαφ. Bar 86 Misc 170* και εν τουτο διαφ. Bar 26 ‖ 14 αρμοσαι] αρμωσαι Bar 26 Laud 39

οἱ εὐαγγελισταί or οἱ ἐπὶ τὸ μνημ. ἐλθ. whom he afterwards seems to divide into two parties, (1) the two Marys and (2) other devout women, the second party coming later than the first.

1. καὶ ὀψὲ σαββάτων κτλ.] The reff. are Matt. xxviii 1, John xx 1, Luke xxiv 1, Mark xvi 2. The first καί must mean 'both,' unless the sentence is begun as if ὡς was not to follow each quotation.

8. *Yet there is no need to suppose*

that they are really at variance and contradictory.

10. ἀλλ᾽ εἰ καί...προθυμήθ.] 'but even if there seem to be some small dispute' (cf. τοῖς ἀκριβολογ. below) 'upon the matter of your inquiry, (that is to say) if, though all agree that the Light of the world our Lord arose on that night, they differ about the hour, yet (ἀλλ᾽) let us be anxious fairly and faithfully to harmonize what is said.' For τοῦ κόσμ. φῶς cf. John ix 5, etc.

A. LETTERS

Τὸ μὲν οὖν ὑπὸ τοῦ Ματθαίου λεχθὲν οὕτως ἔχει· Ὀψὲ
cαββάτων, τῇ ἐπιφωσκούcῃ εἰc μίαν cαββάτων, ἦλθε Μαρία ἡ
Μαγδαληνὴ καὶ ἡ ἄλλη Μαρία θεωρῆcαι τὸν τάφον. καὶ ἰδοὺ
cειcμὸc ἐγένετο μέγαc· ἄγγελοc γὰρ Κυρίου καταβὰc ἐξ οὐρανοῦ
καὶ προcελθὼν ἀπεκύλιcε τὸν λίθον καὶ ἐκάθητο ἐπάνω αὐτοῦ. 5
ἦν δὲ ἡ ἰδέα αὐτοῦ ὡc ἀcτραπὴ καὶ τὸ ἔνδυμα αὐτοῦ λευκὸν
ὡcεὶ χιών. ἀπὸ δὲ τοῦ φόβου αὐτοῦ ἐcείcθηcαν οἱ τηροῦντεc
καὶ ἐγενήθηcαν ὡcεὶ νεκροί. ἀποκριθεὶc δὲ ὁ ἄγγελοc εἶπε ταῖc
γυναιξί· Μὴ φοβεῖcθε ὑμεῖc, οἶδα γὰρ ὅτι Ἰηcοῦν τὸν ἐcταυρω-
μένον ζητεῖτε· οὐκ ἔcτιν ὧδε, ἠγέρθη γὰρ καθὼc εἶπε. 10
τοῦτο δὲ τὸ λεχθὲν ὀψὲ οἱ μέν τινες οἰήσονται κατὰ τὴν
κοινότητα τοῦ ῥήματος τὴν ἑσπέραν δηλοῦσθαι τοῦ σαββά-

1 μεν] νυν Bar 26 || ουν] om Bar 185·158 || οψε]+δε Laud 39 Bar 185 || 2 επιφωσκ.] επιφοσκ. Bar 26 -ουσι Misc 170* || 3 θεωρησαι] θεωρισαι Bar 26 || 5 και προσελθων] om και Bar 185 Coisl 37 et 122 και προελθων Bar 86 || 6 ιδεα] ειδεα Bar 26 et 86 || 7 ωσει] ως Laud 39 Bar 185 || χιων] χιον Bar 26 || 8 εγενηθησαν Bar 26 196 185 Laud 39 εγενοντο Bar 86 Routh || 10 ζητειτε] ζητεισθε Bar 196 post Ιησουν Bar 86 158 || ουκ εστιν—ειπε] ηγερθη, ουκ εστιν ωδε Misc 170 || 11 το λεχθεν] λεχθεν το Bar 158 || τινες οιησ.] οιησ. τινες Bar 86 || 12 δηλουσθαι] δηλουντος Misc 170* δηλουν Routh

1. *St Matthew's record discussed with special reference to his use of* ὀψέ, *whether it means* ἡ ἑσπέρα *or more scientifically* (σοφώτερον) νὺξ βαθεῖα.

ib. Τὸ μὲν οὖν ὑπὸ τοῦ Ματθ. κτλ.] D. now proceeds briefly to discuss the marks of time given by each Evangelist, with a view to showing that they do not contradict one another: for he thinks St Matthew's account (with which St John's tallies) speaks of the two Marys coming to look at the tomb about midnight on Easter eve or morning, while St Luke and St Mark mention certain women who arrived at the tomb with spices somewhat later when the sun had just risen: but the difficulty here is that one at least of the Marys mentioned by St Matthew is identical with one of these mentioned by St Mark and apparently by St Luke. I am not sure, however, that D. does not mean that the two Marys took part in both visits to the tomb (ἥκον οὔπω κτλ.). The student will find modern attempts at harmonizing the accounts in many commentaries (e.g. Dr Westcott on St John and Dr Swete on St Mark).

11. τὴν κοινότητα τ. ῥήμ.] 'the common acceptation of the word.' As to D.'s interpretation of ὀψέ first in its 'ordinary sense' of 'the evening' and then with due regard to the circumstances of the case as equivalent to νυκτὸς βαθείας, we may take it that the former meaning was current in his time and country, though that proves nothing

του, οἱ δὲ σοφώτερον ἐξακούοντες οὐ τοῦτο ἀλλὰ νύκτα
βαθεῖαν ἐροῦσιν εἶναι, βραδύτητα καὶ μακρὸν χρόνον τοῦ
ῥήματος τοῦ ὀψὲ δηλοῦντος. καὶ ὅτι νύκτα λέγει καὶ οὐχ
ἑσπέραν, ἐπήγαγε τῇ ἐπιφωσκογςη εἰς Μίαν ϲαββάτων, καὶ
5 ἦκον οὔπω, ὡς οἱ λοιποί φασι, τὰ ἀρώματα φέρογϲαι ἀλλὰ
θεωρῆϲαι τὸν τάφον· καὶ εὗρον τὸν σεισμὸν γεγονότα καὶ
καθήμενον τὸν ἄγγελον ἐπὶ τοῦ λίθου, καὶ ἀκηκόασι παρ'
αὐτοῦ· Ογκ ἔϲτιν ὧδε· ἡγέρθη. ὁμοίως· Ἰωάννης· Ἐν μιᾷ τῶν
ϲαββάτων, φησί, Μαρία ἡ Μαγδαληνὴ ἦλθε πρωὶ ϲκοτίαϲ ἔτι
10 ογϲηϲ εἰϲ τὸ μνημεῖον, καὶ βλέπει τὸν λίθον ἠρμένον ἀπὸ τογ
μνημείογ. πλὴν παρὰ τοῦτο ϲκοτίαϲ ογϲηϲ ἔτι πλὴν τὸ πρὸς

3 και οτι] οτι δε Bar 26 Misc 170 ‖ 4 εσπεραν] εσπερα Bar 26 ‖ επηγαγεν] επιγαγεν Bar 26 ‖ 5 ουπω] ουτω Bar 26 ‖ φασι] om Misc 170 ‖ φερουσαι]+αι γυναικες Bar 158 ‖ 6 θεωρησαι] -ισαι Bar 26 ‖ γεγονοτα] γινομενον Bar 26 et 86 γενομενον Misc 170 ‖ 7 λιθου και] om ου και Bar 26* add ου Bar 26² ‖ 8 ομοιως]+και ο Coisl 37 et 122 (teste Routh)+ο Bar 196 ‖ 9 ηλθε] post ουσης Bar 86 ‖ σκοτιας ετι] ετι σκοτιας Bar 26 et 185 Laud 39 Misc 170 om ετι Bar 158 ‖ 10 απο] εκ Laud 39 Bar 196 158 Misc 170 ‖ 11 πλην παρα τουτο] om πλην Routh πλιν παρα τ. Bar 26 ‖ πλην το προς εω Laud 39 Bar 185 Misc 170 πλιν το προς εω Bar 26 πριν (ex corr) του π. ε. Bar 86 πλην προς εω Bar 196 om Bar 158

as to St Matthew's use of the word and we may observe, as Routh has pointed out, that the 89th Canon of the Council *in Trullo* (A.D. 680) has accepted his second meaning without question and in fact adopted his ruling on the point raised in this letter *in toto*: cf. Fragm. Euseb. (Mai *Anecd. Gr.* ii 62) quoted by Routh p. 243 εἰ γὰρ μὴ τοῦτο ἦν (h.e. *ni 'sero' vocabulo ὀψέ significaretur*) ἐχρῆν ἡμᾶς τῇ ἡμέρᾳ τοῦ σαββάτου, μετὰ ἡλίου δυσμάς, εὐθέως ἑσπέρας γενομένης, ἀπονηστίζεσθαι· ἀλλ' οὐχ οὕτως ἡ συνήθεια ἐν ταῖς ἐκκλησίαις τοῦ θεοῦ κεκράτηκεν, ἀλλ' ἢ νυκτὸς ἐπιλαβούσης ἢ αὐτῷ μεσονυκτίῳ ἢ περὶ ἀλεκτόρων βοάς.

2. βραδύτητα] 'lateness': βραδύς is so used in the Classics: see Liddell and Scott *s. v.*

3. ὅτι νύκτα λέγει] 'because he means night.'

5. ἦκον οὔπω] Does this imply that they were among those who came later on or not?

7. ἀκηκόασι] As usual in D.'s writings no stress can be laid on the tense.

8. *St John's account seems nearly to tally with S. Matthew's.*

11. πλὴν παρὰ τοῦτο...προελήλ.] The second πλήν is as well supported in the MSS as the first which seems to condition ὁμοίως above: if we retain both, the sense must be: 'however by this account, when it was still dark, although (πλήν) towards dawn, He had already come forth from the tomb.' The subject of προελήλ. is ὁ

A. LETTERS

ἔω τοῦ μνημείου προεληλύθει. ὁ δὲ Λουκᾶς φησί· Τὸ μὲν
cάββατον ἡcύχαcαν κατὰ τὴν ἐντολήν, τῇ Δὲ μιᾷ τῶν cαββάτων
ὄρθρογ βαθέοc ἐπὶ τὸ μνῆμα ἦλθον φέρογcαι ἃ ἡτοίμαcαν
ἀρώματα. εὗρον Δὲ τὸν λίθον ἀποκεκγλιcμένον ἀπὸ τοῦ
μνημείογ. ὁ βαθὺς ὄρθρος ἴσως προυποφαινομένην αὐγὴν 5
ἑωθινὴν ἐμφανίζει τῆς μιᾶς τῶν σαββάτων. διὰ τοῦτο,
παρῳχηκότος ἤδη τελείως σὺν τῇ μετ' αὐτὸ νυκτὶ πάσῃ τοῦ
σαββάτου καὶ ἑτέρας ἀρχομένης ἡμέρας, ἦλθον τὰ ἀρώματα
καὶ τὰ μύρα φέρουσαι, ὅτε δῆλον ὡς ἀνειστήκει πρὸ πολλοῦ.
τούτῳ κατακολουθεῖ καὶ ὁ Μάρκος λέγων· Ἠγόραcαν ἀρώ- 10
ματα ἵνα ἐλθοῦcαι ἀλείψωcιν αὐτόν. καὶ λίαν πρωΐ τῆc μιᾶc
cαββάτων ἔρχονται ἐπὶ τὸ μνημεῖον, ἀνατείλαντος τοῦ ἡλίογ.

1 του μνημειου Bar 26 196 185 86* Laud 39 Misc 170 τω μνημειω
Bar 86² et Routh εις το μνημειον Ped om Bar 158 ‖ προεληλυθει] ελη-
λυθει Bar 86(?) ‖ 3 βαθεος] βαθεω (s evanuit) Bar 26 ‖ ηλθον] ante επι
τ. μ. Bar 86 ‖ 4 απο] εκ Bar 86 158 ‖ 5 ο βαθυς]+ουν. Bar 26 86
Misc 170 ‖ 6 εωθινην] εωθηνην ημεραν Bar 86 ‖ εμφανιζει Bar 26 et
196 εμφαινιζει Laud 39 Bar 185 Routh ‖ των σαββ.] om των Laud
39 Bar 196 185 ‖ δια τουτο παρῳχηκοτος Laud 39 Bar 185 Misc 170²
Coisl 37 et 122 δια το παρῳχηκεναι Bar 26 Misc 170* et Ped δια το
παροχηκεναι Bar 86 δια τουτο παρωχηκεναι Bar 158 ‖ 7 μετ αυτο] μετ
αυτου Bar 86 158 ‖ πασῃ] παντος Bar 26 86 Misc 170* παν Bar 158 ‖
του σαββατου] το σαββατον Bar 158 ‖ 8 ετερας αρχ. ημ.] ετεραν αρχ. ημεραν
Bar 158 ‖ ηλθον] οτε ηλθον Bar 26 86 Misc 170 ‖ 9 οτε] οτι Bar 86 Misc
170² οθεν Bar 158 Coisl 37 122 ‖ ανειστηκει] ανιστηκει Laud 39 ανεστηκει
Bar 196 86 ‖ 10 τουτω] τουτο Laud 39 ‖ ο Μαρκος] om ο Bar 158 ‖ 11 αυτον]
τον Ιησουν Bar 158 Misc 170 ‖ της μιας] om της Bar 26 185 Misc 170
Laud 39 μια Bar 196 ‖ 12 σαββατων] -ου Misc 170

Ἰησοῦς : through not understanding this and referring the verb to Μαρία ἡ Μαγδ., Bar 86² has altered τοῦ μνημείου to τῷ μνημείῳ and Ped. to εἰς τὸ μνήμειον.

1. *St Luke's account evidently refers to a later visit when He had been some time risen.*

ib. Τὸ μὲν σάββ. κτλ.] Luke xxiii 56, xxiv 1, 2.

9. ὅτε...πρὸ πολλοῦ] 'at which time (it is) clear that He had risen long before' : the readings ὅθεν and ὅτι are obviously attempts at correcting the passage.

10. *And St Mark's words seem to refer to the same incident as St Luke's.*

11. τῆς μιᾶς] (τῇ) μιᾷ W. and H.

12. ἀνατείλ. τ. ἡλ.] No doubt these words of St Mark are the most difficult element in the narrative : see Swete *in loc.*

λίαν μὲν γὰρ πρωὶ καὶ οὗτος εἶπεν, ὅπερ ταὐτόν ἐστι τῷ
βαθέος ὄρθρου· καὶ ἐπήγαγεν ἀνατείλαντοσ τοῦ ἡλίου. ἡ
μὲν γὰρ ὁρμὴ καὶ ἡ ὁδὸς αὐτῶν δῆλον ὡς ὄρθρου βαθέος
καὶ λίαν πρωὶ κατήρξαντο· παρέτειναν δὲ κατά τε τὴν
5 πορείαν καὶ περὶ τὸ μνημεῖον διατρίβουσαι μέχρις ἀνατολῆς
ἡλίου. καὶ λέγει καὶ τότε ταύταις ὁ νεανισκὸς ὁ λευχείμων·
Ηγέρθη· ογκ ἔcτιν ὧδε.

Τούτων οὕτως ἐχόντων, τοῦτο τοῖς ἀκριβολογουμένοις
ἀποφαινόμεθα κατὰ ποίαν ὥραν, ἢ καὶ ποῖον ἡμιώριον, ἢ
10 ὥρας τέταρτον, ἄρχεσθαι προσῆκε τῆς ἐπὶ τῇ τοῦ κυρίου
ἡμῶν ἐκ νεκρῶν ἀναστάσει χαρᾶς· τοὺς μὲν λίαν ἐπι-
ταχύναντας καὶ πρὸ νυκτὸς ἐγγὺς ἤδη μεσούσης ἀνιέντας

1 μεν γαρ πρωι] πρωι μεν γαρ Bar 185 ‖ οπερ] οτι Misc 170 ‖ τω] το Bar 26 Misc 170 Laud 39 του Bar 86 ‖ 2 επηγαγεν] επιγαγεν Bar 26 και επηγ Misc 170 ‖ του ηλιου] om του Laud 39 Bar 196 ‖ 3 η οδος] om η Laud 39 Bar 196 et 86 Misc 170 ‖ 4 κατηρξαντο] -ατο Bar 196 et 185 κατηρθη Bar 158 κατηρχθη Ped Routh ‖ δε] τε Bar 26 Misc 170 ‖ κατα τε] om τε Misc 170 ‖ 5 πορειαν] πορρειαν Bar 26 ‖ μεχρις] μεχρης Bar 26 ‖ 6 ηλιου] του ηλ. Bar 158 ‖ ταυταις] ταυταιs Bar 86 ‖ λευχειμων] λευχημων Bar 26 ‖ 7 ηγερθη· ουκ εστ. ωδε] ουκ εστ. ωδε αλλ ηγερθ. Misc 170 ‖ 9 αποφαινομεθα] απολογουμεθα Bar 158 Ped ‖ και ποιον] om και Bar 158 ‖ 11 λιαν] λειαν Bar 26 ‖ επιταχυναντας] -οντας Bar 185 Misc 170 επιτυγχανοντας Bar 196 ‖ 12 προ] om Misc 170 ‖ εγγυς ηδη] ηδη εγγυs Bar 26 ‖ μεσουσης] εγγιζουσης Bar 196

3. ἡ ὁρμή] 'their start': this nom. and the following (ὁδός) go with κατήρξαντο, for which κατήρχθη is an unnecessary correction.

4. παρέτειναν] abs., to be taken with διατρίβ. 'they had gone on spending time both on the road and around the tomb': see Liddell and Scott s. v. and for a similar use cf. Joseph. de bell. Jud. vi 5. 3 παρατείνας ἐπ' ἐνιαυτὸν κομήτης ... καὶ τοῦτο παρέτεινεν ἐφ' ἡμίσειαν ὥραν quoted by Eus. H. E. iii 8. 2, 3. Διατρίβουσαι (sc. χρόνον), 'spending time' as often.

6. καὶ τότε ταύταις] 'on this occasion also to these (women),' i.e. as on the former occasion mentioned by St Matt. and St Mk.

8. The decision: (1) those who are in haste to end the fast before midnight we blame as remiss and wanting in self-restraint. (2) Those who wait till the fourth watch we approve of for their noble earnestness. (3) Those who adopt a middle course are not wholly to be blamed.

ib. τοῦτο...ἀποφαινόμεθα] 'we pronounce this judgement': cf. Eus. H. E. v 8. 6; 13. 5; vi 25. 13: so we have ἀποφάσεις p. 35.

9. κατὰ ποίαν ὥραν κτλ.] to be joined with τοῖς ἀκριβολογ.

12. ἐγγύς] qualifies ἤδη μεσ. 'before midnight though near it' (for which at least they might have waited).

ib. ἀνιέντας] sc. τὴν νηστείαν.

A. LETTERS

ὡς ὀλιγώρους καὶ ἀκρατεῖς μεμφόμεθα, παρ' ὀλίγον προ-
καταλύοντας τὸν δρόμον, λέγοντος ἀνδρὸς σοφοῦ· Οὐ μικρὸν
ἐν βίῳ τὸ παρὰ μικρόν. τοὺς δὲ ἐφυστερίζοντας καὶ
διαρκοῦντας ἐπὶ πλεῖστον καὶ μέχρι τετάρτης φυλακῆς
ἐγκαρτεροῦντας, καθ' ἣν καὶ τοῖς πλέουσιν ὁ σωτὴρ ἡμῶν 5
περιπατῶν ἐπὶ τῆς θαλάσσης ἐπεφάνη, ὡς γενναίους καὶ
φιλοπόνους ἀποδεξόμεθα. τοῖς δὲ μεταξὺ ὡς ἐκινήθησαν ἢ
ὡς ἠδυνήθησαν ἀναπαυσαμένοις μὴ πάνυ διοχλῶμεν· ἐπεὶ
μηδὲ τὰς ἐξ τῶν νηστειῶν ἡμέρας ἴσως μηδὲ ὁμοίως πάντες

1 παρ ολιγ.] ως π. ο. Bar 158 ‖ 2 λεγοντος]+του λογου Bar 26 Misc 170 ‖
4 επι]+το Bar 86 ‖ 7 αποδεξομεθα Laud 39 Bar 196 185 -χομεθα Bar 26 et 86
Routh ‖ 8 διοχλωμεν Bar 26 196 158 Misc 170 Laud 39 διωχλωμεν Bar 86
διενοχλ. Bar 185 Coisl 37 et 122 Routh ‖ 9 μηδε τας] μη δε τας Bar 86 ‖
μηδε ομοιως] μη δε ομ. Bar 196 μη ομ. Bar 86

The pres. part. here seems to suggest that the reading ἐπιταχύνοντας of Bar. 185 above is correct: cf. Fragm. Eus. (quoted above p. 98).
  1. ὀλιγώρους] 'careless,' 'remiss.'
  ib. παρ' ὀλίγ. προκαταλ. τ. δρ.] 'dropping out of the race just before the end' (lit. 'within a little stopping the course beforehand').
  2. Οὐ μικρὸν ἐν β. τὸ παρὰ μικρ.] The saying is equivalent to our 'a miss is as good as a mile' (lit. 'that which is within a little is not little'). It would be interesting to discover who the wise author of the saying is. The Pedalion Graecorum (quoted by Routh) says τὸ γνωμικὸν τοῦτο τὸ λέγον· τὸ μικρὸν ἐν βίῳ οὐ παραμικρόν, αὐτολέξει ἀναφέρει καὶ ὁ μέγας Βασίλειος ἐν τῇ ἀρχῇ τοῦ περὶ βαπτίσματος δευτέρου λόγου, λέγων ὅτι εἶπε τοῦτό τις τῶν παρ' ἡμῖν σοφῶν. τίς δὲ ὁ σοφὸς οὗτος, ἡμῖν ἄδηλον. Basil probably refers to Dionysius. But the turn given to the aphorism by Basil is different, 'the small things in life are not insignificant.' Τὸ παρὰ μικρόν, 'a matter of no moment,' Arist. Phys. 2. 5. 9; Pol. 3. 5. 10 (Lidd. and Scott).
  3. ἐφυστερίζοντας] 'putting off till later': not a classical usage.
  4. διαρκοῦντας ἐπὶ πλεῖστον] 'enduring to the furthest': cf. Luc. Hist. Conscr. 21 ἄσιτος (ὢν) ἐς ἑβδόμην διαρκεῖν (quoted by Liddell and Scott).
  6. περιπατ. ἐπὶ τῆς θαλ.] Cf. Matt. xiv 26.
  7. ὡς ἐκινήθησαν] 'as they were moved' (as we too say).
  8. μὴ π. διοχλῶμεν] 'let us not treat altogether severely.'
  ib. It depends very much on how men have kept the six preceding days of the fast, whether they can last out to the end or not: some keep all six with the utmost strictness and some not even one; and those who fail just at the last in their high ideal are much more excusable than those who are lax all through the week and yet last out till dawn on Easter morning.
  9. μηδὲ ... ἴσως μηδὲ ὁμοίως] 'neither equally nor similarly,' cf. τὴν ἴσην ἄθλησιν below. Ἴσως refers to the length of the fast, viz. some six days, some two and so on, while ὁμοίως refers to the manner or

διαμένουσιν· ἀλλ' οἱ μὲν καὶ πάσας ὑπερτιθέασιν ἄσιτοι διατελοῦντες, οἱ δὲ δύο, οἱ δὲ τρεῖς, οἱ δὲ τέσσαρας, οἱ δὲ οὐδεμίαν. καὶ τοῖς μὲν πάνυ διαπονηθεῖσιν ἐν ταῖς ὑπερθέσεσιν, εἶτα ἀποκάμνουσι καὶ μόνον οὐκ ἐκλείπουσι, 5 συγγνώμη τῆς ταχυτέρας γεύσεως. εἰ δέ τινες, οὐχ ὅπως οὐχ ὑπερτιθέμενοι ἀλλὰ μηδὲ νηστεύσαντες ἀλλὰ καὶ τρυφήσαντες τὰς προαγούσας τέσσαρας, εἶτα ἐλθόντες ἐπὶ τὰς τελευταίας δύο καὶ μόνας αὐτὰς ὑπερτιθέντες, τήν τε παρασκευὴν καὶ τὸ σάββατον, μέγα τι καὶ λαμπρὸν ποιεῖν
10 νομίζουσιν, ἂν μέχρι τῆς ἕω διαμείνωσιν, οὐκ οἶμαι τὴν ἴσην ἄθλησιν αὐτοὺς πεποιῆσθαι τοῖς τὰς πλείονας ἡμέρας προησκηκόσι. ταῦτα μὲν οὖν, ὡς φρονῶ, συμβουλεύων περὶ τούτων ἔγραψα.

(β') Περὶ δὲ τῶν ἐν ἀφέδρῳ γυναικῶν, εἰ προσῆκεν

3 ουδεμιαν] ουδε μιαν Bar 185 ‖ τοις μεν] om μεν Bar 158 ‖ 4 εκλειπουσι] επιλειπ. Laud 39 ‖ 5 ταχυτερας] παχυτ. Bar 86 ‖ ει δε τινες] οι δε τινες Bar 26 Misc 170* οιδε Bar 86 ‖ 6 ουχ υπερτιθεμενοι] ουχ υπερθεμ. Laud 39 om ουχ Bar 86 ‖ νηστευσαντες] νιστευσ. Bar 26* ‖ αλλα και] η και Bar 158 Routh ‖ 7 ελθοντες] -ας Bar 26 ‖ 8 τελευταιας] τελευτεας Bar 26 ‖ μονας αυτας Laud 39 Bar 196 158 Misc 170 om αυτας Bar 26 185 86 μονας ημερας, αυτας Routh ‖ 10 διαμεινωσιν]+ους Bar 26² 86 Misc 170* διαμαν. ους Bar 26* ‖ 11 αθλησιν] ασκησιν Bar 26 86 Misc 170 ‖ αυτους] om Bar 26 86 158 Misc 170* ‖ 12 προησκηκοσι] -οασι Bar 86 ‖ μεν ουν] om ουν Bar 26(?) Misc 170 ‖ φρονω] και φρ. Misc 170 ‖ συμβουλευων] και συμβουλευω Laud 39 Bar 185 ‖ 14 αφεδρω] αφαιδρω Bar 185

degree of it, some till cockcrow, some till evening, etc.
ib. τὰς ἐξ τ. ν. ἡμέρ.] viz. from Monday to Saturday in Holy Week.
1. ὑπερτιθέασιν] Ὑπερτιθέναι (Lat. *superponere* or *continuare*) 'to exceed' or 'to delay' is the technical term for continuing the fast until cockcrow, whereas the ordinary fast ended at 6 p.m. and that of the station days (Wednesdays and Fridays) at 3 p.m. (Tert. *de ieiun.* 13): see Eus. *H. E.* v. 24. 12, Bingham *Antiqq.* Bk xxi chap. i § 25 and Gunning *on Lenten Fast passim.*

7. τρυφήσαντες] 'living luxuriously': cf. p. 160.
8. τὰς τελευτ. δύο] Cf. *Apost. Const.* v 18 and Bingham *l.c.* § 33.
11. ἄθλησιν] 'discipline ' or ' exercise': the word occurs in Heb. x 32.
ib. τοῖς τὰς πλείον. ἡμ. προησκ.] 'as those who have practised it also during the foregoing days.'
14. *Menstruous women ought of their own accord to absent themselves from the Holy Communion though they will not neglect what opportunities they have for other prayers.*
ib. τῶν ἐν ἀφέδρῳ γυν.] Cf. Lev. xv 19, 20, 33; Ezek. xviii 6. For

A. LETTERS 103

αὐτὰς οὕτω διακειμένας εἰς τὸν οἶκον εἰσιέναι τοῦ θεοῦ, περιττὸν καὶ τὸ πυνθάνεσθαι νομίζω. οὐδὲ γὰρ αὐτὰς οἶμαι, πιστὰς οὔσας καὶ εὐλαβεῖς, τολμήσειν οὕτω διακειμένας ἢ τῇ τραπέζῃ τῇ ἁγίᾳ προσελθεῖν, ἢ τοῦ σώματος καὶ τοῦ αἵματος τοῦ χριστοῦ προσάψασθαι. οὐδὲ γὰρ ἡ 5 τὴν δωδεκαετῆ ῥύσιν ἔχουσα πρὸς τὴν ἴασιν σπεύδουσα ἔθιγεν αὐτοῦ, ἀλλὰ μόνου τοῦ κρασπέδου. προσεύχεσθαι μὲν γὰρ ὅπως ἂν ἔχῃ τις, καί, ὡς ἂν διάκειται, μεμνῆσθαι τοῦ δεσπότου, καὶ δεῖσθαι βοηθείας τυχεῖν, ἀνεπίφθονον· εἰς δὲ τὰ ἅγια καὶ τὰ ἅγια τῶν ἁγίων ὁ μὴ πάντη καθαρὸς 10 καὶ ψυχῇ καὶ σώματι προσιέναι κωλυθήσεται.

(γ') Αὐτάρκεις δὲ καὶ οἱ γεγαμηκότες ἑαυτῶν ὀφεί-

3 και ευλαβ.] om και Misc 170 ‖ 4 η τη τραπ.] εν τη τραπ. Laud 39 Bar 196 ‖ 5 του αιμ.] om του Laud 39 Bar 196 Misc 170 ‖ χριστου] κυριου Bar 158 ‖ 6 σπευδουσα] om Bar 196 185 158 ‖ 7 προσευχ.—δεσποτου] om Misc 170* ‖ 8 εχη] ευχη Bar 26 ‖ μεμνησθαι]+τε Bar 26 ‖ 10 τα αγια και] om Bar 86 ‖ καθαρος και]+αμιαντος Misc 170 ‖ 12 γεγαμηκ.] γεγηρακοτες Bar 158

similar regulations to those here we may compare *Can. Hipp.* §§ 93, 95, 100 and (in regard to Holy Baptism) 107 and Tim. Alex. *Resp. Canon.* vii in Beveridge *Synodikon* vol. II p. 166 ἐὰν γυνὴ ἴδῃ τὸ κατ' ἔθος τῶν γυναικείων αὐτῆς, ὀφείλει προσέρχεσθαι τοῖς μυστηρίοις ἢ οὔ; Οὐκ ὀφείλει ἕως οὗ καθαρισθῇ.
ib. προσῆκεν] Cf. p. 104 below for the tense, which in each case suggests that D. is quoting the exact words of Basilides's inquiry.
1. τὸν οἶκον...τοῦ θεοῦ] The expression in O. and N. T. usually refers to the Temple : but cf. 1 Tim. iii 15. See too *Canon. Hipp.* § 88 *neve omnino loquantur in ecclesia, quia est domus Dei* and § 96. So τὰ ἅγια, etc., below.
4. ἢ...προσελθεῖν ἢ...προσάψασθαι] Two stages in the same service are here referred to and therefore ἢ...ἢ are strictly inaccurate. Cf. p. 58 τραπέζῃ παραστάντα...καὶ τοῦ σώματος καὶ τοῦ αἵματος...μετασχόντα. The 44th Canon of the Council of Laodicea (4th cent.) forbade any but the clergy to approach the altar itself at the time of communion. Up till then it appears to have been the custom for both male and female communicants to do so: ὡς ἔοικε δέ, τὸ παλαιὸν εἰσήρχοντο γυναῖκες εἰς τὸ θυσιαστήριον καὶ ἀπὸ τῆς ἁγίας τραπέζης μετελάμβανον (Balsamon).
5. ἡ τὴν δωδ. ῥύσιν ἔχ. κτλ.] Cf. Matt. ix 20, Luke viii 44.
7. ἔθιγεν αὐτοῦ] sc. τοῦ χριστοῦ.
ib. προσεύχεσθαι κτλ.] Cf. p. 59 μόλις παρακαλ. συνεστάναι ταῖς προσευχαῖς ἀνέχεται.
8. διάκειται] subj., for which διακέηται is the correct form: see Matth. *Gr. Gr.* § 240.
10. τὰ ἅγια κτλ.] another Temple phrase (see Heb. *passim*) here applied to a Christian church. Τὰ ἅγια corresponds to the nave and τὰ ἅγια τ. ἀγ. to the sanctuary.
12. *Married folk ought to be their own judges about conjugal abstinence.*
ib. καὶ οἱ γεγαμ.] i.e. married

λουσιν εἶναι κριταί. ὅτι γὰρ ἀπέχεσθαι προσῆκον ἀλλήλων ἐκ cγμφώνογ πρὸc καιρὸν ἵνα cχολάcωcι τῇ προcεγχῇ καὶ πάλιν ἐπὶ τὸ αγτὸ ὦcιν, ἀκηκόασι Παύλου γράφοντος.

(δ´) Οἱ δὲ ἐν ἀπροαιρέτῳ νυκτερινῇ ῥύσει γενόμενοι, καὶ
5 οὗτοι τῷ ἰδίῳ συνειδότι κατακολουθησάτωσαν, καὶ ἑαυτούς, εἴτε διακρίνονται περὶ τούτου εἴτε μή, σκοπείτωσαν. ὡς ἐπὶ τῶν βρωμάτων ὁ Διακρινόμενοc, φησιν, ἐὰν φάγῃ, κατακέκριται, καὶ ἐν τούτοις εὐσυνείδητος ἔστω καὶ εὐπαρρησίαστος κατὰ τὸ ἴδιον ἐνθύμιον πᾶς ὁ προσιὼν τῷ θεῷ.
10 Ταῦτα σὺ μὲν τιμῶν ἡμᾶς, οὐ γὰρ ἀγνοῶν, ἀγαπητέ, τὰ

1 προσηκ. αλληλ.] αλληλ. προσηκ. Bar 158 || 2 σχολασωσι]+τη νηστεια και Misc 170 || 3 αυτο] αυτω Bar 26* || γραφ.] λεγοντος Misc 170 || 4 εν] εν͡ Bar 26 || 5 ιδιω] οικειω Laud 39 Bar 196 || κατακολουθησατωσαν Laud 39 Bar 196 et 185 -θητωσαν Bar 86 -θειτωσαν Bar 26 Routh || 6 περι τουτου] om Laud 39 Bar 196 περι τουτο Bar 185 || διακρινονται] -ωνται Bar 158 || σκοπειτωσαν] -πητωσαν Bar 26 et 86 || 8 ευπαρρησ.]+πας Bar 158 || 9 προσιων] προσιον̅ Bar 26 || 10 ταυτα συ μεν—ευχομαι] desunt Bar 158 || ου] ουδε Bar 86

couples as well as (καὶ) αἱ ἐν ἀφ. γυν. The early edd. read γεγηρακότες against the MSS and the sense. Can. Hipp. § 242 contains no such prohibition as this in regard to ordinary services of prayer, but no doubt this inquiry was (like the last) in connexion with (Easter?) communion.

1. προσῆκον] for the tense see note on προσῆκεν above.

2. ἐκ συμφ....ὦσιν] Cf. 1 Cor. vii 5.

4. Conscience will also decide in the case of those qui in non voluntario nocturno fluxu fuerint.

ib. ἀπροαιρέτῳ] Cf. p. 141.

5. τῷ ἰδίῳ συνειδότι] 'their own conscience': the neut. part. used as a subst. is a well-known classical usage; for this particular instance cf. Lit. of St Mark ἐν καθαρᾷ καρδίᾳ καὶ καθαρῷ συνειδότι.

6. διακρίνονται] 'are in doubt': this use of διακρίνεσθαι occurs several times in N. T.; e.g. Rom. xiv 23 which D. proceeds to quote in the next sentence.

ib. ὡς ἐπὶ τ. βρ....καὶ ἐν τούτ.] 'as in the case of foods..., so in these things, etc.'

8. εὐπαρρησίαστος] Cf. Just. Mart. quoted by Eus. H. E. iv 13. 5 οἱ μὲν οὖν (Χριστιανοὶ) εὐπαρρησιαστότεροι γίγνονται πρὸς τὸν θεόν.

9. κατὰ τὸ ἴδιον ἐνθύμιον] 'in his own judgement'; cf. Rom. xiv 5 ἐν τῷ ἰδίῳ νοΐ. This use of ἐνθύμιον is late: cf. Ps. lxxv (lxxvi) 11. Suidas acc. to Schleusner gives κατὰ τὸν νοῦν as one of the meanings of the phrase.

ib. ὁ προσιὼν τῷ θεῷ] The verb in this connexion in the Ep. to the Hebrews is always προσέρχεσθαι (e.g. vii 25, xi 6, etc.).

10. We have answered your enquiries in no didactic spirit but in the desire to throw out suggestions for your consideration. Send us a reply. Farewell.

ib. οὐ γὰρ ἀγνοῶν] sc. ταῦτα τὰ πύσματα: 'not because you were

A. LETTERS

πύσματα ἡμῖν προσήγαγες, ὁμόφρονας ἡμᾶς, ὥσπερ οὖν
ἐσμέν, καὶ ἰσοψύχους ἑαυτῷ παρασκευάζων. ἐγὼ δὲ οὐχ ὡς
διδάσκαλος, ἀλλ' ὡς μετὰ πάσης ἁπλότητος προσῆκον
ἡμᾶς ἀλλήλοις διαλέγεσθαι, εἰς κοινὸν τὴν διάνοιαν ἐμαυτοῦ
ἐξέθηκα. ἣν ἐπικρίνας καὶ σύ, συνετώτατέ μου υἱέ, ὅ τι ἄν 5
σοι φανῇ βέλτιον, ἢ καὶ οὕτως ἔχειν δοκιμάζῃς, περὶ αὐτῶν
ἀντιγράψῃς. ἐρρῶσθαί σε, ἀγαπητὲ υἱέ μου, ἐν εἰρήνῃ
λειτουργοῦντα τῷ κυρίῳ εὔχομαι.

1 ημας] τινας Misc 170 ‖ 2 εαυτω] σεαυτω Bar 196 ααυτω Bar 185 (?) ‖
3 διδασκαλος] om -καλος Laud 39 (ex paginae versura) + καλος Misc 170² ‖
4 ημας] om Bar 86 ‖ 5 συνετωτατε] νυνετωτατε Bar 26 ‖ 6 φανη] + δικαιον και
Bar 158 Ped Routh ‖ η] ει Bar 86 Ped Routh ‖ 7 αντιγραψης] -εις Edd ‖
ερρωσθαι—ευχομαι] om Misc 170

ignorant of the subjects of your inquiry.'

1. ὁμόφρ.... παρασκευάξ.] 'making us of one mind and soul with thyself, as indeed we are.' For the epithets cf. 1 Pet. iii 8 and Phil. ii 20. Ἑαυτῷ = σεαυτῷ. Παρασκευάζειν in act. (as well as mid.) is used of 'procuring' witnesses, partisans, etc., though usually in a bad sense, and that in a good sense may be the significance of the word here: otherwise it means simply 'to render.'

2. οὐχ ὡς διδάσκ. κτλ.] This is of a piece with D.'s usual gentleness and consideration for others.

3. προσῆκον] neut. part. used abs.

7. ἀντιγράψῃς] 'thou mayest write me word in return' (cf. Thucyd. i 129). The reading of the edd. (-εις) is rightly rejected by Routh in favour of the MSS reading (-ῃς). The subj. is here jussive (a non-classical usage except with negative).

8. λειτουργοῦντα τῷ κυρίῳ] Cf. Acts iii 2.

B. Περὶ Ἐπαγγελιῶν

(Eus. *H. E.* vii 24 and 25)

This was a carefully-prepared[1] treatise in two books directed against the Chiliastic views propounded by Nepos, who had apparently been Bishop of Arsenoe in Egypt, in a composition entitled Ἔλεγχος Ἀλληγοριστῶν[2]. That this was the purpose of the treatise is acknowledged by Jerome (*de virr. ill.* 69), though in his Commentary on Isaiah (*praefat. lib.* xviii) he says that Dionysius wrote it against Irenaeus, by which he can only have meant that the Chiliastic opinions of Irenaeus were refuted incidentally by the περὶ Ἐπαγγελιῶν of Dionysius. Like most of Dionysius's compositions, it was apparently addressed to some particular individual, whose name, however, is not given (ὡς οἶδας, p. 111). Of Nepos himself Dionysius speaks in his usual liberal and large-hearted way: he recognises his faith, laborious life, biblical studies, and hymn writings, which had cheered the hearts of the brethren: he mentions also that he had gone to his rest before Dionysius undertook to correct his errors, and that this in itself led him to treat his memory with respect. But evidently Nepos's treatise had stirred up many others to advocate his views: for Dionysius speaks of διδάσκαλοί τινες who were leading astray the simpler brethren and causing him anxiety, and mentions by name the man who was apparently their ringleader, Coracion (p. 113). Hence, finding himself on one occasion in the nome of Arsenoe, where the evil was most rife and where it had in some cases

[1] σπουδάζεται αὐτῷ, p. 108.

[2] The title no doubt denotes that it was Origen's fanciful interpretations of Scripture which led Nepos to desire more literal interpretations.

B. Περὶ Ἐπαγγελιῶν 107

affected whole churches, he took the opportunity to call together the clergy, teachers, and laity of the district for a debate upon the question; in which, after a free discussion conducted in a fair and friendly spirit on both sides, a satisfactory and orthodox conclusion was arrived at. The present work, we may suppose, is the outcome and embodiment of that conclusion, set forth in Dionysius's own words for the instruction and edification of the province. The nature of Nepos's treatment of the subject of Chiliasm we can only gather in a general way. Eusebius tells us in the passage where he introduces his extracts from the περὶ Ἐπαγγελιῶν that "he taught that the promises made to the saints in the Scripture will be fulfilled in a Jewish sense[1], and maintained that there will be a thousand years of carnal enjoyments upon this earth[2], and so thinking to support his hypothesis from the Revelation of John he wrote his Refutation of the Allegorists, which was an argument he had composed on the subject." Of the two books in which Dionysius replied to his arguments, the first contained Dionysius's own views about the fulfilment of God's promises and the second dealt with the Revelation of St John. The long extracts preserved for us by Eusebius all came from the second book, and it is somewhat remarkable that the only other fragments that remain or have hitherto been discovered, are likewise said to come from that book: these are three (possibly only two) in number, quite inconsiderable in bulk and very different in character from the Eusebian extracts[3].

In the extract which treats of the Revelation Dionysius first deals with the position of those who entirely rejected the Johannine authorship of that book: these are thought to have been the class of biblical students whom Epiphanius styled the Alogi (*Haer.* li 3). They "attributed not only the Apocalypse but also the Gospel and the writings of St John generally to

[1] Ἰουδαικώτερον: "the transition from Judaizing views to Chiliasm is very simple," Westcott *Hist. of N. T. Canon* p. 274: cf. Jerome *in Isaiam praefat. lib.* xviii. *Apocalypsin Ioannis si iuxta litteram accipimus, iudaizandum est: si spiritualiter, ut scripta est, multorum veterum videbimur opinionibus contraire*: cf. 2 Cor. iii 6: Rom. ii 27.

[2] ἐπὶ τῆς ξηρᾶς ταύτης (sc. γῆς), a curious expression in this connexion.

[3] Reprinted from Holl *Fragmente vornicänischer Kirchenväter* in *Texte und Untersuchungen* vol. v pp. 148 and 155 (=Cod. Vat. 1553): given also by Mai *Nova Collectio* vol. vii pp. 99 and 108.

Cerinthus," as Dionysius here informs us, "and this on purely internal grounds[1]." Cerinthus had held gross material views as to Christ's return to reign on earth, and a literal interpretation of the Apocalypse may be held to favour such views: hence the conjecture of the Cerinthian authorship. But, says Dionysius, the literal interpretation cannot be held[2]: much of the book is indeed beyond my comprehension, but in these parts faith accepts what the reason fails to grasp. And that it was written by some holy and inspired person called John it is impossible to doubt, though to identify him with the author of the Fourth Gospel and "the Catholic Epistle" is almost equally impossible. The suggestion is that he is another Asiatic disciple (τῶν ἐν Ἀσίᾳ γενομένων) of that name, and one of the two Johns whom tradition recorded as being buried at Ephesus. Dionysius advances three arguments in support of his conclusion, each again wholly from internal evidence: (1) from the difference in character (ἦθος) of the two writers as shown in the free use of his name by the one and the constant suppression of it by the other; (2) from the different ideas and expressions employed by them; and (3) from the absence of ungrammatical forms of speech and syntax in the one and the prevalence of them in the other. The method of treatment throughout, time and circumstances considered, is entirely admirable, and Bishop Westcott is undoubtedly justified in thinking that there is no "other piece of pure criticism in the early Fathers to compare with it for style and manner[3]."

[1] Westcott *op. cit.* p. 276.
[2] ἀδύνατον αὐτὴν κατὰ τὴν πρόχειρον νοεῖσθαι διάνοιαν, p. 116.
[3] *op. cit.* p. 362, note 3.

Ἐπὶ τούτοις ἅπασι σπουδάζεται αὐτῷ καὶ τὰ περὶ ἐπαγγελιῶν δύο συγγράμματα. ἡ δὲ ὑπόθεσις αὐτῷ Νέπως ἦν, ἐπίσκοπος τῶν κατ' Αἴγυπτον, Ἰουδαικώτερον τὰς ἐπηγγελμένας τοῖς ἁγίοις ἐν ταῖς θείαις γραφαῖς ἐπαγγελίας ἀποδοθήσεσθαι διδάσκων καί τινα χιλιάδα ἐτῶν τρυφῆς σωματικῆς ἐπὶ τῆς ξηρᾶς ταύτης ἔσεσθαι ὑποτιθέμενος. δόξας γοῦν οὗτος ἐκ τῆς ἀποκαλύψεως Ἰωάννου τὴν ἰδίαν κρατύνειν ὑπόληψιν, ἔλεγχον ἀλληγοριστῶν, λόγον τινὰ περὶ τούτου συντάξας ἐπέγραψε. πρὸς ὃν ὁ Διονύσιος ἐν τοῖς περὶ ἐπαγγελιῶν ἐνίσταται, διὰ

B. Περὶ Ἐπαγγελιῶν 109

μὲν τοῦ προτέρου τὴν αὐτοῦ γνώμην ἣν εἶχε περὶ τοῦ δόγματος παρατιθέμενος, διὰ δὲ τοῦ δευτέρου περὶ τῆς ἀποκαλύψεως Ἰωάννου διαλαμβάνων, ἔνθα τοῦ Νέπωτος κατὰ τὴν ἀρχὴν μνημονεύσας ταῦτα περὶ αὐτοῦ γράφει·

(1) Ἐπεὶ δὲ σύνταγμά τι προκομίζουσι Νέπωτος, ᾧ 5
λίαν ἐπερείδονται ὡς ἀναντιρρήτως ἀποδεικνύντι τὴν τοῦ
χριστοῦ βασιλείαν ἐπὶ τῆς γῆς ἔσεσθαι, ἐν ἄλλοις μὲν
πολλοῖς ἀποδέχομαι καὶ ἀγαπῶ Νέπωτα, τῆς τε πίστεως
καὶ τῆς φιλοπονίας καὶ τῆς ἐν ταῖς γραφαῖς διατριβῆς καὶ
τῆς πολλῆς ψαλμῳδίας, ᾗ μέχρι νῦν πολλοὶ τῶν ἀδελφῶν 10
εὐθυμοῦνται, καὶ πάνυ δι' αἰδοῦς ἄγω τὸν ἄνθρωπον ταύτῃ
μᾶλλον, ᾗ προανεπαύσατο, ἀλλὰ φίλη γὰρ καὶ προτιμοτάτη
πάντων ἡ ἀλήθεια, ἐπαινεῖν τε χρὴ καὶ συναινεῖν ἀφθόνως,

1 αὐτου] αὐτου C Schw ‖ 6 αποδεικν.] υποδεικν. A Steph ‖ 10 ᾗ ORab Stroth Schw Lr ἣ Fb om Ea ἢ cett codd et edd *quia* Ruf

5. *I have a great regard for Nepos in many other respects and the more so now that he is dead, but in the interests of truth I cannot refrain from criticizing and correcting his views which have been put forward on the millennium.*
ib. σύνταγμά τι] 'a composition': σύγγραμμα is used below. For a different use of the word see p. 15.
8. ἀποδέχ. καὶ ἀγαπῶ Νέπ.] A good instance of D.'s large heartedness. Cf. 1 Cor. xiii 4—7.
10. τῆς πολλῆς ψαλμ.] This appears to mean hymns of Nepos's own composition (ψαλμοὶ ἰδιωτικοί) and not his care that the Psalms of David should be regularly used in Church, though we learn from Cassian (*Instit.* ii 4) that the Psalter formed a large part of both vespers and nocturns among the Egyptian monks, who are supposed to have taken their rise about this very time. Cf. Eus. *H. E.* v 28. 5 where an author is quoted who asks ψαλμοὶ δὲ ὅσοι καὶ ᾠδαὶ ἀδελφῶν ἀπ' ἀρχῆς ὑπὸ πιστῶν γραφεῖσαι τὸν λόγον τοῦ θεοῦ τὸν χριστὸν ὑμνοῦσι θεολογοῦντες;

Cf. Eph. v 19; Col. iii 16; Plin. *Ep.* x 97 etc. The use of private and uninspired hymns in service was condemned by the Council of Laodicea (A.D. 361).
11. εὐθυμοῦνται] Cf. James v. 13.
ib. πάνυ δι' αἰδοῦς ἄγω] 'I hold in great respect': quite a classical expression, see Liddell and Scott *s.v.* ἄγειν.
ib. ταύτῃ μᾶλλ. ᾗ προανεπαύσ.] Ruf. is probably right in rendering the phrase *inde magis quia iam praecessit ad deum* 'the more because he has gone to his rest before us.' Ταύτῃ...ᾗ might mean 'for the way in which' but the fem. adv. often lost its original meaning in later Gk.; see Liddell and Scott *s.v.* οὗτος.
12. προτιμοτάτη...ἡ ἀλήθ.] Cf. Eus. *H. E.* iv 16. 6 where is quoted a reference in Justin Martyr to Plato (*Rep.* x 595) οὔ τί γε πρὸ τῆς ἀληθείας τιμητέος ἀνήρ: a sentiment which Aristotle (*Eth. Nic.* i 6. 1) has applied to Plato himself; ἀμφοῖν γὰρ ὄντοιν φίλοιν ὅσιον προτιμᾶν τὴν ἀλήθειαν.

εἴ τι ὀρθῶς λέγοιτο, ἐξετάζειν δὲ καὶ διευθύνειν, εἴ τι μὴ
φαίνοιτο ὑγιῶς ἀναγεγραμμένον. καὶ πρὸς μὲν παρόντα
καὶ ψιλῷ λόγῳ δογματίζοντα αὐτάρκης ἦν ἂν ἡ ἄγραφος
ὁμιλία, δι' ἐρωτήσεως καὶ ἀποκρίσεως πείθουσα καὶ συμ-
5 βιβάζουσα τοὺς ἀντιδιατιθεμένους· γραφῆς δὲ ἐκκειμένης,
ὡς δοκεῖ τισί, πιθανωτάτης, καί τινων διδασκάλων τὸν μὲν
νόμον καὶ τοὺς προφήτας τὸ μηδὲν ἡγουμένων καὶ τὸ τοῖς
εὐαγγελίοις ἕπεσθαι παρέντων καὶ τὰς τῶν ἀποστόλων
ἐπιστολὰς ἐκφαυλισάντων, τὴν δὲ τοῦ συγγράμματος
10 τούτου διδασκαλίαν ὡς μέγα δή τι καὶ κεκρυμμένον
μυστήριον κατεπαγγελλομένων, καὶ τοὺς ἁπλουστέρους
ἀδελφοὺς ἡμῶν οὐδὲν ἐώντων ὑψηλὸν καὶ μεγαλεῖον
φρονεῖν οὔτε περὶ τῆς ἐνδόξου καὶ ἀληθῶς ἐνθέου τοῦ
κυρίου ἡμῶν ἐπιφανείας οὔτε τῆς ἡμετέρας ἐκ νεκρῶν

1 δε] τε AE^aF^bO Steph δε cett vero Ruf ‖ 2 φαινοιτο] -εται K ‖ 5 εκκει-
μενης] εγκειμ. nonnulli

2. *If he were still alive and we
could discuss the matter in conversation, there would be no need of my
writing, but as he has left a written
treatise which has had a great effect
on many in leading them to disregard
the teaching of the Old and New Tes-
taments, as to our Lord's appearing
and our rising from the grave to
meet Him, we are forced to deal
with the matter as we can.*

3. ψιλῷ λόγῳ] lit. 'in bare
words': Vales. is probably right in
translating the phrase *viva voce*, and
the distinction drawn is between
spoken and *written* words. In Eus.
H. E. vii 30. 11 λόγῳ ψιλῷ is
opposed to ἐξ ὧν ἐπέμψαμεν ὑπομνη-
μάτων (i.e. as 'mere assertion' to
'the memoranda of the proceedings
we sent'). Ψιλὸς λόγος in the
Classics often means 'prose' as opposed to 'poetry' but the words
below (γραφῆς ἐκκειμένης) seem de-
cisive against supposing that D. is
here making a half humorous allusion
to Nepos's πολλὴ ψαλμῳδία mentioned above.

6. τινων διδασκ.] The plural
shows that Nepos had not been
alone in his opinions and teaching.

9. ἐκφαυλισάντων] 'having de-
preciated': cf. Judith xiv 5 ἵνα ἰδὼν
ἐπιγνοῖ τὸν ἐκφαυλίσαντα τὸν οἶκον
τοῦ Ἰσραήλ.

ib. τὴν δὲ τοῦ συγγράμ....κατε-
παγγ.] Perhaps this means 'making
parade of the teaching of this book
as if it were some great and hidden
mystery': cf. 1 Tim. ii 10, vi 21
where the simpler compound ἐπαγ-
γέλλεσθαι is used in this kind of
sense. On the other hand Vales.
assigns to κατεπάγγ. its ordinary
sense ('to make promises or en-
gagements') and illustrates it by the
habit of the heathen hierophants,
who made out to their neophytes
that they would one day have some
great and wonderful mystery revealed to them (as Tert. *contra Val.*
chap. 1 says) *ut opinionem ac re-
verentiam suspendio cognitionis aedi-
ficarent*.

13. ἐνδόξου...ἐπιφανείας] Cf. Tit.
ii 13; 2 Thess. ii 8 etc.

B. Περὶ Ἐπαγγελιῶν   111

ἀναστάσεως καὶ τῆς πρὸς αὐτὸν ἐπισυναγωγῆς καὶ ὁμοιώ-
σεως, ἀλλὰ μικρὰ καὶ θνητὰ καὶ οἷα τὰ νῦν ἐλπίζειν
ἀναπειθόντων ἐν τῇ βασιλείᾳ τοῦ θεοῦ, ἀναγκαῖον καὶ
ἡμᾶς ὡς πρὸς παρόντα τὸν ἀδελφὸν ἡμῶν διαλεχθῆναι
Νέπωτα.   5

Τούτοις μεθ' ἕτερα ἐπιφέρει λέγων·

(2) Ἐν μὲν οὖν τῷ Ἀρσενοείτῃ γενόμενος, ἔνθα, ὡς οἶδας,
πρὸ πολλοῦ τοῦτο ἐπεπόλαζε τὸ δόγμα, ὡς καὶ σχίσματα
καὶ ἀποστασίας ὅλων ἐκκλησιῶν γεγονέναι, συγκαλέσας
τοὺς πρεσβυτέρους καὶ διδασκάλους τῶν ἐν ταῖς κώμαις 10
ἀδελφῶν, παρόντων καὶ τῶν βουλομένων ἀδελφῶν, δημοσίᾳ
τὴν ἐξέτασιν ποιήσασθαι τοῦ λόγου προετρεψάμην. καὶ
τοῦτό μοι προσαγόντων τὸ βιβλίον ὥς τι ὅπλον καὶ τεῖχος

2 ἐλπίζειν] -ομενα A Steph -ομενα ἐλπίζειν B ∥ 3 αναπειθ.] πειθ. A ∥
7 Ἀρσενοειτη BCDKR^{ab} Steph Val Schw Ἀρσενοιτη AE^aF^{ab}GHO Nic
L^r Ruf and Hein. Ἀρσινοειτη cett ∥ 13 προσαγοντων] προσαγαγοντων R^{ab}

1. πρὸς αὐτ. ἐπισυναγ.] Cf. 2 Thess.
ii 1: the word occurs in Eus. H. E.
viii 1. 5 τὰς μυριάνδρους ἐκείνας ἐπι-
συναγωγάς and in the Liturgy of
St Mark τὰς ἐπισυναγωγὰς ἡμῶν
εὐλόγησον.
  ib. ὁμοιώσεως] Cf. 1 John iii 2.
  7. So when I was in Arsenoe where
the heresy has long been prevalent, I
called together the elders and teachers
of the district and held a public discussion which lasted the whole of
three days. It was this book that
was brought forward and I tried to
correct its statements.
  ib. τῷ Ἀρσενοείτῃ] sc. νομῷ. This
district (the chief town of which was
Arsenoe Crocodilopolis) is in Middle
Egypt, due S. of Memphis. Arsenoe
was a frequent name among the
Ptolemaean princesses: the one who
gave her name to this district was
the daughter of Ptolemy I, who on
the death of her first husband,
Lysimachus King of Thrace, was
married to her half-brother Ptolemy

Ceraunus and lastly in 279 B.C. to
her own brother Ptolemy II Phila-
delphus.
  ib. ὡς οἶδας] It does not appear
to whom D. addressed this treatise.
  8. ἐπεπόλαζε] either 'came to
the surface,' 'appeared,' or 'spread,'
'prevailed': see Liddell and Scott
s.v.: cf. p. 51.
  10. πρεσβυτ. καὶ διδασκ.] Here
the two offices are conjoined as in
1 Tim. v 17. In the Διδαχὴ τῶν
ιβ′ ἀποστόλων (xiii 1, 2, xv 1, 2)
the ἐπίσκοποι and διάκονοι are put
together and the διδάσκαλοι and
προφῆται, no mention being made
of πρεσβύτεροι. In the Canons of
Hippolytus (xii 68, xvii 92 and 99
ed. Achelis) we find the doctor ecclesiae: likewise the γραμματικός.
In the Const. Apost. viii and the
Egyptian Church Order (c. 44 La-
garde) it is stated that ὁ διδάσκων
may be λαϊκός.
  13. προσαγόντων] sc. αὐτῶν. For
the genitive absolute cf. pp. 27 and 39.

ἄμαχον, συγκαθεσθεὶς αὐτοῖς τριῶν ἑξῆς ἡμερῶν ἐξ ἕω
μέχρις ἑσπέρας, διευθύνειν ἐπειράθην τὰ γεγραμμένα.
ἔνθα καὶ τὸ εὐσταθὲς καὶ τὸ φιλάληθες καὶ τὸ εὐπαρα-
κολούθητον καὶ συνετὸν ὑπερηγάσθην τῶν ἀδελφῶν, ὡς
5 ἐν τάξει καὶ μετ' ἐπιεικείας τὰς ἐρωτήσεις καὶ τὰς ἐπα-
πορήσεις καὶ τὰς συγκαταθέσεις ἐποιούμεθα, τὸ μὲν ἐκ
παντὸς τρόπου καὶ φιλονείκως τῶν ἅπαξ δοξάντων περιέ-
χεσθαι, εἰ καὶ μὴ φαίνοιντο ὀρθῶς ἔχοντα, παραιτησά-
μενοι, μήτε δὲ τὰς ἀντιλογίας ὑποστελλόμενοι, ἀλλ' ἐς
10 ὅσον οἷόν τε τῶν προκειμένων ἐπιβατεύειν καὶ κρατύνειν

1 αμαχον AE^a(OR^{ab}) Steph L^r ακαταμαχητον cett ‖ 7 και φιλον.
CF^aGHKOR^{ab} om και cett ‖ 8 ει και μη AE^aF^bO ει μη BCDF^aKR^{ab} ει δε
μη GH *cum quid esset in vero patuisset* Ruf quasi (cum Val et Zimmermanno)
ει και legisset ‖ φαινοιντο] -οιτο AF^b Steph

1. τριῶν ἑξῆς ἡμερῶν] 'for three days in succession': for this use of the gen. cf. p. 24.
2. διευθύνειν...τὰ γεγραμ.] 'to correct the statements made in the book' (i.e. to give them the correct view of the matters discussed in the book): see above p. 110 and below p. 125.
3. *I was much struck with the fairness and reasonableness with which we were able most methodically to raise and answer difficulties: all were ready to abandon positions that had been shown wrong and strove to understand the subject and to arrive at the truth about it.*
ib. εὐσταθές] = βέβαιον (Hesych.), hence here 'steadiness,' 'stability': cf. Eus. *H. E.* iv 15. 9 εὐσταθὲς τὸ ἦθος καὶ ἀκίνητον φυλάξαντα and again § 13 τῷ σεμνῷ καὶ εὐσταθεῖ τοῦ τρόπου.
ib. εὐπαρακολούθητον] usu. passive 'easily followed' or 'understood': here active, as Hesych. explains it, ὀξεῖς εἰς τὰ πράγματα καὶ οὐ νωχελεῖς.
5. μετ' ἐπιεικείας] acc. to St Paul's exhortation (Phil. iv 5) τὸ ἐπιεικὲς ὑμῶν γνωσθήτω πᾶσιν ἀνθρώποις: a distinguishing mark of Christ (2 Cor. x 1). Cf. also James iii 17.
ib. ἐπαπορήσεις] 'freshly raised difficulties.'
6. συγκαταθέσεις] 'points of agreement': cf. Cic. *Acad. Quaest.* i 12 *de assensione atque approbatione quam Graeci συγκατάθεσιν vocant*. Down below συγκαταβάσει and συνδιαθέσει occur together.
ib. τὸ μὲν ἐκ παντὸς...παραιτ.] 'avoiding (the mistake of) holding jealously at any cost to what they had once thought, even though it should (now) be shown to be wrong.' Περιέχεσθαί τινος ('to cleave to, be fond of a person or thing') is common in Herodotus. For ἐκ παντὸς τρόπου cf. Xen. *Mem.* iii 1. 43. The unclassical use of the plural verb φαίνοιντο with ὀρθῶς ἔχοντα is to be noted: cp. pp. 211 and 219.
9. ὑποστελλ.] either 'shrinking from' or 'suppressing': cf. Acts xx 20 and 27.
ib. ἐς ὅσον οἷόν τε] sc. ἦν, 'so far as (was) possible.'
10. ἐπιβατεύειν] = ἀμφισβητεῖν, ζητεῖν (Hesych.); *firmiter tenere* (Hein.); *eniti ad ea de quibus instituta erat disputatio* (Vales.);

Β. Περὶ Ἐπαγγελιῶν

αὐτὰ πειρώμενοι, μήτε, εἰ λόγος αἱρεῖ, μεταπείθεσθαι καὶ συνομολογεῖν αἰδούμενοι, ἀλλ' εὐσυνειδήτως καὶ ἀνυποκρίτως καὶ ταῖς καρδίαις πρὸς τὸν θεὸν ἡπλωμέναις τὰ ταῖς ἀποδείξεσι καὶ διδασκαλίαις τῶν ἁγίων γραφῶν συνιστανόμενα καταδεχόμενοι. καὶ τέλος ὅ τε τῆς διδαχῆς 5 ταύτης ἀρχηγὸς καὶ εἰσηγητής, ὁ καλούμενος Κορακίων, ἐν ἐπηκόῳ πάντων τῶν παρόντων ἀδελφῶν ὡμολόγησε καὶ διεμαρτύρατο ἡμῖν, μηκέτι τούτῳ προσέξειν μηδὲ διαλέξεσθαι περὶ τούτου, μηδὲ μεμνῆσθαι μηδὲ διδάξειν, ὡς ἱκανῶς ὑπὸ τῶν ἀντιλεχθέντων ᾑρημένος· τῶν τε 10

1 αιρει] αιροι E^aF^bG*H ‖ 2 και ανυποκρ.] om και K ‖ 3 και ταις κ.] om και R^{ab} ‖ 9 διαλέξεσθαι] -ασθαι CF^bK Val Hein ‖ 10 ηρημενος] ειρημενων nonnulli *sufficere quod erratum est* Ruf

penetrare in etc. (Schwegler). But the word seems rather, in connexion with κρατύνειν, to imply 'grappling with and mastering the proposition in hand': the metaphor is from a man who mounts a horse (ἐπιβάτης) and breaks it in. In Greg. Nyss. *Cat. Or.* 10 (p. 55 Srawley) the word is used in a more general sense of setting foot on: ἡ ψυχὴ... τῶν ἀβύσσων ἐπιβατεύουσα.

1. εἰ λόγος αἱρεῖ] *si ratio evincit* 'when the argument convinced us': quite a classical phrase.

2. εὐσυνειδήτως] 'conscientiously': cf. Clem. Alex. *Strom.* vii 7 § 48 ἀνεπιλήπτως καὶ εὐσυνειδήτως τὰ παρ' ἑαυτοῦ πάντα ἐκπληροῦν, *ibid.* vi 14 § 113 and Eus. *H. E.* v 1. 43.

3. ταῖς καρδ. π. τ. θ. ἡπλωμ.] 'with hearts spread open before God.' In Eus. *H. E.* ix 8. 8 we have πρηνεῖς ἡπλωμένοι ('with bodies stretched prone upon the ground') and in viii 7. 4 τὰς χεῖρας ἐφαπλοῦντες εἰς σταυροῦ τύπον. Schleusner quotes Job xxii 3 where some MSS. read ἁπλώσῃς (-εις) for ἀπώσῃς τὴν ὁδόν σου and also Symm. Is. xxxiii 23, xxv 11 and Job xi 13 ἁπλώσεις (ordinary reading ὑπτιάζεις) πρὸς αὐτὸν τὰς παλάμας σου.

5. At last their leader Coracion confessed that he was convinced and renounced his former opinions, and many of the brethren rejoiced at the agreement which had resulted from the conference.

6. ἀρχηγὸς καὶ εἰσηγητής] Coracion (of whom we know nothing otherwise) was the champion and mouthpiece of the doctrine on that occasion or since Nepos's death.

7. ἐν ἐπηκόῳ] 'in the hearing of': Liddell and Scott give εἰς ἐπήκ., ἐξ ἐπηκ., though not actually ἐν ἐπηκ.

8. τούτῳ...περὶ τούτου] sc. this opinion : the true antecedent is τῆς διδαχῆς ταύτης.

9. διαλέξεσθαι] Hein. reads the aor. -ασθαι to keep μεμνῆσθαι in countenance as it were, but, as they are still preceded and followed by a future, the difficulty is in no way lessened. As no MS appears to read anything but μεμνῆσθαι (which may mean either 'to remember' or 'to mention') we must leave the difficulty unexplained.

10. ᾑρημένος] 'convicted (of being wrong).'

ἄλλων ἀδελφῶν οἱ μὲν ἔχαιρον ἐπὶ τῇ κοινολογίᾳ καὶ
τῇ πρὸς πάντας συγκαταβάσει καὶ συνδιαθέσει.

Εἶθ' ἑξῆς ὑποβὰς περὶ τῆς ἀποκαλύψεως Ἰωάννου ταῦτά φησι·

(3) Τινὲς μὲν οὖν τῶν πρὸ ἡμῶν ἠθέτησαν καὶ ἀνεσκεύ-
ασαν πάντῃ τὸ βιβλίον, καὶ καθ' ἕκαστον κεφάλαιον διευθύνοντες ἄγνωστόν τε καὶ ἀσυλλόγιστον ἀποφαίνοντες,
ψεύδεσθαί τε τὴν ἐπιγραφήν. Ἰωάννου γὰρ οὐκ εἶναι
λέγουσιν· ἀλλ' οὐδ' ἀποκάλυψιν εἶναι, τὴν σφοδρῷ καὶ
παχεῖ κεκαλυμμένην τῷ τῆς ἀγνοίας παραπετάσματι·
καὶ οὐχ ὅπως τῶν ἀποστόλων τινά, ἀλλ' οὐδ' ὅλως

1 οι μεν ACC^{a}F^{a}R^{ab}L^r οι παροντες cett *omnes vero reliqui fratres* Ruf ||
5 και καθ] add και CGHR^{ab} Schw om cett || 8 ουδ] om R^a || σφοδρω
CF^{ab}G^{2}KR^{ab} Val Schw σφοδρα cett || 9 αγνοιας] αγνωσιας Nic

1. οἱ μὲν ἔχαιρον] The reading παρόντες (for μέν) is no doubt only the conjecture of copyists who did not understand either that Eus. had broken off his quotation in the middle of the sentence or that D. uses οἱ μέν simply in the sense of 'certain'; possibly τινὰ μέν is so used below p. 122.

ib. κοινολογίᾳ] 'conference': cf. 2 Macc. xiv 22 τὴν ἁρμόζουσαν ἐποιήσαντο κοινολογίαν.

2. συγκαταβάσει] either 'his accommodating spirit towards all' (as Hein. who compares Chrysost. *de Sacerdot.* vi 4. 529 πολλῆς χρεία καὶ συγκαταβάσεως καὶ ἀκριβείας) or 'the reconciliation effected between all parties' as Vales.

ib. συνδιαθέσει] either 'his help in settling the matter' or 'their harmonious arrangement.' Lobeck (*Phryn.* 398) objects to the word as *vox Graecis incognita* (acc. to Hein.) but the vb. συνδιατιθέναι is often used to mean 'to help in arranging' or 'disposing.'

4. *Certain people before now have rejected this book denying that it is by John (the Apostle) or any Christian writer and even that it is a true Revelation at all and holding that* Cerinthus the heretic wrote it, because its contents agree with his views of an earthly and carnal millennium.

ib. Τινὲς...ἠθέτησαν] The allusion is apparently to the Ἄλογοι, as Epiphanius (*Haer.* li 3) called them, of the 2nd cent., who were great opponents of Chiliasm as well as of Montanism, and not to Caius of Rome, as has been thought: see Westcott *Hist. of N.T. Canon* p. 276.

ib. ἀνεσκεύασαν] *a canone scripturarum sacrarum abiciendum putarunt* (Ruf.), 'upset': cf. Acts xv 24. Cf. above p. 95.

6. ἄγνωστον] 'unintelligible': so below prob. ἀγνοίας means 'unintelligibility.' The reading of Niceph. here (ἀγνωσίας) evidently shows that he connected the two words.

ib. ἀσυλλόγιστον] 'inconclusive,' 'unreasonable.'

8. ἀποκάλυψιν...παραπετάσματι] one of D.'s favourite playings with words. 'It cannot be an unveiling (Revelation) because of the heavy, thick veil of unintelligibility (or nonsense) which covers it.'

10. οὐχ ὅπως] *non modo non* here: sometimes (e.g. p. 86) it means 'not only.'

B. Περὶ Ἐπαγγελιῶν

τῶν ἁγίων ἢ τῶν ἀπὸ τῆς ἐκκλησίας τούτου γεγονέναι ποιητὴν τοῦ γράμματος, Κήρινθον δὲ τὸν καὶ ἀπ' ἐκείνου κληθεῖσαν Κηρινθιανὴν συστησάμενον αἵρεσιν, ἀξιόπιστον ἐπιφημίσαι θελήσαντα τῷ ἑαυτοῦ πλάσματι ὄνομα· τοῦτο γὰρ εἶναι τῆς διδασκαλίας αὐτοῦ τὸ δόγμα, ἐπίγειον ἔσεσθαι 5 τὴν τοῦ χριστοῦ βασιλείαν, καὶ ὧν αὐτὸς ὠρέγετο φιλοσώματος ὢν καὶ πάνυ σαρκικός, ἐν τούτοις ὀνειροπολεῖν ἔσεσθαι, γαστρὸς καὶ τῶν ὑπὸ γαστέρα πλησμοναῖς, τουτέστι σιτίοις καὶ ποτοῖς καὶ γάμοις, καὶ δι' ὧν εὐφημότερον ταῦτα ᾠήθη ποριεῖσθαι, ἑορταῖς καὶ θυσίαις καὶ ἱερείων 10 σφαγαῖς. ἐγὼ δὲ ἀθετῆσαι μὲν οὐκ ἂν τολμήσαιμι τὸ

2 γράμματος] συγγραμμ. nonnulli ‖ 9 ευφημοτερον] ευθυμωτερον nonnulli

1. τῶν ἁγίων ἢ τῶν ἀπὸ τῆς ἐκκλ.] The passage certainly seems to make some distinction here between οἱ ἅγιοι and the ordinary members of the Church, unless τῶν ἀπὸ τῆς ἐκκλ.=ἐκκλησιαστικῶν ἀνδρῶν in the sense of 'clerical persons' (as in Eus. *H. E.* ii 25. 6 etc.), in which case τῶν ἁγίων has its usual sense of 'the faithful,' though the order is hardly what one would expect. For the form of phrase οἱ ἀπὸ τ. ἐκκλ. cf. Eus. *H. E.* vi 19. 12 οἱ ἀπὸ τῶν Ἑλληνικῶν μαθημάτων and vii 32. 27 οἱ ἀπὸ παιδείας.

ib. ποιητήν] 'author' in a general sense.

2. Κήρινθον δὲ...σφαγαῖς] This passage is given again by Eus. *H. E.* iii 28. 4 and 5, where the opinions of St John (acc. to Irenaeus) and of Caius of Rome are also recorded about Cerinthus. Κήρ. δὲ...ὄνομα 'but that C., the founder of the heresy that was called Cerinthian from him, (was the author), who desired to attribute his own composition to a name that would carry weight': the lexicons give instances of the late use of ἐπιφημίζειν in this sense.

5. τῆς διδασκ....τὸ δόγμα] 'the formulated substance of his teaching.'

7. ὀνειροπολεῖν] The inf. still depends on λέγουσι above and is co-ordinate with τοῦτο εἶναι. Vales.'s emendations ὀνειροπολεῖ or ᾠνειροπόλει are needless.

8. ἔσεσθαι] sc. τὴν τ. χ. βασιλείαν. Cf. Rom. xiv 17.

9. δι' ὧν] The relative refers to ἑορταῖς κ. θυσ. κ. ἱερ. σφ. 'and in such things as he thought would be the means to provide himself more plausibly with these (pleasures).'

ib. εὐφημότερον] *ut aliquid sacratius dicere videretur* (Ruf.). The reading (εὔφημ.) is confirmed by Eus. *H. E.* iii 28. 5.

11. *I myself should not venture to reject the book considering how many of the brethren hold strongly by it: I only think that much of its meaning is beyond my comprehension and must be accepted by faith rather than by reason.*

ib. ἀθετῆσ....οὐκ ἂν τολμήσ.] as opposed to the τινὲς μέν above who did. The ἀθετῆσαι here refers to the contents rather than to the authorship of the book, with regard to which see below.

8—2

βιβλίον, πολλῶν αὐτὸ διὰ σπουδῆς ἐχόντων ἀδελφῶν,
μείζονα δὲ τῆς ἐμαυτοῦ φρονήσεως τὴν ὑπόληψιν τὴν περὶ
αὐτοῦ λαμβάνων, κεκρυμμένην εἶναί τινα καὶ θαυμασιω-
τέραν τὴν καθ' ἕκαστον ἐκδοχὴν ὑπολαμβάνω. καὶ γὰρ
5 εἰ μὴ συνίημι, ἀλλ' ὑπονοῶ γε νοῦν τινὰ βαθύτερον ἐγκεῖ-
σθαι τοῖς ῥήμασιν, οὐκ ἰδίῳ ταῦτα μετρῶν καὶ κρίνων
λογισμῷ, πίστει δὲ τὸ πλέον νέμων, ὑψηλότερα ἢ ὑπ'
ἐμοῦ καταληφθῆναι νενόμικα, καὶ οὐκ ἀποδοκιμάζω ταῦτα,
ἃ μὴ συνεώρακα, θαυμάζω δὲ μᾶλλον, ὅτι μὴ καὶ εἶδον.

10 Ἐπὶ τούτοις τὴν ὅλην τῆς ἀποκαλύψεως βασανίσας γραφήν,
ἀδύνατον δὲ αὐτὴν κατὰ τὴν πρόχειρον ἀποδείξας νοεῖσθαι διάνοιαν,
ἐπιφέρει λέγων·

(4) Συντελέσας δὴ πᾶσαν, ὡς εἰπεῖν, τὴν προφητείαν,
μακαρίζει ὁ προφήτης τούς τε φυλάσσοντας αὐτήν, καὶ

7 το πλεον BCDF^{ab}GHKR^{ab} Nic Schw πως OL^r om το cett || υψη-
λοτερα η] υψηλοτεραν nonnulli

4. τὴν καθ' ἕκ. ἐκδοχ.] 'the way
of taking (or interpreting) each
point.' Liddell and Scott quote
several instances of this use of
ἐκδοχή in Polybius and it is a
favourite word with Origen (e.g.
Philocal. v 46 ed. Robinson) ἡ γὰρ
πᾶσα γραφή ἐστιν ἡ δηλουμένη διὰ
τῆς βίβλου, ἔμπροσθεν μὲν γεγραμ-
μένη διὰ τὴν πρόχειρον αὐτῆς ἐκδοχήν,
ὄπισθεν δὲ διὰ τὴν ἀνακεχωρηκυῖαν
καὶ πνευματικήν (in reference to Rev.
v 1).

7. πίστει δὲ τὸ πλέον νέμων] 'but
giving the preference to faith,' i.e.
reckoning that it is a matter where
faith rather than reason ought to
act: the rendering 'giving more
weight to (the author's) trustworthiness' which Hein. prefers would
seem to require τῇ πίστει, if not τῇ
πίστει αὐτοῦ.

9. ἃ μὴ συνεώρακα] 'which I have
not taken in at a glance,' or 'as
others appear to do': for the meaning of συνορᾶν see Dr Hort's note
on p. 71.

ib. ὅτι μὴ καὶ εἶδον] either 'because I have not even seen (the
visions),' in which case the καί
marks the contrast between εἶδον
and συνεώρακα, or 'because I have
not also seen (them),' in which case
the καί connects εἶδον with θαυμάζω:
the former alternative is more likely.

13. *I would admit that it is the
work of some inspired person named
John but could not easily agree that
he is the Apostle of that name who
wrote the Gospel and the General
Epistle. The Evangelist never mentions his own name or proclaims
himself.*

ib. ὡς εἰπεῖν] loosely used for
σχεδὸν εἰπεῖν. The phrase qualifies
πᾶσαν. Cf. Eus. *H. E.* vi 27 and
other instances quoted by Hein. in
his footnote 22 on Eus. *H. E.* vii
11. 12.

14. ὁ προφήτης] The use of this
word to describe the author, though
suggested by the language of the
quotation, is noticeable: the author
never describes himself by this title.

B. Περὶ Ἐπαγγελιῶν 117

δὴ καὶ ἑαυτόν. Μακάριοc γάρ, φησιν, ὁ τηρῶν τοὺc λόγουc τῆc προφητείαc τοῦ βιβλίου τούτου, κἀγὼ Ἰωάννηc ὁ βλέπων καὶ ἀκούων ταῦτα. καλεῖσθαι μὲν οὖν αὐτὸν Ἰωάννην, καὶ εἶναι τὴν γραφὴν Ἰωάννου ταύτην, οὐκ ἀντερῶ. ἁγίου μὲν γὰρ εἶναί τινος καὶ θεοπνεύστου συναινῶ, οὐ μὴν 5 ῥᾳδίως ἂν συνθοίμην τοῦτον εἶναι τὸν ἀπόστολον, τὸν υἱὸν Ζεβεδαίου, τὸν ἀδελφὸν Ἰακώβου, οὗ τὸ εὐαγγέλιον τὸ κατὰ Ἰωάννην ἐπιγεγραμμένον καὶ ἡ ἐπιστολὴ ἡ καθολική. τεκμαίρομαι γὰρ ἔκ τε τοῦ ἤθους ἑκατέρων καὶ τοῦ τῶν λόγων εἴδους καὶ τῆς τοῦ βιβλίου διεξαγωγῆς 10

6 συνθοιμην BCDF^{a}KR^{ab} Val Schw συνθαιμην F^b συνθειμην cett ∥ τουτον ειναι] ειν. τουτ. F^{a}KR^{ab}

D., in common with Eusebius, speaks throughout with caution as to the authorship of the book, whereas Origen, his former master, a strong anti-chiliast, attributes it to St John the Evangelist acc. to Eus. *H. E.* vi 25. 9. In the letter to Hermammon (p. 71) Rev. xiii 5 is quoted with the words καὶ τῷ Ἰωάννῃ ὁμοίως ἀποκαλύπτεται, very much as it is quoted by Clem. Alex., Origen's master and likewise an anti-chiliast, *Strom.* vi 13 § 106 ὥς φησιν ἐν τῇ ἀποκαλύψει Ἰωάννης, but see further on for D.'s suggestion as to the identity of the John.

1. Μακάριος κτλ.] Rev. xxii 7, 8. D. is no doubt wrong in joining the clause (κἀγὼ Ἰωάννης κτλ.) to the preceding one: the construction is ἐγὼ Ἰ. (εἰμί) ὁ ἀκούων κτλ.

6. συνθοίμην] This (the Attic) form of the 2nd aor. mid. is frequently found in Thucyd., Demosth. and Xen.: see Matthiae *Gk Gr.* 213 § 3.

8. ἡ ἐπιστ. ἡ καθολ.] i.e. the First Ep. of St John: see Westcott *Epp. of St John* p. xxviii, who shows that the epithet (καθολικὴ 'general' in its address or application) occurs "from the close of the second century onwards" in connexion with the Epistles of SS. James, Peter, John and Jude, and quotes Œcumenius *Praef. ad comm. in Ep. Jac.* καθολικαὶ λέγονται αὗται οἱονεὶ ἐγκύκλιοι κτλ. The 2nd and 3rd John were at first (and correctly) not so characterised.

9. τεκμαίρ. γ. ἐκ τοῦ ἤθους κτλ.] These seem to be the three heads of his argument against John the Evang. being the author of the Revelation. (1) ἐκ τοῦ ἤθους ἑκατέρων: here ἑκατ. appears to be masc. = 'the two Johns'; if so, ἦθους = 'character,' as shown in the use or suppression of the name: others take ἑκατ. to mean 'both writings,' but it is doubtful whether ἦθος can be so applied in the sense of 'style' and all the succeeding section deals with the use of the *name.* (2) ἐκ...τοῦ τῶν λόγων εἴδους = ἀπὸ τῶν νοημάτων... ῥημάτων καὶ τῆς συντάξ. αὐτ. p. 121. (3) ἐκ...τῆς τ. βιβ. διεξαγωγῆς 'conduct' or 'arrangement' (οἰκονομία Hein.), a rhetorical expression for which D. almost apologizes (λεγομένης) and which on p. 124 becomes τῆς φράσεως τὴν διαφοράν. Διεξάγειν occurs several times in LXX = 'to manage' (see Schleusner *s. v.*) and so Suidas: διεξάγοντας· διοικοῦντας. It is quite possible however that τῆς τ. β. διεξαγ. represents the τῆς συντάξεως of the

λεγομένης μὴ τὸν αὐτὸν εἶναι. ὁ μὲν γὰρ εὐαγγελιστὴς οὐδαμοῦ τὸ ὄνομα αὐτοῦ παρεγγράφει, οὐδὲ κηρύσσει ἑαυτόν, οὔτε διὰ τοῦ εὐαγγελίου, οὔτε διὰ τῆς ἐπιστολῆς. Εἶθ' ὑποβὰς ταῦτα λέγει πάλιν·

5 (5) Ἰωάννης δὲ οὐδαμοῦ οὐδὲ ὡς περὶ ἑαυτοῦ οὐδὲ ὡς περὶ ἑτέρου· ὁ δὲ τὴν ἀποκάλυψιν γράψας εὐθύς τε ἐν ἀρχῇ ἑαυτὸν προτάσσει· Ἀποκάλγψις Ἰηcoῦ Χριcτoῦ, ἣν ἔΔωκεν αὐτῷ Δεῖξαι τοῖc Δούλοιc αὐτοῦ ἐν τάχει, καὶ ἐσήμανεν ἀποστείλαc Διὰ τοῦ ἀγγέλου αὐτοῦ τῷ Δούλῳ αὐτοῦ Ἰωάννη, ὃc
10 ἐμαρτύρηcε τὸν λόγον τοῦ θεοῦ καὶ τὴν μαρτυρίαν αὐτοῦ, ὅcα εἶΔεν. εἶτα καὶ ἐπιστολὴν γράφει· Ἰωάννηc ταῖc ἑπτὰ ἐκκληcίαιc ταῖc ἐν τῇ Ἀcίᾳ, χάριc ὑμῖν καὶ εἰρήνη. ὁ δέ γε εὐαγγελιστὴς οὐδὲ τῆς καθολικῆς ἐπιστολῆς προέγραψεν ἑαυτοῦ τὸ ὄνομα, ἀλλὰ ἀπερίττως ἀπ' αὐτοῦ τοῦ μυστη-
15 ρίου τῆς θείας ἀποκαλύψεως ἤρξατο· Ὃ ἦν ἀπ' ἀρχῆc, ὃ ἀκηκόαμεν, ὃ ἑωράκαμεν τοῖc ὀφθαλμοῖc ἡμῶν. ἐπὶ ταύτῃ γὰρ τῇ ἀποκαλύψει καὶ ὁ κύριος τὸν Πέτρον ἐμακάρισεν εἰπών· Μακάριος εἶ, Σίμων Βὰρ Ἰωνᾶ, ὅτι cὰρξ καὶ αἷμα

5 ως] εως R^a || 6 εν αρχη εαυτον BCDF^aGHKOR^abNic Schw L^r εαυτ. εν αρχ. cett || 14 εαυτου] αυτου AE^a Steph || απεριττως] περιττως OL^r

second head and that the third argument is not referred to at all here.

5. *But while St John is silent about himself, the writer of the Revelation begins by putting himself forward: and again in the letter to the Seven Churches.* So also in the General Epistle the Evangelist omits his own name and starts at once upon the Revelation which he had received. Even in the short Second and Third Epistles he calls himself not John but the Elder, whereas the author of Revelation is not content with once mentioning his name but repeats it several times.

ib. οὐδὲ ὡς περὶ ἑαυτ. οὐδὲ ὡς π. ἑτέρου] i.e. neither in the first person nor in the third.

7. Ἀποκάλυψις...εἶδεν] Rev. i 2.

D.'s text omits ὁ θεός and ἃ δεῖ γενέσθαι and substitutes τὴν μαρτυρίαν αὐτοῦ for τὴν μαρτ. Ἰησοῦ Χριστοῦ. It appears that D. understood Ἰησ. Χρ. to be the subject of ἔδωκεν and αὐτῷ to mean 'to John': this would make the αὐτοῦ after μαρτ. = Ἰησοῦ Χριστοῦ.

11. Ἰωάννης...εἰρήνη] Rev. i 4.

14. ἀπερίττως] 'without any superfluous words' (*absque ambage* Schwegler).

15. τῆς θείας ἀποκαλύψεως] used to contrast the real 'revelation' to the Evangelist with that which D. believed not to be so: cf. ἀποκαλύψει below.

ib. Ὃ ἦν...ἡμῶν] 1 John i 1.

18. Μακάριος...οὐράνιος] Matt. xvi 17. D.'s text substitutes οὐράνιος for ἐν τοῖς οὐρανοῖς.

B. Περὶ Ἐπαγγελιῶν

οὐκ ἀπεκάλυψέ coι, ἀλλ' ὁ πατήρ μου ὁ οὐράνιος. ἀλλ' οὐδὲ ἐν τῇ δευτέρᾳ φερομένῃ Ἰωάννου καὶ τρίτῃ, καίτοι βραχείαις οὔσαις ἐπιστολαῖς, ὁ Ἰωάννης ὀνομαστὶ πρόκειται, ἀλλὰ ἀνωνύμως ὁ πρεσβύτερος γέγραπται. οὗτος δέ γε οὐδὲ αὔταρκες ἐνόμισεν, εἰς ἅπαξ ἑαυτὸν ὀνομάσας διηγεῖσθαι 5 τὰ ἑξῆς, ἀλλὰ πάλιν ἀναλαμβάνει· Ἐγὼ Ἰωάννης, ὁ ἀδελφὸς ὑμῶν καὶ ϲυγκοινωνὸϲ ἐν τῇ θλίψει καὶ βαϲιλείᾳ καὶ ἐν ὑπομονῇ Ἰηϲοῦ, ἐγενόμην ἐν τῇ νήϲῳ τῇ καλουμένῃ Πάτμῳ, διὰ τὸν λόγον τοῦ θεοῦ καὶ τὴν μαρτυρίαν Ἰηϲοῦ. καὶ δὴ καὶ πρὸς τῷ τέλει ταῦτα εἶπε· Μακάριος ὁ τηρῶν τοὺϲ λόγουϲ 10 τῆϲ προφητείαϲ τοῦ βιβλίου τούτου, κἀγὼ Ἰωάννης ὁ βλέπων καὶ ἀκούων ταῦτα. ὅτι μὲν οὖν Ἰωάννης ἐστὶν ὁ ταῦτα γράφων, αὐτῷ λέγοντι πιστευτέον. ποῖος δὲ οὗτος, ἄδηλον. οὐ γὰρ εἶπεν ἑαυτὸν εἶναι, ὡς ἐν τῷ εὐαγγελίῳ πολλαχοῦ, τὸν ἠγαπημένον ὑπὸ τοῦ κυρίου μαθητὴν οὐδὲ 15 τὸν ἀναπεσόντα ἐπὶ τὸ στῆθος αὐτοῦ οὐδὲ τὸν ἀδελφὸν Ἰακώβου, οὐδὲ τὸν αὐτόπτην καὶ αὐτήκοον τοῦ κυρίου γενόμενον. εἶπε γὰρ ἄν τι τούτων τῶν προδεδηλωμένων,

4 ανωνυμως] -ος GH ǁ ουδε] ουτε CFᵃGHRᵃᵇ ǁ 5 εις απαξ] απαξ BCDFᵃRᵃᵇ Val Schw ǁ 12 μεν ουν] μεν γαρ CFᵃGHKRᵃᵇ

2. ἐν τῇ δευτ. φερομένῃ] Φέρεσθαι Lat. *exstare* 'to be extant' or 'in use': cf. Eus. *H. E.* iii 25. 2 and 4 where we have first one of the ὁμολογούμενα (viz. 1 John) mentioned as τὴν φερομένην Ἰωάννου προτέραν and then ἐν τοῖς νόθοις ἡ φερομένη Βαρνάβα ἐπιστολή: cf. also Orig. *in Ev. Joan.* i 2 (p. 4 ed. Brooke) τῶν τοίνυν φερομένων γραφῶν καὶ ἐν πάσαις ἐκκλησίαις θεοῦ πεπιστευμένων εἶναι θείων. The School of Alexandria generally accepted 2 and 3 John as canonical: see Westcott *Hist. of N.T. Canon* p. 364.

4. οὗτος] sc. the author of Revelation.

6. Ἐγὼ Ἰωάννης...μαρτυρίαν Ἰησοῦ] Rev. i 9: for ἐν ὑπομονῇ Ἰησ. W. and H. read ὑπομονῇ ἐν Ἰησ.

10. Μακάριος ὁ τηρ....ἀκούων ταῦτα] Rev. xxii 7.

12. We must then believe that the writer was one John but who he was is doubtful. For he does not call himself as in the Gospel the beloved disciple and so forth: and he would have done so, if he had wished to reveal his identity. He only says he is our brother and partner and the like.

John (like Paul and Peter) was a common name among Christians, who liked the associations of the name with the Apostle. There is another John in the Acts whose surname was Mark. There was another John among those who were in Asia.

17. αὐτόπτην] as in 1 John i 1 and 3.

18. τούτων τῶν προδεδηλ.] 'of these aforesaid descriptions.'

σαφῶς ἑαυτὸν ἐμφανίσαι βουλόμενος. ἀλλὰ τούτων μὲν οὐδέν, ἀδελφὸν δὲ ἡμῶν καὶ συγκοινωνὸν εἶπε καὶ μάρτυρα Ἰησοῦ καὶ μακάριον ἐπὶ τῇ θέᾳ καὶ ἀκοῇ τῶν ἀποκαλύψεων. πολλοὺς δὲ ὁμωνύμους Ἰωάννῃ τῷ ἀποστόλῳ
5 νομίζω γεγονέναι, οἳ διὰ τὴν πρὸς ἐκεῖνον ἀγάπην, καὶ τῷ θαυμάζειν καὶ ζηλοῦν, ἀγαπηθῆναί τε ὁμοίως αὐτῷ βούλεσθαι ὑπὸ τοῦ κυρίου, καὶ τὴν ἐπωνυμίαν τὴν αὐτὴν ἠσπάσαντο, ὥσπερ καὶ ὁ Παῦλος πολὺς καὶ δὴ καὶ ὁ Πέτρος ἐν τοῖς τῶν πιστῶν παισὶν ὀνομάζεται. ἔστι
10 μὲν οὖν καὶ ἕτερος Ἰωάννης ἐν ταῖς πράξεσι τῶν ἀποστόλων ὁ ἐπικληθεὶς Μᾶρκος, ὃν Βαρνάβας καὶ Παῦλος ἑαυτοῖς ϹΥΜΠΑΡΕΛΑΒΟΝ, περὶ οὗ καὶ πάλιν λέγει· Εἶχον δὲ καὶ Ἰωάννην ὑπηρέτην. εἰ δὲ οὗτος ὁ γράψας ἐστίν, οὐκ ἂν φαίην· οὐδὲ γὰρ ἀφῖχθαι σὺν αὐτοῖς εἰς τὴν Ἀσίαν γέ-
15 γραπται, ἀλλὰ ἀναχθέντες μέν, φησιν, ἀπὸ τῆς Πάφου οἱ περὶ τὸν Παῦλον ἦλθον εἰς Πέργην τῆς Παμφυλίας. Ἰωάν-

6 τω BCDF^aOR^{ab} το cett ‖ 8 και post δη om (B)C(D)F^aHKR^{ab} Schw add cett ‖ 16 τον Παυλον CF^bGHR^{ab} Schw om τον cett

4. πολλοὺς δὲ...ὀνομάζεται] 'I suppose that there were many that bore the same name as the Apostle John, who because of their love for him and from their admiration and emulation of him and desire to be loved by the Lord as he was, gladly took the same name with him, just as many a one among the children of the faithful is called Paul or Peter' (lit. 'as Paul and Peter too is often named among the children of the faithful'). Ἐπωνυμίαν Lat. *cognomen* 'surname': whether this refers strictly to the baptismal name is uncertain, for, though from the earliest times the receiving of a name has been connected with Baptism, yet it did not become such an important part of the rite itself till much later than this.

8. πολὺς...ὀνομάζεται] This use of πολύς with the verb is quite common,

cf. p. 122. With regard to the practice referred to, Vales. quotes the example in Chrysostom's writings of the name Meletius being so given: cf. also Chrys. *Hom. ad Gen.* xxi where parents are exhorted not simply to give children their grandparents' or ancestors' names but to choose those whose examples will inspire them: cf. Eus. *de mart. Pal.* xi 7 τοῦτο δὲ πρὸς αὐτῶν ἐγίγνετο, ἀντὶ τῶν πατρόθεν αὐτοῖς ἐπιπεφημισμένων εἰδωλικῶν ὄντων, εἰ τύχοι, μετατεθεικότων ἑαυτοῖς τὰς προσηγορίας.

11. ὁ ἐπικληθεὶς Μᾶρκος κτλ.] Acts xiii 1, 5.

13. οὐκ ἂν φαίην] 'I should say not.' For the form of sentence cf. πρὸς Νοουᾶτον p. 38 εἰ ἄκων, ὡς φῄς, ἤχθης, δείξεις.

15. ἀναχθέντες...εἰς Ἱεροσόλυμα] Acts xiii 13.

B. Περὶ 'Επαγγελιῶν

νης δὲ ἀποχωρήσας ἀπ' αὐτῶν ὑπέστρεψεν εἰς Ἱεροσόλυμα. ἄλλον δέ τινα οἶμαι τῶν ἐν Ἀσίᾳ γενομένων, ἐπεὶ καὶ δύο φασὶν ἐν Ἐφέσῳ γενέσθαι μνήματα, καὶ ἑκάτερον Ἰωάννου λέγεσθαι.

Καὶ ἀπὸ τῶν νοημάτων δὲ καὶ ἀπὸ τῶν ῥημάτων καὶ 5 τῆς συντάξεως αὐτῶν εἰκότως ἕτερος οὗτος παρ' ἐκεῖνον ὑποληφθήσεται. συνᾴδουσι μὲν γὰρ ἀλλήλοις τὸ εὐαγγέλιον καὶ ἡ ἐπιστολή, ὁμοίως τε ἄρχονται. τὸ μέν φησιν· Ἐν ἀρχῇ ἦν ὁ λόγος· ἡ δὲ Ὃ ἦν ἀπ' ἀρχῆς. τὸ μέν φησι· Καὶ ὁ λόγος σὰρξ ἐγένετο, καὶ ἐσκήνωσεν ἐν 10 ἡμῖν, καὶ ἐθεασάμεθα τὴν δόξαν αὐτοῦ, δόξαν ὡς μονογενοῦς παρὰ πατρός· ἡ δὲ τὰ αὐτὰ σμικρῷ παρηλλαγμένα Ὃ ἀκηκόαμεν, ὃ ἑωράκαμεν τοῖς ὀφθαλμοῖς ἡμῶν, ὃ ἐθεασάμεθα, καὶ αἱ χεῖρες ἡμῶν ἐψηλάφησαν, περὶ τοῦ λόγου τῆς ζωῆς, καὶ ἡ ζωὴ ἐφανερώθη. ταῦτα γὰρ προανακρούεται 15

5 απο των ρημ. BCDF^{ab}GHKOR^{ab} Schw L^r om cett ‖ 7 υποληφθησεται AF^bH (marg) Steph L^r υπονοηθησεται cett

2. δύο φασίν] Cf. Eus. *H. E.* iii 39. 4—6, where a passage is quoted from Papias in which ὁ πρεσβύτερος Ἰωάννης is mentioned among the Lord's disciples as well as (the Apostle) John and then the historian draws our attention to the fact and adds δύο τε ἐν Ἐφέσῳ γενέσθαι μνήματα καὶ ἑκάτερον Ἰωάννου ἔτι νῦν λέγεσθαι: cf. Jerome *de virr. ill.* 9. Archdeacon Lee (*Speaker's Comment.* vol. iv pp. 420, 440 ff.) has an interesting discussion on the points raised: cf. Harnack *Chronologie der altchr. Litt.* p. 660 ff., Zahn in Hauck's *Realencyclopädie* ix 275 ff., Lightfoot *Essays on Supernatural Religion* p. 143 ff.

5. *The Gospel and the Epistle agree with each other in their exordiums. Thus the writer of these books keeps consistently to his propositions discussing the same topics and using the same terms all through, a few instances of which we proceed to give. From this it is clear that the* characteristics of the two books are the same. On the other hand the style of the Revelation has nothing in common with the Gospel and Epistle, nor does the Revelation refer to the Epistle, or vice versa.

ib. Καὶ ἀπὸ τῶν νοημάτων κτλ.] Here begins the 2nd argument from the thoughts and actual words used.

6. συντάξεως] 'collocation' (Salmond following Vales. who adduces the title of Dion. Halic.'s book περὶ συντάξεως ὀνομάτων as meaning this), but 'arrangement' or 'disposition' would be a better translation (cf. Eus. *H. E.* iv 29. 6 τὴν τῆς φράσεως σύνταξιν), unless the word actually means 'syntax' and D. is anticipating his 3rd argument.

9. Ἐν ἀρχῇ ἦν ὁ λόγος] John i 1.
ib. Ὃ ἦν ἀπ' ἀρχῆς] 1 John i 1.
10. Καὶ ὁ λόγ. σὰρξ ἐγέν. κτλ.] John i 14.
12. Ὃ ἀκηκ....ἐφανερώθη] 1 John i 1, 2.
15. προανακρούεται] lit. 'strikes

122 DIONYSIUS OF ALEXANDRIA

διατεινόμενος, ὡς ἐν τοῖς ἑξῆς ἐδήλωσε, πρὸς τοὺς οὐκ ἐν ϲαρκὶ φάϲκονταϲ ἐληλυθέναι τὸν κύριον. δι' ἃ καὶ συνῆψεν ἐπιμελῶς· Καὶ ἑωράκαμεν καὶ μαρτυροῦμεν καὶ ἀπαγγέλλομεν ὑμῖν τὴν ζωὴν τὴν αἰώνιον, ἥτιϲ ἦν πρὸϲ τὸν
5 πατέρα καὶ ἐφανερώθη ἡμῖν· ὃ ἑωράκαμεν καὶ ἀκηκόαμεν, ἀπαγγέλλομεν καὶ ὑμῖν. ἔχεται αὐτοῦ καὶ τῶν προθέσεων οὐκ ἀφίσταται, διὰ δὲ τῶν αὐτῶν κεφαλαίων καὶ ὀνομάτων πάντα διεξέρχεται· ὧν τινὰ μὲν ἡμεῖς συντόμως ὑπομνήσομεν, ὁ δὲ προσεχῶς ἐντυγχάνων εὑρήσει ἐν ἑκατέρῳ
10 πολλὴν τὴν ζωήν, πολὺ τὸ φῶς, ἀποτροπὴν τοῦ σκότους,

2 δι α] διο nonnulli ‖ 3 και εωρακαμεν CF^aGHR^{ab} Schw add ο post και cett ‖ και μαρτυρουμεν] add και CF^aGHKR^{ab} Schw om cett ‖ 6 και υμιν] add και BCDE^aF^aKOR^{ab} Schw L^r om cett ‖ 8 υπομνησομεν AE^aF^bGHO Val Stroth L^r -ματισομεν Nic υπεμνησαμεν DF^a Schw υπεμνησωμεν BCKR^{ab}

up by way of prelude' and so 'begins by saying': the compound is used literally in musical matters (see Liddell and Scott *s. v.*).

1. διατεινόμενος...πρός] 'as he is dealing with.'
2. ἐν σαρκὶ...ἐληλυθ.] Cf. 1 John iv 2.
3. συνῆψεν ἐπιμελῶς] 'is careful to add.'
ib. Καὶ ἑωράκαμεν ... καὶ ὑμῖν] 1 John i 2, 3.
6. ἔχεται αὐτοῦ] 'he is consistent with himself.' The Berlin editor reads αὑτοῦ, though αὐτοῦ is found in two of his MSS, and suggests that the words are a corruption of ἵν' ἔχητε αὐτοῦ κοινωνίαν, a free quotation of the words that follow καὶ ὑμῖν in 1 John, which run ἵνα καὶ ὑμεῖς κοινωνίαν ἔχητε μεθ' ἡμῶν.
7. κεφαλαίων καὶ ὀνομάτων] 'subjects (topics) and terms': so above καθ' ἕκαστον κεφάλαιον διευθύνοντες, p. 114. Ὄνομα (Lat. *nomen*) in grammar = 'noun' but here it means rather the expressions by which certain ideas are denoted (such as those in the list he proceeds to give, ζωή, φῶς etc.).
8. ὧν τινὰ μὲν ἡμεῖς συντ. ὑπο- μνήσομεν] 'certain of which we will briefly recall.' Τινὰ μὲν ἡμεῖς seems to be answered by ὁ δὲ προσεχῶς ἐντυγχάνων, as if D. meant to say: we now can only give a brief and incomplete list of these κεφάλαια and ὀνόματα which occur both in the Gospel and the Epistle, but, if any one took the trouble to go through it carefully, he would be able to make a fuller list (which would of course include those D. gives). The reading ὑπομνήσωμεν is as well supported as -ομεν and it is doubtful which is to be preferred: the reading of DF^a (ὑπεμνήσαμεν) adopted by Schwegler would refer to the instances of consistency in treatment he has already given and would make the passage easier. It is possible that τινὰ μέν only means 'certain' (see note above p. 114) and that ὁ δὲ προσ. ἐντυγχ. only carries out the undertaking implied in ὑπομνήσωμεν. For ἐντυγχάνων ('perusing') cf. p. 52.
10. πολλὴν τ. ζ., πολὺ τ. φ.] See above p. 120.
ib. ἀποτρ. τ. σκ.] Such a phrase occurs nowhere in the N.T., the nearest to it is Acts xxvi 18 ἐπι-

B. Περὶ Ἐπαγγελιῶν 123

συνεχῆ τὴν ἀλήθειαν, τὴν χάριν, τὴν χαράν, τὴν σάρκα
καὶ τὸ αἷμα τοῦ κυρίου, τὴν κρίσιν, τὴν ἄφεσιν τῶν ἁμαρ-
τιῶν, τὴν πρὸς ἡμᾶς ἀγάπην τοῦ θεοῦ, τὴν πρὸς ἀλλήλους
ἡμᾶς ἀγάπης ἐντολήν, ὡς πάσας δεῖ φυλάσσειν τὰς ἐν-
τολάς· ὁ ἔλεγχος τοῦ κόσμου, τοῦ διαβόλου, τοῦ ἀντι- 5
χρίστου, ἡ ἐπαγγελία τοῦ ἁγίου πνεύματος, ἡ υἱοθεσία
τοῦ θεοῦ, ἡ διόλου πίστις ἡμῶν ἀπαιτουμένη, ὁ πατὴρ
καὶ ὁ υἱὸς πανταχοῦ· καὶ ὅλως διὰ πάντων χαρακτηρί-
ζοντας ἕνα καὶ τὸν αὐτὸν συνορᾶν τοῦ τε εὐαγγελίου καὶ
τῆς ἐπιστολῆς χρῶτα πρόκειται. ἀλλοιοτάτη δὲ καὶ 10
ξένη παρὰ ταῦτα ἡ ἀποκάλυψις, μήτε ἐφαπτομένη μήτε
γειτνιῶσα τούτων μηδενί, σχεδὸν ὡς εἰπεῖν μηδὲ συλλαβὴν
πρὸς αὐτὰ κοινὴν ἔχουσα. ἀλλ' οὐδὲ μνήμην τινὰ οὐδὲ
ἔννοιαν οὔτε ἡ ἐπιστολὴ τῆς ἀποκαλύψεως ἔχει (ἔα
γὰρ τὸ εὐαγγέλιον), οὔτε τῆς ἐπιστολῆς ἡ ἀποκάλυψις, 15

14 ἔα GH ἐᾷ CEᵃ ἐῶ Hein || 15 το] om A Val

στρέψαι ἀπὸ σκότους εἰς φῶς: further σκότος occurs but once in St John's Gospel (iii 19) and once in 1 John (i 6), though σκοτία is found eight times in the former and five times in the latter; hence, if the phrase is genuine and not a marginal gloss which has crept into the text, it is one of the νοήματα, not the ῥήματα in D.'s argument. It is to be noted also that ἀποτροπήν is the only noun in the list without the article and that we should have expected πολλὴν τὴν ἀποτρ.; as it is, therefore, the phrase ἀποτρ. τ. σκ. stands in apposition to φῶς.

1. συνεχῆ] 'constantly occurring,' the adj. is used in the same way as πολλήν and πολύ.

2. ἄφεσιν τῶν ἁμαρτ.] only once in St John's Gospel (xx 23) and twice in 1 John (i 9 and ii 12: cf. v 16).

5. ὁ ἔλεγχος κτλ.] The nominatives are out of construction with the foregoing accusatives. The conviction of the world and of the devil are not very frequently mentioned but cf. John xvi 8, vi 70, viii 44 (and iii 20), 1 John iii 8 and 10.

ib. ἀντιχρίστου] The word occurs four times in 1 John (and once in 2 John) but nowhere in the Gospel.

6. υἱοθεσία τ. θ.] a νόημα, not a ῥῆμα: cf. John i 12, xi 52 and 1 John iii 1, 2, 10, v 2.

7. ἡ διόλου π. ἡμ. ἀπαιτ.] 'the faith which is everywhere required of us.'

8. καὶ ὅλως ... πρόκειται] 'and generally throughout, in describing the character of the Gospel and Epistle, one and the same complexion is to be observed in both.' χαρακτηρίζει· σημαίνει τοὺς χαρακτῆρας (Hesych.). For χρῶτα, which is here used like the Lat. *color*, cf. Eus. *H. E.* vi 14. 2 τὸν αὐτὸν χρῶτα εὑρίσκεσθαι...ταύτης τῆς ἐπιστολῆς (τῆς πρὸς Ἑβραίους) καὶ τῶν πράξεων. For συνορᾶν cf. p. 71 and p. 116.

14. ἔα γὰρ τὸ εὐαγγ.] I have

Παύλου διὰ τῶν ἐπιστολῶν ὑποφήναντός τι καὶ περὶ τῶν
ἀποκαλύψεων αὐτοῦ, ἃς οὐκ ἐνέγραψε καθ' αὐτάς.

Ἔτι δὲ καὶ διὰ τῆς φράσεως τὴν διαφορὰν ἔστι τεκ-
μήρασθαι τοῦ εὐαγγελίου καὶ τῆς ἐπιστολῆς πρὸς τὴν
5 ἀποκάλυψιν. τὰ μὲν γὰρ οὐ μόνον ἀπταίστως κατὰ τὴν
τῶν Ἑλλήνων φωνήν, ἀλλὰ καὶ λογιώτατα ταῖς λέξεσι,
τοῖς συλλογισμοῖς, ταῖς συντάξεσι τῆς ἑρμηνείας γέγραπται. πολλοῦ γε δεῖ βάρβαρόν τινα φθόγγον ἢ σολοικισμὸν
ἢ ὅλως ἰδιωτισμὸν ἐν αὐτοῖς εὑρεθῆναι. ἑκάτερον γὰρ
10 εἶχεν, ὡς ἔοικε, τὸν λόγον, ἀμφοτέρους αὐτῷ χαρισαμένου

2 αυτου] εαυτου AE^{a}F^b Steph Stroth L^r ∥ 3 δια E^{a}F^{b}GH Steph Stroth
om cett ∥ 6 των CF^{a}GHOR^{ab} L^r om cett ∥ λογιωτατα] -ταις CGHR^{ab}
Nic ∥ 8 σολοικισμον] σολικ. KO ∥ 10 τον λογον] add την γνωσιν AE^a G (marg)
H Nic Steph ∥ αμφοτερους ACF^{ab}GHKR^{ab} Schw -ρα cett

accepted the Berlin editor's reading, though that of Hein. (ἐῶ) is more obvious: the reading ἐᾷ is meaningless here.

1. Παύλου...καθ' αὐτάς] 'whereas Paul in his epistles gave some indication even about those revelations, which he has not described in themselves.' The reference is to 2 Cor. xii 1 ff.; Gal. i 12, ii 2; Eph. iii 3 etc.

3. *The Gospel and the (First) Epistle are written in irreproachable Greek without barbarisms, solecisms, and provincialisms: whereas genuine as the visions and prophecies of the author of Revelation no doubt are, yet I see numerous instances of bad grammar in his writing. But I will not expatiate upon this, lest I be thought to scoff at him.*

ib. Ἔτι δὲ καὶ διὰ τῆς φράσεως κτλ.] Here begins the 3rd argument from the grammatical constructions etc.

6. λογιώτατα] *eruditissime* (Schwegler) as in Eus. *H. E.* v 21. 4 λογιωτάτην ἀπολογίαν: *disertissime* (Hein.): but in the present context the meaning assigned by Vales. *cum summa elegantia* =

'most skilfully or artistically' seems most appropriate. λόγιος (applied to Apollos, Acts viii 24) is a favourite epithet in Eusebius, usually applied to persons, not things, and the shades of meaning probably vary according to context.

7. τοῖς συλλογισμοῖς] 'their reasonings' (in a general sense, not in the technical logical sense of 'syllogisms').

ib. ταῖς συντάξεσι τῆς ἑρμηνείας] 'the arrangements of expression' (not of course 'of translation'): for συντάξεσι see note above p. 121.

8. βάρβαρον φθόγγον, σολοικισμόν, ἰδιωτισμόν] technical terms of grammar (1) barbarous words, (2) faulty sentences, (3) phrases peculiar to the author or provincialisms. For the solecisms of the Revelation the student may consult Winer *Gram. of N.T. Gk* § lxix 11 and also Lee (*Speaker's Comment.* vol. iv pp. 454—461).

9. ἑκάτερον...τὸν λόγον] D. appears to make here a loose reference to 1 Cor. xii 8, though the substitution of τῆς φράσεως for St Paul's σοφίας is somewhat bold (see apparatus criticus). If this is so, it

B. Περὶ Ἐπαγγελιῶν 125

τοῦ κυρίου, τόν τε τῆς γνώσεως, τόν τε τῆς φράσεως. τούτῳ
δὲ ἀποκάλυψιν μὲν ἑωρακέναι καὶ γνῶσιν εἰληφέναι καὶ
προφητείαν, οὐκ ἀντερῶ, διάλεκτον μέντοι καὶ γλῶσσαν
οὐκ ἀκριβῶς Ἑλληνίζουσαν αὐτοῦ βλέπω, ἀλλ' ἰδιώμασί
τε βαρβαρικοῖς χρώμενον, καί που καὶ σολοικίζοντα. 5
ἅπερ οὐκ ἀναγκαῖον νῦν ἐκλέγειν· οὐδὲ γὰρ ἐπισκώπτων,
μή τις νομίσῃ, ταῦτα εἶπον, ἀλλὰ μόνον τὴν ἀνομοιότητα
διευθύνων τῶν γραφῶν.

(6) Holl *Fragmente* 367 p. 148.

τὸν πρὸς ἀνάγκην ἐπιβληθέντα ζυγὸν ἀποσείονται 10
ῥᾳδίως οἱ ἀνειμένοι· βαρὺ γὰρ πᾶν τὸ ἀπροαίρετον καὶ
ὅπερ δαμασθέντες ὑπέστησαν ῥᾳστωνεύσαντες.

(7) *ibid.* 368.

συμβαίνει πολλάκις καὶ τῶν σοφῶν τινὰς παρορᾶν
τινά, τὰς ἰδίας διανοίας κρίσει, μᾶλλον δὲ οἰήσει, φιλαυτίας 15
ῥέποντας.

1 τον τε της γνωσ. τον τε της φρασ.] τον τε της σοφιας και τον της γνωσ.
AEᵃO Nic Steph ‖ τουτω] -ον FᵃGHKRᵃᵇ Nic Val Schw -ω cett ‖ 2 αποκαλυψιν] -εις Eᵃ Nic Lʳ ‖ 5 τε] μεν AEᵃK Steph Val Stroth ‖ σολοικιζοντα] σολικ. K ‖ 8 διευθυνων] add τουτων KORᵃᵇLʳ ‖ 12 ραστωνευσ.] Holl ραστωσαντες (vox nihili)

is hardly necessary to seek (with Hein.) to explain D.'s use of λόγος as equivalent to the Lat. *res* the 'matter' or 'subject' and the following genitives (τόν τε τῆς γνώσεως, τόν τε τῆς φράσεως) as genitives of definition (cf. Eus. *Vita Const.* i 10. 4 ὁ τῆς φράσεως λόγος); still less to adopt the suggestion of Vales., that Philo's distinction between λόγος ἐνδιάθετος (the conception) and λόγος προφορικός (the expression) is involved in the passage. Εἶχεν sc. ὁ Ἰωάννης.

1. τούτῳ] The dat. is due to οὐκ ἀντερῶ: the reading τοῦτον is an obvious correction.

2. ἀποκάλ....γνῶσιν...προφητ.] Cf. 1 Cor. xiv 6: and for ἰδιώμ. βαρβ. *ibid.* 8, while the use of the tongue (γλῶσσα) is frequently referred to in the context.

8. διευθύνων] 'correcting men's views about' or 'setting forth the correct view about': so above διευθύν. τὰ γεγραμμένα p. 112.

10. *The dissolute* (οἱ ἀνειμένοι) *will not brook any compulsion.*

ib. τὸν...ζυγόν.] The masc. form ζυγός is often used, esp. in later writers.

11. τὸ ἀπροαίρετον] 'that which has not been freely chosen by them.' In the περὶ Φύσεως the word is used in its earlier and more accurate sense: cf. pp. 142 and 147.

12. ῥᾳστωνεύσ.] 'after acting as mere idlers.'

14. συμβαίν. πολλ....ῥέποντας] 'it often happens that even certain of the wise overlook (or misjudge) certain things, because they allow

(8) *ibid.* 392.

ἀλλὰ πέπεισται ὡς ἁπάντων χαλεπώτατον αὐτὸν
γινώσκειν καὶ θεραπεύειν διὰ τὸ προσπεφυκέναι ἀνθρώποις
τὸ φίλαυτον, καὶ κλέπτειν τὴν τοῦ ἀληθοῦς κρίσιν ἑκάστου
5 τῇ περὶ ἑαυτοῦ προσπαθείᾳ.

2 αὐτον] Mai αὐτον ‖ 4 κρισιν] Mai κρισειν

their private opinions to be influenced by the decisions or rather the impressions of self-love': *ρέποντας* seems to be used trans. here, unless τὰς ἰδ. διαν. is accus. of respect after it.

2. *Man's natural self-love is a great hindrance to his knowing and curing himself.*

ib. πέπεισται] impers. 'it is admitted,' or perhaps pers. 'he is persuaded.'

ib. αὐτὸν γιν. καὶ θεραπ.]'to know and heal oneself': cf. the saying of the Delphic oracle γνῶθι σεαυτόν (Juv. *Sat.* xi 27) and the proverb quoted by our Lord ἰατρέ, θεράπευσον σεαυτόν (Luke iv 23).

3. προσπεφυκ.] 'grows upon,' 'is contracted by,' not the same as ἐμπεφυκ. would be.

4. κλέπτειν] The subject is τὸ φίλαυτον: 'and steals from a man the judgement of the truth (i.e. his power of true judgement) through his strong affection for himself.'

5. προσπαθείᾳ] cf. ἀπροσπαθῶς p. 163.

Γ. Περὶ Φύσεως
Πρὸς τοὺς κατ' Ἐπίκουρον

(Eus. *Praep. Evang.* xiv 23—27)

The two principal extracts from Dionysius's treatise of this name we owe to Eusebius, who quotes them in the 14th book of his *Praeparatio Evangelica* in company with similar extracts from Plato, Aristotle, and others. The treatise was addressed to Timothy, ὁ παῖς (see General Introduction p. xii), and its object, or at least the object of that portion of it from which the Eusebian quotations are made[1], was to meet the theories of Epicurus[2] from the Christian point of view. For this, as Eusebius implies, Dionysius was peculiarly well fitted by his position as Bishop of Alexandria, his philosophical temperament and his sincerity as a Christian (τῆς κατὰ Χριστὸν φιλοσοφίας ἐπισκόπου ἀνδρός—an admirably terse description of the man). No doubt at Alexandria, the home of thought and culture, and especially of Neo-platonism, the meeting-point of Greek and Latin civilization, Dionysius would frequently be confronted among others with thinkers who had espoused the views of Epicurus and whose influence upon the adherents of Christianity would always be peculiarly

---

[1] Dr H. Jackson points out to me that the words in which Eusebius introduces his quotations (p. 131) are ambiguous and may mean either "I will lay before you a few extracts from the περὶ Φύσεως written against E." or "from the π. Φ. I will produce a few of the criticisms of E."

[2] Epicurus, a native of Samos, had taken up his residence at Athens in 306 B.C., where in his famous garden he propounded his philosophy for more than 30 years.

dangerous[1]: on the scientific side, because of the plausible account the school could give of the problems of creation and natural phenomena; on the moral side, because of its hedonistic tenets, which the refinements of Epicurus only rendered the more subtly attractive and misleading. Dionysius no doubt entitled his treatise περὶ Φύσεως in reference to Epicurus's own great work in 37 books[2], which bore that name, but of which only a few fragments remain.

The Eusebian extracts, which appear to be fairly continuous throughout, deal (1) with the atomistic portion of the Epicurean philosophy, and (2) with the more strictly 'theological' portion of it, the references to the hedonistic doctrine being only slight and passing[3].

Dionysius begins by remarking that, of the various hypotheses which have been started as to the origin of the universe, one of the least satisfactory is that of Epicurus, viz. that it is the result of a chance concourse of an infinite number of atoms as they rush through space.

He then proceeds to show by a series of illustrations taken from human workmanship that mere chance could never produce the wonderful results that we see all around us. So too from the study of the heavens the same inference must be drawn.

His next point appears to be that the difference in durability, which Epicurus postulates for the various bodies produced by atoms, goes to upset his main theory. If some products (*e.g.* the gods) are eternal[4] and some are short-lived, what determines the difference? Some of the senseless atoms themselves must be gifted with powers of directing, arranging, and ruling. But if it is mere chance still, then Epicurus asks us, who study the order and the phenomena of earth and heaven, to believe the impossible.

---

[1] Origen's opponent Celsus is stated by Eus. (*H. E.* vi 36. 2) to have been an Epicurean.

[2] The title of Lucretius's poem *de rerum natura* is a translation of the Greek title, which was a favourite one with the philosophers: for instance the treatises of Parmenides and Empedocles, and apparently those of Heraclitus and Xenophanes, were so called. The word φύσις here = *universum*: cf. Cic. *de Nat. Deor.* ii: *sunt qui naturae nomine rerum universitatem intellegunt.*

[3] *E.g.* pp. 158 ff.

[4] Or at least μακραίωνα: see p. 138 and note.

Γ. Περὶ Φύσεως

The same conclusion is arrived at by the study of man, whose mere body is a machine so marvellous that some have emerged from the study of it with a belief that Φύσις is herself a deity. The higher powers, too, of man, his mind, and reason and skill, all point in the opposite direction to Epicurus's solution of the problem. It cannot surely be the atoms rather than the Muses, which are responsible for the arts and sciences.

The half-humorous allusion to these heaven-born personages of heathen mythology leads Dionysius to attack the Epicurean theory of the gods. According to Epicurus, the gods in no way concerned themselves with mundane matters, but spent a serene existence without labour or exertion of any kind. But such an existence, says Dionysius, is so repugnant to the very idea and instinct of man that it must be absolutely false with regard to divine beings.

At this point occurs a short passage in which the inconsistency of Democritus, from whom Epicurus had confessedly borrowed his physics, *mutatis mutandis*, is criticized, though it has only a general bearing upon the line of argument. Democritus, he says, who professed that he would have given the world in exchange for the discovery of one good cause (αἰτιολογία), yet in putting forward his idea of Chance as a cause could not have been more absurd: he sets up Τύχη as the sovereign cause of the Universe and yet banishes her as a power from the life of men[1].

The truth is that, while practical men and even philosophers find their highest pleasure in benefiting others, by this theory the gods are to be kept from any share in such pleasure.

One other inconsistency in the Epicurean writings Dionysius proceeds to deal with, and that is Epicurus's own constant use of oaths and adjurations, in which the names of those very gods occur whose influence upon the affairs of men he so depreciates. This in Dionysius's opinion is due to his fear of being put to death by the state for atheism, as Socrates had been: though here he is apparently doing Epicurus a wrong[2].

The extracts end with a repetition of the appeal to the wonders of the heaven and of the earth as a conclusive contradiction of Epicurus's views.

[1] A not over lucid quotation from the Ὑποθῆκαι of Democritus is given in his text by D. (p. 156).
[2] See note on p. 161.

For the text of this section and of the section Ἔλεγχος καὶ Ἀπολογία, so far as it is contained in Eus. *Praepar. Evangel.*, I am indebted to the Rev. Dr Gifford, who kindly lent me the proof-sheets of it, as his edition was passing through the press. The two oldest and best MSS., called by him A and H, do not contain the Dionysian extracts: of the rest the principal authorities are as follows:

B = Parisiensis 465 *bombycinus*; many lacunae; of the xiii cent. with xv cent. additions; the readings are taken from Gaisford's collation.

I = Venetus Bibl. Marc. 341 *chartaceus*, of the xv cent.; newly collated by Dr Redpath.

O = Bononiensis, in two different hands, of which the earlier is of the xiii cent.; collated for the first time by Dr Redpath and Mr Bate.

F = Florentinus Bibl. Medic. Plut. vi 6; of the xv cent.
G = ,, ,, ,, Plut. vi 9; of the xiv cent.
G is a copy of O and F of G.

C = Par. 466 Bibl. Reg. (Nat.); of the xiv cent., mostly agrees with F and G.

Viger's edition of Eus. *Praepar. Evang.* is dated Paris, 1628, and Routh's best edition of the fragments περὶ Φύσεως appeared at Oxford, 1846, in the *Rell. Sacr.* tom. iv. Of the MSS. which the latter used, he lays most stress on one at St John's Coll. Oxon., but Dr Gifford informs me that it 'is quite worthless': he has 'looked at it but with no advantage.'

The four short extracts which are found elsewhere than in Eusebius are of no great importance. The first draws attention to the fact that the workman is naturally anterior to his handiwork. The second compares the world to a workshop, theatre, school, or gymnasium, in which with much labour we are to attain to a knowledge of the truth. The third, which begins in the middle of a sentence, is rather longer than the other two: it draws attention to the truth that it is easier to arrive at a sense of one's duty by ascertaining what is the duty of others than by the more direct route. The fourth is obscurely expressed but contains the undoubted truth that it is as difficult to have knowledge of the small facts of the world as of the large. The thoughts contained in all four fragments are quite admirable, but their style does not impress one with a certainty that they are by Dionysius.

The text of these extracts is taken from that of Holl

Γ. Περὶ Φύσεως 131

Fragmente pp. 147 and 148. Before his edition they had appeared, the first in Pitra's *Anal. Sacr.* vol. II p. xxxvii; the second and third in Mai *Nova Collectio* vol. vii pp. 98 and 108; and the fourth in Le Quien's *Sacr. Parall. Rupefuc. S. Joan. Dam.* vol. ii p. 752. The last three were also printed by Routh *Rell. Sacr.* vol. iv pp. 418 and 419.

In preparing this section of the book I am much indebted to the valuable notes and suggestions of Dr Henry Jackson, of Trinity College, Cambridge, not only where his name appears but in many other places.

Ταῦτα ὁ Πλάτων. ἐγὼ δέ σοι καὶ Διονυσίου, τῆς κατὰ Χριστὸν φιλοσοφίας ἐπισκόπου ἀνδρός, ἀπὸ τῶν περὶ φύσεως βραχέα τῶν πρὸς Ἐπίκουρον ἀντειρημένων παραθήσομαι. σὺ δὲ λαβὼν ἀνάγνωθι τὰς τοῦτον ἐχούσας αὐτοῦ τὸν τρόπον φωνάς·

Πρὸς τοὺς κατ' Ἐπίκουρον, πρόνοιαν μὲν ἀρνουμένους, ἀτόμοις 5
δὲ σώμασιν ἀνατιθέντας τὸ πᾶν.

(1) Πότερον ἕν ἐστι συναφὲς τὸ πᾶν, ὡς ἡμῖν τε καὶ τοῖς σοφωτάτοις Ἑλλήνων Πλάτωνι καὶ Πυθαγόρᾳ καὶ

7—p. 134, l. 3 ποτερον...το ονομα] om B

7. *Is the universe one or dual or composed of an infinite number of molecules rushing blindly through space?* Each of these theories has been held, and of those who hold the last Democritus and Epicurus called the molecules ἄτομοι, while Diodorus is said to have called them ἀμερῆ σώματα and Heraclides ὄγκοι. The main difference in detail between the systems of Epicurus and Democritus is that the former thought all the atoms were minute in size and therefore imperceptible, the latter thought some atoms were quite large.

ib. Πότερον ἕν ἐστι συναφὲς κτλ.] 'This reminds me of Plato *Sophist* 242 C and 245 E: also κατακερματίζειν occurs three times in the same dialogue 255 B, 257 C, 258 D. I think that Plato's passage has suggested D.'s classification: but it is hardly to be regarded as a quotation. See also Isocrates *Antid.* § 258 ὁ μὲν ἄπειρον τὸ πλῆθος ἔφησεν εἶναι τῶν ὄντων, Ἐμπεδοκλῆς δὲ τέτταρα καὶ νεῖκος καὶ φιλίαν ἐν αὐτοῖς, Ἴων δ' οὐ πλείω τριῶν, Ἀλκμαίων δὲ δύο μόνα, Παρμενίδης δὲ καὶ Μέλισσος ἕν, Γοργίας δὲ παντελῶς οὐδέν. Possibly this may serve to interpret ἢ δύο, ὡς ἴσως τις ὑπέλαβεν.' (H. Jackson.)

8. Πλάτωνι καὶ Πυθαγόρᾳ] For the influence of these two philosophers at Alexandria see Zeller (*Stoics, Epicureans, and Skeptics,* p. 28): 'At Alexandria accordingly there arose towards the beginning of the first century before Christ a School calling itself at first Platonic, afterwards Pythagorean, which later still in the shape of Neoplatonism gained the ascendancy over the whole domain of philosophy.'

9—2

τοῖς ἀπὸ τῆς Στοᾶς καὶ Ἡρακλείτῳ φαίνεται, ἢ δύο, ὡς ἴσως
τις ὑπέλαβεν, ἢ καὶ πολλὰ καὶ ἄπειρα, ὥς τισιν ἄλλοις
ἔδοξεν, οἳ πολλαῖς τῆς διανοίας παραφοραῖς καὶ ποικίλαις
προφοραῖς ὀνομάτων τὴν τῶν ὅλων ἐπεχείρησαν κατα-
5 κερματίζειν οὐσίαν, ἄπειρόν τε καὶ ἀγέννητον καὶ ἀπρονόητον ὑποτίθενται; οἱ μὲν γὰρ ἀτόμους προσειπόντες
ἄφθαρτά τινα καὶ σμικρότατα σώματα, πλῆθος ἀνήριθμα,
καί τι χωρίον κενόν, μέγεθος ἀπεριόριστον, προβαλόμενοι,

2 τις] om I ‖ ἢ καὶ] om και O ‖ 3 και ποικ. προφορ.] om I ‖ 4 επεχει-
ρησαν] -ισαν O ‖ 6 γαρ ατομ.] om γαρ I ‖ 7 ανηριθμα] αναριθμα O ‖ 8 προβα-
λομενοι] προβαλλομενοι IO

1. τοῖς ἀπὸ τῆς Στοᾶς] For the
cosmology of the Stoics see Zeller,
op. cit. pp. 182 ff.

ib. Ἡρακλείτῳ] sc. τῷ Σκοτεινῷ:
see *ibid.* p. 134.

ib. ἢ δύο] D. disdains to mention
any name in connexion with this
theory, which appeared to him so
unphilosophical. Perhaps he had
in view the Manichees; but Dittrich
Dionys. d. Gr. p. 20 connecting
this passage with the extract from
the Ἔλεγχος given on pp. 182 ff.
maintains that he was thinking of the
Dualism of the Hellenic Gnostics or
of the later Pythagoreans and Neoplatonists. See also Dr Jackson's
note above.

2. ἢ καὶ πολλά] viz. the various
kinds of Epicureans, whom he proceeds to describe, and perhaps others
as well.

3. παραφοραῖς] 'goings astray,'
'delusions.'

4. προφοραῖς] lit. 'utterances.'
There is a kind of play of words
between παραφ. and προφορ. D.
proceeds to bring out the variety of
nomenclature employed.

ib. τὴν τῶν ὅλων...οὐσίαν] 'the
substance of the universe.'

ib. κατακερματίζειν] lit. 'to cut
up coins into small bits for change';
hence in the transitional sense of
'giving small change' the κερμα-
τισταί, John ii 14: here metaphorically as in Plat. *Rep.* 395 B
φαίνεται εἰς σμικρότερα κατακεκερ-
ματίσθαι ἡ τοῦ ἀνθρώπου φύσις. See
Dr Jackson's note above.

5. ἀπρονόητον] 'not governed by
Providence (πρόνοια)' or perhaps
'not the result of forethought (but
of accident)': 'The Epicurean *natura* is at one and the same time
blind chance' (i.e. absence of design) 'and inexorable necessity,
vi 31 *seu casu seu vi quod sic
natura parasset*,' Munro *Lucret.*
vol. i pp. 571—2.

6. ἀτόμους] 'The ancients attribute the words ἄτομοι, ἄτομα to
Leucippus and Democritus, and
ἄτομα occurs in the fragments of
Democritus, whose Διάκοσμος came
out in 420 B.C.' (H. Jackson.) The
germ of the theory is found in the
famous dictum of Anaxagoras ὁμοῦ
πάντα χρήματα ἦν, ἄπειρα καὶ πλῆθος
καὶ σμικρότητα: see Ritter and Preller
Hist. Phil. §§ 120 ff., 147 ff., 375 ff.

8. καί τι χωρίον κενόν...προβαλ.]
'and assuming a void space, unlimited in size': μέγεθος qualifies
ἀπεριόρ. just as πλῆθος qualifies
ἀνήριθ. above. X. κενόν: this is the
χώρα, τόπος, ἀναφὴς φύσις which it
was necessary for Epicurus to assume in order that his atoms might
have motion: cf. Lucr. i 334 ff.
*locus est intactus inane vacansque,
Quod si non esset, nulla ratione
moveri Res possent.*

Γ. Περὶ Φύσεως

ταύτας δή φασι τὰς ἀτόμους, ὡς ἔτυχεν ἐν τῷ κενῷ
φερομένας, αὐτομάτως τε συμπιπτούσας ἀλλήλαις διὰ
ῥύμην ἄτακτον, καὶ συμπλεκομένας διὰ τὸ πολυσχήμονας
οὔσας ἀλλήλων ἐπιλαμβάνεσθαι, καὶ οὕτω τόν τε κόσμον
καὶ τὰ ἐν αὐτῷ, μᾶλλον δὲ κόσμους ἀπείρους ἀποτελεῖν. 5
ταύτης δὲ τῆς δόξης Ἐπίκουρος γεγόνασι καὶ Δημόκριτος·
τοσοῦτον δὲ διεφώνησαν, ὅσον ὁ μὲν ἐλαχίστας πάσας καὶ
διὰ τοῦτο ἀνεπαισθήτους, ὁ δὲ καὶ μεγίστας εἶναί τινας
ἀτόμους ὁ Δημόκριτος ὑπέλαβεν. ἀτόμους δὲ εἶναί φασιν
ἀμφότεροι, καὶ λέγεσθαι διὰ τὴν ἄλυτον στερρότητα. 10
οἱ δὲ τὰς ἀτόμους μετονομάσαντες ἀμερῆ φασιν εἶναι
σώματα, τοῦ παντὸς μέρη, ἐξ ὧν ἀδιαιρέτων ὄντων συντί-
θεται τὰ πάντα καὶ εἰς ἃ διαλύεται. καὶ τούτων φασὶ
τῶν ἀμερῶν ὀνοματοποιὸν Διόδωρον γεγονέναι. ὄνομα

2 αυτοματως] -ους I ‖ 3 πολυσχημονας ουσας O πολυσχημονουσας I πολυ-
σχημον vulgo ‖ 9 ο Δημοκρ.] om Routh ‖ 11 μετονομ.] μεν ονομ. I ‖ 12 συντι-
θεται] -ενται O ‖ 14 αμερων] μερων O

1. ὡς ἔτυχεν] 'i.e. "without design" not "without antecedent cause": so αὐτομάτως in the next line "without purpose" not "voluntarily."' (H. Jackson.)
2. διὰ ῥύμην ἄτακτον] 'because of an ungoverned rushing movement' (not 'in a whirl' as Salmond). The natural motion of the atoms was sheer downwards (κίνησις κατὰ στάθ-μην), then there was the slight sideward motion (κίνησις κατὰ παρέγ-κλισιν), and, when they impinged, the motion upwards by blows and tossings (ἄνω κατὰ πληγὴν καὶ παλ-μόν), which produced the shapes of things: see Munro *Lucr.* vol. i pp. 415 and 426.
3. πολυσχήμονας] The variety of shapes in the atoms (some being smooth and some rough or hooked, and so on) was supposed to produce the differences in taste, smell, hearing, touch, appearance of substances: see Lucr. ii 330 and foll.

7. τοσοῦτον δὲ διεφών.] See Munro *Lucr.* vol. i p. 435, who shows that Leucippus and Democritus (acc. to Aristotle) taught their atoms ἄπειρα καὶ τὸ πλῆθος εἶναι καὶ τὰς μορφάς. Lucr. (ii 482) argues that, if this were so, some of them would have to be of infinite size (*esse infinita debebunt corporis auctu*) which is impossible: whereas Epicurus taught that the number of shapes of atoms is finite and only the number of atoms themselves infinite: see Zeller *op. cit.* p. 443.
8. ἀνεπαισθήτους] 'imperceptible': lower down the word is used actively 'without sensation.'
12. ἀδιαιρέτων] 'indivisible' i.e. not made up of component parts.
14. Διόδωρον] of Iasus (surnamed Kronos as well as his master Apollonius), circ. 320 B.C.; he was called ἀμερής because of this theory: see Diog. L. ii 111 and Zeller *Socratic Schools* 253 note 1, 270.

δέ, φασιν, αὐτοῖς ἄλλο Ἡρακλείδης θέμενος ἐκάλεσεν ὄγκους, παρ' οὗ καὶ Ἀσκληπιάδης ὁ ἰατρὸς ἐκληρονόμησε τὸ ὄνομα.

Ταῦτ' εἰπὼν ἑξῆς ἀνασκευάζει τὸ δόγμα διὰ πολλῶν, ἀτὰρ καὶ διὰ τούτων.

Ἀπὸ τῶν ἐν ἀνθρώποις ὑποδειγμάτων.

(2) Πῶς αὐτῶν ἀνασχώμεθα τυχηρὰ λεγόντων εἶναι συμπτώματα τὰ σοφὰ καὶ διὰ τοῦτο τὰ καλὰ δημιουργήματα; ὧν ἕκαστόν τε καθ' ἑαυτὸ γενόμενον ὤφθη τῷ προστάξαντι γενέσθαι καλόν, καὶ συλλήβδην ὁμοίως ἅπαντα· Καὶ εἶδε γάρ, φησιν, ὁ θεὸς τὰ πάντα ὅσα ἐποίησε, καὶ ἰδοὺ καλὰ λίαν. ἀλλ' οὐδὲ ἀπὸ τῶν μικρῶν τῶν συνήθων καὶ παρὰ πόδας νουθετοῦνται παραδειγμάτων,

7 ανασχωμεθα] -ομεθα BI || 8 τουτο] -ου I || τα καλα] om τα O || 9 εκαστον τε] om τε O add και Routh || 11 ειδε] ιδε I || τα παντα] om τα BO || 13 νουθετουνται] -ντων vulgo

1. Ἡρακλείδης] sc. Ποντικός. He was a candidate for the headship of the Academy in 339 B.C. See Diog. L. v 86.

2. ὄγκους] 'molecules' or 'masses': cf. Sext. Emp. *Math.* ix 363 : Zeller *Stoics* p. 415 n. 4.

ib. Ἀσκληπιάδης] a physician of Bithynia, who went to live at Rome, contemporary with Lucretius : often mentioned by Galen and Plutarch : 'no genuine Epicurean, though connected with the Epicurean school,' Zeller *op. cit.* p. 415 : Sext. Emp. *Math.* vii 201.

7. *The conditions under which human operations are performed should have guarded them against the mistake of thinking that chance rules the universe: such operations as cloth-making, house-building, ship-building, waggon-making. All these operations should have suggested the truth that the Divine Mind makes and governs all things. It is absurd to speak of κόσμος produced by ἀκοσμία or of orderly movements by a disorderly rush or of* heavenly harmony by discordant instruments.

ib. τυχηρὰ...συμπτώματα] 'the results of a fortuitous concourse of atoms.' There may be a play upon the ordinary and the technical meanings of σύμπτωμα. The Epicureans sought to distinguish between συμβεβηκότα (*coniuncta* in Lucr.) and συμπτώματα (*eventa*), the former being the essential qualities of things, the latter their accidents (e.g. time) though they often used σύμπτωμα indiscriminately for either: cf. Munro *Lucr.* i 363 and 4; Zeller *op. cit.* p. 439. 'But more probably D. uses συμπτώματα, as Aristotle does constantly, to mean "coincidences," results not of design, but of the intersection of lines of causation."' (H. Jackson.)

11. Καὶ εἶδε...λίαν] Gen. i 31.

13. νουθετοῦνται] this reading, which Viger had conjectured and Routh had restored from six of his MSS, is now established by Dr Gifford's MSS (BIO).

Γ. Περὶ Φύσεως 135

ἐξ ὧν δύνανται μανθάνειν, ὅτι χρειῶδες μὲν καὶ πρὸς
ὠφέλειαν ἔργον οὐδὲν ἀνεπιτηδεύτως οὐδὲ συμβατικῶς
ἀπεργάζεται, ἀλλὰ χειρουργούμενον εἰς τὴν πρέπουσαν
ὑπηρεσίαν καταρτίζεται. ὅταν δὲ εἰς ἄχρηστον μετα-
πίπτῃ καὶ ἀνωφελές, τότε διαλυόμενον ἀορίστως καὶ 5
ὡς ἂν τύχῃ διασκίδναται, ἅτε μηκέτι μεταχειριζομένης
μηδὲ διατατούσης αὐτὸ τῆς σοφίας, ᾗ τοῦ συνεστάναι
τοῦτο ἔμελεν. ἱμάτιόν τε γὰρ οὐ χωρὶς ἱστουργοῦ
συνισταμένων τῶν στημόνων, οὐδὲ τῆς κρόκης αὐτομάτως
παρεμπλεκομένης, ἀνυφαίνεται· εἰ δὲ κατατριβείη, τὰ λα- 10
κισθέντα διαρριπτεῖται ῥάκη. οἰκία τε ἀνοικοδομεῖται
καὶ πόλις, οὐ τοὺς μέν τινας δεχομένη θεμελίοις αὐτομολοῦντας λίθους, τοὺς δὲ ἀναπηδῶντας εἰς τὰς ἐπιβολάς,
ἀλλὰ κατὰ χώραν ὁ τοιχοδόμος τοὺς εὐθέτους ἐπιφέρει·
καταρριφθείσης δέ, ὡς ἂν παρείκῃ, κατενεχθεὶς ἕκαστος 15

4 μεταπιπτη] -ει O || 7 αυτο] -ω O* (-ο O²) || ᾗ] ἦ I || 8 εμελεν] εμελλεν O || ου] om BIO || 10 λακισθεντα] σχισθεντα I || 11 διαρριπτειται] διαριπτ. O || 12 πολις] μολις I || ου...απεσφαλη] om B || 15 καταρριφθ.] καταρεφθ. I || παρεικη] -ικη I

2. οὐδὲν ἀνεπιτηδεύτως κ.τ.λ.]
'D.'s argument is, I suppose, that the production of what conduces to an end implies a deliberate process towards that end; whereas in decay design is conspicuously absent; e.g. the construction of a house is the result of design, but there is no design in its decay. Whence it would seem that the cosmos, which maintains its order, course, is intelligently directed.' (H. Jackson.)

8. ἱμάτιόν τε...ἀνυφαίνεται] 'for a garment is woven not because the woof stands up without a weaver, nor yet because the warp weaves itself of its own accord.' οὐ χωρίς: the negative, though absent in BIO, is necessary to the sense. χωρὶς ἱστουργοῦ is best taken with the gen. abs. συνιστ. τῶν στημ. and corresponds to αὐτομάτως ('without purpose') in the next clause. The στήμων was the set of upright threads in a loom and the κρόκη the thread in the shuttle which was shot to and fro through the στήμων.

12. θεμελίοις] The dative, which is loosely used for εἰς τὰ θεμ., is in construction with δεχομένη rather than with αὐτομολοῦντας; and so is εἰς τὰς ἐπιβολάς in the next clause.

ib. αὐτομολ.] in its literal sense 'going of themselves.' Liddell and Scott quote instances of this for αὐτόμολος but not for αὐτομολεῖν.

13. τὰς ἐπιβολάς] 'the layers' or 'courses': cf. Thucyd. iii 20 ταῖς ἐπιβολαῖς τῶν πλίνθων.

14. κατὰ χώραν] 'in proper order': it is rather an extension of its classical use, to join this phrase with a verb of action like ἐπιφέρει: we have κατὰ χ. εἶναι, ἔχειν, ἐᾶν, etc., but not κατὰ χ. τιθέναι or the like.

15. ὡς ἂν παρείκῃ] impers. 'in

ἀπεσφάλη. καὶ κατασκευαζομένης νεὼς οὐχ ἡ μέν τις
ὑπέβαλεν ἑαυτὴν τροπίς, ὁ δὲ κατὰ μέσην ἑαυτὸν ἱστὸς
ὤρθωσε, καὶ τῶν ἄλλων ἕκαστον ξύλων ἦν ἔτυχεν ἐξ
ἑαυτοῦ θέσιν κατέλαβεν· οὐδὲ τὰ λεγόμενα ἑκατὸν τῆς
5 ἁμάξης ξύλα, καθ' ὃν εὗρε κενὸν τόπον ἕκαστον, συνεπάγη·
ἀλλ' ὁ τέκτων ἑκατέρας συνεκόμισε καίριον. εἰ δὲ
διαλυθείη ἡ ναῦς ἐνθαλασσεύουσα, ἢ φερομένη κατὰ γῆν
ἅμαξα, ὅπῃ τύχῃ τὰ ξύλα, τὰ μὲν ὑπὸ τῶν κυμάτων,
τὰ δὲ ὑπὸ τῆς συντόνου ῥύμης διασπείρεται. οὕτως
10 ἂν ἁρμόζοι λέγειν αὐτοῖς, καὶ τὰς ἀτόμους, ἀργὰς μενούσας

1 απεσφαλη] αποσφ. I ‖ 2 υπεβαλεν] υπεβαλλεν I ‖ εαυτην] αὐτὴν BO*
αὐτὴν O² ‖ τροπις] τροπ cum lacuna I ‖ ιστος] add -ο IO ‖ 3 ωρθωσε]
ορθωσεν I ‖ 4 εκατον] εκαστον I ‖ 6 εκατερας] -ερα conj Routh

whichever direction there is nothing to obstruct it,' cf. Greg. Naz. *Theol. Or.* ii 26 (p. 62 Mason) ὅπη παρείκοι. The clause goes with κατενεχθεὶς ἕκαστος (λίθος) not with καταρριφθείσης (τῆς οἰκίας ἢ πόλεως).

1. ἀπεσφάλη] 'falls to the ground.' Liddell and Scott quote Plut. *Per.* 13 ἀποσφαλεὶς ἐξ ὕψους ἔπεσεν for the literal sense ('slipping').

2. τροπίς] 'the keel' (of a vessel).

ib. κατὰ μέσην] sc. τὴν ναῦν.

4. τὰ λεγ. ἑκατόν] The reference is to Hesiod Ἔργ. κ. Ἡμ. 554 νήπιος, οὐδὲ τό γ' οἶδ' ἑκατὸν δέ τε δούραθ' ἁμάξης. The Greeks often used 100 for a large indefinite number: hence ἑκατόμπυλοι Θῆβαι, ἑκατόμποδες Νηρηίδες, ἑκατόμβαι and so forth.

5. κενὸν τόπον] in allusion to the theory mentioned above p. 132.

6. ὁ τέκτων ἑκατέρας (sc. νεὼς ἢ ἁμάξης) συνεκόμ. καίριον (sc. ξύλον)] 'the constructor of each puts the timber together suitably': the sentence is condensed but Routh's conjecture ἑκάτερα (neut. pl.) and καίριον (adv.) is needless.

7. ἐνθαλασσεύουσα] 'when at sea': the compound, which is found in late writers, seem to means the same as the simple θαλασσεύειν which is found in Thucyd. vii 12 and elsewhere.

ib. φερομένη κατὰ γῆν] 'when driven along on land.'

9. ὑπὸ τῆς συντόνου ῥύμης] 'by the violent rapid motion': ῥύμη in allusion to the use of the word on p. 133; cf. Xen. *Cyr.* vii 1. 31 τοὺς μὲν ὀρθοὺς τῇ ῥύμῃ τῇ τῶν ἵππων παίοντες ἀνέτρεπον.

ib. οὕτως ἂν ἁρμόζοι κτλ.] 'in the same way it would befit them to say that the atoms also which, when they are stationary and are not worked by hands, are inoperative, are also useless when they move at random.' 'The point here is that movement which is useful implies design: as by assumption there is no design in the movement of the atoms, it cannot be useful. In fact it is the adjectival predicate (ἀχρήστους) and not the verb (φέρεσθαι) which is emphatic, as we so often find.' (H. Jackson.) Εἰκῇ φέρεσθαι was the common phrase in use among the Epicureans to describe the motion of the atoms: so above ὡς ἔτυχεν p. 133.

Γ. Περὶ Φύσεως

καὶ ἀχειροποιήτους, καὶ ἀχρήστους εἰκῆ φέρεσθαι. ὁράτωσαν γὰρ τὰς ἀθεάτους ἐκεῖνοι, καὶ τὰς ἀνοήτους νοείτωσαν, οὐχ ὁμοίως ἐκείνῳ, ὃς φανερωθὲν ἑαυτῷ τοῦτο ὑπὸ τοῦ θεοῦ πρὸς αὐτὸν ὁμολογεῖ· Τὸ ἀκατέργαϲτόν ϲογ εἴΔοϲΑΝ οἱ ὀφθΑλΜοί Μογ. ὅταν δὲ καὶ ἅ φασιν ἐξ ἀτόμων 5 ὑφάσματα γίνεσθαι, τὰ εὐήτρια ταῦθ᾽ ὑπ᾽ αὐτῶν ἀσόφως καὶ ἀναισθήτως αὐτουργεῖσθαι λέγωσι, τίς ἀνέξεται τὰς ἀτόμους ἀκούων ἐρίθους, ὧν καὶ ὁ ἀράχνης ἐστὶ σοφώτερος, χειροτεχνῶν ἐξ ἑαυτοῦ;

1 αχειροπ.] χειροπ. I ‖ 2 νοειτωσαν] ει sup ras I νοητ. O ‖ 5 ειδοσαν] ειδον BO ιδωσαν I ‖ α φασιν] αφεσιν O* (α φασιν O²) ‖ 6 ευητρια] ευιτρ. BO ‖ 8 εριθους] αριθμους I αρρυθμους Vig

1. ἀχειροποιήτους] Cf. χειρουργούμενον κτλ. above.

2. τὰς ἀθεάτους] sc. ἀτόμους. Viger strangely wants to read ἀθέτους and supply φύσεις ('those disorderly natures'). D. is still turning the Epicureans' ideas against themselves. 'Let them look to those viewless (atoms) of theirs and perceive those imperceptible (ones)': better-instructed people, like the Psalmist, cannot do it, except by revelation. Cf. Lucr. i 599, 600: *extremum quodque cacumen Corporis illius quod nostri cernere sensus Iam nequeunt* and ii 865 foll. *ea quae sentire videmus cumque necessest Ex insensilibus tamen omnia confiteare Principiis constare*.

4. πρὸς αὐτόν] sc. τὸν θεόν.

ib. Τὸ ἀκατέργ....μου] Ps. cxxxviii (cxxxix) 16 'my eyes beheld thy unfinished work.' The reading in the text is that of B: other readings are μου for σου and σου for μου, and εἶδον or ἴδον for εἴδοσαν. Chrysostom seems to have read τὸ ἀκατεργ. μου which he paraphrases ἀμόρφωτόν με τουτέστι μηδένα λαβόντα τύπον, ἔτι ὑφαινόμενον· καὶ οὕτω με ἴδον σαφῶς κτλ. D.'s application of the text as he read it is a little obscure: he apparently means that the Psalmist recognized that the hidden processes of the Divine working had been revealed to him, whereas the Epicureans claimed to know them without any such revelation on the one hand or any scientific observation on the other.

6. ὑφάσμ....τὰ εὐήτρια] Cf. Plat. *Rep.* 310 E εὐήτριον ὕφασμα. Ἦτριον is properly the 'warp' (=στήμονες above) in a web of cloth and then comes to mean 'cloth of a fine web.' Αὐτουργός is 'one who works with his own hands': hence αὐτουργεῖν, which is used with a direct accus. of the thing so wrought. Here the passive is used in a slightly different sense 'to be self-wrought,' the result of spontaneous production. The original idea of αὐτουργός is perhaps caught up again in ἐρίθους below.

8. ἐρίθους] 'day labourers for hire,' esp. 'weavers' (see Liddell and Scott *s.v.*). Suidas quotes a line from Sophocles, which applies the word to the spider πάντα δ᾽ ἐρίθων ἀραχνᾶν βρίθει. Viger's conjecture ἀρρύθμους is needless.

9. χειροτεχνῶν ἐξ ἑαυτοῦ] 'who spins his web out of himself' (lit. 'exercises his handicraft'). D. says that even the spider has more notion of design and purpose than your atoms can have: the sarcasm is hardly to the point.

Ἀπὸ τῆς τοῦ παντὸς συστάσεως.

(3) Ἡ τὸν μέγαν τοῦτον οἶκον τὸν ἐξ οὐρανοῦ καὶ γῆς συνεστῶτα, καὶ διὰ τὸ μέγεθος καὶ πλῆθος τῆς ἐπιφαινομένης αὐτῷ σοφίας καλούμενον κόσμον, ὑπὸ τῶν σὺν οὐδενὶ κόσμῳ φερομένων ἀτόμων κεκοσμῆσθαι, καὶ γεγονέναι κόσμον ἀκοσμίαν; πῶς δὲ κινήσεις καὶ ὁδοὺς εὐτάκτους ἐξ ἀτάκτου προσάγεσθαι φορᾶς; πῶς δὲ τὴν παναρμόνιον τῶν οὐρανίων χορείαν ἐξ ἀμούσων καὶ ἀναρμόστων συνᾴδειν ὀργάνων;

Τίνα δὲ τρόπον, μιᾶς οὔσης καὶ τῆς αὐτῆς ἁπασῶν οὐσίας καὶ τῆς αὐτῆς ἀφθάρτου φύσεως, πλὴν τῶν μεγεθῶν, ὥς φασι, καὶ τῶν σχημάτων, τὰ μέν ἐστι θεῖα καὶ ἀκήρατα καὶ αἰώνια, ὡς αὐτοὶ φήσαιεν ἄν, σώματα, ἢ μακραίωνά γε κατὰ τὸν οὕτως ὀνομάσαντα, φαινόμενά τε καὶ ἀφανῆ·

2 η τον μεγαν—p. 148, l. 8 τον παροντα λογον om B ‖ 3 επιφαιν.] επιφερ. I ‖ 5 κεκοσμησθαι] -εισθαι I ‖ 7 προσαγεσθαι] προαγ. O ‖ 8 χορειαν] χωρειαν I ‖ 10 τινα δε] add και Routh ‖ 10 αυτης] om O ‖ 12 ως φασι] om I ‖ 13 γε κατα] τε κατα IO ‖ 14 τε και αφαν. φαινομ.] om I

2. Ἡ τὸν μέγαν...ἀκοσμίαν] sc. τίς ἀνέξεται ἀκούων (from the last sentence of the last paragraph) : and so with the succeeding sentences. There is no break in the argument here as is suggested by Eusebius's heading ἀπὸ τ. τ. παντ. συστάσ.

ib. τὸν μέγ. τ. οἶκον] For the idea we may compare Heb. iii 4 and Min. Fel. Octav. xviii 4 in hac mundi domo.

4. καλούμενον κόσμον] Cf. Plat. Gorg. 508 A τὸ ὅλον τοῦτο διὰ ταῦτα κόσμον καλοῦσιν.

7. τὴν παναρμόν. τ. οὐρ. χορ.] The music of the spheres was a favourite Platonic notion, cf. Plat. Rep. 617 B, Epin. 982 E. Dr Gifford translates χορείαν 'dance music' here and quotes Pratinas i 6 ἄκουε τὰν ἐμὰν Δοριὰν χορείαν and Ar. Ran. 247 ἐν βυθῷ χορείαν αἰολὰν ἐφθεγξάμεσθα. For τὰ οὐράνια ('heavenly bodies') cf. Xen. Mem. i 1 § 11.

10. If the essence and eternal nature of all atoms is the same except as to size and shape, how is it that the bodies composed of them differ so greatly in durability, some being (as they affirm) eternal, others short-lived? Their answer will be that such differences arise from the differences in the combination of atoms, some combinations being much closer and more durable than others.

ib. ἁπασῶν] sc. τῶν ἀτόμων.

12. τὰ μέν...ὀνομάσαντα] '(1) I think that the σώματα of which D. speaks are not atoms, but bodies aggregated of atoms and including spaces. His argument seems to be "if existence is eternal, one and the same, except so far as the size and the shape of the atoms make differences, how does Epicurus with his eternal atoms account for the difference commonly recognized between (a) bodies which are either eternal or quasi-eternal, (b) bodies which are long-lived, and (c) bodies which are

Γ. Περὶ Φύσεως 139

φαινόμενα μὲν ἥλιος καὶ σελήνη καὶ ἀστέρες, γῆ τε καὶ
ὕδωρ, ἀφανῆ δὲ θεοί τε καὶ δαίμονες καὶ ψυχαί,—ταῦτα
γὰρ οὐδὲ θέλοντες ὑπάρχειν ἀρνήσασθαι δύνανται·—τὰ δὲ
μακροβιώτατα ζῷά τε καὶ φυτά· ζῷα μέν, ἕν τε ὄρνισιν,
ὥς φασιν, ἀετοὶ κόρακές τε καὶ φοίνικες, ἕν τε χερσαίοις 5
ἔλαφοί τε καὶ ἐλέφαντες καὶ δράκοντες, ἐν δὲ τοῖς ἐνύδροις

2 θεοι τε] om τε O

short-lived? D.'s statement would
have been clearer if he had plainly
distinguished between (a¹) ἀίδια,
gods, etc. and (a²) μακραίωνα, sun,
moon, stars, etc. (2) Μακραίωνα appears to be a word which is preferred by some one (not necessarily
an Epicurean) who does not like to
call that which is material by the
name αἰώνιον. Now in the *Timaeus*
(37 D) Plato declines to call the
sensible universe αἰώνιον: nevertheless (38 B, C) it exists throughout time,
and (41 A, B), although the stars are
not of their own nature immortal
or indissoluble, the creator guarantees
them against mortality and dissolu-
tion. Similarly the author of the
epinomis attributes to the stars
either indestructibility and immortality or μακραίωνα βίον 'an age-long
life': δυοῖν δὲ αὐτοῖς μοιρῶν τὴν
ἑτέραν χρὴ δόξῃ μεταδιδόναι σχεδόν·
ἢ γὰρ ἀνώλεθρόν τε καὶ ἀθάνατον
ἕκαστον αὐτῶν εἶναι καὶ θεῖον τὸ
παράπαν ἐξ ἀπάσης ἀνάγκης ἤ τινα
μακραίωνα βίον ἔχειν ἱκανὸν ἑκάστῳ
ζωῆς, ἧς οὐδέν τι πλείονος ἂν προσ-
δεῖσθαί ποτε 981 E. The word
μακραίων occurs fairly often in the
Tragedians: but except in this place
I do not know it in philosophical
writings. It seems to me highly
probable that in κατὰ τὸν οὕτως
ὀνομάσαντα D. was thinking of the
passage from the *epinomis* which
I have referred to above.' (H. Jackson.) According to Lucretius (ii
646 ff., v 146 ff.) though the gods are
immortal, yet earth, water, air, and
fire are mortal and therefore the
world of which these are the parts
is mortal: hence D. seems to have
so far misrepresented the Epicurean
position.

2. ψυχαί] If this means 'souls'
here, it is to be noted that, acc. to
Epicurus, they were no more immortal than the φαινόμενα of the
last clause; see Lucr. iii *passim*:
and if D. uses the word in the Homeric sense of 'ghosts' or 'shades
of the departed,' it is doubtful
whether Epicurus recognized their
existence at all.

5. ὥς φασιν] 'as we are told' not
by the Epicureans but (e.g.) by Hes.
Fr. ccxiii Göttl. ἐννέα τοι ζώει γενεὰς
λακέρυζα κορώνη Ἀνδρῶν ἡβώντων·
ἔλαφος δέ τε τετρακόρωνος· Τρεῖς
δ' ἐλάφους ὁ κόραξ γηράσκεται. αὐτὰρ
ὁ φοίνιξ Ἐννέα τοὺς κόρακας· δέκα δ'
ἡμεῖς τοὺς φοίνικας Νύμφαι ἐυπλόκαμοι
κοῦραι Διὸς αἰγιόχοιο. The longevity
of eagles which Hesiod does not
mention in this curious fragment is
alluded to by Ter. *Hautont.* 3. 2.
10 as proverbial: *aquilae senectus*.
For the phoenix cf. Herod. ii 73.
The elephant is classed (with man)
among long-lived animals by Arist.
de long. et brev. vitae chap. ii, who
maintains that, generally speaking,
length of life is to a great extent a
question of size: and this perhaps
is the reason why D. includes δράκοντες (the larger kinds of snakes)
and τὰ κήτη here; for Aristotle
expressly mentions in the same
chapter the size to which οἵ τε ὄφεις
καὶ αἱ σαῦραι καὶ τὰ φολιδωτά grow
in warm climates.

τὰ κήτη· δένδρα δέ, φοίνικες καὶ δρύες καὶ περσέαι; καὶ
τῶν γε δένδρων τὰ μέν ἐστιν ἀειθαλῆ, ἃ καὶ καταριθμήσας
τις εἶπεν εἶναι τεσσαρακαίδεκα, τὰ δὲ πρὸς καιρὸν ἀνθεῖ
καὶ φυλλορροεῖ· τὰ δὲ πλεῖστα τῶν τε φυομένων καὶ τῶν
5 γεννωμένων ἐστὶν ὠκύμορα καὶ βραχυτελῆ, ὧν ἐστι καὶ
ὁ ἄνθρωπος, ὡς εἶπέ τις ἁγία περὶ αὐτοῦ γραφή· Βροτὸc
Δὲ ϲεννητὸc ϲυναικὸc ὀλιϲόβιοc; ἀλλὰ τοὺς συνδέσμους
φήσουσι τῶν ἀτόμων διαλλάττοντας αἰτίους γίνεσθαι
τῆς περὶ τὴν διαμονὴν διαφορᾶς. τὰ μὲν γὰρ ὑπ' αὐτῶν
10 πεπυκνῶσθαι καὶ κατεσφίγχθαι λέγεται, ὡς ταῦτα παντελῶς δυσαπάλλακτα γεγονέναι πιλήματα, τὰ δὲ μανωτέραν
καὶ χαλῶσαν τὴν συνάφειαν τῶν ἀτόμων ἐπ' ἔλαττον ἢ
πλέον ἐσχηκέναι, ὡς ἢ θᾶττον ἢ μετὰ πολὺ τῆς κοσμήσεως
αὐτῶν ἀφίστασθαι· καὶ τὰ μὲν ἐκ τοιῶνδε καὶ ὧδέ πως
15 ἐσχηματισμένων· τὰ δὲ ἐξ ἑτέρων ἑτεροίως διακειμένων
συμμεμίχθαι.

Τίς οὖν ὁ φυλοκρινῶν, συναγείρων τε καὶ ἀναχέων,

1 περσέαι] -αιαι O ‖ 2 a] om I ‖ 4 φυλλορροει] φυλλοροει IO ‖ των γεννωμ.]
om των I ‖ 8 διαλλαττ.] διαλαττ. O ‖ 9 διαφορας F διαφθορας IO ‖ 10 πεπυκν.
και κατεσφ.] κατεσφιχθαι και πεπυκν. O ‖ λεγεται Vig λεγειν IO ‖ ως ταυτα
I Vig ωστ αυτα O ‖ 13 η μετα] μη μετα O ‖ κοσμησεως I Vig κολλησεως O ‖
15 τα δε] τας δε O ‖ 17 φυλοκρ. IO Vig φιλοκρ. F Routh ‖ αναχεων] διαχ. O

1. φοίνικες] 'date palms.' They
are specially mentioned as long-
lived by Arist. *de long. et brev. vitae*
chap. ii.
 ib. δρύες] are of course proverbial
for longevity: hence Hor. *Od.* iv
13. 10 compares old men to *aridae
quercus.*
 ib. περσέαι] an Egyptian fruit
tree often confused with the 'peach':
cf. Theophr. *Hist. Pl.* iv 2. 1 ἐν
Αἰγύπτῳ γάρ ἐστιν ἴδια δένδρα πλείω,
ἥ τε συκάμινος καὶ ἡ περσέα καλουμένη: *ibid.* 5 τῷ σχήματι δὲ πρόμακρος
ἀμυγδαλώδης.
 2. ἀειθαλῆ] Theophr. *Hist. Pl.* i 9
enumerates more than fourteen.
 6. βροτὸς...ὀλιγόβιος] Job xiv 1
(D. reads δέ for γάρ).
 9. τῆς π. τ. διαμ. διαφορᾶς] 'of

the difference in the matter of their
continuance.' This, the reading of
F, is adopted by Dr Gifford and
was conjectured by Viger; the reading διαφθορᾶς does not suit the
argument.
 ib. ὑπ' αὐτῶν] sc. 'by the Epicureans' (to be taken with λέγεται).
 11. πιλήματα] 'closely packed
masses': cf. Arist. *Mund.* 4. 17
πίλημα νέφους, and Athen. 535
πίλημα λαμβάνων τῆς πολυτελεστάτης
πορφύρας.
 17. *Who then is it that directs
these combinations? Whether they
be unconscious and involuntary or
the reverse, it is impossible to conceive
of the results we see as brought about
in this way.*
 ib. φυλοκρινῶν] It is difficult to

Γ. Περὶ Φύσεως 141

καὶ τάσδε μὲν οὕτω συντάττων εἰς ἥλιον, τάσδε δὲ ὡδί,
ἵνα ἡ σελήνη γένηται, καὶ ἕκαστα συμφέρων κατὰ τὴν
οἰκειότητα πρὸς ἑκάστου φαῦσιν ἀστέρος; οὔτε γὰρ αἱ
ἡλιακαὶ τοσαίδε καὶ τοιαίδε καὶ ὡδέ πως ἑνωθεῖσαι πρὸς
ἐργασίαν σελήνης ἂν καταβεβήκεσαν, οὔτ᾽ ἂν αἱ τῶν 5
σεληνιακῶν ἀτόμων πλεκτάναι γεγόνεσάν ποτε ἥλιος·
ἀλλ᾽ οὐδὲ Ἀρκτοῦρος, εἰ καὶ λαμπρός ἐστι, τὰς Ἑωσφόρου
μεγαλοφρονήσαιτό ποτε ἂν ἀτόμους ἔχειν, οὐδὲ τὰς
Ὠρίωνος αἱ Πλειάδες. καλῶς γὰρ ὁ Παῦλος διέστειλεν
εἰπών· Ἄλλη δόξα ἡλίου, καὶ ἄλλη δόξα σελήνης, καὶ ἄλλη 10
δόξα ἀστέρων· ἀστὴρ· γὰρ ἀστέρος διαφέρει ἐν δόξῃ. καὶ εἰ
μὲν ἀνεπαίσθητος αὐτῶν ὡς ἀψύχων ἡ σύμπηξις ἐγένετο,
ἐπιστήμονος αὐταῖς ἔδει δημιουργοῦ· εἰ δὲ ἀπροαίρετος

1 ωδι] ωδε O ‖ 2 εκαστα I Vig εκαστας O ‖ συμφερων pro I ‖ 4 τοσαιδε] τοσαιδε IO ‖ και τοιαιδε] και bis script I ‖ 5 εργασιαν] add και I ‖ αν] om IO ‖ 6 γεγονεσαν] γεγονασι IO ‖ 13 απροαιρετος] -οις I

say whether this or φιλοκρινῶν (or φιλοκρίνων) is the proper form : the same confusion occurs in Eus. *H. E.* viii 4. 13 and x 4. 61 (cf. Basil *de Spir. Sancto* c. 29) as well as in Thucyd. vi 18 and other classical writers. Liddell and Scott prefer the form φιλοκρινεῖν 'at least in the earlier and more correct writers.'

ib. ἀναχέων] 'pouring abroad,' 'making diffuse,' the opposite of συναγείρων.

3. φαῦσιν] 'light-giving power,' cf. Gen. i 15 ἔστωσαν εἰς φαῦσιν... ὥστε φαίνειν ἐπὶ τῆς γῆς : the older reading was φύσιν for which there is no authority.

4. πρὸς ἐργ. σελ. ἂν καταβεβ.] 'they would never have condescended to form a moon.'

6. πλεκτάναι] 'intertwinings' (as of a rope or wreath, etc.).

8. μεγαλοφρονήσαιτο] 'would plume himself': used in much this sense by Plat. *Rep.* 528 B but not as here with an infinitive : οὐκ ἂν πείθοιντο οἱ περὶ ταῦτα ζητητικοὶ μεγαλοφρονούμενοι.

10. Ἄλλη δόξα...ἐν δόξῃ] 1 Cor. xv 41.

11. εἰ μὲν ἀνεπαίσθητος κτλ.] 'I understand the argument of this passage to be this : (1) if the combination of atoms was unintelligent, they wanted an intelligent artist to put them together; (2) if the junction was the result of necessity, and not of purpose (on their part), a wise ruler brought them together and presided over them; and (3) if they have been linked together to do voluntarily willing service, there was a wonderful master-craftsman who assigned to them their parts ; or, shall we say, a skilful general, who did not leave his army in confusion but arranged his troops in an orderly fashion.' (H. Jackson.)

12. ἀνεπαίσθητος] 'unintelligent' (act.): ὡς ἀψύχων gives the reason for the absence of intelligence, 'as being void of soul.' The αὐτῶν = τῶν ἀτόμων, not τῶν ἀστέρων.

13. ἀπροαίρετος] 'without pur-

καὶ κατ' ἀνάγκην, ὡς ἀλόγων, ἡ σύνερξις, σοφός τις αὐτὰς ἀγελάρχης συνελαύνων ἐπεστάτησεν· εἰ δὲ ἑκουσίως ἐθελουργῆσαι συγκέκλεινται, θαυμάσιός τις αὐτῶν ἀρχιτέκτων ἐργοδοτῶν προηγήσατο· ἢ καθάπερ εὔτακτος στρατηγὸς οὐ συγκεχυμένην εἴασε τὴν στρατιάν, καὶ πάντα ἀναμίξ, ἀλλ' ἐν μέρει μὲν τὴν ἵππον, ἰδίᾳ δὲ τοὺς ὁπλίτας, τούς τε ἀκοντιστὰς καθ' ἑαυτούς, καὶ χωρὶς τοὺς τοξότας καὶ τοὺς σφενδονήτας, ἔνθα ἐχρῆν διετάξατο, ἵνα ἀλλήλοις οἱ ὁμόσκευοι συμμαχοῖεν. εἰ δὲ τοῦτο χλεύην οἴονται τὸ παράδειγμα, διὰ τὸ μεγάλων σωμάτων με πρὸς τὰ ἐλάχιστα ποιεῖσθαι σύγκρισιν, ἐπὶ τὰ σμικρότατα μεταβησόμεθα.

Εἶτα τούτοις ἑξῆς ἐπιλέγει·

(4) Εἰ δὲ μήτε λέξις, μήτε ἐκλογή, μήτε τάξις αὐταῖς ἄρχοντος ἐπικέοιτο, αὐταὶ δὲ ἐφ' ἑαυτῶν αὐτὰς ἐκ τῆς

3 συγκεκλεινται I -ηνται O ‖ αρχιτ. εργοδοτ.] εργοδοτ. αρχιτ. O ‖ 5 συγκεχυμενην] συγκεχωρημενην vulgo ‖ 6 παντα] -ας IO ‖ 8 σφενδονητας] -ιτας Vig ‖ ινα] ιν O ‖ 15 αυτας] εαυτας O

pose,' cf. p. 147: here again ὡς ἀλόγων accounts for the want of purpose, 'as being void of reason.'

2. ἀγελάρχης] either 'the leader of a herd,' or 'the captain of a company,' the former being the more probable meaning here: cf. συναγελάζ. below.

ib. ἑκουσ. ἐθελουργ. συγκέκλ.] 'they have been linked together in order to perform a voluntary work.' Ἑκουσίως ἐθελουργῆσαι is a somewhat pleonastic expression. Συγκλείειν is used of the close array of soldiers with locked shields, but the military metaphor does not seem to begin till ἢ καθάπερ κτλ. and therefore συγκέκλ. probably has no technical sense here.

3. ἀρχιτέκτων ἐργοδοτῶν] 'a master builder who gives out work to be done' (by his men).

5. συγκεχυμένην] 'in confusion':

the older reading συγκεχώρημ. which puzzled the editors has no MS support.

9. οἱ ὁμόσκευοι] 'those who carry the same weapon.'

ib. συμμαχοῖεν] 'may fight side by side,' not 'be allies' as the word is usually to be rendered.

14. *Their answer may be that it is by natural affinity that the atoms combine, and so they conceive of a marvellous kind of democracy at work among them by which the various celestial phenomena are produced.*

ib. Εἰ δὲ μήτε λέξις κτλ.] Here the emphatic word is ἄρχοντος: these atoms have no rulers to speak to them (λέξις) or to choose them (ἐκλογή) or to arrange them (τάξις). Viger renders λέξις by *nomen*, but this is impossible, and 'word' (as Salmond) seems to be the right meaning.

Γ. Περὶ Φύσεως 143

πολλῆς κατὰ ῥύσιν τύρβης διευθύνουσαι, καὶ τὸν πολὺν
τῶν συμπτώσεων διεκπερῶσαι κυδοιμόν, αἱ ὅμοιαι πρὸς
τὰς ὁμοίας οὐχ ὑπὸ τοῦ θεοῦ κατὰ τὸν ποιητὴν ἄγοιντο,
συντρέχοιεν δὲ καὶ συναγελάζοιντο, γνωρίζουσαι τὰς συγ-
γενεῖς, θαυμαστή γε τῶν ἀτόμων ἡ δημοκρατία, δεξιουμένων 5
τε ἀλλήλας τῶν φίλων καὶ περιπλεκομένων, εἰς μίαν τε
κατασκηνοῦν συνοικίαν ἐπειγομένων· καὶ τῶν μὲν ἀποτε-
τορνευμένων αὐτομάτων εἰς ἥλιον ΦωϲΤῆρα ΜέΓαΝ, ἵνα
ποιήσωσι τὴν ἡμέραν, τῶν δὲ εἰς πολλὰς ἴσως πυραμίδας
ἀστέρων ἀναπεφλεγμένων, ἵνα καὶ ὅλον στεφανώσωσι τὸν 10
οὐρανόν, τῶν δὲ περιτεταγμένων, ἵνα αὐτὸν εἰκῆ στερεώ-
σωσι καὶ καμαρώσωσι τὸν αἰθέρα εἰς τὴν τῶν φωστήρων

8 αυτοματον]-ως edd

1. κατὰ ῥύσιν] Cf. διὰ ῥύμην above p. 133 and ὑπὸ τ. συντ. ῥύμης p. 136.
ib. τύρβης] 'mêlée,' 'tumult': the word is connected with θόρυβος and Lat. *turba*; cf. Polyb. i 67 ἦν ἀμιξίας καὶ θορύβου καὶ τῆς λεγομένης τύρβης.
ib. διευθύνουσαι] in the literal sense 'directing,' not as in the περὶ Ἐπαγγελιῶν, pp. 110, 112 and 125.
2. συμπτώσεων] cf. συμπτώματα, p. 134, where see note.
ib. κυδοιμόν] an Homeric word affected by late prose-writers 'din of battle,' 'uproar.'
3. κατὰ τὸν ποιητήν] Hom. *Od.* xvii 218 ὡς αἰεὶ τὸν ὁμοῖον ἄγει θεὸς ὡς τὸν ὁμοῖον, a proverb used by Plat. *Gorg.* 510 B and Arist. *Eth. Nic.* viii 1. 3, ix 1. 6.
4. συναγελάζοιντο] used of both animals and men like ἀγελάρχης above.
7. ἀποτετορνευμένων] 'having rounded themselves off' (as if on a lathe).
8. αὐτομάτων] the adj. instead of the adv. (which the older editors read), as often in Gk.

ib. φωστῆρα μέγαν] Cf. Gen. i 6.
9. τῶν δὲ...ἀναπεφλεγμ.] 'and some likewise lighted up into many pyramids of stars.' 'I fancy that D. is thinking of *Timaeus* 56 B, where Plato supposes the pyramid to be the geometrical form of fire, which is the principal constituent of the bodies of the stars, 40 A.' (H. Jackson.)
10. στεφανώσωσι τὸν οὐρ.] Cf. Hom. *Il.* xviii 485.
11. περιτεταγμένων] 'ranged around' (the sky): *in orbem digestae* (Viger): περιτάσσειν is not given by Liddell and Scott (1890).
ib. ἵνα αὐτὸν...τὸν αἰθέρα|] 'in order that they may—albeit unde- signedly—make the heaven (αὐτόν) firm and form an arch over the atmosphere.' Εἰκῆ is inserted by D. to keep his readers in mind of the absurdity of the Epicurean hypothesis. Στερεώσωσι seems to be a reminiscence of the στερέωμα (firmament) mentioned in Gen. i 6, 7, 8, 14, 15, 17; cf. Is. xlv 12, li 6 (LXX). No doubt the ancients thought the vault of heaven was solid.

ἐπιβάθραν, ἐπιλέξωνταί τε ἑαυταῖς αἱ συνωμοσίαι τῶν χυδαίων ἀτόμων μονάς, καὶ διακληρώσωνται τὸν οὐρανὸν εἰς οἴκους ἑαυταῖς καὶ σταθμούς.

Εἶτα μεθ' ἕτερά φησιν·

5 (5) Ἀλλ' οὐδὲ τὰ φανερὰ ὁρῶσιν οὗτοι οἱ ἀπρονόητοι, πολλοῦ γε δέουσι συνορᾶν καὶ τὰ ἀφανῆ. ἐοίκασι γὰρ μηδὲ ἀνατολὰς ἐποπτεύειν τεταγμένας καὶ δύσεις, μήτε τῶν ἄλλων, μήτε τὰς ἐκπρεπεστάτας ἡλίου· μηδὲ χρῆσθαι ταῖς δι' αὐτῶν δεδωρημέναις ἀνθρώποις ἐπικουρίαις, ἀνα-
10 πτομένῃ μὲν εἰς ἐργασίαν ἡμέρᾳ, ἐπηλυγαζούσῃ δὲ νυκτὶ πρὸς ἀνάπαυλαν. Ἐξελεύσεται γὰρ ἄνθρωπος, φησιν, ἐπὶ τὸ ἔργον αὐτοῦ καὶ ἐπὶ τὴν ἐργασίαν αὐτοῦ ἕως ἑσπέρας.

1 συνωμοσίαι] συνομοσιαι I συνομολογιαι vulgo ‖ 5 ουτοι] αυτοι I ‖ 7 εποπτευειν] υποπτ. I ‖ 9 αναπτομενη O² συναπτομενης O* ανεπομενη I ‖ 10 ημερα O² -ας O* ‖ 11 ανθρωπος φησιν] φησιν ανθρ. O

1. ἐπιβάθραν] lit. 'scaling ladder'; so here of the 'graduated ascent' (Salmond) on which the stars seem to be mounted.

ib. αἱ συνωμοσίαι τῶν χυδαίων ἀτόμ.] 'the confederations of these helter-skelter atoms.' Χυδαίων (fr. χύδην promiscuously) seems used here rather (like εἰκῆ, above) in contrast to συνωμοσίαι than in the sense of 'common,' 'ordinary,' which it sometimes bears: as if D. said, such confused things as atoms are not likely to form confederations and yet that is what the Epicurean theory suggests. The reading συνομολογίαι is the conjecture of some one who did not understand συνωμοσίαι.

5. It is no wonder they fail to account for the invisible parts of creation, when they fail to see even the visible parts to any purpose: the rising and setting of the sun and moon which cause night and day or the succession of the seasons. Atoms cannot produce such effects as these: such atoms would deserve divine honours.

ib. οἱ ἀπρονόητοι] 'the deniers of Divine providence' like the ἄλογοι, ἀκέφαλοι, etc.

6. συνορᾶν] see p. 71 note.

7. ἀνατολὰς ... δύσεις] Epicurus refused to dogmatise about any natural phenomena. Possibly, he said, the sun and the stars may be extinguished at setting and be lighted afresh at rising: it is however equally possible that they may only disappear under the earth and reappear again or that their rising and setting may be due to yet other causes. See Zeller op. cit. p. 436, who quotes Diog. Laert. 88, 92—95. The reading ὑποπτεύειν ('to suspect') is nearly as good as ἐποπτ. ('to consider').

9. ἀναπτ. ... ἡμέρᾳ, ἐπηλυγ. δὲ νυκτί] in apposition to ἐπικουρίαις. The reading ἀναπτομένη is evidently the right one, though it depends only on a correction of O. For ἐπηλυγαζ. cf. p. 77.

11. Ἐξελεύσεται...ἑσπέρας] Ps. ciii (civ) 23.

Γ. Περὶ Φύσεως

ἀλλ' οὐδὲ τὴν ἑτέραν ἐπισκοποῦσιν ἀνακύκλησιν αὐτοῦ,
καθ' ἣν ὡρισμένας ὥρας καὶ καιροὺς εὐκαίρους καὶ τροπὰς
ἀπαρατρέπτους ἀποτελεῖ, ὑπὸ τῶν ἐξ ὧν ἐστὶν ἀτόμων
ὁδηγούμενος. ἀλλὰ κἂν μὴ θέλωσιν οἱ δείλαιοι, ὡς δ'
οὖν πιστεύουσιν οἱ δίκαιοι, Μέγας Κύριος ὁ ποιήσας ἀυτὸν 5
καὶ ἐν λόγοις ἀυτοῦ κατέσπευσε πορείαν. ἄτομοι γὰρ ὑμῖν
χειμῶνα φέρουσιν, ὦ τυφλοί, καὶ ὑετούς, ἵνα ἡ γῆ τροφὰς
ὑμῖν τε καὶ πᾶσι τοῖς ἐπ' αὐτῆς ζῴοις ἀνῇ; θέρος τε
ἄγουσιν, ἵνα καὶ τοὺς ἀπὸ δένδρων εἰς τρυφὴν καρποὺς
λάβητε; καὶ διὰ τί μὴ ταῖς ἀτόμοις προσκυνεῖτε καὶ 10
θύετε ταῖς ἐπικάρποις; ἀχάριστοί γε, μηδὲ ἀπαρχὰς
αὐταῖς ὀλίγας τῶν πολλῶν δωρεῶν, ἃς παρ' αὐτῶν ἔχετε,
ἀφιεροῦντες.

Καὶ μετὰ βραχέα φησίν·

(6) Ὁ δὲ πολυεθνὴς καὶ πολυμιγὴς δῆμος τῶν ἀστέρων, 15

6 κατεσπευσε O² κατεπαυσε O* LXX^{Nc. a} ‖ 8 επ αυτης] επ αυτη I επ αυτοις vulgo ‖ 12 εχετε] -ουσιν IO

1. τὴν ἑτέραν...ἀνακύκλησιν] i.e. the yearly revolution of the sun (as opp. to the daily).
2. τροπὰς ἀπαρατρέπτους] lit. 'turnings which cannot be turned aside,' i.e. the winter and summer solstices, which are regular in their occurrence.
4. ὁδηγούμενος] sc. ὁ ἥλιος. Of course D. is only accepting the Epicureans' view of the sun's composition against themselves.
ib. ἀλλὰ κἂν μὴ θέλ. κτλ.] Routh's translation is probably correct: *Verum quamvis nolint miseri isti, tamen quemadmodum credunt iusti, Magnus est Dominus* etc., although there is no other instance in these extracts of οἱ δίκαιοι meaning 'Christians.' Viger identifies οἱ δείλαιοι with οἱ δίκαιοι and translates: *at enim vero, velint nolint homines reapse miseri, quomodo tamen sibi persuadent aequissimi: Magnus ille Dominus* etc. But D. is not here attacking any ethical doctrine as such a rendering would suggest. For δ' οὖν cf. p. 52.
5. Μέγας Κύριος κτλ.] Ecclus. xliii 5.
10. διὰ τί μή] The negative would of course be οὐ in classical Gk; cf. p. 24.
11. ταῖς ἐπικάρποις] 'the guardians of earth's fruits' (Salmond). This form of the adjective is not given by Liddell and Scott (1890). Dr Jackson suggests that we should read ταῖς ἐπὶ καρποῖς.
13. ἀφιεροῦντες] 'dedicating': usually the middle is used in this sense, cf. Aesch. *Eum.* 451 ταῦτ' ἀφιερώμεθα: but Hesych. gives ἀφιέρωσε· τῷ θεῷ ἀνέθηκε: cf. 4 Macc. xiii 13 ἑαυτοὺς τῷ θεῷ ἀφιερώσομεν. Eus. *H. E.* x 4. 20 and 3. 1 ἀφιερώματα and ἀφιερώσεις occur in the sense of 'offerings.'
15. *Perhaps they think that the stars take their position by mutual*

οὓς αἱ πολυπλανεῖς καὶ ἀεὶ διαρριπτούμεναι συνέστησαν
ἄτομοι, χώρας ἑαυτοῖς κατὰ συνθήκας ἀπεδάσαντο, ὥσπερ
ἀποικίαν ἢ συνοικίαν ἀνελόμενοι, μηδενὸς οἰκιστοῦ μηδὲ
οἰκοδεσπότου προεστηκότος· καὶ τὰς πρὸς τοὺς πλησιοχώ-
5 ρους γειτνιάσεις ἐνωμότως καὶ μετ' εἰρήνης φυλάττουσιν,
οὐχ ὑπερβαίνοντες οὓς κατειλήφασιν ἐξ ἀρχῆς ὅρους,
ὥσπερ ὑπὸ τῶν βασιλίδων ἀτόμων νομοθετούμενοι. ἀλλ'
οὐκ ἄρχουσιν ἐκεῖναι. πῶς γὰρ αἱ μηδ' οὖσαι; ἀλλὰ θείων
λογίων ἐπακούσατε· Ἐν κρίϲει Κυρίου τὰ ἔργα αὐτοῦ ἀπ'
10 ἀρχῆϲ, καὶ ἀπὸ ποιήϲεωϲ αὐτῶν διέϲτειλε μερίδαϲ αὐτῶν·
ἐκόϲμηϲεν εἰϲ αἰῶνα τὰ ἔργα αὐτοῦ, καὶ τὰϲ ἀρχὰϲ αὐτῶν εἰϲ
γενεὰϲ αὐτῶν.

Καὶ μετὰ βραχέα φησίν·

(7) *Ἡ τίς οὕτως εὔτακτος πεδιάδα γῆν διώδευσε
15 φάλαγξ, οὐ προθέοντος οὐδενός, οὐκ ἐκτρεπομένου, οὐκ

5 και μετ] om και O ‖ 6 κατειληφ.] και ειληφ. I pr και O* (reprob O²) ‖
7 ατομων] ατε I ‖ 8 αρχουσιν] αρκουσιν I ‖ μηδ ουσαι] μηδεουσαι I μη δε ουσαι
O ‖ 10 μεριδας αυτων] μερ. αυτου O ‖ 12 γενεας αυτων] εργα αυτου I ‖ 14 ευτακ-
τος] -ως I Vig

compact, but this implies the presence of law among the atoms which they have not.

ib. δῆμος] Cf. δημοκρατία above.

2. κατὰ συνθ. ἀπεδάσαντο] 'have apportioned according to agreements.' Ἀποδατεῖσθαι is an Hom. word adopted by D.

3. συνοικίαν] 'a community' or 'household' (*sodalitas*, Viger) under an οἰκοδεσπότης in contrast to ἀποικία 'a colony' under its οἰκιστής ('founder'). At Athens συνοικία was used of a tenement let out in flats (Lat. *insula*) but that can hardly be the sense here. Possibly D. may have had in his mind the fact that in astrology the star that 'ruled' the οἶκος was called οἰκοδεσπότης.

ib. ἀνελόμενοι] 'setting up for themselves': or perhaps 'choosing,' the compound being used in the sense of the simple verb.

5. γειτνιάσεις] 'nearness of position,' and so here 'duties of neighbourhood,' *viciniae iura* (Viger), 'border laws' (Gifford).

ib. ἐνωμότως] 'according to oath' (i.e. by compact with the other stars): cf. the συνωμοσίαι above, p. 144.

7. τῶν βασιλίδων ἀτόμ.] i.e. as if some of the atoms were regal in power.

8. αἱ μηδ' οὖσαι] See note on p. 77.

9. Ἐν κρίσει...γενεὰς αὐτ.] Ecclus. xvi 26, 27 where BN* read διέστελλε (for διέστειλε). Τὰς ἀρχ. αὐτ. εἰς γεν. αὐτ., i.e. from their beginnings throughout their generations.

14. *They account for the regular courses of the stars, etc. by the side-motions and upward motions of the atoms: but can such disorderly clashings produce such results?*

15. ἐκτρεπομένου] 'falling out (of the ranks).'

Γ. Περὶ Φύσεως

ἐμποδοστατοῦντος, οὐκ ἀπολειπομένου τῶν συμπαρα-
τεταγμένων, ὡς ἰσόστοιχοι καὶ συνασπιδοῦντες ἀεὶ
προΐασιν, ὁ συνεχής τε καὶ ἀδιάστατος ἀόχλητός τε
καὶ ἀνεμπόδιστος τῶν ἄστρων στρατός; ἀλλ' ἐγκλίσεσι
καὶ ταῖς εἰς πλάγιον ἐκνεύσεσι γίνονταί τινες αὐτῶν 5
ἄδηλοι τροπαί. καὶ μὴν ἀεὶ καιροφυλακοῦσι καὶ προ-
ορῶνται τὰς χώρας, ὅθεν ἕκαστος ἄνεισιν, οἱ τούτοις
προσεσχηκότες. εἰπάτωσαν οὖν ἡμῖν οἱ τῶν ἀτόμων
τομεῖς καὶ τῶν ἀμερῶν μερισταὶ καὶ τῶν ἀσυνθέτων
συναγωγεῖς καὶ τὰ ἄπειρα περινοοῦντες, πόθεν ἡ κυκλο- 10
φορικὴ τῶν οὐρανίων συνοδία καὶ περιοδία, οὐχ ἑνὸς
παραλόγως ἀτόμων πήγματος οὕτω σφενδονηθέντος, ἀλλὰ
τοσούτου κυκλικοῦ χοροῦ κατὰ ῥυθμὸν ἴσα βαίνοντος καὶ
συμπεριδινουμένου; πόθεν ἀδιάτακτοι καὶ ἀπροαίρετοι
καὶ ἀγνῶτες ἀλλήλων συνέμποροι παμπληθεῖς συνανε- 15
στράφησαν; καλῶς τε ὁ προφήτης ἐν τοῖς ἀδυνάτοις

1 εμποδοστ.] εμποδιστ. I ‖ 2 ισοστοιχοι] ισοστιχοι O ‖ 5 εκνευσεσι]
νευσεσι I ‖ 6 τροπαι] -οι I ‖ 7 ανεισιν] ανιησι I ‖ 11 και περιοδια] om O om και
tantum I ‖ 13 κυκλικου] κυκλιου I

1. ἐμποδοστατ.] 'obstructing (his comrades' course).'
  ib. τῶν συμπαρατεταγ.] gen. after ἀπολειπ. 'falling behind his comrades.'
4. ἀλλ' ἐγκλίσεσι κτλ.] Ἀλλά, like *at* in Latin, introduces a fresh difficulty raised by D. 'Yet with all this wonderful regularity, we are told that we must allow for certain obscure deviations.' It is answered by καὶ μὴν...προσεσχηκότες. For the terms employed see note on p. 133 above.
10. πόθεν ἡ κυκλοφορικὴ κτλ.] As was said above p. 144, Epicurus held very vague views on these and similar astronomical questions: see Zeller pp. 449 and 450, who quotes the following passages as to his teaching on the rising and setting, the revolution and deviation of the heavenly bodies, Diog. Laert.

92, Lucr. v 509 ff. and Cleomed. *Met*. p. 87.
11. συνοδία καὶ περιοδία] 'a journey round (the heavens) in company.' Συνοδία is a well-attested word for 'a journey in company' or 'a caravan.' Liddell and Scott (1890) quote Epicurus *ap.* Diog. L. x 83 for περιοδία in the sense of 'going through a subject,' 'diligent study.'
  ib. οὐχ ἑνὸς...σφενδονηθέντος] 'not because a single combination of atoms has been without rhyme or reason hurled as if from a sling in this particular way.' Πῆγμα, 'a framework' (Lat. *compages*): cf. 4 Macc. ix 21 τὸ τῶν ὀστέων πῆγμα.
13. χοροῦ] Cf. above χορείαν, p. 138.
14. ἀπροαίρετοι] 'without purpose': cf. p. 142.

καὶ ἀνενδέκτοις ἔταξε τὸ ξένους κἂν δύο συνδραμεῖν·
Εἰ πορεγ́coνταί, φησι, Δγ́ο ἐπὶ τὸ αγ̓τὸ καθόλογ, ἐὰν μὴ
γνωρίcωcιν ἑαγτογ́c;

Ταῦτ' εἰπών, μυρία τε ἄλλα τούτοις ἐπαγαγών, ἑξῆς κατασκευάζει
5 διὰ πλειόνων τὸ πρόβλημα, ἀπό τε τῶν κατὰ μέρος στοιχείων τοῦ
παντός, ἀπό τε τῶν ἐν τούτοις παντοδαπῶν ζῴων, καὶ δὴ καὶ ἀπὸ
τῆς τἀνθρώπου φύσεως. ἐξ ὧν ἔτι βραχέα τοῖς εἰρημένοις προσθεὶς
καταπαύσω τὸν παρόντα λόγον.

'Από τῆς ἀνθρώπου φύσεως.

10 (8) Καὶ οὔτε ἑαυτοὺς οὔτε τὰ περὶ ἑαυτοὺς ὁρῶσιν. εἰ
γάρ τις τῶν ἀρχηγετῶν τοῦ τῆς ἀσεβείας ταύτης δόγματος
ἑαυτὸν ὅστις ἐστὶ καὶ ὅθεν ἀνελογίζετο, ἐφρόνησεν ἂν
ἅπερ συνῃσθημένος ἑαυτοῦ καὶ εἶπεν ἂν οὐ πρὸς τὰς
ἀτόμους ἀλλὰ πρὸς τὸν πατέρα καὶ ποιητὴν αὐτοῦ· Αἱ
15 χεῖρέc coy ἔπλαcάν με καὶ ἐποίηcάν με· καὶ προσεπεξειργά-
σατο ἂν ὡς ἐκεῖνος τὸν θαυμάσιον τῆς ποιήσεως ἑαυτοῦ

1 το ξεν. καν δυο συνδρ.] ους και δυο συνδραμων I || 13 απερ] οπερ I add ο
BIO ωσπερ Vig || και ειπεν...προσκαλεσαμενη om B || 15 προσεπεξειργ.]
προσεπεξεργ. I || 16 ως] om Vig || εαυτου] αυτου O

2. Εἰ πορεύσονται ... ἑαυτούς]
Amos iii 3.
10. *Let them consider the construction of their own bodies. Let Epicurus reflect upon the process of his formation in his mother's womb. Every part of the process whether for utility or for beauty argues Providence, not chance. The head and other parts of the human frame likewise reveal design and purpose. In fine, could a crowd of atoms make the human body? Why, they could not even fashion an earthen figure, or a wooden statue or a metal idol. Yes (Epicurus would say), but figures are produced by human arts and crafts. True, D. replies, then who gave men the mental and spiritual powers that they possess? it surely cannot be the atoms who played the part of the Gods and Muses of Greek legend, if they are unable themselves* (as you acknowledge) *to practise these arts and crafts*.

12. ἐφρόνησεν ἂν...εἶπεν ἄν] 'he would have formed opinions about himself, which when he had perceived, he would also have said,' etc.; for this use of φρονεῖν cf. Acts xxviii 22 ἀξιοῦμεν δὲ παρὰ σοῦ ἀκοῦσαι ἃ φρονεῖς.

14. πατέρα καὶ ποιητήν] Cf. Plato *Timaeus* 28 C.

ib. Αἱ χεῖρες...ἐποίησάν με] Job x 8, where ℵA give the two verbs in the reverse order: cf. Ps. cxviii (cxix) 73.

15. προσεπεξειργ. ἄν] 'he would have gone on to investigate (or work out) thoroughly.' This compound is found in Polybius and Porphyrius, but apparently in a slightly different sense: ἐπεξεργάζεσθαι 'to work at,' 'investigate,' occurs below, p. 151.

16. ὡς ἐκεῖνος] 'as he (viz. Job)

Γ. Περὶ Φύσεως 149

τρόπον· Ἡ οὐχ ὥσπερ γάλα με ἤμελξας, ἐτύρευσας δέ με ἴσα τυρῷ; δέρμα καὶ κρέας με ἐνέδυσας, ὀστέοις δὲ καὶ νεύροις με ἔνειρας· ζωὴν δὲ καὶ ἔλεος ἔθου παρ' ἐμοί, ἡ δὲ ἐπισκοπή σου ἐφύλαξέ μου τὸ πνεῦμα. πόσας γὰρ ἀτόμους ὁ Ἐπι- κούρου πατὴρ καὶ ποταπὰς ἐξ ἑαυτοῦ προέχεεν, ὅτ' ἀπε- 5 σπέρμαινεν Ἐπίκουρον; καὶ πῶς εἰς τὴν μητρῴαν αὐτοῦ καταβληθεῖσαι γαστέρα συνεπάγησαν, ἐσχηματίσθησαν, ἐμορφώθησαν, ἐκινήθησαν, ηὐξήθησαν; καὶ πολλὰς ἡ βραχεῖα ῥανὶς τὰς Ἐπικούρου ἀτόμους προσκαλεσαμένη τὰς μὲν ἐπημφίεσεν αὐτῶν δέρμα καὶ σάρκα γενομένας, 10 ταῖς δὲ ὀστεωθείσαις ἠνώρθωται, ταῖς δὲ συνεδέθη νευ- ρορραφούμενος; τά τε ἄλλα πολλὰ μέλη καὶ σπλάγχνα καὶ ἔγκατα καὶ αἰσθητήρια, τὰ μὲν ἔνδοθεν, τὰ δὲ θύραθεν ἐφήρμοσε, δι' ὧν ἐζωογονήθη τὸ σῶμα; ὧν οὐδὲν ἀργὸν οὐδὲ ἀχρεῖον προσετέθη· ἐπεὶ μηδὲ τὰ φαυλότατα, μήτε 15 τρίχες μήτε ὄνυχες, πάντα δέ, τὰ μὲν πρὸς τὸ τῆς συστά- σεως ὄφελος, τὰ δὲ πρὸς τὸ κάλλος τῆς ὄψεως συντελεῖ.

1 ετυρευσας] -ωσας Vig ‖ 6 αυτου] εαυτου IO ‖ 7 καταβληθεισαι] κατακλη- θεις I κατακλεισθεισαι Vig ‖ 8 ηυξηθησαν correxit Gifford ηυξυνθησαν vulgo ηυξηνθησαν I om O ‖ 10 επημφιεσεν] -αν I επαμφιεσεν BO ‖ αυτων] -ον BIO ‖ 11 ηνωρθωται] ανορθωται I ‖ νευροραφουμενος BIO -ενη edd ‖ 14 εφηρμοσε] -ωσεν I ‖ 17 το καλλος] om το O

did.' The older editions omitted ὡς, which would have made ἐκεῖνος = τις τῶν ἀρχ. mentioned above, although Viger translated it *quemadmodum alter ille*.

1. Ἡ οὐχ ὥσπερ...πνεῦμα] Job x 10—12, where for ἐτύρευσας B reads -ωσας (as Viger here), but A ἔπηξας.

7. καταβληθ.] Cf. εἰς καταβολὴν σπέρμ. Heb. xi 11.

ib. ἐσχηματίσθ. ἐμορφώθ.] The two words are probably here used without scientific accuracy as almost synonymous: but for the philo- sophical distinction between μορφή (the specific character) and σχῆμα (the external shape) see Lightfoot's *Excursus to Phil.* pp. 127—133

and Trench *N. T. Syn.* § xv.

9. ῥανίς] *semen virile*.

11. ἠνώρθωται] Note the double augment here: see Matthiae *Gk Gr.* § 170, who quotes Dem. 329, 2 ἐπηνώρθωται, etc. The subject of ἠνώρθ and συνεδέθη is changed from ῥανίς to Ἐπίκουρος.

ib. νευρορραφ.] lit. 'being stitched with sinews': the verb, which is used of mending shoes with νεῦ- ροι, is here cleverly adapted to its special signification.

14. ὧν οὐδὲν ἀργ. οὐδὲ ἀχρεῖον] D. still persists in showing the evidences of design here as before.

15. μηδὲ τὰ φαυλότατα] sc. ἀργὰ ἢ ἀχρεῖά ἐστι.

16. πρὸς τὸ τ. συστ. ὄφ....συντελεῖ]

οὐ γὰρ τῆς χρείας μόνης, ἀλλὰ καὶ τῆς ὥρας ἐπιμελὴς ἡ
πρόνοια. ἔρυμα μὲν γὰρ καὶ σκέπασμα πάσης τῆς
κεφαλῆς ἡ κόμη, εὐπρέπεια δὲ ὁ πώγων τῷ φιλοσόφῳ.
τήν τε τοῦ ὅλου σώματος τοῦ ἀνθρωπείου φύσιν ἐκ τῶν
5 μερῶν ἀναγκαίων πάντων ἥρμοσε, καὶ τοῖς μέλεσι πᾶσι
τήν τε πρὸς ἄλληλα κοινωνίαν περιέβαλε, καὶ τὴν παρὰ
τοῦ ὅλου χορηγίᴀν ἐπεμέτρησεν. ὧν τὰ μὲν ὁλοσχερῆ
καὶ τοῖς ἰδιώταις ἐκ τῆς πείρας ἣν ἔχει δύναμιν πρόδηλα·
κεφαλῆς ἡγεμονία καὶ περὶ τὸν ἐγκέφαλον ὥσπερ ἄρχοντα

2 πασης] πασι BO ‖ 4 του ανθρ.] om του O ‖ ανθρωπειου] -ιου I ‖
5 ηρμοσε] -ῶσε I

'contribute to the benefit of the fabric, and others to the beauty of the appearance.' Συντελεῖν εἰς was used of classes of ratepayers in classical times: here we have the phrase used metaphorically.

1. οὐ γὰρ τῆς χρείας κτλ.] a really great saying, lifting up Horace's dictum *omne tulit punctum, qui miscuit utile dulci* from earth to heaven. Ὥρα strictly means only the beauty of freshness and vigour, but here it evidently bears a more general sense.

3. ὁ πώγων τῷ φιλοσόφῳ] No doubt this is something of an *argumentum ad hominem*. The philosophers affected beards long after the practice of shaving had come in: hence such proverbs as ἐκ πώγωνος σοφός, πωγωνοτροφία φιλόσοφον οὐ ποιεῖ quoted by Bekker (*Charicles* Exc. iii p. 458). The Emperor Julian wrote a satire, which he called Μισοπώγων, 'an ironical confession of his own faults and a severe satire of the licentious and effeminate manners of Antioch,' the title being an allusion to 'the insolent songs which derided...even the *beard* of the emperor,' Gibbon *Decline and Fall* chap. xxiv.

4. *The parts of the human head* show that there is design and purpose in each.

5. ἀναγκαίων πάντων] 'all of which are necessary': the words contain an argument, which D. proceeds to develope.

ib. τοῖς μέλ....περιέβαλε] 'imposed upon all the limbs the common bond of interdependence.'

6. τὴν παρὰ ... ἐπεμέτρησεν] 'assigned the supply which the whole should contribute.' Cf. Eph. iv 16. This and the last clause balance each other: there is the duty of each to all, the benefit of all to each.

7. ὁλοσχερῆ] 'principal,' 'important'; this is the later meaning of the word (e.g. often in Polybius), the older writers using it in the sense of 'whole,' 'complete.'

9. κεφαλ. ἡγεμ. κτλ.] in rough apposition to τὰ μὲν ὁλοσχ. above.

ib. τὸν ἐγκέφαλον ὥσπερ ἄρχοντα] Cf. Plat. *Phaed.* 96 B, where a similar preeminence is said to be assigned to the brain by some, probably the Pythagoreans: so Diog. Laert. viii 30 εἶναι τὴν ἀρχὴν τῆς ψυχῆς ἀπὸ καρδίας μέχρις ἐγκεφάλου, καὶ τὸ μὲν ἐν τῇ καρδίᾳ μέρος αὐτῆς ὑπάρχειν θυμόν, φρένας δὲ καὶ νοῦν τὰ ἐν τῷ ἐγκεφάλῳ.

Γ. Περὶ Φύσεως

ἐν ἀκροπόλει τῶν αἰσθήσεων ἡ δορυφορία· προιοῦσαι μὲν ὄψεις, ἀναγγέλλουσαι δὲ ἀκοαί, ἐδωδὴ δ' ὥσπερ φορολογοῦσα, ὄσφρησις καθάπερ ἀνιχνεύουσα καὶ διερευνωμένη, καὶ ἁφὴ πᾶν διατάττουσα τὸ ὑπήκοον. (κεφαλαιωδῶς γὰρ νῦν ὀλίγα τῶν τῆς πανσόφου προνοίας ἔργων ἐπιδρα- 5 μούμεθα, μετ' ὀλίγον ἀκριβέστερον τοῦ θεοῦ διδόντος ἐπεξεργασόμενοι, ὅταν πρὸς τὸν δοκοῦντα λογιώτερον ἀποτεινώμεθα.) χειρῶν διακονία, δι' ὧν ἐργασίαι τε παντοῖαι καὶ πολυμήχανοι τελοῦνται τέχναι, ταῖς κατὰ μέρος δυνάμεσιν εἰς μίαν συνεργίαν διηρθρωμένων· ὤμων 10 τε ἀχθοφορίαι, καὶ κατοχαὶ δακτύλων, ἀγκώνων τε καμπαί, πρός τε τὸ σῶμα εἴσω στρεφόμεναι καὶ πρὸς τὸ ἐκτὸς ἀπονεύουσαι, ἵνα ἐφέλκεσθαί τε καὶ ἀπωθεῖσθαι δύνωνται·

1 προιουσαι coniec Vig προσιουσαι vulgo ‖ 2 εδωδη...διερευνωμενη om B ‖ εδωδη] add δ O ‖ 4 αφη] pr η O ‖ παν O² παντα BO* ‖ 5 των] om I ‖ 6 μετ ολιγ....εκτιθεμενη om B ‖ 13 απωθεισθαι] αποθ. I

1. *ἐν ἀκροπόλει*] Cf. Plato *Timaeus* 70 A and Cic. *De Nat. Deor.* ii 56 *in capite tamquam in arce.* 'For the words ἀκρόπολις and δορυφορία in this connexion cf. also Plato *Rep.* 560 B, 573 E, and 587 C: but the parallels are not exact.' (H. Jackson.)

ib. προιοῦσαι] Viger's conjecture ('acting as advance-guard') is adopted by Dr Gifford and seems to suit the sense better than προσιοῦσαι, 'encountering objects': cf. Cic. *op. cit. oculi tanquam speculatores.*

2. *ἐδωδὴ ὥσπ. φορολογ.*] 'the taste which is, as it were, the tribute-gatherer' (Salmond); but perhaps ἐδωδή (usually 'food') should rather be translated 'the organs of eating' here.

4. *πᾶν...τὸ ὑπήκοον*] 'all that comes under its command': the phrase is adopted from a regular Thucydidean use.

7. *ἐπεξεργ.*] See above προσεπεξεργ.

ib. τὸν δοκοῦντα λογιώτερον] Dittrich (p. 13) thinks that some Stoic philosopher is referred to.

Epicurus was, as Routh says, considered to be *indisertus*: he despised learning (see Cic. *de Fin.* i 21. 71, ii 4. 12). For the Stoic view of God's Providence see Zeller *op. cit.* pp. 149 ff. and the authorities there quoted, e.g. Chrysippus, ὅτι δ' ἡ κοινὴ φύσις καὶ ὁ κοινὸς τῆς φύσεως λόγος εἱμαρμένη καὶ πρόνοια καὶ Ζεύς ἐστιν οὐδὲ τοὺς ἀντίποδας λέληθε· πανταχοῦ γὰρ ταῦτα θρυλεῖται ἀπ' αὐτῶν.

8. *ἀποτεινώμεθα*] · 'deal at length,' or perhaps simply 'proceed to deal.'

ib. χειρῶν...διηρθρωμένων] 'the service of the hands which are articulated and endued with powers in every part with a view to mutual cooperation.'

11. *κατοχαὶ δακτ.*] 'the grasping powers of the fingers.'

ib. ἀγκ. καμπαί] 'the bendings of the arms': ἀγκών is itself the 'bent arm' or the 'elbow,' and Liddell and Scott quote examples of this particular phrase from Aristotle and Hippocrates.

ποδῶν ὑπηρεσία, δι' ὧν πᾶσα ἡμῖν ὑποπέπτωκεν ἡ
περίγειος κτίσις, βάσιμος ἡ γῆ, πλωτὴ ἡ θάλασσα,
περάσιμοι οἱ ποταμοί, καὶ πάντων πρὸς πάντα ἐπιμιξία·
γαστὴρ ταμιεῖον τροφῶν, πᾶσι τοῖς συντεταγμένοις μέλεσιν
5 ἐξ ἑαυτῆς ἐν μέτρῳ τὸ σιτηρέσιον διανέμουσα, καὶ τὸ
περιττεῦον ἐκτιθεμένη· καὶ τὰ ἄλλα δι' ὅσων ἐμφανῶς
ἡ διοίκησις τῆς ἀνθρωπείου μεμηχάνηται διαμονῆς, ὧν
ὁμοίως τοῖς ἄφροσιν ἔχοντες οἱ σοφοὶ τὴν χρῆσιν οὐκ
ἴσχουσι τὴν γνῶσιν. οἱ μὲν γὰρ εἰς ἣν ἂν οἰηθῶσιν
10 θεότητα τὴν ἐπιστημονικωτάτην περὶ πάντων καὶ τὴν
εἰς ἑαυτοὺς εὐεργετικωτάτην ἀναφέρουσιν οἰκονομίαν,
κρείττονος καὶ θείας ὄντως φρονήσεώς τε καὶ δυνάμεως

3 παντα] pr τα I παντας O ‖ επιμιξια] -ιαι I ‖ 4 ταμιειον] ταμεια O ‖
7 ανθρωπειου] -ιου I ‖ διαμονης] διανομης vulgo ‖ 8 χρησιν] κρισιν vulgo ‖
10 θεοτητα] coniec Vig approb Routh ἀθεότητα MSS ‖ την εις εαυτ.] om την
I ‖ 11 εις εαυτους] εις αυτους G εις εα periit sed υ manet in O

3. πάντων πρὸς πάντα ἐπιμιξία]
This is generally taken as coordinate
with the other clauses under the
relative δι' ὧν ('the general intercourse of mankind,' as in Greg.
Naz. *Theol. Or.* ii 27, p. 64 Mason),
but the absence of the article (ἡ)
and the neuter πάντων πρὸς πάντα
make it probable that the phrase is
coordinate with ποδῶν ὑπηρεσία and
that it means 'the intercourse (so
to speak) of all the parts of the body
(μέρη or μέλη) with one another,'
and introduces therefore a fresh
thought.

5. τὸ σιτηρέσιον] Cf. note on
p. 89.

7. διαμονῆς] is now established
as the right reading. Viger, who
first suggested it, well renders the
phrase thus: *quorum vi humanae
firmitatis et conservationis ratio
continetur*; cf. p. 140 τῆς περὶ τὴν
διαμονὴν διαφορᾶς.

ib. ὧν ὁμοίως...ἀνατιθέασι] We
all alike have the use of this body of
ours whether we attribute its crea-

tion to the true cause or not.

8. τοῖς ἄφροσιν...οἱ σοφοί] 'the
foolish' (like us Christians)...'the
wise' (like the Epicureans): of
course the epithets are sarcastically
applied.

ib. χρῆσιν] is again a reading
which, first proposed by Viger, is
now proved correct.

ib. οὐκ ἴσχουσι] with οὐκ here
ὁμοίως must be supplied.

10. θεότητα] Yet another conjecture of Viger's, which is almost
certainly right ('godhead, whatever their notions of godhead may
be'). The attempts, which have
been made to extract sense from
ἀθεότητα, are not successful (e.g.
that the subject of οἰηθῶσιν is οἱ
Ἐπικούρειοι not οἱ μέν, or that the
clause κρείττονος ... πιστούμενοι is
closely connected with ἣν ἂν οἰηθ.
ἀθεότ. 'some power which they
deem indeed to be no divinity,
though they believe it to be the
work of a wisdom and power which
is higher and truly divine').

Γ. Περὶ Φύσεως

ἔργον αὐτὴν εἶναι πιστούμενοι· οἱ δὲ συντυχίᾳ καὶ συμπτώσει τῶν ἀτόμων ἀσκόπως τὴν θαυμασιωτάτην καλλιεργίαν ἀνατιθέασι. τὴν δὲ ἐναργεστέραν ἔτι τούτων ἐπίσκεψιν καὶ τὴν τῶν ἐνδοσθίων διάθεσιν ἰατροὶ μὲν ἀκριβῶς διερευνησάμενοι, καὶ καταπλαγέντες, ἐξεθείασαν 5 τὴν φύσιν· ἡμεῖς δὲ ὕστερον, ὡς ἂν οἷοί τε γενώμεθα, κἂν ἐπιπολῆς ἀναθεωρήσομεν. καθόλου δὲ καὶ συλλήβδην, ὅλον τοῦτο τὸ σκῆνος τίς τοιοῦτον ἐσκηνοποίησεν ὑψηλόν, ὄρθιον, εὔρυθμον, εὐαίσθητον, εὐκίνητον, εὐεργόν, παντουργόν; ἡ τῶν ἀτόμων ἄλογός, φασι, πληθύς. ἀλλ' 10 οὐδ' ἂν εἰκόνα πηλίνην ἐκεῖναι συνελθοῦσαι πλάσαιεν, οὐδ' ἀνδριάντα λίθινον ξέσαιεν, οὐδ' ἂν εἴδωλον ἀργυροῦν ἢ χρυσοῦν χωνεύσασαι προαγάγοιεν. ἀλλὰ τέχναι καὶ χειρουργίαι τούτων ὑπ' ἀνθρώπων εὕρηνται σωματουργοί.

5 εξεθειασαν] εξεθιασαν I || 7 επιπολης] επι πολης I επι πολλης O || αναθεωρησομεν Vig -σωμεν codd || καθολου δε] καθ. τε BO || 9 ορθιον] ορθριον I ορθον O || παντουργον] πανουργον I || 13 προαγαγ.] προσαγαγ. Vig

1. συμπτώσει] See above p. 134.
2. ἀσκόπως] The word may be from σκοπεῖν ('heedlessly') or from σκοπός ('aimlessly'), but probably the former sense is meant, as the adv. qualifies ἀνατιθέασι, of course not συντ. καὶ συμπτ. τῶν ἀτόμων.
4. ἐπίσκεψιν] Supply ποιησάμενοι or the like from διερευνησ. which properly only goes with διάθεσιν, or possibly there is a kind of zeugma, ἐπισκ. being a sort of cognate accus. after διευρ.
ib. ἐνδοσθίων] This form is found in Ecclus. ix 9, and is given by Hesych.; the usual form is ἐντόσθια.
ib. ἰατροὶ...ἐξεθείσας. τ. φύσ.] It is not clear who these are.
6. ὕστερον] 'in another part of this treatise,' according to Dittrich op. cit. p. 13.
7. ἐπιπολῆς] There is nothing to be said for Viger's emendation ἐπὶ πολλοῖς (sc. λόγοις).

ib. ἀναθεωρήσ.] 'we will review (their theory)'; the object has to be supplied from the ἐπίσκεψιν and διάθεσιν of the last sentence.
8. σκῆνος] This form of the word is found in 1 Cor. v 1, Wisd. ix 15. 'It also has plenty of classical authority, especially for the body as tabernacle of the soul: see Liddell and Scott s.v.' (H. Jackson.)
9. παντουργόν] 'adapted to all purposes': cf. Soph. Ai. 445 φωτὶ παντουργῷ φρένας.
13. ἀλλὰ τέχναι...σωματ.] 'but arts and handicrafts for the production of such bodies have been invented by men.' Τούτων (neut. pl.) must be taken with σωματουργαί (for which the old reading was σωματουργῶν agreeing with ἀνθρ.). The adj. σωματουργός (here used not of living bodies but their imitations) is not given by Liddell and Scott.

154 DIONYSIUS OF ALEXANDRIA

ὧν δὲ ἀπεικασίαι καὶ σκιαγραφίαι δίχα σοφίας οὐκ ἂν
γένοιντο, πῶς τὰ ἀληθῆ καὶ πρωτότυπα τούτων αὐτομάτως
συμβέβηκε; ψυχὴ δὲ καὶ νοῦς καὶ λόγος πόθεν ἐγγέγονε
τῷ φιλοσόφῳ; ἢ παρὰ τῶν ἀψύχων καὶ ἀνοήτων καὶ
5 ἀλογίστων ἀτόμων ταῦτ' ἠρανίσατο; κἀκείνων αὐτῷ τί
ἑκάστη νόημα καὶ δόγμα ἐνέπνευσε; καὶ ὥσπερ ὁ Ἡσιόδου
μῦθος τὴν Πανδώραν φησὶν ὑπὸ τῶν θεῶν, οὕτως ἡ σοφία
τἀνδρὸς ὑπὸ τῶν ἀτόμων συνετελέσθη; καὶ ποίησιν δὲ
πᾶσαν, καὶ πᾶσαν μουσικήν, ἀστρονομίαν τε καὶ γεω-
10 μετρίαν καὶ τὰς ἄλλας ἐπιστήμας, οὐκέτι θεῶν εὑρήματα
καὶ παιδεύματα φήσουσιν Ἕλληνες εἶναι, μόναι δὲ γεγόνασιν ἐμπειρικαὶ καὶ σοφαὶ πάντων αἱ ἄτομοι Μοῦσαι;

1 ων δε...ενεπνευσε] om B ∥ σκιαγραφιαι] σκιογρ. IO ∥ 4 η παρα] om
η IO ∥ 6 ο Ησιοδου] om ο BO ∥ 10 ευρηματα] ευρεμ. BI ∥ 11 και παιδευματα]
om I ∥ μοναι] -οι I ∥ 12 εμπειρικαι] -οι I εμπειροι BO ∥ σοφαι] -οι I

2. τὰ ἀληθῆ καὶ πρωτότυπα] i.e.
the living bodies themselves.
3. συμβέβηκε] See note on p.
134.
ib. ψυχή] See p. 139.
5. ἀλογίστων] 'irrational,' 'un-
calculating,' almost equivalent to
ἄλογος above.
ib. ἠρανίσατο] sc. ὁ φιλόσοφος:
'did he borrow' (or 'procure')?
The metaphor is taken from the
practice of making a collection
(ἔρανος) for a man who had fallen
into adversity: see Becker *Charicles*
p. 40 n. and the authorities there
quoted.
ib. κἀκείνων] sc. τῶν ἀτόμων.
ib. τί ἐκ. νόημ. κ. δόγμ.] The
editors read τι here, but τί makes
better sense and the order of words
suggests it.
6. ὁ Ἡσιόδου μῦθος] The reference is to Ἔργ. κ. Ἡμ. 54—82 and
Θεογ. 570 foll. The well-known
story is that by order of Zeus
Hephaestus made a woman (Pandora) out of earth, and each of the
gods bestowed on her some special
gift or power by which she should

work ruin among men, in revenge
for Prometheus having stolen fire
from heaven.
10. θεῶν εὑρήμ. κ. παιδεύμ.] The
Muses, who were connected with the
arts and sciences, being daughters
of Zeus (or some other god), the
Greeks considered both their origin
and conveyance to man divine, and
the Stoics, in their allegorizing way,
accepted the view, holding definitely that the Muses represented the divine
origin of all culture: see Zeller *op.
cit.* p. 365. 'The philosophical
schools (and, I think, other scholas-
tic establishments) were in the eye
of the law religious foundations
(θίασοι) for the worship of the Muses,
and accordingly they had each a
Μουσεῖον or chapel dedicated to
those divinities. The Muses were
therefore in a special sense the
deities of philosophers.' (H. Jackson.)
12. πάντων] neut. after ἐμπ. κ.
σοφ. 'skilled and wise in all subjects': σοφός is sometimes used
with a genitive, e.g. Aesch. *Suppl.*
453 κακῶν σοφός.

Γ. Περὶ Φύσεως 155

ἡ γὰρ ἐκ τῶν ἀτόμων Ἐπικούρου θεογονία τῶν μὲν
ἀπείρων κόσμων ἐξόριός ἐστιν, εἰς δὲ τὴν ἄπειρον ἀκοσμίαν
πεφυγάδευται.

Ὅτι οὐκ ἐπίπονον τῷ θεῷ τὸ ἐργάζεσθαι.

(9) Ἐργάζεσθαι δέ γε καὶ διοικεῖν καὶ εὐεργετεῖν τε καὶ 5
προκήδεσθαι καὶ τὰ τοιαῦτα τοῖς μὲν ἀργοῖς καὶ ἄφροσι
καὶ ἀσθενέσι καὶ κακούργοις ἴσως ἐπαχθῆ, οἷς ἐγκατέλεξεν
ἑαυτὸν Ἐπίκουρος, τοιαῦτα φρονήσας περὶ τῶν θεῶν· τοῖς
δὲ σπουδαίοις καὶ δυνατοῖς καὶ συνετοῖς καὶ σώφροσιν,
οἵους εἶναι χρὴ τοὺς φιλοσόφους (πόσῳ γε μᾶλλον τοὺς 10
θεούς;), οὐχ ὅπως ἀηδῆ ταῦτα καὶ προσάντη ἀλλὰ καὶ
τερπνότατα καὶ πάντων μᾶλλον ἀσπαστότατα, οἷς τὸ

1 η γαρ] om γαρ I ‖ Επικουρου] -οι I ‖ 2 εξοριος] εξορος Vig ‖ 5 εργαζ.
δε] om δε BO ‖ γε] τε I ‖ 7 και ασθενεσι] om O ‖ 9 και δυνατ.] post και
συνετ. O

1. Ἐπικ. θεογονία] The gods of Epicurus seem to have been created or at least material beings like men, but unlike them immortal and perfectly happy, with bodies analogous to our bodies, ethereal and consisting of the finest atoms: cf. Lucr. v 148, 9 *tenvis enim natura deum longeque remota Sensibus ab nostris*. See Zeller p. 467.

ib. τῶν μὲν ἀπείρων...πεφυγάδ.] 'has indeed (by their theory) been put outside the bounds of their infinite worlds, but (in consequence) is banished to this infinite disorder of theirs.' It is impossible to reproduce the play on κόσμων and ἀκοσμίαν. Epicurus held that the gods had no concern in mundane affairs, but, D. argues, this in conjunction with his other theories makes 'confusion worse confounded.' For ἀπείρων κόσμ. cf. p. 133 κόσμ. ἀπείρ. ἀποτελεῖν.

5. *The truth is that Epicurus has read his own inherent idleness and dislike of exertion into the nature of the Gods as he has pictured them.*

Whereas even Hesiod, let alone the Bible, has shown us that strenuousness and a desire to attain perfection are to be preferred to all temporal advantages. Democritus himself half realized this when he said he would rather discover a single cause than gain the kingdom of Persia: and yet he displayed the strangest inconsistency in asserting that Τύχη *was supreme in all matters but allowing it no place in the affairs of men. For Democritus begins his book entitled* Ὑποθῆκαι *with the statement that men's idea of* Τύχη *is an idle fiction and that* Γνώμη (*judgement*) *overrules* Τύχη. *Practical minded folk seek their pleasure in works of practical beneficence, and philosophers seek it in instructing their fellows in the truth. How then can Epic. and Dem. venture to say that the gods exist at all, if they do not think they take any practical part in the management of the world?*

11. οὐχ ὅπως] 'not only not,' see p. 114.

ἀμελὲς καὶ τὸ μέλλειν τι πράττειν τῶν χρηστῶν ὄνειδος,
ὡς ἐκείνους τε ποιητὴς νουθετεῖ συμβουλεύων,
" μηδ' ἀναβάλλεσθαι ἐς τ' αὔριον,"
καὶ προσεπαπειλῶν,
5 " αἰεὶ δ' ἀμβολιεργὸς ἀνὴρ ἄτῃσι παλαίει."
ἡμᾶς τε σεμνότερον παιδεύει προφήτης, θεοπρεπῆ μὲν
ὄντως ἔργα τὰ κατ' ἀρετὴν ὑπάρχειν λέγων, τὸν δὲ ὀλι-
γωροῦντα τούτων ἐξάγιστον. Ἐπικατάρατος γάρ, φησίν,
ὁ ποιῶν τὰ ἔργα Κυρίου ἀμελῶς. εἶτα καὶ τοῖς μὲν ἀμαθέσιν
10 ἡστινοσοῦν τέχνης, καὶ ἀτελεστέροις διὰ τὸ τῆς πείρας
ἄηθες καὶ τὸ τῶν ἔργων ἀτριβές, κάματος ἐγγίνεται ταῖς
ἐπιχειρήσεσιν· οἱ δὲ προκόπτοντες, καὶ μᾶλλον ἔτι οἱ
τέλειοι, ῥᾳδίως ἃ μετίασι κατορθοῦντες γάννυνται, καὶ
μᾶλλον ἂν ἕλοιντο τὰ εἰωθότα πράττοντες ἀνύειν καὶ
15 τελεσιουργεῖν ἢ πάντα σφίσιν ὑπάρξαι τὰ ἐν ἀνθρώποις
ἀγαθά. Δημόκριτος γοῦν αὐτός, ὥς φασιν, ἔλεγε βούλεσθαι

2 εκεινους] -ον I ‖ 3 ες τ] εις I Vig ‖ 5 αιει δ...αποκηρυττων βιου] om B ‖ αμβολιεργος] αμβολιοεργος I ‖ 7 λεγων] -ειν I ‖ 8 τουτων] -ω I ‖ φησιν] om I Vig ‖ 9 τοις μεν] om μεν Holl ‖ 10 ατελεστεροις] διατελ. Holl ‖ 11 αηθες] αειθες Holl ‖ εργων] -ον I ‖ καματος] καμινος O ‖ 12 ετι οι] αιτιοι I ‖ 13 μετιασι] μετεισι Holl

1. μέλλειν τι πράττειν] 'delay in doing something,' the pres. inf. being the usual construction with μέλλειν in this sense.
2. ἐκείνους τε] sc. the heathen, to whom the poets were to some extent what the Bible is to us: to these are opposed ἡμᾶς τε (viz. the Christians) in the next sentence.
3. μηδ' ἀναβάλλ. κτλ.] Hes. Ἔργ. κ. Ἡμ. 408.
5. αἰεὶ δ' κτλ.] ibid. 411.
7. κατ' ἀρετήν] 'according to the standard of virtue'; the phrase is a reminiscence of Arist. Nic. Eth. passim.
8. ἐξάγιστον] 'accursed': cf. p. 73.
ib. Ἐπικατάρατος κτλ.] Jer. xlviii (xxxi) 10.
9. τοῖς μὲν ... γάννυνται] given

with one or two variants in Holl Fragmente 361 p. 147 from Cod. Vat. 1553.
12. οἱ τέλειοι] 'those who have reached perfection' in a general sense. For a special meaning of the phrase see p. 68.
13. γάννυνται] often spelt γάνυντ. 'are cheered.'
15. τελεσιουργεῖν] 'to bring to perfection,' 'accomplish': cf. Prov. xix 4 (7) ὁ πολλὰ κακοποιῶν τελεσιουργεῖ κακίαν.
16. Δημόκριτος ... ἔλεγε] The 'happiness of the king of Persia' was proverbial. Compare Hor. Od. ii 12. 21, iii 9. 4. In line 1 (p. 157) οἱ = sibi. Αἰτιολογίαν: cf. Eus. H. E. iv 29. 3 τῇ δὲ τοῦ Ἀδὰμ σωτηρίᾳ παρ' ἑαυτοῦ τὴν αἰτιολογίαν ποιησάμενος.

Γ. Περὶ Φύσεως 157

μᾶλλον μίαν εὑρεῖν αἰτιολογίαν ἢ τὴν τῶν Περσῶν οἱ
βασιλείαν γενέσθαι· καὶ ταῦτα μάτην καὶ ἀναιτίως
αἰτιολογῶν, ὡς ἂν ἀπὸ κενῆς ἀρχῆς καὶ ὑποθέσεως
πλανωμένης ὁρμώμενος, καὶ τὴν ῥίζαν καὶ τὴν κοινὴν
ἀνάγκην τῆς τῶν ὄντων φύσεως οὐχ ὁρῶν, σοφίαν δὲ 5
μεγίστην ἡγούμενος τὴν τῶν ἀσόφως καὶ ἠλιθίως συμβαινόντων κατανόησιν, καὶ τὴν τύχην τῶν μὲν καθόλου
καὶ τῶν θείων δέσποιναν ἐφιστὰς καὶ βασιλίδα, καὶ
πάντα γενέσθαι κατ᾽ αὐτὴν ἀποφαινόμενος, τοῦ δὲ τῶν
ἀνθρώπων αὐτὴν ἀποκηρύττων βίου, καὶ τοὺς πρεσβεύον- 10
τας αὐτὴν ἐλέγχων ἀγνώμονας. τῶν γοῦν Ὑποθηκῶν
ἀρχόμενος λέγει· Ἄνθρωποι τύχης εἴδωλον ἐπλάσαντο,
πρόφασιν ἰδίης ἀνοίας· φύσει γὰρ γνώμη τύχῃ μάχεται·
καὶ τὴν ἐχθίστην τῇ φρονήσει ταύτην αὐτὴν ἔφασαν

1 αιτιολογιαν] αποΛ. I ‖ την] om O ‖ των Π.] om των I ‖ 3 ως αν] om
αν IO ‖ 8 εφιστας] επιστας I ‖ 13 ανοιας] -ης BO ‖ γνωμη τυχῃ] γνωμη τυχη
coniec Routh

4. τὴν κοινὴν ἀνάγκην] It is
obvious that D. only uses this expression to describe the supreme
will and purpose of God in contradistinction to the Epicurean theory
of chance and not as a fatalist: cf.
1 Cor. ix 16, etc.

6. τῶν ... συμβαινόντων] See
above.

7. τὴν τύχην...δέσπ....κ. βασιλ.]
Cf. Lucr. v 77 *fortuna gubernans*,
and vi 31 *seu casu seu vi quod sic
natura parasset*. For βασιλίδα cf.
p. 146.

ib. τῶν μὲν καθόλου καὶ τῶν
θείων] 'of things universal and
(even) of things divine,' corresponds
to τοῦ δὲ...ἀποκηρ. βίου 'and yet
warning her off from matters of
human life and conduct.'

11. τῶν ... Ὑποθηκῶν] ' Suggestions' or 'Precepts.' The title
is not included in the list of
Democritus's works, but may be the
same as his Ὑπομνήματα ἠθικά. For
the quotation see Stob. *Ecl. Eth.*
ii c. 7, p. 345, Democr. *Ethical
Fragments*, l. 14 (Mullach i p. 340).

12. τύχης εἴδωλον] 'the figure of
Chance.' Though εἴδωλον is not
here used in a technical sense, yet
we may note in passing that Democritus formulated a theory of εἴδωλα
which was adopted by Epicurus;
see Zeller *op. cit.* pp. 457, 8, and
cf. Lucr. iv 42 ff. *Dico igitur rerum
effigies tenuisque figuras Mittier ab
rebus summo de corpore rerum...
speciem ac formam similem gerit eius
imago Cuius cumque cluet de corpore
fusa vagari.*

13. γνώμη τύχῃ] Routh's conjecture γνώμη τύχη seems probable,
because τύχη is the subject of the
passage not γνώμη. For the sentiment Viger appositely quotes Cic.
pro Marc. § 7 *numquam temeritas
cum sapientia commiscetur nec ad
consilium casus admittitur.*

14. ταύτην αὐτὴν ἔφασαν] The
quotation is usually considered to
end at τὴν τύχην, in which case the

κρατεῖν· μᾶλλον δὲ καὶ ταύτην ἄρδην ἀναιροῦντες καὶ
ἀφανίζοντες ἐκείνην ἀντικαθιστᾶσιν αὐτῆς. οὐ γὰρ εὐτυχῆ
τὴν φρόνησιν, ἀλλ' ἐμφρονεστάτην ὑμνοῦσι τὴν τύχην.
οἱ μὲν οὖν τῶν βιωφελῶν ἔργων ἐπιστάται ταῖς πρὸς τὸ
5 ὁμόφυλον ἐπικουρίαις ἀγάλλονται, ἐπαίνου τε ὀρέγονται
καὶ κλέους ἐφ' οἷς αὐτῶν προκάμνουσιν, οἱ μὲν τρέφοντες,
οἱ δὲ κυβερνῶντες, οἱ δ' ἰώμενοι, οἱ δὲ πολιτευόμενοι· οἱ δέ
γε φιλόσοφοι καὶ σφόδρα παιδεύειν ἐπιχειροῦντες ἀνθρώπους φρυάττονται. ἢ τολμήσουσιν Ἐπίκουρος ἢ Δημό-
10 κριτος εἰπεῖν, ὡς ἀσχάλλουσι φιλοσοφοῦντες; ἀλλ' οὐδὲ
θυμηδίαν ταύτης ἂν ἑτέραν προθεῖντο. καὶ γὰρ εἰ τὸ
ἀγαθὸν ἡδονὴν εἶναι φρονοῦσιν, ἀλλ' αἰδεσθήσονταί γε μὴ

3 εμφρον.] φρο periit in O εμφανεστατην G ‖ 4 οι μεν ουν...πολιτευομενοι
om B ‖ βιωφελων] βιοφ. I ‖ 5 επαινου τε] επαινουνται I ‖ 6 αυτων] αυτοι
coniec Routh ‖ 9 η τολμ....φιλοσοφουντες om B ‖ τολμησουσιν] -ατωσαν O ‖
10 ασχαλλ.] ασχαλ. I ‖ 11 προθεινητο] προσθοιντο I

subject of ἔφασαν, ἀντικαθιστᾶσιν
and ὑμνοῦσι is 'men in general';
but it is possible that the quotation
ends at μάχεται and in that case the
subject of the verbs will be 'the
Epicureans.' It makes little difference whether ταύτην represents
τύχην and αὐτήν represents φρόνησιν or vice versa. 'Men (or the
Epicureans) have said that this
(chance) which is the greatest
enemy of intelligence yet has the
mastery over it.' Κρατεῖν is used
with the accus. as well as with the
gen. (and dat.).

1. ἄρδην] 'utterly': from αἴρειν
and so lit. 'by lifting up bodily.'

3. ὑμνοῦσι τὴν τύχην] We may
compare Soph. O. T. 977—9 Τί δ'
ἂν φοβοῖτ' ἄνθρωπος ᾧ τὰ τῆς τύχης
Κρατεῖ, πρόνοια δ' ἐστὶν οὐδενὸς
σαφής; Εἰκῇ κράτιστον ζῆν ὅπως δύ-
ναιτό τις, and Eur. Alc. 785—9
Τὸ τῆς τύχης γὰρ ἀφανὲς οἷ προ-
βήσεται, Κἄστ' οὐ διδακτόν, οὐδ'
ἁλίσκεται τέχνῃ... Εὔφραινε σαυτόν,
πῖνε, τὸν καθ' ἡμέραν Βίον λογίζου
σόν, τὰ δ' ἄλλα τῆς τύχης.

4. ταῖς πρὸς τὸ ὁμόφ. ἐπικ.]
'measures which advance the interests of their kind.'

6. ἐφ' οἷς] = ἐπὶ τούτοις ἅ, 'for
their labours on behalf of others.'
αὐτῶν (gen. aft. προκάμν.) sc. τῶν
ὁμοφύλων or the like.

ib. τρέφοντες] 'purveyors of ways
and means' (Salmond), but 'rearers
(of families)' is better.

9. φρυάττονται] properly of
horses, 'to neigh and prance,' hence
of men 'to give themselves airs.'
'Yes, and our philosophers plume
themselves greatly on their efforts
to instruct mankind.'

10. ἀσχάλλουσι] 'vex themselves,'
opp. to φρυάττονται above.

ib. ἀλλ' οὐδὲ θυμηδίαν ... προ-
θεῖντο] 'nay, they could not consider any pleasure preferable to
this' (i.e. the pleasure of philo-
sophizing).

11. τὸ ἀγαθὸν ἡδονὴν εἶναι] 'The
only unconditional good, according
to Epicurus, is pleasure... In calling
pleasure the highest object in life
we do not mean...sensual enjoy-

Γ. Περὶ Φύσεως 159

λέγειν ἥδιον αὐτοῖς εἶναι τὸ φιλοσοφεῖν. τοὺς δὲ θεούς,
περὶ ὧν οἱ μὲν ποιηταὶ παρ' αὐτοῖς ᾄδουσι 'δωτῆρας ἐάων,'
οὗτοι δὲ οἱ φιλόσοφοι μετὰ τωθείας εὐφημοῦσι, θεοὶ
πάντων ἀγαθῶν ἀδώρητοί τε καὶ ἀμέτοχοι. καὶ τίνι
τρόπῳ τεκμηριοῦνται θεοὺς εἶναι, μήτε παρόντας καὶ 5
πράττοντάς τι ὁρῶντες (ὡς οἱ τὸν ἥλιον καὶ τὴν σελήνην
καὶ τοὺς ἀστέρας θαυμάσαντες διὰ τὸ θέειν ἔφασαν
κεκλῆσθαι θεούς), μήτε τινὰ δημιουργίαν αὐτοῖς ἢ κατα-
σκευὴν προσνέμοντες, ἵν' ἐκ τοῦ θεῖναι, τοῦτ' ἔστι ποιῆσαι,
θεοποιήσωσιν αὐτούς (τούτου γὰρ ἕνεκα πρὸς ἀλήθειαν ὁ 10

1 ηδιον] ιδιον I || αὐτοις IO αὐτοις vulgo || το φιλοσοφ.] τι του φιλοσ.
BO || 2 περι ων...θαυμασαντες] om B || δωτηρας] δοτ. O || 3 τωθειας] -ιας I ||
4 αδωρητοι τε] om τε I Vig || 6 οἱ Dind vulgo οἵ οσοι O || 7 θεειν] θειν I ||
9 ιν εκ...εξωγραφ. σκιας] om B || 10 ενεκα] ·εν I

ments at all, but the freedom of
the body from pain and the freedom
of the soul from disturbance (ἀτα-
ραξία)... The root from which it
springs and therefore the highest
good is intelligence.' Zeller pp.
473 and 476, but see also pp.
478 foll. for other admissions of
Epicurus.
1. ἥδιον] 'a higher form of
pleasure': the reading is one of
Viger's many conjectures now
proved correct: the older reading
being ἡδὺ ὄν. D. appears to understand ἡδονήν in the ordinary sense
without giving Epicurus credit for
his refinements, and to mean that
even Epic. would say that τὸ φιλοσοφεῖν was ἥδιον (τῆς ἡδονῆς). The
play on the words is quite in his
manner.
ib. τοὺς δὲ θεούς] The accus. is
governed by εὐφημοῦσιν, but the
construction is a little confused
through D.'s loose use of μέν and
δέ.
2. δωτῆρας ἐάων] 'givers of good
gifts,' an Homeric phrase, e.g. Od.
viii 325 and 335.
3. τωθείας] 'scoffing' from τωθά-
ζειν, a curious form for τωθασμός.

ib. εὐφημοῦσι] 'sing their praises,'
said sarcastically.
4. ἀδώρητοι] sc. εἰσί: here act.,
opp. to δωτ. ἐάων. See Zeller
pp. 467 and 8. The sentence looks
like a quotation.
5. τεκμηριοῦνται] Cf. Thucyd.
i 3 and 9: the middle voice here
means 'find evidence,' according to
Dr Gifford.
6. ὡς οἱ... θαυμάσ. ... ἔφασαν]
'even as those who admired the sun,
etc. said.' With the old reading (ὡς
οἵ) the sense would be 'like those
who admiring...said.'
7. διὰ τὸ θέειν...ἐκ τοῦ θεῖναι]
The former derivation is given by
Plato *Cratyl.* 397 C, to which there
is a quite distinct reference in this
passage; the latter by Herod. ii 52
ὅτι κόσμῳ θέντες τὰ πάντα πρήγματα
καὶ πάσας νομὰς εἶχον (both quoted
by Liddell and Scott): cf. Aesch.
Suppl. 80 εἰ θείη θεὸς εὖ παναληθῶς.
This is hardly the place to discuss
the correct etymology: but it is not
unlikely that the root is θε as found
in τίθημι, though Curtius proposes
a root θες = 'to pray': see Peile's
Introd. to Philol. p. 37 (3rd ed.
1875).

τῶν ἁπάντων ποιητὴς καὶ δημιουργὸς μόνος ἐστὶ θεός),
μήτε διοίκησιν ἢ κρίσιν ἢ χάριν αὐτῶν τινὰ πρὸς ἀνθρώπους ἐκτιθέμενοι, ἵνα φόβον ἢ τιμὴν ὀφλήσαντες προσκυ-
νήσωμεν αὐτοῖς;

5   Ἡ τοῦ κόσμου προκύψας Ἐπίκουρος καὶ τὸν οὐράνιον
ὑπερβὰς περίβολον, ἢ διά τινων κρυφίων, ἃς μόνος οἶδεν,
ἐξελθὼν πυλῶν, οὓς ἐν τῷ κενῷ κατεῖδε θεοὺς καὶ τὴν
πολλὴν αὐτῶν ἐμακάρισε τρυφήν; κἀκεῖθεν ἐπιθυμητὴς
γενόμενος τῆς ἡδονῆς καὶ τῆς ἐν τῷ κενῷ ζηλωτὴς διαίτης,
10 οὕτω πάντας ἐπὶ τὴν τοῦ μακαρισμοῦ τούτου μετουσίαν,
ἐξομοιωθησομένους ἐκείνοις τοῖς θεοῖς, παρακαλεῖ, συμπόσιον αὐτοῖς μακάριον, οὐχ ὅπερ οἱ ποιηταί, τὸν οὐρανὸν ἢ
τὸν Ὄλυμπον, ἀλλὰ τὸ κενὸν συγκροτῶν, ἔκ τε τῶν ἀτόμων

6 οιδεν] ειδεν (οι in marg) I ‖ 7 ους] τους coniec Vig ‖ 10 επι την] om
την I ‖ τουτου] om O ‖ 12 αυτοις] -ος I ‖ 13 ατομων] ατμων coniec Vig

3. φόβ. ἢ τιμ. ὀφλήσ.] 'under an obligation of fear or reverence': the accus. here is an extension of its use with ὀφλισκ. for the penalty of conviction, not the charge; the form ὀφλήσ., as if from ὀφλέω, is late and not classical.

5. When did Epicurus catch sight of the lazy, luxurious life of the gods, that he incites us all to imitate their style of living? And how comes it that he so frequently invokes one or other of these gods in his writings, if they have no interest in our concerns? Evidently it was to avoid the charge of being an atheist, which had proved fatal to Socrates. It was not because he looked intelligently either on the heavens or the earth, as writers in the Bible had done. And yet unless these men are quite blind, they must surely see that the Bible account of God's creation is the right one.

ib. τοῦ κόσμ. προκύψας] 'peeping out from (i.e. beyond) the world.'

7. οὓς...τρυφήν] 'pronounced the gods whom he saw in the void and their great enjoyment happy.' Viger's conjecture τούς would perhaps make the sentence run better (and down below we have τῆς ἐν τῷ κενῷ...διαίτης): but it is not necessary if we take both οὓς... θεούς and τὴν π. αὐτ. τρ. as objects after ἐμακάρ. For τρυφήν ('life of enjoyment') cf. Liturg. of St Mark ᾧ καὶ ἐχαρίσω τὴν ἐν παραδείσῳ τρυφήν.

10. ἐπὶ τὴν τοῦ μακαρ. τ. μετουσ.] Some such idea as this was actually in Epicurus's mind in recognizing the existence of gods: see Zeller op. cit. p. 466.

11. συμπόσιον] 'a place of revelry,' not, as more commonly, 'a company of revellers': see Liddell and Scott (1890) s.v.

13. συγκροτῶν] 'hammering together,' 'knocking up': possibly D. uses the word with a humorous reference to the 'clashing' of the atoms.

ib. ἔκ τε τῶν ἀτόμων] Viger's conjecture ἀτμῶν ('vapours') is quite needless.

Γ. Περὶ Φύσεως

τὴν ἀμβροσίαν αὐτοῖς παρατιθείς, καὶ προπίνων αὐτοῖς
ἐξ ἐκείνων τὸ νέκταρ; καὶ δὴ καὶ κατ' ἐκείνων τῶν μηδὲν
πρὸς ἡμᾶς ὅρκους τε καὶ ὀρκισμοὺς μυρίους τοῖς ἑαυτοῦ
βιβλίοις ἐγγράφει, ὀμνύς τε συνεχῶς "μὰ Δία" καὶ "νὴ
Δία," ἐξορκῶν τε τοὺς ἐντυγχάνοντας καὶ πρὸς οὓς δια- 5
λέγοιτο "πρὸς τῶν θεῶν," οὔ τί που δεδιὼς αὐτὸς ἢ
δεδιττόμενος ἐκείνους τὴν ἐπιορκίαν, κενὸν δὲ τοῦτο καὶ
ψευδὲς καὶ ἀργὸν καὶ ἄσημον ἐπιφθεγγόμενος τοῖς λόγοις
αὐτοῦ παράρτημα, οἷον εἰ καὶ χρέμπτοιτο καὶ πτύοι, τό τε
πρόσωπον στρέφοι καὶ τὴν χεῖρα κινοίη. τοιαύτη γὰρ 10
ἀδιανόητος ἦν ἡ παρ' αὐτῷ καὶ ματαία ὑπόκρισις ἡ τῶν
θεῶν ὀνομασία. ἀλλὰ τοῦτο μὲν πρόδηλον, ὅτι μετὰ τὸν

2 και κατ] om και IO ‖ 3 ορκους] -ου I ‖ 4 εγγραφει] -οι I ‖ 5 ους] οις I ‖
6 αυτος] coniec αυτους Vig ‖ 9 παραρτημα] -υμα O ‖ 11 ην] add αὖ I om O

2. κατ' ἐκείν. τ. μηδὲν πρὸς ἡμ.]
Viger translates *iis de rebus quae
nihil ad nos pertineant*: but what
matters are these? Ἐκείνων = τῶν
θεῶν: though the gods according
to Epicurus are 'nothing to us,'
he garnishes his books with frequent
oaths by them. For this use of κατά
cf. Heb. vi 13, 16: it occurs several
times in the LXX; Grimm refers
to Dem. p. 553, 17 and 23, and
quotes Longinus κατὰ πάντων ὤμνυε
τῶν θεῶν. Μηδὲν πρὸς ἡμ. is used as
an indeclinable phrase.

3. ὅρκους τε καὶ ὀρκισμούς] In
LXX the two words seem nearly
synonymous. Ὁρκίζω is used both in
LXX and N.T. (e.g. Mark v 7) in the
sense of to 'adjure,' and probably
ὅρκ. τε κ. ὀρκισμ. means 'oaths and
adjurations' here, ὅρκους corresponding to ὀμνύς, and ὀρκισμούς to ἐξορκῶν.

5. τοὺς ἐντυγχάνοντας] 'his
readers,' cf. p. 52.

ib. πρὸς οὓς διαλέγοιτο] 'with
whomsoever he conversed': the
opt. is iterative.

7. τὴν ἐπιορκίαν] As the text
stands, this must be direct accus. after
δεδιώς and accus. of respect after δε-

διττ. 'neither himself fearing nor
frightening them (sc. τοὺς ἐντυγχάνοντας) as to perjury.' Viger's conjecture αὐτούς (sc. τοὺς θεούς) would
simplify the sentence, 'neither fearing the gods nor frightening his
readers in the matter of perjury.'

9. παράρτημα] 'appendage.' Socrates preferred νὴ τὸν κύνα and the
like expressions to swearing by the
gods.

ib. οἷον εἰ] 'of the same efficacy as
if.' Such actions then as now were
regarded as doing away with the
effect of what had been said.

ib. πτύοι] For superstitious practices in the matter of spitting see
Becker *Charicles* p. 132 n. 2.

10. τοιαύτη γὰρ ... ὀνομασία] 'so
meaningless and empty a pretence
was his naming of the gods': ἡ
παρ' αὐτῷ ('that we find in his
writings') must be taken with ἡ τῶν
θ. ὀνομ.

12. μετὰ τὸν Σωκρ. θάνατ.] As
this occurred in 399 B.C. and Epicurus was not born till 342 B.C.,
D. must greatly exaggerate the
effect of it on Epicurus, to say the
least.

Σωκράτους θάνατον κατεπτηχὼς Ἀθηναίους, ὡς μὴ δοκοίη
τοῦθ᾽, ὅπερ ἦν, ἄθεος εἶναι, κενὰς αὐτοῖς ἀνυποστάτων
θεῶν τερατευσάμενος ἐζωγράφησε σκιάς. οὔτε γὰρ εἰς
οὐρανὸν ἀνέβλεψε νοεροῖς ὀφθαλμοῖς, ἵνα τῆς ἐναργοῦς
5 ἄνωθεν φωνῆς ἀκούσῃ, ἧς ὁ προσεκτικὸς θεατὴς κατακούσας
ἐμαρτύρησεν, ὅτι Οἱ ογρανοὶ Διηγοῦνται Δόξαν θεοῦ, ποίησιν
Δὲ χειρῶν αὐτοῦ ἀναγγέλλει τὸ στερέωμα, οὔτε τῇ διανοίᾳ
κατεῖδεν εἰς τοὔδαφος· ἔμαθε γὰρ ἄν, ὅτι Τοῦ ἐλέους Κυρίου
πλήρης ἡ γῆ, καὶ ὅτι Τοῦ Κυρίου ἡ γῆ καὶ τὸ πλήρωμα αὐτῆς.
10 Καὶ μετὰ ταῦτα γάρ, φησι, Κύριος εἰς τὴν γῆν ἐπέβλεψε καὶ
ἐνέπλησεν αὐτὴν τῶν ἀγαθῶν αὐτοῦ· ψυχὴν παντὸς ζῴου
ἐκάλυψε τὸ πρόσωπον αὐτῆς. εἰ δὲ μὴ σφόδρα τυφλώτ-
τουσιν, ἐπισκεψάσθωσαν τὴν παμποίκιλον τῶν ζῴων
πολυπλήθειαν, τὰ χερσαῖα, τὰ πτηνά, τὰ ἔνυδρα, καὶ
15 κατανοησάτωσαν ὡς ἀληθὴς ἐπὶ τῇ πάντων κρίσει γέγονεν

2 αυτοις] -ων O ‖ 5 ης...οτι] λεγουσης B ‖ 7 τη διαν.] om τη I ‖ 9 και οτι
...γη] om B ‖ 10 και μετα...προσωπον αυτης om B ‖ κυριος] om I ‖ 11 αὐτοῦ]
αὐτοῦ O ‖ ψυχην] -η Vig marg ‖ 13 επισκεψασθ.] επισκεψατωσαν O ‖
14 πολυπληθειαν] -θιαν I ‖ 15 αληθης] -ες I ‖ κρισει] om I κτισει coniec Vig

1. ὡς μὴ δοκοίη κτλ.] 'that he
might not appear to be what he
really was' (i.e.) 'an atheist.' That
the Epicureans were sincere and
not merely opportunists in their
belief about gods see Zeller *op. cit.*
pp. 465 foll.
2. κενὰς ... σκιάς] Cf. Sext.
Math. ix 25 Ἐπίκουρος δὲ ἐκ τῶν
κατὰ τοὺς ὕπνους φαντασιῶν οἴεται
τοὺς ἀνθρώπους ἔννοιαν ἐσπακέναι
θεοῦ. μεγάλων γὰρ εἰδώλων φησὶ
καὶ ἀνθρωπομόρφων κατὰ τοὺς ὕπνους
προσπιπτόντων ὑπέλαβον καὶ ταῖς
ἀληθείαις ὑπάρχειν τινὰς τοιούτους
θεοὺς ἀνθρωπομόρφους: see too Lucr.
ii 1161—1193 etc.
3. τερατευσάμενος] 'making up
fables' (Lat. *portenta loqui*).
4. νοεροῖς ὀφθαλμ.] 'with intelligent eyes': for this use of νοερός
(opp. to ἀσύνετος) Liddell and Scott
quote Sext. *Math.* vii 325. Its

usual meaning is 'intellectual,'
'mental,' and later on it becomes
equivalent to λογικός, 'spiritual,' e.g.
Lit. of St Mark τὸ ἅγιον καὶ ὑπερ-
ουράνιον καὶ νοερὸν σου θυσιαστήριον.
6. Οἱ οὐρανοί...τὸ στερέωμα] Ps.
xviii (xix) 2, where A gives ἀναγ-
γελεῖ and B ἀναγγέλλει.
8. Τοῦ ἐλέους...ἡ γῆ] Ps. xxxii
(xxxiii) 5.
9. Τοῦ κυρίου...αὐτῆς] Ps. xxiii
(xxiv) 1.
10. Καὶ μετὰ τ....αὐτῆς] Ecclus.
xvi 29, 30, where A gives ἐπί and
B εἰς. Viger's marginal suggestion
of ψυχῇ here for ψυχήν is not borne
out by the MSS of LXX: ψυχήν is
2nd accus. after ἐκάλυψε.
15. ἐπὶ τῇ π. κρίσει] 'when
He pronounced judgement on all
things': Viger's conjecture κτίσει is
not needed. The words καὶ πάντα...
καλά are a paraphrase of Gen. i 31.

Γ. Περὶ Φύσεως

ἡ μαρτυρία τοῦ δεσπότου, καὶ πάντα κατὰ τὴν αὐτοῦ πρόσταξιν πέφηνε καλά.

Ταῦτά μοι ἀπὸ πλείστων ἐξήνθισται τῶν πρὸς Ἐπίκουρον Διονυσίῳ τῷ καθ' ἡμᾶς ἐπισκόπῳ πεποιημένων.

(10) Holl *Fragmente* 363 p. 147: Pitra *Anal. Sacr.* II p. xxxvii.

Φύσει κατὰ τὴν πρώτην τάξιν ἐστὶ πρεσβύτερος καὶ πρόγονος ὁ τεχνίτης τῶν τεχνιτευομένων ὑπ' αὐτοῦ.

(11) Holl *Fragm.* 364 p. 147: *Sacr. Parall. Rupefuc.* fol. 55.

Ἐργαστήριον ἀνθρώποις καὶ θέατρον, διδασκαλεῖον καὶ γυμνάσιον ὁ κόσμος ἠνέῳγεν, ἵν' αὐτὸν καὶ τὰ ἐν αὐτῷ πολυπραγμονήσαντες τὸ μέγιστον ἐπὶ τὴν αὐτῶν γνῶσιν ἐφελκώμεθα.

(12) Holl *Fragm.* 365 p. 148: *Sacr. Parall. Rupefuc.* fol. 55.

—ἐπεὶ καὶ σύμβουλος ἀγαθὸς ὤφθη ξένοις ὁ πολλάκις ἐν οἰκείᾳ βούλῃ σφαλών. τυφλώττει μέν τις ἐπὶ πολὺ περὶ τὰ αὐτῷ προσήκοντα διὰ φιλαυτίαν· ἀπροσπαθῶς δὲ καὶ σχολαζούσῃ τῇ διανοίᾳ τοῖς ἐκτὸς προιὼν ῥᾷον αὐτῶν εὐσύνοπτον ἴσχει καὶ καταφανῆ τὴν διάθεσιν.

7 υπ αυτου] om Pitra ‖ 13 συμβουλος] coniec Routh συμβολος Holl ‖ 15 σφαλων] an legendum σφαλεις? ‖ 17 προιων] an legendum προσιων? ‖ 18 αυτων] coniec Routh -ον Holl

6. *The producer is anterior to his productions.*
ib. Φύσει...τεχνιτευομ.] 'for by nature the craftsman is in the first rank, (being) senior to and the progenitor of the things produced by his craft.' The phrase κατὰ τὴν πρ. τ. no doubt refers to something that has gone before. For πρευβύτ. cf. p. 183 and for τῶν τεχνιτ. cf. p. 184.

9. *A study of nature should lead us to knowledge of self.*

10. ἠνέῳγεν] This form of the perf. is not recognized by Liddell and Scott, who give ἀνέῳγα: it is questionable whether the tense is active or passive here (see Liddell and Scott s.v.).

11. τὸ μέγιστον...ἐφελκ.] 'that we may be drawn to the knowledge of ourselves, (which is) of chief importance.' Cf. p. 126. Τὸ μέγιστον is in apposition to the sentence ἐπὶ τὴν...ἐφελκ.

14. *One who has failed to advise himself well, is sometimes a good counsellor to others: for in their case he is not blinded by self-love but exercises a calm and clear judgement, and this very process will make him better acquainted with himself.*

ib. ὤφθη] Perhaps a 'gnomic' aor. but, the sentence being incomplete, we do not know what it gives the reason for.

16. φιλαυτίαν] See p. 126.

ib. ἀπροσπαθῶς] 'without passionate affection': cf. προσπάθεια on p. 126 and Clem. Alex. *Strom.* iv p. 481 ἀπολιπεῖν μὲν γένος τὸ κοσμικόν, ἀπολιπεῖν δὲ οὐσίαν καὶ κτῆσιν πᾶσαν διὰ τὸ ἀπροσπαθῶς βιοῦν.

18. αὐτῶν] sc. τῶν ἐκτός. The

εἶτα ἐκείνοις συγκροτηθεὶς καὶ διαδονισθείς, ἐντρεχέστερος τε νοεῖν γενόμενος, καὶ ἑαυτοῦ ποτὲ συναισθήσεται, εἴ γε καὶ τῆς ἐν τοῖς περικειμένοις ἀληθείας ὀξυδερκὴς ἐπιγνώμων γένοιτο.

5 (13) Holl *Fragm.* 366 p. 148: *Sacr. Parall. Rupefuc.* fol. 55.

Οὐχ ἁπλῶς τῶν μεγίστων τοῦ κόσμου καὶ τῶν ὑπ' αὐτὸν καὶ τοῦ ἀριθμοῦ τοῦ αἰῶνος, ἀλλὰ πάντων καὶ τῶν ἐλαχίστων ἄπειρος καὶ ἀτέλεστος ἀνθρώποις ἡ γνῶσις.

2 συναισθήσεται] συνεσθ. Holl ‖ 6 μεγιστων] μεριστων nonnulli ‖ υπ'] υπερ coniec Routh ‖ 8 απειρος και] om και Routh qui coniecit ατελεστος τε ‖ ανθρωποις] των εν ανθ. Routh

gen. depends on διάθεσιν. The reading αὐτόν makes no sense.

1. συγκροτηθείς] Cf. συγκροτῶν above p. 160.
   ib. διαδονισθείς] from διαδονίζειν, a collateral form of διαδονεῖν ('to toss to and fro').
   ib. ἐντρεχέστερος...νοεῖν] Ἐντρεχής, 'ready,' 'keen,' is a classical word and its construction with an inf. is like δεινὸς λέγειν, ὀξὺς ἐπινοῆσαι, etc.

2. ἑαυτοῦ] Routh's addition of συναισθήσεται (which is found also with the gen. in Arist. *Nic. Eth.* ix 9) is now proved correct.
   ib. εἴ γε...γένοιτο] 'if so be he become a keen discerner also of the truth in things that surround him.'

6. *Human knowledge can never grasp all the facts of the natural world.*

ib. μεγίστων] opp. to ἐλαχίστων: the reading μεριστῶν is due perhaps to an attempt to connect this fragment with the passage on p. 147.
ib. τῶν ὑπ' αὐτόν] sc. τὸν κόσμον: cf. Ecclus. i 3 ὕψος οὐρανοῦ καὶ πλάτος γῆς καὶ ἄβυσσον...τίς ἐξιχνιάσει; The whole sentence indeed seems to be based upon Ecclus. i, *q.v.*

7. τοῦ ἀριθμοῦ τοῦ αἰῶνος] Cf. *ibid.* i 2 ἡμέρας αἰῶνος τίς ἐξαριθμήσει; and again v 9 and v 19 (23).

8. ἄπειρος κ. ἀτέλ. ἀνθ. ἡ γνῶσις] 'knowledge is infinite and without end for men' (i.e. always imperfect and incomplete). Cf. p. 226 οὐδεὶς γὰρ τὰ ἔργα τοῦ θεοῦ ὁλοκλήρως καταλαβεῖν δύναται.

Δ. THE CONTROVERSY BETWEEN THE TWO DIONYSII.

The prominence which after events gave to the utterances of Dionysius on the subject of Sabellianism, and especially to his controversy with Dionysius of Rome in connexion with it, renders a somewhat full discussion of our author's position desirable.

Sabellius was a Libyan of the Pentapolis by birth, and in his native district as well as at Rome his views had been wide-spread some time before we find the Alexandrian Bishop attacking them: in fact Sabellius himself was probably already dead by that time. It was in 257 that Dionysius called the attention of Xystus (or Sixtus) II to this pernicious heresy, which, in laying too much stress on the unity of the Godhead, hopelessly confounded the Three Persons in the Trinity. "I have sent unto you," he says, "with reference to the doctrine which has now arisen at Ptolemais in the Pentapolis, for it is impious and contains much blasphemy about the Almighty God and Father of our Lord Jesus Christ, and much unbelief about His only begotten Son, the First-begotten of all creation, the Incarnate Word, and a want of perception of the Holy Spirit[1]." From this it appears as if Dionysius was unaware that these errors were not of quite recent origin in either the East or the West, and the statement is also important because it shows that this later phase of Sabellianism was seen to endanger the dignity of the Third Person as well as of the First and Second. In Libya the heresy gained such a hold upon the Church that even certain of the Bishops were infected with it and the Son of God was

[1] See pp. 51 f.

no longer preached[1]. Dionysius therefore, feeling his responsibility for the churches under his care[2], became active in trying to eradicate the evil. Eusebius (*H. E.* vii 26. 1) mentions a number of letters which he wrote on the subject "to Ammon, Bishop of the Church at Berenice[3], to Telesphorus, to Euphranor, and again to Ammon and Euporus." In one of these letters, which Athanasius generally speaks of as addressed πρὸς Εὐφράνορα καὶ Ἀμμώνιον[4] (though the title does not exactly tally with any in Eusebius's list) and which was written about the year 260, Dionysius made use of certain illustrations and expressions about the Son of God, which were seized hold of by some members of the Church either at Alexandria or in the Pentapolis as heretical. This letter was apparently one of the later ones of the series; for Athanasius says that it was when Dionysius's earlier overtures had failed to produce any good effect that he felt impelled to write it in order to vindicate the true relation of the Son to the Father by an appeal to Scripture[5].

Dionysius's critics laid a formal complaint against him before his namesake, who had by now succeeded the martyred Xystus II as Bishop of Rome, and in so doing they accused him of having fallen into five errors whilst correcting the false views of the Sabellians:

(1) separating the Father and the Son (διαιρεῖ καὶ μακρύνει καὶ μερίζει τὸν υἱὸν ἀπὸ τοῦ πατρός, Athan. *de sent. D.* 16);

(2) denying the eternity of the Son (οὐκ ἀεὶ ἦν ὁ θεὸς πατήρ, οὐκ ἀεὶ ἦν ὁ υἱός, ἀλλ' ὁ μὲν θεὸς ἦν χωρὶς τοῦ λόγου, αὐτὸς

---

[1] ἐν Πενταπόλει τῆς ἄνω Λιβύης τηνικαῦτά τινες τῶν ἐπισκόπων ἐφρόνησαν τὰ Σαβελλίου καὶ τοιοῦτον ἴσχυσαν ταῖς ἐπινοίαις ὡς ὀλίγου δεῖν μηκέτι ἐν ταῖς ἐκκλησίαις κηρύττεσθαι τὸν υἱὸν τοῦ θεοῦ (Athan. *de sent. D.* 5). Sabellius had invented the word υἱοπάτωρ to designate the Godhead (Athan. *de synod.* 16; Hil. *de Trin.* iv 12; Harnack *Hist. of Dogma* iii pp. 85 ff.).

[2] αὐτὸς γὰρ εἶχε τὴν μέριμναν τῶν ἐκκλησιῶν ἐκείνων (*de sent. D.* 5).

[3] This was one of the five chief cities of the Pentapolis.

[4] *ibid.* 9 and 10: in chap. 6 it is spoken of as πρὸς Ἀμμώνιον only.

[5] The whole sentence in *de sent. D.* 5 runs as follows: ὡς δὲ οὐκ ἐπαύοντο ἀλλὰ καὶ μᾶλλον ἀναιδέστερον ἠσέβουν, ἠναγκάσθη πρὸς τὴν ἀναίδειαν ἐκείνων γράψαι τὴν τοιαύτην ἐπιστολὴν καὶ τὰ ἀνθρώπινα τοῦ Σωτῆρος ἐκ τῶν εὐαγγελίων παραθέσθαι, ἵν' ἐπειδὴ τολμηρότερον ἐκεῖνοι τὸν υἱὸν ἠρνοῦντο καὶ τὰ ἀνθρώπινα αὐτοῦ τῷ πατρὶ ἀνετίθεσαν, οὕτως οὗτος δείξας ὅτι οὐχ ὁ πατὴρ ἀλλ' ὁ υἱός ἐστιν ὁ γενόμενος ὑπὲρ ἡμῶν ἄνθρωπος, πείσῃ τοὺς ἀμαθεῖς μὴ εἶναι τὸν πατέρα υἱόν, καὶ οὕτως λοιπὸν κατ' ὀλίγον ἐκείνους εἰς τὴν ἀληθινὴν ἀναγάγῃ θεότητα τοῦ υἱοῦ καὶ τὴν γνῶσιν τὴν περὶ τοῦ πατρός.

Δ. *THE TWO DIONYSII* 167

δὲ ὁ υἱὸς οὐκ ἦν πρὶν γενηθῇ, ἀλλ' ἦν ποτὲ ὅτε οὐκ ἦν· οὐ γὰρ ἀΐδιός ἐστιν ἀλλ' ὕστερον ἐπεγέγονεν, *ibid.* 14);

(3) naming the Father without the Son and the Son without the Father (πατέρα λέγων οὐκ ὀνομάζει τὸν υἱὸν καὶ πάλιν υἱὸν λέγων οὐκ ὀνομάζει τὸν πατέρα, *ibid.* 16);

(4) virtually rejecting the term ὁμοούσιος as descriptive of the Son (προσφέρουσιν ἔγκλημα κατ' ἐμοῦ ψεῦδος ὃν ὡς οὐ λέγοντος τὸν χριστὸν ὁμοούσιον εἶναι τῷ θεῷ, *ibid.* 18);

(5) speaking of the Son as a creature of the Father and using misleading illustrations of their relation (ποίημα καὶ γενητὸν εἶναι τὸν υἱὸν τοῦ θεοῦ, μήτε δὲ φύσει ἴδιον, ἀλλὰ ξένον κατ' οὐσίαν αὐτὸν εἶναι τοῦ πατρός, ὥσπερ ἐστὶν ὁ γεωργὸς πρὸς τὴν ἄμπελον καὶ ὁ ναυπηγὸς πρὸς τὸ σκάφος. καὶ γὰρ ὡς ποίημα ὢν οὐκ ἦν πρὶν γένηται, *ibid.* 4).

Upon receiving this complaint Dionysius of Rome appears to have convened a synod which condemned the expressions complained of[1], and the Roman Bishop addressed a letter upon the subject of Sabellianism and the modes of correcting it to the Church of Alexandria (pp. 169 f.). From motives of delicacy he made no actual mention of his Alexandrian brother-bishop in this letter whilst criticising his views, but wrote to him privately asking for an explanation[2]. The extract given on pp. 177 ff. is from the former of these two letters. The Ἔλεγχος καὶ Ἀπολογία was Dionysius's reply to the latter. It was drawn up in four books and is no doubt the work referred to by Eus. *H. E.* vii 26. 1 συντάττει δὲ περὶ τῆς αὐτῆς ὑποθέσεως (sc. κατὰ Σαβελλίου) καὶ ἄλλα τέσσαρα συγγράμματα, ἃ τῷ κατὰ Ῥώμην ὁμωνύμῳ Διονυσίῳ προσφωνεῖ[3]. So far as we can now judge, it appears to have satisfied his critics at the time and was certainly held in high repute by the ancient Church: for

[1] ἀλλά τινων αἰτιασαμένων παρὰ τῷ ἐπισκόπῳ Ῥώμης τὸν τῆς Ἀλεξανδρείας ἐπίσκοπον ὡς λέγοντα ποίημα καὶ μὴ ὁμοούσιον τὸν υἱὸν τῷ πατρί, ἡ μὲν κατὰ Ῥώμην σύνοδος ἠγανάκτησεν (Athan. *de synod.* 43): cf. *ibid.* 45 πρὸ αὐτῶν (sc. the Nicene Fathers) ἦσαν οἱ Διονύσιοι καὶ οἱ ἐν Ῥώμῃ τὸ τηνικαῦτα συνελθόντες ἐπίσκοποι.

[2] ἔγραψεν ὁμοῦ κατά τε τῶν τὰ Σαβελλίου δοξαζόντων...ἴσην καὶ κατὰ διάμετρον ἀσέβειαν εἶναι λέγων τήν τε Σαβελλίου καὶ τὴν τῶν λεγόντων κτίσμα καὶ ποίημα καὶ γενητὸν εἶναι τὸν τοῦ θεοῦ λόγον. ἐπέστειλε δὲ καὶ Διονυσίῳ δηλῶσαι περὶ ὧν εἰρήκασι κατ' αὐτοῦ (*de sent. D.* 13): see Harnack *op. cit.* 89.

[3] D. speaks of ἄλλη ἐπιστολή, which he had sent in his defence either to the Bishop of Rome or to some one else, on p. 188: see note *in loc.* and Basil *de Sp. Sanct.* 29, § 72 (p. 198).

not only does Eusebius quote an important extract from it in his *Praeparatio Evangelica* vii 19 (pp. 182 ff.), but also, when Arius promulgated his views and appealed to Dionysius's statements in support of them[1], especially those contained in the letter πρὸς Εὐφράνορα καὶ 'Αμμώνιον, Athanasius (*de sent. Dion:*) undertook an elaborate defence of his famous predecessor, and in so doing made those extensive quotations from the Ἔλεγχος which now form the bulk of our remaining text. Basil also has preserved for us three other short extracts (pp. 196 and 198) in his work *de Spiritu Sancto* (29 § 72), though his defence of Dionysius here and in his Epistle (1 ix) to Maximus is much more critical and judicious than that of Athanasius. The references to the Ἔλεγχος καὶ 'Απολογία in the controversy between Jerome and Rufinus about the heretical teaching to be found in Origen's writings (Hieronym. *adv. Ruf.* ii 17) are only of a general character and add nothing to our knowledge of its contents[2].

One other short sentence is found in a considerable number of MSS and is given on p. 185.

The Letter of Dionysius of Rome
πρὸς Σαβελλιανούς

The extract given on pp. 177 ff. comes from Athanasius *de decret. Nic. Syn.* 26 (cf. *de sent. Dion.* c. 13). Its contents seem to suggest that it forms the second portion of the letter. It deals with the way in which the school of Alexandria in general, and Dionysius its exponent in particular, met the false teaching of the Sabellians, whilst the first portion probably dealt with the Sabellians themselves. The language of the extract, though very different in style from that of Dionysius of Alexandria, and exhibiting distinct traces of Western modes of thought (in its directness and avoidance of subtleties), is

---

[1] Hence the remark of Gennadius (*de eccl. dogm.* 4) *Dionysius fons Arii.*

[2] e.g. (*scribit Rufinus*) *Dionysium Alexandrinae urbis episcopum, virum eruditissimum, contra Sabellium voluminibus disputantem in Arianum dogma delabi:* cf. n. 1 on p. 173 for other expressions.

excellent Greek in its way and gives no impression that the writer felt hampered by it in expressing his meaning.

Two main points are treated of in the extract. First there is the charge of virtual tritheism, which Dionysius of Rome brings against the Alexandrian Church in opposing the Patripassian views of Sabellius (διαιροῦντας καὶ κατατέμνοντας καὶ ἀναιροῦντας ...τὴν μοναρχίαν εἰς...θεότητας τρεῖς...οἳ κατὰ διάμετρον, ὡς ἔπος εἰπεῖν, ἀντίκεινται τῇ Σαβελλίου γνώμῃ, and again τρεῖς θεοὺς τρόπον τινὰ κηρύττουσιν). This, he says, is the practical result of speaking of τρεῖς ὑποστάσεις ξένας ἀλλήλων, παντάπασιν κεχωρισμένας; for such an expression, which is however stronger than Dionysius of Alexandria himself had used, ignores (*a*) the essential unity that there is between ὁ θεὸς τῶν ὅλων and the Divine Word, (*b*) the indwelling and abiding of the Holy Spirit in God (ἐμφιλοχωρεῖν and ἐνδιαιτᾶσθαι are the verbs used), and (*c*) the summing up and gathering together of both the Word and the Spirit into the Almighty Father (here the verbs are συγκεφαλαιοῦσθαι and συνάγεσθαι). It will be seen when we come to discuss Dionysius of Alexandria's defence that the expressions criticized are somewhat rough reproductions of his own utterances, so far as we can gather them from Athanasius's writings. Dionysius of Rome rather unfairly remarks that the Alexandrian doctrine repeats the perverse error of Marcion as to three ἀρχαί in the Godhead.

Secondly, there is the charge of teaching that the Son was the creature (ποίημα) of the Father. Here again the Roman Bishop gives an unsympathetic turn to at least one expression or set of expressions used by his Alexandrian brother: to attribute the sense of χειροποίητον τρόπον τινά to his statements about the Father as ποιητής is perhaps a strictly fair comment on the illustration of the ναυπηγός and the σκάφος, but it is obvious that few similes will hold beyond a certain point and need to be considered in relation to their setting. It is not clear in what sense Dionysius of Alexandria had spoken of the Λόγος (i.e. whether as the Word in His eternal and essential relations to God or as the Incarnate Word); in any case the Roman Bishop's remarks on the eternity of the Λόγος take no account of the subtle distinctions drawn by Eastern theologians with regard to that doctrine[1]. Little

[1] The Alexandrian School of Theology following upon the lines of later Greek philosophy had sought to distinguish the Word Immanent in the Godhead (ἐνδιάθετος), the Personal Word (ἐνυπόστατος) and the Incarnate Word.

objection can be taken to the difference he seeks to establish between γέγονεν (which would wrongly be applied to the Son, as denying His eternity, but which Dionysius of Rome thinks is involved in calling Him ποίημα) and γεγέννηται (which only suggests His eternal Generation and Sonship); and this is the main argument of this section of the fragment. Yet here again some of the Scriptural quotations, on which the argument is based, are, as the notes will show, to say the least, of doubtful applicability[1].

The extract ends with a brief repetition of the essential unity of the Godhead, which these attempts at separating the Persons tend to destroy, and of the dignity of the Son, which is marred by attributing ποίησις to the Father in regard to Him. The realization of the Scriptural statements "I and the Father are one," and "I in the Father and the Father in Me," is necessary to the preservation of the unity of the Divine Trinity.

The text of the extract is based on that of Routh (*Rell. Sacr.* iii pp. 373 ff.), who quotes the readings of *Codex Regius* on the authority of Montfaucon.

Ἔλεγχος καὶ Ἀπολογία

The first fragment we possess is embedded in Eus. *Praepar. Evang.* vii 19 and deals with the thesis μὴ ἀγένητον εἶναι τὴν ὕλην. Eusebius tells us that it comes from the first book, and, though it is easy to imagine its place in the argument as to the eternal Generation of the Son, yet the passage itself is not directed so much against the Sabellians or against the Roman critics of Dionysius as against the recent theories of some kind of heretics not mentioned by name[2]. These persons had assumed the ἀγενησία of matter and had only attributed the management and disposal of it to God. But this, he says, is impossible: for on the one point it puts matter on a level with God, whilst on the other it subordinates matter to Him. And further the theory only makes God a superior artisan or crafts-

---

[1] See notes on p. 181.

[2] Dionysius himself perhaps recognizes the partial irrelevancy of the discussion at the end of the passage: πολὺς μὲν οὖν καὶ πρὸς τούτους ὁ λόγος, ἀλλ' οὐ νῦν ἡμῖν πρόκειται (p. 185).

Δ. Ἔλεγχος καὶ Ἀπολογία 171

man, moulding and shaping that which He did not originate. Yet this view by which God endowed matter with its proper qualities as according to His infinite wisdom He saw fit is better than others which have been held (see Dr Jackson's notes on pp. 182 and 185). The text of this fragment is mainly Dr Gifford's (see p. 130).

With the exception perhaps of the short sentence given on p. 185, the exact position of which in the argument is not easy to define, though it would seem to belong to some discussion of μοναρχία in its relation to the Trinity, all the other extracts we possess have a direct bearing upon the questions at issue between the two Dionysii and are all derived from Athanasius's writings or (in three instances) from those of Basil.

Let us see how Dionysius defended himself on the five points mentioned above. (1) As to the charge of separating the Father, the Son, and the Holy Ghost, on which the extract from Dionysius of Rome's letter dwells[1], he distinctly denies it: "Each of the names mentioned by me," he says, "is inseparable and indivisible from its neighbour: I say Father and, before I bring in the Son, I signify Him too in the Father. I bring in the Son: even if I had not already mentioned the Father, He would in any case be implied in the Son. I add the Holy Spirit and at once I suggest His Source and Channel." The very names employed imply one another. "How then can I who use them imagine that they are altogether divided and separated from one another?" (p. 192). And again: "Thus each is in each, the one being different from the other: and being two, They are one."

(2) As to the eternity of the Son, Dionysius is equally distinct and emphatic. God was always the Father, and therefore Christ was always the Son, just as, if the sun were eternal, the daylight would also be eternal. The Son derives His being from the Father and is related to the Father as the rays are to the light (see p. 187).

(3) The charge of omitting the Son in speaking of the Father and *vice versa* is refuted in what is said under (1): the one name involves the other.

(4) Dionysius's rejection or non-employment of the term ὁμοούσιος is not so easily disposed of. He practically acknowledges that, as he did not find it anywhere in Scripture, he had not used it, but at the same time he maintains that he had

---
[1] e.g. τρεῖς ὑποστάσεις ξένας ἀλλήλων παντάπασι κεχωρισμένας (p. 178).

employed figures which suggested a similar relationship (συγγένεια), e.g. the figure of parent and child who are ὁμογενεῖς, and seed and root and plant which are ὁμοφυῆ, and again source and stream (p. 189), and in another place ὁ ἐν καρδίᾳ λόγος and ὁ διὰ γλώσσης νοῦς προπηδῶν. But, as Bethune-Baker (*Early History of Christian Doctrine* chap. viii pp. 113 ff.) has pointed out, in considering such epithets as equivalents to ὁμοούσιος, Dionysius of Alexandria shows that he had not grasped the tradition of the West of one *substantia* of Godhead existing in three *personae*: to him it occurred to think of three *personae* of the same *genus* and *natura*, i.e. to acknowledge rather the generic than the essential oneness of the Godhead[1]. And it is noteworthy, as Harnack says[2], that even in the Ἔλεγχος, so far as we can tell, the word ὁμοούσιος is never actually used; and further that Athanasius's attempt to defend Dionysius's doubtful utterances by referring them to the *human* nature of Christ is not warranted by the facts of the case[3].

(5) Perhaps however the most serious misunderstanding naturally arose from Dionysius of Alexandria speaking of the Son as ποίημα and illustrating the word by the γεωργός with his vine and the ναυπηγός with his boat. As we have seen, Dionysius of Rome took strong exception to this, and with some show of reason, if with undue pressing of the figures. Dionysius of Alexandria's defence is that, though he had undoubtedly used such rather unsuitable (ὡς ἀχρειοτέρων) figures somewhat casually (ἐξ ἐπιδρομῆς), yet they were not the only ones employed, but several others more suitable and apposite were immediately adduced (such as those mentioned under (4) above). And he complains that, instead of considering these latter figures, the critics had fastened upon the first two in order to assail him.

In fact, as Athanasius (*de sent. Dion.* 14) tells us, that was the head of his complaint against his accusers generally, that they did not take his utterances as a whole (ὁλοκλήρως) but slashed his writings about (περικόπτοντας αὐτοῦ τὰς λέξεις) and made what sense of them they liked with no good conscience but with an evil intent; he compared them to

---

[1] See further on this matter lower down where the use of ὑπόστασις in the writings of the two Dionysii is discussed (p. 173).

[2] *Hist. of Dogma* iii p. 92 n. 2.

[3] See e.g. *de sent. Dion.* 9 and 10.

Δ. Ἔλεγχος καὶ Ἀπολογία

those who found fault with St Paul's epistles, the reference being apparently to 2 Cor. x 10[1].

With regard to the word ποίημα itself Dionysius points out that the corresponding word ποιητής is used in a great number of different ways (besides that of χειροτέχνης) both in ordinary conversation, e.g. ποιηταὶ καὶ τῶν ἰδίων καλοῦνται λόγων οἱ σοφοί (p. 194), and in the Scriptures, e.g. ποιηταὶ νόμου καὶ κρίσεως καὶ δικαιοσύνης (p. 195), and that he had only used it in close connexion with πατήρ (μετὰ τὸ εἰπεῖν πατέρα ποιητὴν ἐπαγήοχα, p. 193), which showed that he meant to use ποιεῖν as equivalent to γεννᾶν. The figure of the νοῦς and the λόγος therefore seems to please him best: for here οὔτε ὁ νοῦς ἄλογος οὔτε ἄνους ὁ λόγος, ἀλλ' ὅ γε νοῦς ποιεῖ τὸν λόγον ἐν αὐτῷ φανείς, καὶ ὁ λόγος δείκνυσι τὸν νοῦν ἐν αὐτῷ γενόμενος κτλ. (p. 197); and thus the Father has the Son as His Interpreter and Messenger (ἑρμηνέα καὶ ἄγγελον ἑαυτοῦ, p. 197).

Two other phrases, on which Dionysius of Rome had seized for criticism, remain to be considered. (1) Sabellius, according to Athan. *c. Arian.* iv 25, had maintained that ὥσπερ διαιρέσεις χαρισμάτων εἰσί, τὸ δὲ αὐτὸ πνεῦμα, οὕτω καὶ ὁ πατὴρ ὁ αὐτὸς μέν ἐστι, πλατύνεται δὲ εἰς υἱὸν καὶ πνεῦμα. In combating this πλατυσμός (expansion) of Sabellius, which did not sufficiently distinguish the Three Persons of the Trinity, Dionysius of Rome feels that Dionysius of Alexandria had not been careful enough in stating τὴν θείαν τριάδα εἰς ἕνα, ὥσπερ εἰς κορυφήν τινα (τὸν θεὸν τῶν ὅλων τὸν παντοκράτορα λέγω), συγκεφαλαιοῦσθαί τε καὶ συνάγεσθαι. In the Ἔλεγχος (p. 193) the Alexandrian Bishop consents to use both πλατύνειν and συγκεφαλαιοῦσθαι so long as an orthodox sense is given to both terms: if we so expand the Unity into the Trinity as not to divide it (ἀδιαίρετον), we must likewise so sum up the Trinity as not to subtract from it (ἀμείωτον).

(2) The use of the word ὑπόστασις was a yet more distinct source of confusion between them. The Roman Bishop maintains that if you so separate (μερίζειν) the Trinity as to speak of τρεῖς ὑποστάσεις, you at once set up τρεῖς θεότητας (pp. 177 and 181). The Alexandrian Bishop no less stoutly maintains to the end, according to Basil *de Spir. Sancto*, chap. 29 §72 (p. 196), that

---

[1] Cf. Hieron. *adv. Ruf.* ii 17 *de adulteratione librorum Origenis*, where Rufinus is accused of shirking the real issue between them by raising fresh issues, e.g. *Athanasius episcopus sic Dionysii defendit errorem, Apostolorum scripta similiter depravata sunt.*

if by the ὑποστάσεις being three, they say they are separated (μεμερισμένας), three they are, however much the statement is disliked, or else they must completely destroy the Divine Trinity. Here it appears as if only the supposed consequences of the expression were at stake (i.e. the dividing up of the Godhead), but the truth is that the two combatants were using the word ὑπόστασις in rather different senses[1]. To Dionysius of Alexandria ὑπόστασις implied something distinct from οὐσία, whereas to Dionysius of Rome the two were almost interchangeable terms. Οὐσία however could be used in two senses: (1) *particular* existence (almost equivalent to individual or person), and (2) existence *in general*, the essence shared by several things or persons of the same class, and this is the sense attached to οὐσία by Dionysius of Alexandria. So also ὑπόστασις had two possible meanings: (1) that of *individual* attributes and so equivalent to person, and this is how Dionysius of Alexandria as a rule used it; (2) that of οὐσία in the *generic* sense, and so it was used long after the period now under discussion; Dionysius himself seems to use it somewhat in this sense on p. 184. But at Rome the deficiencies of the Latin language increased the confusion. Abstract thought being unsuitable to the Roman mind, *essentia*, the proper translation of οὐσία, never came into use, and *substantia* (with a suggestion of almost material existence) took its place, though this naturally would represent ὑπόστασις. Hence Dionysius of Rome would rather have expected that his native term *persona* (person), which with him had no evil associations, would have been represented in a Greek treatise on the Trinity by πρόσωπον, not by ὑπόστασις, but πρόσωπα (rôles) had been so misapplied by the Sabellians in treating of the Godhead[2] that orthodox Greek thinkers were shy of the word. These facts will explain the misunderstanding of the two Champions of Truth, and it is sad to think that their controversy did little to remove it, and that the Alexandrian Bishop's rather unguarded expressions gave countenance in after days to so much further misunderstanding and difficulty.

It is interesting to compare Basil's defence of Dionysius the Great with that of Athanasius. As we have observed in

---

[1] See above on ὁμοούσιος (p. 172) and cf. Bethune-Baker *op. cit.* pp. 113 ff., to whose lucid explanation I am much indebted here. See also Strong *J. T. S.* vol. iii 36, Liddon *Bampt. Lect.* p. 33, and Schwane *Dogmengeschichte* i 144.

[2] See Harnack *op. cit.* pp. 87 and 88.

Δ. Ἔλεγχος καὶ Ἀπολογία 175

the course of these remarks, the latter is very thorough and unreserved in maintaining his predecessor's orthodoxy: he not only supports Dionysius in his complaints that the critics picked out one or two expressions and pressed them unfairly to the neglect of the general tenour of his argument, but he also urges a defence of those less fortunate expressions which is itself barely defensible[1]. He will not in fact see that anything which Dionysius had said could fairly be alleged in support of Arianism (the rising heresy of his own time).

Basil on the contrary is much more temperate in his defence. There are three passages in which he refers to Dionysius of Alexandria. The first is in *de Spiritu Sancto*, chap. 29 § 72, from which come the three short but important extracts from the Ἔλεγχος given on pp. 196 and 198. In the preceding § 71 Basil had mentioned both the Dionysii as well as Clemens Romanus and Irenaeus amongst those who in the doxology used either the form καί or σὺν τῷ πνεύματι indiscriminately, and quotes the closing sentence of the Ἔλεγχος with the remark that "it is surprising to hear (such honour paid by him to the Holy Spirit)" but adds that "no one can say that it was altered afterwards: for he would not have insisted so much on his having received the formula (from the ancients) if he had said ἐν τῷ πνεύματι, the latter being a common form, whereas it was the former that required defence." The second reference is in *Ep.* I ix to Maximus the Philosopher, who had consulted him as to the orthodoxy of Dionysius the Great. Basil's reply is this: "We do not admire all the man says, some things indeed we distinctly contradict. For he is, so far as we know, the first man who sowed the seed of the impiety now prevailing as to τὸ ἀνόμοιον. Yet I do not think wickedness of purpose to be the cause but his vehement desire to oppose Sabellius." Basil then proceeds to compare Dionysius to a gardener who in trying to straighten the branch of a tree pulls it too much the other way, and continues: "The result is that he exchanges one evil for another and misses the ὀρθότης τοῦ λόγου. Consequently he is very variable in his compositions, sometimes rejecting τὸ ὁμοούσιον, because his opponent had used it to disprove the ὑποστάσεις, and sometimes adopting it where he is answering his namesake[2]. And moreover about the Spirit also he has uttered words which are by no means becoming to the Spirit, banishing Him from the adorable Godhead and

---

[1] See p. 194.   [2] Hardly an accurate statement: see p. 171.

reckoning Him in a lower rank with created and subject nature. Such therefore is the man (as we find him)." It has been thought that Basil here retracts the approval of Dionysius's views, which, as a young man, he had expressed; but the former quotation shows, as much as the latter, that he was always rather suspicious of Dionysius's phraseology, though at heart he believed him to be sound and orthodox. The third reference is in *Ep.* ii 188 to Amphilochius περὶ κανόνων : here again Basil freely criticizes Dionysius's attitude towards heretical baptism, particularly in connexion with the Pepucenes (one of the Montanist heresies). He is surprised that Dionysius κανονικὸς ὤν did not see the blasphemous results of accepting their baptism εἰς πατέρα καὶ υἱὸν καὶ Μοντανὸν ἢ Πρίσκιλλαν : we however must be, he says, careful to avoid his mistake.

Basil's opinion of the Roman Dionysius is a high one : in *Ep.* ii 70 to Damasus (*de synodo*) he speaks of him as ἐκεῖνον τὸν μακαριώτατον ἐπίσκοπον παρ' ὑμῖν ἐπί τε ὀρθότητι πίστεως καὶ τῇ λοιπῇ ἀρετῇ διαπρέψαντα, and refers to a letter of his to the Church of Caesarea (Basil's own see), and to a signal proof of kindness which he had given in bringing about the release of Christian captives in those parts (πέμπειν τοὺς ἀπολυτρουμένους ἐκ τῆς αἰχμαλωσίας τὴν ἀδελφότητα)[1]. Dionysius of Alexandria himself, according to Eus. *H. E.* vii 7. 6, considered his future opponent to be λόγιός τε καὶ θαυμάσιος ἀνήρ, when still only a Roman presbyter (p. 55), and we may well believe that his notorious fair-mindedness and generosity would enable him to retain this good opinion to the end.

The text of the Ἔλεγχος here given is in the main based on that of Routh (*Rell. Sacr.* iii pp. 390 ff.).

Διονυσίου τοῦ κατὰ Ῥώμην πρὸς Σαβελλιανοὺς Ἐπιστολή

(Athan. *de decret. Nic. Syn.* c. 26)

"Ὅτι δὲ οὐ ποίημα οὐδὲ κτίσμα ὁ τοῦ θεοῦ λόγος, ἀλλὰ ἴδιον τῆς τοῦ πατρὸς οὐσίας γέννημα ἀδιαίρετόν ἐστιν, ὡς ἔγραψεν ἡ μεγάλη σύνοδος, ἰδοὺ καὶ ὁ τῆς Ῥώμης ἐπίσκοπος Διονύσιος, γράφων κατὰ τῶν τὰ τοῦ Σαβελλίου φρονούντων, σχετλιάζει κατὰ τῶν ταῦτα τολμώντων λέγειν, καί φησιν οὕτως·

[1] See note on p. 45.

Δ. DIONYSIUS OF ROME'S LETTER 177

Ἑξῆς δ' ἂν εἰκότως λέγοιμι καὶ πρὸς τοὺς διαιροῦντας καὶ κατατέμνοντας καὶ ἀναιροῦντας τὸ σεμνότατον κήρυγμα τῆς ἐκκλησίας τοῦ θεοῦ, τὴν μοναρχίαν, εἰς τρεῖς δυνάμεις τινὰς καὶ μεμερισμένας ὑποστάσεις καὶ θεότητας τρεῖς. πέπυσμαι γὰρ εἶναί τινας τῶν παρ' ὑμῖν κατη- 5
χούντων καὶ διδασκόντων τὸν θεῖον λόγον ταύτης ὑφηγητὰς τῆς φρονήσεως· οἳ κατὰ διάμετρον, ὡς ἔπος εἰπεῖν,

1 διαιρουντας] καταδιαιρ. Cod Reg

1. *In opposing the doctrine of Sabellius who says that the Father and the Son are the same, certain of you have been led into a kind of tritheism akin to Marcion's heresy of three principles in the Godhead, thus destroying the Unity of the Trinity and contradicting the Scriptures.*
ib. διαιρ. καὶ κατατέμν. καὶ ἀναιρ.] 'dividing and dissecting and thus destroying': for διαιρεῖν cf. διαιρεῖ καὶ μακρύνει καὶ μερίζει τὸν υἱὸν ἀπὸ τοῦ πατρός (Athan. *de sent. Dion.* 16) and Greg. Naz. *Theol. Or.* i 6 (p. 10 Mason) τί...ἀκούει...τομὴν καὶ διαίρεσιν καὶ ἀνάλυσιν; iii 8 (p. 84) κατάβαλέ σου...τὰς διαιρέσεις καὶ τὰς τομάς.
3. τὴν μοναρχίαν] See note on πολυαρχία p. 185.
ib. τρεῖς δυνάμεις τινάς] The use of the word δύναμις in this connexion is an unusual one, and D. of R. himself seems to be conscious of this and to apologize for it by adding τινάς. D. of A. appears to have used no language which justified the insinuation: so far as we know, he had only quoted 1 Cor. i 24, where Christ is called δύναμις θεοῦ, and Wisdom vii 25, where σοφία is described as ἀτμὶς τῆς τοῦ θεοῦ δυνάμεως: see pp. 186 and 187.
4. μεμερισμένας] See p. 196.
ib. ὑποστάσεις] See Introduction, pp. 173 f. and n. on p. 196. Acc. to Jerome (*ad Dam.* x 4) *D. Rom. cum tota saecularium schola nihil*

aliud hypostasim nisi usiam (οὐσίαν) *novit.* Orig. *in Joh.* tom. ii (p. 71 Brooke) on the other hand speaks of his belief in τρεῖς ὑποστάσεις, and *c. Cels.* viii 12 (p. 229 Kötschau) describes the Father and the Son as δύο τῇ ὑποστάσει πράγματα, where the word means 'person' rather than 'being': cf. *in Joh.* tom. x (p. 231 Brooke). Dionysius of Rome understood D. of A. as if he had meant the word in the sense of ' essence' not ' person.'
ib. θεότητας τρεῖς] Lower down tritheism of a certain kind is definitely attributed to the Alexandrian Church (τρεῖς θεοὺς τρόπον τινὰ κηρύττουσιν): here the abstract term θεότητας in combination with the two other abstract terms δυνάμεις and ὑποστάσεις is not meant to be quite equivalent to θεούς but rather suggests 'grades' or 'kinds of Godhead.'
5. πέπυσμαι] See Introduction p. 166 for the way in which he had gained this information.
ib. παρ' ὑμῖν] sc. the Alexandrian Church in general: see Introduction p. 167.
ib. κατηχούντων] 'giving oral instruction' (to catechumens and others): cf. Luke i 4 and Gal. vi 6.
6. τὸν θεῖον λόγον] here bears its more ordinary meaning of 'Christian teaching,' i.e. theology in general.
ib. ταύτης ὑφηγητὰς τῆς φρονήσεως] 'who instil this notion.'
7. κατὰ διάμετρον...ἀντίκεινται]

F.   12

ἀντίκεινται τῇ Σαβελλίου γνώμῃ. ὁ μὲν γὰρ βλασφημεῖ, αὐτὸν τὸν υἱὸν εἶναι λέγων τὸν πατέρα, καὶ ἔμπαλιν· οἱ δὲ τρεῖς θεοὺς τρόπον τινὰ κηρύττουσιν, εἰς τρεῖς ὑποστάσεις ξένας ἀλλήλων, παντάπασι κεχωρισμένας, 5 διαιροῦντες τὴν ἁγίαν μονάδα. ἡνῶσθαι γὰρ ἀνάγκη τῷ θεῷ τῶν ὅλων τὸν θεῖον λόγον· ἐμφιλοχωρεῖν δὲ τῷ θεῷ καὶ ἐνδιαιτᾶσθαι δεῖ τὸ ἅγιον πνεῦμα. ἤδη καὶ τὴν θείαν τριάδα εἰς ἕνα, ὥσπερ εἰς κορυφήν τινα (τὸν θεὸν τῶν ὅλων τὸν παντοκράτορα λέγω), συγκεφαλαιοῦσθαί τε καὶ 10 συνάγεσθαι πᾶσα ἀνάγκη· Μαρκίωνος γὰρ τοῦ ματαιόφρονος δίδαγμα εἰς τρεῖς ἀρχὰς τῆς μοναρχίας τομὴν καὶ διαίρεσιν, παίδευμα ὂν διαβολικόν, οὐχὶ δὲ τῶν ὄντως

12 διαιρεσιν] add διορίζει Routh e coniec

'are diametrically opposed' as we say, though the addition of ὡς ἔπος εἰπεῖν suggests that the phrase was still usually employed in its geometrical, not metaphorical, sense: cf. Athan. *de sent. D.* c. 13 (p. 167 n. 2) where this sentence is referred to. Lidd. and Sc. quote Luc. *Catapl.* 4 ἐκ διαμέτρου ἀντικεῖσθαι.
4. ξένας ἀλλήλ. παντάπ. κεχωρισμ.] a much stronger statement than μεμερισμένας above. We gather from Athan. *de sent.* D. c. 4 that D. of A. had used some such phrase as οὐ φύσει ἴδιος ἀλλὰ ξένος κατ' οὐσίαν τοῦ πατρός. See p. 192, where his defence is given, πῶς...μεμερίσθαι ...καὶ ἀφωρίσθαι παντελῶς ἀλλήλων οἴομαι;
6. τὸν θεῖον λόγον] 'the Divine Word' (sc. the Son).
ib. ἐμφιλοχωρεῖν] 'to love to dwell in': the word is used (e.g.) by Cyril of Alexandria *in Joh.* v (lib. ii p. 2057) ἐμφιλοχωρεῖ τοῖς εὐγνώμοσιν ὁ χριστός and Greg. Naz. *Theol. Or.* v 22 (p. 172 Mason) but neither ἐμφιλοχ. nor ἐνδιαιτᾶσθαι (to live in) is ordinarily used of the Holy Spirit. D. of A. uses a different figure on p. 192 ἐν ταῖς χερσὶν αὐτῶν ἐστὶ τὸ πνεῦμα.
7. ἤδη καὶ...πᾶσα ἀνάγκη] In speaking of the Second and Third Persons in the last sentence D. has urged the necessity (ἀνάγκη and δεῖ) of maintaining their Unity with the Almighty Father. Now, he says, it is still further absolutely essential that They should be summed up and gathered into Him. This absolute identification of the term 'the Almighty God' with the Person of the Father is archaic and biblical and might seem to go some way towards justifying the language used by D. of A.
8. εἰς ἕνα...συγκεφαλαιοῦσθαι] The way in which Dionysius of Alexandria consented to accept these phrases in his reply is given on p. 193 τὴν τριάδα συγκεφαλαιούμεθα εἰς τὴν μονάδα, but so that the Trinity remains ἀμείωτος.
10. Μαρκίωνος γὰρ...μαθήμασιν] It is evident that in this sentence D. of R. suggests a parallel between the teaching which he is impugning and that of Marcion, but the grammatical construction of the sentence is not quite certain. Unless some word like διορίζει, which Routh

Δ. DIONYSIUS OF ROME'S LETTER

μαθητῶν τοῦ χριστοῦ καὶ τῶν ἀρεσκομένων. τοῖς τοῦ
σωτῆρος μαθήμασιν. οὗτοι γὰρ τριάδα μὲν κηρυττομένην
ὑπὸ τῆς θείας γραφῆς σαφῶς ἐπίστανται, τρεῖς δὲ θεοὺς
οὔτε παλαιὰν οὔτε καινὴν διαθήκην κηρύττουσαν.

Οὐ μεῖον δ' ἄν τις καταμέμφοιτο καὶ τοὺς ποίημα τὸν 5
υἱὸν εἶναι δοξάζοντας, καὶ γεγονέναι τὸν κύριον, ὥσπερ
ἕν τι ὂν τῶν γενομένων, νομίζοντας, τῶν θείων λογίων
γέννησιν αὐτῷ τὴν ἁρμόττουσαν καὶ πρέπουσαν, ἀλλ'
οὐχὶ πλάσιν τινὰ καὶ ποίησιν προσμαρτυρούντων. βλάσ-
φημον οὖν οὐ τὸ τυχόν, μέγιστον μὲν οὖν, χειροποίητον 10
τρόπον τινὰ λέγειν τὸν κύριον. εἰ γὰρ γέγονεν υἱός, ἦν
ὅτε οὐκ ἦν· ἀεὶ δὲ ἦν, εἴ γε ἐν τῷ πατρί ἐστιν, ὡς αὐτός

6 δοξάζοντας] δοξάσαντας Cod Reg ‖ 7 ὂν τῶν] ὄντως Cod Reg

proposes, has fallen out, the sentence must depend on ἀνάγκη (in a kind of *oratio obliqua*): 'because the division and separation of the μοναρχία into three ἀρχαί (is) the perverse Marcion's doctrine, a diabolical tenet indeed, unknown to Christ's true disciples who are content to accept the Saviour's teaching.' The better known heresy of Marcion was that there were two principles, a good and a bad. The idea that there were three was apparently a later developement of his school: see Eus. *H. E.* v 13. 3 and 4, where these words of Rhodon are quoted, ἕτεροι δὲ καθὼς καὶ αὐτὸς ὁ ναύτης Μαρκίων δύο ἀρχὰς εἰσηγοῦνται..., ἄλλοι δὲ πάλιν ἀπ' αὐτῶν (sc. Potitus and Basilicus who agreed with Marcion) ἐπὶ τὸ χεῖρον ἐξοκείλαντες οὐ μόνον δύο ἀλλὰ καὶ τρεῖς ὑποτίθενται φύσεις, ὧν ἐστιν ἀρχηγὸς καὶ προστάτης Σύνερως. Routh also quotes Cyril of Jerusalem *Cat.* 6. 16, Epiph. *Haer.* 42. 3 and Aug. *de haer.* 22.

1. ἀρεσκομένων] 'acquiescing in,' 'joyfully accepting': this use of the middle of ἀρέσκειν is not uncommon: see Liddell and Scott s.v.

2. οὗτοι γὰρ] sc. οἱ ὄντως μαθηταὶ τ. χ.

5. *Not less reprehensible are those who speak of the Son as in any sense 'made' and 'having become.' They seem to have neglected the teaching of Scripture on His eternal generation.*

ib. Οὐ μεῖον δὲ κτλ.] Here begins the discussion of the second point in D. of A.'s recent utterances, to which D. of R. objects (ποίημα τὸν υἱὸν εἶναι δοξάζοντας). For D. of A.'s defence see pp. 193 ff., but the exact phrase γεγονέναι τὸν κύριον is nowhere actually discussed.

7. ὂν τῶν] The ordinary reading is ὄντως, but, if this is correct, the addition of τῶν (or even ὂν τῶν) before it is required, and the meaning, in accordance with the context, can only be 'of those things which really came into existence' (i.e. from non-existence) not 'which came into real existence.' I have adopted therefore the reading in the text which yields a much more obvious and satisfactory sense: 'as being one of those things which came into existence' or 'were made.'

12. ἐν τῷ πατρί] John xiv 11.

12—2

φησι, καὶ εἰ λόγος καὶ σοφία καὶ δύναμις ὁ χριστός (ταῦτα γὰρ εἶναι τὸν χριστὸν αἱ θεῖαι λέγουσι γραφαί, ὥσπερ ἐπίστασθε), ταῦτα δὲ δυνάμεις οὖσαι τοῦ θεοῦ τυγχάνουσιν· εἰ τοίνυν γέγονεν ὁ υἱός, ἦν ὅτε οὐκ ἦν ταῦτα.
5 ἦν ἄρα καιρός, ὅτε χωρὶς τούτων ἦν ὁ θεός· ἀτοπώτατον δὲ τοῦτο. καὶ τί ἂν ἐπὶ πλέον περὶ τούτων πρὸς ὑμᾶς διαλεγοίμην, πρὸς ἄνδρας πνευματοφόρους καὶ σαφῶς ἐπισταμένους τὰς ἀτοπίας τὰς ἐκ τοῦ ποίημα λέγειν τὸν υἱὸν ἀνακυπτούσας; αἷς μοι δοκοῦσι μὴ προσεσχηκέναι
10 τὸν νοῦν οἱ καθηγησάμενοι τῆς δόξης ταύτης, καὶ διὰ τοῦτο κομιδῇ τοῦ ἀληθοῦς διημαρτηκέναι, ἑτέρως ἢ βούλεται ταύτῃ ἡ θεία καὶ προφητικὴ γραφὴ τὸ Κύριος ἔκτισέ με ἀρχὴν ὁδῶν αὐτοῦ ἐκδεξάμενοι. οὐ μία γὰρ ἡ τοῦ

10 ταύτης Cod Reg om cett || 11 ἢ] Cod Reg ῇ || 12 ταύτῃ] αὐτή Routh e coniec

1. λόγ. κ. σοφ. κ. δύν.] 1 Cor. i 24, see p. 186.

3. δυνάμεις οὖσαι] Here used in a different and more ordinary sense than above p. 177.

4. ἦν ὅτε οὐκ ἦν] 'there was a period when He was not': see pp. 185 ff. This was the phrase which the Arians afterwards took up as describing the γέννησις of Christ: they avoided the word χρόνος as they wished to imply that His Sonship was before all time.

5. καιρός] A strange word to use in this connexion, if it retains any of its earlier meaning of 'season' or 'occasion': but see Dr Hort's note on 1 Pet. i 11.

ib. ἀτοπώτατον δὲ τοῦτο] D. of R. shows but slight appreciation of the Alexandrians' position: they would all have agreed with what he here says, but, as Harnack remarks, "the subtle distinction between Logos and Logos he leaves wholly out of account" (iii p. 94 n.). See Introduction p. 169.

7. πνευματοφόρους] not 'bearing the spirit' but 'borne by the spirit': applied to prophets by Hos. ix 7 and Zeph. iii 4 (LXX): cf. 2 Pet. i 21 and Gal. v 18; and to N.T. writers as well by Theophilus of Antioch *ad Autol.* ii 22, iii 12; cf. Sanday *Inspiration* p. 31.

9. ἀνακυπτούσας] used of objects that emerge from the surface of water or the like.

12. ταύτῃ] If this is the right reading, it apparently means 'by this line of argument,' but it is out of place where it stands in the middle of the clause ἑτέρως...... γραφή and hardly required. Routh's emendation αὐτή makes better sense.

ib. τὸ Κύριος...αὐτοῦ] Prov. viii 22: grammatically the quotation is the object after ἐκδεξ.

13. ἐκδεξάμενοι] 'interpreting': cf. the use of the noun ἐκδοχή p. 116.

ib. οὐ μία κτλ.] Cf. πρὸς Βασιλείδην p. 97 for a similar discussion.

Δ. DIONYSIUS OF ROME'S LETTER

ἔκτιcεν, ὡς ἴστε, σημασία· ἔκτιcε γὰρ ἐνταῦθα ἀκουστέον
ἀντὶ τοῦ ἐπέστησε τοῖς ὑπ' αὐτοῦ γεγονόσιν ἔργοις,
γεγονόσι δὲ δι' αὐτοῦ τοῦ υἱοῦ. οὐχὶ δέ γε τὸ ἔκτιcεν
νῦν λέγοιτ' ἂν ἐπὶ τοῦ ἐποίησε· διαφέρει γὰρ τοῦ ποιῆσαι
τὸ κτίσαι. ογκ αγτὸc ογτὸc coγ πατὴρ ἐκτὴcατό cε, καὶ 5
ἐποίηcέ cε καὶ ἔκτιcέ cε; τῇ ἐν τῷ Δευτερονομίῳ μεγάλῃ
ᾠδῇ ὁ Μωσῆς φησί. πρὸς οὓς καὶ εἴποι ἄν τις· ὦ
ῥιψοκίνδυνοι ἄνθρωποι, ποίημα ὁ πρωτότοκοc πάcηc κτίcεωc, ὁ ἐκ γαcτρὸc πρὸ ἑωcφόρογ γεννηθείc, ὁ εἰπὼν ὡς
σοφία, Πρὸ δὲ πάντων Βογνῶν γεννᾷ με; καὶ πολλαχοῦ 10
δὲ τῶν θείων λογίων γεγεννῆσθαι, ἀλλ' οὐ γεγονέναι, τὸν
υἱὸν λεγόμενον εὕροι τις ἄν. ὑφ' ὧν καταφανῶς ἐλέγχονται τὰ ψεύδη περὶ τῆς τοῦ κυρίου γεννήσεως ὑπολαμβάνοντες οἱ ποίησιν αὐτοῦ τὴν θείαν καὶ ἄρρητον γέννησιν
λέγειν τολμῶντες. 15

Οὔτ' οὖν καταμερίζειν χρὴ εἰς τρεῖς θεότητας τὴν

---

1. ἔκτισε γὰρ ἐνταῦθα] Perhaps D. of R. does not mean that ἔκτισε is equivalent to ἐπέστησε but that the whole expression ἐπέστ....ἔργοις represents the sense of the whole expression ἔκτισε...ὁδὸν αὐτοῦ.

3. οὐχὶ δὲ...ἐποίησε] 'yes, and the word ἔκτισεν could not in the case before us (νῦν) be used for ἐποίησε.'

4. διαφέρει τοῦ ποιῆσαι τὸ κτίσαι] The Septuagint uses these two verbs in various ways: κτίζειν often represents the Hebrew *bârâ* (*creare*), in Is. xliv 2 it stands for Heb. *âsâh* (*facere*), here in Prov. viii 22 it represents *qânâh* (*possidere*), where ἐκτήσατο seems more natural. On the other hand ποιεῖν represents *bârâ* and *âsâh* and other words. For a discussion of the patristic interpretation of this text see Schwane *Dogmengeschichte* ii 109 ff. and Mason *Greg. Naz.* p. 110.

5. οὐκ αὐτὸς...ἔκτισέ σε;] Deut. xxxii 6: here ἐκτήσατο represents the word which in Prov. viii 22 above is rendered ἔκτισεν, while ἔκτισεν stands for Heb. *kûn*; but D. of R. quotes the passage to show that the Scriptures distinguish between ποιεῖν and κτίζειν, as well as to show that both verbs are applied to the begetting of sons.

7. πρὸς οὕς] sc. τοὺς καθηγησαμένους τῆς δόξης ταύτης.

8. ῥιψοκίνδυνοι] 'running needless risks' (of Divine wrath).

ib. ὁ πρωτότ. π. κτ.] Col. i 15.

9. ἐκ γαστ. ... γενν.] Ps. cix (cx) 3.

10. πρὸ δὲ π....με] Prov. viii 25.

12. ἐλέγχονται...ὑπολαμβ.] 'are convicted of holding that which is false about the Lord's generation.'

16. *Both these errors must be avoided: we must believe in the Three Persons but also maintain Their essential Unity.*

ib. Οὔτ' οὖν καταμερίζ. κτλ.] This is the final decision upon the two points raised in the extract.

θαυμαστὴν καὶ θείαν μονάδα, οὔτε ποιήσει κωλύειν τὸ ἀξίωμα καὶ τὸ ὑπερβάλλον μέγεθος τοῦ κυρίου, ἀλλὰ πεπιστευκέναι εἰς Θεὸν πατέρα παντοκράτορα καὶ εἰς Χριστὸν Ἰησοῦν τὸν υἱὸν αὐτοῦ καὶ εἰς τὸ ἅγιον πνεῦμα· 5 ἡνῶσθαι δὲ τῷ θεῷ τῶν ὅλων τὸν λόγον. Ἐγὼ γάρ, φησι, καὶ ὁ πατὴρ ἓν ἐσμεν· καὶ ἐγὼ ἐν τῷ πατρὶ καὶ ὁ πατὴρ ἐν ἐμοί. οὕτω γὰρ ἂν καὶ ἡ θεία τριὰς καὶ τὸ ἅγιον κήρυγμα τῆς μοναρχίας διασώζοιτο.

Ἔλεγχος καὶ Ἀπολογία

1. (Eus. *Praep. Evang.* vii 19)

11 Θήσω δὲ οὐκ ἐμὰς φωνὰς τῶν δὲ πρόσθεν ἡμῶν τὸ δόγμα διηκριβωκότων καὶ πρώτου γε Διονυσίου ὃς ἐν τῷ πρώτῳ τῶν πρὸς Σαβέλλιον αὐτῷ γεγυμνασμένων τάδε περὶ τοῦ προκειμένου γράφει·

Οὐδ' ἐκεῖνοι μὲν γὰρ ὅσιοι, οἱ τὴν ὕλην ὡς ἀγένητον

1 κωλυειν] ? κολουειν Routh e coniec

1. ποιήσει κωλύειν] 'to hinder (or impair) by the idea of "making"': Routh's emendation κολούειν is unnecessary.
5. Ἐγὼ...ἐσμέν] John x 30.
6. ἐγὼ...ἐμοί] *ibid.* xiv 11.
7. οὕτω...διασώζοιτο] i.e. by an acknowledgement of the mystery, not by attempts to reconcile the Triad and the Monarchia logically.
14. *Those are to be reprehended who hold that Matter is unoriginate but subject to the disposition and modification of God. For this makes Matter like yet unlike God, and lands them in the difficulty of maintaining that there can be two things equally unoriginate, and moreover that One of these is active and unchangeable, the other passive and changeable.*
ib. Οὐδ' ἐκεῖνοι...τῷ θεῷ] 'for neither are those pious, who hand over matter to God as a thing without beginning for His orderly disposition.' 'In this part of the *Praepar. Evangel.* Eusebius apparently opposes to the view which he accepts two heresies, (1) κακίας πηγὴν τὴν ὕλην εἶναι ἀγένητόν τε ὑπάρχειν, (2) τῇ μὲν οἰκείᾳ φύσει ἄποιον καὶ ἀσχημάτιστον, τῇ δὲ τοῦ θεοῦ δυνάμει τὸν κόσμον αὐταῖς ποιότησι προσειληφέναι, of which (2) is much to be preferred to (1). D. here discusses (2). Down to χειροκμ. τ. θεόν he states objections to it: but from εἰ δὲ οἴαν onwards he commends it in comparison with (1).'' (H. Jackson.) Cf. Greg. Naz. *Theol. Or.* iii 11 (p. 88 Mason) οὐκ ἂν μὲν συγχωρήσαιεν εἶναι μόνου Θεοῦ τὸ ἀγέννητον οἱ καὶ τὴν ὕλην καὶ τὴν ἰδέαν συνεισάγοντες ὡς ἀγέννητα. These however are the Platonists, whereas

Δ. Ἔλεγχος καὶ Ἀπολογία

ὑποχείριον εἰς διακόσμησιν διδόντες τῷ θεῷ· παθητὴν γὰρ
αὐτὴν καὶ τρεπτὴν ὑπάρχουσαν εἴκειν ταῖς θεοποιήτοις
ἀλλοιώσεσι. καὶ πόθεν γὰρ ὑπάρχει καὶ τῷ θεῷ καὶ τῇ ὕλῃ
τό τε ὅμοιον καὶ τὸ ἀνόμοιον διασαφήτωσαν. ἑκατέρου
γὰρ δεῖ τινὰ ἐπινοῆσαι κρείττονα, ὃ μηδὲ θεμιτὸν ἐν- 5
νοῆσαι περὶ τοῦ θεοῦ. τό τε γὰρ ἀγένητον, ὅμοιον ἐν
ἀμφοτέροις λεγόμενον, καὶ ἕτερον νοούμενον παρ' ἑκάτερον, πόθεν ἐν αὐτοῖς ἐγένετο; εἰ μὲν γὰρ αὐτοαγένητόν
ἐστιν ὁ θεός, καὶ οὐσία ἐστὶν αὐτοῦ, ὡς ἂν εἴποι τις,
ἡ ἀγενησία, οὐκ ἂν ἀγένητον εἴη ἡ ὕλη· οὐ γὰρ ταυτόν 10
ἐστιν ἡ ὕλη καὶ ὁ θεός. εἰ δὲ ἑκάτερον μέν ἐστιν ὅπερ
ἐστὶν ἡ ὕλη καὶ ὁ θεός, πρόσεστι δὲ ἀμφοτέροις τὸ
ἀγένητον, δῆλον ὡς ἕτερόν ἐστιν ἑκατέρου, καὶ ἀμφοτέρων
πρεσβύτερόν τε καὶ ἀνωτέρω. ἀνατρεπτικὴ δὲ παντελῶς
καὶ τοῦ ταῦτα συνυπάρχειν, μᾶλλον δὲ τοῦ τὸ ἕτερον 15

2 και τρεπτην] om BO ‖ 3 και τω θεω] om και IO ‖ 4 το τε] om το BO ‖ διασαφητωσαν] -ειτωσαν BO ‖ 6 του θεου] om του BO ‖ 8 αυτοαγενητον] αυτο αγεννητ. edd ‖ 10 αγενησια] αγενν. O ‖ 11 η υλη και ο θεος] ο θεος και η υλη I ‖ 11 ει...αγενητων] om B ‖ οπερ εστιν] om O ‖ 15 του το] τουτο edd

D. seems to be attacking rather the Gnostics of various kinds or the Manichees or the theories of Hermogenes the Stoic (so Gallandius), as we have them described by Tertullian in his treatise against him.

ib. ἐκεῖνοι μέν] Dionysius is not very strict in his use of μέν, but perhaps there was another class of misbelievers mentioned in the next section to this.

4. ἑκατέρου ... κρείττονα] 'for someone must be imagined superior to either,' i.e. there must have been some agent who gave to them both that property of ἀγενησία.

6. τό τε γὰρ ἀγέν....ἐγένετο;] 'for whence came it that there is in them both the being without beginning, which is what is said to be "like" in both, and which is also conceived of as different from both

(ἕτερον παρ' ἑκάτ.)?' The ἀγενησία is not the very essence of either.

9. οὐσία ἐστὶν αὐτοῦ] 'His very essence.' This position is combated by Greg. Naz. *Theol. Or.* iii 10 (pp. 87 and 88 Mason).

11. εἰ δὲ ἑκάτ....ἀνωτέρω] 'but if each is what it is independently and to both belongs in addition the attribute of being without beginning, clearly the being without beginning is different from either and older and higher than both.' For πρεσβύτερον cf. p. 163.

15. ταῦτα] viz. God and matter.

ib. μᾶλλον δὲ τοῦ τὸ κτλ.] Both Dr Mason and Dr Jackson have independently suggested the restoration of the right reading τοῦ τό for τοῦτο (retained by Dr Gifford) here.

αὐτῶν τὴν ὕλην ἐφ' ἑαυτῆς ὑπάρχειν, καὶ ἡ τῆς ἐναντίας
ἕξεως διαφορά. εἰπάτωσαν γὰρ τὴν αἰτίαν, δι' ἥν, ἀμφοτέρων ὄντων ἀγενήτων, ὁ μὲν θεὸς ἀπαθής, ἄτρεπτος,
ἀκίνητος, ἐργαστικός, ἡ δὲ τὰ ἐναντία παθητή, τρεπτή,
5 ἄστατος, μεταποιουμένη.

Καὶ πῶς ἥρμοσαν καὶ συνέδραμον; πότερον κατὰ τὴν
τῆς ὕλης φύσιν ἐξοικειώσας ἑαυτὸν ἐτεχνίτευσεν αὐτὴν
ὁ θεός; ἀλλὰ τοῦτό γε ἄτοπον, ὁμοίως ἀνθρώποις χρυσοχοεῖν καὶ λιθουργεῖν, καὶ κατὰ τὰς ἄλλας τέχνας, ὅσας
10 αἱ ὗλαι μορφοῦσθαι καὶ τυποῦσθαι δύνανται, χειροκμητεῖν τὸν θεόν.

Εἰ δὲ οἵαν αὐτὸς ἐβούλετο κατὰ τὴν ἑαυτοῦ σοφίαν
ἐποίωσε τὴν ὕλην, τὸ πολύμορφον καὶ παμποίκιλον τῆς δη-
μιουργίας ἑαυτοῦ σχῆμα καὶ τύπον ἐνσφραγιζόμενος αὐτῇ,
15 καὶ εὔφημος καὶ ἀληθὴς οὗτος ὁ λόγος, καὶ προσέτι καὶ
τὴν ὑπόστασιν τῶν ὅλων τὸν θεὸν ἀγένητον εἶναι κρατύνει.

1 εφ] αφ O ‖ 4 τα εναντια] om BO ‖ 9 οσας] ως I ‖ 10 αι] om BO ‖
μορφουσθαι και] om BO ‖ τυπουσθαι] τυπουσι BO ‖ δυνανται] om BO ‖
13 εποιωσε BDFI -ησε O edd ‖ 14 εαυτου σχημα] αυτου σωμα BO

1. τὴν ὕλην] in apposition to τὸ
ἕτερον αὐτῶν.
6. *How did Matter and God
come in contact and combine?* Surely
not as the human artificer works upon
the material of his art.
ib. Καὶ πῶς ἥρμ. κ.συνέδρ.;] This
is a new objection: 'Again, how is
it that there is that intimate connexion and harmony between God
and matter that we observe?' Ἥρμοσαν is intrans. here: cf. p. 96.
ib. πότερον...ὁ θεός;] 'did God
adapt (or 'assimilate') Himself to
match (κατά) the nature of matter
and exercise His craft upon it?'
For ἐξοικειώσας cf. p. 255, and for
ἐτεχνίτευσεν cf. p. 163.
9. ὅσας] Κατά must be supplied
from the preceding words.
10. χειροκμητεῖν] apparently a
word coined by D. from the adj.
χειρόκμητος ('handwrought': fr. χείρ
and κάμνειν).
12. *And yet the view that God has
imposed on Matter the manifold qualities which His own wisdom has deter-
mined is so far to be preferred that
by it the Nature of God which is the
basis of the universe is preserved*.
ib. Εἰ δὲ οἵαν...κρατύνει] 'but, if
according to His own wisdom He
endowed matter with such qualities
as He Himself wished, impressing
on it, as with a seal, the multiform
and diverse shape and fashion of
His own workmanship, this account
of it is both proper and true, and yet
further proves that God who is the
fundamental principle (ὑπόστασις)
on which the universe exists is
without beginning.' Ἐποίωσε 'gave
qualities (ποιότητες) to': the reading
ἐποίησε is against the context as
well as against the MSS; for D. is
still using his opponents' position

Δ. Ἔλεγχος καὶ Ἀπολογία

τῷ γὰρ εἶναι ἀγένητον ἅμα καὶ τὸ πῶς εἶναι προσῆψε. πολὺς μὲν οὖν καὶ πρὸς τούτους ὁ λόγος, ἀλλ' οὐ νῦν ἡμῖν πρόκειται· συγκρίσει δὲ τῇ πρὸς τοὺς ἀθεωτάτους πολυθέους εὐφημότεροι οὗτοι.

Ταῦτα μὲν οὖν καὶ ἀπὸ τῶν Διονυσίου.

2. (Holl *Fragmente* 362 p. 147: Mai *Coll. vett. script.* vol. vii p. 96)

Ἀναρχία μᾶλλον καὶ στάσις ἡ ἐξ ἰσοτιμίας ἀντιπαρεξαγομένη πολυαρχία.

3. (Athan. *de sent. Dion.* 14 and 15)

Φασκόντων τοίνυν ἐκείνων φρονεῖν τὸν Διονύσιον· "Οὐκ ἀεὶ ἦν ὁ θεὸς πατήρ, οὐκ ἀεὶ ἦν ὁ υἱός. ἀλλ' ὁ μὲν θεὸς ἦν χωρὶς τοῦ λόγου, αὐτὸς δὲ ὁ υἱὸς οὐκ ἦν πρὶν γεννηθῇ. ἀλλ' ἦν ποτὲ ὅτε οὐκ ἦν. οὐ γὰρ ἀΐδιός ἐστιν ἀλλ' ὕστερον ἐπεγέγονεν," ὅρα πῶς ἀποκρίνεται· τὰ μὲν οὖν πλεῖστα τῶν αὐτοῦ ῥημάτων, ἅπερ ἢ ζητῶν ἐξετάζει, ἢ συλλογιζόμενος συνάγει ἢ ἐρωτῶν ἐλέγχει, ἢ τοὺς κατειρηκότας αἰτιᾶται, ταῦτα παρεὶς διὰ τὸ μῆκος τῶν λόγων μόνα τὰ πρὸς τὴν κατηγορίαν ἀναγ-

3 δὲ γὰρ Cod Vat 1996 f. 78

against themselves. Σχῆμα 'outward shape,' τύπος 'the impress of a seal' (σφραγίς): cf. p. 149. Εὔφημος, sc. not blasphemous against God: so below.

1. τῷ γὰρ...προσῆψε] 'for He added to its ἀγένητον εἶναι (or ἀγενησία) also τὸ πῶς εἶναι,' i.e. it was of itself ἀγένητος and He qualified it. "Thus in so far this doctrine secures to God the proper supremacy and is better than the doctrine of the ἀθεώτατοι, e.g. the upholders of (1)." (H. Jackson.) The subject of προσῆψε is ὁ θεός and τὸ πῶς εἶναι means 'to bear certain qualities,' as suggested by the ἐποίωσε above.

3. συγκρίσει δὲ τῇ...οὗτοι] 'yet these are more proper in their language in comparison with the absolutely atheistical polytheists.' The play on words is just in D.'s style. Εὐφημότεροι refers back first to εὔφημος...ὁ λόγος and then to οὐδ' ἐκεῖνοι...ὅσιοι at the beginning of the passage. Οὗτοι viz. the maintainers of the particular form of dualism which D. has been combating.

8. *The multiplication of co-ordinate principles leads to nothing but confusion and disorder.*

ib. ἡ ἐξ ἰσοτιμ. ἀντιπαρεξ. πολυαρχία] 'the plurality of principles (or deities, ἀρχαί) on an equal footing with which they (the heathen) confront us.' Πολυαρχία is opposed to μοναρχία for which see the Ep. of D. of R. p. 177, and Coustant's note quoted by Routh *Rell. Sacr.* vol. iii p. 385 ff. For a clear statement of the distinction between ἀναρχία (atheism), πολυαρχία and μοναρχία see Greg. Naz. *Theol. Or.* iii 2 (pp. 74—77 Mason): cf. Harnack *op. cit.* iii p. 11 ff.

καῖα τίθημι. ἀπολογούμενος τοίνυν πρὸς ἐκεῖνα γράφει ταῖς λέξεσι ταύταις ἐν τῷ πρώτῳ τῷ ἐπιγραφομένῳ 'Ἐλέγχου καὶ 'Ἀπολογίας μεθ' ἕτερα οὕτω·

Οὐ γὰρ ἦν ὅτε ὁ θεὸς οὐκ ἦν πατήρ.

5 Καὶ τοῦτο οἶδεν ἐν τοῖς ἑξῆς·

ἀεὶ τὸν χριστὸν εἶναι, λόγον ὄντα, καὶ cοφίαν καὶ δύναμιν—οὐ γὰρ δὴ τούτων ἄγονος ὢν ὁ θεὸς εἶτα ἐπαιδοποιήσατο—ἀλλ' ὅτι μὴ παρ' ἑαυτοῦ ὁ υἱός, ἀλλ' ἐκ τοῦ πατρὸς ἔχει τὸ εἶναι.

10 καὶ μετ' ὀλίγα πάλιν περὶ τοῦ αὐτοῦ φησίν·

'Ἀπαύγαcμα δὲ ὢν φωτὸc ἀϊδίου, πάντως καὶ αὐτὸς ἀΐδιός ἐστιν. ὄντος γὰρ ἀεὶ τοῦ φωτός, δῆλον ὡς ἔστιν ἀεὶ τὸ ἀπαύγασμα. τούτῳ γὰρ καὶ ὅτι φῶς ἐστί, τῷ

12 εστιν αει] και Cod Vat ‖ 13 τουτω] Routh coniec τουτο ut in Cod Vat 1996 f. 78

4. *The eternity of the Son as well as of the Father is shown by the examples employed.* For if the Father is compared to the sun, and the Son to the light, then the one being eternal, the other must also be: for we cannot conceive of the one without the other: and so with parent and child, πνεῦμα and ἀτμίς.

ib. Οὐ γὰρ ἦν κτλ.] 'for there never was a time when God was not Father. That (D.) knows this is shown also in what follows, viz. that Christ exists eternally, being the Word and Wisdom and Power. For of course it is not to be supposed that God was once in a state in which He had not produced these things and then afterwards begot them. What is meant is that the Son hath His being not from Himself but from the Father.' Λόγ. ὄντα κ. σοφ. κ. δύν.: cf. D. of R. p. 180.

8. ἀλλ' ὅτι μὴ κτλ.] It seems as if the construction is changed from the accus. and inf. in the former clause (ἀεὶ τὸν χρ. εἶναι). It is possible that in neither clause Athan. gives D.'s exact words.

11. Ἀπαύγασμα ... φωτὸς ἀϊδίου] Wisdom vii 26 (cf. Heb. i 3). This was a common biblical reference in this connexion among the Fathers: e.g. Orig. *in Jer.* ix 4 (Klostermann p. 70); *c. Cels.* v 10, 30; viii 14. The following sentences (ἀπαύγ. δὲ ὢν...ἀειγενές, ὄντος οὖν...ἐκ φωτὸς ὢν and φωτὸς μὲν οὖν...λέγεται) are practically identical with an excerpt given in Vat. Cod. 1996 f. 78 (circ. x cent.), which only adds at the beginning τὸ δὲ εἰμί (in John viii 12) τὸ ἀΐδιον τῆς ὑποστάσεως σημαίνει (with γάρ instead of δὲ after ἀπαύγ. and καὶ between ἀεί and τὸ ἀπαύγ.).

13. τούτῳ γὰρ κτλ.] 'for in this, viz. in shining, lies the very conception of light, and light cannot exist, if it give no light.' Τούτῳ = τῷ καταυγάζειν: if we adopt Routh's emendation τοῦτο, then τοῦτο = καὶ ὅτι φῶς ἐστί: but it would give little meaning to the καί.

Δ. Ἔλεγχος καὶ Ἀπολογία

καταυγάζειν, νοεῖται, καὶ φῶς οὐ δύναται μὴ φωτίζον εἶναι. πάλιν γὰρ ἔλθωμεν ἐπὶ τὰ παραδείγματα· εἰ ἔστιν ἥλιος, ἔστιν αὐγή, ἔστιν ἡμέρα· εἰ τοιούτων μηδὲν ἔστι, πολύ γε δεῖ καὶ παρεῖναι ἥλιον. εἰ μὲν οὖν ἀίδιος ὁ ἥλιος, ἄπαυστος ἂν ἦν καὶ ἡ ἡμέρα. νῦν δέ, οὐ γάρ ἐστι, ἀρξα- 5 μένου τε ἤρξατο, καὶ παυομένου παύεται. ὁ δέ γε θεὸς αἰώνιόν ἐστι φῶς, οὔτε ἀρξάμενον, οὔτε λῆξόν ποτε. οὐκοῦν αἰώνιον πρόκειται καὶ σύνεστιν αὐτῷ τὸ ἀπαύγασμα ἄναρχον καὶ ἀειγενές, προφαινόμενον αὐτοῦ, ὅπερ ἐστὶν ἡ λέγουσα σοφία, Ἐγὼ ἤμην ᾗ προσέχαιρε· καθ᾽ 10 ἡμέραν δὲ εὐφραινόμην ἐν προσώπῳ αὐτοῦ ἐν παντὶ καιρῷ.

Καὶ αὖθις ἐπάγει μετ᾽ ὀλίγα περὶ τοῦ αὐτοῦ λέγων·

Ὄντος οὖν αἰωνίου τοῦ πατρός, αἰώνιος ὁ υἱός ἐστι, φῶς ἐκ φωτὸς ὤν· ὄντος γὰρ γονέως, ἔστι καὶ τέκνον· εἰ δὲ μὴ τέκνον εἴη, πῶς καὶ τίνος εἶναι δύναται γονεύς; ἀλλ᾽ 15 εἰσὶν ἄμφω, καὶ εἰσὶν ἀεί.

Εἶτα πάλιν προστίθησι ταῦτα·

Φωτὸς μὲν οὖν ὄντος τοῦ θεοῦ, ὁ χριστός ἐστιν ἀπαύγασμα. πνεύματος δὲ ὄντος—πνεῦμα γάρ, φησιν, ὁ θεός—ἀναλόγως πάλιν ὁ χριστὸς ἀτμὶς λέγεται—ἀτμὶς γάρ, 20 φησίν, ἐστι τῆς τοῦ θεοῦ δυνάμεως.

4. (*ibid.* c. 18)

Εἶτα καὶ αἰτιασαμένων αὐτὸν ὡς ἕνα λέγοντα τῶν γενητῶν εἶναι

2 ελθωμεν] ηλθομεν Cod Vat || 3 ηλιος] ημερα Cod Vat || εστιν ημερα] om Cod Vat || τοιουτων] -ον Cod Vat || 4 και παρειναι] om και Cod Vat || 5 η ημερα] om η Cod Vat || 8 ουκουν αιων. προκ.] om Cod Vat

2. εἰ ἔστιν ἥλιος, ἔστιν αὐγή] Cf. Tert. *Apolog.* 84 *Cum radius ex sole porrigitur, portio ex summa: sed sol erit in radio, quia solis est radius nec separatur substantia sed extenditur:* cf. *adv. Prax.* cap. viii.

8. αἰώνιον πρόκειται] 'is set before Him from all eternity.' So below προφαινόμ. αὐτοῦ 'shining forth before Him.' The thoughts are explained by the quotation from Proverbs which D. proceeds to make.

10. Ἐγὼ ἤμην...καιρῷ] Prov. viii 30.

14. φῶς ἐκ φωτός] a phrase perhaps already incorporated in the Creeds of various Churches.

19. πνεῦμα ὁ θεός] John iv 24.

20. ἀτμὶς γὰρ...δυνάμεως] Wisd. vii 25.

τὸν υἱὸν καὶ μὴ ὁμοούσιον τῷ πατρί, αὐτὸς πάλιν ἐν μὲν τῷ πρώτῳ βιβλίῳ τοὺς τοιούτους διελέγχει λέγων·

Πλὴν ἐγὼ γενητά τινα καὶ ποιητά τινα φήσας νοεῖσθαι, τῶν μὲν τοιούτων ὡς ἀχρειοτέρων ἐξ ἐπιδρομῆς εἶπον παρα-
5 δείγματα· ἐπεὶ μήτε τὸ φυτὸν ταὐτὸν ἔφην τῷ γεωργῷ, μήτε τῷ ναυπηγῷ τὸ σκάφος. εἶτα τοῖς ἱκνουμένοις καὶ προσ-φυεστέροις ἐνδιέτριψα. καὶ πλέον διεξῆλθον περὶ τῶν ἀληθεστέρων, ποικίλα προσεπεξευρὼν τεκμήρια, ἅπερ καί σοι δι' ἄλλης ἐπιστολῆς ἔγραψα· ἐν οἷς ἤλεγξα καὶ
10 ὃ προφέρουσιν ἔγκλημα κατ' ἐμοῦ ψεῦδος ὄν, ὡς οὐ λέγοντος τὸν χριστὸν ὁμοούσιον εἶναι τῷ θεῷ. εἰ γὰρ

5 ταυτον] deest in codd

3. *Some of the figures I used in speaking of the Son were not quite suitable to my purpose, but afterwards I dealt with several more appropriate figures, and in so doing disposed of the objection that I would not use the term ὁμοούσιος which is not to be found in the Scriptures. I cannot recal my exact words but I remember to have spoken of the relation of a plant to its seed or root, and of a river to its source. But these later arguments of mine they wilfully ignore.*

4. τῶν μὲν τοιούτων κτλ.] Cf. p. 167. 'I did indeed casually mention examples of such things, recognizing that they (i.e. the whole class, not merely the particular examples) were not very useful for my purpose (ὡς ἀχρειοτέρων): for instance I said that neither was the plant the same as the husbandman nor the boat as the shipwright.' I have inserted ταὐτόν in the text as necessary to the sense, though it does not appear in the MSS.

6. τοῖς ἱκν. καὶ προσφ. ἐνδιέτρ.] 'I dwelt at length (opp. to ἐξ ἐπιδρομῆς) upon examples which were to the point and more cognate to the subject.' For this use of ἱκνεῖ-σθαι see L. and Sc. s.v.

9. καί σοι δι' ἄλλης κτλ.] This passage down to τὸ ἐκ τῆς πηγῆς ὕδωρ is quoted again by Athan. *de decr. Syn. Nic.* 25 but without σοι before δι' ἄλλης. Eus. *H. E.* vii 7. 6 and 9. 6 mentions two (other) letters of our Dionysius to Dionysius of Rome, viz. the fourth περὶ βαπτίσματος and ἄλλη τις...ἡ περὶ Λουκιανοῦ. The letter here referred to was probably different from either of these and was apparently unknown to Eusebius: but there is some doubt whether σοι should stand in the text here; see Harnack *Altchr. Litt.* i 416.

10. οὐ λέγοντος τὸν χρ. ὁμοούσ. εἶναι] Athanasius himself, as Harnack points out (*Hist. of Dogma* vol. iii p. 140 n. 2 Eng. Trans.), "always made a sparing use of the catchword ὁμοούσιος in his works. The formula was not sacred to him, but only the cause which he apprehended and established under cover of the formula": cf. also *ibid.* p. 229. Moreover even the synod of Antioch (A.D. 264) "expressly rejected the term as being liable to misconstruction," *ibid.* p. 94: cf. pp. 51 f.

Δ. Ἔλεγχος καὶ Ἀπολογία

καὶ τὸ ὄνομα τοῦτό φημι μὴ εὑρηκέναι μηδ' ἀνεγνωκέναι που τῶν ἁγίων γραφῶν, ἀλλά γε τὰ ἐπιχειρήματά μου τὰ ἑξῆς, ἃ σεσιωπήκασι, τῆς διανοίας ταύτης οὐκ ἀπᾴδει. καὶ γὰρ ἀνθρωπείαν γονὴν παρεθέμην, δῆλον ὡς οὖσαν ὁμογενῆ· φήσας πάντως τοὺς γονεῖς μόνον ἑτέρους εἶναι 5 τῶν τέκνων, ὅτι μὴ αὐτοὶ εἶεν τὰ τέκνα, ἢ μήτε γονεῖς ἀναγκαῖον ὑπάρχειν εἶναι μήτε τέκνα. καὶ τὴν μὲν ἐπιστολήν, ὡς προεῖπον, διὰ τὰς περιστάσεις οὐκ ἔχω προκομίσαι· εἰ δ' οὖν, αὐτά σοι τὰ τότε ῥήματα, μᾶλλον δὲ καὶ πάσης ἂν ἔπεμψα τὸ ἀντίγραφον· ὅπερ, ἂν εὐ- 10 πορήσω, ποιήσω. οἶδα δὲ καὶ μέμνημαι πλείονα προσθεὶς τῶν συγγενῶν ὁμοιώματα· καὶ γὰρ καὶ φυτὸν εἶπον ἀπὸ σπέρματος ἢ ἀπὸ ῥίζης ἀνελθὸν ἕτερον εἶναι τοῦ ὅθεν ἐβλάστησε, καὶ πάντως ἐκείνῳ καθέστηκεν ὁμοφυές· καὶ ποταμὸν ἀπὸ πηγῆς ῥέοντα ἕτερον σχῆμα καὶ ὄνομα 15 μετειληφέναι, μήτε γὰρ τὴν πηγὴν ποταμὸν μήτε τὸν

15 ποταμον] add ειπον catena

1. τὸ ὄνομα τοῦτο] 'this word' (sc. ὁμοούσιος). For the history of the word in the 3rd century cf. Harnack *Hist. of Dogm.* vol. i 257 ff., ii 352 ff., iii 45 ff., 88 ff., Liddon's *Bampt. Lect.* pp. 430 ff., Bethune-Baker *Texts and Studies* vol. vii no. 1.

ib. φημί] sc. in the letter to Euphranor.

3. τῆς διανοίας ταύτης] 'this conception' (sc. of the Homoousion).

4. ἀνθρωπείαν γονὴν κτλ.] 'I used the comparison of human generation, which is clearly a transmission of the parent's own nature.' For D.'s use of ὁμογενῆ here see p. 172.

8. διὰ τὰς περιστάσεις] 'owing to circumstances': the phrase suggests that the present treatise was written when D. was in exile.

9. προκομίσαι] 'lay my hands on,' 'produce,' or perhaps 'despatch.'

ib. εἰ δ' οὖν...ποιήσω] 'otherwise I would have sent you my exact words or rather a copy of the whole (letter): and I will do so, if I have opportunity.' For this use of εἰ δ' οὖν ('if it were not so') cf. Soph. *Ant.* 722 εἰ δ' οὖν, φιλεῖ γὰρ τοῦτο μὴ ταύτῃ ῥέπειν, Καὶ τῶν λεγόντων εὖ καλὸν τὸ μανθάνειν.

11. οἶδα ... μέμνημαι ... προσθείς] The construction is the classical one: 'I know and remember that I added several illustrations from things kindred to one another.'

ib. οἶδα δὲ...ἐκ τῆς πηγῆς ὕδωρ] This passage is given in Cramer's *Catena* (vii p. 362) as from Dionysius. In the *Panoplia* of Euthymius Zigabenus it runs thus, καὶ φυτὸν ἀπὸ ῥίζης ἀνελθὸν ἕτερον μέν ἐστι τοῦ ὅθεν ἐβλάστησεν, ἔστι δὲ ἐκείνῃ ὁμοφυές. καὶ ποταμὸς ἀπὸ πηγῆς ῥέων ἕτερον μέν ἐστι παρ' αὐτήν· μήτε γὰρ ποταμὸν πηγὴν μήτε τὴν πηγὴν ποταμὸν λέγεσθαι, ἓν δὲ ἀμφό-

ποταμὸν πηγὴν λέγεσθαι, καὶ ἀμφότερα ὑπάρχειν, καὶ
τὴν μὲν πηγὴν οἱονεὶ πατέρα εἶναι, τὸν δὲ ποταμὸν εἶναι
ἐκ τῆς πηγῆς ὕδωρ. ἀλλὰ ταῦτα μὲν καὶ τὰ τοιαῦτα μηδὲ
ὁρᾶν γεγραμμένα ἀλλ' οἱονεὶ τυφλώττειν ὑποκρίνονται·
5 τοῖς δὲ δυσὶ ῥηματίοις ἀσυνθέτοις, καθάπερ λίθοις,
μακρόθεν ἐπιχειροῦσί με βάλλειν, ἀγνοοῦντες ὡς τῶν
ἀγνοουμένων καὶ προσαγωγῆς εἰς ἐπίγνωσιν δεομένων οὐ
μόνον ἀλλοῖα πολλάκις ἀλλὰ καὶ ὑπεναντία τεκμήρια
γίνεται τῶν ἐπιζητουμένων δηλώματα.

10   5. (*ibid.* c. 23)

Ἐπειδὴ δὲ...αὐχεῖ (ὁ Ἄρειος) παρὰ τοῖς ἀγνοοῦσιν ὡς καὶ ἐν
τούτοις ἔχων ὁμόδοξον τὸν Διονύσιον, ὅρα καὶ τὴν περὶ τούτων
πίστιν τοῦ Διονυσίου καὶ πῶς μάχεται ταῖς τοιαύταις Ἀρείου
κακονοίαις. γράφει γὰρ ἐν μὲν τῷ πρώτῳ οὕτω·

15 Προείρηται μὲν οὖν, ὅτι πηγὴ τῶν ἀγαθῶν ἁπάντων
ἐστὶν ὁ θεός· ποταμὸς δὲ ὑπ'. αὐτοῦ προχεόμενος ὁ υἱὸς

2 ειναι] add το catena || 16 υπ] Routh coniec απ

τερα ὑπάρχειν ὁμολογοῦμεν [ἔστι]κατὰ
τὴν φύσιν καὶ ὁμοούσια, καὶ τὴν μὲν
πηγὴν οἱονεὶ πατέρα νοεῖσθαι, τὸν δὲ
ποταμὸν εἶναι τὸ ἐκ τῆς πηγῆς γεν-
νώμενον. Tertullian (*adv. Prax.*
cap. viii) makes use of three similar
illustrations of the relation of Father
and Son, viz. *sol* and *radius, fons*
and *fluvius, radix* and *frutex*; see
also *Apolog.* 84 quoted above.

1. καὶ ἀμφότερα ὑπάρχειν] 'and
that both these things exist' (i.e.
that each of the two is itself and
not the other): cf. above ἢ μήτε
γονεῖς ἀναγκαῖον ὑπάρχειν εἶναι μήτε
τέκνα. The reading of Euthymius
above, ἐν δὲ ἀμφ. ὑπ., misses the
point of the argument, as directed
against Sabellian views.

4. γεγραμμένα] i.e. in D.'s letter.

5. τοῖς δὲ δυσὶ ῥημ. ἀσυνθ.] 'with
those two poor phrases of mine, ill-
fitting (as I acknowledge them to
be),' i.e. about the φυτόν and the
σκάφος, for which he has already

apologized as ἀχρειότερα.

ib. καθάπερ λίθοις...βάλλειν] Cf.
p. 46 καταλεύσωμεν.

6. μακρόθεν] 'from a distance'
(*eminus*), i e. they had gone or sent
to Rome in order to attack him.

ib. ἀγνοοῦντες...δηλώματα] 'failing to recognize that where the
subject of enquiry is obscure and
requires to be brought within our
understanding (προσαγωγῆς εἰς
ἐπίγν.), not only do diverse but
even quite contradictory illustrations (τεκμήρια) very often convey
the meaning required.' For τεκμήρια
see above.

15. *As has been said, the Father
is the Source and the Son is the
stream flowing forth from Him.
And so we may compare the former
to the human νοῦς, and the latter to
the λόγος which issues forth by means
of the tongue. Here again the Unity
of the Father and the Son is set
forth.*

Δ. Ἔλεγχος καὶ Ἀπολογία 191

ἀναγέγραπται. Ἀπόρροια γὰρ νοῦ λόγος καί, ὡς ἐπ' ἀνθρώπων εἰπεῖν, ἀπὸ καρδίας διὰ στόματος ἐξοχετεύεται, ἕτερος γενόμενος τοῦ ἐν καρδίᾳ λόγου ὁ διὰ γλώσσης νοῦς προπηδῶν. ὁ μὲν γὰρ ἔμεινε προπέμψας, καὶ ἔστιν οἷος ἦν· ὁ δὲ ἐξέπτη προπεμφθεὶς καὶ φέρεται πανταχοῦ. 5 καὶ οὕτως ἐστὶν ἑκάτερος ἐν ἑκατέρῳ, ἕτερος ὢν θατέρου· καὶ ἕν εἰσιν, ὄντες δύο. οὕτω γὰρ καὶ ὁ πατὴρ καὶ ὁ υἱὸς ἓν καὶ ἐν ἀλλήλοις ἐλέχθησαν εἶναι.

6. (*ibid.* c. 15)

Καὶ ἐκ τοῦ δευτέρου πάλιν φησί· 10

Μόνος δὲ ὁ υἱὸς ἀεὶ συνὼν τῷ πατρί, καὶ τοῦ ὄντος πληρούμενος, καὶ αὐτὸς ἔστιν, ὢν ἐκ τοῦ πατρός.

7. (*ibid.* c. 16 and 17: Holl *Fragmente*, 359, p. 146)

Καὶ πρὸς τὴν ἄλλην ὑποψίαν τῶν λεγόντων ὅτι πατέρα λέγων Διονύσιος οὐκ ὀνομάζει τὸν υἱὸν καὶ πάλιν υἱὸν λέγων οὐκ ὀνο- 15 μάζει τὸν πατέρα ἀλλὰ διαιρεῖ καὶ μακρύνει καὶ μερίζει τὸν υἱὸν ἀπὸ τοῦ πατρός, ἀποκρίνεται καὶ δυσωπεῖ τούτους λέγων ἐν τῷ δευτέρῳ βιβλίῳ·

Τῶν ὑπ' ἐμοῦ λεχθέντων ὀνομάτων ἕκαστον ἀχώριστόν

---

1. ἀναγέγραπται] 'is described' (i.e. in Scripture) or possibly 'is involved' (in the mention of πηγὴ ὁ θεός): cf. προσγέγραπται below p. 193.
ib. Ἀπόρροια] Cf. Wisd. vii 25: cf. Orig. *in Joann.* xiii 25. A similar description of νοῦς and λόγος, reminding us very forcibly, as Harnack (*Hist. of Dogm.* iii p. 91) says, of Porphyry and the Neoplatonists, is given below p. 197.
2. ἐξοχετεύεται] 'is let out' as through a sluice (ὀχετός).
3. ὁ διὰ γλ. νοῦς προπηδῶν] 'the mind that finds expression by means of the tongue': cf. p. 197 below. Προπηδᾶν is applied to ἀγάπη on p. 91.
8. ἐλέχθησαν] sc. in D.'s letter to Euphranor: cf. John x 30, xvii 11, 21, 22.
11. *The Son alone, being ever with the Father and being filled with Him that is, has absolute existence, being from the Father.*
ib. Μόνος δὲ ὁ υἱὸς κτλ.] Cf. above p. 187.
19. *The very titles employed are inseparable from one another. Father implies Son, and Son Father. And Holy Spirit implies the Source from which, and the Medium by which, it proceeds forth. Thus there can be no absolute separation between them. If we expand the Unity, it is without dividing it, and if we sum up the Trinity it is without subtracting from it.*
ib. Τῶν ὑπ' ἐμοῦ...στέρεσθαι] This

ἐστι καὶ ἀδιαίρετον τοῦ πλησίον. πατέρα εἶπον, καὶ πρὶν
ἐπαγάγω τὸν υἱόν, ἐσήμανα καὶ τοῦτον ἐν τῷ πατρί.
υἱὸν ἐπήγαγον· εἰ καὶ μὴ προειρήκειν τὸν πατέρα, πάντως ἂν ἐν τῷ υἱῷ προείληπτο. ἅγιον πνεῦμα προσέθηκα·
5 ἀλλ' ἅμα καὶ πόθεν καὶ διὰ τίνος ἦκεν ἐφήρμοσα. οἱ δὲ
οὐκ ἴσασιν ὅτι μήτε ἀπηλλοτρίωται πατὴρ υἱοῦ ᾗ πατήρ,
—προκαταρκτικὸν γάρ ἐστι τῆς συναφείας τὸ ὄνομα,—
οὔτε ὁ υἱὸς ἀπῴκισται τοῦ πατρός· ἡ γὰρ πατὴρ προσ-
ηγορία δηλοῖ τὴν κοινωνίαν. ἔν τε ταῖς χερσὶν αὐτῶν
10 ἐστὶ τὸ πνεῦμα, μήτε τοῦ πέμποντος μήτε τοῦ φέροντος
δυνάμενον στέρεσθαι. πῶς οὖν ὁ τούτοις χρώμενος τοῖς
ὀνόμασι μεμερίσθαι ταῦτα καὶ ἀφωρίσθαι παντελῶς
ἀλλήλων οἴομαι;

2 και τουτον] om και Holl ‖ τω πατρι] om τω Holl ‖ 3 ει και μη] και ει
μη Holl ‖ 11 δυναμενον στερεσθαι] δυναμενων υστερεισθαι Holl

passage is given by Holl *Fragmente* 359 p. 146 from the *Sacr. Parall. Rupefuc.* fol. 17 with the important variation of δυναμένων ὑστερεῖσθαι ('neither the Sender nor the Bearer being able to be left destitute of Him') for δυνάμενον στέρεσθαι ('the Spirit not being able to be deprived of either the Sender or the Bearer'); the reading στέρεσθαι is supported by στέρονται below p. 197. In the first sentence of the passage (τῶν ὑπ' ἐμοῦ...πλησίον) D. insists that each title (Father, Son, and Spirit) is meaningless without the other: 'each of the titles used by me is indivisible and inseparable from its neighbour.'

5. ' καὶ πόθεν καὶ διὰ τίνος] i.e. from the Father and through the Son: a view of the procession of the Holy Spirit, which D. appears to have derived from his master, Origen: see Swete *Hist. of Doctr. of Process.* p. 65. It will be observed, however, that in the context D. is thinking rather of what is called the Mission of the Spirit than of the eternal and necessary relations of the Trinity (see πέμποντος, φέροντος immediately below).

7. προκαταρκτικὸν γάρ κτλ.] 'for the title (Father) denotes the establishment of the connexion' (with a Son).

8. οὔτε ὁ υἱός] corresponds with μήτε ἀπηλλοτρ. πατήρ, so that we should have expected μήτε here, but D. has forgotten that the sentence is oblique.

9. ἔν τε ταῖς χερσὶν αὐτῶν] a striking expression, which Athanasius apparently borrows from D. in his *Expositio of the Faith* c. 4 (Migne xxv 208 ff.), τὸ ἅγιον πνεῦμα ἐκπόρευμα ὂν τοῦ πατρὸς ἀεί ἐστιν ἐν ταῖς χερσὶ τοῦ πέμποντος πατρὸς καὶ τοῦ φέροντος υἱοῦ. The phrase ('to be the object of their dealings') may be taken as a kind of passive of the phrase ἐν χερσὶν ἔχειν 'to be occupied with': cf. the classical phrase τὰ ἐν ποσί 'the things at hand.' The word φέροντος is used of the Son in this connexion as the Medium (διὰ τίνος) by which the Holy Spirit is conveyed to the world.

12. μεμερίσθαι...ἀλλήλων] Cf. p.

Δ. Ἔλεγχος καὶ Ἀπολογία

Καὶ μετ' ὀλίγα ἐπάγει λέγων·

Οὕτω μὲν ἡμεῖς εἴς τε τὴν τριάδα τὴν μονάδα πλατύνομεν ἀδιαίρετον, καὶ τὴν τριάδα πάλιν ἀμείωτον εἰς τὴν μονάδα συγκεφαλαιούμεθα.

8. (*ibid.* c. 20)

Ὅτι γὰρ οὐ κτίσμα οὐδὲ ποίημα φρονεῖ τὸν υἱὸν εἶναι,—καὶ γὰρ καὶ ἐν τούτῳ τεθρυλλήκασιν αὐτόν—οὕτως ἐν τῷ δευτέρῳ βιβλίῳ φησίν·

Ἐὰν δέ τις τῶν συκοφαντῶν, ἐπειδὴ τῶν ἁπάντων ποιητὴν τὸν θεὸν καὶ δημιουργὸν εἶπον, οἴηταί με καὶ τοῦ χριστοῦ λέγειν, ἀκουσάτω μου πρότερον πατέρα φήσαντος αὐτόν, ἐν ᾧ καὶ ὁ υἱὸς προσγέγραπται. μετὰ γὰρ τὸ εἰπεῖν πατέρα ποιητὴν ἐπαγήοχα· καὶ οὔτε πατήρ ἐστιν ὧν ποιητής, εἰ κυρίως ὁ γεννήσας πατὴρ ἀκούοιτο·

---

196. 'The complete dividing and separating' of the Father from the Son was one of the charges which D. of R. had brought against his namesake (see p. 178), and D. repels it as a calumny, though, without the obnoxious παντελῶς, he would not have ventured wholly to discard the position: see Harnack *l.c.* p. 92.

2. Οὕτω μὲν ... συγκεφαλαιούμ.] 'thus do we (Catholics) expand the Unity into the Trinity without dividing it, and again sum up the Trinity in the Unity without subtracting from it.' Both ἀδιαίρετον and ἀμείωτον are parts of the predicate. Πλατύνειν (πλατυσμός) was a term adopted in one phase of Sabellianism to explain God's mode of revealing Himself: see Introduction p. 173. What D. means is that, when we consent to use the words πλατύνειν and συγκεφαλαιοῦσθαι, we do not intend either to divide the Substance or to confound the Persons. "It is a process, which does not depend upon the wants of the creature but which is immanent in the eternal life of God." Swete *op. cit.* p. 46. Cf.

Dorner *Person of Christ* Div. I. Vol. 2 p. 156 (Eng. Trans.). For συγκεφαλαιούμεθα cf. p. 178.

9. *I did not use the word 'Maker' of the Father in respect of the Son in the sense in which I used it of Him in respect of the universe. Both words are used in profane and sacred literature in various senses.*

ib. τις τῶν συκοφαντῶν] 'one of my false accusers': cf. p. 14 ἐσυκοφαντήθη.

10. καὶ τοῦ χριστοῦ] sc. ποιητὴν καὶ δημιουργόν.

12. ἐν ᾧ] 'in which (name).'

ib. προσγέγραπται] 'is included': cf. n. on ἀναγέγρ. p. 191.

ib. μετὰ γάρ] 'for (not till) after.'

13. ἐπαγήοχα] 'I added': cf. p. 33 ἀπαγήοχεν.

ib. καὶ οὔτε πατὴρ κτλ.] 'and neither is He Father in cases where He is Maker, if (only) he that begat is properly called father (for the full breadth of the term 'father' we will deal with hereafter): nor is the Father Maker, if only the manufacturer is called maker.' Cf. p. 148.

14. ἀκούοιτο] The passive is here

τὴν γὰρ πλατύτητα τῆς τοῦ πατρὸς προσηγορίας ἐν τοῖς
ἑξῆς ἐπεξεργασόμεθα· οὔτε ποιητὴς ὁ πατήρ, εἰ μόνος ὁ
χειροτέχνης ποιητὴς λέγοιτο· παρ' "Ελλησι γὰρ ποιηταὶ
καὶ τῶν ἰδίων καλοῦνται λόγων οἱ σοφοί, καὶ ΠΟΙΗΤΗΣ,
5 ὁ ἀπόστολος εἶπε, ΝΟΜΟΥ· καὶ τῶν ἐγκαρδίων γὰρ ἀρετῆς
ἢ κακίας ποιηταὶ καθίστανται, ὡς εἶπεν ὁ θεός· ἜΜΕΙΝΑ
ΤΟΥ̂ ΠΟΙΗ̂ΣΑΙ ΚΡΊΣΙΝ, ἘΠΟΊΗΣΕ ΔῈ ἈΝΟΜΊΑΝ.

9. (*ibid.* c. 21)

Ἐπειδὴ ἀσυνειδήτως τινὲς ἐπήγαγον αὐτῷ ὅτι ποιητὴν εἶπε τὸν
10 θεὸν τοῦ χριστοῦ, διὰ τοῦτο ποικίλως ἀπολογούμενός φησι μηδ' οὕτως
ἐπιλήψιμον εἶναι τὸν λόγον· εἰρηκέναι γὰρ ποιητήν φησι διὰ τὴν
σάρκα, ἣν ἀνέλαβε, γενητὴν οὖσαν αὐτήν, ὁ Λόγος. εἰ δὲ καὶ περὶ
τοῦ Λόγου τις ὑπονοήσοι τοῦτο λελέχθαι, καὶ οὕτως ἔπρεπεν αὐτοὺς
ἀφιλονείκως ἀκοῦσαι·

13 ὑπονοησοι] -ει codd nonnulli

used instead of the more classical active, which is itself used as pass. of καλεῖν. We might have expected to find the classical in D.: see p. 91 where εὖ πάσχειν (as pass. of εὖ ποιεῖν) occurs.

3. παρ' "Ελλησι γάρ] The γάρ introduces instances to show that it is not only ὁ χειροτέχνης who can be called ποιητής.

4. τῶν ἰδίων λόγων] Christ as λόγος τοῦ θεοῦ stands in a somewhat similar relation to the Father as οἱ ἴδιοι λόγοι to οἱ σοφοί, and the word ποιεῖν might not improperly be used of Him in a somewhat similar sense.

ib. οἱ σοφοί] often used of poets in Gr. and imitated in Lat. by the word *doctus*, e.g. Tib. i 4. 61, Hor. *Od.* i 1. 29 etc.: so again below.

ib. ποιητής...νόμου] James iv 11, Rom. ii 13.

5. τῶν ἐγκαρδίων] So below τῶν ἀπὸ καρδίας κινημάτων.

6. Ἔμεινα ... ἀνομίαν] Is. v. 7. Apparently D. understood such an expression as ποιῆσαι κρίσιν as meaning 'to make,' not 'to do judgement.'

11. διὰ τὴν σάρκα] There is much truth in Harnack's remark (*op. cit.* p. 92 n. 2), "the attempt of Athanasius to explain away the doubtful utterances of Dionysius by referring them to the *human* nature of Christ is a makeshift born of perplexity." For even if the words εἰ δὲ καὶ... δυνατόν imply that Dionysius would have been glad to escape from his difficulty by a reference to the Incarnation, yet he very soon retires from that ground; and surely Athanasius would have quoted any other passages in the Ἔλεγχος that proved his point more directly than this does, if he could. D.'s real defence seems to have been that he used the word (ποιητής) in a general sense, and to some extent even inaccurately, of the Father's relation to the Son, if he used it at all. It must be remembered that D. had not a copy of his words by him at the time of writing.

12. εἰ δέ...λέγουσα] This passage

Δ. Ἔλεγχος καὶ Ἀπολογια

Ὡς γὰρ οὐ ποίημα φρονῶ τὸν Λόγον, καὶ οὐ ποιητὴν ἀλλὰ πατέρα τὸν θεὸν αὐτοῦ λέγω· κἂν ἐξ ἐπιδρομῆς εἴπω ποιητὴν τὸν θεόν, διηγούμενος περὶ τοῦ υἱοῦ· ἀλλὰ καὶ οὕτως ἀπολογήσασθαι δυνατόν. ποιητὰς γὰρ τῶν ἰδίων λόγων Ἑλλήνων μὲν οἱ σοφοί φασι, καίτοι πατέρας 5 ἑαυτοὺς ὄντας τῶν ἰδίων λόγων. ἡ δὲ θεία γραφὴ καὶ τῶν ἀπὸ καρδίας κινημάτων ποιητὰς ἡμᾶς διαγορεύει, ποιητὰc νόμου καὶ κρίcεωc καὶ Δικαιοcύνηc λέγουσα.

Ὥστε πανταχόθεν τὸν μὲν υἱὸν μὴ εἶναι κτίσμα μηδὲ ποίημα, ἑαυτὸν δὲ ἀλλότριον τῆς Ἀρειανῆς κακοδοξίας ἀποδείκνυσιν. 10

10. (*ibid.* c. 25)

Ὅτι...πάλιν ὁ Διονύσιος ἀνθίσταται καὶ διαβάλλει τὴν τοιαύτην κακοδοξίαν, ὅρα πάλιν πῶς ἐν τῷ δευτέρῳ βιβλίῳ γράφει περὶ τούτων οὕτω·

Ἐν ἀρχῇ ἦν ὁ λόγοc· ἀλλ' οὐκ ἦν λόγος ὁ τὸν λόγον 15 προέμενος. ἦν γὰρ ὁ λόγοc πρὸc τὸν θεόν. cοφία γεγένηται ὁ κύριος· οὐκ ἦν σοφία ὁ τὴν σοφίαν ἀνείς· ἐγὼ γὰρ ἤμην, φησίν, ᾗ προcέχαιρεν. ἀλήθειά ἐστιν ὁ χριστός· εὐλογητὸc δέ, φησίν, ὁ θεὸc τῆc ἀληθείαc.

11. (Basil *de Spir. Sancto* c. 29 § 72) 20

Ὅς γε (sc. ὁ Διονύσιος) καὶ κατὰ μέσον που τῆς γραφῆς οὕτως εἴρηκε πρὸς τοὺς Σαβελλιανούς·

from Athan. *de sent. Dion.* 21 is not printed by Routh, presumably because it covers nearly the same ground as the last passage.

1. *My expressions about* '*making*' *in reference to the* Λόγος *may be defended by the use made of the word by poets and in Scripture.*

2. ἐξ ἐπιδρομῆς] Cf. above p. 188.

3. διηγούμενος περὶ τ. υἱ.] 'while discoursing about the Son.'

7. ποιητὰς ... δικαιοσύνης] e.g. 1 John ii 29, iii 7 etc.

15. *Scripture uses* show *that there is no identity between Christ and the Father.*

ib. Ἐν ἀρχῇ κτλ.] John i 1.

16. σοφία γεγένηται] 1 Cor. i 24, 30.

17. ὁ τ. σοφ. ἀνείς] 'He that put forth wisdom' (sc. from His immediate Presence): see above p. 187 where the succeeding quotation has already been employed.

ib. ἐγὼ...προσέχαιρεν] Prov. viii 30.

18. ἀλήθεια] John xiv 6.

19. εὐλογητὸς...τῆς ἀληθείας] 1 Esdr. iv 40. Though this quotation is strictly speaking hardly apposite, the point of it for D. is obvious, viz. that to say that God is the God of

DIONYSIUS OF ALEXANDRIA

Εἰ τῷ τρεῖς εἶναι τὰς ὑποστάσεις μεμερισμένας εἶναι
λέγουσι, τρεῖς εἰσί, κἂν μὴ θέλωσιν, ἢ τὴν θείαν τριάδα
παντελῶς ἀνελέτωσαν.

Καὶ πάλιν·

5 Θειοτάτη γὰρ διὰ τοῦτο μετὰ τὴν μονάδα καὶ ἡ τριάς.

12. (Athan. *de sent. Dion.* 18)

Ἐν δὲ τῷ τρίτῳ βιβλίῳ φησίν·

Ζωὴ ἐκ ζωῆς ἐγεννήθη, καὶ ὥσπερ ποταμὸς ἀπὸ
πηγῆς ἔρρευσε, καὶ ἀπὸ φωτὸς ἀσβέστου λαμπρὸν φῶς
10 ἀνήφθη.

13. (*ibid.* 23)

Ἐν δὲ τῷ τετάρτῳ βιβλίῳ οὕτως λέγει·

Ὡς γὰρ ὁ ἡμέτερος νοῦς ἐρεύγεται μὲν ἀφ' ἑαυτοῦ

---

truth indicates that God and truth are not identical.

1. *There are three ὑποστάσεις in the Trinity, whether they think this involves division or not. And the Trinity is an undeniable fact about the Godhead as well as is the Unity.*

ib. Εἰ τῷ τρεῖς...ἀνελέτωσαν] 'if, because there are three hypostases, they maintain that they are separated, three they are, whether they like it or not, or they must absolutely annul the Trinity.' Cf. the Letter of D. of R. p. 177. For the confusion between the various meanings of ὑπόστασις, which gave rise to the dispute, see Introduction pp. 173 f.

ib. μεμερισμέναs] see pp. 177 f. and cf. Greg. Naz. *Theol. Or.* v 14 (p. 163 Mason), ἀμέριστος ἐν μεμερισμένοις ἡ θεότης. The passage of Gregory is instructive as showing that by A.D. 380 theologians were content to accept contradictory expressions in describing the mystery of the Godhead: see Harnack *Hist. of Dogm.* iii p. 100.

5. Θειοτάτη] 'altogether Divine' (i.e. descriptive of, or in accordance with, the Divine Nature).

ib. μετὰ τὴν μονάδα] 'besides the Unity,' not of course 'after' in point of time.

8. *He was begotten, Life from Life, and as river flows from source and light shines from light.*

ib. Ζωὴ ἐκ ζωῆs] a phrase found in the Creed of Eusebius (Ath. *de decr. Syn. Nic.*) but not adopted into the Creed of Nicaea: cf. Epiph. *Haer.* cxxiv 7 ζωὴ δὲ ὅλος ὁ θεός, οὐκοῦν ζωὴ ἐκ ζωῆς ὁ υἱός· ἐγὼ γάρ εἰμι ἡ ἀλήθεια καὶ ἡ ζωή.

ib. ἐγενν., ἔρρευσε, ἀνήφθη] The subject of the verb in each case is the Son.

ib. ποταμὸς ἀπὸ πηγῆς] See above p. 189.

9. ἀπὸ φωτὸς...φῶς] See above p. 187.

13. *The human νοῦς occupies its own place in the heart, and the λόγος its own place on the tongue and in the mouth, and yet though they are different they are not separated from each other, but the one implies the other; the one is, as it were, father to the other. So the Almighty Father has the Son (the Λόγος) as His Interpreter and Messenger.*

ib. Ὡς γάρ] The apodosis does

Δ. Ἔλεγχος καὶ Ἀπολογία

τὸν λόγον, ὡς εἶπεν ὁ προφήτης· Ἐξηρεύξατο ἡ καρδία
μου λόγον ἀγαθόν, καί ἐστι μὲν ἑκάτερος ἕτερος θατέρου,
ἴδιον καὶ τοῦ λοιποῦ κεχωρισμένον εἰληχὼς τόπον, ὁ μὲν
ἐν τῇ καρδίᾳ, ὁ δὲ ἐπὶ τῆς γλώττης καὶ τοῦ στόματος
οἰκῶν τε καὶ κινούμενος, οὐ μὴν διεστήκασιν, οὐδὲ καθάπαξ 5
ἀλλήλων στέρονται, οὐδέ ἐστιν οὔτε ὁ νοῦς ἄλογος, οὔτε
ἄνους ὁ λόγος, ἀλλ' ὅ γε νοῦς ποιεῖ τὸν λόγον ἐν αὐτῷ
φανείς, καὶ ὁ λόγος δείκνυσι τὸν νοῦν ἐν αὐτῷ γενόμενος, καὶ ὁ μὲν νοῦς ἐστὶν οἷον λόγος ἐγκείμενος, ὁ δὲ
λόγος νοῦς προπηδῶν, καὶ μεθίσταται μὲν ὁ νοῦς εἰς τὸν 10
λόγον, ὁ δὲ λόγος τὸν νοῦν εἰς τοὺς ἀκροατὰς ἐγκυκλεῖ,
καὶ οὕτως ὁ νοῦς διὰ τοῦ λόγου ταῖς τῶν ἀκουόντων
ψυχαῖς ἐνιδρύεται, συνεισιὼν τῷ λόγῳ, καί ἐστιν ὁ μὲν
οἷον πατὴρ ὁ νοῦς τοῦ λόγου, ὢν ἐφ' ἑαυτοῦ, ὁ δὲ καθάπερ
υἱὸς ὁ λόγος τοῦ νοῦ, πρὸ ἐκείνου μὲν ἀδύνατον, ἀλλ' 15
οὐδὲ ἔξωθέν ποθεν σὺν ἐκείνῳ γενόμενος, βλαστήσας δὲ
ἀπ' αὐτοῦ· οὕτως ὁ πατὴρ ὁ μέγιστος καὶ καθόλου
νοῦς πρῶτον τὸν υἱὸν λόγον ἑρμηνέα καὶ ἄγγελον ἑαυτοῦ
ἔχει.

not come till οὕτως ὁ πατήρ at the end of the extract.

1. Ἐξηρεύξατο...ἀγαθόν] Ps. xliv (xlv) 1.

7. ποιεῖ] See above p. 194.

9. λόγος ἐγκείμ. ... προπηδῶν] The same thought less fully developed has already occurred on p. 191. D.'s language is based on Philo's discussion of the λόγος ἐνδιάθετος and the λόγος προφορικός *de vita Mosis* p. 230 Cohn.

11. ἐγκυκλεῖ] Hesych. gives ἐγκυκλήσω· ἐγκαλύψω, but perhaps the meaning is simply 'to roll in' (trans.), i.e. 'to introduce': cf. ἐπεισκυκλεῖν p. 55. Coustant's translation *in circumstantes auditores transmittit* can hardly be right.

14. ὢν ἐφ' ἑαυτοῦ] 'though it has an independent existence.'

15. πρὸ ἐκείνου κτλ.] 'an impossibility prior to the mind, yet not brought into association with it from any outside source, but springing from the mind itself.' Ἐκείνου, ἐκείνῳ and αὐτοῦ all refer to ὁ νοῦς. Ἀδύνατον is in a sort of apposition to ὁ λόγος: the neuter is to be explained like Virgil's *triste lupus stabulis*.

17. οὕτως ὁ πατήρ] corresponds to ὡς γάρ above. 'Even so the Father who is the Almighty and Universal Mind has His Son, the Word, as the Chief Interpreter and Messenger of Himself.' Τὸν υἱὸν λόγον here forms one expression, as ὁ θεὸς λόγος frequently does, and πρῶτον goes with ἑρμηνέα καὶ ἄγγελον ἑαυτοῦ. For ἄγγελον we may compare such passages as Is. ix 6 (LXX).

14. (Basil *de Spir. Sancto* c. 29 § 72)

Καὶ ὁ Ἀλεξανδρεὺς Διονύσιος, ὃ καὶ παράδοξον ἀκοῦσαι, ἐν τῇ δευτέρᾳ πρὸς τὸν ὁμώνυμον ἑαυτοῦ ἐπιστολῇ περὶ Ἐλέγχου καὶ Ἀπολογίας οὕτω τὸν λόγον ἀνέπαυσε· γράψω δὲ ὑμῖν αὐτὰ τοῦ
5 ἀνδρὸς τὰ ῥήματα·

Τούτοις πᾶσιν ἀκολούθως καὶ ἡμεῖς, καὶ δὴ παρὰ τῶν πρὸ ἡμῶν πρεσβυτέρων τύπον καὶ κανόνα παρειληφότες, ὁμοφώνως τε αὐτοῖς προσευχαριστοῦντες, καὶ δὴ καὶ νῦν ὑμῖν ἐπιστέλλοντες, καταπαύομεν· τῷ δὲ θεῷ πατρί,
10 καὶ υἱῷ τῷ κυρίῳ ἡμῶν Ἰησοῦ Χριστῷ, σὺν τῷ ἁγίῳ πνεύματι, δόξα καὶ κράτος εἰς τοὺς αἰῶνας τῶν αἰώνων. ἀμήν.

Καὶ ταῦτα οὐκ ἄν τις εἴποι μεταγεγράφθαι. οὐ γὰρ ἂν οὕτω διετείνετο, τύπον καὶ κανόνα παρειληφέναι λέγων, εἴπερ ἐν τῷ πνεύματι
15 εἰρηκὼς ἦν· ταύτης γὰρ τῆς φωνῆς ἡ χρῆσις πολλή, ἀλλ' ἐκεῖνο ἦν τὸ τῆς ἀπολογίας δεόμενον.

6. *In accordance with the formula which we have received from our forefathers we now end and say,* To God the Father and to His Son our Lord Jesus Christ with the Holy Spirit be glory and power for ever and ever. *Amen.*

ib. Τούτοις ... καταπαύομεν] 'in accordance with all this we too having indeed received a form and rule (of doxology) from the elders that went before us conclude our present communication just as we habitually conclude our (Eucharistic) thanksgiving in conformity with them.' Τούτοις πᾶσιν is prob. neut., though it might be masc. ('these authorities quoted'). Αὐτοῖς = τοῖς πρὸ ἡμ. πρεσβ. Καταπαύομεν (intrans. as often) to be taken with the participles προσευχαρ. and ἐπιστέλλ.

10. σὺν τῷ ἁγίῳ πνεύματι] For this variation of the doxology see Hooker *Eccl. Pol.* v 42, and Bingham *Antiqq.* Bk xiv chap. 2 § 1. In the words preceding our extract Basil includes Dionysius of Rome with Dionysius of Alexandria, Irenaeus and Clement of Rome amongst those who οἱ μὲν τῇ προθέσει (sc. σύν), οἱ δὲ τῷ συνδέσμῳ (sc. καί), κατὰ τὴν δοξολογίαν τὸν λόγον ἐνώσαντες οὐδὲν διάφορον δρᾶν ὥς γε πρὸς τὴν ὀρθὴν τῆς εὐσεβείας ἔννοιαν ἐνομίσθησαν. Cf. Theodoret i 24 and Sozomen iv 19 to whom Hooker *l. c.* refers, and see Introduction p. 175.

E. EXEGETICAL FRAGMENTS.

I

[ἐκ τῶν κατ' Ὠριγενοῦς]

Anast. Sinait. *Quaest. in Gen.* ii 8, 9 (p. 266 ed. Gretseri)

A similar but by no means identical passage is ascribed to Hippolytus Romanus in John Dam. *Sacr. Parall.* (Le Quien p. 787): the concluding words (πεφύτευται—ἐκλογῆς) are the same. Harnack (*Altchrist. Lit.* i 422) considers this passage genuinely Dionysian. See further General Introduction, pp. xxv f.

Ἐὰν δὲ τὸν παράδεισον μὴ τοῦ κόσμου μέρος εἶναι λέγοις μηδὲ ἐν αὐτῷ γεγονέναι μηδὲ σὺν τοῖς ἄλλοις καὶ περὶ αὐτοῦ κατέπαυcεν ὁ θεὸc γεγράφθαι ἀλλ' ὑπερκόσμιον χωρίον, πῶς τὸν γήινον ἐκεῖ πλάσας τὸν ἄνθρωπον εἰσήγαγεν; πῶς δὲ ἐκεῖ ἔπλαcεν ὁ θεὸc ἔτι ἐκ τῆc γῆc 5

1. *Unless Paradise were a place on earth, how could God have put Adam there, who was made of earth? and how could Eve and the animals and the death-bringing tree and the serpent have been found there?*
ib. Ἐὰν...λέγοις] For the construction cf. pp. 34 and 53. Orig. (*Comment. in Gen.*) does not think Paradise can be anything but an earthly place.

2. μηδὲ σὺν κτλ.] '(if you say) that the statement "God rested" (Gen. ii 2) was not written about it in common with the other (works) but that (it is) a supermundane place, how did He set the man of the ground (*ibid.* 7) there, whom He had formed?'

5. ἔπλασεν...αὐτά] Gen. ii 19.

πάντα τὰ θηρία τοῦ ἀγροῦ καὶ τὰ πετεινὰ τοῦ οὐρανοῦ ὅπου
τὸν ἄνθρωπον καὶ τὴν γυναῖκα καὶ ἤγαγεν αὐτὰ πρὸς
αὐτόν, ἰδεῖν τί καλέσει αὐτά; ποῦ ξύλον θανατηφόρον
καὶ ἀπατεὼν ὄφις ἐκεῖ; οὐκοῦν λογιζέσθω πᾶς ὅτι οὐκ
5 εἰς τὸν οὐρανὸν ἀλλ' ὄντως καὶ ἐν τῇ γῇ πεφύτευται·
ἔστι γὰρ τόπος ἀνατολῆς καὶ χωρίον ἐκλογῆς.

3 που]? πως

1. ὅπου τ. ἀνθρ.] Supply ἔπλασεν.
2. καὶ τὴν γυναῖκα] is probably coordinate with πάντα τὰ θηρ. and τὰ πετ. τ. οὐρ. not with τὸν ἀνθρώπων (cf. v. 22). But the difficulty of this is that Eve was not brought with the rest to see what Adam would call her.
3. ξύλον θανατηφ.] Cf. v. 17.
6. τόπος ἀνατολῆς] Cf. v. 8.
ib. χωρίον ἐκλογῆς] 'a chosen spot': cf. Acts ix 15 σκεῦος ἐκλογῆς.

II

Εἰς Ἰώβ

These comments on Job were printed by Dr Routh in the *Reliquiae Sacrae* (vol. iv pp. 439—447, ed. 1846) from the Catena of Nicetas of Heraclea (xi cent.), published in A.D. 1637 by Patrick Junius[1]. Routh's text however is a revision of that of Junius based on five Bodleian MSS. (176, 178, 195, 201, 701), only two of which (probably 176 and 201) had been used by the older editor: 195 and 201 are the earliest MSS. Harnack mentions several other continental MSS. Junius ascribed five sections to Dionysius, but the first was not printed by Routh in his last edition, and it has since been discovered that it consists of quotations partly from the "Hierarchy" of Dionysius the Areopagite and partly from a treatise of Basil[2]. The other four sections, in spite of their being attributed to Dionysius in some of the MSS, are of doubtful authenticity: for no one has ever ascribed any work on Job to him, while the Codex Neapolit. 61 assigns the third section (ὁ μὲν θεὸς κτλ.) to Chrysostom and the fourth (μία γὰρ κτλ.) to Dionysius of Halicarnassus! In Harnack's opinion there is no internal evidence against their genuineness,

[1] A Latin version by the Jesuit Comitolus had appeared in A.D. 1586 under the name of Olympiodorus.
[2] See Harnack *Altchrist. Lit.* i 420.

but to the present editor the style of treatment in the third extract certainly seems not quite consistent with that of the second, whereas the fourth is rather more like the first and second[1] than the third is: on the other hand the fourth extract contains one or two words or phrases, the use of which is not altogether like the genuine Dionysius, e.g. ἡ σοφὴ βίβλος, ὁμοθυμαδόν (= ὁμοῦ), μονοειδές (= 'unique,' not 'uniform'), γόνιμος (of place), and perhaps γράμμα (= γραφή). On the whole one is tempted to maintain that the first and second extracts are with greater probability attributed to our author than either the third or the fourth. Bardenhewer (*Altkirch. Lit.* ii 176) agrees with Harnack in thinking the authorship still an open question.

[1] E.g. ἀνέφικτον occurs in both (2) and (4), but most of the resemblances are less direct than this. It may be noticed that Job is called μακάριος in (2), θαυμάσιος in (3), σοφὸς καὶ ἅγιος in (4), while both μακάριος and θαυμάσιος occur in different connexions in (4): cf. also p. 40.

Τὸ δέ· "Ὥσπερ μίὰ τῶν ἀφρόνων ἐλάλησάς, τινες εἰς τὴν Εὔαν ἐξέλαβον.

(1) Ἐκείνην, φησίν, ἐμιμήσω τὴν πρώτην δεξαμένην τῆς ἁμαρτίας τὸ βέλος, καὶ συμβουλαῖς ὁμοίαις παρακρουσαμένην τὸν εἰκόνι θεοῦ τετιμημένον ἐκεῖνον καὶ 5

1 το δε ωσπερ...ελευθερον] haec verba in nonnullis codicibus excerpto cuidam Chrysostomi sec Routh assignantur et excerptum nostrum incipit cum ηγνοησε ‖ 4 βελος] νεφος nonnulli

1. Ὥσπερ μία...ἐλάλησας] Job ii 10: the commentator omits γυναικῶν after ἀφρόνων.
ib. τινές...ἐξέλαβον] 'certain have accepted as referring to Eve': for this use of ἐκλαμβάνειν, cf. p. 227, τοὺς ἐξειληφότας. The words τὸ δὲ ...ἐξέλαβον are probably the words of the author of the Catena, and if so, τινές includes D. as he proceeds to show. Routh quotes a similar interpretation from '*Auctor in Jobum apud S. Chrysostomi op. tom.* v p. 962 *ed. Savilii*: ὡς μία τῶν ἀφρόνων. ὡς εἴ τις ἔλεγεν, ὡς ἡ Εὔα ἐλάλησας.'
ib. *Job's words to his wife have been thought to refer to Eve, who through ignorance of Satan's wiles was the instrument in his hands for leading Adam astray.*
3. φησίν] sc. ὁ Ἰώβ.
4. τῆς ἁμαρτίας τὸ βέλος] Cf. Eph. vi 16 τὰ βέλη τοῦ πονηροῦ. Routh quotes a remark of Chrysostom from p. 100 of this Catena, μυρία βέλη δεχόμενος οὐκ ἐνεδίδου. The reading νέφος makes less good sense.
ib. παρακρουσαμένην] 'having led astray': cf. Gen. xxxi 7 ὁ δὲ πατὴρ ὑμῶν παρεκρούσατό με: see below p. 203.
5. τὸν εἰκόνι θεοῦ τετιμ. ἐκ.] sc. Ἀδάμ: the reference is obviously to Gen. i 26, 27.

πάσης κακίας ἐλεύθερον. ἠγνόησε γὰρ τοῦ ὄφεως τὰ πολύπλοκα καὶ σκολιὰ νοήματα, καὶ τὴν ἀγρίαν καὶ ἀτίθασον φρόνησιν, δι' ἣν οὐκ ἀνθρώπων φρονιμώτερος λέλεκται· οὐδὲ γὰρ ἂν δύναιτο τῶν δικαίων ὁ ἄδικος, 5 τῶν τοῦ θεοῦ παρέδρων ὁ ἀποστάτης. εἰ δὲ τοὺς ἄφρονας καὶ ἀνοήτους κατασοφίζεται, τῷ πηλῷ καὶ τῇ πλινθείᾳ γοητεύων, καὶ τοὺς οὐκ ἀναβοῶντας πρὸς τὸν θεόν, διὰ τὸ μὴ τῆς ἐπιβουλῆς αὐτοῦ συναισθέσθαι, εἰκότως ἐν τοῖς θηρίοις ἐκεῖνοι λογισθεῖεν, ὧν μόνον φρο-
10 νιμώτερος εἶναι λέλεκται. ἀτελὴς γὰρ ἦν ἔτι καὶ ὁ ὑπ' αὐτοῦ πρῶτος ἀπατηθεὶς ὁ Ἀδάμ, εἰς ψυχὴν ζῶσαν μόνον, μηδέπω δὲ καὶ εἰς πνεῦμα ζωοποιοῦν γενόμενος, καὶ ἔτι γε πρὸ αὐτοῦ ἡ πλευρὰ οἰκοδομηθεῖσα εἰς γυναῖκα. οὕτω

3 ατιθασον] -ασσον Routh || δι ην] add θηριων coniec Routh || 4 δυναιτο] δυναται των αγιων vulgo || 5 ει δε τους...ανοητους] om cod 195 || 7 και τους ουκ αναβ...συναισθ.] και επιβουλης αυτου συνεσθεσθαι nonnulli || 9 μονον] μονων coniec Routh

1. ἠγνόησε] sc. ἡ Εὖα.
3. οὐκ ἀνθρ. φρονιμ. λέλεκται] Gen. iii 1: the addition of θηρίων before οὐκ ἀνθρ. suggested by Routh is not needed.
4. οὐδὲ γὰρ ἂν δύν.] sc. φρονιμώτερος εἶναι, as below on p. 203.
5. τῶν τοῦ θεοῦ παρέδρων] 'the assessors of God's Majesty'; cf. p. 18 where οἱ νῦν τοῦ χριστοῦ πάρεδροι are οἱ θεῖοι μάρτυρες.
6. κατασοφίζεται] 'overcomes by subtlety': the verb is constructed with the accus. several times in the Bible. Here, from the context, there appears to be a reference to Exod. i 10.
ib. τῷ πηλῷ καὶ τῇ πλινθείᾳ] Exod. i 14. The word γοητεύων probably contains an allusion to the magicians of Egypt.
7. ἀναβοῶντ. π. τ. θεόν] Cf. Exod. ii 23. It is evident from the references given above that the author is illustrating his argument from the history of Israel in Egypt: if they had not called unto the Lord in their trouble when the devil used Pharaoh as his agent to overcome them by subtlety, they would have succumbed; but then we should have had to reckon them among 'the beasts of the field,' which cannot resist his craft, and not among men.
9. λογισθεῖεν] used passively: the omission of ἄν is not without parallel in these fragments: cf. p. 235.
10. ἀτελής] 'incomplete,' opp. to τέλειος ἄνθρωπος ἐν Χριστῷ (Col. i 28) and ἀνὴρ τέλειος (Eph. iv 13). This conception of Adam's 'imperfection' at the time is to be noted, and also the curious view, which seems to be implied, that Adam himself was destined to become πνεῦμ. ζωοπ.
11. εἰς ψυχὴν ζῶσαν] Gen. ii 7.
12. εἰς πνεῦμα ζωοπ. γεν.] Cf. 1 Cor. xv 45.
13. πρὸ αὐτοῦ] sc. ἀτελὴς ἦν: cf. 1 Tim. ii 14, where St Paul argues that Adam was not deceived himself.
ib. ἡ πλευρὰ οἰκοδομ. εἰς γυναῖκα] Cf. Gen. ii 22.

E. EXEGETICAL FRAGMENTS

μὲν οὖν οὐ φρονιμώτερος ἀνθρώπων, ἀλλ' οὐδὲ ἀγγέλων·
πῶς γὰρ ὁ εἰς τὸ καταπαίζεσθαι ὑπ' αὐτῶν γενόμενος;
οὐκ αὐτῶν δὲ μόνων ἀλλὰ καὶ εἴ τις τῶν ἐνταῦθα ἰσάγγελος, ὥσπερ ὁ Ἰώβ, ὃς περιγενόμενος αὐτοῦ, καὶ κατα-
κρατήσας ἑκατέρωθεν, καὶ μήτε διὰ τὴν εὐθηνίαν καὶ 5
τὴν εὐπραγίαν ἁλοὺς ἢ παρακρουσθεὶς ὑπ' αὐτοῦ, ἀλλὰ
διαμείνας, ὡς μαρτυρεῖται ὑπὸ τοῦ θεοῦ, ἄμεμπτος, μήτε
διὰ τὴν ἀνύποιστον νόσον καὶ τὸ ἀνήκεστον καὶ ὁλο-
σχερὲς ἕλκος ἐνδούς, ἀλλὰ πάντα ὑποστάς, ἵνα ἡ περὶ
αὐτὸν τελειωθῇ τοῦ κυρίου πρόνοια καὶ δίκαιος ἀναφανῇ· 10
οὗτος γέρας τοῦτον καὶ ἆθλον λαμβάνει· Λήψῃ, φησίν,
ἀυτὸν δοῦλον ἀιώνιον, παίξῃ δὲ ἀυτῷ ὥσπερ ὀρνέῳ.

(2) Εἶδες οἷα περὶ θεοῦ λέγει ὁ μακάριος Ἰώβ.

11 τουτον και αθλον Routh ex cod 195 τουτων και αθλων vulgo ‖ 12 παιξη δε] add εν Junius ex LXX ‖ ορνεω] ορνω vulgo

1. οὐ φρον. ἀνθρ.] For Adam and Eve were not yet, acc. to our writer, fully human beings.
2. πῶς γὰρ...γενόμενος] 'for how could he (be wiser than the angels) having been made to be their sport?' καταπαίζεσθαι ὑπ' αὐτῶν (sc. τῶν ἀγγέλων) is a reference to Job xl 14 (19) acc. to the LXX version. Behêmôth there (the hippopotamus) is frequently treated by the early interpreters as a figure of Satan. The present Heb. text is translated 'He only that made him can make his sword approach unto him.'
3. τῶν ἐνταῦθα] 'of men on earth': cf. p. 60.
ib. ἰσάγγελος] Cf. Luke xx 36.
5. ἑκατέρωθεν] explained by μήτε...μήτε.
6. παρακρουσθείς] See above p. 201.
7. ἄμεμπτος] Job i 8: also i 1.
8. ὁλοσχερές] Cf. note on p. 150.
11. οὗτος...λαμβάνει] The text, as usually printed, is corrupt. The clause is a completion of the relative clause that began with ὅς and so I have accepted Routh's reading, and treat οὗτος as resumptive ('he receives him, sc. Satan, as his reward and prize'). The sense in which Job can be thus said to have 'received Satan as a reward and prize' is explained by the quotation which follows.
ib. Λήψῃ...ὀρνέῳ] Job xl 23, 24, where the two clauses are properly interrogative, though not so applied in this passage. The LXX version appears to represent a very different text from the present Heb. one.
13. Not only are the works of God infinite in number and exceeding wondrous, as Job says, but God Himself is likewise beyond description and praise, as other scriptures proclaim.
ib. Εἶδες] either the person unknown to whom the commentary was addressed or the general reader: see p. 216 θεωρεῖς, and p. 220 γνώσῃ.

πολλὰ γὰρ κατὰ μέρος ἐπιθειάσας αὐτὸν καὶ δοξο-
λογήσας, πάλιν συγκεφαλαιωσάμενος ἔφη· Ὁ ποιῶν μεγάλα καὶ ἀνεξιχνίαστα, ἔνδοξά τε καὶ ἐξαίσια, ὧν οὐκ ἔστιν
ἀριθμός. εἰ γὰρ καὶ ἀναρίθμητος ὁ ἀριθμός ἐστι, καὶ
5 τέλος οὐδὲν ἴσχει, ἐπαύξησιν ἀεὶ καὶ προσθήκην εἰς
ἑαυτὸν δεχόμενος, ἐπ' ἄπειρόν τε καταριθμούμενος, ἀλλ'
ὑπερβάλλει, φησί, σύμπαντα τὸν ἀδιεξόδευτον ἀριθμὸν
τὰ ἔργα τοῦ θεοῦ. εἰ δὲ τὰ ἔργα, πόσῳ μᾶλλον αὐτός;
ὃ γάρ ἐστιν ἀνέφικτον παντὶ καὶ ἀτελεύτητον, τοῦτ'
10 ἐλάχιστόν ἐστι παρὰ τῷ θεῷ, κατά τε ποσότητα, ὡς
ἐνταῦθα εἴρηται, καὶ κατὰ μέγεθος ὡς ὁ ψαλμὸς ὑπερ-
μεγέθη φησὶν αὐτὸν εἶναι, λέγων· Μέγας Κύριος καὶ αἰνετὸς
σφόδρα, καὶ τῆς μεγαλωσύνης αὐτοῦ οὐκ ἔστι πέρας.
πάσης γὰρ αἰνέσεώς ἐστιν ἀνώτερος, παντὸς θαυμασ-
15 μοῦ θαυμασιώτερος, καὶ πάσης δόξης ἐνδοξότερος καὶ
παντὸς ὑψώματος ὑψηλότερος· ὡς γέγραπται· Φοβερὸς Κύριος καὶ σφόδρα μέγας καὶ θαυμαστὴ ἡ δυναστεία
αὐτοῦ· Δοξάζοντες Κύριον ὑψώσατε καθ' ὅσον ἂν δύνησθε,

1 επιθειασας] επιθαυμασας cod 176 Junius ‖ 2 παλιν] παλαι codd 178 et
201 ‖ 9 παντι] τω παντι nonnulli ‖ 14 ανωτερος] αινετωτερος coniec Junius

1. κατὰ μέρος] 'in detail,' opp. to συγκεφαλαιωσ. below ('summing up').
ib. ἐπιθειάσας] properly 'to adjure by the name of God,' but here the sense more nearly approaches the word ἐκθειάζειν (as used on p. 153), 'to address as God.'
2. Ὁ ποιῶν...ἀριθμός] Job ix 10.
4. εἰ γὰρ...τὰ ἔργα τοῦ θεοῦ] 'for if number is itself unnumbered and has no end, ever receiving increase and addition to itself and being reckoned to infinity, yet (ἀλλ') the works of God, saith he, exceed all the unlimited extent of number.'
Ὁ ἀριθμός means 'the idea of number' in general; no number is so great but what the addition of one more makes it greater until infinity is reached. So far the argument of the text is correct, but it is a needless refinement to say that God's works exceed infinity.
8. πόσῳ μ. αὐτός] Cf. Wisd. xiii 3, 4.
9. ἀνέφικτον] 'out of reach': cf. 3 Macc. ii 15 τὸ μὲν γὰρ κατοικητήριόν σου οὐρανὸς τοῦ οὐρανοῦ ἀνέφικτος ἀνθρώποις ἐστίν: also below p. 206 and Greg. Naz. *Theol. Or.* ii 11 (p. 39 ed. Mason).
10. ὡς ἐνταῦθα εἴρηται] viz. in the quotation from Job ix 10 given above.
12. Μέγας...πέρας] Ps. cxliv (cxlv) 3: ὁ κύριος B.
14. ἀνώτερος] 'higher than,' 'above': it is hardly necessary to adopt Junius's conjecture αἰνετώτερος.
16. Φοβερὸς...καὶ ἔτι] Ecclus xliii 29, 30.

ὑπερέξει γὰρ καὶ ἔτι. καὶ πολὺ ἔργον ἂν εἴη τοὺς ἀπὸ τῶν θειῶν γραφῶν παμμεγέθεις ὕμνους ἐκλέγοντα παρατίθεσθαι, ὧν πάντων ὑπεραινετὸς καὶ ὑπερυψούμενός ἐστιν ὁ θεός.

Νυνὶ δὲ ἐπὶ τὰ ἐχόμενα τῆς ἑρμηνείας ἴωμεν.

(3) Ὁ μὲν θεὸς ἔστιν ἀεὶ καὶ σύμπας ὁ αἰὼν ἐνέστηκεν ὅλος αὐτῷ καὶ πάρεστιν, ἡμῖν δὲ ὃ λέγεται τὸ νῦν καὶ τὸ παρὸν οὔτε δύναται μένειν, οὔθ᾽ ὅλως ὑφέστηκεν, ἅμα δὲ τῷ λεχθῆναι, τάχα δὲ καὶ πρὶν νοηθῆναι, παρῆλθε καὶ οὐκ ἔστι ποτέ, οὐδ᾽ ἂν κατάσχοι τις τῇ διανοίᾳ τὸ νῦν. φεῦγον γὰρ καὶ ὑπεξιὸν οἴχεται· τὸ δὲ ἀποδιδράσκον καὶ φροῦδον ἀεὶ πῶς ἂν εἴποι τις παρεῖναι; ἀλλὰ καὶ τὸ ἐσόμενον μικρὸν φανησόμενον, καὶ εὐθέως ἀφανισθησόμενον, οὐδέπω μὲν ἔστι, σπεύδει δὲ κἀκεῖνο πρὸς τὸ μηκέτι εἶναι. ὅθεν καὶ ὁ θαυμάσιος Ἰὼβ τὸ ἀκρατὲς καὶ ἄστατον ἐδήλωσε τοῦ χρόνου, φήσας περὶ ἑαυτοῦ· Εἰς γὰρ τὰ πρῶτα πορεύσομαι καὶ οὐκέτι εἰμί, τὰ δὲ ἐπ᾽ ἐσχάτοις τί οἶδα; δεικνὺς ὅτι κατὰ τὸ ἐνεστὸς ζῶμεν οἱ ἄνθρωποι, τὸ δὲ παρελθὸν ἀπωλέσαμεν καὶ τὸ μέλλον οὔπω ἔχομεν.

(4) Μία γὰρ ἡ τῆς σοφίας πηγὴ ὁ θεός, ἧς τῆς

5 ερμηνειας] προφητειας cod 195 ‖ 8 ολως] ολος vulgo ‖ 13 αφανισθ. ουδεπω μεν εστι] αφανισθησομενος (-ον ?) μικρον μεν εστηκεν αλλ ουδεπω εστι cod 195

5. Νυνὶ δὲ...ἴωμεν] Routh is probably right in attributing this sentence to the author of the Catena and in considering the reading of cod. 195 προφητείας to be a correction of one who thought it was part of the extract itself.

6. *God is eternal and unaffected by time, but we men are never free from the limitations which time imposes on us.*

ib. ἐνέστηκεν...ὑφέστηκεν] The first word is nearly equivalent to πάρεστιν, the second = 'subsists.'

10. καὶ οὐκ ἔστι ποτέ] 'and never actually exists.'

13. μικρόν] adv. 'for a little while.'

15. τὸ ἀκρατὲς καὶ ἄστατον...τοῦ χρόνου] 'that time can neither be fixed nor stayed'; ἀκρατές is here equivalent to ἀκράτητον.

17. Εἰς γὰρ τὰ ..τί οἶδα,] Job xxiii 8: the LXX rendering καὶ οὐκέτι εἰμί does not represent the present Heb. text (v'ênenu) which means 'He is not (there).'

21. *God is the sole source of true wisdom, after which Job yearns, and He imparts it, as He does all His other good gifts, only to those that seek it from Him: of all His gifts wisdom is the best.*

ib. Μία γάρ] It is hardly necessary to point out that the γάρ does

εὑρέσεως καὶ ὁ Ἰὼβ ὀρέγεται, λέγων πολλάκις· Ἡ δὲ
ϲοφίⲁ πόθεν εὑρέθη; ποῖοϲ δὲ τόποϲ ἐϲτὶ τῆϲ ϲυνέϲεωϲ;
καὶ τὸ ἀνέφικτον αὐτῆς καὶ ἀπερινόητον τοῖς πολλοῖς
διαγράφων προστίθησι· λέληθε πάντα ἄνθρωπον. ὅτι δὲ
5 μόνοις ἐστὶ τοῖς ἁγίοις γνώριμος, συνεὶς ἐπιλέγει· Ὁ Κύριοϲ
ϲυνέϲτηϲεν ⲁὐτῆϲ τὴν ὁδὸν κⲁὶ τὰ ἑξῆϲ. ποῦ δὲ καὶ πόθεν
ἐστὶν αὕτη, πάλιν λέγει· Πⲁρ' ⲁὐτῷ ϲοφίⲁ κⲁὶ δύνⲁμιϲ,
ⲁὐτῷ βουλὴ κⲁὶ ϲύνεϲιϲ. εἰς οὖν ὁ τῆς σοφίας γενεσι-
ουργὸς καὶ δοτήρ, καὶ εἴ τις αὐτῆς μετέσχεν, ἔχει παρ'
10 ἐκείνου λαβών· Ὅτι Κύριοϲ δίδωϲι ϲοφίⲁν, καὶ ἀπὸ προϲ-
ώπου ⲁὐτοῦ γνῶϲιϲ κⲁὶ ϲύνεϲιϲ, ὡς ἡ σοφὴ βίβλος ἐμή-
νυσε, καὶ ὡς ἕτερον ὅμοιον γράμμα ἐδίδαξε, φῆσαν· Ὅτι
ⲁὐτόϲ κⲁὶ τῆϲ ϲοφίⲁϲ ὁδηγόϲ ἐϲτι, κⲁὶ τῶν ϲοφῶν διορθωτήϲ.
ἐν γὰρ χειρὶ ⲁὐτοῦ κⲁὶ ἡμεῖϲ κⲁὶ οἱ λόγοι ἡμῶν, πᾶϲⲁ τε
15 φρόνηϲιϲ κⲁὶ ἐργⲁτειῶν ἐπιϲτήμη. οὐ γὰρ ἄλλοθέν ποθεν
ἧκεν εἰς ἡμᾶς τῶν ἀγαθῶν καὶ θαυμασίων οὐδέν· ἀλλ'
εἴ τι ἀγⲁθόν, ⲁὐτοῦ, κⲁὶ εἴ τι κⲁλόν, πⲁρ' ⲁὐτοῦ, φησὶν
ὁ Ζαχαρίας. τό τε σύστημα καὶ τὸ πλήρωμα τῶν

5 συνεις] coniec συνεσις Routh sed perperam ‖ 12 ομοιον] om codd nonnulli ‖ 15 εργατειων] -τιων codd nonnulli ‖ 16 αγαθων] αγαστων codd nonnulli

not connect this extract with the
last: see Introduction p. 200.
1. Ἡ δὲ σοφία...συνέσεως] Job
xxviii 20 (cf. 12 etc.).
3. τὸ ἀνέφικτον αὐτῆς] 'its un-
attainableness': see above p. 204.
4. διαγράφων] Lat. describens:
cf. p. 235.
ib. Λέλ. π. ἄνθρ.] ibid. 21.
ib. ὅτι δὲ...ἐπιλέγει] 'and understanding that (wisdom) is only to be
known by the saints, (Job) adds.'
5. Ὁ κύριος συνέστ. κτλ.] ibid. 23:
LXX add εὖ before συνέστ.
7. Παρ' αὐτῷ...σύνεσις] Job xii 13.
8. ὁ τῆς σοφίας γενεσιουργός] 'the
Author of wisdom': the word is
used in the later philosophers and
in Wisd. xiii 5 (cf. also v. 3).
10. Ὅτι Κύριος...σύνεσις] Prov. ii. 6.

11. ἡ σοφὴ βίβλος] an unusual
title for the Proverbs: cf. Melito,
Bp of Sardis (A.D. 180), quoted by
Eus. H.E. iv 26 Σολομῶνος παροιμίαι
ἢ καὶ σοφία.
12. γράμμα]=γραφή: as on p.
225.
ib. Ὅτι αὐτὸς...ἐπιστήμη] Wisd.
vii 15, 16.
17. εἴ τι ἀγαθὸν ... παρ' αὐτοῦ]
Zech. ix 17: the commentator appears to take the verse as meaning
'if (there is) any good, (it is) His,
and if (there is) any beauty, (it is)
from Him,' whereas in the original
and prob. in the LXX text, His
(αὐτοῦ) and from Him (παρ' αὐτοῦ)
go closely with ἀγαθόν and καλόν
respectively and do not form separate
clauses.

E. EXEGETICAL FRAGMENTS

ἀρετῶν ἐξέκυψε καὶ προεφάνη παρ' αὐτοῦ. διὸ καὶ πάσας ὁμοθυμαδὸν περιλαμβάνοντες, καὶ καθ' ἑκάστην διορίζοντες, ἀνατιθέασιν αὐτῷ, καὶ πρώτην γε τὴν σοφίαν, ἣ πρεσβυτάτη καὶ προηγουμένη τῶν ἄλλων ἐν ἡμῖν γίνεται ὥσπερ θεμέλιος, τοῖς λοιποῖς ἐποικοδομουμένοις 5 ὑποκειμένη. ὡς γὰρ μόνος ἀγαθός ἐστιν, οὕτω καὶ σοφός· Εἶς γάρ, φησιν, ἐςτὶ Δυνατός, coφὸc cφόδρα, καθήμενος ἐπὶ θρόνου αὐτοῦ. καὶ τὴν αἰτίαν, δι' ἣν τὸ ἐξαίρετον αὐτῷ τοῦτο καὶ μονοειδὲς ἀνῆψεν ὄνομα, προσέθηκεν εἰπών· Κύριος αὐτὸς ἔκτισεν αὐτὴν καὶ ἐξηρίθμησεν αὐτὴν 10 καὶ ἐξέχεεν αὐτὴν ἐπὶ πάντα τὰ ἔργα αὐτοῦ.

Καὶ ἐπὶ ταύτην ἡμᾶς τὴν μακαρίαν ἐπίγνωσιν ὁ Βαροὺχ παρεκάλει λέγων· Μάθε ποῦ ἐςτὶ φρόνηςις, ποῦ ἐςτὶν ἰςχύς, ποῦ ἐςτὶ ςύνεςις, τοῦ Γνῶναι ἅμα ποῦ ἐςτὶ μακροβίωςις καὶ ζωή, ποῦ ἐςτὶ φῶς ὀφθαλμῶν καὶ εἰρήνη. 15 τίς εὖρε τὸν τόπον αὐτῆς; καὶ τίς εἰςῆλθεν εἰς τοὺς θηςαυροὺς αὐτῆς; τόπος γὰρ ὁ γόνιμος αὐτῆς καὶ θησαυρὸς ὅθεν πρόεισι καὶ τοῖς δεξαμένοις ἐπιμετρεῖται ὁ θεός

12 και επι] om και nonnulli || ο Βαρουχ] και ο Βαρ. vel και Βαρ. nonnulli

1. διὸ...ἀνατιθ. αὐτῷ] 'wherefore when they group them all together and when they take each separately, (men) refer (them) to Him.' Ὁμοθυμαδόν is used loosely for ὁμοῦ: lit. 'with one consent.'
4. πρεσβυτάτη] Cf. pp. 163 and 183.
5. τοῖς λοιποῖς...ὑποκειμ.] 'underlying the rest which are built thereupon.' Τοῖς λοιποῖς ἐποικ. refers to the virtues and therefore should strictly be fem. (not neut.).
6. μόνος ἀγαθός] Cf. Luke xviii 19 and Rom. xvi 27.
7. Εἶς...θρόνου αὐτοῦ] Ecclus i 8: LXX have σοφός, φοβερός for δυν., σοφ.
8. τὸ ἐξαίρ....ὄνομα] 'he ascribed this excellent and unique name to Him.' Μονοειδές (lit. 'uniform') used here in the sense of 'unique.' Lidd. and Sc. quote Sext. Emp. Math. i 226 where μονοείδεια is taken to mean 'singularity.'
10. Κύριος...αὐτοῦ] ibid. 9, LXX add καὶ ἴδεν after ἔκτ. αὐτ.
12. Baruch also incites to the search for wisdom; as to the nature of which, others have interpreted it in different ways, but Job seems to me to suggest that while man by wisdom makes all his inventions and discoveries, yet he can never find wisdom itself: it is wholly the gift of God.
13. Μάθε...θησ. αὐτῆς;] Bar. iii 14, 15.
17. τόπος...ὁ γόνιμος αὐτῆς] 'the place that produced it' or simply 'its birthplace.'
18. ἐπιμετρεῖται] 'is dispensed': cf. p. 236.

ἐστί. διὸ καὶ προητιάσατο τοὺς οὐ μεταλαμβάνοντας αὐτοῦ. Ἐγκατέλιπες γάρ, φησι, τὴν πηγὴν τῆς σοφίας. τῇ ὁδῷ τοῦ θεοῦ εἰ ἐπορεύθης, κατῴκεις ἂν ἐν εἰρήνῃ τὸν αἰῶνα. ταῦτα μὲν διὰ μακροῦ τοῖς ἄλλοις ἡρμήνευται, 5 σοφίαν νοοῦσιν ἤτοι τὴν τῶν ὄντων γνῶσιν καὶ θεωρίαν ἢ τὴν θεοσέβειαν, ἐγὼ δὲ τὸ δοκοῦν μοι περὶ τῆς λεγομένης ἐνταῦθα σοφίας συντόμως καὶ σαφῶς παραστήσω. ἡγοῦμαι γὰρ τὸν σοφὸν καὶ ἅγιον Ἰὼβ τοιοῦτόν τι λέγειν· "Ὅτι τὰ μὲν ἄλλα διὰ τῆς σοφίας εὗρεν ὁ ἄνθρωπος, οἷον 10 ὕλας μεταλλικάς, τέχνας, ἐπιστήμας καὶ ὅσα μετὰ θαύματος αὐτὸς ἀπηριθμήσατο, αὐτὴν δὲ τὴν σοφίαν πόθεν εὗρε; μήποτε γῆν ἀνώρυξεν ἢ θαλάττης ὑπέδυ μυχούς, ἵνα ταύτην εὕρῃ; ἄπαγε· θεοῦ γὰρ δῶρον τὸ χρῆμα.

13 δωρον] το δωρον codex unus

2. Ἐγκατέλιπες...τὸν αἰῶνα] *ibid.* 12, 13.

4. τοῖς ἄλλοις...θεοσέβειαν] 'has been interpreted by others who conceive of wisdom as either the knowledge and investigation of things that are or godliness.' Τοῖς ἄλλοις dat. of agent.

10. ὕλας μεταλλικάς] 'materials found in mines.'

11. αὐτός] Routh is probably right in referring this to Job rather than to ὁ ἄνθρωπος, the allusion being to Job xxviii 1 ff.

13. τὸ χρῆμα] sc. ἡ σοφία.

III

Εἰς τὴν ἀρχὴν τοῦ Ἐκκλησιαστοῦ

Eusebius (*H. E.* vii 26. 3), followed by Jerome (*de virr. ill.* 69), tells us that Dionysius in writing to Basilides, Bishop of Pentapolis[1], mentions his having composed an exposition upon the beginning of Ecclesiastes[2]: but he does not as usual inform us to whom the work was addressed[3]. Procopius of Gaza

[1] See p. 91.

[2] φησὶν ἑαυτὸν εἰς τὴν ἀρχὴν ἐξήγησιν πεποιῆσθαι τοῦ ἐκκλησιαστοῦ.

[3] These fragments contain two possible indications that they were addressed to some individual, viz. θεωρεῖς, p. 216, and γνώσῃ, p. 220, but the inference is uncertain.

E. EXEGETICAL FRAGMENTS 209

(*Comment. in Gen.* cap. iii) also refers to this work and says that in it Dionysius rejected the allegorical interpretation of that chapter of Genesis (esp. ver. 21)[1].

The fragments here printed consist chiefly of those first edited in the *Bibliotheca vett. patrum* of Gallandius, appendix to vol. xiv, from the Codex Venetus xxii, which contains among other things a catena of Procopius on Ecclesiastes from Dionysius, Gregory of Nyssa, Origen and others. It seems not improbable that many of these extracts are genuine, but in the case of three (ἡ ἀκολουθία κτλ. p. 220, παροδικὰ κτλ. p. 222, and τῷ ὄντι κτλ. p. 223) the marginal note Διονυσίου καὶ Νείλου renders it uncertain which comes from Dionysius and which from Nilus[2].

Two other short passages will be found on pp. 210 f. and 227; they were printed by Pitra (*Spic. Solesm.* i 17) from a Commentary on Ecclesiastes (wrongly ascribed to Greg. Nyss.), which he found in the Codex Coislin. 157 (xii cent.), where they are in the margin marked as quotations from Dionysius. But the style of these is so very different from the style of the other extracts that they can hardly be by the same author, especially as one of the two extracts professes to deal with a verse already commented upon in the other MS.

As the notes will testify, the Greek text set as the heading of each section is a strange one, and in certain cases the commentator himself does not follow it. The comments made on the text are consistent with what we know of Dionysius's position as a loyal but not uncritical pupil of Origen in the interpretation of Scripture[3]. Except in the second of Pitra's extracts, the author, in spite of the attitude attributed to him by Procopius (see above), accepts the allegorical interpretation rather than the literal. In so doing he hardly carries us with him in his attempts to make out that the pleasure-seeking of Solomon was only part of his noble-minded pursuit of true and lasting wisdom. Some of the reflexions on the text are not without merit for their spiritual insight, but the general impression left on the reader will be that he is here in presence

---

[1] A fragment on Gen. ii 8, 9 is given on pp. 199 f., where allegorical treatment is also rejected.

[2] The *Peristeria* of Nilus, sectio IX, cap. vii, contains a passage on the ἀνωμαλία βίου and a reference to Eccl. v 11 (see p. 220), which suggests that the first (ἡ ἀκολουθία κτλ.) is from that author.

[3] See General Introduction, pp. xxv ff.

F. 14

of a mind which is either not yet matured or altogether of a lower order than that of the author of the commentary on the Passion (pp. 231 ff.), or of the treatise περὶ Ἐπαγγελιῶν (pp. 109 ff.). If these extracts therefore are mostly genuine, perhaps Bardenhewer[1] is right in thinking that they were written before Dionysius became Bishop of Alexandria (A.D. 247).

[1] *Altkirch. Lit.*, vol. ii p. 176.

Κεφ. Α΄

Στίχ. α΄ Υἱοῦ Δαβὶδ Βασιλέως Ἰσραὴλ ἐν Ἱερουσαλήμ.

Οὕτω καὶ Ματθαῖος υἱὸν Δαβὶδ ὀνομάζει τὸν κύριον.

Στίχ. γ΄ Τίς περισσεία τῷ ἀνθρώπῳ ἐν παντὶ μόχθῳ
5 αὐτοῦ, ᾧ μοχθεῖ ὑπὸ τὸν ἥλιον;

Τίς γὰρ ἐκ τῆς τῶν γηίνων ἐργασίας πλουτήσας, δίπηχυς ὑπάρχων, τρίπηχυς ἐγένετο, ἢ τυφλὸς ὤν, ἀνέβλεψεν; οὐκοῦν ὑπὲρ τὸν ἥλιον τοὺς πόνους πεμπτέον. ἐκεῖ γὰρ οἱ μόχθοι τῶν ἀρετῶν διαβαίνουσι....

10 Ἄλλοι δὲ τὸ ὑπὸ τὸν ἥλιον δηλοῦν ᾠήθησαν καὶ τὴν γεωργικὴν ἐπιμέλειαν καὶ φιλεργίαν—λέξεσιν αὐταῖς

2. βασιλέως Ἰσραήλ] So LXX, but neither the present Heb. text nor Vulg. has the word 'of Israel.'

3. υἱὸν Δαβίδ] Cf. Matt. i 1: but in connexion with our Lord the title obviously means 'descendant of David,' whereas in Eccl. i 1 it no less obviously means strictly 'son of David,' sc. Solomon. It is possible that the quotation implies that D. interpreted the ἐκκλησιαστής to be Christ. The question of authorship does not properly come in here, but doubtless D., in common with Melito of Sardis circ. A.D. 170 (Eus. *H. E.* iv 26. 14), Origen (Eus. *H. E.* vi 26. 2) and the whole ancient church, ascribed the book to Solomon.

6. *Mere earthly labour is unprofitable: our affections must be set on things above.*

7. δίπηχυς ὑπ. τρίπ. ἐγεν.] The reference is evidently to Matt. vi 27, and perhaps it is more than a mere coincidence that Σολομὼν ἐν πάσῃ τῇ δόξῃ αὐτοῦ is mentioned shortly afterwards in that passage. D.'s amplification of our Lord's μεριμνῶν into ἐκ τῆς τῶν γηίν. ἐργ. πλουτήσας is somewhat bold.

8. ὑπὲρ τὸν ἥλιον] i.e. εἰς οὐρανόν opp. to ὑπὸ τ. ἥλ. (= ἐπὶ γῆς).

9. ἐκεῖ...διαβαίνουσι] 'for there do the toils of virtue penetrate': cf. Matt. vi 21 etc. Ἐκεῖ put loosely for ἐκεῖσε.

10. *Interpretations which confine the passage to the labours of the husbandmen or condemn strenuousness in general are to be rejected.*

ib. Ἄλλοι δὲ...καθυποβεβλ. κτλ.] This passage is one of the two extracts (see Introduction, p. 209) from Pitra *Spic. Solesm.* i 17 assigned as a comment of D. on Eccl. i 3, and

E. EXEGETICAL FRAGMENTS

εἰπόντες, τὰς περὶ τὴν γῆν ἐργασίας φασίν. οὐδετέραν γὰρ ἐκδοχὴν προσίεται τῆς ἀληθείας ὁ λόγος. τὰ γὰρ ὑπὸ τοῦ δημιουργοῦ γεγονότα πάντα καλὰ λίαν ἐμαρτυρήθησαν· καὶ οὔτε τῷ λόγῳ τῆς θείας γραφῆς οἷόν τέ ἐστιν ἀντιφάσκειν, οὔτε τὴν διεγνωσμένην καὶ κατειλημ- 5 μένην χρησιμότητα καὶ καλλονὴν καὶ τάξιν τῆς φύσεως τῶν ὄντων καὶ φαινομένων ὁπωσοῦν ἐνδιαβάλλειν προσῆκεν. ἀλλὰ καὶ τοὺς τὰς γεωργικὰς ἐπιμελείας καὶ γηπονίας καὶ φιλεργίας ἐσχηκότας ἀνθρώπους παλαιοὺς καὶ νέους κατασεμνυνομένους εὑρίσκομεν ὑπὸ τῆς θείας γραφῆς· ὡς 10 ἔμπαλιν τοὺς ἀμελεῖς καὶ ἀργοὺς καὶ ῥᾳθύμους μέμψεσι πολλαῖς καθυποβεβλημένους κτλ.

Στίχ. δ´ Γενεὰ πορεύεται καὶ γενεὰ ἔρχεται, ἡ δὲ γῆ εἰς τὸν αἰῶνα ἕστηκε.

so I have inserted it here. But, if it is part of the same treatise as the rest, it must either be part of a longer passage that came before τίς γὰρ...διαβαίνουσι, or there must be a lacuna between διαβαίνουσι and ἄλλοι δέ. The author must have mentioned one interpretation of the 'labour under the sun' which either connected it in some way with God's creation of the world or condemned strenuousness in earthly affairs in general; if the latter, then the last words of the extract (ὡς ἔμπαλιν κτλ.) again refer to it, for they cannot refer to husbandry only. At all events this interpretation together with that of ἄλλοι, who confined the phrase to works of husbandry and agriculture, is rejected as contrary to the word of truth and the Scriptures. This discussion may well have come either before or after the words τίς γὰρ...διαβαίνουσι in which the passage is commented on in a sound though rather fantastic way. We take the first sentence thus: 'But others have thought that the phrase "under the sun" describes also the attention and laboriousness of the husbandman—saying so in so many words, (for) they speak of "the works upon the land".' For λέξεσιν αὐταῖς see note on αὐτῆς ὥρας p. 24.

1. οὐδετέραν...ὁ λόγος] 'for the word of truth admits neither interpretation.' Ἐκδοχήν, see note on p. 116. Τῆς ἀλ. ὁ λόγος, cf. Eph. i 13; 2 Tim. ii 15, etc.

3. ἐμαρτυρήθησαν] For the plural verb with neuter subj. cf. p. 219.

5. τὴν διεγν. καὶ κατειλ. χρησ. κτλ.] 'the usefulness etc. which we have known and proved.'

7. ἐνδιαβάλλειν] 'to include in their calumniations': the word occurs several times in LXX (e.g. Num. xxii 22).

9. παλαιοὺς καὶ νέους] 'of old time and more recently.'

10. κατασεμνυνομένους...ὑπὸ τῆς θ. γρ.] 'highly praised by Holy Writ,' e.g. Ecclus vii 15 μὴ μισήσῃς ἐπίπονον ἐργασίαν καὶ γεωργίαν ὑπὸ Ὑψίστου ἐκτισμένην.

ib. ὡς ἔμπαλιν...καθυποβεβλ.] 'even as on the other hand (we find) the careless and idle and sluggish subjected to many reproaches,' e.g. Prov. vi 6—11.

14—2

Ἀλλ' οὐκ εἰς τοὺς αἰῶνας.

Στίχ. ιϛ' Ἑλάλησα ἐγὼ ἐν καρδίᾳ μου τοῦ λέγειν· Ἰδοὺ
ἐγὼ ἐμεγαλύνθην καὶ προσέθηκα σοφίαν ἐπὶ πᾶσιν οἳ ἐγένοντο
ἔμπροσθέν μου ἐν Ἱερουσαλήμ· καὶ ἡ καρδία μου εἶδε πολλὴν
5 σοφίαν καὶ γνῶσιν.

Στίχ. ιζ' Παραβολὰς καὶ ἐπιστήμην ἔγνων· ὅτι καί γε
τοῦτο προαίρεσις πνεύματος.

Στίχ. ιη' Ὅτι ἐν πλήθει σοφίας πλῆθος γνώσεως, καὶ
ὁ προστιθεὶς γνῶσιν προστίθησιν ἄλγημα.

10 Ἐφυσιώθην μάτην καὶ προσέθηκα σοφίαν, οὐχ ἣν
ἔδωκεν ὁ θεὸς ἀλλὰ περὶ ἧς φησὶν ὁ Παῦλος· Ἡ σοφία
τοῦ κόσμου τούτου μωρία παρὰ τῷ θεῷ. Σολομῶν γὰρ
καὶ ταύτην ἐπεπαίδευτο ὑπὲρ τὴν φρόνησιν πάντων τῶν
ἀρχαίων. δείκνυσιν οὖν ταύτης τὸ μάταιον, ὡς δηλοῖ
15 καὶ τὰ ἑξῆς· Καὶ ἡ καρδία μου εἶδε τὰ πολλά· σοφίαν
καὶ γνῶσιν, παραβολὰς καὶ ἐπιστήμας ἔγνων· σοφίαν δὲ καὶ

13 επεπαιδευτο] -ευετο ed ‖ φρονησιν] +υπερ MS ‖ 15 ειδε] ειπε MS

1. Ἀλλ' οὐκ εἰς τοὺς αἰῶνας] D. takes εἰς τὸν αἰῶνα to mean 'for the present age' or 'aeon' and not 'for eternity' (εἰς τοὺς αἰῶνας). The original (l'ôlâm) and the LXX equivalent εἰς τὸν αἰῶνα mean eternity quite as much as the plural forms do: a glance at a concordance will show the great variety of ways in which ôlâm and αἰών are used in the Bible.

2. τοῦ λέγειν· Ἰδοὺ ἐγώ] is the reading of ℵ, τῷ λέγ. ἐγὼ ἰδού of ABC.

4. πολλὴν] Πολλὰ is the reading of the LXX, and D. also seems to have read it really: see below εἶπε τὰ πολλά.

6. Παραβολάς] Before this clause LXX reads a clause here omitted καὶ ἔδωκα καρδίαν μου τοῦ γνῶναι σοφίαν καὶ γνῶσιν.

7. τοῦτο] τοῦτο ἐστιν LXX: and so D. reads below.

10. Solomon discovered that mere human knowledge puffs up, and brings no real satisfaction.

ib. Ἐφυσιώθην] anticipates the reference below to 1 Cor. viii 1.

11. Ἡ σοφία...τῷ θεῷ] 1 Cor. iii 19.

13. καὶ ταύτην ἐπεπαίδευτο] As there is no verb ἐπιπαιδεύειν, the correction of -εύετο into -ευτο is practically certain : ταύτην (sc. τὴν σοφίαν) is cogn. accus. after ἐπεπαίδ.

ib. ὑπὲρ τὴν φρόν. π. τ. ἀρχ.] Cf. 1 (3) Kings iv 26, from which passage it is clear that the second ὑπὲρ should be omitted here. The confusion prob. arose from the scribe joining ταύτην to φρόν. and omitting the first ὑπέρ.

15. εἶδε τὰ πολλά] I have corrected the reading of the MS here, though what follows makes it just possible that εἶπε is what D. wrote.

E. EXEGETICAL FRAGMENTS

γνῶcιν, οὐ τὴν ἀληθῆ, ἀλλ᾽ ἥτις κατὰ Παῦλον φγcιοῖ. εἶπε δέ, καθὰ γέγραπται, καὶ τριcχιλίαc παραβολάc, ἀλλ᾽ οὐ τὰς ἐν πνεύματι, ἀλλ᾽ οἷαι τῇ κοινῇ πολιτείᾳ τῶν ἀνθρώπων ἁρμόττουσιν, οἷον περὶ ζῴων ἢ φαρμάκων. διὸ καὶ ἀποσκώπτων ἐπήγαγεν· Ἔγνων ὅτι καί γε τοῦτό ἐcτι 5 προαίρεcιc πνεγματοc. πλῆθος δὲ γνώcεωc, οὐ τοῦ ἁγίου πνεύματος, ἀλλ᾽ ὅπερ ὁ ἄρχων ἐνεργεῖ τογτογ τογ κόcμογ, καὶ ἐπιπέμπει σκελίζεσθαι τὰς ψυχάς, πολυπραγμονῶν οὐρανοῦ μέτρα, γῆς θέσιν, θαλάσσης πέρατα. ἀλλ᾽ ὁ προcτιθεὶc τούτων γνῶcιν, προcτίθηcιν ἄλγημα. ἐρευνῶσι 10 γὰρ τὰ τούτων βαθύτερα τίς ἡ χρεία τοῦ τὸ πῦρ ἄνω χωρεῖν, τὸ δὲ ὕδωρ κάτω· καὶ μαθόντες ὅτι τὸ μὲν ὡς κοῦφον, τὸ δὲ ὡς βαρύ, προστιθέασιν ἄλγημα· καὶ διατί μὴ ἀνάπαλιν.

Κεφ. Β′

Στίχ. α′ Εἶπον ἐγὼ ἐν καρδίᾳ μογ· Δεῦρο, πείρασαί ὡc ἐν εὐφροςύνῃ, καὶ ἴδε ἐν ἀγαθῷ· καί γε τοῦτο ματαιότης.

1. φυσιοῖ] Cf. 1 Cor. viii 1.
2. τρισχιλίας παραβολάς] Cf. 1 (3) Kings iv 28 where εἶπε is represented in the LXX by ἐλάλησεν. The original words for the παραβολὰς καὶ ἐπιστήμην of the LXX in Eccl. i 17 (*hîlêlôth v'siklôth*) mean 'madness and folly' (*erroresque et stultitiam* Vulg.).
3. τῇ κοινῇ πολιτείᾳ τ. ἀνθ.] 'men's manner of life as members of a commonwealth or nation.' This use of πολιτεία is found in the classics: cf. also Eph. ii 12 (and Phil. iii 20).
4. οἷον περὶ ζῴων ἢ φαρμάκων] Cf. 1 (3) Kings iv 29 and Wisd. vii 20.
6. προαίρεσις πνεύματος] 'the choice of the spirit.' The original phrase (*ra'yôn ruach*) more probably means 'striving after wind' than 'vexation of spirit' (*afflictio spiritus* Vulg.).

7. ὁ ἄρχων...τούτ. τ. κ.] Cf. John xiv 31, xvi 11.
8. σκελίζεσθαι] The word is used (in the act.) in Jer. x 18 where the Hebrew word signifies 'to sling out' (*proiciam* Vulg.), while Theodotion uses it in Prov. xix 3 (LXX λυμαίνεται), and Aquila in Job viii 3 (LXX ἀδικήσει); in both these cases Vulg. has *supplantat*. Liddell and Scott assign the same meaning as ὑποσκελίζειν has, 'to trip up,' 'subvert,' which suits well enough here.
13. καὶ διατί μὴ ἀνάπαλιν] Though detached from its sentence by προστ. ἄλγ., this clause belongs to μαθόντες, 'having learned that fire is light, etc., and why not the reverse'; or it may be coordinate with the clause τίς ἡ χρεία κτλ.
16. Δεῦρο...ματαιότης] LXX read δεῦρο δὴ πειράσω σε ἐν εὐφρ. καὶ ἴδε ἐν ἀγ.· καὶ ἰδοὺ καί γε τ. ματ.

Πείρας γὰρ ἕνεκα καὶ κατὰ συμβεβηκὸς ἀπὸ τοῦ σεμνοτέρου καὶ κατεσκληκότος βίου ἦλθεν εἰς τὴν ἡδονήν. εὐφροcγ́νην δέ φησιν, ἣν ὀνομάζουσιν ἄνθρωποι. ἐν ἀγαθῷ δὲ ἃ καλοῦσιν ἀγαθά, ἅπερ οὐχ ἱκανὰ ζωοποιεῖν
5 τὸν κτησάμενον, ἃ ματαιοῖ τὸν πράττοντα.

Στίχ. β' Τῷ γέλωτι εἶπον περιφορὰν καὶ τῇ εὐφροcγ́νη,
Τί τοῦτο ποιεῖc;

Διπλῆν ὁ γέλως ἔχει περιφοράν· ὅτι δὴ περιφορὰ γεννᾷ γέλωτας, καὶ πενθεῖν οὐ συγχωρεῖ τὰς ἁμαρτίας, καὶ ὅτι
10 οὗτος περιφέρεται, καιροὺς καὶ τόπους ἐναλλάττων καὶ πρόσωπα. φεύγει γὰρ τοὺς πενθοῦντας. καὶ τῇ εὐφροcγ́νη,
Τί τοῦτο ποιεῖc; τί πορεύῃ πρὸς οὓς οὐ θέμις εὐφραίνεσθαι; πρὸς τοὺς μεθύσους καὶ πλεονέκτας καὶ ἅρπαγας; διὰ τί δὲ ὡc οἶνον; ἐπειδὴ τὴν καρδίαν οἶνος εὐφραίνει·

2 κατεσκληκοτος] κατεσχλ. Migne || 5 κτησαμενον] κτισ. MS || 8 δη] δε MS

1. *His experiences in a life of pleasure yielded no better results.*
   ib. Πείρας γὰρ ἕνεκ. καὶ κατὰ συμβεβ. κτλ.] 'for it was only by way of experiment and incidentally that he came from the nobler and austere life to (a life of) pleasure.' D. means that Solomon's career of royal splendour and luxury was not sought for its own sake, but for the sake of the wisdom that comes through experience. Κατεσκληκότος an intrans. perf. of κατασκέλλεσθαι (to be dried up): Liddell and Scott quote its use in Philostr. 508 in the sense of 'to be austere' as here: the form ἀπεσκληκέναι occurs twice in Eus. *H. E.* (ii 23. 6 of St James's knees hardened like a camel's by constant kneeling, and ix 8. 8 of persons worn to a shadow by famine and disease).

3. εὐφροσύνην] According to Milton (*L'Allegro* 11—13) this 'goddess fair and free' was 'in Heav'n ycleap'd Euphrosyne, And by men heart-easing Mirth': few sinister associations gather round her in the classics.

5. ματαιοῖ] 'befool': the verb is always used in the pass. in the Bible, e.g. 2 (4) Kings xvii 15 and Rom. i 21.

6. εἶπον] LXX εἶπα.

8. *The folly of laughter is that it hinders repentance and removes good influences. Pleasure seeking brings us into bad company. Yet the moderate indulgence of the flesh rejoices the heart like wine.*
   ib. Διπλῆν ὁ γέλ. ἔχ. περιφορ. κτλ.] 'laughter has a twofold distraction: (first) indeed because madness engenders laughter and permits not to mourn one's sins, and (then) because he that loves laughter (οὗτος) seeks distraction by changing seasons and places and persons. For he flees from those that mourn.' Περιφοράν: the original word (*m'hôlâl*) is from the same root as that mistranslated παραβολάς in i 17 above: the Vulg. again translates it *errorem*. One would have thought that παραφορά (madness) would have better represented it than περιφορά (distraction).

13. διὰ τί δὲ ὡc οἶνον;] 'why (does he use the expression) ὡc

E. EXEGETICAL FRAGMENTS 215

πραυθύμους γὰρ τοὺς ἀνθρώπους ἐργάζεται· εὐφραίνει δὲ
αὐτὴν καὶ ἡ σάρξ, εὔτακτα κινουμένη καὶ μέτρια.

Στίχ. γ′ Καὶ ἡ καρδία μου ὡδήγησεν ἐν σοφίᾳ, καὶ τοῦ
κρατῆσαι ἐπὶ εὐφροσύνῃ, ἕως οὗ εἰδῶ ποῖον τὸ ἀγαθὸν τοῖς
υἱοῖς τῶν ἀνθρώπων, ὃ ποιήσουσιν ὑπὸ τὸν ἥλιον, ἀριθμὸν 5
ἡμερῶν ζωῆς αὐτῶν.

Ὁδηγηθείς, φησιν, διὰ σοφίας κατεκράτησα τῶν ἡδονῶν
ἐπὶ εὐφροσύνῃ· σκοπὸς δέ μοι τῆς γνώσεως τὸ ἐπὶ μηδενὶ
ματαίῳ τὴν ζωὴν ἀσχολῆσαι, εὑρεῖν δὲ τὸ ἀγαθόν, οὗ τις
τυχὼν οὐχ ἁμαρτάνει τῆς τοῦ συμφέροντος κρίσεως, ὃ 10
διαρκές ἐστι καὶ πρόσκαιρον, τῇ δὲ ἁπάσῃ ζωῇ παρα-
τείνεται.

Στίχ. δ′ Ἐμεγάλυνα ποίημά μου· ᾠκοδόμησά μοι οἴκους·
ἐφύτευσά μοι ἀμπελῶνας.

Στίχ. ε′ Ἐποίησά μοι κήπους καὶ παραδείσους. 15

1 πραυθυμους] ? ραθυμους

οἶνον?': he is quoting from v. 3, which runs καὶ κατεσκεψάμην εἰ ἡ καρδία μου ἑλκύσει ὡς οἶνον τὴν σάρκα μου ('I considered if my heart shall draw my flesh, like wine'). This does not represent the original, which R.V. trans. 'I searched in my heart how to cheer my flesh with wine.' The ἑλκύσει of LXX seems to be used with a reference to the sense of 'quaffing' (Lat. *ducere*). If for πραυθύμους, which can only mean 'meek tempered' (cf. Prov. xiv 30, xvi 19), we read ῥαθύμους, D.'s interpretation is ingenious and sensible, though hardly justified by the text. 'Because, as wine cheers the heart (for it makes men good tempered), so the flesh also cheers it, when exercised in an orderly and measured fashion (e.g. in dancing).'

3. καρδία] LXX ἡ καρδ.
4. εἰδῶ] LXX ἴδω: D. paraphrases εἰδῶ below as σκοπὸς τῆς γνώσεως.
7. *I sought, he says, to find if* there were any lasting benefits *in a life of pleasure*.

ib. κατεκράτησα τῶν ἡδ. ἐπὶ εὐφρ.] 'I laid hold of pleasures for the sake of mirth': D. is apparently right in thus paraphrasing τοῦ κρατῆσαι ἐπὶ εὐφροσ.

8. τὸ ἐπὶ...ἀσχολῆσαι] 'that one's life should be occupied over nought that is vain.'

10. τῆς τοῦ συμφέρ. κρίσεως] 'of a right judgement as to what is expedient.'

ib. ὃ διαρκές ἐστι...παρατείνεται] 'which is satisfactory and seasonable and extends over all one's life.' Ὁ sc. τὸ συμφέρον. The clause is intended as an explanation of ἀριθμὸν...αὐτῶν ('throughout the number of their days'). Πρόσκαιρον is here used in the sense of 'suited to the occasion,' down below it bears its more ordinary sense of 'temporary.'

15. παραδείσους] LXX add καὶ ἐφύτευσα ἐν αὐτοῖς ξύλον πᾶν καρποῦ.

Στίχ. ς΄ Ἐποίηςά μοι κολγμβήθρας ὑδάτων, τοῦ ποιῆςαι ἀπ' αὐτῶν δργμὸν Βλαστῶντα ξύλα.

Στίχ. ζ΄ Ἐκτηςάμην δούλογς καὶ παιδίςκας καὶ οἰκογενεῖς ἐγένοντό μοι. καί γε κτῆςις Βογκολίογ καὶ ποιμνίογ ἐγένετό 5 μοι πολλή, ὑπὲρ πάντας τοὺς γενομένογς ἔμπροςθέν μογ ἐν Ἱερογςαλήμ.

Στίχ. η΄ Сγνήγαγόν μοι καί γε ἀργύριον, καί γε χργςίον, καὶ περιογςιαςμοὺς τῶν Βαςιλέων καὶ τῶν χωρῶν. ἐποίηςά μοι ᾄδοντας καὶ ᾀδούςας καὶ τργφήματα τοῦ γἱοῦ τοῦ ἀνθρώ-
10 πογ, οἰνοχόας καὶ οἰνοχύον.

Στίχ. θ΄ Καὶ ἐμεγαλύνθην, καὶ προςέθηκα παρὰ πάντας οἳ ἐγένοντο ἔμπροςθέν μογ ἐν Ἱερογςαλήμ. καί γε ςοφία ἐςτάθη μοι.

Στίχ. ι΄ Καὶ πᾶν ὃ ᾔτηςαν οἱ ὀφθαλμοί μογ, οὐκ ἀφεῖλον
15 ἀπ' αὐτῶν. οὐκ ἀπεκώλγςα τὴν καρδίαν μογ ἀπὸ πάςης εὐφροςύνης.

Θεωρεῖς ὅπως πλῆθος οἴκων καὶ ἀγρῶν καὶ τῶν λοιπῶν, ὧν φησὶν ἀριθμήσας, εἶτα μηδὲν ἐν τούτοις ἐπικερδὲς εὑρών (οὐδὲ γὰρ τὴν ψυχὴν ἐξ αὐτῶν βελτίων ἐγένετο,
20 οὐδὲ διὰ τοῦτο τὴν πρὸς θεὸν οἰκείωσιν ἐκτήσατο), ἀναγκαίως ἐπὶ τὸν ἀληθῆ πλοῦτον καὶ τὴν βεβαίαν ὕπαρξιν τὸν λόγον μετατίθησιν. δεῖξαι τοίνυν βουληθεὶς ποῖα τῶν κτημάτων ἵσταται τῷ κτησαμένῳ, μένει τε αὐτῷ

1. ποιῆσαι] LXX ποτίσαι.
2. ξύλα] om. B.
5. πολλή] before ἐγένετό μοι LXX.
8. τῶν βασιλέων] LXX om. τῶν.
9. τρυφήμ.] LXX ἐντρύφ.
ib. τοῦ υἱοῦ τοῦ ἀνθρώπου] υἱῶν ἀνθρώπων B, υἱῶν τοῦ ἀνθ. ℵA.
10. οἰνοχόας καὶ οἰνοχόον] LXX οἰνοχόον καὶ οἰνοχόας.
12. οἳ ἐγένοντο] LXX τοὺς γενομένους.
ib. σοφία] + μου LXX.
16. εὐφροσύνης] + μου LXX.
17. So too in great riches he found no permanent gain: for only wisdom abides with a man. Nor is there any real profit in the labours of men whereby they gain their livelihood. If we seek enduring results, we must toil for things above the skies.
ib. Θεωρεῖς] addressed to the reader or possibly to the person (unknown) to whom this commentary was dedicated: cf. γνώσῃ below (see Introduction).
20. τὴν πρὸς θεὸν οἰκείωσιν] 'affinity' or 'adaptation to God': we have the verb οἰκειοῦν on p. 233 and ἐξοικειοῦσθαι on p. 256 similarly used.
23. ἵσταται] 'stand firm': opp. to ἀφίσταται 'depart,' below.

E. EXEGETICAL FRAGMENTS 217

διηνεκῶς καὶ σώζεται, ἐπήγαγε· Καί γε cοφία ἐcτάθη μοι.
μόνη γὰρ αὕτη μένει, τὰ δ' ἄλλα φεύγει καὶ ἀφίσταται,
ὅσα φθάσας ἠρίθμησε. cοφία τοίνυν ἐcτάθη μοι, κἀγὼ δι'
αὐτὴν ἐστάθην. ἐκεῖνά τε γὰρ πίπτει, καὶ πεσεῖν ποιεῖ
τοὺς αὐτοῖς ἐπιτρέχοντας. ἀλλὰ γὰρ σύγκρισίν θεῖναι τῆς 5
σοφίας καὶ τῶν ὑπ' ἀνθρώπων ἀγαθῶν νομιζομένων βουλόμενος, ταῦτα ἐπήγαγε· Καὶ πᾶν ὃ ἤτηcαν οἱ ὀφθαλμοί
μογ, ογκ ἀφεῖλον ἀπ' ἀγτῶν καὶ τὰ ἑξῆς· οὐ μόνον τούτοις
κακίζων τοὺς μόχθους οὓς οἱ ἐν εὐφροσύνῃ τρυφῶντες
πάσχουσι μοχθοῦντες ἀλλὰ καὶ οὓς πρὸς ἀνάγκην καὶ 10
βίαν οἱ ἄνθρωποι μοχθοῦντες ὑπομένουσι, τροφῆς ἕνεκεν
τῆς ἐφημέρου, ἐν ἱδρῶτι τοῦ προcώπογ τὰς τέχνας ἐργα-
ζόμενοι. ὁ μὲν γὰρ μόχθος πολύς, φησιν, ἡ δὲ τέχνη
ἡ ἐκ τοῦ μόχθου πρόσκαιρος, οὐδὲν προτιθεῖσα τῶν τερ-
πομένων χρήσιμον. διόπερ τὸ κέρδος οὐδέν. ἔνθα γὰρ 15
ογκ ἔcτι περιccεία, οὐδὲ κέρδος. εἰκότως τοίνυν ΜΑΤΑΙΌΤΗϹ
τὰ σπουδασθέντα καὶ προαίρεcιc πνεγματοc. πνεῦμα δὲ
τὴν ψυχὴν ὀνομάζει. ἡ γὰρ προαίρεσίς ἐστι ποιόν, οὐ

6 των υπ' ανθρ.] την ανθρ. MS

3. ὅσα φθάσας ἠρίθμησε] 'all that he has just enumerated,' viz. in vv. 4—8.
5. τοὺς αὐτοῖς ἐπιτρέχ.] ' those who run after them.'
6. τῶν ὑπ' ἀνθρ.] This is a necessary emendation of the text: Gallandius reads τὴν (or τῶν) ἀνθρ.
9. κακίζων] 'depreciating,' i.e. in the words which follow in v. 11 τὰ πάντα ματαιότης κτλ.
12. ἐν ἰδρ. τ. προσώπ.] Gen. iii 19.
ib. τὰς τέχνας] sc. such arts and handicrafts as are the result of toil and practice : see next sentence.
14. πρόσκαιρος] See above p. 215. In what sense is ἡ ἐκ τοῦ μόχθου τέχνη 'transitory'? The reason given is that 'it proposes nothing useful though it does propose what gratifies, and therefore there is no real or lasting gain: for there must be a surplus, if there is to be gain.' In this rendering τῶν τερπ. depends on οὐδ. χρήσ. 'nothing useful of the things enjoyed': we might however take τῶν τερπ. as governed by προτιθ.; 'it prefers nothing useful to what gratifies.' The point appears to be that a man who labours for his livelihood must be always renewing his labours: it is like trying to fill a bottomless pitcher: he can make no store on which to draw for any length of time.
16. οὐκ ἔστι περ.] Eccl. ii 11.
17. τὰ σπουδασθέντα] 'the works he has taken so much pains over.'
18. ἡ γὰρ προαίρ....κίνησις] 'for the choice here spoken of is a quality, not a motion': by denying that προαίρεσις is a κίνησις the author wishes to express that the phrase implies not the literal action of the

κίνησις. καὶ ὁ Δαβίδ· Εἰc χεῖράc coγ παρατίθημι τὸ πνεῦμά μοy. καί γε ἀληθῶς coφίa ἐcτάθη μοι, ὅτι με γνῶναι καὶ συνιέναι πεποίηκε τοῦ λέγειν πᾶν ὅτι ογκ ἐcτὶ περιccεία ὑπὸ τὸν ἥλιον. εἰ τοίνυν ἀγαθοῦ κέρδους ἐπιθυμοῦμεν, 5 εἰ περισσείαν θέλομεν, εἰ ἄφθαρτοι ζητοῦμεν εἶναι, μοχθήσωμεν μόχθους τοὺς ὑπὲρ τὸν ἥλιον τρέχοντας. ἐν τούτοις γὰρ οὐκ ἔστι ματαιότης, οὐδὲ προαίρεσις τοῦ εἰκαίου καὶ μάτην ὧδε κἀκεῖ περισπωμένου πνεύματος.

Στίχ. ιβ´ Καὶ ἔβλεψα ἐγὼ τοῦ ἰδεῖν coφίαν καὶ περιφορὰν 10 καὶ ἀφροcγνην· ὅτι τίc ἄνθρωπος, ὃc ἐλεγcεται ὀπίcω τῆc Βογλῆc cγμπαντα ὄca ἐποίηcεν αγτη;

Σοφίαν φησὶν τὴν παρὰ θεοῦ, ἣ καὶ αὐτῷ ἐστάθη· περιφορὰν δὲ καὶ ἀφροσγνην, τοὺς ἀνθρωπίνους μόχθους, καὶ τὴν ἐπ᾽ αὐτοῖς τέρψιν εἰκαίαν καὶ ἀνόητον. ταῦτα 15 διαγνούς, καὶ τί τὸ μέσον αὐτῶν καὶ τῆς ἀληθοῦς σοφίας, μακαρίζων ἐπήγαγεν· Ὅτι τίc ἄνθρωπος, ὃc ἐλεγcεται ὀπίcω τῆc Βογλῆc; αὕτη γὰρ ἡ βουλὴ ἡμᾶς σοφίαν τὴν

---

wind (πνεῦμα), i.e. atmospheric disturbance, but a mental process.

1. Εἰς χεῖρας...τὸ πν. μου] Ps. xxx (xxxi) 6: D. reads παρατίθημι instead of παραθήσομαι. In Luke xxiii 46 W. and H. read παρατίθεμαι.

3. τοῦ λέγειν...τὸν ἥλιον] 'so as to say that in no case (πᾶν) is there any superabundance (i.e. advantage) under the sun'; i.e. my wisdom gained by large and varied experience enables me to say what is worth doing and what is not (acc. to the explanation of περισσεία given above). The construction τοῦ λέγειν is an imitation of the common LXX construction suggested by καὶ τοῦ κρατῆσαι in v. 3.

5. ἄφθαρτοι] Cf. Rom. ii 7, 1 Cor. xv 52 etc.

6. μ. τοὺς ὑπὲρ τὸν ἡλ. τρέχ.] See above p. 210.

9. ἔβλεψα] LXX ἐπέβλεψα.

ib. περιφοράν] אA: παραφοράν B.

10. ἐλεύσεται] ἐπελεύσ. AB, ἀπελεύσ. א[c.a].

11. σύμπαντα ὅσα ἐποίησεν αὕτη] τὰ ὅσα ἐποί. αὐτήν B, σὺν ὅσα ἐποί. αὕτη א[c.a(vid)], τὰ ὅσα ἐποίησαν αὐτήν A. This obscure phrase is not touched by D.'s comments: it is accus. of respect after ἐλεύσεται, as it stands in D.'s text.

12. *True wisdom is from God, and man must seek it from Him only.*

15. τί τὸ μέσον κτλ.] 'what is the difference between them and the true wisdom'; this clause depends on διαγνούς as does ταῦτα.

16. μακαρίζων] intrans. here 'congratulating himself.'

17. ὀπίσω τῆς βουλῆς] For βωλῆς the Vulg. and other versions agree in reading 'king,' which clearly represents the present Heb. text (*hammelech*). D. understands βουλῆς to be 'the counsel of God.'

ὄντως διδάσκει, περιφορᾶς τε καὶ ἀφροσύνης ἀπαλλαγὴν χαρίζεται.

Στίχ. ιγ΄ Καὶ εἶδον ἐγὼ ὅτι περισσεία ἐστὶ τῇ σοφίᾳ ὑπὲρ τὴν ἀφροσύνην, ὡς περισσεία τοῦ φωτὸς ὑπὲρ τὸ σκότος.

Οὐ κατὰ σύγκρισιν τοῦτό φησιν· ἀσύγκριτα γὰρ τὰ 5 ἐναντία, καὶ ἄλληλα φθείρονται· ἀλλ᾽ ὅτι τὸ μὲν αἱρετικὸν ἔγνω, τὸ δὲ φευκτόν. τοιοῦτον καὶ τό· Ἠγάπησαν οἱ ἄνθρωποι τὸ σκότος μᾶλλον ἢ τὸ φῶς. τὸ γὰρ μᾶλλον τῆς αἱρέσεως τοῦ ἀγαπήσαντος, οὐ τῆς τῶν πραγμάτων συγκρίσεως.   10

Στίχ. ιδ΄ Τοῦ σοφοῦ οἱ ὀφθαλμοὶ ἐν κεφαλῇ αὐτοῦ καὶ ὁ ἄφρων ἐν σκότει πορεύεται.

Κάτω νεύων ἀεὶ καὶ ἐσκοτισμένον ἔχων τὸ ἡγεμονικόν. καὶ μὴν πάντες οἱ ἄνθρωποι ἐν τῇ κεφαλῇ τοὺς ὀφθαλμοὺς κεκτήμεθα, κατὰ τὴν τοῦ σώματος θέσιν. ἀλλὰ περὶ 15 τῶν τῆς διανοίας ὀφθαλμῶν λέγει. ὥσπερ γὰρ οἱ ὀφθαλμοὶ τοῦ χοίρου εἰς οὐρανὸν οὐκ ἀνανεύουσι, διὰ τὸ

6 αιρετικον] ? αιρετεον vel αιρετον

3. περισσεία ἐστί] ℵ: ἐστὶ περισσ. AB.
5. *Opposites are not here compared, but we are told to choose the one and flee the other.*
ib. ἀσύγκριτα γὰρ ... φθείρονται] 'for opposites cannot be compared; they destroy one another.' For the plural verb cf. above p. 211.
6. ἀλλ᾽ ὅτι...φευκτόν] 'but (he says it) because he knew that the one (sc. σοφία) is to be chosen and the other (sc. ἀφροσύνη) is to be avoided.' Αἱρετικόν is probably a copyist's error for αἱρετέον or αἱρετόν.
7. Ἠγάπησαν...τὸ φῶς] John iii 19.
8. τὸ γὰρ μᾶλλον κτλ.] 'for the word μᾶλλον implies the choosing of him that loves, not the comparing of the things.'
11. οἱ ὀφθαλμοί] + αὐτοῦ LXX.
13. *The eyes of our mind are to be ever directed upwards to Christ, who is 'the way,' not downwards like those of the lower animals.*
ib. Κάτω νεύων καὶ...ἔχων] The construction is continued from πορεύεται.
ib. ἐσκοτισμένον...τὸ ἡγεμονικόν] Cf. Eph. iv 18, Rom. i 21. Τὸ ἡγεμονικόν· ὁ νοῦς Hesych.: cf. Zeno apud Diog. L. vii 159 and Cic. *de Nat. Deor.* ii 11 *principatum id dico quod Graeci* ἡγεμονικὸν *vocant, quo nihil in quoque genere nec potest nec debet esse praestantius*: also Greg. Naz. *Theol. Or.* i 3 (p. 5 Mason) and ii 19 (p. 51).
15. κατὰ τὴν τοῦ σώματος θέσιν] Cf. pp. 150 f.
ib. περὶ τῶν τῆς διανοίας ὀφθαλμῶν] Cf. Eph. i 18, where however W. and H. read τῆς καρδίας, which is also the reading in Clem. Rom. *ad Cor.* i 36.

φυσικῶς πεπλάσθαι ἐπὶ γαστέρα νεύειν, οὕτως ὁ νοῦς τοῦ ἅπαξ ἐγγλυκανθέντος ταῖς ἡδοναῖς δυσαποσπάστως ἐκεῖθεν ἔχει διὰ τὸ μὴ ἐπιβλέπειν ἐπὶ πάcac τὰc ἐντολὰc τοῦ κυρίου. καὶ πάλιν· Ἡ κεφαλὴ τῆc ἐκκληcίαc ὁ χριcτόc ἐcτι. σοφοὶ
5 δὲ οἱ τῇ ὁδῷ αὐτοῦ πορευόμενοι, διὰ τοῦ εἰπεῖν αὐτόν· Ἐγώ εἰμι ἡ ὁδόc. δεῖ οὖν πάντοτε τοὺς τῆς διανοίας ὀφθαλμοὺς τὸν σοφὸν εἰς αὐτὸν τείνειν τὸν χριστόν, ἵνα ἐπὶ μηδενί, μήτε ἐπὶ εὐημερίᾳ πράγματος ἐπαίρηται μήτε ἐπὶ κακοπραγίᾳ ὀλιγωρεῖν, τῷ τὰ κρίματα αὐτοῦ ἀβύccουc
10 εἶναι, ὅπερ ἀκριβέστερον γνώσῃ ἐκ τῶν ἑπομένων.

Στίχ. ιδ´ Καὶ ἔγνων καί γε ἐγώ, ὅτι cυνάντημα ἓν cυναντήcεται πᾶcιν αὐτοῖc.

Στίχ. ιε´ Καὶ εἶπα ἐγὼ ἐν καρδίᾳ μου ὡc· cυνάντημα τοῦ ἄφρονοc cυναντήcεταί μοι, καὶ ἵνα τί ἐcοφιcάμην ἐγώ;

15 Ἡ ἀκολουθία τοῦ λόγου διὰ τῶν ἑπομένων θεραπεύει

5 δια του ειπ.] ? δια το ειπ. ‖ 8 ευημερια] -ας MS ‖ 10 et 15 επομενων] εσομ. MS

2. ἐγγλυκανθέντος τ. ἡδ.] 'enervated by (lit. 'sweetened in') pleasures': the word is used in a very different connexion in Eus. *H. E.* v 1. 46 ἐγγλυκαίνοντος (sweetening their thoughts) τοῦ τὸν μὲν θάνατον τοῦ ἁμαρτωλοῦ μὴ βουλομένου ἐπὶ δὲ τὴν μετάνοιαν χρηστευομένου θεοῦ.

ib. δυσαποσπάστως ἐκεῖθεν ἔχει] 'finds it difficult to tear itself away from them': the phrase δυσαποσπ. ἔχειν occurs in other authors, see Liddell and Scott.

3. ἐπιβλέπειν...τὰς ἐντολάς] Ps. cxviii (cxix) 6.

4. Ἡ κεφαλὴ...χριστός ἐστι] Eph. v 23.

6. Ἐγώ εἰμι ἡ ὁδός] John xvi 6.

7. ἵνα...εἶναι] The construction is somewhat involved: ὀλιγωρεῖν is epexegetic inf. after ἐπαίρ. and πράγματος is gen. after ὀλιγ. ('so as to despise any matter'). Τῷ...εἶναι ('by remembering that etc.'?) is a somewhat curious expression: the reference is to Ps. xxxv (xxxvi) 7, and the point of it is that great steadfastness of gaze upon Christ is necessary, because He 'moves in a mysterious way, His wonders to perform.'

10. γνώσῃ] so above θεωρεῖς p. 216.

12. πᾶσιν] LXX τοῖς πᾶσιν.

13. ἐγώ] om. ABC.

ib. τοῦ ἄφρονος] + καί γε ἐμοὶ LXX.

15. *The little-minded are disquieted at the anomalies of life; the wise man often suffers as much as or more than the fool. But Solomon condemns such thoughts, and comes to the conclusion that there is an essential difference between the wise man and the fool.*

ib. Ἡ ἀκολουθία κτλ.] Διονυσίου καὶ Νείλου is written in the margin of the MS here, as applying to this and the next two passages (παροδικὰ κτλ. and τῷ ὄντι κτλ.): see Introduction p. 209. 'The course of the argument in what follows deals with τοὺς μικροψύχως διακειμένους περὶ ταύτην τὴν ζωήν, οἷς χαλεπόν τι τὸ τοῦ θανάτου νομίζεται, καὶ αἱ σωματικαὶ ἀνωμαλίαι, καὶ διὰ τὸ μηδὲν διαφέρειν ἐν τοῖς συμπτώμασι τούτοις ἐπὶ σοφοῦ τε καὶ ἄφρονος. τῆς περιφορᾶς οὖν ῥήματα λέγει ῥεψάσης ἐπὶ τὴν ἀφροσύνην, ὅθεν καὶ 5 ἐπιφέρει ὅτι· Ἄφρων ἐκ περιccεύματοc λαλεῖ, ἄφρονα ἑαυτὸν ἢ καὶ πάντα τὸν οὕτω λογιζόμενον εἰπών. καταγινώcκων οὖν τῆς ἀτόπου ἐννοίας ταύτης—διὸ καὶ ἐν καρδίᾳ ὑποστελλόμενος εἶπεν αὐτήν, δεδοικὼς πάντως τὴν ἐκ τῶν ἀκούεσθαι μελλόντων δικαίαν κατάγνωσιν—ἐπὶ λογισμῷ 10 λύει τῆς ἀπορίας τὴν ἔνστασιν. τὸ γὰρ Ἵνα τί ἐcοφιcάμην ἐνδυάζοντος ἦν, καὶ ἀμφιβάλλοντος, εἰ καλῶς τῇ σοφίᾳ ἢ μάτην προσανάλωμα, εἴ γε τοῦ ἄφρονος οὐδὲν διαφέρει πλεονεκτήματα τοῖς αὐτοῖς ἐν τῷ νῦν αἰῶνι ὁμοίως αὐτῷ πάθεσιν ὑποκείμενος. διὰ δὲ τοῦτο Περιccόν, φησιν, ἐλά- 15

1 μικροψυχως] -ους MS ‖ 12 ει καλως] η καλως MS
 ‖ 13 ει γε] η γε MS

those who are timidly disposed about this life, to whom the matter of death appears something hard and (likewise) the unfair distribution of bodily advantages; and because there is no difference made in this distribution between the wise and the unwise.' Possibly we should omit the διά before τὸ μηδὲν διαφ. For the subject of the passage compare Nilus *Peristeria* sectio ix cap. vii ἀλλὰ τοσαύτη νῦν ἀνωμαλία συγκατέχει τοῦ βίου ὡς τοὺς μὲν μὴ ἐπαρκεῖν ταῖς φροντίσι πλούτου μηδ' ἔχειν τῇ πολλῇ μερίμνῃ τῶν κτημάτων ὕπνου καιρὸν κατὰ τὸν λέγοντα τῷ ἐμπλησθέντι τοῦ πλουτῆσαι οὐκ ἔστιν ἀφίων αὐτὸν τοῦ ὑπνῶσαι (Eccl. v 11).

4. τῆς περιφορᾶς ... ἀφροσύνην] 'he mentions therefore words of madness, which inclines to folly.'

6. ὅτι Ἄφρων...λαλεῖ] v. 15. Ἐκ περισσεύματος, 'to excess.'

8. ὑποστελλόμενος] 'shrinking back' (i.e. afraid to give the thought utterance).

9. δεδοικὼς...κατάγνωσιν] 'greatly fearing the just condemnation that would follow upon such words being heard.'

10. ἐπὶ λογ....ἔνστασιν] 'by a course of reasoning he relieves the pressure of his difficulty.'

11. τὸ γὰρ...ὑποκείμενος] 'for the words "to what purpose was my wisdom?" were (the words) of one who hesitated and doubted whether that which was spent on wisdom (was) wisely (spent) or in vain, when as a matter of fact he (Solomon) differs nothing from the unwise as to advantages, being subject to the same sufferings as he is in the present life.' Ἐνδυάζ. collateral form of ἐνδοιάζ. With προσανάλωμα we should rather have expected the article (τό).

15. Περισσὸν...ἐν καρδ. μου] v. 16.

λΗϲΑ ἐν κΑρΔίᾳ ΜΟΥ, μηδὲν νομίσας εἶναι μέσον σοφοῦ καὶ ἄφρονος.

Στίχ. ιϛ' Ἐπειδὴ ογκ ἔϲτι ΜνεῖΑ τοῦ ϲοφοῦ ΜετΑ τοῦ ἄφρονοϲ εἰϲ τὸν ΑἰῶνΑ.

5 Παροδικὰ μὲν γὰρ τὰ τοῦ βίου συμπτώματα, εἴτε καθέστηκε λυπηρά, περὶ ὧν φησίν· ΚΑθότι ἥΔΗ τὰ πάντΑ ἐπελήϲθΗ, ἐπειδὴ χρόνου μικροῦ παραδραμόντος λήθῃ τὰ συμβαίνοντα βιωτικὰ τοῖς ἀνθρώποις σβέννυται. καὶ αὐτοὶ δὲ οἷς ταῦτα συμβέβηκεν, οὐχ ὁμοίως μνημονεύονται,
10 εἰ καὶ συμπτώμασι βιωτικοῖς παραπλησίως ὑπήντησαν. οὐδὲ γὰρ ἀπὸ τούτων μνημονεύονται, ἀλλ' ὥσπερ ἂν σοφίας ἔσχον ἢ ἀφροσύνης, ἀρετῆς ἢ κακίας. τούτων γὰρ αἱ μνῆμαι τοῖς ἀνθρώποις διὰ τὰς ἐπ' αὐτοῖς ἀμοιβὰς οὐ σβέννυνται. διὰ τοῦτο ἀκολούθως ἐπήγαγε· ΚΑὶ πῶϲ

1. μηδὲν νομ...ἄφρονος]'considering that there is no difference between the wise and the unwise': see above τί τὸ μέσ. αὐτ. p. 218.
3. Ἐπειδὴ οὐκ ἔστι μνεία] LXX ὅτι οὐκ ἔ. μνήμη.
5. *As the circumstances of life soon pass away, so the memories of men tend to pass away too; but those are remembered best and longest who have met the trials of life both in prosperity and in adversity with the greatest wisdom and virtue. This is one point in the essential difference between the wise man and the fool.*
ib. Παροδικά] fr. ἐν παρόδῳ 'transitory.'
ib. εἴτε...λυπηρά] εἴτε μή is to be supplied.
6. Καθότι...ἐπελήσθη] v. 16: αἱ ἡμέραι ἐρχόμεναι omitted before τὰ πάντα.
8. καὶ αὐτοὶ δὲ κτλ.] The argument is 'The circumstances of life vanish, and the men themselves (καὶ αὐτοὶ δὲ) are not (all) alike remembered.'
11. ἀπὸ τούτων] sc. τῶν βιωτ. συμπτωμ. 'Men are not remembered (merely) for the fortunes which befel them in this life but for the amount of wisdom or folly, virtue or vice they displayed.' Ὡς ἔχειν with the gen. is a common construction in Greek; ὥσπερ ἂν...ἔσχον here means 'according as they may have had.'
12. τούτων γὰρ αἱ μνῆμαι κτλ.] 'for the remembrance of such things is not extinguished among men because of the consequences that follow upon them': τούτων and ἐπ' αὐτοῖς both refer to σοφίας ἢ ἀφροσύνης, ἀρετῆς ἢ κακίας. The argument is : a man is not remembered only because he had more misfortunes or successes than others : the question of how he encountered them has to be considered ; for a display of wisdom and virtue under prosperity or adversity meets with our approbation which remains long after death, whereas one who easily succumbs to trials is soon forgotten. This is a nobler view than Antony's, when he says ironically "the evil that men do lives after them ; the good is oft interred with their bones." (*Jul. Caes.* Act III, Sc. 2.)
14. Καὶ πῶς...ἄφρονος;] v. 16.

ἀποθανεῖται ὁ σοφὸς μετὰ τοῦ ἄφρονος; θάνατος μὲν γὰρ
ἁμαρτωλῶν πονηρός. μνήμη δὲ δικαίου μετ᾽ ἐγκωμίων
γίνεται, ὄνομα δὲ ἀσεβοῦς σβέννυται.

Στίχ. κβ′ Ὅτι γίνεται τῷ ἀνθρώπῳ ἐν παντὶ μόχθῳ.

Τῷ ὄντι γὰρ τοῖς εἰς τὸν περισπασμὸν τοῦ βίου τὴν 5
ψυχὴν ἀσχολοῦσιν ἐπαλγὴς μὲν ἡ ζωή, οἷόν τισι κέντροις,
ταῖς τῶν πλειόνων ἐπιθυμίαις τὴν καρδίαν μαστίζουσα.
ἐπώδυνος δὲ ἡ περὶ τὴν πλεονεξίαν σπουδή, οὐ τοσοῦτον
οἷς ἔχει εὐφραινομένη, ὅσον ἀλγυνομένη τοῖς λείπουσι·
καὶ τῆς μὲν ἡμέρας δαπανωμένης ἐν μόχθοις, τῆς δὲ νυκτὸς 10
ἀποπεμπούσης τῶν ὀμμάτων τὸν ὕπνον ταῖς τοῦ κέρδους
φροντίσι. ματαία οὖν ἡ σπουδὴ τοῦ πρὸς ταῦτα βλέ-
ποντος.

Στίχ. κδ′ Καὶ οὐκ ἔστιν ἀγαθὸν ἀνθρώπου, εἰ μὴ ὃ
φάγεται καὶ πίεται· καὶ δείξει τῇ ψυχῇ αὐτοῦ ἀγαθὸν ἐν μόχθῳ 15
αὐτοῦ. καί γε τοῦτο εἶδον ἐγώ, ὅτι ἀπὸ χειρὸς θεοῦ ἐστίν.

Στίχ. κε′ Ὅτι τίς φάγεται καὶ πίεται παρ᾽ αὐτοῦ;

Ὅτι μὴ περὶ αἰσθητῶν βρωμάτων ὁ λόγος, νῦν αὐτὸς

The commentator interprets the question as an indignant denial.

1. θάνατος...πονηρός] Ps. xxxii (xxxiii) 22.
2. μνήμη...σβέννυται] Prov. x 7.
4. τῷ ἀνθρώπῳ] This is the reading of ℵAC; 'because it (viz. ματαιότης or the like) happeneth to a man (thus) in all his labour.' B reads ἐν τῷ ἀνθρ.
5. There is more toil and pain than delight or profit in the pursuit of pleasure or riches.
ib. περισπασμόν] 'distraction': cf. ὧδε κἀκεῖ περισπωμένου p. 218. The word occurs four times in Eccl. (i 13, ii 23, 26, viii 16) and is variously translated in Vulg. occupationem, aerumnis (?), afflictionem and distensionem.
6. οἷόν τισι...μαστίζουσα] 'lashing the heart as it were with the stinging lust after more.' Μαστίζουσα (an Epic word used in late prose) is inaccurately applied to κέντρα (oxgoads); the latter word is often used of physical desire (cf. Plat. Phaedr. 251 D, E κεντουμένη...ἡ ψυχή...κέντρων...ἔληξεν), but here specially refers to auri sacra fames.
10. δαπανωμένης] Cf. p. 89.
11. ἀποπεμπούσης...ὕπνον] Cf. Eccl. ii 23, viii 16.
14. Καὶ οὐκ ἔ. ἀγ. ἀνθ. εἰ μὴ ὅ] LXX om. καί; εἰ μὴ om. AB, πλὴν ℵc.a.
15. πίεται] ὃ πίεται ℵBC.
ib. δείξει] ὃ δείξ. LXX.
16. θεοῦ] τοῦ θ. LXX.
17. πίεται παρ᾽ αὐτοῦ] τίς π. παρὲξ αὐτοῦ; LXX and so the commentator himself below.
18. This passage speaks of the joys of spiritual food (i.e. of seeking wisdom from God), not of satisfying the carnal appetites.
ib. Ὅτι μὴ...ἐποίσει] 'that the argument is not about actual foods, (the author) will now show by

ἐποίσει· Ἀγαθὸν πορευθῆναι εἰς οἶκον πένθους ἢ εἰς οἶκον πότου καὶ ἃ τοῖσδε νῦν ἐπήγαγε· Καὶ δείξει τῇ ψυχῇ αὐτοῦ ἐν μόχθῳ αὐτῆς. καίτοι οὐκ ἀγαθὸν τῇ ψυχῇ αἰσθητὸν βρῶμα ἢ πόμα. ἡ γὰρ σὰρξ προστρεφομένη πολεμεῖ τῇ
5 ψυχῇ καὶ συστασιάζει κατὰ τοῦ πνεύματος. πῶς δὲ καὶ οὐ παρὲκ θεοῦ ἀσωτία βρωμάτων καὶ μέθη; οὐκοῦν περὶ μυστικῶν φησί. πνευματικῆς γὰρ τραπέζης οὐδεὶς μεταλήψεται, μὴ παρ᾽ αὐτοῦ κεκλημένος, καὶ σοφίας ἀκούσας· Ἐλθὲ καὶ φάγε.

10 Κεφ. Γ´

Στίχ. γ´ Καιρὸс τοῦ ἀποκτεῖναι καὶ καιρὸс τοῦ ἰάсαсθαι.
Ἀποκτεῖναι τὸν ἀσύγγνωστα πταίοντα, ἰάσασθαι τὸν ἔχοντα πληγὴν ἀνεξομένην φάρμακον ἐπιδέξασθαι.
Στίχ. δ´ Καιρὸс τοῦ κλαῦсαι καὶ καιρὸс τοῦ γελάсαι.

2 α] τα MS ‖ 6 ασωτια βρωμ.] ασωτων βρωμ. MS

adding (in chap. vii 3 (2)) It is good etc.' The sense of v. 24 suggested by introducing εἰ μή before ὅ (though not expressed in the Heb.) is accepted by Vulg. and Eng. R.V., but it is hard to see how the attempt to give it a non-literal application is justified by the context or even by the quotation from chap. vii 3 (2).

2. ἅ] The reading (τά) of the MS is untranslateable.

ib. τῇ ψυχῇ] The commentator here gives the word a sense not meant by the writer of the text.

4. ἡ γὰρ σάρξ...πνεύματος] 'for the flesh being highly nurtured wars against the soul and revolts against the spirit': cf. Gal. v 17 etc. Προστρεφομένη: the only instance of the verb given in Liddell and Scott is Aesch. *Ag.* 735, where it means simply 'brought up in' (δόμοις προσεθρέφθη), but here the πρός must mean either 'additionally' (i.e. 'highly') or 'in opposition to (the soul).' Συστασιάζειν lit. 'to be a fellow rebel,' but here the force of the prefix is lost.

5. πῶς δὲ...μέθη;] The MS here reads ἀσώτων which is impossible: 'but how can there be dissolute feastings and carousings, which are not apart from God?' The reference is to verse 25, where the commentator now reads παρέξ not παρ'. His argument is that in the literal sense the text (with παρέξ) is absurd. The present Heb. text (*mimmenē*) means 'more than I,' i.e. 'who has had more opportunity than I have had of knowing what feasting means?'

8. μὴ παρ᾽ αὐτοῦ κεκλημ.] 'if not invited by Him.'

9. Ἐλθὲ καὶ φάγε] Cf. Prov. ix 5: for πνευμ. τραπέζ. cf. p. 58, where τράπεζα is used of the Christian altar.

11. Καιρὸς κτλ.] *All action is to be guided by a regard for times and seasons.*

12. Ἀποκτεῖναι...ἐπιδέξασθαι] The time (καιρός) in this case is apparently considered to be in God's hand, not man's, though the reference may possibly be to Church discipline.

E. EXEGETICAL FRAGMENTS

Καιρὸς τοῦ κλαῦσαι, ὅτε ὁ καιρὸς τοῦ πάθους, λέγοντος τοῦ κυρίου· Ἀμὴν λέγω ὑμῖν, ὅτι κλαύσετε καὶ θρηνήσετε· γελάσαι δὲ περὶ τῆς ἀναστάσεως· Ἡ γὰρ λύπη ὑμῶν, φησίν, εἰς χαρὰν γενήσεται.

Στίχ. δ´. Καιρὸς τοῦ κόψασθαι καὶ καιρὸς τοῦ ὀρχεῖσθαι. 5
Ὅταν λογίσηταί τις τὸν θάνατον, ὅνπερ ἡ τοῦ Ἀδὰμ παράβασις ἐπήνεγκε, κόψασθαι· πανηγυρίσαι δέ, ὅταν εἰς νοῦν λάβωμεν ἣν προσδοκῶμεν διὰ τὸν νέον Ἀδὰμ ἐκ νεκρῶν ἀνάστασιν.

Στίχ. ς´ Καιρὸς τοῦ φυλάξαι καὶ καιρὸς τοῦ ἐκβαλεῖν. 10
Καιρὸς τοῦ φυλάξαι τὴν γραφὴν ἐπὶ τοῖς ἀναξίοις, ἐκβαλεῖν δὲ τοῖς ἀξίοις. ἢ καὶ τὸ νομικὸν γράμμα πρὸ τῆς ἐπιδημίας καιρὸς ὑπῆρχε φυλάττεσθαι, ἐκβληθῆναι δέ, ἡνίκα ἤνθησεν ἡ ἀλήθεια.

---

1. ὅτε ὁ καιρὸς τοῦ πάθους] 'during the period of the Passion' opp. to περὶ τῆς ἀναστάσεως in the next clause: this limitation of the apophthegm is curious.

2. Ἀμὴν...θρηνήσετε] John xvi 20: cf. Luke vi 25.

3. Ἡ...λύπη κτλ.] *ibid.*

5. ὀρχεῖσθαι] LXX ὀρχήσασθαι.

6. ἡ τοῦ Ἀδὰμ παράβ.] Cf. Rom. v 14.

7. πανηγυρίσαι] of general rejoicing, apparently a late sense, as Liddell and Scott give Ael. *V. H.* 13, 'to enjoy oneself.'

8. τὸν νέον Ἀδάμ] Cf. 1 Cor. xv 45: the exact phrase occurs in Greg. Naz. *Theol. Or.* iv 1 (p. 108 Mason).

11. τοῦ φυλ. τ. γραφ. ἐπὶ τ. ἀναξ. ἐκβαλ. δὲ τ. ἀξ.] 'to guard the Scripture in the case of the unworthy and to put it forth for the worthy' (i.e. to keep the Scriptures out of the hands of those who would misuse them or had forfeited their right to them, and to give the faithful every opportunity of profiting by them). Οἱ ἀνάξιοι would include the unbeliever and the maker of charms (see Bingham *Antiqq.* Bk xvi chap. v § 6) and the excommunicate. For the use of the Bible by οἱ ἄξιοι (lay as well as clerical) cf. *Hipp. Can.* §§ 217 and 232: the latter section is specially interesting: *quocunque die in ecclesia non orant somnum scripturam ut legas in ea. sol conspiciat matutino tempore scripturam super genua tua.* Τὴν γραφήν is here equivalent to τὰς γραφάς, usually 'some particular passage of the Bible.'

12. τὸ νομικὸν γράμμα] sc. the Law; γράμμα = γραφή is a late usage.

ib. πρὸ τῆς ἐπιδημίας] 'before the sojourning (of our Lord on earth),' i.e. before the Incarnation: a common use of the word in the Fathers; cf. Eus. *H. E.* vi 33. 1 πρὸ τῆς εἰς ἀνθρώπους ἐπιδημίας, and iv 3. 2.

14. ἤνθησεν ἡ ἀλήθεια] For the general idea we may compare John i 17, and for the metaphor we may refer to Ps. lxxxiv (lxxxv) 11 ἀλήθεια ἐκ τῆς γῆς ἀνέτειλεν. It is perhaps needless to remark that this second interpretation of the text is only capable of a very partial ac-

Στίχ. ζ′ Καιρὸς cιγᾶν καὶ καιρὸc τοῦ λαλεῖν.

Καιρὸς τοῦ λαλεῖν, ὅταν ὦσιν οἱ τὸν λόγον δεχόμενοι ἀκροαταί· τοῦ δὲ σιγᾶν, ἡνίκα διαστρέφοντες τὸν λόγον οἱ ἀκροώμενοι, ὥς φησιν Παῦλος· Αἱρετικὸν ἄνθρωπον μετὰ μίαν καὶ δευτέραν νουθεσίαν παραιτοῦ.

Στίχ. ι′ Εἶδον οὖν τὸν περιcπαcμόν, ὃν ἔδωκεν ὁ θεὸς τοῖς υἱοῖς τῶν ἀνθρώπων, τοῦ περιcπᾶcθαι ἐν αὐτῷ·

Στίχ. ια′ Τὰ cύμπαντα ἃ ἐποίηcε καλὰ ἐν καιρῷ. καὶ γε cύμπαντα τὸν αἰῶνα ἔδωκεν ἐν καρδίᾳ αὐτῶν ὅπωc μὴ εὕρῃ ἄνθρωπος τὸ ποίημα, ὃ ἐποίηcεν ὁ θεόc, ἀπ᾿ ἀρχῆc καὶ μέχρι τέλους.

Καὶ τοῦτο ἀληθές ἐστιν. οὐδεὶς γὰρ τὰ ἔργα τοῦ θεοῦ ὁλοκλήρως καταλαβεῖν δύναται. ποίημα δὲ τοῦ θεοῦ ὁ κόσμος. τούτου οὐδεὶς εὑρεῖν τὸ ἀπ᾿ ἀρχῆc καὶ μέχρι τέλους, τοῦτ᾿ ἔστι τὸν τεταγμένον αὐτῷ χρόνον καὶ τὴν ὁρισθεῖσαν ἐπ᾿ αὐτῷ προθεσμίαν, δύναται, ἐπειδήπερ ἄγνοιαν ὁ θεὸς cύμπαντα τὸν αἰῶνα ἐν ταῖc καρδίαιc ἡμῶν ἔδωκεν, ὥς φησί τις· Τὴν ὀλιγότητα τῶν ἡμερῶν μου ἀνάγγειλόν μοι. οὕτω πρὸς τὸ συμφέρον ἡμῖν τὸ τέλος τοῦ αἰῶνος τούτου, δηλαδὴ τῆς παρούσης ζωῆς, ἠγνόηται.

oeptation in view of our Lord's own words (Matt. v 17).

3. διαστρέφοντες τὸν λόγον] 'misinterpret (or misapply) the word': διαστρέφειν is not so used in the Bible; but cf. 2 Pet. iii 16. The misuse of Scripture by heretics (e.g. Marcion and Cerinthus) is well known.

4. Αἱρετικὸν...παραιτοῦ] Tit. iii 10.
6. οὖν] σὺν πάντα B.
ib. περισπασμόν] πειρασμόν A.
8. ἐν καιρῷ] + αὐτοῦ B, + αὐτῶν ℵc.a.

12. *It is greatly to our advantage that God who made the world has kept times and seasons hidden from us.*
ib. οὐδεὶς γὰρ κτλ.] Cf. p. 164.
13. ποίημα...κόσμος] Cf. p. 160.
15. τὴν ὁρισθ. ἐπ᾿ αὐτ. προθεσ-

μίαν] 'the limit assigned to it,' i.e. the time when ὁ κόσμος shall pass away. Ἡ προθεσμία (sc. ἡμέρα) in Greek law was the day appointed beforehand as a limit for the performance or non-performance of an action: the word occurs in Gal. iv 2.

17. σύμπαντα τὸν αἰῶνα] is here considered to be not the object of ἔδωκεν but the accus. of duration of time, and the clause ὅπως μὴ εὕρῃ κτλ. is taken as the object after ἔδωκεν and paraphrased by the single word ἄγνοιαν. As on chap. i. v. 4, the commentator evidently interprets αἰών of 'the present age' or 'world.'

18. Τὴν ὀλιγ....μοι] Ps. ci (cii) 24.
19. δηλαδή] 'namely' (Lat. scilicet): this is a later use of the adverb.

E. EXEGETICAL FRAGMENTS

Κεφ. Δ΄

Στίχ. θ΄, ι΄ Ἀγαθοὶ οἱ δύο ὑπὲρ τὸν ἕνα, οἷς ἐστὶ μισθὸς ἀγαθὸς ἐν μόχθῳ αὐτῶν· ὅτι ἐὰν πέσωσιν, ὁ εἷς ἐγερεῖ τὸν μέτοχον αὐτοῦ.

Ταῦτα μὲν οὖν οὕτω κατὰ τὸ γράμμα νοήσαντες, οὐ προσιέμεθα τοὺς ἐξειληφότας ἐπὶ τῆς ψυχῆς καὶ τοῦ 5 σώματος τὴν ἐκδοχὴν τῶν εἰρημένων, ὡς ἥκιστα σωζομένην. ἡ μὲν γὰρ ψυχὴ τὸ κῦρος ἔχει τῆς ἡγεμονίας καὶ κυβερνήσεως ὅλης καὶ τῆς ἰδίας καὶ τῆς τοῦ σώματος, τὸ δὲ σῶμα δοῦλόν ἐστι τῆς ψυχῆς, ἐπὶ πᾶσι ταῖς κρίσεσιν αὐτῆς ἐξυπηρετούμενον καὶ θητεῦον. ἐὰν οὖν ἡ ψυχὴ 10 κατανεύσῃ πρὸς τὸ φαῦλον καὶ πονηρόν, καὶ παραρρυῇ τῶν κρειττόνων ἐνθυμήσεων καὶ διαλογισμῶν, οὐχ οἷόν τέ ἐστιν αὐτὴν τὸ σῶμα διανιστᾶν, καὶ πρὸς τὸ βέλτιον ἐπανάγειν· οὐ γὰρ πέφυκε. καὶ πάλιν κτλ.

7 κυρος] κυνος MS

4. We accept the literal interpretation of this verse, and reject the interpretation of those who take it of the soul and body: for, since the soul is naturally the governing power and the body its slave, if the soul yields to lower thoughts and desires, the body cannot lift it to higher things.

ib. Ταῦτα μὲν οὖν...κ. πάλιν κτλ.] This is the second extract from Pitra Spic. Solesm. i 17 : see p. 209.

ib. οὕτω κατὰ τὸ γράμμα νοήσ.] 'as we understand it thus according to the letter' (i.e. literally). Τὸ γράμμα is here used as in 2 Cor. iii 6 and not as above p. 225.

ib. οὐ προσιέμ....τὴν ἐκδοχήν] Cf. above p. 211 οὐδετέραν ἐκδοχ. προσίεται.

5. τοὺς ἐξειληφότας] 'those who have accepted': ἐκλαμβάνειν is used in this sense in Plat. Legg. 807 D and elsewhere: cf. εἰς τὴν Εὔαν ἐξέλαβ. p. 201.

6. ὡς ἥκιστα σωζομένην] 'as not being justified' or 'sound,' a very unusual use of σώζεσθαι.

7. τὸ κῦρος...τῆς ἡγ. κτλ.] 'entire control over the ruling and governing both of itself and of the body.'

9. ἐπὶ πᾶσι...θητεῦον] 'being subservient and enthralled to it in all its decisions' (or 'judgements'). Ἐξυπηρετεῖσθαι : the act. rather than the middle is in general use.

11. παραρρυῇ] 'become careless of': cf. Clem. Alex. Paed. iii 11 (Migne P. G. viii 632) μὴ παραρρυῶσιν (αἱ γυναῖκες) τῆς ἀληθείας διὰ χαυνότητα : the verb is used abs. in Heb. ii 1.

13. διανιστᾶν] 'to restore': a late form of the inf. (for διανιστάναι).

14. πέφυκε] sc. τὸ σῶμα : 'it is not in the nature of the body' (to do so : i. e. διανιστᾶν καὶ ἐπανάγειν τὴν ψυχήν).

15—2

IV

On the Song of Solomon

(Pitra *Anal. Sol.* iii. 597 : Cod. Vatic. 2022)

We cannot be sure of the authenticity of this fragment nor say from which work it came. Its method of allegorically interpreting two texts from the Song of Solomon (viii 5 and i 5, 6) is quite in character with the method of Origen and his school, and therefore Dionysius may not impossibly be the author, though Eusebius mentions no work of his from which it is very likely to have come. Apart from a certain extravagance of interpretation the thoughts of the passage are not unworthy of Dionysius; they are briefly these, (1) that at the Resurrection the soul of the faithful will shine white in the light of the Saviour who receives it, though on earth it was 'black, even if comely'; and (2) Christ who is our Peace clothes us with His robe of righteousness which we lost at Adam's fall.

Τὴν γὰρ τοιαύτην ψυχὴν ἀνισταμένην καὶ ὑπὸ τοῦ Σωτῆρος ἀναλαμβανομένην, φωτοειδῆ προσιοῦσαν ὁρῶντες, ἐροῦσιν οἱ ἅγιοι ἄγγελοι· Τίς αὕτη ἡ ἀναβαίνουσα λελευκανθισμένη, καὶ ἐπιστηριζομένη ἐπὶ τὸν ἀδελφιδὸν αὐτῆς;
5 οὐ γὰρ ἦν ἐξ ἀρχῆς λευκὴ ἡ λέγουσα· Μέλαινά εἰμι καὶ καλή, θυγατέρες Ἱερουσαλήμ, ὡς σκηνώματα Κηδάρ, ὡς δέρρεις Σολομών. μὴ βλέψητέ με, ὅτι ἐγώ εἰμι μεμελανωμένη. ἔστω γὰρ ἐντεῦθεν ἤδη καλή, κἂν ἔτι μέλαινα ᾖ· ἀνάγκη γὰρ εἶναι τοιαύτην ὡς τὰ σκηνώματα Κηδάρ,
10 ἐν αὐτοῖς γε οὖσαν· συσκοτασμὸς γὰρ ἡ Κηδὰρ ἑρμη-

1 ανισταμενην] ? ανιπταμ. ‖ 2 προσιουσαν] προσειουσαν Pitra ‖ 3 αὕτη] αὐτή Pitra ‖ 4 τον αδελφιδὸν] -ων -ων Pitra ‖ 7 βλεψητε] βλεψετε Pitra ‖ 8 καν] και Pitra

1. Τὴν τοιαύτην] The context no doubt has described what the soul must be which receives the Angels' greeting.
3. Τίς αὕτη...αὐτῆς;] Cant. viii 5. τὸν ἀδελφ. αὐτῆς: Heb. *dôdah* 'her beloved.'
5. Μέλαινα...μεμελαν.] *ibid.* i 5, 6.
7. δέρρεις] 'hides of animals' used as curtains or screens: Heb. *yrî'ôth* is quite a general term for such curtains.
8. ἐντεῦθεν] 'even in this life.'
10. συσκοτασμὸς κτλ.] Heb. *qêdar*

νεύεται. οἱ δὲ ἐν τῷ κόσμῳ τούτῳ καὶ ἐν τῷ ϹΚΗΝΕΙ
μένοντες ἐν ὑποζόφῳ διατρίβουσιν, ὥσπερ ἐν σπηλαίῳ
τινί, ἐν ᾧ καὶ βραδύνων τις ὀδύρεται λέγων· ΟἶΜΟΙ ὅτι
ἡ παροικίΑ ΜΟΥ ἐΜΑΚΡΎΝΘΗ, ΚΑΤΕϹΚΉΝΩϹΑ ΜΕΤΑ τῶν ϹΚΗΝΩ-
ΜΆΤΩΝ ΚΗΔΆΡ. ΔΈΡΡΕΙϹ δὲ ϹΟΛΟΜῶΝ ὁ δερμάτινος ἔοικεν 5
εἶναι χιτὼν ἐπιρραφεὶς καὶ ἐπιταθεὶς τῷ προτέρῳ καὶ
καθαρῷ σώματι, ὃν ὁ εἰρηνικὸς καὶ εἰρηνοποιὸς κύριος
ἡμῶν τὸν ἄνθρωπον ἐνέδυσεν—τοῦτο γὰρ Σολομὼν ἑρμη-
νεύεται—ὃν διὰ μὲν τῆς παρακοῆς ἐνδυσάμενος ἄνθρωπος
ἐξεβλήθη τοῦ παραδείσου. εἰ δὲ εἰσιέναι μέλλοι πάλιν, 10
ἀποδύεται, ἀμείψας τὸ τῆς δικαιοσύνης ἔνδυμα, ὅπερ
ἐνδυσάμενος τούτου γυμνὸς εὑρίσκεται.

8 ενεδυσεν] ενδυσεν Pitra ‖ 9 ενδυσαμενος] εκδυσ. Pitra

appears to come from a root which signifies 'dark' and 'gloomy' of colour, though here of course it is the proper name of an Arab tribe often mentioned in the Old Testament.

1. ἐν τῷ σκήνει] 2 Cor. v 4. See n. on p. 153.
3. οἴμοι ... Κηδάρ] Ps. cxix (cxx) 5.
8. τοῦτο γὰρ Σολ. ἑρμην.] *Shalôm* means 'peace,' 'safety.'
9. διὰ μὲν τῆς παρακ. κτλ.] Origen in his comments on Gen. iii 21 refuses to interpret the 'coats of skin' literally and mentions two other interpretations: (1) that they represent the fleshly body with which God clothed Adam and Eve; but this they already had and therefore it is preferable to interpret the coats (2) as representing the liability to die (νέκρωσις) which they then incurred. This view is evidently in the mind of our author here, who, in common with others, held that Adam had at his creation received the gift of immortality. Cf. Srawley's Greg. Nyss. *Or. Cat.* 8 (p. 42) and the authorities there cited; also pp. xx ff. of the same edition.
12. τούτου] sc. τοῦ δερματ. χιτῶνος.

V

Exegesis of Luke xxii 42 ff.

The sources of this cento of fragments are the Codex Venetus (in St Mark's Library) 494 fol. 56 and the Codex Vaticanus 1611 fol. 291 and fol. 292 *b*. The first named MS contains the whole exegesis, except that the comments on *v*. 42 and on *vv*. 45 and 46 are much shortened by omissions.

The second contains a much fuller commentary on those verses. Against the passage (ἀλλὰ ταῦτα—ἐχώμεθα, pp. 231 ff.) in the Vatican MS stand the words Διονυσίου Ἀλεξανδρείας πρὸς Ὠριγένη, which is evidently an attempt to identify it with the treatise περὶ μαρτυρίου addressed to his master by Dionysius, mentioned by Eusebius (*H. E.* vi 46. 2)[1]. This identification both Harnack (*Altchrist. Lit.* i 421) and Bardenhewer (*Altkirch. Lit.* ii 177) are ready to accept, and likewise the assigning of the passage (ὅπερ καὶ αὐτὸς—χειραγωγεῖ, pp. 245 ff.) to the same treatise. In so doing the former compares the close and careful examination of the various Gospel-accounts here with the very similar treatment to which they are submitted in the letter πρὸς Βασιλείδην (pp. 94 ff.). It is clear that the subject-matter of these portions is appropriate enough in such a connexion: on the other hand the more direct allusions to martyrdom[2] occur in the comments on *vv.* 43 and 44 (παροιμία—ἐξ ἀλογίας, pp. 241 ff.) which are found in Cod. Ven. 494 only. On internal grounds however we should hesitate to ascribe the last named passage to Dionysius. For (1) its literary style throughout is very different from that of his acknowledged writings: (2) its exegetic methods are more fanciful and far fetched: and (3) two passages occur at the end which are obviously out of place in their present position and which are out of harmony with the interpretation of *v.* 42 given in the earlier portion of the Commentary (see notes on pp. 233 and 244).

The discussion on *vv.* 45 and 46 contained in the passage ὅπερ καὶ—χειραγωγεῖ, pp. 245 ff., is fairly consistent with that on *v.* 42 and ends with comments on James i 13 which assort well with the short extract on the same text given on p. 251.

With regard to the passage which deals with *vv.* 47 and 48 (βαβαὶ—κέρδος) there can be little doubt that it is from the writings of Chrysostom or one of his imitators.

Altogether the Dionysian authorship of any of these extracts must be considered very doubtful. The long discussions on the will of Christ certainly suggest that the bulk of them belong to some author of the Monothelete times (VII cent.) who was himself not a Monothelete, whilst one or two passages are due to other writers later than our Dionysius. The composite

---

[1] ἐν τούτοις ἐστὶ καὶ ἡ περὶ μαρτυρίου πρὸς τὸν Ὠριγένην γραφεῖσα.

[2] πρὸς τοὺς τοῦ μαρτυρίου μεγ. ἀθλ. and τῶν ὑπὲρ εὐσεβ. ἀγώνων οἱ ἀθλεῖν μέλλ. τοὺς ἱερ. ἄθλους, p. 243.

nature of the Commentary thus suggested will be the less surprising if we remember that the chief of the extracts come from the end of a Catena of Nicetas of Heraclea on St Luke, seven of the earlier extracts being taken, as Sickenberger[1] (quoted by Bardenhewer *loc. cit.*) has shown, either from Dionysius the Areopagite or from some other Dionysius. The words which have given rise to the most discussion are those on p. 241, περὶ μὲν τούτων—ἐχώμεθα. Harnack is disinclined to consider them as the words of the compiler of the Catena, and suggests that in them Dionysius himself refers to remarks of his (α) which he has made on St Matthew's and St John's accounts of the Passion earlier in this same treatise, and (β) which he intends to make on St Mark's account, when he has finished with St Luke. But Sickenberger's explanation seems much simpler and easier, that they are the words of Nicetas himself, who here remarks that he has made similar Catenas on St Matthew and on St John, and promises to make a fourth on St Mark when he has completed the present one.

In the present edition I have pieced all the fragments together into a continuous commentary, but the reader should not study them as a whole without bearing in mind what I have said as to their comparative claims to authenticity. The passages taken from Cod. Ven. 494 were printed in Gallandi's *Biblioth. vett. patr.* xiv App. pp. 115—118, and those from Cod. Vat. 1611 by Mai *Biblioth. Nova Patr.* vi 1. 165, 166. My text has been prepared from Migne's reprint (*Patr. Gr.* x 1589—1602).

[1] *Die Lukaskatene der Niketas von Herakleia*, Leipzig, 1902.

Εἰς τοῦ ἁγίου Εὐαγγελίου κατὰ Λουκᾶν

κεφ. κβ′ στίχ. μβ′ κτλ.

(ex codd. Veneto 494 et Vaticano 1611)

Στίχ. μβ′ Πάτερ, εἰ βούλει παρενεγκεῖν τὸ ποτήριον τοῦτο ἀπ᾽ ἐμοῦ· πλὴν μὴ τὸ θέλημά μου ἀλλὰ τὸ σὸν γενέσθω. 5 Ἀλλὰ ταῦτα μὲν εἰρήσθω περὶ τοῦ θελήματος. τό

6. *The petition that the cup may pass implies that it will come to Him before it passes away. Hence His distress at its approach and*

γε μὴν Παρελθέτω τὸ ποτήριον οὐκ ἔστι Μὴ προσελθέτω
ἡ ἐγγισάτω μοι. τὸ γὰρ παρερχόμενον πάντως κατ᾽
ἐκεῖνον γίνεται πρότερον, καὶ πρόσεισιν αὐτῷ, ὅνπερ
παρέρχεται. εἰ γὰρ μὴ πλησιάσοι, οὐκ ἂν παρέλθοι.
5 ὡς γοῦν ἤδη παρόντος αἰσθόμενος, ἤρξατο λυπεῖσθαι
καὶ ἀδημονεῖν καὶ ἐκθαμβεῖσθαι καὶ ἀγωνίζεσθαι, καί,
ὡς ἐγγὺς ὂν καὶ προκείμενον, οὐχ ἁπλῶς φησὶ τὸ ποτήριον ἀλλὰ δείκνυσι τοῦτο. ὡς οὖν τὸ παρερχόμενον οὔτε
ἀπρόσιτόν ἐστιν οὔτε καταμένον, οὕτω καὶ ὁ Σωτὴρ
10 ἠρέμα καὶ ἐξ ἐπιπολῆς προσελθόντα τὸν πειρασμόν,
καὶ κούφως προσομιλήσαντα, παρωσθῆναι τὴν πρώτην
ἀξιοῖ. καὶ τοῦτο πρῶτον εἶδός ἐστι τοῦ μὴ εἰς πειρασμὸν
ἐμπεσεῖν, ὅπερ συμβουλεύει καὶ τοῖς ἀσθενεστέροις
προσεύχεσθαι, τὸ τὸν μὲν πειρασμὸν προσελθεῖν (δεῖ
15 γὰρ ἐλθεῖν τὰ σκάνδαλα), αὐτοὺς δὲ μὴ εἰς τὸν πειρασμὸν
πεσεῖν. ὁ δὲ τελειότατος τοῦ μὴ εἰς πειρασμόν ἐστιν

1 μηην Ven μεν Vat ‖ μη] add δε Vat ‖ 3 ονπερ] οπερ Vat Ven ‖ 4 πλη-
σιασοι] -η Ven ‖ 5 ως γουν...το των ανθρωπων] om Ven

His desire that it may soon be removed.

1. Παρελθέτω τὸ ποτ.] Matt. xxvi 39.
2. τὸ γὰρ παρερχ....παρέρχεται] 'for that which passes by, certainly is first at hand to him and approaches him whom it passes by.' The reading of both MSS ὅπερ παρέρχ. is certainly wrong, as the phrase would merely repeat the sense of the words τὸ παρερχόμενον.
4. πλησιάσοι] For the fut. opt. with εἰ, cf. below p. 235 εἰ μὴ...ἁρμόσοιμι.
5. παρόντος] sc. τοῦ ποτηρίου: so below ἐγγὺς ὂν καὶ προκείμ.
ib. ἤρξατο λυπ. κτλ.] Cf. Matt. xxvi 37 and Mark xiv 33.
9. ἀπρόσιτον] used actively here.
10. ἐξ ἐπιπολῆς] lit. 'on the surface' and so, as it were, 'on tiptoe,' 'lightly.'
11. τὴν πρώτην] an adv. use, 'the first time'; see note on p. 24.
12. *The not entering into temptation means* (1) *that temptation should come to us and not we go to it and still better* (2) *perfect resignation to the Father's will, who is the dispenser of nothing that is not good.*
ib. τοῦτο πρῶτον κτλ.] 'this is the first kind of not falling into temptation, which He advises the weaker (brethren) also to make the subject of their prayers, viz. that temptation should indeed come—for "it must needs be that offences come"—but that they themselves may not fall into temptation.'
ib. εἰς πειρασμόν] Cf. Matt. xxvi 40.
14. δεῖ γὰρ ἐλθ. τὰ σκ.] Matt. xviii 7 (D. puts δεῖ for ἀνάγκη).

E. EXEGETICAL FRAGMENTS

εἰσελθεῖν τρόπος, ὅνπερ αἰτεῖ δεύτερον οὐχ ἁπλῶς· Οὐχ
ὡς ἐγὼ θέλω ἀλλ' ὡς cύ. ὁ γὰρ θεὸς ἀπείραστός ἐστιν
κακῶν· θέλει δὲ τὰ ἀγαθὰ διδόναι ἡμῖν ὑπερεκπερισσοῦ
ὧν αἰτούμεθα ἢ νοοῦμεν.

Τὸ μὲν οὖν θέλημα αὐτοῦ τὸ τέλειον αὐτὸς ὁ ἀγα- 5
πητὸς ἠπίστατο, καὶ τοῦτο ἐληλυθέναι πολλάκις φησὶ
ποιήσων, οὐ τὸ αὐτοῦ, τοῦτ' ἔστι τὸ τῶν ἀνθρώπων.
οἰκειοῦται γὰρ τὸ πρόσωπον τῶν ἀνθρώπων, ὡς γενόμενος
ἄνθρωπος. διόπερ καὶ τότε, τὸ μὲν ἑαυτοῦ, τὸ ἔλαττον,
παραιτεῖται ποιεῖν, αἰτεῖ δὲ τὸ τοῦ πατρός, τὸ μεῖζον, 10
γενέσθαι, τὸ θεικὸν θέλημα, ὅπερ πάντως κατὰ τὴν
θεότητα ἓν θέλημα τὸ αὐτοῦ καὶ πατρός. τὸ γὰρ πατρικὸν θέλημα, τὸ διὰ πειρασμοῦ παντὸς ἐπισκῆψαν
διελθεῖν, διάγοντος αὐτὸν θαυμασίως αὐτοῦ τοῦ πατρὸς
μὴ μέχρι τοῦ πειρασμοῦ, μηδὲ εἰς αὐτὸν εἰσελθεῖν, ἀλλ' 15

5 αγαπητος] om ο Vat ‖ 7 αυτου] αὐτοῦ Migne ‖ 9 το μεν] add το Ven ‖
10 το του πατρος] om το Vat ‖ 11 παντως Vat παλιν Ven ‖ 12 αυτου] αυτου
Migne ‖ 13 επισκηψαν] επισκηψαντος Vat επισκη (sic) Ven (sec Migne)

2. ὁ γὰρ θεὸς κτλ.] James i 13.
3. θέλει δὲ κτλ.] cf. *ibid.* 17.
ib. ὑπερεκπ. κτλ.] Eph. iii 20. The connexion of thought between these quotations is that, if under temptation we resign ourselves to God's will, the result will be not only that we escape the evil, but that we gain more good than we can ask or think, because God is altogether unaffected by evil and overrules it for good.
5. *It was our Lord's human will that submitted itself to the will of God, with which His Divine will was at one. And the Father's will was able to bring the Son not only, as was necessary, face to face with temptation, but above and beyond it.*
ib. τὸ θέλημα αὐτ. τὸ τέλ.] Cf. Rom. xii 2.
6. πολλάκις φησί] Cf. John vi 38, Heb. x. 7, Ps. xxxix (xl) 8.
8. οἰκειοῦται] 'He appropriates': cf. ἐξοικειοῦται, p. 255.
ib. τὸ πρόσωπον] 'the character.'

The word is used in its earlier, dramatic, not in its later, theological, sense of 'person.' So Greg. Naz. *Theol. Or.* iv 6 uses the word δραματουργεῖται of Christ's sufferings, where see Dr Mason's note (p. 115).
11. ὅπερ πάντως ... καὶ πατρός] 'which of course, according to the Godhead, is one will, His own and the Father's.'
12. τὸ γὰρ πατρικὸν...γενέσθαι] 'for (it was) the Father's will which enjoined that He should go through every temptation, the Father Himself wonderfully bringing Him, not (merely) as far as the temptation, nor yet that He should enter into it, but that He should rise above the temptation and pass beyond it.' Ἐπισκῆψαν is almost a certain correction of the Vat. reading ἐπισκήψαντος. Μετ' αὐτόν, 'after (i.e. beyond) it,' as opp. to κατ' ἐκεῖνον 'at it,' above p. 232.

ὑπεράνω τοῦ πειρασμοῦ καὶ μετ' αὐτὸν γενέσθαι· ὅλως
δὲ οὐδὲ ἀδύνατον, οὐδὲ ἄπρακτον οὐδ' ὑπεναντίον τῷ
βουλήματι τοῦ πατρὸς τὸν Σωτῆρα αἰτεῖν. ἔστι δὲ
δυνατόν, ὡς ὁ Μάρκος ἀπεμνημόνευσε λέγοντος αὐτοῦ·
5 Ἀββᾶ ὁ πατήρ, πάντα coι Δγνατά· καὶ δυνατὰ εἰ βούλοιτο,
ὡς Λουκᾶς φησὶν αὐτὸν εἰρηκέναι· Πάτερ, εἰ Βογλει,
παρένεγκε τὸ ποτήριον τοῦτο ἀπ' ἐμοῦ.

Τὸ οὖν πνεῦμα τὸ ἅγιον εἰς τοὺς εὐαγγελιστὰς κατανεμηθὲν τὴν πᾶσαν τοῦ Σωτῆρος ἡμῶν διάθεσιν ἐκ τῆς
10 ἑκάστου φωνῆς συντίθησιν. οὔτε γάρ τι αἰτεῖται παρὰ
τοῦ πατρός, ὃ μὴ ὁ πατὴρ βούλεται. τὸ γὰρ Εἰ βογλει
ὑποταγῆς καὶ ἐπιεικείας ἐστίν, οὐκ ἀγνοίας, οὐδὲ ἀμφι-
βολίας ἦν δήλωμα· ὥσπερ καὶ ἡμεῖς εἰώθαμεν παρὰ
πατρὸς ἢ ἄρχοντος ἢ διδασκάλου ἤ τινος ὧν θερα-
15 πεύομεν ἀξιοῦντές τι τῶν ἐκείνῳ καταθυμίων λέγειν
Εἴ σοι φίλον, οὐχ ὡς ἀμφιγνοοῦντες. οὕτως καὶ ὁ Σωτὴρ

2 τω βουλήματι] του βουληματος Ven ‖ 4 ο Μαρκος] add αυτου Ven ‖
λεγοντος αυτου] om αυτου Ven ‖ 5 ο πατηρ] ο πατερ Ven (sec Migne) ‖
βουλοιτο] -εται Ven ‖ 10 τι αιτειται] om τι Ven ‖ 13 δηλωμα] δηλωτικον Ven ‖
ωσπερ και...δυνατον αυτω] om Ven

1. ὅλως δὲ...αἰτεῖν] This clause further explains what τὸ πατρικὸν θέλημα is: 'and generally that the Saviour should ask neither what is impossible, nor what is impracticable, nor what is opposed to the Father's will.' Οὐδέ in this clause is put for μηδέ. Αἰτεῖν is coordinate with the infinitives in the previous sentence.

3. ἔστι δὲ δυνατόν] sc. τὸ παρελ-θεῖν τὸ ποτήριον, and so we must expand the next clause καὶ δυνατὰ (sc. πάντα), εἰ βούλοιτο (sc. ὁ πατήρ).

5. Ἀββᾶ ὁ πατ. κτλ.] Mark xiv 36.

8. The Holy Spirit brings out the various sides of the Saviour's character by means of the different gospel-records; St Luke's 'If Thou art willing' implies submission, not ignorance, as St Mark's 'All things are possible to Thee' shows, while St Matthew's 'If it be possible' suggests humble-mindedness, not that anything is impossible with God except what He does not will.

ib. Τὸ οὖν πνεῦμα...συντίθησιν] For other instances of similar views of almost 'verbal' inspiration of the New Testament in the early Church see Sanday Inspiration pp. 34–36. Διάθεσιν, 'disposition,' 'character': cf. Plat. Rep. 489 A φιλοσόφους τὴν διάθεσιν.

12. ἀμφιβολίας] 'uncertainty': cf. Plut. 2. 756 C, 1050 A.

14. ὧν θεραπεύομεν] 'of those whom we respect': ὧν = τούτων οὕς.

15. τῶν ἐκείνῳ καταθυμίων] 'of the things acceptable to such an one.'

16. Εἴ σοι φίλον] rather an archaic

E. EXEGETICAL FRAGMENTS

ἔλεγεν Εἰ βούλει, οὐχ ἕτερόν τι βουλόμενον εἰδὼς εἶτα τοῦτο πυνθανόμενος, ἀλλ' ἀκριβῶς εἰδὼς ὅτι βούλεται παρενεγκεῖν ἀπ' αὐτοῦ τὸ ποτήριον, ἠπίστατο δικαίως ὃ βούλεται δυνατὸν αὐτῷ. διὰ τοῦτο ἡ ἑτέρα γραφή φησιν· Πάντα coi δυνατά. καὶ τοῦτο πάντως τὸ εἰκτὸν 5 καὶ ταπεινόφρον ὁ Ματθαῖος διαγράφει, Εἰ δυνατόν ἐcτι λέγων. εἰ γὰρ μὴ οὕτως ἁρμόσοιμι τὴν διάνοιαν, τάχα τινὲς ἐκδέξοιντο ἀσεβῶς τὸ Εἰ δυνατόν ἐcτι, ὥς τινος ὄντος ἀδυνάτου τῷ θεῷ ποιῆσαι, πλὴν μόνου οὗ μὴ βούλεται. οὐκ αὐθέκαστον οὖν οὐδὲ αὐτῷ μόνῳ δοκοῦσαν 10 ἢ ἀντικειμένην τῇ βουλῇ τοῦ πατρὸς ἐποιεῖτο τὴν ἀξίωσιν, ἀλλὰ καὶ τῷ θεῷ συνδοκοῦσαν.

Καὶ μὴν φήσει τις ὅτι ἀναγκάζεται καὶ μετανοεῖ καὶ ἕτερον εὐθὺς οὐ τὸ πρότερον αἰτεῖ, οὐκέτι τὸ αὑτοῦ κρατύνει, τὸ δὲ τοῦ πατρὸς ἵστησι βούλημα. ναί· ἀλλ' 15

5 και] καν Ven ‖ παντως Vat παλιν Ven ‖ εικτον Vat εικτικον Ven ‖
7 γαρ μη Vat μη γαρ Ven ‖ ουτως] ουτε Ven ‖ αρμοσοιμι Ven αρμοσαιμεν Vat ‖
8 τινος οντος αδυν.] -ων -ων -ων Ven ‖ 10 ουκ αυθεκαστον...ταχιστα παρελθ.
απ αυτ. το ποτ. om Ven

or poetical expression for εἰ βούλει, frequent in Homer: cf. Herod. i 108, iv 97.

1. οὐχ ἕτερόν τι...δυνατὸν αὐτῷ] 'not because He knew that He (sc. τὸν πατέρα) willed something else, and then made this enquiry (sc. εἰ βούλ.); but, knowing for certain that He willed to take away the cup from Him, He was perfectly aware that what He willeth is possible for Him.' Δικαίως is used loosely for ἀκριβῶς and qualifies ἠπίστατο.

5. καὶ τοῦτο πάντως...διαγράφει] 'and it is just (πάντως) this submissiveness and humility that Matthew describes.' Εἰκτόν (fr. εἴκειν 'yield') is not given by Liddell and Scott.

7. ἁρμόσοιμι τὴν διάνοιαν] 'make the sense (or thought) harmonize': for the fut. opt. with εἰ see above p. 232.

8. ἐκδέξοιντο] For the omission of ἂν cf. p. 202; the tense is very unusual.

9. πλὴν...βούλεται] 'besides that only which He willeth not.' οὗ = τούτου ὅ.

10. αὐθέκαστον] The epithet when applied to persons means 'outspoken' (e.g. Arist. Eth. Nic. iv. 7. 4): when used of style it means 'rough,' 'inartificial,' Hesych. αὐθέκαστα· ἁπλᾶ, αὐστηρά. Perhaps 'independent' (Salmond) best represents it here.

13. *It is true then in a sense that the Son under compulsion forgoes His own desire and carries out the Father's will, but only because He acknowledges that the latter way is higher and better. He does not substitute 'Let it not pass' for 'Let it pass.'*

15. ἵστησι] 'sets up.'

οὐκ ἀνθ' ἑτέρου πάντη πράγματος ἕτερον μεταλαμβάνει, τῆς
δὲ αὐτῆς ἀμφοτέροις ἀρεσκούσης πράξεως, ὁδὸν ἑτέραν καὶ
ἀλλοιότερον τρόπον ἀσπάζεται, ἀντὶ τοῦ μικροτέρου καὶ
ἀπαρέσκειν αὐτῷ δοκοῦντος τὸν μείζονα καὶ θαυμασιώ-
5 τερον ἐπιμετρούμενον ὑπὸ τοῦ πατρός. παρελθεῖν μὲν
γὰρ πάντως αἰτεῖ τὸ ποτήριον· πλͱν ογχ ὡc ἐΓώ, φησι,
θέλω ἀλλ' ὡc cγ́. ὠδίνει μὲν ἑκατέρως παρελθεῖν, ἄμεινον
δὲ ὡς ὁ πατὴρ βούλεται. οὐ γὰρ τὸ μὴ παρελθεῖν ἀντὶ
τοῦ παρελθεῖν μετῄτησεν, ἀλλὰ προκειμένου τοῦ παρελ-
10 θεῖν ὡς ὁ πατὴρ βούλεται, τοῦτο γενέσθαι μεταλαμβάνει.

Διττὴ γὰρ ἡ τοῦ παρερχομένου δύναμίς ἐστιν· ἡ
παραφανὲν ἢ προσαψάμενον, εὐθὺς διωχθὲν ἢ παραδραμὸν
οἴχεσθαι, ὥσπερ οἱ παραξέοντες ἀλλήλους δρομεῖς· ἢ
συμβιῶσαν καὶ διατρίψαν καὶ προσκαθίσαν, καθάπερ

1 ετερον] -ου Vat (sec Migne) ‖ 13 αλληλους] -ως Vat (sec Migne)

1. οὐκ...πάντη...ἕτερ. μεταλαμβ.]
'He does not take up a wholly new thing': μεταλαμβ. occurs again below.

3. ἀλλοιότερον] This comparative is found several times in the classics (e.g. Thucyd. iv 106 and Herod. vii 212) and appears to have much the same force as the positive. With ἀντὶ τοῦ μικρ. κτλ. supply τρόπον and with τὸν μείζ. καὶ θαυμ. supply τρόπον.

5. ἐπιμετρούμ.] 'marked out for Him': cf. p. 14 ὑπέρθεσιν εἰς μετάνοιαν...ἐπιμετρεῖν and p. 207.

7. ὠδίνει...βούλεται] 'in both cases He longs painfully that (the cup) should pass; but the better way (is that it should pass) as the Father willeth.' Ἑκατέρως, sc. εἰ δυνατὸν κτλ. and πλὴν οὐχ ὡς ἐγὼ κτλ. Ἄμεινον may be taken either as an adv. coordinate with ἑκατέρως and explained by ὡς ὁ π. βούλ. or as an adj. with simply ἐστίν understood.

11. 'Passing' implies one of two things, either a short, transitory action or the relinquishing of a project after considerable lapse of time spent upon it. The former was the sense

in which the Saviour first used the petition, but He was immediately enabled to adopt the latter, i.e. to endure the long and bitter struggle before relief and victory came.

ib. Διττὴ γὰρ κτλ.] D. proceeds to show that there are two senses in which παρέρχεσθαι may be used; the one (ἡ παραφανὲν...δρομεῖς) illustrated by the case of a runner in a race who comes up behind and rushes past a competitor, the other (ἢ συμβιῶσαν...παρέρχονται) illustrated by the case of a body of brigands or soldiers, which, after being encamped in the neighbourhood of another body, is defeated and goes away unsuccessful and in disgrace.

13. οἱ παραξέοντες ἀλλ.] 'those who graze one another in passing': the word is so used in Heliod. v 32 and the Anthologia Palatina vii 478 (acc. to Liddell and Scott). Ἀλλήλους is a necessary correction of Migne's text.

14. προσκάθισαν] 'having laid siege to (a place)': the middle is more usual in this connexion, but cf.

E. EXEGETICAL FRAGMENTS 237

ληστρικὸν ἢ στρατόπεδον, εἶτα ἡττηθὲν καὶ μηδὲν λαβὸν
μόλις ἄπρακτον ἀπελθεῖν· εἰ μὲν γὰρ ἕλοιεν, οὐκ ἂν
παρεληλύθασιν, ἀλλὰ συναπήγαγον ἑαυτοῖς οὓς ἐχειρώ-
σαντο, εἰ δὲ κρατῆσαι μὴ δυνηθεῖεν, καταισχυνθέντες
παρέρχονται. ἐβούλετο μὲν γὰρ κατὰ τὸν πρότερον τύπον 5
ἐλθεῖν εἰς χεῖρας αὐτοῦ καὶ ἐν τάχει ποθὲν ῥᾷστα καὶ
τάχιστα παρελθεῖν ἀπ' αὐτοῦ τὸ ποτήριον. ἀλλ' ἅμα τε
εἶπε καὶ παραχρῆμα ἐπιρρωσθεὶς κατὰ τὴν ἀνθρωπότητα
ὑπὸ τῆς πατρικῆς θεότητος ἀσφαλεστέραν ποιεῖται τὴν
αἴτησιν καὶ οὐκέτι οὕτω βούλεται, ἀλλ' ὡς ἀρέσκει τῷ 10
πατρὶ ἐνδόξως καὶ καρτερῶς καὶ πλῆρες πιεῖν. τοῦτο
γὰρ ἤκουσεν Ἰωάννης αὐτοῦ λέγοντος ὁ τὰ μεγαλειότατα
καὶ θειότατα τῶν τοῦ Σωτῆρος λόγων καὶ ἔργων ὑπομνη-
ματισάμενος· Τὸ ποτήριον ὃ δέδωκέ μοι ὁ πατήρ μου, οὐ
μὴ πίω αὐτό; πιεῖν δὲ ἦν τὸ ποτήριον, πληρῶσαι τὴν 15
διακονίαν καὶ πᾶσαν τοῦ πειρασμοῦ τὴν οἰκονομίαν
ἀνδρείως ἐχόμενον τοῦ πατρὸς διανύσαι καὶ ὑπερ-

1 μηδεν λαβον] om μηδεν Vat ‖ 2 ουκ αν] ου γαρ Vat (sec Migne) ‖
7 αλλ αμα τε ειπε και] αλλα cum lacuna Ven ‖ 8 κατα την] om την Ven ‖
10 ουτω] αυτο Ven ‖ 11 πιειν] ποθεν Vat Ven ‖ 14 το ποτηριον] pr και
Ven ‖ 16 την οικονομ.] om την Vat ‖ 17 τ. πατρος] add ελομενου Vat Ven

Polyb. i 12. 4 προσκαθίσαντα πολιορ-
κεῖν.
1. ληστρικόν] 'a band of brigands':
the form ληστρικός is found equally
with ληστικός; cf. Thucyd. ii 69 τὸ
ληστικόν.
ib. μηδὲν λαβόν] I have added
μηδέν, some such word being required for the sense, unless λαβόν
itself is corrupt (? for σφαλέν).
5. ἐβούλετο] sc. ὁ Σωτήρ.
6. ποθέν] loosely used for πως
('somehow').
11. πλῆρες] The neut. adj. is used
for the adv. here.
ib. πιεῖν] sc. βούλεται. The MSS
reading ποθεν yields no satisfactory
sense.
12. τὰ μεγαλειότατα] 'the most

sublime': τὰ μεγαλεῖα is used as a
noun in Acts ii 11 ('mighty works'):
cf. Ps. lxx (lxxi) 19: and the comp.
adv. is found in Plat. *Theaet.* 128 C
and Xen. *Hell.* iv 1. 9.
14. Τὸ ποτήριον...αὐτό;] John xviii
11.
15. πιεῖν δὲ...τὰ δεινά] 'now to
drink the cup was to fulfil the
ministry (cf. Acts xii 25) and bravely
accomplish the whole dispensation of
temptation, adhering to the Father,
and overcome its terrors.' The
word ἑλομένου, which both MSS give
after τοῦ πατρός, hopelessly encumb-
ers the construction of the sentence
and is probably only a copyist's error
derived from ἐχόμενον. We could
however omit ἐχόμενον instead and

βῆναι τὰ δεινά. ἐκεῖνος γὰρ δι' ὧν αὐτὸς ἠξίου ταῦτα καταλιμπάνων—παρέρχεσθαι γὰρ λέγεται ἑκάτερον ἀφ' ἑκατέρου, καὶ τὸ μένον τοῦ ἀπιόντος καὶ τὸ ἀπιὸν τοῦ μένοντος. ὁ δὲ Ματθαῖος σαφέστατα ἐδήλωσεν, ὅτι
5 παρελθεῖν μὲν τὸ ποτήριον ᾔτει, μὴ μὴν ὡς αὐτός, ἀλλ' ὡς ὁ πατὴρ ἐβούλετο, τοῦτο γενέσθαι ἠξίου. ἁρμοστέον ἀκολούθως καὶ τὰ διὰ Μάρκου καὶ Λουκᾶ ῥήματα· ὁ μὲν γὰρ Μάρκος Ἀλλ' οΫ τί ἐΓὼ θέλω φησὶν ἀλλά τί cΥ θέλεις, ὁ δὲ Λουκᾶς Πλὴν Μὴ τὸ θέλΗΜΆ Μογ ἀλλὰ τὸ cὸν
10 ΓινέcΘω. ἔλεγε μὲν γὰρ αὐτὸς καὶ ἤθελε ταχέως λωφῆσαι καὶ πεπαῦσθαι τὸ πάθος, ἤθελε δὲ αὐτὸν ὁ πατὴρ λιπαρῶς καὶ διαρκῶς τὸν ἀγῶνα πληρῶσαι. πάντα οὖν τὰ προσπίπτοντα παρέσχετο· καὶ ὥσπερ σιδηροῖς καὶ ἀρρήκτοις ὅπλοις προσρασσόμενα βέλη, μᾶλλον δέ, ὡς ἀπὸ
15 στερρᾶς πέτρας, τὰ μὲν ἐθραύετο, τὰ δὲ ἀνεκρούετο, ῥαπίσ-

1 εκεινος γαρ...ανεκραγε προς τον πατ.] om Ven ‖ 2 καταλιμπανων vel corrupta est lectio vel anacoluthon est vel etiam deest nonnihil (e.g. δῆλος ἦν)

make τοῦ πατρ. ἐλομ. absolute and parenthetical.

1. ἐκεῖνος γὰρ...καταλιμπάνων] Unless the text is corrupt, we must either supply some phrase like δῆλος ἦν ('by the terms of His own prayer He clearly left all this behind') or consider that the sentence is broken off and not resumed after what is intended to be a parenthesis (beginning with παρέρχεσθαι γάρ) till the words πάντα οὖν κτλ. Ταῦτα, sc. both the decision and τὰ δεινά just mentioned.

2. παρέρχ. γὰρ κτλ.] 'for either may be said to pass away from either, that is to say both that which remains from that which departs and that which departs from that which remains.' These words are added to explain how the Saviour could be said ταῦτα καταλιμπάνειν. He dismissed it from His mind and therefore it 'passed away.'

4. ὁ δὲ Ματθαῖος κτλ.] D. proceeds to show from the three Synoptic Gospels that he is justified in appealing to the Saviour's own prayer (δι' ὧν αὐτὸς ἠξίου) for his interpretation of the passage (viz. that He καταλιμπάνει ταῦτα). Μὴ μήν, 'not however.'

8. Ἀλλ' οὐ τί...θέλεις] Mark xiv 36.

10. ἔλεγε μὲν γὰρ αὐτός] '(for this is what) He said Himself.' The stress is again on αὐτός, as above in αὐτὸς ἠξίου.

12. λιπαρῶς καὶ διαρκῶς] 'thoroughly and completely.' Λιπαρῶς is from λιπαρής (earnest) not λιπαρός (bright).

ib. τὸν ἀγῶνα πληρ.] Cf. τὴν διακον. πληρ. above.

ib. πάντα οὖν τὰ προσπίπτ. παρέσχ.] 'He (sc. ὁ Σωτήρ) submitted to all the things that fell upon Him (sc. τὸν Σωτῆρα).' The metaphor of τὸν ἀγῶνα is continued. Παρέχεσθαι is here used in the sense of 'letting them come on.'

13. καὶ ὥσπερ...ἀνεκρούετο] 'And the shafts were either shivered in

E. EXEGETICAL FRAGMENTS 239

ματα, ἐμπτύσματα, μάστιγες, θάνατος, καὶ τοῦ θανάτου
τὸ ὕψωμα.

Καὶ τούτων ἐπιτελουμένων ἐϲιώπα καὶ διεκαρτέρει,
ὥσπερ οὐδὲν πάσχων ἢ ὡς ἤδη τεθνεώς. μηκυνομένου
δὲ θανάτου καὶ ὑπὲρ δύναμιν αὐτὸν ἤδη δαμάζοντος, 5
ἀνέκραγε πρὸς τὸν πατέρα. τὸ δὲ Τί με ἐγκατέλιπες;
ἦν ἄρα οἷς προηξίωσεν ἀκόλουθον· τί μοι μέχρι νῦν ὁ
θάνατος συνέζευκται καὶ οὔπω τὸ ποτήριον παραφέρεις;
τί δὲ οὐκ ἔπιον αὐτὸ ἤδη καὶ ἀνήλωσα; ἀλλὰ δέος
μὴ ὑπ' αὐτοῦ πλήρης ἐπικειμένου καταποθείην· ὃ 10
γένοιτ' ἂν εἴ με ἐγκατέλιπες. τὸ μὲν παραμενεῖ πε-
πληρωμένον, ἐγὼ δὲ οἰχήσομαι κεκενωμένος. ἤδη ποτὲ
τετελέσθω τὸ Βάπτιϲμα, ὡς καὶ πρὸ πολλοῦ ϲυνειχόμην,
ἕωϲ ὅτου τελεϲθῇ. ταύτην τοῦ Σωτῆρος τὴν διάνοιαν ἐν

6 το δε] ante τι με εγκατ. Ven post Vat ∥ 8 παραφερεις Vat περιφερω Ven ∥ 9 τι δε ουκ...τελεσθη] om Ven ∥ τι] ει Vat

pieces or recoiled (upon the foe) as if they beat upon resistless steel armour or rather as if they rebounded from hardest rock.'

1. τοῦ θανάτ. τὸ ὕψωμα] 'the uplifting in death' sc. the crucifixion. The expression is suggested by such passages as John iii 14, etc.

3. *The cry which burst forth from Him after silence on the cross 'Why hast Thou forsaken me?' is consistent with His former petition: God did not forsake Him; for He drank the cup straightway, and so it passed.*

ib. τούτ. ἐπιτελ. ἐσιώπα] Cf. Mark xiv 61.

4. ὥσπερ οὐδὲν π.] Cf. Ev. Petri § 4 αὐτὸς δὲ ἐσιώπα ὡς μηδὲν πόνον ἔχων, but the words here have no Docetic tendency as they have there.

5. ὑπὲρ δύναμιν...δαμάζοντ.] a condensed expression : 'was now overcoming Him (being) beyond His strength,' i.e. when His human powers of resisting death were failing.

6. Τί με ἐγκατέλιπες;] Matt. xxvii 46, Mark xv 34.

7. οἷς προηξ. ἀκόλ.] 'in accordance with His former petitions.'

ib. μοι...συνέζευκται] For the metaphor cf. Eur. *Hipp.* 1389 οἴᾳ ξυμφορᾷ ξυνεζύγης and *Hel.* 255 τίνι πότμῳ συνεζύγην.

9. ἀνήλωσα] 'finished it,' as we say. Τί for εἰ is a necessary correction.

ib. ἀλλὰ δέος...καταποθ.] 'nay but my fear is lest I be swallowed up by its coming in full force upon me.' Cf. Is. xxv 8. For the use of πλήρης indeclinable see Mr C. H. Turner's note on John i 14 in *J.T.S.* vol. i pp. 120 ff. and 561 ff.

11. τὸ μὲν] sc. ποτήριον.

13. βάπτισμα...συνειχ. ἕως ὅτ. τελ.] Cf. Luke xii 50. The metaphor τὸ βάπτισμα takes the place of τὸ ποτήριον, perhaps through the word καταποθείην which may have suggested it. Cf. Mark x 38.

14. ταύτην τοῦ Σωτ. κτλ.] 'this I surmise was the Saviour's meaning

τῇ συντόμῳ φωνῇ τεκμαίρομαι γεγονέναι καὶ ἀληθῆ γε ἔλεγε καὶ οὐκ ἐγκαταλέλειπται, ἀλλὰ εὐθὺς ἐξέπιεν ὡς ἠξίωσε καὶ παρελήλυθε.

Καὶ τούτου μοι δοκεῖ τὸ προσενεχθὲν ὄξος αὐτῷ
5 γεγονέναι σύμβολον. ὁ γὰρ ἐντροπίας οἶνος διεσήμαινεν ἴσως τὴν ὀξεῖαν αὐτοῦ τροπὴν καὶ μεταβολὴν ἣν κατεδέξατο, ἀντὶ τοῦ πάθους τὴν ἀπάθειαν, καὶ ἀντὶ τοῦ θανάτου τὴν ἀθανασίαν, καὶ ἀντὶ τῆς φθορᾶς τὴν ἀφθαρσίαν, καὶ ἀντὶ τοῦ κρίνεσθαι τὸ κρίνειν,
10 καὶ ἀντὶ τοῦ τυραννεῖσθαι τὸ βασιλεύειν μεταλαβών. ὅ τε γὰρ σπόγγος, ὡς οἶμαι, τὴν ὅλην δι' ὅλου τοῦ ἁγίου πνεύματος ἐν αὐτῷ γενομένην ἀνάκρασιν ἀνέφηνε· καὶ ὁ κάλαμος τὸ βασίλειον σκῆπτρον καὶ τὸν θεῖον νόμον ὑπέφησεν. ὁ δὲ ὕσσωπος τὴν ζωτικὴν

2 ελεγε] -εν Ven ‖ 4 τουτου] τουτο Ven ‖ προσενεχθ.] παρενεχθ. Ven ‖ 8 του θανατου] om του Vat ‖ και αντι της φθορ. την αφθ.] om Ven ‖ 9 κρινειν και] om και Ven ‖ 12 ανεφηνε] ενεφ. Ven ‖ 14 υπεφησεν] υπεφηνεν Ven

in the short utterance' (viz. τί με ἐγκατέλιπες;).

2. οὐκ ἐγκαταλέλειπται] Cf. Theophylact *in Marc.* xv 34 ἡμεῖς μὲν γὰρ οἱ ἄνθρωποι ἦμεν οἱ ἐγκαταλελειμμένοι, ἐκεῖνος δὲ οὐκ ἐγκατελείφθη ποτὲ παρὰ τοῦ πατρός· ἄκουε γὰρ αὐτοῦ τί φησιν· Οὐκ εἰμὶ μόνος ὅτι ὁ πατὴρ μετ' ἐμοῦ ἐστίν.

ib. ὡς ἠξίωσε] 'even as He had prayed,' i.e. without delay or protest (εὐθύς): cf. προηξίωσεν above.

3. παρελήλυθε] sc. τὸ ποτήριον: this explains why οὐκ ἐγκατελέλειπται.

4. The wine turned to vinegar seems to me a symbol of the change from suffering to absence of pain, from death to life, which Christ then obtained. The sponge signifies the immanence of the Holy Spirit in Christ, the reed His royalty and jurisdiction, the hyssop His life-giving resurrection.

5. ἐντροπίας οἶνος] 'turned or sour wine.' Hesych. ἐντροπίας· εὐμετάβολος, ὀξίνης. The forms ἐκτροπίας and τροπίας also occur: e.g. Aristoph. fr. 13 ταχύ νυν πέτου καὶ μὴ τροπίαν οἶνον φέρε.

6. τροπήν] used of wine turning sour, Plut. *Mor.* ii 939 F.

10. μεταλαβών] Cf. above p. 236.

11. τὴν ὅλην...ἀνάκρασιν] 'the complete infusion of the Holy Spirit that was throughout in Him.' Δι' ὅλου is the adverbial expression and τοῦ ἁγ. πν. is gen. after ἀνάκρασιν. The allusion is to such passages as Luke iv 1. For the interpenetration of spirit and matter generally we may compare Greg. Nyss. *Cat. Or.* 6 (pp. 30 f. Srawley).

14. ὑπέφησεν] 'expressed': the Lexicons give ὑποφήτης, etc. but not ὑπόφημι: hence perhaps Cod. Ven. is right in reading ὑπέφηνεν.

ib. ὁ δὲ ὕσσωπος] Hyssop was used in the purificatory rites connected with leprosy (Lev. xiv 4 ff.)

καὶ σωτήριον ἔγερσιν αὐτοῦ, δι' ἧς καὶ ἡμᾶς ὑγίασεν, ἔδειξεν.

Ἀλλὰ περὶ μὲν τούτων ἱκανῶς καὶ ἐν τῷ Ματθαίῳ καὶ ἐν τῷ Ἰωάννῃ διήλθομεν· τὰ δὲ καὶ [ἐν] τῷ Μάρκῳ διδόντος θεοῦ ἐροῦμεν. νῦν δὲ τῶν ἑξῆς ἐχώμεθα. 5

Στίχ. μγ´ Ὤφθη δὲ αὐτῷ ἄγγελος ἀπ' οὐρανοῦ ἐνισχύων αὐτόν.

Στίχ. μδ´ Καὶ γενομενος ἐν ἀγωνίᾳ ἐκτενέστερον προσ-ηύχετο. ἐγένετο δὲ ὁ ἱδρὼς αὐτοῦ, ὡσεὶ θρόμβοι αἵματος καταβαίνοντες ἐπὶ τὴν γῆν. 10

Παροιμία λέγεται ἐπὶ τῶν σφόδρα λυπουμένων καὶ ἀγωνιώντων αἵματος ἵδρωσις, ὥσπερ καὶ ἐπὶ τῶν πικρῶς ὀδυρομένων αἵματα κλαίει, ὅτι ὡσεὶ θρόμβοι αἵματος.

1 ὑγίασεν] ὑγία Ven per errorem ‖ 3 αλλα περι μεν...εχωμεθα] om Ven ‖ 11 παροιμια λεγεται...εξ αλογιας] om Vat

and defilement from the dead (Num. xix 6 ff., 18 ff.): hence in Ps. l (li) 9 *ῥαντιεῖς με ὑσσώπῳ καὶ καθαρισ-θήσομαι.* Thus its ancient associations under the Mosaic Law suggest its symbolical meaning here.

1. ὑγίασεν] 'restored to health,' possibly with reference again to the uses of hyssop after leprosy (see above).

3. Ἀλλὰ περὶ μὲν...ἐχώμεθα] For a discussion of these words see Introduction, p. 231. I have printed them as the words of the compiler of the Catena, not of D., in accordance with Sickenberger's view. So above, p. 205.

11. *The bloody sweat is not to be taken literally: it describes the reality and intensity of Christ's agony, which produced so great a flow of perspiration.*

12. αἵματος ἵδρωσις] Livy gives as prodigies *scuta duo sanguine sudasse* xxii 1: cf. *id.* xxvii 4. The noun ἵδρωσις is not given by Liddell and Scott.

13. αἵματα κλαίει] The phrase αἵματι κλαίειν was proverbial: Suidas καθ' ὑπερβολήν, οὐ δάκρυσιν· ἐφ' ὧν μὴ δύναιντο πεῖσαι πάντα πράττοντες, οὕτως ἔλεγον οἱ ἀρχαῖοι· οὐδ' ἂν πείσῃ αὐτὸν οὐδ' αἵματι κλαίων· οὐδ' ἂν αἵματι στένων πείσειαν. Heliodorus *Aeth.* iv 8 speaks of a woman ἣν ἀπὸ δακρύων τῶν ἐπὶ σοὶ καὶ αἵματος ἐχάραττον.

ib. ὅτι ὡσεὶ θρόμβοι κτλ.] These words explain why the author takes the phrase metaphorically, as is also the case with the proverbial saying, which he has cited: 'because when he said "as it were drops of blood" he did not mean actually drops of blood, for then he would not have spoken of the sweat under this similitude' (τούτων = τῶν θρόμβων αἵματος): 'for this is the force of "as it were drops"' (i.e. ὡσεὶ θρ. αἵμ. is καθ' ὁμοιότητα). Παρίστησι ('suggests,' 'describes') is an ordinary classical use. The MS reads ἱδρῶτος after οὐ θρόμβους, but it is probably due to a copyist's error and its omission greatly aids the meaning. For a good account of the genuineness of vv. 43 and 44 the reader may consult Scrivener *Introd.* 2nd ed. pp. 521 ff., as well as Westcott and Hort *in loc.*

εἰπών, οὐ θρόμβους ἀπεφήνατο αἵματος. οὐ γὰρ ἂν
καθ' ὁμοιότητα τούτων εἴρηκε γενέσθαι τοὺς ἱδρῶτας.
τοῦτο γὰρ ὡσεὶ θρόΜBοι παρίστησι. θέλων δὲ μᾶλλον
δηλῶσαι, ὡς οὐχὶ λεπταῖς τισὶ νοτίσι, καὶ οἷον ἐνδείξεως
5 χάριν ἐπιφαινομέναις, τὸ δεσποτικὸν ἐνοτίζετο σῶμα,
ἀλλ' ὡς ἀληθῶς ἁδρῶν σταγόνων δίκην ὅλον τοῖς ἱδρῶσι
περιεστάζετο, τοὺς τῶν αἱμάτων θρόμβους εἰς εἰκόνα
τοῦ γεγενημένου παρείληφεν. ἐδήλου δὲ ἄρα, ὥσπερ καὶ
διὰ τῆς ἐντεταμένης προσευχῆς καὶ τῆς πολλῆς ἀγωνίας,
10 οὕτω καὶ διὰ τῆς τῶν ἱδρώτων παχύτητος, ὡς φύσει καὶ
ἀληθῶς, ἀλλ' οὐκ ἐπιδείξει καὶ φαντασίᾳ, ἄνθρωπός τε
ἐχρημάτισεν ὁ Σωτὴρ καὶ τοῖς φυσικοῖς τῶν ἀνθρώπων
καὶ ἀδιαβλήτοις ὑπηρετήσατο πάθεσι.

Τὸ μέντοι Ἐξογcίαn ἔχω θεῖnαι τὴn ψγχήn μογ, καὶ
15 ἐξογcίαn ἔχω πάλιn λαβεῖn αὐτήn, ἐν τούτοις δηλοῖ ἑκούσιον
εἶναι τὸ πάθος· καὶ ἔτι, ὡς ἄλλη μὲν ἡ τιθεμένη καὶ
λαμβανομένη ψυχή, ἄλλη δὲ ἡ τιθεῖσα καὶ λαμβάνουσα
θεότης. καὶ ὥσπερ σαρκὶ τὸν θάνατον ὑπομείνας ἑκὼν

1 ου θρομβους] add ιδρωτος Ven

4. οἷον ἐνδείξ. χάρ. ἐπιφαιν.]
'appearing on Him as it were for
the sake of display.' The author
seems to be thinking of Docetic
notions in this passage: see below
ὡς φύσει...φαντασίᾳ and cf. Chrysost.
in Matt. xxvi 39 ἵνα μὴ δόξῃ ὑπόκρισις
εἶναι τὸ πρᾶγμα, οἱ ἱδρῶτες ἐπιρρέου-
σιν...καὶ ἵνα μὴ τοῦτο εἴπωσιν αἱρε-
τικοί, ὅτι ὑποκρίνεται τὴν ἀγωνίαν,
διὰ τοῦτο καὶ ἱδρῶτες ὡς θρόμβοι
αἵματος...καὶ μυρία τεκμήρια, ἵνα μή
τις εἴπῃ τὰ ῥήματα πεπλασμένα.

5. τὸ δεσποτικὸν...σῶμα] 'the
Master's body.' The use of δεσπότης
of Christ is said to indicate the end
of the 4th century—esp. the Cappa-
docian divines (Holl Amphilochius
p. 127): but cf. Jude 4 and Eus.
H. E. i 7. 14.

7. περιεστάζετο] 'was bedewed
all round': cf. Anth. Pal. vii 36.

11. ἄνθρωπός τε ἐχρημάτισεν]
'passed for a man': cf. Acts xi 26
and Rom. vii 3; the verb χρηματίζειν
lit. 'to transact business' came in
later Greek to signify simply 'to be
called' or 'to pass for.'

12. τοῖς φυσικοῖς...πάθεσι] 'was
subject to the natural and innocent
sensations of men.' The middle
use of ὑπηρετεῖν does not occur till
later Greek: see above pp. 82 and 227.

14. *His sufferings were voluntarily endured and have nerved many
to become martyrs. Even the bloody
sweat may be mystically considered
to signify this.*

ib. Ἐξουσίαν ἔχω...αὐτήν] John x
18.

15. ἐν τούτοις] sc. in the instances
mentioned (ἱδρώς, ἀγωνία, etc.).

16. ἄλλη μὲν...θεότης] The inter-
polation of the compiler of the
Catena here well expresses the
meaning: ἄλλην δὲ καὶ ἄλλην ἔφη,

E. EXEGETICAL FRAGMENTS 243

ἐν αὐτῇ τὴν ἀφθαρσίαν ἐφύτευσεν, οὕτω καὶ τὸ τῆς
δουλείας βουλήσει προσηκάμενος πάθος αὐτῇ τὸ θάρσος
καὶ τὴν ἀνδρείαν ἐνέσπειρεν, ἐξ ἧς τοὺς πιστεύοντας εἰς
αὐτὸν πρὸς τοὺς τοῦ μαρτυρίου μεγάλους ἄθλους ἐνεύρισε.
ταύτῃ τοι καὶ θρόμβοι ἱδρῶτος αὐτοῦ παραδόξως οἷα 5
σταγόνες αἵματος ἀπέρρεον, ἵνα τῆς ἡμετέρας φύσεως
ὥσπερ ἀναξηράνῃ καὶ ἐξοικίσῃ τὴν τῆς δειλίας πηγήν.
ἐπεὶ εἰ μὴ τοῦτο ἦν ὡς ἐν ΜΥCΤΗΡΊῼ πραττόμενον, οὐδὲ εἰ
σφόδρα δειλότατός τις καὶ ἀγενέστατος ὑπῆρχεν, αἵματος
ἔμελλεν νοτίσιν ἐξ ἀγωνίας μόνον ὥσπερ ἰκμάσιν ἱδρῶτος 10
παρὰ φύσιν ὑγραίνεσθαι.

Τοιοῦτόν ἐστι κἀκεῖνο τὸ εἰρημένον, ὡς ἄΓΓελος ἦν
παρεστηκὼς τῷ Σωτῆρι καὶ ἐνιϲχύων αὐτόν. καὶ τοῦτο
γὰρ τῆς περὶ ἡμᾶς ἕνεκεν οἰκονομίας ἐπράττετο. τῶν
γὰρ ὑπὲρ εὐσεβείας ἀγώνων οἱ ἀθλεῖν μέλλοντες τοὺς 15
ἱεροὺς ἄθλους ἀγγέλους ἐξ οὐρανοῦ ἐπικουροῦντας αὐτοῖς
ἔχουσι.

2 δουλειας] δειλιας coniec Migne ‖ 8 ει 2°] coniec Migne pro ἡ

οὐκ εἰς δύο πρόσωπα διαιρῶν ἀλλὰ
τῶν δύο φύσεων δεικνὺς τὸ διάφορον.
1. τὴν ἀφθ. ἐφύτ.] Perhaps 1 Cor.
xv 42-44 is in the commentator's
mind.
  ib. τὸ τῆς δ....πάθος] 'having of
His own will submitted to the
sufferings of a slave'; cf. Phil. ii
7, 8. Migne's conjecture however,
δειλίας (for δουλείας), is not improbable.
4. ἐνεύρισε] Νευρίζειν is not given
in Liddell and Scott but it is apparently a collateral form to νευροῦν
'to strengthen,' 'to tighten the
nerves.'
5. ταύτῃ] adv. 'in this way.'
6. τῆς ἡμετέρας φύσεως] dep. on
τῆς δειλίας.
7. ἐξοικίσῃ] 'might remove'; a
strange word to use in combination
with ἀναξηράνῃ and τὴν πηγήν.
8. ἐπεὶ εἰ μὴ...ὑγραίνεσθαι] 'for

unless this were being done as in a
mystery' (i.e. with a mystical meaning: cf. 1 Cor. ii 7), 'not even some
absolutely cowardly and ignoble
person was likely to be so unnaturally bathed in a flow of blood
like the moisture of sweat merely
from the agony he suffered.' We
should have expected αἵματος and
ἱδρῶτος to exchange places in the
sentence (as indeed Salmond has
translated it). But the commentator
seems to condense two arguments
into one: (1) the mystic interpretation explains the meaning of the
'Bloody Sweat,' and (2) the greatest
cowardice in the world could not
account for actual blood flowing instead of sweat.
  12. *The appearing of 'an angel
strengthening Him' was for our sake
to assure us of similar aid in times
of need.*

Τάχα δὲ τό· Πάτερ, παρένεγκε τὸ ποτήριον οὐχ ὡς δεδιὼς τὸν θάνατον ἔφησεν, ἀλλ' ἵνα διὰ τούτων προσκαλέσηται τὸν διάβολον πῆξαι αὐτῷ τὸν σταυρόν. ῥήμασι δολεροῖς ἠπάτησεν ἐκεῖνος τὸν Ἀδάμ, ῥήμασι
5 δειλοῖς ἀπατηθήτω ὁ δολερός.

Ἀλλ' οὐδὲ ἄλλο θέλημα τοῦ υἱοῦ, καὶ ἄλλο τοῦ πατρός. ὁ γὰρ θέλων ὃ θέλει ὁ πατὴρ εὑρίσκεται ἔχων τὸ θέλημα τοῦ πατρός. σχήματι οὖν λέγει· Μὴ τὸ ἐμὸν ἀλλὰ τὸ cόν· οὐ γὰρ θέλει αὐτὸ παρενεχθῆναι, ἀλλὰ τῷ βουλή-
10 ματι τοῦ πατρὸς ἀναπέμπει τὸ ἐκ τοῦ πάθους κατόρθωμα, ὡς ἀρχὴν τιμῶν τὸν πατέρα. εἰ γὰρ γνώμην τὴν διάθεσιν καλοῦσιν οἱ πατέρες, γίνεται δὲ διάθεσις

5 δειλοις] θεικοις Ven

1. *Perhaps the prayer (to remove the cup) was not from fear of death but in order to cheat the devil into setting up the cross.*

ib. Τάχα δὲ ... ὁ δολερός] This passage is based on a sermon by Amphilochius of Iconium, recently recovered by Holl. See Holl *Amphilochius von Ikonium* (Tübingen 1904) p. 98 ῥήμασιν ἐκείνοις δολεροῖς ἠπάτησεν τὸν Ἀδάμ, ῥήμασιν ἐγὼ (sc. ὁ Σωτήρ) δειλοῖς ἀπατῶ τὸν δολερόν.

5. ἀπατηθήτω ὁ δολερός] This idea that Satan was deceived by the Humanity of Christ at the Crucifixion is traced as far back as Ignatius, *Eph.* § 19, and may have been suggested by 1 Cor. ii 8. See Srawley's note, Greg. Nyss. *Cat. Or.* p. 89 (cf. p. 97) and Mason's note, Greg. Naz. *Theol. Or.* iv p. 117.

6. *The Son's will was one with the Father's. The Son had no desire apart from His.*

ib. Ἀλλ' οὐδὲ ἄλλο...ἐξ ἀλογίας;] This passage also seems to bear no relation to what is being discussed. See Introduction p. 230.

7. ὁ γὰρ θέλων κτλ.] The commentator here maintains that the Son's will did not differ from the Father's, because as a matter of fact He willed to receive the cup, whereas the author of the passage on p. 233 has distinctly stated that in that respect the Son abandoned His own (human) will in favour of the Father's and that it was only κατὰ τὴν θεότητα that there was unity of will between the Father and the Son. The two passages therefore can hardly be from the same hand.

8. σχήματι] 'for a show' or 'pretence' as in the previous paragraph.

10. ἀναπέμπει...κατόρθωμα] 'attributes the successful result of the passion.' Ἀναπέμπειν here bears the meaning of 'tracing up' (as of a pedigree, ἀναπέμπειν γένος εἴς τινα, Diod. iv 83).

11. ὡς ἀρχὴν τιμῶν τὸν πατέρα] Cf. p. 178. Cf. Greg. Naz. *Theol. Or.* iv 12 (pp. 125–8 Mason).

ib. γνώμην τὴν διάθ. καλ. οἱ πατέρες] Hesych. γνώμη· διάθεσις ποιά τις καὶ ἐπιστήμη. Suidas: γνώμη· ἡ προαίρεσις, ἡ βουλή: cf. Arist. *Eth.* (*Eud.*) vi 11. 1 ἡ καλουμένη γνώμη ... ἡ τοῦ ἐπιεικοῦς ἐστὶ κρίσις ὀρθή. Οἱ πατέρες, 'our fathers,' the ancients.

12. γίνεται...βουλεύσεως] 'disposition is formed secretly, of set purpose, as after deliberation.'

E. EXEGETICAL FRAGMENTS

πρὸς τὸ κρυβὲν ἐμφρόνως ὡς ἀπὸ τῆς βουλεύσεως, πῶς φασί τινες τὸν κύριον, τὸν ὑπὲρ ταῦτα πάντα, θέλημα φέρειν γνωμικόν; ἢ δῆλον ἐξ ἀλογίας;

Στίχ. με΄ Καὶ ἀναστὰς ἀπὸ τῆς προσευχῆς, ἐλθὼν πρὸς τοὺς μαθητὰς εὗρεν αὐτοὺς κοιμωμένους ἀπὸ τῆς λύπης. 5

Στίχ. μς΄ Καὶ εἶπεν αὐτοῖς· Τί καθεύδετε; ἀναστάντες προσεύχεσθε, ἵνα μὴ εἰσέλθητε εἰς πειρασμόν.

Ὅπερ καὶ αὐτὸς προσηύχετο, πολλάκις πίπτων ἐπὶ πρόσωπον, καὶ δι' ἀμφοτέρων τὸ μὴ εἰσελθεῖν εἰς πειρασμὸν αἰτῶν, τοῦ τε Εἰ δυνατόν, παρελθέτω τὸ ποτήριον, 10 καὶ τοῦ Οὐχ ὡς ἐγὼ θέλω, ἀλλ' ὡς σύ. τὸ γὰρ μὴ εἰσελθεῖν εἰς πειρασμὸν ἔλεγε, καὶ τοῦτο ᾔτει, οὐ τὸ μηδὲ ὅλως πειραθῆναι περιστάσεως ἢ ἐν δυσχερίᾳ τινὶ μὴ γενέσθαι καθάπαξ. καὶ γὰρ ἀδύνατον μάλιστα μὲν ἴσως παντὶ ἀνθρώπῳ τὸ παντελῶς ἄγευστον χαλε- 15 ποῦ τινὸς διαβιῶναι. Ὅλος γάρ, φησιν, ὁ κόσμος ἐν τῷ

1 βουλευσεως] ? legendum βουλησεως ‖ 8 οπερ και...καθαπαξ] om Ven ‖ 13 ἢ] ἢν Vat ‖ δυσχερια] ? legendum δυσχερεια ‖ 15 παντι] και παντι Vat ‖ 16 διαβιωναι Vat διαμειναι Ven

1. πῶς φασί τινες κτλ.] ' how say some that the Lord, who is above all these things, exercises a deliberately formed desire (θέλ. γνωμ.)? Surely it is only from defective reasoning?' The argument appears to be that the phrase θέλ. γνωμ. applied to our Lord by some writers unknown (in connexion with the Agony) is illogical, because γνώμη is here equivalent to διάθεσις and διάθεσις is a human characteristic, which has to act imperfectly as best it can, while our Lord is above all such limitations.

8. *The Saviour prayed for Himself, not that He might not encounter adversity, nor that He should escape from the curse pronounced upon Adam at the Fall; for this is the common lot of man and especially of the righteous. But His prayer was that He might be delivered from His affliction and ' overcome the world.'*

ib. Ὅπερ] i.e. μὴ εἰσελθεῖν εἰς π.

9. δι' ἀμφοτέρων] ' by both (petitions),' sc. τοῦ τε Εἰ δυν. κτλ. καὶ τοῦ Οὐχ ὡς ἐγὼ κτλ.

11. τὸ γὰρ μὴ κτλ.] 'For what He meant by "not entering," etc. and what He prayed for was not that He should have no experience of adversity or that He should never be in any difficulty at all.' Περιστάσεως, 'difficult circumstances,' 'critical times.' Cf. p. 189.

14. μάλιστα μὲν ἴσως παντὶ ἀνθ.] 'in the first instance perhaps for mankind in general ': to this corresponds μάλιστα δὲ τοῖς ἁγίοις below. The first μάλιστα therefore is used in a different sense from the second. For the argument cf. the discussion in Hooker *Eccl. Pol.* v 48.

16. Ὅλος...ὁ κόσμ....κεῖται] 1 John v 19.

πονηρῷ κεῖται καὶ τὸ πλέον τῶν ἡμερῶν τοῦ ἀνθρώπου κόπος καὶ πόνος· ὡς καὶ αὐτοὶ λέγουσιν· ὀλίγος ἐστὶ καὶ λυπηρὸς ὁ βίος ἡμῶν. ἀλλ' οὐδὲ εἰκὸς ἦν αὐτὸν κελεύειν εὔχεσθαι μὴ πληροῦσθαι τὴν ἀρὰν τὴν λέγουσαν· Ἐπι-
5 κατάρατος ἡ γῆ ἐν τοῖς ἔργοις coy· ἐν λύπαις φαγῇ αὐτὴν πάσας τὰς ἡμέρας τῆς ζωῆς coy· ἢ τὸ Γῆ εἶ καὶ εἰς γῆν ἀπελεύσῃ. δι' ἣν καὶ ποικίλως αἱ θεῖαι γραφαί, τὸ περιπαθὲς τοῦ βίου δεικνῦσαι, κοιλάδα κλαυθμῶνος αὐτὸν καλοῦσιν. μάλιστα δὲ τοῖς ἁγίοις ἐπαλγὴς ὁ κόσμος,
10 πρὸς οὓς ἀθέμιτον αὐτῷ ψεύδεσθαι λέγοντι· Ἐν τῷ κόcμῳ τούτῳ θλίψιν ἕξετε· καὶ ὁμοίως διὰ τοῦ προφήτου· Πολλαὶ αἱ θλίψεις τῶν δικαίων. ἀλλὰ τὸ μὴ εἰς πειρασμὸν εἰσελθεῖν λέγειν αὐτὸν ὑπολαμβάνω τὸ ῥυσθῆναι μὲν κατὰ τὸν προφήτην τῶν θλίψεων· Ἐκ πασῶν γὰρ
15 αὐτῶν φησὶ ῥύcεται αὐτοὺc ὁ κύριος· ὡς δὲ τὸ αὐτοῦ ῥῆμα ὑπισχνεῖται, κρατῆσαι τῶν θλίψεων, καὶ τῆς νίκης, ἧς ὑπὲρ ἡμῶν ἐνίκησε, μετασχεῖν· μετὰ γὰρ τὸ εἰπεῖν Ἐν τῷ κόcμῳ θλίψιν ἕξετε, ἐπήγαγεν· Ἀλλὰ θαρcεῖτε, ἐγὼ ἐνίκηcα τὸν κόcμον.
20 Καὶ προσεύχεσθαι δὲ πάλιν ἐδίδασκε μὴ ἐμπεσεῖν

2 ως και αυτοι...απο του πονηρου] om Ven ‖ 15 αὐτοῦ ρῆμα]? αὐτοῦ ρ. ‖ 18 αλλα] και Vat ‖ 19 ενικησα] νενικηκα apud Joann xvi 33

1. τὸ πλέον...κόπος καὶ πόνος] Cf. Ps. lxxxix (xc) 10.
2. ὀλίγος...ἡμῶν] Wisd. ii 1.
4. Ἐπικατάρατος...ζωῆς σου] Gen. iii 17.
6. Γῆ εἶ...ἀπελεύσῃ] ibid. 19.
7. τὸ περιπαθὲς τ. β.] 'the grievous sufferings of life.'
8. κοιλάδα κλαυθμῶνος] Ps. lxxxiii (lxxxiv) 7.
9. ἐπαλγής] 'a source of grief.'
10. αὐτῷ] sc. our Lord, whose prayer is here under discussion.
ib. Ἐν τῷ κόσμῳ...ἕξετε] John xvi 33: where τούτῳ is omitted and ἔχετε stands for ἕξετε: the commentator himself omits τούτῳ below.

12. Πολλαί...δικαίων] Ps. xxxiii (xxxiv) 20.
13. τὸ ῥυσθῆναι μὲν κτλ.] To this corresponds the next clause ὡς δὲ τὸ αὐτ. κτλ.
14. Ἐκ πασῶν...αὐτούς] Ps. xxxiii (xxxiv) 20.
20. *He has taught us also to pray not only* 'Lead us not into temptation' *but also* 'Deliver us from the Evil One.' *There is a difference between* 'being tempted' *and* 'falling into temptation.' *The devil tempts us and we may either resist by God's help or yield: in the latter case we* 'fall into temptation.' *God also Himself is said to tempt* (i.e. to try)

E. EXEGETICAL FRAGMENTS 247

εἰς πειρασμόν· καὶ δὴ καὶ ΜΗ ΕἰϹΕΝΈΓΚΗϹ ἩΜᾶϹ ΕἰϹ ΠΕΙ-
ΡΑϹΜΌΝ, τοῦτ' ἔστι Μὴ ἐάσῃς ἡμᾶς ἐμπεσεῖν εἰς πειρασμόν.
ὅτι δὲ τοῦτο ἦν οὐ τὸ μὴ πειρασθῆναι, ῥυσθῆναι δὲ ἀπὸ
τοῦ πονηροῦ, προσέθηκεν· Ἀλλὰ ῥῦϹΑΙ ἩΜᾶϹ ἈΠΌ ΤΟΫ͂
ΠΟΝΗΡΟΫ͂. ἀλλὰ τί διενήνοχεν, ἴσως ἐρεῖς, τὸ πειρασθῆναι 5
καὶ τὸ εἰς πειρασμὸν ἐμπεσεῖν ἤτοι εἰσελθεῖν; ὁ μὲν γὰρ
ἡττηθεὶς ὑπὸ τοῦ πονηροῦ (ἡττηθήσεται δέ, εἴπερ μὴ
ἀγωνίζοιτο, ὑπερασπίζοι δὲ αὐτοῦ καὶ ὁ θεός) εἰς πειρασμὸν οὗτος ἐνέπεσε καὶ εἰς πειρασμὸν εἰσῆλθε καὶ
ἔστιν ἐν αὐτῷ καὶ ὑπ' αὐτὸν ὥσπερ ἀχθεὶς αἰχμάλωτος· 10
ὁ δὲ ἀντισχὼν καὶ ὑπομείνας, πεπείρασται μὲν οὗτος,
οὐ μὴν εἰς πειρασμὸν εἰσῆλθεν ἤτοι ἐνέπεσεν. ἈΝΉΧΘΗ
γοῦν ὁ Ἰηςοῦς ὑπὸ τοῦ πνεύματος οὐκ εἰς πειρασμὸν εἰσελθεῖν ἀλλὰ πειρασθῆναι ὑπὸ τοῦ διαβόλου. καὶ ὁ Ἀβραὰμ
οὐκ εἰς πειρασμὸν εἰσῆλθεν, ἀλλ' οὐδὲ εἰς πειρασμὸν 15
ἦγεν ὁ θεός, ἀλλὰ ἐπείραζεν, οὐκ ἐνέβαλεν αὐτὸν εἰς
πειρασμόν. καὶ αὐτὸς δὲ ὁ κύριος ἐπείραζε τοὺς μαθητάς.
ὁ μὲν γὰρ πονηρὸς πειράζων εἰς τοὺς πειρασμοὺς καθέλκει,
οἷα πειραστὴς κακῶν, ὁ δὲ θεὸς πειράζων τοὺς πειρασμοὺς παραφέρει ὡς ἀπείραστος κακῶν· ὁ γὰρ θεός, φησιν, 20

8 υπερασπιζοι] -ει Ven || εις πειρ. ουτ. ενεπεσε] om Ven || 11 πεπειρασται]
πειραται Ven || 14 πειρασθηναι] πειραθηναι Ven || 16 ενεβαλεν] ενεβαλε δε
Ven || 20 παραφερει] περιφ. Ven

us, but in that case He provides a way to escape, whereas the devil tempts us to our ruin.

ib. μὴ ἐμπεσ. εἰς πειρ.] viz. in the words of *v.* 46: cf. above p. 233.

1. καὶ μὴ εἰσεν....πειρασμόν] Matt. vi 13, Luke xi 4.

5. τί διενήνοχεν;] 'what difference was there between?' The answer to the question begins with ὁ μὲν γὰρ κτλ.

8. ὑπερασπίζοι] 'cover him with a shield'; usually with an accus., sometimes with gen. as here: cf. Gen. xv 1 ἐγὼ ὑπερασπίζω σου.

12. οὐ μήν] 'not however': cf. μὴ μήν above p. 238.

ib. ἀνήχθη...διαβόλου] Cf. Matt. iv 1.

16. ὁ θεὸς...ἐπείραζεν] Gen. xxii 1.

17. ἐπείρ. τοὺς μαθ.] Cf. John vi 6.

20. παραφέρει] 'takes (the temptations) away from us,' as opposed to the violent methods of Satan who drags us (καθέλκει) into them. For παραφέρει cf. above p. 235 βούλεται παρενεγκεῖν τὸ ποτ., and p. 239 οὔπω τὸ ποτ. παραφέρεις;

ib. ὁ γὰρ θ....ἀπείρ. κακ.] James i 13: for other discussions of this text see pp. 233 and 252.

ἀπείραστος κακῶν. ὁ μὲν γὰρ διάβολος ἐπ' ὄλεθρον ἕλκων βιάζεται, ὁ δὲ θεὸς ἐπὶ σωτηρίαν γυμνάζων χειραγωγεῖ.

Στίχ. μζ΄ Ἔτι αὐτοῦ λαλοῦντος, ἰδοὺ ὄχλος καὶ ὁ λεγόμενος Ἰούδας, εἷς τῶν δώδεκα, προήρχετο αὐτοὺς καὶ ἤγγισε
5 τῷ Ἰησοῦ, φιλῆσαι αὐτόν.

Στίχ. μη΄ Ὁ δὲ Ἰησοῦς εἶπεν αὐτῷ· Ἰούδα, φιλήματι τὸν υἱὸν τοῦ ἀνθρώπου παραδίδως;

Βαβαὶ τῆς ἀνεξικακίας τοῦ δεσπότου, τοῦ καὶ φιλήσαντος τὸν προδότην, καὶ τοῦ φιλήματος ἁπαλώτερα
10 ῥήματα φθεγξαμένου. οὐ γὰρ εἶπεν· ὦ μιαρὲ καὶ παμμίαρε καὶ προδότα, ταύτας ἡμῖν ἀποδίδως τὰς ἀμοιβὰς τῆς τοσαύτης εὐεργεσίας; ἀλλὰ πῶς; Ἰούδα, τὸ κύριον ὄνομα τιθείς, ὃ μᾶλλον ταλανίζοντος ἦν καὶ ἀνακαλοῦντος ἢ ὀργιζομένου. καὶ οὐκ εἶπε· τὸν διδάσκαλόν σου, τὸν
15 δεσπότην, τὸν εὐεργέτην, ἀλλὰ τὸν υἱὸν τοῦ ἀνθρώπου,

2 σωτηριαν] -ας Ven ‖ χειραγωγει] hic desinit fragmentum in Vat codice ‖ 4 προηρχετο] προσηρχ. Migne ‖ 5 φιλησαι] -ησας Migne ‖ 12 το κυριον] τὸν κ. Migne

2. γυμνάζων χειραγ.] 'leads us by the hand, as He trains us for salvation,' i.e. God does not leave us alone in the midst of our trials. For χειραγ. cf. Greg. Nyss. *Cat. Or.* 32 (p. 120 ed. Srawley) δι' ἀκοῆς ἡμᾶς πρὸς τὴν τῆς θεότητος χειραγωγεῖσθαι.

8. *How wondrous is the Lord's forbearance towards Judas and how terrible is Judas's treachery in kissing Him. Surely the Lord's example should at least keep us from betraying the brethren. For when once a man sacrifices another for his own selfish ends, he becomes deaf to all advice and falls like Judas. Christ therefore omitted nothing which might warn us against such conduct.*

ib. Βαβαὶ τῆς ἀνεξικακ.] 'how wondrous is the Master's long-suffering.' Βαβαί in the classics usually expresses a semi-humorous surprise; here it is used seriously enough. Hesych. βαβαί· θαυμαστικὴ φωνή. For τῆς ἀνεξικακίας cf. Wisd. ii 19 ὕβρει καὶ βασάνῳ ἐτάσωμεν αὐτόν, ἵνα... δικάσωμεν τὴν ἀνεξικ. αὐτοῦ. The whole of this last passage is much in the style of Chrysostom's *Comment. in Matt.* xxvi 49: βαβαὶ πόσην ἐδέξατο πονηρίαν ἡ τοῦ προδότου ψυχή;... ποίῳ στόματι ἐφίλει; ὦ μιαρᾶς γνώμης... ποῖον σύμβολον ἔδωκε τῆς προδοσίας; ὃν ἂν φιλήσω, φησίν. ἐθάρρει τῇ ἐπιεικείᾳ τοῦ διδασκάλου· ὃ μάλιστα πάντων ἱκανὸν ἦν αὐτὸν ἐντρέψαι καὶ πάσης αὐτὸν ἀποστερῆσαι συγγνώμης ὅτι τὸν οὕτως ἥμερον παρεδίδου κτλ.

12. τὸ κύρ. ὄνομα] 'his proper name.'

13. ταλανίζοντος] 'commiserating,' lit. to call oneself or (as here) another τάλας, like σχετλιάζειν and μακαρίζειν. Hesych. ταλανίζει· θρηνεῖ.

ib. ἀνακαλοῦντος] 'calling to' (by way of encouragement): cf. Thucyd. vii 70 ἀνακαλοῦντες ὀνομαστὶ τὸν τριήραρχον.

E. EXEGETICAL FRAGMENTS 249

τοῦτ' ἔστι τὸν ἥμερον, τὸν πρᾶον. εἰ γὰρ μὴ διδάσκαλος
ἦν μηδὲ δεσπότης μηδὲ εὐεργέτης, τὸν οὕτως ἀπλάστως,
τὸν οὕτως ἡμέρως πρός σε διακείμενον, ὡς ἐν τῷ καιρῷ
τῆς προδοσίας σε φιλεῖν καὶ ταῦτα τοῦ φιλήματος συμ-
βόλου τῆς προδοσίας ὄντος, τοῦτον παραδίδως; εὐλο- 5
γητὸς εἶ, Κύριε· πόσης ἀνεξικακίας, πόσης ταπεινο-
φροσύνης ὑπόδειγμα ἡμῖν γέγονας. οὐ μὴν ἀλλὰ καὶ
τοῦ μὴ ἀφίστασθαι τῆς πρὸς τοὺς ἀδελφοὺς συμβουλῆς,
κἂν μηδὲν πλέον ἐκ τῶν ἡμετέρων ῥημάτων γίνηται, ὑπόδειγμα τοῦτο πεποίηκεν ὁ δεσπότης. καθάπερ γὰρ τὰ 10
ἀνίατα τῶν τραυμάτων, οὐδὲ τοῖς αὐστηροῖς τῶν φαρμάκων, οὐδὲ τοῖς γλυκαίνειν αὐτὰ δυναμένοις, οὕτω καὶ
ψυχή, ἐπειδὰν ἅπαξ αἰχμάλωτος γένηται, καὶ ἑαυτὴν
ἐπιδῷ ὁτιοῦν πλημμελήματι, καὶ μὴ βούληται τὸ ἑαυτῆς
συμφέρον συνιδεῖν, κἂν μυρία τις ἐνηχῇ, οὐδὲν κερδαίνει, 15
ἀλλά, καθάπερ νεκρὰς ἀκοὰς κεκτημένη, οὐδεμίαν ἀπὸ
τῆς παραινέσεως δέχεται τὴν ὠφελείαν, οὐκ ἐπειδὴ μὴ
δύναται, ἀλλ' ἐπειδὴ μὴ βούλεται. τοῦτο καὶ ἐπὶ τοῦ
Ἰούδα γέγονεν. ὁ δὲ χριστὸς καὶ ταῦτα πάντα προειδὼς
οὐ διέλιπεν ἐξ ἀρχῆς μέχρι τέλους τὰ παρ' ἑαυτοῦ πάντα 20

12 ουτω coniecit Migne: MS ουτε ‖ 14 οτιουν] coniecit ωτινιουν Migne

2. ἀπλάστως] 'unaffectedly,' 'simply': cf. Gen. xxv 27 Ἰακὼβ δὲ ἦν ἄνθρωπος ἄπλαστος.
3. ὡς...σε φιλεῖν] 'as to kiss thee': the Gospel record does not say or suggest that the Saviour returned the kiss.
7. οὐ μὴν ἀλλὰ...ὁ δεσπότης] i.e. the incident is not only a proof of His own goodness but is also a practical lesson to us.
9. κἂν μηδὲν κτλ.] 'even if no other good come from our words': so below κἂν μυρία τις ἐνηχῇ and κἂν μηδὲν...κέρδος.
10. τὰ ἀνίατα τ. τραυμ.] Οὐδὲν κερδαίνει must be supplied from the end of the sentence: Migne pro-

poses to add ἰαθῆναι δύναται but it is not necessary.
14. ὁτιοῦν] unless we adopt Migne's emendation ᾠτινιοῦν, must be a sort of cognate accus. after ἐπιδῷ: 'and give herself up in any thing to wrong doing.'
15. συνιδεῖν] 'to take in at a glance,' 'to comprehend.' Cf. p. 71 n.
ib. κἂν μυρία τις ἐνηχῇ] 'even if we din a thousand things in its ears.'
17. οὐκ ἐπειδὴ ... βούλεται] 'not because it cannot but because it will not.'
20. ἐξ ἀρχῆς μέχρι τέλους] Cf. Eccl. iii 11.
ib. τὰ παρ' ἑαυτοῦ π. ἐπιδ.]

ἐπιδεικνύμενος. ἃ καὶ ἡμῶν εἰδότων ῥυθμίζειν χρὴ τοὺς ἠμελημένους διὰ παντός, κἂν μηδὲν ἐκ τῆς συμβουλῆς γίνηται κέρδος.

'setting forth all that was at His command (i.e. by way of counsel or example).' Τὰ παρ' ἑαυτ. lit. 'all that proceeded from Himself.'

1. ῥυθμίζειν χρή] 'we must unceasingly (endeavour to) regulate the careless.' For ῥυθμίζειν cf. Plat. *Phaedr.* 253 B πείθοντες καὶ ῥυθμίζοντες (αὐτοὺς) εἰς τὸ ἐκείνου (sc. τοῦ θεοῦ) ἐπιτήδευμα καὶ ἰδέαν ἄγουσιν. Ἠμελημένους must here be deponent: the adv. (-ως) is used for 'carelessly,' e.g. Xen. *Mem.* iii 11. 4 οὐδὲ ταύτας ἠμελημένως ἐχούσας.

Z. MISCELLANEOUS FRAGMENTS.

I

In Act. Apost. v 4

This extract comes from Cod. lviii (of the 13th cent.) at New Coll. Oxf. and MS Coisl. xxv: it is given in Cramer's *Catena* iv p. 85.

Ἀγαθὸν τὸ μὴ εὔξασθαί σε ἢ τὸ εὔξασθαι καὶ μὴ ἀποδοῦναι. οὐδὲν γὰρ ὁ θεὸς ἐξ ἀνάγκης οὐδὲ ἐκ λύπης βούλεται. ἐπειδήπερ οὔκ ἐστι σά, ἄπερ ἅπαξ διὰ τῆς ἐν ταῖς εὐχαῖς ἐπαγγελίας ἀνέθηκας.

2 βουλεται]+η το ευξασθαι σε και μη αποδουναι Cramer

1. *Promises voluntarily made in prayer must be fulfilled.*
ib. Ἀγαθὸν...ἀποδοῦναι] Eccl. v.

4. The passage is apparently applied to the case of Ananias.

II

In Rom. xi 26

This extract is given in Cramer's *Catena* (iv p. 418) from the Codex Monacensis and by Routh (*Rell. Sacr.* iv p. 447) as *ex Œcumenii Catena* from the Bodleian MS 202.

Καὶ οὕτως πᾶς Ἰσραὴλ σωθήσεται· Διονυσίου Ἀλεξανδρείας Ἀντὶ τοῦ οἱ πλείονες.

2. Ἀντὶ τοῦ οἱ πλείονες] i.e. πᾶς Ἰσραὴλ is equivalent to 'most Israelites.' If genuine, the extract is interesting as a slight indication of D.'s reasonable methods of interpreting Scripture: see General Introduction, p. xxv ff.

III

In S^{ti} Iac. Ep.

1

This extract is possibly out of the περὶ Πειρασμῶν, one of the πολυεπεῖς λόγοι mentioned by Eus. *H. E.* vii 26. 2 in conjunction with the περὶ Φύσεως. That work was dedicated to Euphranor: see General Introduction, p. xxx. According to Cramer, who gives the extract in his *Catena* (v p. 5), one MS ascribes the fragment to Dionysius of Alexandria, but another to Origen.

Ὅτι ὁ θεὸς πειράζων ἐπ᾽ ὠφελείᾳ πειράζει, οὐκ ἐπὶ τῷ κακοποιῆσαι· διὸ καὶ ἐλέχθη ὅτι ὁ θεὸς ἀπείραστός ἐστι κακῶν.

Καὶ μετ᾽ ὀλίγα·

5 Ὁ οὖν φέρων τοὺς πειρασμοὺς γενναίως στεφανοῦται. ἄλλο δέ ἐστιν ἐπὶ τοῦ διαβόλου· ἐκεῖνος γὰρ πειράζει, ἵνα τοὺς πειθομένους αὐτῷ θανατώσῃ. καὶ ὁ μὲν ἀγνοῶν τὸ ἐσόμενον, ὁ δὲ θεὸς εἰδὼς μὲν τὸ ἐσόμενον, πλὴν διδοὺς τῷ ἀνθρώπῳ πράττειν ὃ θέλει διὰ τὸ αὐτεξ-
10 ούσιον.

1. *God tries us for our good, not for our ruin.*
    ib. ὁ θεὸς...κακῶν] James i 13. The same passage is discussed on p. 247. Apparently both there and here ἀπείραστος κακῶν is understood actively 'does not tempt men with evil.'
5. *The devil tempts us in order to destroy us. But he knows not what the result will be, while God does, though He leaves our wills free.*
    ib. στεφανοῦται] Cf. *ibid.* i 12.
    7. ἵνα...θανατώσῃ] Cf. p. 248.

2

This extract is given by Simon de Magistris p. 200 from Cod. Vall. F 9 p. 26 and in Cramer's *Catena* (v p. 25) from Coisl. MS xxv. By both authorities it is ascribed to our Dionysius.

Z. MISCELLANEOUS FRAGMENTS

Δείκνυσιν ὡς κἂν ὑποπλάττωνται λόγον διδασκαλικόν, ὅλοι σαρκικοί εἰσι καὶ τὰ χαλεπώτατα πράττουσι. τοῦτο δὲ ὁ Παῦλος ὠνείδιζεν· Ὅπου ϝὰρ ἐν ὑμῖν, λέγει, ζῆλοϲ καὶ ἔριϲ, οὐχὶ ϲαρκικοί ἐϲτε; ὁ μὲν γὰρ ἀγρὸν ἀρκοῦντα κεκτημένος, ἐπειδὴ μείζονα θεωρεῖ τὸν τοῦ γείτονος, αὐξῆσαι τὸν ἑαυτοῦ φιλονεικεῖ· ὡσαύτως καὶ ποιῆσαι τὸν οἶκον ὑψηλότερον.

1 ὑποπλαττωνται] -ονται Simon || λογον διδασκαλικον] -οι -οι Simon || 2 χαλεπωτατα] -οτατα Simon || 7 ποιησαι] -ειται Simon || ὑψηλοτερον] add του γειτονος θεωρουμενος Simon

1. *Even when men presume to teach others, their real nature often comes out in their jealousy towards their neighbours.*

ib. Δείκνυσιν] sc. ὁ Ἰάκωβος.

ib. κἂν ὑποπλάττ. λόγ. διδασκ.] 'even if they make a parade of instructive words.' The reference seems to be to James iii 1. For διδασκαλικόν cf. p. 105. Ὑποπλάσσεσθαι ('to pretend') is a rare word, not found in the classics.

2. ὅλοι σαρκ. εἰσι] The idea is explained by the quotation which follows.

3. Ὅπου γὰρ...ἐστε;] 1 Cor. iii 3: cf. James iv 2.

IV

In Apocal. xxii 3

This fragment is not attributed to Dionysius of Alexandria by Cramer, who prints it in his *Comment. in Revel.* p. 491. The Areopagite is sometimes called ὁ μέγας.

...καὶ ὄψεται τὸν θεὸν πρόϲωπον πρὸϲ πρόϲωπον οὐ δι' αἰνιγμάτων ἀλλ' ὥσπερ τοῖς ἁγίοις ἀποστόλοις,

ὥϲ φηϲιν ὁ μέγαϲ Διονύϲιοϲ.

1. πρόσωπ. π. πρόσωπ.] Cf. 1 Cor. xiii 12: the phrase δι' αἰνιγμ. is a combination of δι' ἐσόπτρου and ἐν αἰνίγματι of the same passage.

V

Πρὸς Ἀφροδίσιον

Nothing is known of the treatise from which these six extracts come nor of the person to whom they are addressed. Eus. *H. E.* vi 46. 5 tells us that ἄλλοις πλείοσιν ὁμοίως διὰ γραμμάτων ὁμιλήσας, ποικίλας τοῖς ἔτι νῦν σπουδὴν περὶ τοὺς λόγους αὐτοῦ ποιουμένοις καταλέλοιπεν (Διονύσιος) ὠφελείας: and in vii 22. 11 he says φέρεται δέ τις (ἐπιστολὴ) αὐτοῦ καὶ περὶ σαββάτου καὶ ἄλλη περὶ γυμνασίου. It is possible that one of these two last-named epistles was addressed to Aphrodisius; and, as the same MS (Cod. Vat. 1553), which is one of several which give the six extracts under this heading, gives also another extract under the heading περὶ Γυμνασίου (*q.v.*), it is perhaps more likely that περὶ Σαββάτου was addressed to him than the other: at the same time the extracts themselves have no close connexion with the subject of the Sabbath. They are found in vol. ii of Leontius and Johannes *Res Sacrae* and were printed by Mai *Nova Collectio* vii 96, 98, 99, 102 and 107. Since then (in 1899) they have been critically edited by Holl *Fragmente vornicänischer Kirchenväter* in *Texte und Untersuchungen* (*Neue Folge*), vol. v pp. 149 and 150.

(1) Τὸ ἀνεπίσκοπον καὶ ἀπρονόητον ἐγκαταλειφθῆναι ὑπὸ θεοῦ πάντων ὀλεθριώτατον, καὶ ἡ ἐπὶ τοῖς μεγίστοις ἀδικήμασι μεγίστη τιμωρία αὕτη, τὸ ἔρημον καὶ ὀρφανὸν γενέσθαι θεοῦ· ὁ γὰρ ξένος τοῦ βοηθοῦ καὶ σωτῆρος
5 γενόμενος ὑπὸ τοῖς ἐχθροῖς καὶ τοῖς λησταῖς εὐθύς ἐστιν.

1 ανεπισκ. και απρον.] απρον. και ανεπισκ. Cod Vat et Mai ‖ 2 υπο]+του Mai ‖ 3 τιμ. αυτη, το] τιμ.˙αυτη· το Holl ‖ ερημον] ειρημενον Cod Vat et Mai ‖ 4 θεου]+ποιει Cod Vat et Mai ποιει θεον Holl απο θεου cod unus om ποιει alter

1. *To be left without the Divine protection would be the most serious punishment for wrong doing: we should at once be at the mercy of the enemy.*
ib. ἀνεπίσκοπον] 'not superintended' by God: cf. Eus. *H. E.* viii 1. 8 οἷά τινες ἄθεοι ἀφρόντιστα καὶ ἀνεπίσκοπα τὰ καθ' ἡμᾶς ἡγούμενοι.
ib. ἀπρονόητον] pass. here, 'destitute of (God's) Providence (πρόνοια)': usually act. 'without foresight'; but see p. 132.
2. καὶ ἡ...τιμωρία] 'and this (is) the greatest punishment for the greatest iniquities, viz. the being

forsaken and bereft of God.' For the construction cf. pp. 6, 52 and 71; and for the phrase ὀρφ. θεοῦ cf. Lam. v 5 and John xiv 18. The omission of ποιεῖ from the text removes all difficulty from the sentence and renders the various corrections that have been proposed (see *appar. crit.*) unnecessary.
4. ξένος τ. βοηθ. κ. σωτ.] 'a stranger to help and safety': cf. Soph. *O. T.* 219, 220 ξένος μὲν τοῦ λόγου τοῦδ'...ξένος δὲ τοῦ πραχθέντος and Plat. *Apol.* 17 D ξένως ἔχω τῆς ἐνθάδε λέξεως.
5. ὑπὸ τ. ἐχθροῖς...ἐστιν] 'he is at the mercy of his enemies': cf.

Z. MISCELLANEOUS FRAGMENTS

(2) Πᾶσιν ἀνθρώποις ἐναντίως διακειμένοις, καὶ τοῖς μὲν κακοῖς, τοῖς δὲ ἀγαθοῖς οὖσιν, τὰ αὐτὰ ὁμοίως ἀδύνατον εἶναι φίλα.

(3) Οὐχ ἱκανὴ προτροπὴ τὸ καθήμενον ἐξ ὑπερδεξίου καθάπερ θεατὴν Ἀνδρίζου λέγειν, ἀλλὰ τὸ συναποδύντα καὶ συγκονισάμενον ἑαυτὸν ἀπομιμεῖσθαι κελεύειν.

(4) Οὐ σχολὴ τῇ κατωδύνῳ ψυχῇ τὸ τοῦ κολάζοντος ἐκλογίζεσθαι φρόνημα, οὐδὲ δύναται κλυδωνιζομένη καὶ συγκεχυμένη τὴν ἀτάραχον καὶ γαληνιῶσαν τοῦ κρείττονος ἐνορᾶν διάνοιαν.

(5) Τὸ μὲν ἐκ τῶν ὄντων αἰσχρῶν ὑγιεῖ κρίσει πρὸς τὰ ἀληθῆ καὶ σεμνὰ χωρεῖν ἔπαινος· τὸ δὲ τοῖς οὐκ ὀρθῶς ὑπειληφόσι βουλόμενον ἀρέσκειν ἀπὸ τῶν κρειττόνων ἐκκλίνειν πρὸς τὰ φαῦλα δι' ἔπαινον ψόγος.

6 συγκονισάμενον] συγκομισ. Cod Vat Mai Holl ‖ 7 σχολη] σχολει Cod Vat Mai Holl ‖ κατωδυνω] κατοδ. Cod Vat Mai Holl ‖ 11 αισχρων] αισχρον Cod Vat Mai Holl ‖ 13 απο] υπο Mai ‖ 15 ψογος] om Mai

ὑπὸ τοῖς στρατιώταις γενόμ. (p. 25) and Thucyd. i 32 μέγας ὁ κίνδυνος, εἰ ἐσόμεθα ὑπ' αὐτοῖς.

1. Men's desires differ according to the goodness or the badness of their dispositions.

4. It is not sufficient incitement to sit on high like a spectator and say Play the man; but what is needed is that one should strip and wrestle with him and bid him do, as he himself does.

5. συναποδύντα] We should expect -υάμενον.

6. συγκονισάμενον] For this word see Lidd. and Sc. s.v.: the reading of the MS yields no satisfactory sense.

7. The soul that is racked with pain is not free to consider the purpose of his corrector.

9. τοῦ κρείττονος] 'of the Higher Being' i.e. God. Οἱ κρείσσονες often occurs in classical Greek and sometimes is applied to the gods (e.g. Eur. Or. 710).

11. To-pass from base to noble acts is praiseworthy, but to decline from good to evil ways from the love of praise is reprehensible.

ib. Τὸ μὲν ἐκ τῶν ὄντ. αἰσχρ.] The reading αἰσχρόν makes no good sense, but the phrase τῶν ὄντων αἰσχρῶν for τῶν αἰσχρ. ὄντ. is unusual; perhaps we should read ὄντως for ὄντων.

12. τὰ ἀληθῆ καὶ σεμνά] Cf. Phil. iv 8 ὅσα ἐστὶν ἀληθῆ, ὅσα σεμνά...εἴ τις ἔπαινος, ταῦτα λογίζεσθε.

13. τοῖς οὐκ ὀρθῶς ὑπειληφ.] Cf. Plat. Gorg. 458 E ἴσως γάρ τοι σοῦ ὀρθῶς λέγοντος ἐγὼ οὐκ ὀρθῶς ὑπολαμβάνω.

15. ψόγος] is the reading of Holl without comment. Mai omits the word and prints the sentence as if it was unfinished in the MS from which he quotes.

(6) Καταγέλαστον ἀνθρώπῳ τῷ τῶν ἰδίων ἀφει-
δήσαντι παιδεύειν ἐπιχειρεῖν τοὺς ξένους.

1. *It is ridiculous for one who neglects his own folk to try to correct strangers.*
ib. τῶν ἰδίων ἀφειδ.] Ἀφειδεῖν properly means 'to be unsparing,' but is sometimes used as here (e.g. Soph. *Ant.* 414 and Apoll. Rhod. ii 89 and 869) as equivalent to φείδεσθαι 'to neglect.'

VI

περὶ Γυμνασίου

This extract is given by Mai *Nova Collectio* vii 98 and by Holl *Fragmente* 376 p. 151: see General Introduction, p. xxxii.

The meaning of the title and the probable subject of the letter are illustrated by the expression in Dionysius's letter to the brethren at Alexandria (p. 82), which occurs in the same chapter of Eusebius as that in which this treatise is referred to (*H. E.* vii 22. 6), ἡμῖν δὲ οὐ τοιοῦτο μὲν γυμνάσιον δὲ καὶ δοκίμιον οὐδενὸς τῶν ἄλλων ἔλαττον.

Ὥσπερ ἐν νόσοις, ἐκ διαστημάτων γινομέναις κατὰ
περίοδον, οὐκ ἂν διὰ τὰς ἀνέσεις ὑγιαίνειν τις λέγοιτο
ἀλλὰ διὰ τὰς ἐπιτάσεις νοσεῖν, οὕτως οὐκ εὐδαίμων ὁ
βίος, ἐπεί ποτε τῶν ὀδυνῶν ἀποπαύεται, ἐπίμοχθος δὲ
5 πᾶς πᾶσιν ἐπεὶ πολλάκις τοῖς ὀδυνηροῖς ἐξοικειοῦται.

1 κατα περιοδον] om Mai ‖ 3 επιτασεις] επιστασεις Mai

1. *Life as a whole is full of toils and pains in spite of occasional happiness, just as in intermittent diseases a man is not reckoned well because of the periods of relief.*
2. ἄνεσις, ἐπίτασις] are medical terms for the cessation and recurrence of attacks.
5. τοῖς ὀδυνηροῖς] Cf. p. 91 τοῖς ἰδ. ἀλγεινοῖς.
ib. ἐξοικειοῦται] Cf. pp. 184 and 233.

VII

περὶ Γάμων

This treatise is not mentioned either by Eusebius or by Jerome. The latter however (*Ep.* 49. 3) mentions Dionysius among several writers *qui latissime hanc epistolam* (sc. 1 Cor.)

interpretati sunt (i.e. on the subject of marriage e.g. vii 7), which may be a reference to this treatise (see General Introduction, p. xxviii). The extract appears in Mai *Nova Collectio* vii 102 and Holl *Fragmente* 375 p. 151 (from Cod. Vat. 1553 and other MSS).

Τὰς συμφορὰς ἐλεεῖν οὐ μισεῖν προσῆκεν.

ου μισειν] μισειν ουν ου codex unus

It becomes us to pity men's misfortunes, not to abhor them.

VIII

From works unspecified.

(1) Holl *Fragmente* 379 p. 152: Cod. Hieros. *SS. Parall.* f. 286.

Τοῦ ἐλεεῖν καὶ εὐεργετεῖν οὔτε προτιμότερον οὔτε φιλανθρωπότερόν ἐστιν ἡμῖν τι ἕτερον, ἐπεὶ μηδὲ τῷ θεῷ.

3 προτιμοτερον Holl -ωτερον nonnulli

3. *Mercy and kindness, being dear to God, are peculiarly becoming in ourselves.* The sentiment is similar to that of such passages as Matt. v 7, Luke vi 36 and Heb. xiii 16.

(2) Holl *Fragmente* 381 p. 152: *Sacr. Parall. Rupefuc.* ii p. 780 (Le Quien).

Πρὸς μὲν τοὺς ἀπειθεῖς καὶ βεβήλους ἀπὸ τῶν ἔξωθεν καὶ τῶν κοινῶν ἐννοιῶν καὶ λογισμῶν τὰς τῶν λόγων ἐπιχειρήσεις ποιούμεθα, ἡμᾶς δὲ αὐτοὺς καὶ τοὺς ὁμόφρονας ἐκ τῶν θείων λογίων ἐπιστηρίζειν πειρώμεθα.

3. *We argue with unbelievers on general principles but we try to confirm ourselves and fellow believers by an appeal to Scripture.* The rule here laid down is similar to that which Basil says he imposed upon himself (*Hom. de Fide* tom. ii p. 224 ed. Benedict.).
ib. βεβήλους] Cf. 1 Tim. i 9.

ib. ἀπὸ τῶν ἔξωθεν] Cf. *ibid.* iii 7, but there it is masc. while here it is neut.
4. τῶν κοινῶν ἐννοιῶν] 'ideas which are the common property of mankind.' Gregory of Nyssa wrote a treatise περὶ κ. ἐνν. Cf. note on Greg. Nyss. *Or. Cat.* 5 (p. 50 Srawley).

(3) Holl *Fragmente* 382 p. 152 : *Sacr. Parall.* f. 274.

Ὁ δέ γε ἐρρωμένος καὶ ἀκριβὴς λόγος καὶ τὰ πικρὰ εἶναί φησι τῶν γλυκέων ἐφόδια, καὶ γίνεσθαι καρποὺς τῶν πόνων τὰς ἡδονάς. ἀκμητὶ γὰρ οὐδὲν δύναται παραγενέσθαι.

3 γλυκεων] -ειων Holl

2. *It is a true saying that bitter ofttimes produces sweet and pleasure is the result of toil. Nothing can succeed without trouble.*

3. ἐφόδια] properly 'provisions for a journey,' here 'means of obtaining.'

4. παραγενέσθαι] 'reach perfection,' like the French 'arriver.'

(4) Holl *Fragmente* 383 p. 153 : *Sacr. Parall.* f. 266.

Two of the MSS in which this extract is found assign it to the Letter to Philemon, but this claim is rejected by Holl. The sentiment, however, for which we may compare 1 Tim. v 24, 25, might well occur in that letter from what we know of its contents (see pp. 52 ff.).

Τὴν προφανῆ κακίαν φυλάξασθαι ῥᾴδιον, τὴν δὲ ἐγκεκρυμμένην ἐκτρέπεσθαι δύσκολον.

1. *It is easy to guard against an open evil but difficult to avoid that which is concealed.*

(5) *Sacr. Parall.* ii p. 674 (Le Quien).

This extract is not included in the lists of either Harnack or Holl among the Dionysian fragments.

Μηδὲν τῶν συμβαινόντων χωρὶς ἂν γενέσθαι θεοῦ πεπεῖσθαι χρή· εἶναι δὲ ἀγαθὰ παρ' αὐτοῦ πάντα κἂν ἀλγεινὰ ᾖ.

1. *We ought to feel sure that nothing happens without God and that all things are good as being from Him, even if they be painful.* For the sentiment Rendel Harris in his edition of the Διδαχὴ τῶν ιβ´ ἀποστ. (p. 39) well compares iii 10 of that treatise τὰ συμβαίνοντά σοι ἐνεργήματα ὡς ἀγαθὰ προσδέξῃ. He also suggests that the extract comes from the περὶ Φύσεως.

(6) Holl *Fragmente* 384 p. 153.

The following extract is assigned to some Dionysius in *Florileg. Monac.* 81, but Holl considers it is more likely to come from some ascetic writer than from our author. He also

Z. MISCELLANEOUS FRAGMENTS

prints five other extracts quoted in the Sacred Parallels, which are almost certainly to be assigned to Dionysius the Areopagite, not to Dionysius of Alexandria.

Ἡ λέγε σιγῆς τι κρεῖσσον ἢ σιγὴν ἔχε.

(7) Pitra *Anal. Sacr.* iii 598.

These questions and answers, as Pitra informs us, are written in an eleventh century hand on the last page of the Cod. Palatinus 431, where they are ascribed to our Dionysius. Loofs (*Theol. Litzg.* 1884, col. 554) notices that one of them occurs in a Bodleian MS with the note against it, *cacodoxi cuiusdam quaestio ad Dionysium Magnum*; perhaps here again (as on p. 253) there is a confusion between the Alexandrian and the Areopagite. Harnack (*op. cit.* 425) considers that the first question rather points to a post-Nicene date. In any case the authenticity of the passage as a whole and in its present form is extremely doubtful.

αʹ ἐρώτησις. Πότερον αὐτὸς ἑαυτὸν ἐγέννησεν ὁ υἱὸς ἢ ἐκ τοῦ πατρὸς ἐγεννήθη;

ἀπόκρισις. Ἐκ τοῦ πατρὸς γεγέννηται καὶ οὐκ αὐτὸς ἐγέννησεν ἑαυτὸν ὁ υἱός.

βʹ. Ὄντα οὖν ἐγέννησεν ἢ μὴ ὄντα; 5

Ὧν ἅμα καὶ γεγεννημένος ἐστὶ καὶ οὐκ ἦν πρὸ τοῦ γεννηθῆναι αὐτὸν τὸ μὴ εἶναι, οὐδ' εἶχεν πρὸ τῆς γεννήσεως αὐτοῦ χρόνον, ἵνα ἤρξατο.

γʹ. Ἄναρχον λέγεις ἐξ ἀνάρχου;

Οὐκ ἄναρχον ὡς γέννημα, τὸν πατέρα δὲ ἄναρχον ὡς 10 ἀγέννητον.

δʹ. Βουλήσει τῇ ἐκ πατρὸς γεγέννηται ὁ υἱὸς ἢ ἀβούλητος;

†Τῇ ὑπερβουλήσει τῆς γνώσεως†.

εʹ. Ἐπαύσατο γεννῶν ὁ πατὴρ ἢ ἐπιγεννᾷ; 15

15 επιγεννα] an legendum ετι γεννα?

8. ἵνα ἤρξατο] ἵνα is here used as a temporal conjunction.
13. ἀβούλητος] pass. 'without (the Father's) will.'
14. †Τῇ ὑπερβ. τ. γνώσ.†] The passage must be corrupt. Perhaps we should read τῇ ὑπερβαλλούσῃ τῆς γνώσεως ἀγάπῃ τοῦ πατρός with a reference to Eph. iii 19.
15. ἐπιγεννᾷ] 'continues to be-

Οὐκ ἐπαύσατο, ἐπεὶ μηδὲ ἤρξατο.

ϛ'. Ὁ ὢν τὸν ὄντα γεννᾷ ἢ τὸν μὴ ὄντα;
Ὁ ὢν ἀΐδιος τὴν οὐσίαν, δύναμιν ἀϊδίως ἐγέννησε.

ζ'. Τί ἐστι γέννησις;

Ὕπαρξίς τινος ἔκ τινος· καὶ τὸ μὲν ἀϊδίως ὂν ἀϊδίως γεννᾷ, τὸ δὲ ἐν χρόνῳ, χρόνῳ.

5 ον] ων Pitra

get': but this compound seems to occur elsewhere only in the passive. On p. 185 ἐπεγέγονεν means 'was begotten in addition.'

3. τὴν οὐσίαν] acc. of respect qualifying ἀΐδιος.

ib. δύναμιν] Cf. 1 Cor. i 24 Χριστὸν Θεοῦ δύναμιν: see pp. 180 and 186.

5. Ὕπαρξις ... χρόνῳ] 'existence derived by one thing from another; and that which is eternal, eternally begets, whilst that which exists in time, (begets) in time.'

LIST OF BIBLICAL QUOTATIONS AND REFERENCES.

GENESIS

i 6 ff.	143
i 15	141
i 26, 27	201
i 31	134, 162
ii 2, 7, 8, 9, 17, 19	199 f.
ii 7	202
ii 10 ff.	88
ii 22	202
iii 1	202
iii 17, 19	246
iii 19	217
iii 21	229
xv 1	247
xix 17	39
xxii 1	247
xxv 27	249
xxxi 7	201

EXODUS

i 10, 14	202
ii 23	202
vii 11 ff.	72
vii 20, 21	88
xii 30	80
xiv 21, 22	86
xx 5	76

LEVITICUS

xiv 4 ff.	240
xv 19, 20, 33	102
xvi 29	95
xxiv 13–16	47

NUMBERS

xix 6 ff.	241
xix 18 ff.	241
xxii 22	211

DEUTERONOMY

xix 14	55
xxxii 6	181

1 (3) KINGS

iv 26	212
iv 28, 29	213
xxii 17	63

2 (4) KINGS

xvii 15	214

JOB

i 1, 8	203
ii 10	201
viii 3	213
ix 10	204
x 8	148
x 10 ff.	149
xi 13	113
xii 13	206
xiv 1	140
xxii 3	113
xxiii 8	205
xxviii 1 ff.	208
xxviii 12, 20, 23	206
xl 14 (19), 23, 24	203

PSALMS

iv 5	64
xxiii (xxiv) 1	162
xxx (xxxi) 6	218
xxxii (xxxiii) 5	162
xxxii (xxxiii) 22	223
xxxiii (xxxiv) 9	61
xxxiii (xxxiv) 20	246
xxxiv (xxxv) 13	95
xxxv (xxxvi) 7	220

xxxix (xl) 8	233
xliv (xlv) 1	197
l (li) 9	241
lxx (lxxi) 19	237
lxxv (lxxvi) 11	104
lxxvi (lxxvii) 15	87
lxxxiii (lxxxiv) 7	246
lxxxiv (lxxxv) 11	225
lxxxix (xc) 10	246
ci (cii) 24	226
ciii (civ) 23	144
cix (cx) 3	181
cxviii (cxix) 6	220
cxviii (cxix) 73	148
cxix (cxx) 5	229
cxxxv (cxxxvi) 4	87
cxxxviii (cxxxix) 16	137
cxliv (cxlv) 3	204

PROVERBS

ii 6	206
vi 6–11	211
viii 22	180
viii 25	181
viii 30	187, 195
ix 5	224
x 7	223
xiv 30	215
xvi 19	215
xix 3	213

ECCLESIASTES

i 1, 3	210
i 4	211
i 13	223
i 16, 17, 18	212
ii 1	213
ii 2	214
ii 3, 4, 5	215
ii 6–10	216
ii 11	217
ii 12	218
ii 13, 14	219
ii 14, 15	220
ii 16, 17	221, 222
ii 22, 24, 25	223
ii 23, 26	223
iii 3, 4	224
iii 4, 6	225
iii 7, 10, 11	226
iii 11	249
iv 9, 10	227

v 4	251
v 11	221
vii 3 (2)	224
vii 17	64
viii 16	223

SONG OF SONGS

i 5, 6	228
viii 5	228

ISAIAH

v 7	194
ix 6	197
xxv 8	239
xxv 11	113
xxxiii 23	113
xlii 9	77
xliv 2	181
xlv 12	143
xlix 8	66
li 6	143
lxvi 3, 4	75

JEREMIAH

x 18	213
xlviii (xxxi) 10	156

LAMENTATIONS

v 5	254

EZEKIEL

xiii 3	74
xviii 6	102
xviii 23	18
xxxiii 11	18
xxxiv 6	63

DANIEL

vii 8, 25	71

AMOS

iii 3	148

ZECHARIAH

ix 17	206

WISDOM

ii 1	246
vii 15, 16	206
vii 20	213

BIBLICAL QUOTATIONS AND REFERENCES

vii 25	187, 191	
vii 26	186	
ix 15	153	
xi 4	87	
xiii 3, 4	204	
xiii 3, 5	206	

ECCLESIASTICUS

i 2, 3	164
i 8, 9	207
i 12	90
vii 15	211
ix 9	153
xvi 26, 27	146
xvi 29, 30	162
xliii 5	145
xliii 29, 30	204

BARUCH

iii 12, 13	208
iii 14, 15	207

TOBIT

iv 15	53
vi 6	63
xii 7	28

JUDITH

xiv 5	110

I ESDRAS

vi 23	30

II MACCABEES

xiv 22	114

III MACCABEES

ii 15	204

IV MACCABEES

ix 21	147
xiii 13	145

MATTHEW

i 1	210
iii 12	11
iii 17	60
iv 1	247
v 6	54
v 7	257
v 11	12
v 17	226
vi 13	247
ix 20	103
x 32	21
xiv 26	101
xvi 17	118
xviii 7	232
xix 23, 25	10
xix 28	18
xxiv 24	9
xxvi 37, 39, 40	232
xxvi 50	27
xxvii 38	14
xxvii 46	239
xxviii 1	96 ff.

MARK

v 7	161
vi 36	257
vii 12	53
x 38	239
xiii 22	9
xiii 35	94
xiv 33	232
xiv 36	234, 238
xiv 52	27
xiv 61	239
xv 27	14
xv 34	239
xvi 2	96 ff.

LUKE

i 35	54
ii 14	60
iv 1	240
iv 23	126
vi 22	12
vi 25	225
viii 44	103
x 4 ff.	63
x 21	24
xi 4	247
xii 50	239
xv 4 ff.	63
xviii 13	58
xviii 19	207
xxii 42	231
xxii 43, 44	241
xxii 45, 46	245
xxii 47, 48	248

xxiii 33	14
xxiii 46	218
xxiii 56	99
xxiv 1	96 ff.
xxiv 1, 2	99

JOHN

i 1	121, 195
i 12	123
i 14	121
i 17	225
iii 14	239
iii 19	122, 219
iii 20	123
iv 24	187
vi 6	247
vi 38	233
vi 70	123
viii 12	186
viii 44	123
ix 5	96
x 11	63
x 18	242
x 30	182, 191
xi 52	123
xiv 6	195
xiv 11	179, 182
xiv 18	254
xiv 27	81
xiv 31	213
xvi 6	220
xvi 8	123
xvi 11	213
xvi 20	225
xvi 33	246
xvii 11, 21, 22	191
xviii 11	237
xix 18	14
xx 1	96 ff.
xx 23	123

ACTS

ii 9, 10	45
ii 11	237
iii 2	105
iii 19	21
v 4	251
v 29	29
v 33	15
vii 54	15
viii 24	124
ix 15	200
x 24	114
xii 25	33, 237
xiii 1, 5, 13	120
xiv 15	33
xvi 20, 35	65
xvii 22	6
xix 13	73
xx 20, 27	112
xxi 16	57
xxv 12	15
xxvi 18	122
xxviii 22	148

ROMANS

i 21	214, 219
ii 7	218
ii 13	194
v 14	225
viii 35	36
xi 26	251
xii 2	15, 233
xiv 1, 3	18
xiv 5	104
xiv 17	115
xiv 23	104
xvi 1	18
xvi 27	207

I CORINTHIANS

i 24	180, 186, 260
i 24, 30	195
ii 6	68
ii 8	244
iii 3	253
iii 19	213
iv 13	83
v 1	153
v 3	33
v 7, 8	50, 78
vi 2	18
vi 11	50
vii 5	104
viii 1	213
ix 16	157
xii 8	124
xiii 1	26
xiii 4 ff.	109
xiii 12	253
xiv 6, 8	125
xiv 16	58
xiv 20	68
xv 41	141

BIBLICAL QUOTATIONS AND REFERENCES

xv 42–44 243
xv 45 ... ... 202, 225
xv 52 218

II CORINTHIANS

i 2 51
ii 14 16
iii 1 18
iii 6 227
v 4 229
v 20 70
vi 2 66
x 1 112
xi 1, 17, 21 ... ... 28, 36
xii 1 ff. 124
xii 6, 11 ... ... 28, 36

GALATIANS

i 12 124
i 20 23
ii 2 124
ii 9 11
iv 2 226
v 17 224

EPHESIANS

i 3 51
i 18 219
ii 12 213
iii 3 124
iii 19 259
iii 20 233
iv 6 74
iv 13 202
iv 16 150
iv 18 219
v 19 109
v 23 220
vi 16 201
vi 20 70

PHILIPPIANS

ii 7, 8 243
ii 10 105
iii 8 84
iii 15 68
iii 20 213
iv 5 112
iv 8 255

COLOSSIANS

i 15 ... ... 51, 181
i 17 74

i 28 ... ... 68, 202
ii 15 16
iii 16 109
iv 3 33
iv 5 62
iv 12 68

I THESSALONIANS

i 9 33
iv 12 62
v 21 53

II THESSALONIANS

ii 1 111
ii 8 110

I TIMOTHY

i 9 257
ii 2 31
ii 10 110
ii 14 202
iii 5 103
iii 7 ... ... 62, 257
v 7 62
v 17 111
v 10, 16 45
vi 11 72
vi 21 110

II TIMOTHY

iii 17 72

TITUS

ii 13 110
iii 10 226

PHILEMON

12 86

HEBREWS

i 3 186
ii 1 227
iii 4 138
v 14 68
vi 13, 16 161
vii 25 104
ix 1 54
x 7 233
x 32 102
x 34 ... ... 8, 35

xi 6	104
xi 38	16
xiii 16	257

JAMES

i 4	68
i 12	251
i 13	233, 247, 252
i 17	233
ii 2	32
iii 1	253
iii 2	68
iii 17	112
iv 2	253
iv 11	194
v 13	109

I PETER

i 3	51
i 14	15
ii 3	56, 61
iii 8	105
v 1	28

II PETER

i 21	72
iii 9	18
iii 16	226

I JOHN

i 1	118, 121
i 1, 3	119
i 1, 2	121
i 2, 3	122
i 9	123
ii 12	123
ii 29	195
iii 1, 2, 10	123
iii 2	111
iii 7	195
iii 8, 10	123
iv 2	122
v 2	123
v 16	123
v 19	245

JUDE

4	242

REVELATION

i 1, 2, 4	118
i 9	119
iii 21	18
xiii 5	71, 117
xxii 3	253
xxii 7	119
xxii 7, 8	117

Incerti auctoris	53

PROPER NAMES.

Adam 200, 202 f., 225, 229, 244; the new A. 225
Aelia (Capitolina) 44
Aemilian (1) the Emperor xviii; 28, 70
Aemilian (2) the Prefect xix, xxiii; 22 f., 28 ff.
Alexander (1) an Alexandrian martyr 12
Alexander (2) Bishop of Jerusalem 39 f., 55
Alexander Severus the Emperor xv; 72
Alexandria xiii, xvi ff.; 4, 5 ff., 22 ff., 65, 72, 79 ff., 85 ff., 127, 165 ff.
Alogi 107, 114
Ammon a Christian soldier 15
Ammonarion a virgin martyr 12 f.
Ammonius Bp of Berenice 52, 166, 167
Amphilochius of Iconium 242, 244
Anastasius Sinaita xii; 199
Apostolic Constitutions 94, 111
Aquila an Alexandrian Christian 67
Antinoia 39
Arabia xiii; 41, 45, 229
Arabian mountain 17
Arcturus 141
Arianism xxx; 51, 168, 180
Aristotle quoted or referred to xxiv; 101, 109, 127, 143, 156
Armenians xxxi; 62
Arsenoe (the nome) xxiii, xxvi; 106 ff., 111
Asclepiades the physician 134
Asia Minor 40, 43, 108
Ater (Asterius) an Egyptian martyr 13
Athanasius xi, xxi, xxxii; 166, 168, 172, 174 f., 188, 194

Balsamon 92, 94
Baruch 207
Basil the Great xi, xxi; 41, 101, 168, 173, 174 ff., 198, 257
Basilides xxii, 91 ff., 230
Bethune-Baker, Dr 172, 174 n.
Besas a Christian soldier 12
Bithynia 45

Caesarea (in Palestine) xxv; 44
Caesarea (in Cappadocia) 41, 45, 176
Canons of Hippolytus xxx; 37, 94, 103, 104, 111
Cappadocia 41, 45, 50, 242 n.
Carthage xii, xxix f.; 5, 40, 54
Celsus (the philosopher) 128
Censor, office revived xviii
Cephro xix; 20, 33 f.
Cerinthus 108 ff.
Chaeremon (1) Bp of Nilopolis 16 f.
Chaeremon (2) an Alexandrian deacon 28
Chiliasm xxvi; 106 ff.
Chronicon Orientale xii, xiii, xv
Chrysostom 200, 230, 248
Cicero quoted 128, 151, 219
Cilicia 45, 50
Colluthion xix; 23, 34
Conon 59 ff.
Consistentes 59
Coracion 106, 113
Cornelia Salonina xviii; 78
Cornelius Bp of Rome xxxi; 5, 39, 40
Council of Antioch xiii, xxi; 37, 51, 188
Council *in Trullo* 91, 98
,, of Laodicea 103

Cronion (Eunus) an Alexandrian martyr 11
Cyprian xii, xxix f.; 5, 40, 50, 54

Decius xvi ff.; 3 ff., 22 ff., 36, 69
Demetrian Bp of Antioch 39
Demetrius (1) Bp of Alexandria xiii, xv, xxv; 39
Demetrius (2) a presbyter of Alexandria 67
Democritus xxiv; 129 ff., 156, 158
Didymus 3, 22, 64 ff.
Diodorus (of Iasus) 133
Dionysia an Alexandrian martyr 13
Dionysius the Areopagite xi *n.*, xii; 200, 231, 253, 259
Dionysius (of Halicarnassus) 64, 200
Dionysius (of Rome) xxi; 42, 43, 50, 55 f., 165 ff.
Dioscorus (1) an Alexandrian boy confessor 13 f.
Dioscorus (2) an Alexandrian presbyter 67
Docetists 239, 242
Domitius 3, 22, 64 ff.

Easter 64, 65, 69, 78, 79, 80, 84, 92
Eden 88: *see* Paradise
Egypt 33, 34, 67, 72
Egyptians xiii, 13, 14, 80, 84, 87
Elenchus Allegoristarum xxvi; 106
Elenchus et Apologia xxi; 91, 182 ff.
Empedocles 128
Ephesus 121
Epicureans xv, xxii; 127 ff.
Epimachus an Alexandrian martyr 12
Epiphanius quoted xxxii; 107
Eunus: *see* Cronion
Euphranor 166, 252
Euporus 166
Eusebius Bp of Laodicea 28, 68
Eve 200, 201 f.
Exorcists 73

Fabius (Fabianus) Bp of Antioch xvi; 3 ff., 62
Father, God the 51, 148, 165 ff., 233 ff., 259 f.
Faustinus an Alexandrian Christian 67

Faustus a companion of Dionysius 27, 28, 67
Firmilian Bp of Caesarea (Cappadocia) 41, 45, 50

Gaius a companion of Dionysius 27, 67
Galatia 50
Gallienus the Emperor xviii ff.; 31, 32, 69, 77, 78
Gallus the Emperor xvii f.; 69
Gennadius 168 *n.*
Germanus an opponent of Dionysius xii, xvii; 3, 21 ff.
Gifford, Dr 130 ff., 171
Gihon 88
Gnostics 132, 183
Gregory of Nyssa 209, 257

Harris, Dr Rendel 258
Helenus Bp of Tarsus 45, 49
Heliodorus Bp of Laodicea 45
Hellenes 124, 131, 154, 194, 195
Heraclas Bp of Alexandria xv; 43, 54, 57
Heraclides Ponticus 134
Heraclitus ὁ Σκοτεινός 128, 132
Hermammon of Egypt xix; 69 ff.
Hermogenes the Stoic 183
Hermopolis 59
Heron an Egyptian martyr 13
Hesiod quoted xxiv; 136, 154, 156
Hierax an Egyptian Bishop xxiv; 65, 79, 84 ff.
Hippolytus xxvii; 37, 199
Homer quoted xxiv; 143, 159
Hypothecae of Democritus 129, 157

Iconium 40, 42, 50, 55
Ingenes (Ingenuus) a Christian soldier 15
Irenaeus referred to 106
Ischyrion a martyr 16
Isidorus an Egyptian martyr 13
Israel 86, 87

Jackson, Dr H. 127 ff., 171, 182 ff.
Jerome xxviii, xxix, xxxii, xxxv; 39, 41, 59, 62, 106, 168, 208, 256
Jews in Alexandria 72
Job 200 ff.
John the author of the Revelation 71, 117 ff.

John of Damascus xi, xxvii; 199
Julian (1) the Emperor 150
Julian (2) an Alexandrian martyr 11

Kedar 228 f.

Laodiceans xxxi; 45, 62
Larpent, M. 37
Lenten Fast 92 ff., 94 ff.
Libya 12, 31, 67, 165
Liturgy of St Mark 104, 111, 160, 162
Lucian xxix; 188 n.
Lucifer 141
Lucius Bp of Rome xxx
Lucretius 128 ff.

Macar (Macarius) a Libyan martyr 12
Macrianus xix f., xxiii; 70 ff.
Macrianus iunior 75
Manichees 183
Marcellus a Roman Christian 28, 30
Marcion 178
Mareotes (the nome) 34, 67
Marinus Bp of Tyre 44
Maximus Bp of Alexandria 28, 67
Mazabbanes Bp of Aelia 44
Melito of Sardis 206, 210
Mercuria an Alexandrian martyr 13
Meruzanes Bp of Armenia xxxi, xxxv
Mesopotamia 45
Metras an Alexandrian martyr 6
Monasticism, rise of 17
Monotheletes 230
Montanists 41, 114, 176
Morin, Dom xxx; 37
Moses 181
Muses 129, 154

Narcissus Bp of Jerusalem 39
Nemesion an Egyptian martyr 14
Neoplatonism 127, 182
Nepos Bp of Arsenoe xxiii, xxvi; 106 ff.
Nicetas of Heraclea xii; 200, 231
Nile 24, 87, 88
Nilopolis 16
Nilus the author 209, 220
Noah 84
Novatianism xxiii; 36 ff., 40 ff.

Novatus (Novatianus) 36 ff., 55 f.

Ocean 88
Oecumenius 251
Olympus 160
Origen xiii, xv, xvi, xxv ff.; 4, 8, 39, 45, 106, 128, 168, 209, 210, 228 f., 230, 252
Orion 141

Pandora 154
Papyri Oxyrhynchus 12, 13
  ,, Amherst 13
Paradise 198, 229
Paraetonium 67
Paschal Fast 92, 94: *see* Lenten Fast
Paschal Letters xxiii, xxiv, xxxi; 64 ff.
Paul a common Christian name 120
Paul (1) a companion of Dionysius 27, 67
Paul (2) of Samosata xxi f.; 51
Pentapolis 51, 91, 165 f., 208
Pepucenes 176
Persian King 159
Peter a common Christian name 120
Peter (1) a companion of Dionysius 27, 67
Peter (2) Bp of Alexandria xi, xvii
Philemon a Roman presbyter xiv; 42, 43, 52 ff., 258
Philippus Arabs the Emperor xv; 3, 32
Plato 109, 127, 131, 139, 159
Pleiads 141
Pontus 45
Priscilla 176
Procopius of Gaza xxvii f., 208 f.
Ptolemaeus a Christian soldier 15
Ptolemais 51, 165 f.
Pythagoras 131

Quietus son of Macrian 75
Quinta an Alexandrian martyr 7

Red Sea 87
Roman Church 5, 28, 37, 39, 41, 45, 52, 55, 56, 94, 165 ff.
Rufinus xxx, 37, 168, 173

Sabaita xii, xiii

Sabinus the Prefect xvii; 22, 24, 36
Sabellianism xxi, xxiii; 43, 51, 165 ff.
Sabellius xvii *n.*; 165
Salmon, Dr 45
Sanday, Dr xxviii; 234
Saracens 17
Sarapion (1) an Alexandrian martyr 8
Sarapion (2) an Alexandrian penitent 5, 19 f.
Sixtus II: *see* Xystus II
Socrates, death of 161
Solomon 210, 212, 228 f.
Spirit, the Holy 52, 56, 123, 178, 182, 192, 238
Stephen Bp of Rome 40, 44 f., 47, 49, 50
Stephen Gobar xxvi
Stoics 132, 151
Synnada 40, 42, 50, 55
Syria 41, 45

Taposiris xxii, 22
Tarsus 45
Telesphorus 166
Tharsicius 20

Thelymidres Bp of Laodicea xxxi, xxxv; 45
Theoctistus Bp of Caesarea (Palestine) 39
Theophilus an Alexandrian martyr 15
Theotecnus Bp of Caesarea xxvi
Thucydides quoted xxiv; 82, 255
Timotheus ὁ παῖς xiv; 25 f., 127
Tyre xvi, xxvi; 45

Valerian the Emperor xviii ff.; 4, 31, 70 ff.

Westcott, Bp 97, 107 f.
Whytford's *Martiloge* xxxiii; 13, 15
Word, the 52, 121, 169 ff., 182, 195, 197
Wordsworth, Bp Christ. 37

Xenophanes 128
Xystus (Sixtus) II 42, 43, 57, 165 f.

Zeno a Christian soldier 15
Zonaras 75, 92, 94

GREEK WORDS.

ἀβούλητος 259
ἀγαπᾶν 109
ἀγάπη 82, 91, 123
ἄγγελος 63, 97, 98, 197, 228, 243
ἀγελάρχης 142
ἀγενής (ignoble) 243
ἀγενησία 183
ἀγέννητος (ἀγένητος) 132, 183, 184, 185, 259
ἅγια τά 103
ἅγιοι οἱ 115
ἅγιον τό 54
ἀγκών 51
ἄγονος 186
ἄγραφος 110
ἀγράφως 30
ἀγωνιᾶν 241
ἀδιάβλητος 242
ἀδιαίρετος 192, 193
ἀδιανόητος 161
ἀδιάστατος 147
ἀδιάτακτος 147
ἀδιεξόδευτος 204
ἀδρός 242
ἀδώρητος (act.) 159
ἀειγενής 187
ἀειθαλής 140
ἀθανασία 240
ἀθέατος 137
ἀθεεί 24
ἄθλησις 102
ἀίδιος 186, 260
αἷμα τοῦ κυρίου 123; αἷμ. (τοῦ) χριστοῦ 58, 103
αἵματα κλαίειν 241
αἵρεσις 50, 54, 115
αἱρετικός 50, 52, 57; (? = αἱρετέος) 219
αἰσθητήριον 149
αἰσθητός (visible) 32 (cf. 223 f.)

αἰτιολογεῖν 157
αἰτιολογία 157
αἰχμάλωτος 247
αἰώνιος 138, 187
ἀκαλλιέρητος 73
ἀκμητί 258
ἀκολουθία 220
ἀκοντιστής 142
ἀκοσμία 138
ἀκρατής (=ἀκράτητος) 205
ἀκριβολογεῖσθαι 100
ἀκρόπολις 151
ἀκύμαντος 87
ἀλαλάζειν 26
ἀλεκτοροφωνία 94
ἀλήθεια 109, 123, 225
ἀληθεύειν (trans.) 13
ἀλιτήριοι δαίμονες 73
ἀλλὰ γάρ 6, 109
ἀλλοῖος 123, 190; ἀλλοιότερος 236
ἀλλοίωσις 183
ἀλογία 245
ἀλόγιστος 154
ἄλογος 90, 142, 153, 197
ἄλυτος 133
ἀμείωτος 193
ἀμερής 133, 147
ἀμέτοχος 159
Ἀμήν τό 58
ἄμουσος 138
ἄμπελος 167
ἀμφιβολία 234
ἀμφιγνοεῖν 234
ἀναβαπτίζειν 50
ἀναγράφειν 95, 110, 191
ἀναθυμίασις 88
ἀναισθησία 28, 52
ἀναισθησία (act.) 19, 31
ἀναισθήτως 137
ἀνακαθαίρειν 77

ἀνακαλεῖν 248
ἀνακύκλησις 145
ἀνακύπτειν 180
ἀναλίσκειν 239
ἀνάλογον 11
ἀναλόγως 187
ἀναμάσσειν 82
ἀναμίξ 142
ἀναντιρρήτως 109
ἀναπέμπειν (attribute) 244
ἀνάπηρος 75
ἀναρίθμητος 204
ἀνάρμοστος 138
ἀναρριπίζειν 6
ἀναρχία 185
ἄναρχος 187, 258
ἀνασκευάζειν 19, 58, 114, 134
ἀνάστασις 95, 100, 111, 225
ἀνασφάλλειν (intrans.) 20
ἀνατέλλειν 96
ἀνατολή 86, 144
ἀνατρεπτικός 183
ἀναφέρειν (intrans.) 21
ἀνδριάς 153
ἀνδρίζεσθαι 255
ἀνειμένος 90, 125
ἀνεμπόδιστος 147
ἀνένδεκτος 148
ἀνεξικακία 248, 249
ἀνεπαισθητος (act.) 141; (pass.) 133
ἀνεπίσκοπος 254
ἀνεπιτηδεύτως 135
ἀνεπίφθονος 103
ἄνεσις 256
ἀνέφικτος 204, 206
ἀνηλεής 56
ἄνθρωποι τοῦ θεοῦ 72
ἀνθυπάγειν 61
ἀνίατος 249
ἀνιέναι 100, 145
ἀνίμησις 88
ἀνιχνεύειν 151
ἀνόητος 137, 154
ἀνόμοιος 175, 183
ἀνομοιότης 125
ἀνοσιουργία 6
ἀντιγράφειν 105
ἀντίγραφον 52, 189
ἀντιδιατίθεσθαι 54, 110
ἀντικαθιστάναι 158
ἀντιλογία 112
ἀντιπαρεξάγειν 185
ἀντίχριστος 123
ἄνυδρος 87

ἀνύποιστος 203
ἀνυποκρίτως 113
ἀνυπόστατος 162
ἀνωμαλία 221
ἀορασία 24
ἀορίστως 135
ἀόχλητος 147
ἀξίωμα 35, 182
ἀξίωσις 235
ἀπάθεια 240
ἀπαθής 184
ἀπακριβοῦν 95
ἀπαλλάττειν 21; ἀπαλλάττεσθαι (τοῦ βίου) 20
ἀπαράτρεπτος 145
ἀπατεών 200
ἀπαύγασμα 186
ἄπαυστος 187
ἀπεικασία 154
ἀπείραστος (act.) 233 (?), 247, 252
ἄπειρος 132 ff., 164, 204; (=ἀπέρατος) 86
ἀπεοικότως 29
ἀπερινόητος 206
ἀπεριόριστος 132
ἀπερίττως 118
ἀπλάστως 249
ἁπλότης 105
ἁπλοῦν (spread out) 113
ἀπὸ τῆς ἐκκλησίας οἱ 115
ἀπὸ τῆς Στοᾶς οἱ 132
ἀποβρέχειν 21
ἀποδατεῖσθαι 146
ἀποδειλιᾶν 15
ἀποικία 146
ἀποκαλύπτειν 71
ἀποκάλυψις 114, 118, 120, 123
ἀπολύειν 20
ἀπονηστίζεσθαι 94
ἀπόρροια 191
ἀποσκυβαλίζεσθαι 84
ἀποσμήσσειν 88
ἀποσπερμαίνειν 149
ἀποστασία 111
ἀποστέλλειν 61
ἀποστῆναι 32, 54
ἀπόστολος 110, 114, 194, 253
ἀποτελεῖν 133, 145
ἀποτορνεύειν 143
ἀποφαίνειν 61, 100, 114, 159
ἀπόφασις 35
ἄπρακτος (act.) 237; (pass.) 234
ἀπροαίρετος 104, 125, 141, 147
ἀπρονόητος 132, 144, 253

GREEK WORDS

ἀπρόσιτος (act.) 232
ἀπροσπαθῶς 163
ἀπταίστως 124
ἀρά 74, 246
ἀράχνης 137
ἀργός 136, 149
ἀριθμός 164, 204
ἀριστεύειν 12
Ἀρκτοῦρος 141
ἁρμόζειν (trans.) 150, 235; (intrans.) 96, 184; (impers.) 136
ἀρχή 178, 244
ἀρχηγέτης 148
ἀρχηγός 113
ἀρχισυνάγωγος xix; 72
ἀρχιτέκτων 142
ἄρχων 16, 142, 150
ἄρωμα 99
ἀσάλευτος 31
ἄσβεστον πῦρ 11, 12
ἄστατος 184, 205
ἀστήρ 139, 141, 143, 145, 159
ἄστρον 147
ἀστρονομία 154
ἄστρωτος 26
ἀσύγγνωστος 224
ἀσύγκριτος 219
ἀσυλλόγιστος 114
ἀσύνθετος 147, 190
ἀσχάλλειν 158
ἀσχολεῖν 215, 223
ἀσχολία 9
ἀσωτία 224
ἄτακτος 133, 138
ἀτάραχος 255
ἀταράχως 34
ἄταφος 84
ἀτέλεστος 164
ἀτελεύτητος 204
ἀτελής 156, 202
ἀτμίς 187
ἀτμός 88
ἄτομος 132 ff.
ἄτρεπτος 184
αὐθέκαστος 235
αὐτάρκης 66, 103, 110, 119
αὐτεξούσιος 251
αὐτήκοος 119
αὐτῆς ὥρας 24 (cf. 17 and 211)
αὐτοαγένητος 183
αὐτόματος 143
αὐτομάτως 133, 135, 154
αὐτομολεῖν 135
αὐτόπτης 119

αὐτουργεῖν 137
ἀφανισμός 89
(ἐν) ἀφεδρῷ 102
ἀφειδεῖν (not to spare) 82; (to neglect) 256
ἄφεσις 60, 123
ἀφθαρσία 240, 243
ἀφιέναι 20, 60
ἀφιεροῦν 145
ἄφιξις (arrival) 24
ἀφιστάναι 122, 140
ἀφορίζειν 192
ἀφορισμός 62, 98
ἀφυλάκτως 82
ἄφωνος 19
ἀχειροποίητος 137
ἀχθοφορία 151
ἀχώριστος 191
ἄψυχος 141, 154

βαβαί 248
βάθρον 15
βάπτισμα 57
βαρβαρικός 125
βάρβαρος 125
βάσανος 8, 14
βασιλεία 74, 75, 77; βασ. τοῦ θεοῦ 111; βασ. τοῦ χριστοῦ 115
βασιλεύς 72, 74, 76, 77
βασιλικός 5, 78
βασιλίς 146, 157
βάσιμος 8, 152
βδελυκτός 73
βδελύττεσθαι 7
βιβλίον 111, 114, 116, 117
βιωφελής 158
βλασφημία 51, 55, 57
βόρβορος 53
βουλευτικός 35
βραδύνειν 229
βραδύτης (lateness) 98
βριχυτελής 140

γαληνιᾶν 255
γαληνός 87
γαμεῖν 103
γάμος 115, 256
γάννυσθαι 156
γαστήρ 115, 152, 220
γειτνιᾶν 123
γειτνίασις 146
γενεσιουργός 206
γεῦσις 102
γεωμετρία 154

γεωργικός 210, 211
γεωργός 167, 172, 188
γηπονία 211
γλυκαίνειν 249
γνώμη 19, 57, 244
γνωμικός 245
γνῶσις 125, 152
γοητεύειν 202
γονεύς 187
γονή 189
γόνιμος 207
γράμμα 86, 115, 227; (=γραφή) 206, 225
γυμνάζειν 248
γυμνάσιον 82, 163, 256
γυμνός 27, 229

δαίμων 64, 73, 139
δαπανᾶν 89, 223
δειλός 243, 244
δεισιδαιμονία 6
δερμάτινος χιτών 229
δεσμωτήριον 81
δεσμώτης 60, 66
δεσπότης (of Christ) 248, 249
δεσποτικός 242
δεξιοῦσθαι 143
δήλωμα 190, 234
δήμευσις 35
δημιούργημα 134
δημιουργία 159, 184
δημιουργός 141, 160, 193, 211
δημοκρατία 143
δῆμος 145
δημοσίᾳ 14, 54, 111
δημοσιεύειν (intrans.) 10
δημώδης 82
δι' αἰδοῦς ἄγειν 109
διὰ σπουδῆς ἔχειν 116
διαδονίζειν 164
διάδοσις 84
διάθεσις 153, 163, 234, 244
διαιρεῖν 177, 178
διαίρεσις 178
διακληροῦν 144
διακονία 151
διακονικός xxx; 37
διάκονος 28, 83
διακρίνεσθαι 104
διάλεκτος 125
διαλλάττειν (intrans.) 140
διαλύειν 135, 136
διαμονή 140, 152
διαναπαύειν 69

διαπαννυχίζειν 26
διαρθροῦν 151
διαρκεῖν 101
διαρκής 14, 215
διαρκῶς 238
διαρριπτεῖν 135, 146
διασκιδνάναι 135
διάστημα 256
διατείνειν 122
διαχέειν 12
διδασκαλεῖον 163
διδασκαλία 110, 113, 115
διδασκαλικός 52, 253
διδάσκαλος 72, 105, 110, 111, 234, 248, 249
διδαχή 113
διεκπερᾶν 143
διεξαγωγή 117
διεξέρχεσθαι 122
διέπειν τὴν ἡγεμονίαν 30, 31
διευθύνειν 110, 112, 114, 125, 143
διηνεκῶς 31
δικάζοντες οἱ 15
δίκαιοι οἱ 145
δικαίως (=ἀκριβῶς) 235
δικαστήριον 11, 15
δικαστής 12
διοδεύειν 86, 146
διόλου 123, 240
διοχλεῖν 101
δίπηχυς 210
διωγμός 5, 24
δόγμα 51, 111, 115, 148, 154
δογματίζειν 110
δοκιμαστής 19
δοκίμιον 82, 256
δολερός 244
δοξολογεῖν 204
δορυφορία 151
δ' οὖν 52, 145
δράκων 139
δρῦς 140
δύναμις 177, 180, 186, 187
δυσαπάλλακτος 140
δυσαποσπάστως ἔχειν 220
δύσις 144
δυσμή 25, 86
δυσφορεῖν (with dat.) 91
δυσχερία 245
δωδεκαετής 103

ἐγγλυκαίνειν 220
ἐγγράφειν 124, 161
ἔγερσις 241

GREEK WORDS

ἐγκάρδιος 194
ἐγκαρτερεῖν 14, 101
ἔγκατα 149
ἐγκαταλέγειν 155
ἐγκαταλείπειν 208, 239, 240, 254
ἐγκέφαλον 150
ἔγκλισις 147
ἐγκυκλεῖν 197
ἐθελουργεῖν 142
ἔθνη τά 82, 84
εἰ δ' οὖν (otherwise) 189
εἴ σοι φίλον 234
εἰδωλεῖον 7
εἰδωλολατρεῖν 38
εἴδωλον 33, 153, 157
εἰκῆ 137
εἰκτός 235
εἰλικρινής 88
εἰρήνη 44, 64; εἰρ. χριστοῦ 81
εἰρηνικός 229
εἰρηνοποιός 229
εἰς ἀνήνυτον 13
εἰς πλάγιον 147
εἰσηγητής 113
ἑκατόνταρχος 14, 67
ἐκδέχεσθαι 180, 235
ἐκδοχή 116, 211, 227
ἐκθειάζειν 153
ἐκκλησία 72, 75, 86, 111, 177
ἐκκλησιάζειν 34
ἐκκύπτειν 207
ἐκλαμβάνειν 201, 227
ἔκνευσις 147
ἑκουσίως 142
ἐκφαυλίζειν 110
ἐλαύνειν (banish) 70, 81
ἔλεγχος 123
ἔλεος (τοῦ Θεοῦ) 75
ἐλλαμπρύνεσθαι 14
Ἑλληνίζειν 125
ἐμπνεῖν 73
ἐμποδοστατεῖν 147
ἐμπομπεύειν 16
ἐμφανίζειν 99, 120
ἐμφιλοχωρεῖν 178
ἐν ἐπηκόῳ 113
ἐναγωνίως 68
ἐνανθρωπεῖν 52
ἐνδιαβάλλειν 211
ἐνδιαιτᾶσθαι 178
ἐνδιατρίβειν 188
ἐνδόσθια 153
ἐνδυάζειν 221
ἐνευφραίνεσθαι 81

ἐνηλλαγμένος 95
ἐνηχεῖν 249
ἐνθαλασσεύειν 136
ἔνθεος 110
ἐνθύμησις 52
ἐνθύμιον 104
ἐνοῦν 44, 141, 178, 182
ἐνόχλησις 32
ἔνστασις 221
ἐνσφραγίζειν 184
ἐντεταμμένος 242
ἐντεῦθεν (= ἐνταῦθα) οἱ (men on earth) 60 (cf. 203)
ἐντροπίας οἶνος 240
ἐντυγχάνειν 52, 53, 122, 161
ἔνυδρος 139, 162
ἐνωμότως 146
ἐξ ἐπιδρομῆς 188, 195
ἐξ ἐπιπολῆς 232
ἐξ ὑπαρχῆς 58
ἐξ ὑπερδεξίου 255
ἐξάγιστος 73, 156
ἐξανδραποδίζειν 17, 26
ἐξαφανίζειν 77
ἐξέτασις 111
ἐξοικειοῦν 184, 256
ἐξοικίζειν 243
ἐξομοιοῦν 160
ἐξομοργνύναι 76
ἐξόριος 155
ἐξοχετεύειν 191
ἐξυπηρετεῖσθαι 227
ἔξωθεν 62, 257
ἐπ' ἐμαυτοῦ βάλλεσθαι 23
ἐπαγγελία 123, 251
ἐπαλγής 246
ἐπαληθεύειν (trans.) 75
ἐπαμφιεννύναι 149
ἐπανατέλλειν 77
ἐπαοιδός 73
ἐπαπόρησις 112
ἐπαρκεῖν 45
ἐπαρτᾶν 52
ἔπειξις 26
ἐπεισκυκλεῖν 55
ἐπεξεργάζεσθαι 151, 194
ἐπηλυγάζειν 77, 144
ἐπιβάθρα 144
ἐπιβατεύειν 112
ἐπιβολή 135
ἐπίγειος 115
ἐπιγεννᾶν 259
ἐπιγίγνεσθαι 167, 185
ἐπιγνώμων 164

18—2

ἐπιγράφειν 117
ἐπιγραφή 114
ἐπιδημία 225
ἐπιείκεια 112, 234
ἐπιθειάζειν 204
ἐπίκαρπος 145
ἐπικατασκήπτειν 81
ἐπίκλην 11
ἐπικλύζειν 87
ἐπικουρεῖν 91
ἐπιμαίνεσθαι 75
ἐπιμετρεῖν 14, 150, 207, 236
ἐπιμιξία 34, 152
ἐπιπολάζειν 111
ἐπιπολῆς 153 (cf. 232)
ἐπιστάζειν 21
ἐπιστατεῖν 142
ἐπιστολιμαῖος 86
ἐπιστρεπτικός xxxi; 61
ἐπιστρέφεια 32
ἐπιστροφή 15, 61
ἐπισυναγωγή 111
ἐπίτασις 256
ἐπιταχύνειν 100
ἐπιφημίζειν 115
ἐπιχώριος 6
ἐποπτεύειν 144
ἐποχεῖσθαι 11
ἑπταετηρίς 78
ἐρανίζεσθαι 154
ἐργασία 141, 210, 211
ἐργαστήριον 163
ἐργαστικός 184
ἐργοδοτεῖν 142
ἔριθος 137
ἑρμηνεία 124
ἑρμηνεύς 197
ἐρώτησις 110, 112
ἑστίασις 18
ἑτεροδιδασκαλεῖν 54
ἑτεροίως 140
ἑτέρως (=κακῶς) 61
εὖ πάσχειν 91
εὐαίσθητος 153
εὐάλωτος 34
εὐγνωμόνως 96
εὐδοκία 60
εὐένδοτος 14
εὐεργός 153
εὐήτριος 137
εὔθετος 135
εὐθηνία 203
εὐθυμεῖσθαι 109
εὐκίνητος 153

εὐλαβής 103
εὐπαράγωγος 14
εὐπαρακολούθητος 112
εὐπαρρησίαστος 104
εὐπραγία 203
εὐπρέπεια 150
εὕρημα 154
εὔρυθμος 153
εὐσταθής 112
εὐσυνείδητος 104
εὐσυνειδήτως 113
εὐσύνοπτος 163
εὔτακτος 138, 142, 146
εὔφημος 115, 184, 185
εὐφροσύνη 95, 215
εὐχαριστία 58; (the consecrated bread) 20
εὐωχεῖσθαι 26, 81
ἐφέστιος 8
ἐφήμερος 217
ἐφόδιον 258
ἐφυστερίζειν 101
ἔχειν (intrans.) 25
Ἑωσφόρος 141

ζυγός (masc.) 125
ζύμη 50
ζωγραφεῖν 162
ζωή 122, 196
ζωογονεῖν 149
ζῷον 139, 145, 213
ζωοποιεῖν 202, 214
ζωτικός 240

ἡγεμονία 30, 31, 150, 227
ἡγεμονικός 35; τὸ ἡγεμ. 219
ἡγεμών (Prefect) 13
ἡγούμενος (Prefect) 14, 68
ἦθος 117
ἡλιακός 77, 141
ἡλικιώτης 89
ἥλιος 77, 139, 141, 143, 159, 187
ἠμελημένος 250
ἤμην 27
ἡμιθνής 84
ἡμιώριον 100
ἠνέῳγα 163
ᾐσθημένως 95

θανατηφόρος 200
θανατοῦν 81, 251
θεά 120
θεατής 162, 254
θέατρον 163

GREEK WORDS

θέλημα χριστοῦ 231, 232, 244, 245
θεογονία 155
θεόπεμπτος 53
θεόπνευστος 117
θεοποιεῖν 159
θεοποίητος 183
θεοπρεπής 14, 60, 156
θεότης 152, 177, 237, 242
θεοφιλής 31
θεραπεύειν 82, 126
θέσις 136, 213, 219
θητεύειν 227
θολοῦν 88
θριαμβεύειν 16
θυγατριδοῦς 20
θύειν 10, 16, 19
θυμηδία 158
θύραθεν 149
θυσία 115

ἴασις 103
ἰατρός 134, 153
ἰδίωμα 125
ἰδιώτης 66, 150
ἰδιωτισμός 124
ἴδρωσις 241
ἱερεῖον 115
ἱεροί (ἄνδρες) 70 ·
ἱερουργία 73
ἱκνούμενος (apposite) 188
ἱππήλατος ἡ 87
ἴσα βαίνειν 147
ἰσάγγελος 203
ἰσόστοιχος 147
ἰσοτιμία 185
ἰσόψυχος 105
ἰχώρ 88

καθαρός 73, 103, 229
καθάρσιος 88
κάθαρσις 58
καθολικός xi ; 74, 75, 117, 118
καθόλου 18, 74, 197; ὁ ἐπὶ τῶν καθόλου λόγων xix ; 74
καθυποβάλλειν 211
καίριος 136
καιρός 145, 224, 225
καιροφυλακεῖν 147
κακίζειν (depreciate) 217
κάλαμος 7, 240
καλλιεργία 153
καμαροῦν 143
καμπή 151
κανονικός xi ; 176

κανών 53, 59, 91, 198
κατ' ἀρετήν 156
κατὰ διάμετρον 167 n., 177
κατὰ μέρος 35, 151, 204
κατὰ νοῦν 70
κατὰ φύσιν 30
κατὰ ῥυθμόν 147
κατὰ χώραν 135
καταβοᾶν 87
καταβόησις 35
καταβροχθίζειν 21
καταδρομή 34
καταθύμιον 234
κατακερματίζειν 132
καταλεύειν 7, 46
καταλιθοβολεῖν 7
κατανύσσειν 57
καταξαίνειν 14, 68
καταποντισμός 87
καταρτίζειν 135
κατασεμνύνεσθαι 211
κατασκευάζειν 95
κατασκηνοῦν 143
κατασφίγγειν 140
κατατέμνειν 177
καταυγάζειν 187
καταχορδεύειν 74
κατεπαγγέλλεσθαι 61, 110
κατεσχληκώς 214
κατόρθωμα 38, 244
κατοχή 151
κενὸν τό 133, 160 (cf. 132)
κεφάλαιον 114, 122
κεφαλαιωδῶς 151
κήρυγμα 8, 177, 182
κληρονομεῖν 134
κλυδωνίζεσθαι 255
κοιμητήριον 32
κοινὴ ἔννοια 257
κοινολογία 114
κοινότης 97
κοινωνεῖν 18, 50
κοινωνία 57, 58, 84, 150, 192
κοινωνός 27
κόσμησις 140
κόσμος 123, 133, 154, 160, 163, 199, 226
κουφισμός 60
κράσπεδον 103
κραταιοῦν 11
κρατύνειν 112, 184, 235
κρίσις 18, 19, 60, 74, 123, 125, 126, 160, 255
κριτής 104

κριτικός 64
κρόκη 135
κυδοιμός 143
κυκλικός 147
κυκλοφορικός 147
κῦρος 227
κωλυτής 73

λακίζειν 135
λέξις 124, 142
λευχείμων 100
λεώφορος 8, 87
λῆξις 63
λῃστής 14
λῃστρικόν 237
Λιβυκός 33
λιθοβολεῖν 33, 46
λιθόστρωτον 7
λιθουργεῖν 184
λιμήν 87, 88
λιμός 81
λιπαρία 69
λιπαρῶς 82, 238
λόγιος 94, 124, 151, 176
λόγος 154, 197
Λόγος ὁ 52, 121, 169 ff., 182, 195, 197
λόγος αἱρεῖ 113
λοιμός 88
λουτρόν 56, 83
λωφᾶν 91

μαγγανεία 73
μάγος 72
μακαρίζειν 116, 118, 160, 218
μακάριος 68, 120, 160, 203, 207
μακαρισμός 160
μακραίων 138
μακρόβιος 139
μακρόθεν 190
μανός 140
μάντις 6
μαρτυρία (testimony) 163; (martyrdom) 16, 38
μαρτύριον 83, 243
μάρτυς 11, 16, 27, 68, 81, 120
μαστίζειν 223
μάστιξ 12, 14, 66
ματαιόφρων 198
μεγαλεῖος 110, 237
μεγαλοφρονεῖσθαι 141
μερίζειν 177, 192, 196
μεριστής 147
μέσον τό (the difference) 218, 222

μεταλλικός 208
μετάνοια 14, 62
μετασκηνοῦν 34
μεταχειρίζειν 135
μετέωρος 11
μετονομάζειν 133
μηδ' εἶναι 77, 146
μικρολογία 96
μισθοδότης 16
Μισοπώγων 150 n.
μοναρχία 177, 182
μονάς 178, 182, 193, 196
μονή 144
μονογενής 51
μονοειδής (unique) 207
μουσική 154
μυλιαῖος 7
μυστήριον 28, 47, 110, 118

ναυπηγός 167, 169, 172, 188
ναῦς 136
νεανισκός 100
νεογενής 74
νευρίζειν 243
νευρορραφεῖν 149
νηστεύειν 102
νοερός 162
νόημα 121, 154
νομοθετεῖν 146
νοσοκομεῖν 82
νόσος 68, 81, 82, 89
νοσφίζειν 7

ξηρός 87, 107 n.
ξυστήρ 12

ὁδηγεῖν 145, 215
οἴησις 125
οἰκειότης 141
οἰκειοῦν 233
οἰκείωσις 216
οἰκήτωρ 89
οἰκιστής 146
οἰκοδεσπότης 146
οἰκονομεῖν 34
οἰκονομία 28, 152, 237, 243
οἶκος (=κόσμος) 138; οἶκ. τοῦ θεοῦ 103
ὅλα τά (the universe) 178, 182, 184
ὀλίγωρος 101
ὁλοκλήρως 172, 226
ὁλοσχερής 150, 203
ὁμογενής 189
ὁμογνώμων 18

GREEK WORDS

ὁμοθυμαδόν (=ὁμοῦ) 207
ὁμοίωμα 189
ὁμοίωσις 111
ὁμολογεῖσθαι 21
ὁμολογητής 68
ὁμολογία 35, 56
ὁμόνοια 38
ὁμοούσιος 172, 188
ὁμόσκευος 142
ὁμόσκηνος 86
ὁμόφρων 44, 105
ὁμοφυής 189
ὁμόφυλος 158
ὀνειροπολεῖν 115
ὄνομα 122, 132
ὀνομάζεσθαι 78
ὀνομαστί 10, 66
ὄξος 240
ὀξυδερκής 164
ὁπλόμαχος 12
δραμα 53
ὄρθιος 153
ὅρος 95, 146
ὀστεοῦν 149
οὐ μὴν ἀλλά 249
οὐσία 132, 138
ὄφις 200, 202
ὄχλησις 91
ὀψέ 96, 97, 98

παγγενῆ 76
παθητός 183
παιδοποιεῖν 186
παῖς 25, 51
παλαμναῖοι δαίμονες 64
πᾶν τό 131, 133
παναρμόνιος 138
πανδοχεῖον 81
πανηγυρίζειν 225
πανηγυρικός 81
πάνσοφος 151
παντοκράτωρ 51
παντουργός 153
πάπας 54
παρὰ βραχύ 9
παρὰ μικρόν τό 101
παρ' ὀλίγον 101
παρ' πόδας 134
παρὰ φύσιν 30, 243
παράδειγμα 134; παράδ. τοῦ χριστοῦ 14
παραδόξως 243
παράδοσις 52
παραδοχή 58

παραιτεῖσθαι 64, 91, 112
παρακρούεσθαι 201, 203
παραλλάττειν 121
παραλόγως 147
παραξέειν 236
παραπέτασμα 114
παραπολαύειν 81
παραρρυῆναι 227
παράρτημα 161
παρασκευή ἡ 102
παρατείνειν (intrans.) 100
παραφορά 132
παρεγγράφειν 118
πάρεδρος τοῦ χριστοῦ 18; π. τοῦ Θεοῦ 202
παρείκειν (impers.) 135
παρεισάγειν 54
παρεμπλέκειν 135
παρθένος 12
παροδικός 222
παροικεῖν 85
παροιμία 241
παρορμᾶν 6
παχύτης 242
πεδιάς 146
πειραστής 247
περὶ ἡλίου δυσμάς 25
περίγειος 152
περιηχεῖν (trans.) 80
περιοδία 147
περίοδος 256
περιορίζειν 64
περιπαθής 246
περισπασμός 223
περιστάζειν 242
περίστασις 189, 245
περιστολή 68, 83
περιτάσσειν 143
περιττεύειν 152
περιφανέστεροι οἱ 10, 45
περιφορά 214, 218, 219, 221
περίψημα 83
περσέα 140
πεῦσις 14
πηγή 189, 190, 196, 205
πῆγμα 147
πηλινός 153
πίλημα 140
πλάσμα 74, 115
πλατύνειν 193
πλατύτης 194
πλεκτάνη 141
(τὸ) πλέον νέμειν 116
πληθύς 153

πλημμυρεῖν 87
πλήρης (indecl.) 239
πλήρωμα 206
πλησιόχωρος 146
πλησμονή 115
πλωτός 152
ποδαγρός 11
ποίημα 179, 181, 195, 226
ποίησις 148, 154, 179
ποιητής 6, 115, 143, 148, 159, 160, 193, 194, 195
ποιοῦν 184
πολίχνιον 27
πολυαρχία 185
πολυετής 145
πολύθεος 185
πολυμήχανος 151
πολυμιγής 145
πολύμορφος 184
πολύπαις 13
πολυπλανής 146
πολυπλήθεια 162
πολύπλοκος 202
πολυσχήμων 133
πονηρός ὁ 246, 247
ποσότης 204
ποταμός 24, 87, 88, 189, 190, 196
πράξεις al 10
πραΰθυμος 215
πρεσβεύειν 70, 157
πρεσβύτερος (an elder) 20, 28, 83, 111, 119, 198; (of things) 163, 183, 207
πρεσβῦτις 66
πρίεσθαι 15
πρὸ πολλοῦ 99, 111, 239
προαίρεσις 217, 218
προανακρούεσθαι 121
προαναπαύεσθαι 109
προανατέλλειν 77
προαξιοῦν 239
προαποφαίνεσθαι 12
προάστειον 7, 33
πρόγραμμα 52
προγραφή 35
προηγουμένως 29
προθεσμία 226
προκαταλύειν 101
προκαταρκτικός 192
προκατηχεῖσθαι 50
προκεῖσθαι 119, 123
προκομίζειν 109, 189
προκύπτειν 160
πρόμαχος ἡ 13

πρόνοια 25, 74, 150, 151, 203
προπηδᾶν 91, 191, 197
πρόρρησις 10, 76
πρόρριζος 76
πρὸς ἕω τό 98
πρὸς καιρόν 140
πρὸς τὸ κρυβέν (secretly) 245
προσάγεσθαι (induci) 12, 68
προσαγωγή 190
προσανάλωμα 221
προσαναπνεῖν 9
προσαράσσειν 7 (cf. 238)
προσεγγράφειν 89
προσεπεξεργάζεσθαι 148
προσεπεξευρίσκειν 188
προσευχαριστεῖν 198
προσευχή 18, 59, 70, 242
πρόσκαιρος 215, 217
προσπάθεια 126
προσπελάζειν 77
προσπεφυκέναι 126
προσράσσειν 238 (cf. 7)
πρόσταγμα 5
πρόσωπον (dramatic character) 233
προυποφαίνεσθαι 99
προφητεία 116, 125
προφήτης 110, 116, 147, 156, 197, 246
πρωτότοκος 80
πρωτότυπος 154
πυκνοῦν 140
πυραμίς 143
πύσμα 105
πώγων 150

ῥαίζειν 61
ῥανίς 149
ῥᾳστωνεύειν 125
ῥημάτιον 190
ῥίζα 157, 189
ῥιψοκίνδυνος 181
ῥυθμίζειν 250
ῥύμη 133, 136
ῥύσις 103, 104, 143

σάββατον 97 ff.
σαρκικός 115, 253
σάρξ 149, 242; σ. τοῦ κυρίου 123
σεβαστός (augustus) 31
σελήνη 139, 141, 159
σεληνιακός 141
σκανδαλίζειν 9
σκάφος 167, 169, 188
σκελίζεσθαι 213
σκέπασμα 150

GREEK WORDS

σκῆνος 153, 229
σκηνοποιεῖν 153
σκῆπτρον 240
σκιαγραφία 154 (cf. 162)
σκίμπους 26
σιαγών 8
σιτηρέσιον 89, 152
σολοικίζειν 125
σολοικισμός 124
σοφία 135, 138, 154, 180, 181, 187, 195, 205, 207, 208, 217, 218, 222
σοφός (of a poet) 194
σπόγγος 240
σταγών 242
σταυρός 244
στενωπός 8
στέργειν 91
στεφανοῦν 251
στήμων 135
στοιχεῖον 88
στρατηγός 67, 142
στρατιώτης 11, 66, 67
στρατιωτικός 15
συγγενής 143, 189
συγκατάβασις 114
συγκατάθεσις 112
συγκαταλέγειν 89
συγκεφαλαιοῦσθαι 178, 193, 204
συγκοινωνός 120
συγκονίεσθαι 255
σύγκρισις 185, 217, 219
συγκροτεῖν 33, 160, 164
συκοφαντεῖν 14, 56
συκοφάντης 193
συλλαβή 123
συλλογισμός 124
συμβαίνειν 81, 154
συμβατικῶς 135
σύμβιος ἡ 17
συμπαρατάσσειν 147
συμπεριδινεῖν 147
συμπίπτειν 133
συμπρεσβύτερος 28, 50
σύμπτωμα 134
σύμπτωσις 143, 153
συμπόσιον (place of revelry) 160
σύμψηφος 18
σύμψυχος 86
συνάγειν 6, 18, 29, 32, 54, 178
συναγελάζειν 143
συναγωγεύς 147
συναγωγή 32, 35, 57
συναναστρέφειν 147
συνανομολογεῖν 77

συναπαλλάττειν 82
συναποδῦναι (intrans.) 255
συνασπιδοῦν 147
συνάφεια 140, 192
συναφής 131
συνδημεῖν 33
συνδιάθεσις 114
συνδιαφέρειν 81
συνδικάζειν 18
συνδοκεῖν 235
σύνεδρος 15
συνειδός τό 104
συνεκφωνεῖν 8
συνεπιφθέγγεσθαι 58
συνεργία 151
συνιστάναι 18, 61, 146
συνίστασθαι 59, 113, 115, 135
συννοεῖν 71
συνοδία 147
σύνοδος 26, 50, 55
συνοικία 143, 146
σύνοικος 14
συνορᾶν 71 n., 116, 123, 144
σύνταγμα (band) 15; (composition) 52, 109
σύνταξις 121, 124
συντελεῖν εἴς τι 149
συσκοτασμός 228
συστασιάζειν 224
σύστημα 206
συσχηματίζεσθαι 15
σφάλμα 38
σφενδονᾶν 147
σφενδονήτης 142
σχῆμα 138, 184, 189, 244
σχηματίζειν 140, 149
σχίσμα 111
σώζεσθαι (to be sound) 227
σῶμα χριστοῦ 58, 103
σωματουργός 153

ταλανίζειν 248
τάξις 19, 112, 142, 163, 211
ταπεινόφρων 235
τάχιον 95
τεκμηριοῦσθαι 159
τέλειος 68, 81, 156
τελεσιουργεῖν 156
τελετή 73
τερατεύεσθαι 162
τεσσαρακοντούτης 89
τεχνιτεύειν 163, 184
τεχνίτης 163
τοιχοδόμος 135

τομεύς 147
τοξότης 142
τράπεζα (altar) 58, 59, 103, 224
τρεπτός 183
τριάς 179, 182, 193, 196
τρίπηχυς 210
τροπή 145, 147, 240
τροπίς 136
τρυφᾶν 102, 217.
τρυφή 145, 160
τύπος 53, 184, 198, 237
τυραννεῖσθαι 240
τύρβη 143
τύχη 129 ff.

ὑγιάζειν 241
ὑγιαίνειν 256
ὑγιής 255
υἱοθεσία 123
ὕλη 182, 183, 184, 208
ὑπεναντίος 190, 234
ὑπεξιέναι 205
ὑπεράγασθαι 112
ὑπεραινετός 205
ὑπερασπίζειν 247
ὑπέργηρως 16
ὑπέρθεσις (reprieve) 14, 32; (superpositio) 92
ὑπερκόσμιος 199
ὑπερόριος 86
ὑπερτιθέναι 66, 102
ὑπερυψοῦν 205
ὑπεύθυνος 18
ὑπηρεσία 135
ὑπηρετεῖσθαι 82, 242
ὑπηρετής 25, 67
ὑπιδέσθαι 74
ὑπό (with dat.) 25, 26
ὑπὸ γαστέρα 115
ὑποδοχή 58
ὑπόζοφος 229
ὑπομνηματίζειν 30, 237
ὑποπαραιτεῖσθαι 8
ὑποπλάττεσθαι 253
ὑπόστασις 173, 174, 177, 196
ὑποστέλλεσθαι 112
ὑποχείριος 183
ὕσσωπος 240
ὑφηγητής 177
ὑφίεσθαι 36
ὕψωμα 204, 239

φάλαγξ 146

φαῦσις 141
φέρεσθαι (exstare) 119
φιλαδελφία 82
φιλαλήθης 112
φιλανθρωπία 30, 60
φιλάνθρωπος 257
φιλαυτία 125, 163
φίλαυτος 126
φιλεργία 210, 211
φίλημα 248, 249
φιλόθεος 78
φιλονεικεῖν 253
φιλοπονία 109
φιλόπονος 101
φιλοσοφεῖν 158, 159
φιλόσοφος 150, 154, 155, 158
φιλοσώματος 115
φοῖνιξ (bird) 139; (tree) 140
φονᾶν 6
φοράδην 27
φορολογεῖν 151
φράσις 124, 125
φρουμεντάριος xvii; 24
φρυάττεσθαι 158
φυγαδεύειν 56, 75, 155
φυλλορροεῖν 140
φυλοκρινεῖν 140
φυσιοῦσθαι 212
φύσις 138, 153, 157; οἱ κατὰ φ. θεοί 31; οἱ παρὰ φ. (θεοί) 30
φυτόν 139, 188, 189
φῶς 122, 187, 196
φωστήρ 143
φωτοειδής 228

χαρακτηρίζειν 123
χαριστήριον 74
χειραγωγεῖν 248
χειροκμητεῖν 184
χειροποίητος 179
χειροτεχνεῖν 137
χειροτέχνης 194
χειροτονία 48, 57
χειρουργεῖν 135
χειρουργία 153
χερσαῖος 139, 162
χορεία 138
χορηγία 150
χρειώδης 135
χρέμπτεσθαι 161
χρηματίζειν 242
χρησιμότης 211
χρηστεύεσθαι 19
χρυσοχοεῖν 184

χρώς (*color*) 123
χυδαῖος 144
χωνεύειν 153
χωρίζειν 178, 197
χωρικός 26
χωρίον κενόν 132 (cf. 133 and 160)

ψαλμῳδία 109
ψιλὸς λόγος (prose) 110

ψυχή 139, 154, 224, 227, 228, 242, 249

ὠκύμορος 140
ὠμογέρων 89
ὠμοφορεῖν 83
ὥρα 24, 145, 150
ὡς εἰπεῖν 116, 123
ὡς ἔπος εἰπεῖν 177

www.ingramcontent.com/pod-product-compliance
Lightning Source LLC
Chambersburg PA
CBHW071956220426
43662CB00009B/1160